Taking Every Thought Captive

Don W. King

Taking Every Thought Captive

FORTY YEARS OF THE CHRISTIAN SCHOLAR'S REVIEW

Don W. King, editor

Perry L. Glanzer, David A. Hoekema, Jerry A. Pattengale,
Todd C. Ream, Todd P. Steen, co-editors

TAKING EVERY THOUGHT CAPTIVE
FORTY YEARS OF THE CHRISTIAN SCHOLAR'S REVIEW

Copyright 2011 by *Christian Scholar's Review*

ISBN 978-0-89112-547-1
LCCN 2011006293

Printed in the United States of America

ALL RIGHTS RESERVED
No part of this publication may be reproduced, stored in a retrieval system, or transmitted in any form by any means—electronic, mechanical, photocopying, recording or otherwise—without prior written consent.

Scripture taken from the HOLY BIBLE, NEW INTERNATIONAL VERSION®. Copyright © 1973, 1978, 1984 Biblica. Used by permission of Zondervan. All rights reserved.

LIBRARY OF CONGRESS CATALOGING-IN-PUBLICATION DATA
Taking every thought captive : forty years of Christian scholar's review / Don King, editor.
   p. cm.
ISBN 978-0-89112-547-1
1. Theology. 2. Christian universities and colleges. I. King, Don W., 1951- II. Christian scholar's review.
BR50.T32 2011
230.071'1--dc22

2011006293

Cover design by Rick Gibson
Interior text design by Sandy Armstrong

For information contact:
Abilene Christian University Press
1626 Campus Court
Abilene, Texas 79601

1-877-816-4455 toll free
www.abilenechristianuniversitypress.com

Dedicated to the first four editors
of *Christian Scholar's Review*

George Brushaber (1970-79)

Clifton Orlebeke (1979-85)

William Hasker (1985-94)

Roger Olson (1994-99)

Editor

Don W. King is Professor of English at Montreat College and serves as editor of the *Christian Scholar's Review*. His essays and reviews have appeared in many periodicals, including *Books & Culture*, *Christianity and Literature*, and *SEVEN: An Anglo-American Literary Review*; and he contributed articles on Lewis' poetry to *The C. S. Lewis Readers' Encyclopedia* and to *C. S. Lewis—Life, Works, and Legacy*. He is author of *C. S. Lewis, Poet: The Legacy of His Poetic Impulse*, *Hunting the Unicorn: A Critical Biography of Ruth Pitter*, *Out of My Bone: The Letters of Joy Davidman*, and he is currently writing *Yet One More Spring: A Critical Study of Joy Davidman*.

Co-editors

Perry L. Glanzer teaches in the School of Education and the Institute for Church-State Studies at Baylor University. His two most recent books, *Christianity and Moral Identity in Higher Education* and *Christianity and Scholarship in Higher Education*, were coauthored with Todd Ream. He serves as Book Review Co-editor of *Christian Scholar's Review*.

David A. Hoekema is Professor of Philosophy at Calvin College, where he has served as academic dean and as vice president for student life and has just been appointed department chair. His recent teaching and research have focused on philosophy and religion in contemporary Africa. He has served as Publisher of *Christian Scholar's Review* since 1998.

Jerry A. Pattengale serves as the Assistant Provost for Public Engagement at Indiana Wesleyan University, the Director of the Green Scholars Initiative, and the Executive Director of The National Conversations. His books include *Why I Teach* and *Purpose-Guided Education*. He serves as Associate Publisher for *Christian Scholar's Review*.

Todd C. Ream is the Senior Scholar for Faith and Scholarship and Associate Professor of Humanities in the John Wesley Honors College at Indiana Wesleyan University. He and his family live in Greentown, Indiana where they are members of Jerome Christian Church. He serves as Book Review Co-editor of *Christian Scholar's Review*.

Todd P. Steen is the Granger Professor of Economics at Hope College in Holland, Michigan. He received his Ph.D. in economics from Harvard University in 1992. His areas of research interest are labor economics and Christian perspectives on economic thought. Since 1995, he has served as Managing Editor of *Christian Scholar's Review*.

Contents

An Invitation from the Publisher 9
Acknowledgments 10
Introduction 11

I. CHRISTIAN HIGHER EDUCATION AND THE ACADEMIC VOCATION

1. *The Christian Scholar's Task in a Stricken World* 17
   Carl F. H. Henry
2. *Christian Thinking and the Rise of the American University* 31
   Mark A. Noll
3. *Theory and Praxis* 45
   Nicholas Wolterstorff
4. *The State of Evangelical Christian Scholarship* 63
   George Marsden
5. *On Developing Hopeful Virtues* 75
   Stanley Hauerwas
6. *When Faith and Reason Clash: Evolution and the Bible* 87
   Alvin Plantinga
7. *Faith-Learning Integration: An Overview* 109
   William Hasker
8. *Jesus the Logician* 123
   Dallas Willard
9. *Education for Homelessness or Homemaking?*
   The Christian College in a Postmodern Culture 133
   Steven Bouma-Prediger and Brian Walsh
10. *Hospitality and Christian Higher Education* 147
    Elizabeth Newman
11. *Needed: A Few More Scholars/Popularizers/Activists:*
    Reflections on My Journey 165
    Ronald J. Sider

II. DISCIPLINARY AND INTERDISCIPLINARY INTEGRATION

12. *The Concept of Natural Law* (Philosophy) 175
    Arthur F. Holmes
13. *Naturalism in the Natural Sciences:*
    A Christian Perspective (Natural Sciences) 187
    Paul de Vries

14. *Christian Philosophy and Cultural Diversity* (Philosophy) 197
    Richard J. Mouw
15. *Psychology's "Two Cultures": A Christian Analysis* (Psychology) 209
    Mary Stewart Van Leeuwen
16. *The Cult and Culture of Interpretation* (Literature) 227
    Roger Lundin
17. *Traditional Christianity and the Possibility of
    Historical Knowledge* (History) 249
    Mark A. Noll
18. *Christian Scholarship in Sociology: Twentieth Century Trends and
    Twenty-First Century Opportunities* (Sociology) 267
    Nancy T. Ammerman
19. *Michelangelo's Mirrors* (Art) 277
    Luke Reinsma
20. *Rejecting Neutrality, Respecting Diversity:
    From "Liberal Pluralism" to "Christian Pluralism"* (Political Science) 289
    Jonathan Chaplin
21. *A Pietist Perspective on Love and Learning in Cultural Anthropology*
    (Anthropology) 315
    Jenell Williams Paris
22. *Does Mathematical Beauty Pose Problems for Naturalism?*
    (Mathematics) 329
    Russell W. Howell
23. *Mark and Aristotle: The Christ Embodied as Tragic Hero* (Drama) 341
    Norman A. Bert
24. *Money or Business? A Case Study of Christian Virtue Ethics in
    Corporate Work* (Business) 355
    Scott Waalkes

Afterword
    Alister McGrath 378
Contributors 380

An Invitation from the Publisher

From its inception *Christian Scholar's Review* has been a shared endeavor through which the Christian liberal arts colleges of the United States and Canada seek to encourage and disseminate excellent scholarly work. In the articles that we publish, the light of the gospel illuminates important issues in the humanities, social sciences, physical sciences, and professional fields. Without the steadfast support of our sponsoring institutions the life of the journal could not be sustained, and without the regular contributions from faculty members at the same institutions our contents would be much the poorer. Although we welcome submissions from scholars at any educational institution and from independent scholars, much of the best work submitted for our consideration comes from colleagues at our forty-seven member colleges and universities.

If you find this commemorative collection of value in your own intellectual journey, and you are not currently a faculty member at a sponsoring institution, you can ensure that you receive all future issues of *Christian Scholar's Review* in one of three ways. As an individual, you can enter a personal subscription. (There is a subsidized rate for students.) Or you can ask the librarian in your town, at your church, or in your school or business to enter a library subscription. Details are on our Web site, www.csreview.org, under "subscribe/purchase."

If you are a faculty member at a Christian college or university that is not a current sponsoring institution, you can do a service both to your colleagues and to *CSR* by adding your institution to the ranks of our sponsoring institutions. In return for a modest annual subvention, graduated according to institutional enrollment, your college will receive four quarterly issues each year for distribution to all full-time faculty members, and your chief academic officer will be invited to appoint a representative to participate in the journal's Editorial Board. In a time when travel costs are rising and college budgets are shrinking, *CSR* is an exceptionally effective investment in faculty development. For information on the criteria for membership as a sponsoring institution and on the process by which this status is granted, please contact me by telephone or email as indicated below.

While you are savoring the rich buffet of past contributions that we have selected to celebrate the fortieth anniversary of *CSR*, please take the necessary steps to ensure that each future issue will be in your mailbox, four times each year, to carry the conversation forward.

> David A. Hoekema
> Publisher, *Christian Scholar's Review*
> Professor of Philosophy, Calvin College
> email dhoekema@calvin.edu
> telephone (616) 526-6750

Acknowledgments

On behalf of my co-editors, I have several people to thank for helping to bring this book to print. First, I thank my student editorial assistants who were instrumental in preparing the manuscript: Audrey Coffman, Joanna King, Alyssa Klaus, Kayla Newsom, and Rikki Roccanti. Second, I thank Joy Ortiz and Jessica Frey of Hope College and Kim McMurtry of Montreat College who also assisted in preparing the manuscript. Third, I thank Leonard Allen and his staff at Abilene Christian University Press for shepherding this book along; they were all very helpful and eager to assist in whatever ways they could. Finally, I thank the sponsoring institutions of the *Christian Scholar's Review*:

Azusa Pacific University	Greenville College	Regent College
Baylor University	Hope College	Regent University
Bethel College (Indiana)	Houghton College	Roberts Wesleyan College
Bethel University (Minnesota)	Huntington University	Seattle Pacific University
Biola University	Indiana Wesleyan University	Simpson University (California)
Calvin College	John Brown University	Spring Arbor University
Charleston Southern University	Judson University	Taylor University
Cornerstone University	Malone University	Toccoa Falls College
Covenant College	Messiah College	Trinity Christian College
Dordt College	MidAmerica Nazarene University	Trinity International University
Eastern Mennonite University	Montreat College	Union University
Eastern University	Northwestern College (Iowa)	Waynesburg University
Geneva College	Oklahoma Baptist University	Westmont College
George Fox University	Olivet Nazarene University	Wheaton College
Gordon College	Point Loma Nazarene University	Whitworth University
Grove City College	Redeemer University College	

Introduction

Taking Every Thought Captive: Forty Years of the Christian Scholar's Review is an attempt to capture in one volume a representation of the best scholarship to appear in the pages of the *Christian Scholar's Review* from its inception in 1970 through 2010. To do this has been no small task, so I thank my co-editors of this book Perry Glanzer (*CSR* Book Review Editor), David Hoekema (*CSR* Publisher), Jerry Pattengale (*CSR* Associate Publisher), Todd Ream (*CSR* Book Review Editor), and Todd Steen (*CSR* Managing Editor) for working with me to select the articles appearing herein. In general our selection process was driven by one over-riding principle: to select excellent articles in the areas of Christian higher education and academic disciplinary/interdisciplinary faith and learning integration.

I think it is appropriate here to provide a brief historical perspective on *CSR*, so I reproduce below the opening paragraphs of the first words to appear in *CSR*, the editorial by the first editor of *CSR*, George K. Brushaber, "Why Another Journal?":

> New journals appear almost daily. Most of us find time and finance insufficient to keep pace with the ever-growing body of literature in our respective disciplines. In presenting the first issue of the *Christian Scholar's Review*, the editors recognize the need to justify another scholarly periodical.
>
> Three purposes sustain the *Christian Scholar's Review*. First, as scholars who are Christians, we welcome to our areas of competence the enriching perspectives of divine revelation. Our commitment to intellectual integrity, as well as the experience of divine grace in our own lives, requires that we acknowledge the significance which a Christian view of the world and of human existence has for our study. Secondly, the Christian faith can serve as a catalyst by which the fragmented fields of learning are unified into a comprehensive view of man, his world, and his God. In this case, the integration of faith and scholarship occurs on the inter-disciplinary level. Finally, the discovery and reflection of the scholar must always be shared with others and, in return, benefit from the discerning judgment of others upon it. The *Christian Scholar's Review*, we believe, is an appropriate and needed vehicle by which all three of these concerns may be served.[1]

After noting the mission of *CSR* (which I will cite later in this introduction), the editorial concludes:

In May, 1970, an independent editorial board was organized for the purpose of publishing the *Christian Scholar's Review*. Fifteen colleges of the arts and sciences, located from Massachusetts to California, agreed to sponsor the journal because, institutionally, each was committed to the goals of the *Christian Scholar's Review*.[2] The journal, however, is not an official organ of any of these schools. The *Christian Scholar's Review* is successor to the *Gordon Review*, an interdisciplinary journal which was published from 1955-1970.

It is hoped that the *Christian Scholar's Review* will open avenues of fruitful discussion and discovery among Christians of all persuasions and among scholars who confess the faith of Christ and those who do not. The *Christian Scholar's Review* is offered as a servant to all who love the truth, who seek after it, and who obey the truth when they find it.

The goal for the founders of the *Christian Scholar's Review* was simple: create an effective forum whereby robust Christian scholarship would advance and flourish. By any of several measurements this goal has been achieved. First, for instance, even though longevity is not the most important sign of a healthy scholarly journal, it is a clear indication that over the long term many scholars and researchers have been intellectually nourished and challenged by the content they found within the pages of the journal; now entering its fortieth year of continuous publication, *CSR* has consistently proven its mettle in this regard. Second, having published over six hundred scholarly articles and review essays as well as over sixteen hundred book reviews, *CSR* has shaped at least a part of the ongoing conversation about Christian scholarship from 1970 until today. Third, many established Christian scholars today cut their teeth in the early pages of *CSR*, including George Marsden, Mark Noll, Alvin Plantinga, and Nicholas Wolterstorff. Moreover, over the years many other well-known Christian scholars have published in *CSR*, including Michael Boivin, Paul de Vries, C. Stephen Evans, Stanley Hauerwas, Carl Henry, Arthur Holmes, Alan Jacobs, David Livingston, Roger Lundin, Richard Mouw, Jenell Williams Paris, Ron Sider, Mary Stewart Van Leeuwen, Clarence Walhout, and Dallas Willard. Their work, and that of countless others, gives witness to the rigors of the intellectual enterprise found within the pages of the journal and how it has helped to sustain the life of the mind for many Christian scholars.

My own life as a scholar owes much to *CSR*. I was a sophomore at Virginia Tech when the first issue of the *CSR* appeared in Fall 1970. The Beatles were still hot, my favorite band was the Doors, and the first great national rock festival, Woodstock, was still fresh in my mind (although I won't pretend that I'm one of the ten million or so who claim to have been there!). At the time I was not a scholar and certainly not a Christian. But during that fall I went through a conversion experience, and, serendipitously, I shifted my major from civil engineering to literature. I really liked my English professors. They were very bright, they were good teachers, and it was obvious they loved literature. In fact, most of them tended to treat literature as something holy; literary studies for them verged on religious devotion. At the same time they divorced literary study from any sense of divine truth and meaning. Literature may have been holy, but it had no direct connection to God.

I found that quite frustrating because I longed for them to help me make connections between literary studies and my faith. On the one hand, there was my love of literature, including the beauty of the way words sound, the power of metaphor, the complexity and subtleties of language, the orderliness and beauty of literary forms (poetry, drama, fiction), and especially the tender, poignant portrayal of the human condition, including the possibility of discovering truth and meaning, the redemptive nature of human love as well as the destructive force of human selfishness, pride, and deception. On the other hand there was my embryonic faith and the things I was learning about Christianity, including the creation, the fall, my own patterns of sinful living and thinking, and redemption. My love for literature and my emerging love for Christ swirled together, and I longed to meld them into a coherent framework; regrettably—but not surprisingly since I was attending a large state-supported university—my literature professors could not help me think Christianly about literature.

Providentially, I began to encounter literary critics who helped me do this—chief among them was C. S. Lewis, a writer I had known previously only as the author of the Chronicles of Narnia. As a young Christian, I was looking forward to a course on John Milton that featured an extended study of *Paradise Lost*. I had heard *Paradise Lost* was a distinctively "Christian" piece of literature, so I was looking forward to a rich literary experience, assuming that perhaps it would be informed by Milton's Christian experience. In that I was not disappointed. Yet what equally excited me was that I found Lewis there before me. A required supplemental text in the course was Lewis's little masterpiece, *A Preface to Paradise Lost*. I still marvel at Lewis's insights throughout the book, including this one: "The Satan in Milton enables him to draw the character well just as the Satan in us enables us to receive it."[3] There is a depth of literary and spiritual insight throughout Lewis's *Preface* rarely equaled elsewhere. Moreover, Lewis's scholarship modeled for me perhaps the best example of faith and learning integration that I have ever encountered (not that Lewis would have used such terms).

Reading Lewis eventually led me to several scholarly journals that took seriously the idea that one's faith could inform scholarship and vice versa. I realized this the first time I picked up a copy of *CSR*, as I was struck by it two-fold mission:

> The Christian scholar, experiencing the redemptive love of God and welcoming the enriching perspective of divine revelation, accepts as part of his or her vocation the obligation not only to pursue an academic discipline but also to contribute toward a broader and more unified understanding of life and the world. This vocation therefore includes the obligation to communicate such an understanding to the Christian community and to the entire world of learning.
>
> The *Christian Scholar's Review* is intended as a peer-reviewed medium through which Christian scholars may cooperate in pursuing these facets of their tasks. Specifically, *CSR* has as its primary objective the integration of

Christian faith and learning on both the intra- and inter-disciplinary levels. As a secondary purpose, this journal seeks to provide a forum for the discussion of the theoretical issues of Christian higher education. The *Review* is intended to encourage communication and understanding among Christian scholars, and between them and others.

The interdisciplinary nature of *CSR* attracted me then, and it continues to do so today. I enjoy the give and take of academic debate, and I am very thankful to my *CSR* colleagues in other disciplines who help me think more deeply from a biblically informed perspective about economics, philosophy, psychology, biology, history, anthropology, theology, art, literature, mathematics, and so on.

In 1999 I had the privilege of assuming the role of *CSR* editor, something I could not have imagined back in fall 1970. One particular aspect of *CSR* that I have enjoyed since then is working with associate editors and referees; these men and women work diligently (and without pay!) to help scholars sharpen and refine their ideas—and almost without exception an essay is vetted several times before it is ready for publication. I believe this a wonderful service we provide, and over the years many authors have expressed their thanks for the academic insight, scholarly expertise, and collegial support they have received via our review process. This vetting process was also the pattern under the previous editors of *CSR*: George Brushaber (1970-79), Clifton Orlebeke (1979-85), William Hasker (1985-94), and Roger Olson (1994-99).

Taking Every Thought Captive caps our celebrations of the fortieth anniversary year of *CSR* and gives tangible evidence that *CSR* is committed to serving its original mission and to seeking new ways to support, enhance, and promote Christian scholarship for as many years as God directs us to continue publication. I hope what follows is not only a worthy reflection of the sacrifices made by Christian scholars over the course of the last forty years but also an inspiration to each reader's own sense of calling.

Don W. King
Editor, *Christian Scholar's Review*
Montreat College
December 2010

Notes

1. George K. Brushaber, "Why Another Journal?" *Christian Scholar's Review* 1.1 (Fall 1970): 3-4. This issue contained the following articles: "The Christian College and the Transformation of Culture," by Edmund Clowney; "Sidney's 'Leave Me, O Love'": An Interpretation," by Leland Ryken; "On Thinking of God as King," by Merold Westphal; "Responsibility for the Ecological Crisis," by Richard Wright; and "A Question of Color," by Stuart Babbage.

2. These institutions were Anderson College, Barrington College, Bethel College (Minn.), Calvin College, Gordon College, Houghton College, Northwestern College (Iowa), Nyack Missionary College, Spring Arbor College, Taylor University, Trinity Christian College, Trinity College (Ill.), Westmont College, and Wheaton College.

3. C. S. Lewis, *A Preface to Paradise Lost* (Oxford: Oxford University Press, 1942), 101.

I.
CHRISTIAN HIGHER EDUCATION AND THE ACADEMIC VOCATION

1 The Christian Scholar's Task in a Stricken World (1988)

Carl F. H. Henry

The West has lost its epistemic and moral compass.[1] It has done so, moreover, at the very time when the world more than ever is aware of its intellectual and ethical diversity, and when a possibility of nuclear destruction overhangs the cultural crisis. Our awesome imperative as scholars is to address the civilizational turmoil of Euro-American culture.

Western society is now engulfed by neo-pagan naturalists who consider impersonal cosmic processes and events their homeland. These intellectual frontiersmen, as they would like to be known, disdain theological themes as a diversionary concession to abstract word games. Many in our generation are unsure of the sense and worth of human life. They hold in suspense, moreover, distinctive values of Western civilization, such as the ultimacy of God the creator, the equal dignity of human beings, a divine purpose in nature and history, the supreme manifestation of righteousness and love in Jesus of Nazareth, and a final triumph of the good and decisive judgment of evil. These fundamentals and their implications are now vigorously assailed by the radical secularism that formatively influences education, the mass media, and politics.

We are well aware that biblical theism supplied the cognitive supports of Western culture. It adduced a linear view of history; it affirmed the sacredness of human life; it focused man's responsible role as steward of the cosmos; it nurtured the development of modern science; it engendered the compassionate humanitarian movements that differentiated Western society; it shaped the vision of a climactic end-time triumph of the good and of mankind's decisive deliverance from injustice; it offered the practical impetus and a means as well of transforming human existence into a new society that exudes moral and spiritual power.

This formative influence of Judeo-Christian motifs upon the outlook of the Western world is conceded by theistic and non-theistic scholars alike. Political theologian Johannes B. Metz affirms that "the Jewish and Christian Biblical message . . . first recognized the world as history."[2] Marxist philosopher Ernst Bloch grants that "all the utopian aspirations of the great movements of human liberation derive from Exodus and the messianic parts of the Bible."[3] The ultimate basis for belief in individual equality, observes John H. Hallowell, is the emphasis of the biblical creation account on the dignity of all human beings as bearers of the image of God.[4] Alfred North Whitehead acknowledged that the biblical view of nature's creation and preservation by a sovereign rational God contributed essentially to the emergence of modern science. The historian F. A. Foakes-Jackson affirmed that the humanitarian movements of the West all took their rise from the theology of the Cross. One could readily expand this avowal of our deep cultural indebtedness to Christianity.

The Christian view of God and the world, although not disproved, has nonetheless lost its grip on the mind of modernity, and many intellectually formative centers in the erstwhile Christian West now strip it of force. With the emergence of modern philosophy, speculative theists built a case for theism by appealing not to divine rational revelation and biblical disclosure but rather to creative philosophical reasoning. Scientific empiricism, with its growing regard for sensory observation as the only authentic way of knowing, rendered suspect claims for the reality of the supernatural. Modern phenomenological theory stressed the knower's subjective contribution to experience; logical positivism confined truth and meaning to empirically verifiable claims; secular humanism openly proclaimed the modern victory of ancient naturalism. In the beleaguered culture of the West atheistic forces today hold a major initiative in universities, in the mass media and in politics. Atheistic communists rule over most of the earth's land mass; many countries long considered Christian remain under Soviet domination; most European nations claiming Free World status show meager interest in Christianity. In the United States, still the bulwark of global evangelism and missions, the neo-pagan left increasingly prods humanists to embrace an uncompromising naturalism.

Say what one will about its defection from historic Christian theism, the West's fall away from biblical theology proved more costly than its promoters at first recognized. The naturalistic demotion of a supernatural deity to fable and fantasy had of course left a vacuum where medieval philosophers had long spoken confidently of eternal being, objective truth and good, creation, purpose in nature and history, sin and redemption, divine incarnation, spiritual regeneration and universal moral judgment. But that was not all. However gradual, the intellectual transformation of traditional conceptions of cosmic reality and human history was far-reaching, and it produced new theories of man, of religion, of law and ethics, and of much else.

The sacrifice of a personal and purposive Creator and Sustainer of the universe led to new cosmologies that left unsure man's substance and status in the cosmos. The deletion of a divine activity and goal exposed history and nature to unbridled speculation, whether about their creative new possibilities or about their inherent futility. As James H. Moorhead remarks, "Without God to relativize nature, the latter became a closed system of causal order in which human freedom and efficacy were problematic. Likewise, the absence of a God who endowed nature or history with purpose forced people to play gods themselves; and that Promethean quest forms the substance of the dismal stories of nationalism, Marxism, existentialism, and other variants of secular humanism. The result has been a 'blight of meaninglessness' plaguing Western culture."[5]

It has long been recognized that early modern speculative theists and the triumphant naturalists who succeeded them both unwittingly retained from biblical theism some highly important emphases. To be sure, conjectural theism abandoned scriptural revelation, discussed God's existence without reference to Christology and apart from an articulate doctrine of man's sin, fall, and redemption. The cultural theists in the main shared with ancient classic idealism a speculative insistence on the reality of the supernatural, the supra-animality of man, and the objectivity of truth and good. Yet, in contrast with ancient supernaturalists, and under the influence of Christianity, even conjectural theists broke with the theory that matter is evil, and viewed the universe as somehow a divine creation, restated variously in terms of divine emanation, continuous creation, or evolutionary development. They clung also to the future Kingdom of God, although they increasingly grounded this expectation in notions of man's essential goodness and history's inevitable progress toward utopia. Instead of a universe pliable in the hands of its Creator free to act routinely or to work miracles, they spoke of God mainly as a phantom whose presence guaranteed a felicitous end-time.

Detached as it was from the self-disclosing God and from the power of an inscripturated revelation, conjectural theism—for all its retention of other fragments of Judeo-Christian teaching—could not hold the line against naturalism. Whatever their intentions, the theories forged by Kant and Hegel channeled into naturalism. For all his effort to rescue the universal validity of human knowledge, Kant deprived mankind of God's implanted image and allowed theism only postulational significance; whereas by making everything God, Hegel made God nothing. Slowly but surely speculative philosophy in the West collapsed into the theory that nature alone is real, that man is essentially only a complex animal, and that distinctions of truth and the good are temporary and changing.

For all that, the form in which modern exponents first championed naturalism was notably less radical than ancient Greco-Roman materialism. Post-Christian naturalism, no less than post-Christian theism, inadvertently borrowed from the Judeo-Christian heritage aspects of the biblical world view that are logically extraneous to atheistic empiricism. While early modern naturalism indeed affirmed nature to be ultimately real, it was prone to identify nature in terms of Reason, that is, of a mathematically structured system accessible to human observation and verification. It therefore assumed that man is somehow the apex of nature, and indeed permanently so, and also that distinctions of truth and morality, while subject to change, could through empirical confirmation nonetheless gain a relatively durable significance.

The notable point is that the Christian revelational world-life view had so deeply penetrated the mind and conscience of Western man that both modern speculative theism and early modern naturalism, despite their deliberate rejection of Judeo-Christian fundamentals, remained more deeply dependent on unique biblical emphases than either movement suspected. That same haunting indebtedness is true also of contemporary secular humanism; into its naturalistic control-beliefs it infuses a social agenda of durable imperatives including concern for the poor and weak and for universal justice. But if reality reduces ultimately to impersonal, purposeless processes and events, if man is the accidental byproduct of a cosmic explosion, and if man creatively defines and redefines the content of truth and the good, then no consistent place remains for unrevisably fixed ethical norms. Critics often note that while radically secular humanism has sacrificed the metaphysical realities that make sense of moral absolutes, it nonetheless affirms certain absolutes despite their incongruity with naturalistic presuppositions; this it does, moreover, because secular humanism has been unable to divest itself wholly of Judeo-Christian influence. The biblical view of the world, as Thomas Dean observes, has "proved decisive in the subsequent shaping of the Western outlook, both the world of Christendom and the world of modern secular man."[6]

Today radically secular humanism is increasingly placed on the defensive by evangelical criticism on the right and by neo-pagan secularism on the left. Speaking over twenty years ago, Herman Dooyeweerd observed of the European scene that "the Humanistic faith in mankind, and in the power of human reason to rule the world and to elevate man to a higher level of freedom and morality, has no longer any appeal to the mind of the present day mass man.... This modern man ... considers himself cast into a world that is meaningless, and that offers no hope for a better future."[7] A widening tradition of hard-core naturalism shuns the humanist commitment to universal human welfare and finds no basis for confidently viewing man or society as specially important. Those who espouse a purely scientific view of persons, and are prone to explain mind and consciousness in neurophysiological terms, have little basis for insisting on the dignity of humanity.

Revelatory theists have long stressed that secular humanism's social agenda is merely a cut-flower phenomenon doomed to wither for lack of metaphysical roots, and that it cannot logically withstand the rapid deterioration of cultural norms. If impersonal processes comprise reality, naturalism has no consistent basis for identifying man as the evolutionary capstone, let alone for adducing universal and permanent human rights, or for championing the weak and impoverished rather than affirming the survival of the fittest. To take evolution seriously, as did Bertrand Russell, is to concede that eventually the human species will be as insignificant in the context of some yet future emergent as the primal protozoa or single-cell animal is today considered inconsequential; in an atheistic evolutionary context the fixed nature of man and the permanence of present-day human rights seem indefensible. The evolutionary prospect of a superman or super species renders problematic the universality of human rights; in the framework of German National Socialism, Adolph Hitler considered Aryans as inheritors of the future and Jews an inferior species unworthy of preservation. Marxist materialistic metaphysics likewise presumes to account for all physics, history, ethics, politics, and economics. It links with a supposedly altruistic social program its view that the totalitarian state originates all human duties and rights. Not without reason is communism sometimes declared to be a "Christian heresy." Biblical futurism enters into its distortive dogma that history will eventually crest in a proletarian communist utopia. But failure of the Russian Revolution to attain its promised utopia has necessitated a critical revision of the communist dogma that the universe is self-enclosed and governed by inviolable mechanical necessity.

Radical secularism rejects the view of Greek philosophers and of Spinoza and Hegel that the world-process is a self-sufficient totality in which all entities arise through a reorganization of what already exists. Instead, it gratuitously borrows from the Bible the emphasis that the universe is open to transformation, and is not self-enclosed or governed by mechanical determinism. In unwitting dependence on biblical truth, it holds to the possibility of the new creation of an open future. To be sure, secularism discards as myth the biblical doctrine that the universe owes its existence to an independent, transcendent personal Creator. It does not relate cosmic contingency to ontological dependence on a supernatural Creator; rather, it characterizes the universe itself as ungrounded continuous creativity, as free activity capable of being channeled toward a revolutionary humanization of mankind.

Against cosmic and historical determinism, Christian-Marxist dialogue has posed anew the question of human self-transcendence. Many Neo-Marxists now affirm the openness of nature and history to the future, and emphasize that human decision and praxis are necessary to the triumph of the communist dialectic. These neo-Marxists pursue a restatement of the doctrines of nature, man, and history in a dialogue that attests that, even while post-Christian speculation slides ever more deeply into neo-pagan atheism, it nonetheless during this descent clings doggedly to ever-fading remnants of the biblical view.

Across a half generation scholarly exchanges have occurred between secular spokesmen who profess to speak on the one hand for a revised Christian view, and on the other for a critically-restated Marxist view. All these disputants consider themselves secular radicals; one side claims to speak christianly, although that description may be debatable. Both sides repudiate a supernatural ontology and insist on a one-layer finite reality.

Marxism, as we know, considers the Christian doctrine of God to be merely an ideological reflection of man's alienation from his fellow man. In the Christian priority for God Marxism sees a preoccupation with individual redemption, a devaluation of the world, and a passivity concerning the status quo. Atheism is basic to Marxist humanism. It therefore scorns the mediating effort of socially-minded theologians to so revise the biblical view that a supernatural deity supports materialistic humanism and this-worldly priorities.

No less than secular neo-Marxists, the more radical "Christian" secularists also abandon any supernatural reality, and along with this forego the divine creation of the finite cosmos and the center of history in Jesus of Nazareth. In short, they surrender any conceptual equivalent of the supernatural God of the Bible. In contrast to Paul Tillich's Ground of all being, Charles Hartshorne's bipolar divinity, and Gustavo Gutierrez's politicizing of revelatory motifs into a revolutionary eschatology, the "Christian" secularists join Marxists in renouncing every effort to modernize a supernatural reality. Instead, they exchange a theistic ontology outright for a finite world as the ultimate horizon of human life and destiny.

In this so-called Christian-Marxist debate neo-Marxist philosophers diverge, as we have said, from the orthodox communist dogma of materialistic and collectivistic determinism which excludes the new in nature and history. To be sure, neo-Marxism coordinates social revolution with the naturalistic insistence on process, temporality, and change, but it does so in an existential context around which its discussion of theism, atheism, and humanism then revolves. It reintroduces a measure of transcendence, and undergirds revolutionary and utopian expectation by linking human freedom with historical openness to an earthly future.

The radically Christian secularist similarly stresses human autonomy and responsibility for restructuring society amid pervasive anxiety and alienation. He rejects a deterministic reduction of humanity to merely physical or biological data, or even to only psychological and sociological data, and reaches beyond human finitude and existential experience to promote an anthropology that involves a realm of transcendence.

While in Paris and other Continental centers Christian secularists and disenchanted Marxists dialogued over transcendence, radically secular humanists progressively penetrated public education, the media, and government in the Anglo-Saxon West. Secular humanism distanced itself from thoroughgoing naturalism by championing social justice and compassion, and by accommodating all religions and all the gods, supernatural or not—although it stripped the entire panoply of objective significance. To religion it assigned a functional role, one that brought subjective integration to the alienated self, and thus supplied beleaguered human experience with a unifying perspective. According to secular humanism, religion tells the "truth" insofar as it integrates the discordant outlook of the embattled ego, but it lies if it professes to depict the objective nature of reality.

Modern philosophy progressively whittled down the essence of human personhood. The biblical rational-moral self made in God's image gave way to Descartes' doubting ego, and then to Hume's stream of consciousness, until nothing remained but a terminally withered psyche. Conjectural philosophy snared the spiritually arid self in impersonal processes that offered little prospect but mechanical determinism.

Neo-Marxists and radically Christian secularists challenged the ancient doctrine of deterministic recurrence. The neo-Marxist alternative to mechanical determinism combines human creativity with an obscure overriding of cosmic necessity. But the debate over man's cosmic and historical transcendence vis-à-vis an all-encompassing determinism reflects a much deeper disorder. The disavowal of theism invited the decline of both idealism and humanism to unqualified naturalism. Neither the projection of an altruistic society nor the projection of a revolutionary utopia can long outrun a purposeless cosmos and history.

No doubt mankind has a melancholic sense of meaninglessness, a pervasive experience of alienation, a capacity for self-criticism, a haunting awareness of death. No doubt human aspirations and needs reach beyond the socio-economic. But to explain these elements in terms of an ontology of finitude tapers the discussion of man's transcendence to his being-in-this-world without acknowledging his link to the supernatural. If it does not lead to God, the search for an obscure transcendence beyond the self leads only to despair; self-transcendence—or the self beyond itself—is a self in serious psychiatric trouble.

Augustine's confession of a larger spiritual reality—"Thou hast made us for Thyself, O God, and our hearts are ever restless until they find their rest in Thee"—represents the only supreme wisdom about man's ego. Any lesser position forfeits the only referent that can relativize either cosmic recurrence or human decision. For man and society the loss of biblical theism means the loss also of genuine liberation and humanism. The view of radical Christians and revisionary Marxists who contend that Christian theism is theoretically untenable, and of Marxists who contend that Judeo-Christian ontology deforms the essential nature of human life, can only mislead us; for their view of human existence is not only shallow and incomplete, but also false. Promoting naturalistic boundaries of existence, the Christian and Marxist secularists deny that any conceptual-logical framework extends beyond finite realities; their obscure notions of transcendence lack any nonfinite mode of reality. The self-styled radical Christian abandons those very theistic realities that best illumine the borders of the finite at the very edges where naturalism becomes mystical and ambiguous.

The frayed remnant of anthropological transcendence that secularists affirm is but the death rattle of an expiring theism whose strangulation neo-paganism eagerly anticipates. Since its rupture with biblical revelation, secular Western philosophy has progressively stripped away Christianity's arms and legs and head and heart: namely, its transcendent Creator, its purposive universe, its goal in history, and its unique incarnation of the Logos in Jesus Christ. Not even plastic surgery could restore ontic significance to Karl Barth's transcendent revelation once he deemed public reason irrelevant to revelatory truth. Agreeing with Barth that God remains real only in personal decision, Bultmann capitulated outright to the secular world view. Unimpressed by the theological subtleties of European theologians and metaphysicians, hardcore naturalism unqualifiedly repudiated theistic ontology and insistently made scientism its creed.

Western culture today overwhelms all other cultures; its interpreters promote its reductionist world view around the globe. In consequence, as Lesslie Newbigin says, the scientific world view has become "the operative plausibility structure of our modern world."[8] Demanding that all disciplines submit their truth-claims to its judgment, the scientific world-view relativizes all presuppositions but its own. Its restrictive methodology tolerates neither divine revelation nor miracle, neither design in nature nor purpose in history; it thus guarantees that biblical theism will be rejected as a publicly significant option. At the same time scientism is hospitable to Asian religions that reject a Creator/creation distinction and that encourage the theory that all religions are essentially one.

But there is another, and equally important, side to this reductionist assault. It is that Western culture itself, where this reductionist view first took root, is becoming more impervious to Christian influences than are African and Asian cultures. Post-theistic atheism stands guard against any tatters of transcendence that derive genetically and logically from the Judeo-Christian heritage. Stripped of futurist illusions, the reinvigorated pagan spirit collapses even the anthropological transcendence of Christian-Marxist dialogue into historical cycles and cosmic determinism. It regards the biblical inheritance in its totality as antiquated. Christianity is considered destructive of self-fulfillment; its effort to alter human dispositions is deplored as an inexcusable tampering with natural instincts; its commendation of the survival-rights of the weak is declared misleading; sin is considered an illusion whose admission leads to neurosis; and the call to regeneration is regarded as repressive of man's cultural identity.

Over against Christianity, atheistic materialism deliberately sets forth its genius as definitive of the truly civilized mind and energetically thrusts raw naturalism into the cultural mainstream. Rooted in the rebellious spirit of fallen man, nurtured in the past by Greco-Roman materialist cosmology, reinforced by post-Renaissance humanism, neo-naturalism considers the Protestant Reformation an intellectual catastrophe. Claiming to be Europe's authentic heritage, it disparages classic idealism, medieval trinitarianism, and modern philosophical theism, as suppressants of the genius of naturalism.

Ever since Nietzsche, the pagan motif has captivated ardent literary luminaries, among them Hermann Hesse, Julian Huxley, Aldous Huxley, and D. H. Lawrence. In the twentieth-century, the spirit of paganism first scaled the walls of civilization to gain a foothold here and there; today it is deeply entrenched in the cultural enterprise. Ours is, as Newbigin says, no longer "a secular society. It is a pagan society, and its paganism, having been born out of the rejection of Christianity, is far more resistant to the gospel than the pre-Christian paganism with which cross-cultural missions have been familiar."[9]

Martin Heidegger critiques all Western onto-theology, biblical theism no less than the speculative isms, whose destiny in common is from the outset, he says, the cultural death of God conceived as an object. From their beginnings, he protests, Greek metaphysics and Christian theology misguidedly postulated a supreme existence as the basis of everything else, a foundation deeper than the actually given existence of reality. Heidegger invites theology to say what it can on the basis only of revelation as an irreducible event. Although Heidegger does not intend his philosophy to be deployed theologically, it nonetheless carries preconceptions important for theism. Heidegger's questioning of being and search for a non-objectified reality would seem to reduce deity, as Claude Geffre implies, to "the other party without content in an encounter about which nothing can be said."[10]

In Heidegger's aftermath so-called deconstructionist philosophers, paced by Jacques Derrida, demand the dismantling of the entire Western tradition of philosophy and theology, with its emphasis on objectively existing deity. Setting out anew from the pre-Socratic thinkers, they propose an anti-Logos course, under whose influence, notes Geffre, "the theologians themselves eagerly echo such phrases as 'the end of metaphysics,' 'the death of the god of metaphysics,' 'the end of theism,' and 'the beginning of a post-metaphysical age.'"[11]

Karl Barth's elevation of the actuality of God above the logical law of contradiction is welcomed as an unwitting contribution to the deconstructionist effort.[12] Religious ontology is declared lacking in cognitive basis, is derogated as mere human imagination, in the name of a revolution in consciousness that replaces the Judeo-Christian theological heritage by what Lonnie D. Kleiver calls a polysymbolic fictive religiosity. Nietzsche, Heidegger, and Derrida are prime movers in this effort to deconstruct and then to radically reconstruct the very history of Western thought through a new attitude toward reality and a new methodology. The deconstructionists reject the dominance of culture both by mathematico-scientific thought (with its quantitative-atomic approach to reality) and by the "onto-theo-logical" tradition of Western philosophy and theology (with its personal divine object). Hegel's *Phenomenology of Spirit* accelerated interest in a dialogical activity and a new language system in which reality emerges in conversation. Nietzsche displaced supernatural deity by the will to power, and detached the divine image in man from both reason and will. Derrida seeks not only to banish the "Greco-Christian God," but also any eternal and immutable Logos—any "logocentrism"—that permeates the universe. He seeks release from formal logic and from the desire for verification, and projects an evolving fluid logos and open spectrum of verbal signification. The one sure result is a nihilistic assault on the Judeo-Christian heritage; no longer does the word "god" refer to a singularly unique metaphysical being. Max A. Myers proposes to replace the term "theology" by the term "religious thinking."[13] For Myers god is a cluster of linguistic names and images whose meaning waits to emerge within dialogic activity.[14] In Carl A. Raschke's words: "The deconstruction of god coincides with the end of theology.... Reconstruction is the dance of death upon the tomb of God."[15]

We would misread the self-styled deconstructionist movement if we totally disdain its repudiation of Western metaphysical theology. In view of the almost endless succession of new vogues in theology—the anthropological and postpositivist versions of theology in recent modern thought, the endless medieval theorizing about divine Being, the ready Greco-Roman objectification of conflicting deities—have not many of us believed also that for secular philosophy and theology wintertime was overdue? Raschke pointedly describes the vacuity of the modern outlook when he says that "the idols of the secular marketplace have a tinny ring" and that "the logos of our latter-day '-ologies,' including theology, has become naught but a ritualistic and compulsive defense against... 'the void.'"[16] The increasing entrapment of deity in space-time processes, the ongoing religious reductionism bent on compressing deity until God gives up the ghost, the attempt to derive a metaphysics from an analysis of finitude, are these not some of the many elements of a metaphysical menagerie by which Western intellectual thought has brought itself to an impasse? Surely a critical reexamination of metaphysical theorizing was needed, as well as a challenge also to the objectification of conflicting deities, and a reshaping of religious studies and their theological lifeline. The object of Christian theology is simply not Aristotle's Pure Act, Tillich's Ground of all being, or a score of modern alternatives.

Yet a much bolder concern motivates the deconstructionist movement. It considers all traditional metaphysics spurious, including Christian theology; it espouses not simply the deposition of twentieth-century intellectual history but also the liquidation of theology. Over against historic Christianity it sponsors a defection more radical than the renaissance, a break with orthodoxy that requires the cancellation of biblical theism, and the abandonment of the ontological reference of all theological language. We are told that all that has been said about the transcendent Creator-Redeemer God of the Bible needs to be dismantled as a conjectural misconception.

The element of truth in deconstructionism, that the metaphysical and theological tradition of the West calls for radical critique, is nullified by its intended dethronement of biblical theism along with conjectural philosophy, and its deliberate espousal of an atheistic alternative. Neo-paganism counters the reality of the one God, counters confidence in divine creation, counters the Gospel of divine redemption, and counters the singular incarnation of the Logos in Jesus Christ.

The qualitative leap that deconstructionism champions is a life-or-death matter for theology, one that proposes a sweeping dehistoricizing of biblical faith, one that confuses rather than clarifies a plausible system of reference for theological realities, one that substitutes a creative consciousness for intelligible divine disclosure. In the deconstructionist movement atheism no longer entrenches itself as but one dissenting option among others, but rather as the epistemic center of human experience, the primal referent through which absolute emptiness replaces absolute being. Its public prospectus and agenda are ranged over against both scientific rationalism with its technocratic illusion of utopia and the Judeo-Christian heritage.

Neo-paganism rails against mind grounded in the Logos of God, against reason per se as truth and reality. The logos now becomes only a thought form in the human mind, a product of evolution and experience, whose asserted centrality is viewed not only as a disservice to theology but also to man himself. For some deconstructionists logos is simply "a gathering of meaning in a dialogic event." Raschke writes of the transformation of word as *logos* ("representation") into word as *rhema* ("flow").[17]

Seldom is it so openly stated that this promotion of self-sufficient nature as an all-engulfing process strips history of linear meaning and purpose, sunders human life from fixed goals, and rejects universally shared reason. Neo-naturalism rejects all the professedly altruistic cultural and political models that stem from the so-called Christian heresies of communism and socialism. Rejecting the linear view of history as a sham, the neo-pagan spirit sees in Marxism but a secular version of biblical messianism; it reverts to cyclical history and disowns a climax in the historical process. In the dogmatically formulated views of Jacques Monod[18] and Carl Sagan[19] this mechanistic mood speaks for contemporary academe.

Hard-core naturalists herald the repudiation of God, of a purposive creation, and of eternally fixed moral imperatives as the dawning of millennial freedom. "Nature is replete with its own rhythms," says philosopher Reuben Abel; its "periodicities are neither necessary, unique or eternal." He assures us that it is "adolescent folly" to think that "romantic despair, or nihilism, or radical skepticism" ensue "if there are no purposes in nature other than the ones we introduce; if *Homo sapiens* is merely the end product pro tem of random mutations in certain chemicals" or if human personality cannot be clearly differentiated from the body.[20] Yet Abel does not show why his optimism may not also be the byproduct of chemical mutants.

This mindshift from theism to naturalism does not mean that in the shaping centers of contemporary society biblical theology is now a shattered encrustation. For many it remains the only form in which supernatural metaphysics retains credibility as an intellectual option. The two main lessons of twentieth-century theology are, first, that the concept of a personal God is viable only where God makes himself known in self-revelation, and second, that only where the divine will is scripturally encapsulated does divine revelation fully escape mystical generality and ambiguity. This is not to deny universal revelation; the Bible itself insists that every human being has some knowledge of God and his claim on conscience. But, more clearly than ever, the cognitive conflict today reduces to biblical theism or bald naturalism as the real alternatives; the intermediary options continue to collapse into ever fading compromises. Say what one will about Christianity's loose grip on the secular mainstream, it retains herculean educational and ecclesiastical resources—television, radio, literature, professionally trained missionaries and clergy, and vocationally prominent lay leaders in all arenas of work. In the most powerful nation on our planet fifty million persons claim to be "born again" Christians and many have emerged from cultural isolation to remount a public and social witness.

But these advances largely bypass a challenge to the intellectual crisis. The electronic church in America, mass evangelistic crusades, and much pulpit oratory are concerned to challenge the will of contemporary man more than to confront the mind of modernity. Even evangelical colleges respond tardily to the need for competent exposition of the Christian world-life view, and some are becoming so concessive that critics consider them counterproductive in advancing Christian core-beliefs.[21] No great evangelical metropolitan university has emerged to engage secular academe in a cognitive exchange that bristles with intellectual drama.

Yet even within mainstream philosophical circles one discovers a new regard for theistic belief. The Society of Christian Philosophers has enlisted a surprising number of members and its *Faith and Philosophy* journal has won an impressive circulation among professional philosophers. Competent evangelicals hold key philosophy posts on numerous mainline campuses; one of them, Alvin Plantinga, has been invited to give the prestigious Gifford Lectures. Evangelical seminaries are burgeoning with students, evangelical churches are growing, hundreds of their young scholars have earned doctorates from leading universities in biblically-related fields, evangelical divinity professors are returning to maintream professional societies, and more and more are contributing quality books in theological studies.

But lest one fall into grand visions of evangelical awakening it is well to catch one's breath in the secular city. The disconcerting fact, as Lesslie Newbigin writes, is that wherever Western culture now penetrates in the name of modernity, it dissolves faith in the supernatural and in the inherited religious beliefs, and not least of all, in Christian affirmation.[22] Rejoice though we may over Christian resurgence in mainland China despite the Cultural Revolution, or in Third World spiritual growth in South Korea, Kenya and elsewhere, the hard fact remains that over half the Asian population lives under the control of atheistic communism and that no movement in the twentieth century has reflected greater numerical growth than has atheism. In Europe, both on the Continent and in Britain, church attendance is pathetically low. Multitudes remain unreached by evangelical literature even in India, the second most populous nation on our planet and the home of the most English-language literates outside the Anglo-Saxon West.

Anti-theistic humanists hold a driving initiative even in Western culture. Newbigin is speaking not of the Communist world but of Western society when he states that "the most obvious fact that distinguishes our culture from all that have preceded it is that it is—in its public philosophy—atheist."[23]

Merely to gloat over culture-pervasive anxiety, its boredom and loss of meaning, would constitute an unworthy intellectual cop-out. If we aim to win only the psychologically depressed, the suicidal fringe of a neo-pagan society, then Christianity will erase the tough-minded intellectual rebels from its prospect list and grant them cognitive immunity from Christian truth-claims. We dare not imply that Christianity has nothing to say to the unyielding naturalistic ego, and that we can only stand by to await its sure descent into the abyss of meaninglessness.

The fact is, that Christianity says something powerful not only at emotional frontiers, but also and especially at the cognitive zenith of contemporary naturalism. It is quite willing to hear out "the other side," to allow the atheist and relativist plead their cause, and to note how they strain to accommodate and even to promote certain imperatives as inviolable. It is Sidney Hook and Paul Kurtz and others of their intellectual stance to whom the claim of supernatural revelation is to be confidently addressed. It is the humanist in his unsteady humanism, the naturalist in his unjustifiable naturalism, whom we must engage. We must do so, moreover, not simply as crusaders for evangelistic decision, appropriate as that may be in its time and place, but in confrontation of both mindset and willset. We must dispute the axioms of neo-pagan thought, unmask a disposition under no absolute constraint to oppose eternal truth and a fixed good, and exhibit the self-legislated limits within which scientific empiricism lays claim to all truth and reality. We remind a scientific society that modern science owes its very life not to the Greek philosophers or to Chinese, Indian, and Egyptian sages, despite their noteworthy achievements in mathematics. Although self-imposed methodological limits constrain scientists to screen out supernatural reality and purpose, neither the interpretation of nature nor scientific necessity requires suspending them on empirical tolerances. We offer the pagan mind a critique of its illogic, of its incoherence and instability. We offer also a superior alternative, namely, the revelation of the personal Creator of a purposeful universe, and the incarnate Christ manifest in Jesus of Nazareth who stands tallest in the annals of humanity. We affirm this not merely as a matter of heroic courage, but confident that we are on the side of reason, that theistic claims stand the test of publicly shared criteria, and that the Lord battles with us and for us.

The Christian world and life view is staggeringly comprehensive; its grand exposition embraces the whole of existence and life. The emerging naturalism of the West surrendered it stage by stage, unaware that its own quest for human meaning and worth rested upon borrowed premises. Christian theism deserves better from its friends than from its foes. In contemporary society it is the evangelical community that often obscures the comprehensive and cohesive nature of the biblical view. Our colleges must recover the unifying character and explanatory power of revelatory theism. A sociology course that allows the "is" to determine the "ought," a psychology course that merely sprinkles a few Scripture verses atop a secular theory of the self, a science course that views the creation account as poetic myth, soon amputates all the vital parts until the whole is ready for cremation.

In view of mounting financial pressures that threaten the effective survival of many colleges and universities, the fulfillment by the evangelical colleges of their distinctive educational mission becomes a major concern. This is all the more the case as Christian colleges seek to emulate the secular universities as evidence of professional maturity. There are no doubt some aspects of secular learning that faith-affirming institutions may well aspire to duplicate, and other aspects they had best avoid. A highly respected evangelical dean, Dr. Walter Kaiser, asks whether the time may not have come for the formation of an Evangelical Council for Academic Accountability which would function in educational matters much as the Evangelical Council for Financial Accountability functions in respect to promotional and fundraising practices. Such an agency would ideally be independent of the Christian College Coalition and Christian College Consortium. It might be coordinated with the Commission on Higher Education of the National Association of Evangelicals. It would require an annual audit of academic fulfillment or nonfulfillment of publicly announced institutional principles and objectives, and stipulate the availability to the constituency of relevant records.

There is no good reason why the elaboration of Christian world and life postulates should be left to a cadre of gifted evangelical scholars in secular universities. The publications by Christian scholars in the secular world should be looked upon as a welcome stimulus to the entire evangelical academic community, prodding it to a cooperative and corporate confrontation of secular modernity and modern consciousness. We need to wrestle the emerging neopagan agenda as a doomsday decision.

The worst affliction of the modern age is not AIDS, epidemic as it may be; atheism is, for it makes spiritual death unavoidable in this life and the next. For all that, AIDS is a plague that has arisen in a particular pagan era; its almost universal menace is a concomitant of a certain view of human life and its priorities.

The mindset of modernity is but a transitory phenomenon. But it will exploit the illusion of permanence if we do not effectively exhibit its weaknesses and, more importantly, exhibit the superiority of the theistic view. Modernity is but an agonizing moment in the history of civilizations; only a view that has eternal validity can hope to be forever contemporary. The transitional mindset is not worthy of one's soul. It is scientism—not science, or orderly knowledge of the natural world—that disqualifies secular consciousness; it is rationalization—not philosophy, or love of wisdom—that discredits secular consciousness; it is modern mythology—not theology, or the truth of God—that distorts secular consciousness. As the deconstruction of Western metaphysics gains momentum, it should be clear again that the enduring foundations of theology, philosophy and science rest upon the biblical heritage. The loss of that biblical heritage means the loss of one's soul, the loss of a stable society, and the loss of an intelligible universe as well. The intellectual suppression of God in his revelation has precipitated the bankruptcy of a civilization that turned its back on heaven only to make its bed in hell.

Notes

1. This essay first appeared in *CSR* 17.4 (June 1988): 474-88. It is a version of the banquet address given during the Institute for Advanced Christian Studies and the Institute for the Study of American Evangelicals in June 1987.
2. Quoted by Ingo Hermann, "Total Humanism," in Johannes B. Metz, ed., *Is God Dead? Concilium*, Vol. 16 (New York: Paulist Press, 1966), 166.
3. Quoted by Richard Shaull in Carl Oglesby and Shaull, *Containment and Change* (New York: Macmillan, 1969), 214.
4. *Main Currents in Modern Political Thought* (New York: Holt, Rinehart and Winston, 1965), 627.
5. Review of Willis B. Glover, *Biblical Origins of Modern Secular Culture: An Essay in the Interpretation of Western History*, in the *Journal of the American Academy of Religion*, 54.2 (Summer, 1986): 375.
6. *Post-Theistic Thinking: The Marxist-Christian Dialogue in Radical Perspective* (Philadelphia: Temple University Press, 1975), 317.
7. *In the Twilight of Western Thought* (Nutley, N.J.: Craig Press, 1965), 175.
8. *Foolishness to the Greeks: The Gospel and Western Culture* (Grand Rapids, Mich.: Eerdmans, 1986), 14.
9. Ibid., 20.
10. *A New Age in Theology* (New York: Paulist Press, 1974), 60.
11. Ibid., 51.
12. Cf. Robert P. Scharlemann, "The Being of God When God Is Not Being God," in Thomas J. Altizer, et. al., *Deconstruction and Theology* (New York: Crossroad, 1982), 80.
13. "Toward What Is Religious Thinking Underway?" in *Deconstruction and Theology*, 109n.
14. Ibid., 140 ff.
15. "The Deconstruction of God," in *Deconstruction and Theology*, 30, 28.
16. Ibid., 3.
17. In *Deconstruction and Theology*, 109n.
18. *Chance and Necessity* (New York: Random House, 1972).
19. *Cosmos* (New York: Ballantine, 1985).
20. *Man Is the Measure* (New York: Free Press, 1976), 272 ff.
21. Cf. James D. Hunter, *Evangelicalism. The Coming Generation* (Chicago: University of Chicago Press, 1987).
22. "Can the West Be Converted?" *International Bulletin of Missionary Research*, 11.1 (Jan. 1987): 2.
23. *Foolishness to the Greeks*, 65.

2 Christian Thinking and the Rise of the American University (1979)

MARK A. NOLL

As the first president of Stanford University, David Starr Jordan would play a leading role in American higher education during the first years of the twentieth century.[1] Jordan's career, however, began well before higher education assumed its modern form. When he went to the west coast in 1891, with the heady prospect of spending millions of Leland Stanford's dollars in creating a modern university, he carried with him the memory of what college used to be. Two decades earlier, Jordan had begun his career at Lombard College in Galesburg, Illinois, a small institution organized by churchmen for the purpose of outfitting upright American citizens. The nature of the revolution in higher education which Jordan witnessed in his lifetime is suggested by a partial listing of the responsibilities of his first job. In his one year at Lombard, Jordan taught six different courses in natural science, as well as political economy, Christian evidences, Spanish, German, and literature – and he filled up spare moments in the spring by pitching for the college baseball team.[2]

The contrast between Jordan's experience at Lombard and the later shape of higher education in the United States can be illustrated further by quoting from a book on the rise of professional philosophy at Harvard from 1860 to 1930. The author of this study, Bruce Kuklick, notes the sharp distinction between the broadly human concerns of Harvard's first great modern philosophers, William James and Josiah Royce, and the much narrower interests of Harvard philosophers in 1920s. During this latter period, in Kuklick's words, "the order of the day was technical specialized research for technically competent audiences in technical journals, with popularization in all areas of specialization frequently relegated to hacks, incompetents, and has-beens."[3]

This shift from broad and eclectic academic concerns to narrowly specialized ones is, however, only a symptom of the revolution in American higher education taking place between the end of the Civil War and the start of World War I. The revolution is of first importance for Christians today since before it occurred higher education in the United States was securely, if not too competently, Christian; while afterwards university life has been persistently secular. To set the education revolution in the context of economic and intellectual change, as this essay seeks to do, provides an instructive example to those who are concerned about Christian education in the last third of the twentieth century. In order to describe the revolution and its importance for Christians, we will first examine the old-style college, then look at the revolutionary changes which ushered in the new university, and finally offer an explanation for the way in which developmental science and economic Darwinism combined with Christian inflexibility to secularize higher education in American.

Intellectual life in America's colleges before 1870 bears little resemblance to what we know today. The curriculum of the old college consisted of a little mathematics; a great deal of praise for empirical science with, however, only meager opportunities to actually carry out experiments; much drill in the classics; and an exposure to systematic arguments for morality, civic virtue, and the existence of God. Modern languages and literature had no place in the curriculum, and history as a discipline was just beginning to be recognized.[4] Instruction proceeded by recitation. The professor, acting more as scorekeeper than teacher, called upon the students to translate, parse, recapitulate, or summarize.[5] Close discipline, extending well beyond the classroom, was the rule. Teachers were regarded as keepers of the peace. At Harvard in 1827 a financial crisis forced the college to increase teaching loads, consolidate positions, and also extend the parietal responsibilities of the faculty to nightly bed checks of the undergraduates.[6] Not surprisingly, the tedium of the classroom, the rigor of extracurricular discipline, and the natural feistiness of late adolescence led to student unrest. One of the less destructive ways in which students protested their lot was to disrupt the morning devotional at Princeton by herding a compliant cow into the chapel. Student unrest often led to violence as well, including once or twice the murder of professors who had fallen from favor.[7]

Some of the student exuberance noted in the frequent disturbances may have reflected an unconscious awareness of the irrelevance of collegiate instruction. Throughout the nineteenth century a bachelor's degree in the liberal arts remained more an ornament of the upper middle class than a doorway to intellectual growth or economic success. It was not necessary to study the liberal arts before taking up a career in medicine or law, and only some of the country's new seminaries required ministerial candidates to stand a regular four-year undergraduate curriculum. The country's best engineers came not from the liberal arts colleges but from the military academy at West Point.[8]

Nor were the college faculty members the intellectual elite of the country. The faculty at the nation's oldest and most prestigious college, Harvard, was not even the dominant intellectual force in Boston. Henry Adams, reflecting on the Harvard faculty in the years surrounding the Civil War, wrote that "no one took Harvard College seriously."[9] One of the reasons may have been the college's casual regard for scholarship, an attitude seen, for example, when the same Henry Adams was in 1870 appointed professor of medieval history, a subject about which he professed himself "utterly and grossly ignorant."[10]

By 1870 it was clear as well that the old college was not keeping pace with the intellectual needs of the country. In that year the nation's colleges enrolled about 52,000 out of a general population of 40 million (the equivalent of 300,000 students in our present population). And the rate of growth in numbers of college students was falling behind the rate of growth in the country as a whole.[11]

For all of its weaknesses, however, the old-style American college had one important advantage to its credit: with very rare exceptions, it was founded and operated as an avowedly Christian institution. In the great westward expansion of the country before the Civil War, Protestant denominations excelled one another in founding educational institutions.[12] Many of these schools were founded by the efforts of a single clergyman. Most suffered from a surplus of competition and a deficit in financing. But all sought to answer the Protestant need for a literate laity and a learned clergy and the democratic American need for upstanding citizens.

In 1821 Harvard was the largest college in the country with 286 students and 16 faculty. By 1860 it had been joined by Yale and Dartmouth as the largest colleges, numbering 300-400 students and 15-25 faculty.[13] These schools and the many other smaller colleges led a precarious existence, but they did know why they existed. The founders of colleges, and the parents who sent their sons, saw them as places of "intellectual stability and order in fluid society."[14] Edward Everett, president of Harvard, could speak in 1846 of the three purposes for colleges—to acquire knowledge, to train the mind, to prepare good citizens. He went on to say that of these the third was far and away most important.[15] Colleges before the Civil War offered one of the ways for exuberant American society to retain a measure of order and cohesion.

The capstone of the college experience in those days was a year-long course, often taught by the college president, in a subject called "Moral Philosophy" or sometimes "Mental Science."[16] It was a course with vast horizons, including everything having to do with human beings and their social relationships (the subjects studied under this rubric would later become the separate disciplines of psychology, philosophy, religion, political science, sociology, anthropology, economics, and jurisprudence). The course almost always included an investigation of epistemology in general and the epistemological foundations of Christianity in particular. The purpose of the course was to provide final Christian integration for the college career and final exhortations concerning the kind of citizenship good Christians should practice.

In view of what would happen to college education later in the nineteenth century, it is worth pausing to sketch the intentions and methods of Moral Philosophy in some detail. From a modern Christian perspective, the instruction in Moral Philosophy had much to commend. It represented an effort to perceive all bits of knowledge as parts of a comprehensive whole, and to do so within a Christian framework. It was, in modern jargon, a course seeking to integrate faith and learning. Moral Philosophy provided college seniors with a respectable defense of God's existence and the moral law. It offered comprehensive exhortations to live morally in society, to support religion, to put public good above selfish interests, and to work for the coming of God's kingdom in America.

When we look more carefully at American Moral Philosophy, however, some of its luster fades. American Moral Philosophy had grown out of an effort in the late eighteenth century to combat philosophical skepticism and social chaos.[17] Its earliest proponent had been the transplanted Scotsman, John Witherspoon of Princeton, but it was also promoted before 1800 by President Timothy Dwight of Yale and President David Tappan at Harvard. It was securely grounded on a philosophical perspective, Scottish Common Sense Realism, which argued that intuition—universal common sense—was a valid scientific method to prove the reality of the external world and the reliability of Christian morality.

Moral philosophy was useful in holding back atheistic skepticism, promoting democratic republicanism, and encouraging social morality. It nonetheless had at least four deficiencies which made it singularly ill-equipped to meet the social and intellectual crises of the later nineteenth century. First, the Christianity of Moral Philosophy was reductionistic. Textbooks in Mental Science by the Calvinistic Presbyterians Archibald Alexander and James McCosh, the Arminian revivalist Charles Finney, and the Harvard Unitarians James Walker and Andrew Preston Peabody shared similar commitments —to intuition as a defense of morality, to science as the royal road to truth, and to logical arguments as proof for the existence of God. Academics of all Christian varieties, furthermore, often left the impression that their ultimate concern was not so much training in the moral law for its own sake as the preservation of established order in American society.

Second, the ethics of Moral Philosophy was individualistic. Moral Philosophy could inspire collegiate and seminarians to organize individuals in the battles against slavery and drink, but it saw with less clarity that evil could be a property of institutions as well as persons. The ethics of Moral Philosophy called for the recapture of the nearly mythical stability of the Anglo-American past, or urged its adherents to bring in the millennium. But in neither case did it look for more than personal exertion nor encourage an examination of the social and economic structures of American life.

Third, Moral Philosophy was captive to the static categories of Baconian science.[18] It was wholeheartedly committed to science, but its science was conceived in narrowly inductivist terms. "Facts" were unchanging elements of nature, perceived reliably by unbiased sense experience, organized inductively into generalizations, and summarized as natural laws. To suggest that the mind of the scientist predisposed him to see certain things and not others in the facts, or to contend that the construction of scientific laws required hypothetical or unverifiable steps, were ideas scored as speculative, romantic, idealistic, and false.

Finally, the science of Moral Philosophy was also determinedly "doxological."[19] That is, America's leading academicians before the Civil War were convinced, before their investigations even began, that the results of science would confirm traditional Protestant ideas of God, the relationship between God and the world, and the relationship between God and humankind. In particular, they were convinced that proper science would confirm the biblical record of the creation, which the moral philosophers understood in terms of the framework provided by their Baconian conception of truth.

This, then, was the old-time college: intellectually unexciting, small and poorly financed, founded for a combination of Christian and civic purposes, committed to producing good citizens, and wrapping it all together with a comprehensive integration of faith of learning. Merely to list the extensive changes taking place in American higher education from the end of the Civil War to World War I is to chronicle the collapse of the old American college. It is to note the breakdown of Christian learning, the breakdown of integrated learning (among disciplines as well as between religious faith and the intellect), and the breakdown of the old science as the vehicle for learning. The new movements in higher education were so numerous and so profoundly at odds with educational practice before the Civil War that it is difficult to present them in a logical order. It will be necessary, therefore, to describe the educational upheaval in a somewhat disjointed fashion before, at the end, trying to make some sense of it all.

The beginning of the revolution in higher education can be dated from 1869, when the innovative Charles Eliot became president of Harvard, or from 1876, when The Johns Hopkins University was founded with the express intent of providing specialized, graduate instruction on the model of the German seminar.[20] Certainly the years from 1865 to 1900 constituted a time of transition for American education. Beyond Harvard and Johns Hopkins, Cornell University was founded in 1868 under the presidency of Andrew D. White; during the 1880s the University of Chicago, Stanford University, and Clark University came into existence; and in the 1890s Yale, Princeton, and Columbia were all reorganized into universities by the addition of graduate and professional schools. And by the turn of the century, state universities, as in Michigan and Wisconsin, had begun to be recognized as major centers of learning.

It is of the greatest significance that the money for this academic explosion did not come from the churches, which had hitherto been the financial bellwether for American education. Rather, the new universities were thriving on new sources of funds. The federal government, for one, had begun to provide land and money for the practical arts through the Morrill Act of 1862. Much more important, at this stage, were the large sums coming from the new industrialists, from those who had best exploited the postwar expansion of the American economy. Before citing names and numbers, it would be helpful to establish a standard of comparison from the old time college. Harvard enjoyed a $10,000 annual grant from the Massachusetts legislature for the ten years following 1814 and was the envy of struggling academicians everywhere. When Princeton a decade later audaciously sought $100,000 from its alumni, it created a sensation.[21]

The sums contributed to establish the new universities, however, put previous philanthropy in the shade. Ezra Cornell, who made his money in telegraph construction and banking, donated $500,000 to the school which bears his name and managed a Morrill grant for $2,500,000 more. Johns Hopkins, a banker and investor in the Baltimore & Ohio Railroad, left $3,500,000 to the university and an equal sum to establish a teaching hospital. Cornelius Vanderbilt (steamships and railroads) gave an initial gift of $1,000,000 to establish a Harvard of the South and later followed this up with other generous bequests. Leland Stanford, who parlayed political office into control of the Central and Southern Pacific Railroads, left $20,000,000 to establish a university in honor of his son. James Duke, of the American Tobacco Company, assigned the largest part of the income from a

$100,000,000 trust fund to the university that bears his name. And John D. Rockefeller's gifts to establish a great Baptist university in Chicago eventually totaled $45,000,000.[22] From a different, but still dizzying perspective, private donors in the twenty years from 1878 to 1898 gave $140,000,000 to American colleges and universities. What this could do for an individual institution can be seen from the jump in Harvard's permanent endowment from $2,500,000 in 1869 to $20,000,000 in 1909.[23]

The number of students attending colleges and universities grew almost as rapidly as the number of dollars going into higher education. While the country's population nearly doubled (forty million to seventy-six million) from 1870 to 1900, the number of college students leaped nearly fivefold (from 52,000 to 238,000). In 1870, 1.7% of the 18-21-year-old population was in college. By 1930, the figure had reached 12.4%.[24] To again cite the example of Harvard, it grew from a thousand students in 1869 to four thousand in 1909; during the same period its faculty grew even more rapidly, from sixty to six hundred.[25] The surge in attendance was fueled by the growth in public high schools, by growing the number of women seeking higher education, and, very likely, by an increasing desire for higher education by individuals outside of the traditional Anglo-Saxon Protestant sources.

Almost unnoticed in the great influx of dollars and students was the demise of overt Christian characteristics that had marked higher education to this time. Neither the new donors not the new breed of administrators were overly concerned about the orthodoxy of their faculty. Visible signs of this change abounded. At Harvard compulsory chapel ceased in 1886. The opening ceremonies at Johns Hopkins in 1876 contained no prayer, but did feature an address by British evolutionary theorist Thomas Huxley.[26] As money from businessmen increased, so did their concern that boards of trustees and college administrators function in a businesslike way. Thus it was that businessmen replaced clergymen as trustees and laymen replaced ministers as college presidents.[27] In 1839, fifty-one of the fifty-four presidents of American's largest colleges were clergymen (forty of these being Presbyterians or Congregationalists).[28] By the end of the century the number was greatly reduced. Princeton, always conservative, waited until 1902 to name its first lay president, Woodrow Wilson.

One further bit of information shows how the standards of businessmen donors helped to effect the external secularization of the American college. When the Carnegie Foundation (originator of TIAA/CREF) was established in the early twentieth century to provide retirement income for college professors, its programs were originally restricted to nonsectarian colleges. Several colleges, wavering in their allegiance to traditional Christian forms, rapidly cut themselves loose at this inducement.[29]

Another facet of the revolution in higher education was the growing appeal of the German model for academic life.[30] Anglo-American higher education had traditionally stressed character as much as intellectual stimulation; it had paid greater heed to transmitting the old than to experimenting with the new; and it had favored discipline over creativity and novelty. In the last half of the nineteenth century, however, the German emphasis on specialized and advanced scholarship became increasingly attractive.

Germany had early appealed to Americans as an academic mecca, with nearly three hundred American scholars in German universities during the 1850s. Study in a German university had also been one of the convenient ways to avoid the draft during the Civil War. In the 1900 edition of *Who's Who*, three hundred of the seven hundred academics listed had studied in Germany. What appealed most to these scholars was the German emphasis on freedom: freedom for the faculty to teach subjects of their own choice and to pursue sophisticated research. It is at least possible that the practice of laissez-faire in American economic life during this period was promoted by infatuation with the laissez-faire of German academic life.

Under the influence of this German model, the new university took shape rapidly. In the first instance promoters of the new university stressed its freedom from sectarian and paternal control. It became increasingly common to regard the faculty as the essence of the university. Advanced study became the jewel in the university's crown. Undergraduate education also moved into a new era. The elective system, popularized by Eliot at Harvard, fostered competition among the new disciplines and stimulated a thirst for relevance which still remains unslaked a century later. Science, particularly laboratory science, became an increasingly important part of undergraduate work, as did instruction in modern languages and literature. The vocational and scientific requirements of the wider community also received more attention in the colleges. Cornell was one of the first of the new universities to offer agricultural and vocational courses in its regular academic curriculum. John D. Rockefeller was won over to a belief in the value of American universities at least in part because of practical improvements made at Yale in the refining of oil.[31] The need to serve more, and more specialized, scholars led to a rapid growth in libraries as well. At Harvard the library grew from 20,000 volumes in 1820 to 900,000 in 1900.[32] Earlier in the century debating societies often possessed more extensive libraries that their colleges, but this would no longer be the case. Taken as a whole, the German ideal promoted the beginning of professionalization in American higher education.

If the German example was the source of the university's professionalization, the new science was the source of its pride. This new science was popularly, if inaccurately, associated with the name of Charles Darwin, whose *Origin of Species by Means of Natural Selection* had been published in 1859.[33] Darwinism, which one recent scholar has neatly summarized as "a scientifically credible theory of random and purposeless change,"[34] stood for an intellectual perspective which went well beyond questions in biology. It is in fact possible to see three levels of Darwinism: a scientific method, a scientific result, and a philosophical system. At each level, Darwinism both undercut the antebellum scientific world of American higher education and offered the glowing prospect of unprecedented scientific progress.

Superficially considered, the scientific method of Darwinism closely resembled the science championed by American moral philosophers before the Civil War. Both made much of empirical observation, and both generalized from the results of empirical observation, though the newer science did question the earlier confidence in induction.

At a deeper level the doxological character of the old science was being replaced by the agnostic cast of the new. Epistemological realism was giving way to idealism. Baconian inductivism was yielding to a science in which imaginative hypotheses played a larger role. Practitioners of the new science criticized advocates of the old for prejudging questions of scientific fact, for forcing the bedrock data of science into the comfortable but untimely unscientific molds of the past. In Darwin, as they saw it, they possessed the shining example of a true scientist who dared to follow the data wherever they led.

The scientific results of Darwinism were no less offensive to the old scientists. Darwin's principle of "natural selection" contradicted all that Moral Philosophy had sought to prove over the previous century. Random change did not fit into a world where the moral law within, and the laws of nature without, were alike considered images of the law of God. The harmony among nature, man, and God was disrupted if nature operated according to no laws but its own. Darwinists shrugged at these charges, and reminded the old scientists of their commitment to the results of sense experience. We must follow our observations, the Darwinists said, even if they lead us to a universe where the Bible's cosmology (at least as traditionally understood) passes into myth.

It was as a philosophy of life, however, that Darwinism caused the moral philosophers greatest pain. In the *Systematic Philosophy* (1862-1893) of Herbert Spencer, Darwinism appeared as a comprehensive, non-Christian explanation for all of life. According to Spencer, mankind was progressing from simpler to more complex forms, from worse to better modes of existence, from primitive to sophisticated states. One grasped best the nature of things not by delving into divine revelation but by understanding what it meant for the fit to survive.

To many academicians, from old colleges and new universities alike, the three levels of Darwinism seemed bound together inextricably. And virtually all academicians in the new universities accepted one or more of Darwinism's meanings. While Darwinists gloried in the breathtaking discoveries opened up through the new scientific perspective, practitioners of the old science reeled in confusion. It was bad enough that God and the moral law were in danger from Spencer's Social Darwinism. Even worse was the fact that this non-Christian worldview claimed to rest on the kind of scientific explanation that they themselves had championed for so long. Science, once the handmaiden of morality, seemed now to have become an ally of agnosticism. As science was rapidly coming to be understood, it seemed to have passed from defender of the faith to its prosecutor.

As Moral Philosophy collapsed, each of the many disciplines it had gathered in its skirts went its own way—psychology, epistemology, political science, sociology, anthropology, and others. The breakup of Moral Philosophy's integrating force, coming as it did when the appeal of German higher education was reaching its peak, led to a rapid growth of specialization in the new university. Almost overnight the Ph.D. became a new symbol of prestige and the ticket to advancement in university life. Yale had granted the first American doctorate in 1861; in 1880 American universities gave 54 Ph.D.s, and the flow would increase.[35] The Johns Hopkins graduate school rapidly became the model for specialized research at other American universities.

Not surprisingly the years between the Civil War and World War I saw the organization of professional societies to provide outlets for specialized research and extra-institutional stimulation for specialized scholars. Of the forty-two professional societies currently members of the American Council of Learned Societies, twenty of them were founded between 1869 and 1912, including such prominent bodies as the Modern Language Association, the American Historical Associations, and the Society for Biblical Literature. Professional journals proliferated. And in the last third of the century it also became the practice for medical and law schools to require candidates to hold a B.A. degree.

A whole new idea of the faculty member was also coming into existence.[36] The new professional enjoyed certifiable training, and he coveted standing in an academic specialty. He, and gradually she as well, normally went through a probation period as teacher-researcher-scholar. He sought employment at institutions offering specialized instruction. He was committed to publishing the results of his research for scholars outside his own institution. And his scholarly functions and professional reputation became at least as important as his teaching responsibilities or his institutional loyalty. Befitting this new status, faculty members were spared some of the responsibilities they had traditionally exercised. Harvard professors, for example, were relieved of their disciplinary duties over the students in 1870.[37]

Given this intense interest in specialization, the broad training appropriate for undergraduates was criticized. One Harvard scholar in the late nineteenth century argued that "the College [i.e., the undergraduate program] ought to be suppressed or moved out into the country where it would not interfere with the proper work of the University."[38] President Eliot at Harvard did try, but without success, to compress the B.A. program into three years in order to make more room for specialization. Not all of this went down easily, however, even at those institutions leading the charge into the modern era. Harvard philosopher George Santayana, for one, looked around at the turn of the century and reflected that the Harvard faculty was like "an anonymous concourse of coral insects, each secreting out one cell, and leaving that fossil legacy to enlarge the earth."[39]

One of the results of increasing specialization was a concomitant growth in competition among faculty members. The key question for hiring and promotion became not so much orthodoxy, or even friendship, as competence. Less frequently did deans ask, "Who is he?" than "What has he done?"[40] Many schools, even in the years of most rapid expansion, were wary of naming too many full professors, preferring to add on less experienced, but cheaper, instructors and assistant professors. These serfs often abandoned their scruples in scrambling over one another up the feudal ladder. And even the attainment of a coveted professorship could not entirely efface the results of the strain. One Harvard historian, after suffering years of uncertainty before being made a professor, committed suicide a brief year after his triumphant appointment. Reported the *Boston Transcript*: "The cause of death was insanity produced by overwork."[41]

The new professor also adopted a different role in the world at large. Old-time college leaders had spoken to society as a whole, but more as moral cheerleaders and defenders of a public faith. The new academicians achieved their recognition as experts, individuals with extraordinary competence in one or another of the esoteric disciplines cultivated by the new university. The public pronouncements of Oliver Wendell Holmes on the law, Thorsten Veblen on economics, or William James and John Dewey on philosophy were not always followed, but they were heard.

This then was the new university that had emerged by the turn of the century. More than just thirty-five years separated it from the old college as it had existed at the close of the Civil War. The new university was professional; it offered technical training in a wide variety of separate fields; it was funded by large gifts from America's industrial giants; it had laid aside the external marks of Christianity; its professors sought to become well known in their fields and to speak expertly to society as a whole; its new science purported to illumine a better way to truth, progress, and perhaps even happiness; and it was offering its wares to an ever growing part of the American population. With a few exceptions, which it will be important to note shortly, the old American college had given way to the new university.

One of the ways to account for this manifold change is to note the relationships among the new science, Social Darwinism, and the new money. It could be argued that the excess capital generated by industrialists after the Civil War arose from a widespread exploitation of new scientific technology. If there had been no Bessemer process, the railroad would not have expanded so rapidly. If there had been no internal combustion engine, less refined petroleum would have been needed. Furthermore, this excess wealth was generated by individuals who had laid aside the constraints of Christian altruism that Moral Philosophy, for which the new capitalists had no time, had sought to inculcate in its graduates. American industrialists, to one degree or another, seemed to have preferred the kind of Social Darwinism popularized by Herbert Spencer. Perhaps it is better to say that some industrialists (like Andrew Carnegie) found in Spencer's categories convenient rationalization for business practices arising from a more primitive human avarice. Industrial capitalists extended their influence to education because they needed more of the practical science and managerial theory coming from the new universities and less of the moralism coming from the colleges. Through the influence of the industrialists, then, clergymen were replaced by hard-headed businessmen on boards of trustees, ministers were replaced as presidents by educators alert to management ideas and the demands of the new science. These new presidents, in turn, focused much more attention on scholarship than on orthodoxy. Furthermore, the new scholarship which these presidents encouraged had been "liberated" from the old orthodoxies of Moral Philosophy. It was frankly naturalistic in science and pragmatic in philosophy. In turn—and this brings the circle full—the new naturalistic science and the new pragmatic philosophy encouraged industrial giantism by providing training and technique to the capitalists while at the same time offering few criticisms of the new industrial wealth. Against this combination of new money, social Darwinism, and naturalistic science, Moral Philosophy stood almost no chance. Its reductionistic Christianity had little guidance to offer industrialists or the new urban masses. Its individualistic ethics could not comprehend the magnitude of new economics and social developments. Its empiricism had been turned against the traditional verities. And its doxological view of science had become an embarrassment as the now popular science destroyed the traditional faith.

The collapse of Moral Philosophy signaled the collapse of an effort to preserve a unified Christian world view in America. From the point of view of the new university, the effort to view knowledge whole was abandoned under the assumption that discrete parts of truth, discovered through empirical science, could stand on their own. The effort to integrate religious faith with learning was abandoned under the assumption that the pursuit of science carried with it no antecedent commitments to a world view. On another level, Scottish Common Sense Realism, which had bonded the old synthesis, lost its hold on the major centers of American learning. Of this sudden departure Perry Miller has written: "It is a curious fact that one of the most radical revolutions in the history of the American mind took place in the two or three decades after the Civil War without exciting appreciable comment: the philosophy and the philosophers of Scottish Realism vanished from the American colleges, leaving not even a rack behind, and were swiftly replaced by expounders of some form of Idealism."[42]

And yet there were a few places where the pursuit of a unified Christian world view continued. A few old-style colleges and more newly founded ones rejected Darwinism, agnostic science, and Spencerian evolution.[43] At Wheaton College, for example, Moral Philosophy was taught by the president into the 1920s and by regular faculty until after World War II.[44] And at Wheaton and other fundamentalistic-evangelical institutions theologians continued to write under the influence of Scottish Common Sense Realism. But in such institutions and such theologies there was a mentality distinctly at odds with that which had prevailed in the old schools before the Civil War. Now the colleges which clung to Scottish Realism and the pursuit of a Christian world view inhabited an intellectual backwater, relatively out of touch with the mainstream of academic philosophy and academic science in the twentieth century. And thus at the very time when Americans needed most to hear how human learning and the Christian faith could coinhere—when academic professionalism was fragmenting the life of the mind, when urbanization and industrialization were helping to make Protestant ethics a dead letter—the Christian colleges did not rise to the challenge. Many of them could not because, giving in to the spirit of the age, they had ceased to be Christian. Others which retained the faith pictured the relationship between modern learning and Christian belief as a confrontation; these headed for cover to preserve the faith. For the dogged preservation of the faith in these latter institutions we must be sincerely thankful. At the same time it is a cause for regret that the Christian world view had been so tightly circumscribed by the reductionistic faith, individualistic ethics, and Baconian science of the early nineteenth century, for these limiting commitments largely foreclosed opportunities to exploit critically the results of modern learning.

Christians today may well wish to take seriously lessons from the revolution in American higher education. We can, from this distance, see how the self-assurance of Christian Moral Philosophy blinded its practitioners to its internal problems. We can also see, however, that Christian thought and some forms of modern learning did in fact contradict each other radically. And we can see how the chagrin and the defeats at the turn of the century have, after the passage of a generation or two, provided the stimulus for a new approach by some American evangelicals to the life of the mind. In the interim, while Anglo-American evangelicals have been recovering from the revolution in higher education, other Protestants without a commitment to Moral Philosophy—Lutherans, Mennonites, and the Dutch Reformed[45]—have shouldered the major burden in gathering fruits of learning for the kingdom of Christ.[46]

Notes

1. This essay first appeared in *CSR* 9.1 (Fall 1979): 3-16.
2. Richard Hofstadter, "The Revolution in Higher Education," in *Paths of American Thought*, eds. Arthur M. Schlesinger, Jr. and Morton White (Boston: Houghton Mifflin, 1970), 284; and "David Starr Jordan," in *Dictionary of American Biography* (New York: Charles Scribner's Sons, 1928ff.) X: 221 (hereafter DAB). The Hofstadter essay has provided many of the examples and has shaped many of the judgments for this paper.
3. Bruce Kuklick, *The Rise of American Philosophy, Cambridge, Massachusetts, 1860-1930* (New Haven: Yale University Press, 1977), 565.
4. Hofstadter, "Revolution in Higher Education," 270.
5. The scorekeeper image is taken from Robert A. McCaughey, "The Transformation of American Academic Life: Harvard University 1821-1892," *Perspectives in American History*, VIII (1974): 259.
6. Ibid., 255-56.
7. On the cow in chapel: Thomas Jefferson Wertenbaker, *Princeton 1746-1896* (Princeton, N.J.: Princeton University Press, 1946), 136. On student violence: Burton J. Bledstein, *The Culture of Professionalism: The Middle Class and the Development of Higher Education in America* (New York: Norton, 1976), 228-34.
8. Hofstadter, "Revolution in Higher Education," 286-87.
9. McCaughey, "The Transformation of Harvard," 263.
10. Ibid., 279.
11. U.S. Bureau of the Census, *Historical Statistics of the United States: Colonial Times to 1957* (Washington: Department of Commerce, 1960), 211.
12. Winthrop S. Hudson, *Religion in America*, 2nd ed. (New York: Charles Scribner's Sons, 1973), 155n, provides a partial list of colleges founded in this period. See also Timothy L. Smith, "Uncommon Schools: Christian Colleges and Social Idealism in Midwestern America, 1820-1950" (published for the author by the Indiana Historical Society, 1978), for a fuller description of the founding of representative Christian colleges.
13. McCaughey, "The Transformation of Harvard," 246-48; Hofstadter, "Revolution in Higher Education," 271.
14. D. H. Meyer (quoting Stow Persons), *The Instructed Conscience: The Shaping of the American National Ethic* (Philadelphia: University of Pennsylvania Press, 1972), 5.
15. Ibid., 65-66.
16. The next several paragraphs draw from D. H. Meyer's excellent study of American Moral Philosophy before the Civil War (see following note).
17. As such, it represented a domestication of the European, particularly British-Scottish, Enlightenment. On this process, see Donald H. Meyer, *The Democratic Enlightenment* (New York: G. P. Putnam's Sons, 1976); and Henry F. May, *The Enlightenment in America* (New York: Oxford University Press, 1976).
18. For an excellent treatment of Baconianism in America, see Theodore Dwight Bozeman, *Protestants in an Age of Science: The Baconian Ideal and Antebellum American Religious Thought* (Chapel Hill: University of North Carolina Press, 1977).
19. See ibid., 71-100.
20. Hofstadter, "Revolution in Higher Education," 273, opts for 1869, or even 1868 with the opening of Cornell University.
21. McCaughey, "The Transformation of Harvard," 246; Wertenbaker, *Princeton*, 217-19. The fund drive at Princeton did fall a couple of thousand dollars short.
22. Hofstadter, "Revolution in Higher Education," p. 275; "Ezra Cornell," DAB, IV: 445-46; "Johns Hopkins," DAB, IX: 214; "Cornelius Vanderbilt," DAB, XIX: 173; "Leland Stanford," DAB, XVII: 504-505; "James Duke," DAB, V: 498; Peter Collier and David Hororwitz, *The Rockefellers: An American Dynasty* (New York: Holt, Rinehart and Winston, 1976), 50.
23. Hofstadter, "Revolution in Higher Education," 275. It is worth nothing that dollars were actually *growing* in value throughout much of this period.
24. Bureau of Census, *Historical Statistics*, 210-11.
25. Hofstadter, "Revolution in Higher Education," 274.
26. "Charles Eliot," DAB, VI: 74; "Daniel Coit Gilman," DAB, VII: 301.
27. Hofstadter, "Revolution in Higher Education," 278.

28. George M. Mardsen, *The Evangelical Mind and the New School Presbyterian Experience* (New Haven: Yale University Press, 1970), 30.
29. Hofstadter, "Revolution in Higher Education," 279.
30. The following two paragraphs draw heavily on ibid., 280-82.
31. Collier and Horowitz, *The Rockefellers*, 39.
32. Hofstadter,"Revolution in Higher Education," 284-85.
33. On the importance of Darwin's ideas for wider intellectual spheres in Britain and the United States, see Gertrude Himmelfarb, *Darwin and the Darwinian Revolution* (New York: Norton, 1978); and Cynthia Eagle Russett, *Darwin in America: The Intellectual Response, 1865-1912* (San Francisco: W. H. Freeman, 1976).
34. Meyer, *Instructed Conscience*, 128.
35. Bureau of Census, *Historical Statistics*, 212.
36. The following characteristics of academic professionalism are taken from McCaughey, "The Transformation of Harvard," 243.
37. Ibid., 298.
38. Ibid., 306.
39. Ibid., 309.
40. Ibid., 245.
41. Ibid., 303.
42. Perry Miller, ed., *American Thought: Civil War to World War I* (New York: Holt, Rinehart and Winston, 1954), ix.
43. On the newer Christian colleges founded at the turn of the century, see Smith, "Uncommon Schools."
44. Cy Hulse, "The Shaping of a Fundamentalist: A Case Study of Charles Blanchard" (unpublished M. A. Thesis: Trinity Evangelical Divinity School, 1977), 82.
45. See, for example, the educational philosophies and histories contained in the report of the Calvin College Curriculum Study Committee, *Christian Liberal Arts Education* (Grand Rapids: Eerdmans, 1970); and in the study papers issued by professors from six Lutheran institutions of higher learning, *Christian Faith and the Liberal Arts*, ed. Harold Dittmanson, et. al. (Minneapolis: Augsburg, 1960).
46. The first draft of this paper was prepared with the support of the Christian College Consortium for its 1977 Summer Faith-Learning Institute. Subsequent drafts enjoyed helpful critiques from the faculty of Seattle Pacific University and the participants in the 1978 history conference at Trinity College.

3 Theory and Praxis (1980)

Nicholas Wolterstorff

> Just as the socialist system which will finally emerge in the Latin American countries will not be a copy of the existing ones, but a creation related to our reality, so the analysis has to be adequate to this reality and develop its own categories and methods. Such new categories and methods are, moreover, not developed in abstraction or in pure objective contemplation, but in the very effort to overcome the present situation and move forward to a new society.[1]

Two fundamental sorts of decisions face every scholar.[2] He must decide which matters to investigate. And on the matters under investigation, he must decide which views to hold. In my small book, *Reason within the Bounds of Religion*, I addressed myself to the bearing of the Christian faith on the latter of these two sorts of issues. Here I address myself to the bearing of the Christian faith on the former, paying particular attention to the pure-versus-praxis-oriented-theory debate.

Deep in the Christian tradition is the conviction that each of us is not to be the center of his own concerns but rather to love and serve God with all his life, and, in similar fashion, to love his neighbor as himself. One might add to these the conviction that each is also to be a responsible steward of the creation within which God has placed us. To love and serve God in all our ways, to love our neighbors as ourselves, and to be responsible stewards of nature—those are clearly proclaimed in the authoritative Scriptures of the Christian community as the fundamental obligations of mankind.

Deep in the Christian tradition is also the conviction that the fundamental attitude of God himself toward humanity is that of love. It would seem then that the goal God sets for human existence is intimately linked to the service, love, and stewardship he asks of us. It would seem that human fulfillment is to be found in what we experience when we love God with our whole life, when we love our neighbor as ourselves, and when we act as responsible stewards of nature. It would seem that in enjoining us to act thus with respect to Himself, neighbor, self, and nature, God is enjoining us to participate in his own cause of human fulfillment—to be his agents in the world. And I judge that the Christian Scriptures do indeed present the situation thus.

Yet there is within the Christian tradition a strange reluctance—even a refusal—thus to link what God sets as human responsibility and what he sets as the goal toward which he is working in history. For example, the Westminster divines would not disagree with what I have said concerning the fundamental character of human responsibility. Yet in the catechism they composed they said that the end of man is to know God and enjoy him forever. Notice, in this formulation, how nature and neighbor have dropped from the picture. The situation is basically no different if we look, for another example, at Aquinas. He too would not disagree with what I have said concerning the structure of human responsibility. Yet the *beatitudo* which he regarded as the end of human existence differs in its essential marks not at all from what the high Calvinists assembled at Westminster meant by knowing and enjoying God.

I have already suggested that the proclamation of the Christian Scriptures concerning God's goal for mankind is different. I shall try to say what, in my judgment, that goal is. Before I do so, however, it should be remarked that it is a goal which has the character of renewal. Our human situation is not such that a loving God would simply try to bring to fuller development all the tendencies already at work in self and society. For many of those tendencies lead to quite the opposite of love of God, self, and neighbor. They lead to deprivation and oppression. Renewal is needed.

To the question, "What is God's goal for human existence, to which human beings are called to contribute?" many of our brothers and sisters in the Third World, and in the oppressed components of the First and Second worlds, would today say "liberation." Liberation is what God's cause in the world is all about, and which you and I should then commit ourselves to. I can well appreciate why they speak thus. And yet I must say that this does not seem to me an adequate answer. For it leaves unanswered the question, "After liberation, then what?"

I suggest that immediately at hand in the Christian Scriptures is a better concept for describing God's goal for human existence. Admittedly it is a concept which has enjoyed only marginal attention in the Christian tradition. But it seems to me a concept well worth taking note of. The concept I have in mind is the concept of peace—in Hebrew, *shalom*, in Greek, *eirenē*.

The goal of human existence is that man should dwell at peace in all his relationships: with God, with himself, with his fellows, with nature, a peace which is not merely the absence of hostility, though certainly it is that, but a peace which at its highest is enjoyment. To dwell in shalom is to enjoy living before God, to enjoy living in nature, to enjoy living with one's fellows, to enjoy life with oneself. A condition of shalom is justice, and a component in justice is liberation from oppression. Never can there be shalom without justice. Yet shalom is more than justice. Justice can be grim. In shalom, there is delight.

It comes as a surprise to us that the prophets, those of all the biblical writers who speak most emphatically and intensely about justice, are also the ones who speak most concretely and explicitly about shalom. Isaiah hears God speaking thus:

> Then justice shall make its home in the wilderness,
> and the righteousness dwell in the grassland;
> when righteousness shall yield peace
> and its fruit be quietness and confidence for ever.
> Then my people shall live in a tranquil country,
> dwelling in peace, in houses full of ease. (Isa. 32:16-18)

And in the best known passage of all, Isaiah describes the anticipated shalom with a multiplicity of images of harmony, harmony among the animals, harmony between man and animal:

> Then a shoot shall grow from the stock of Jesse,
> and a branch shall spring from his roots.
> The spirit of the Lord shall rest upon him,
> a spirit of wisdom and understanding,
> a spirit of counsel and power,
> a spirit of knowledge and the fear of the Lord
> ....
> Then the wolf shall live with the sheep,
> and the leopard lie down with the kid;
> the calf and the young lion shall grow up together,
> and a little child shall lead them;
> the cow and the bear shall be friends,
> and their young shall lie down together.
> The lion shall eat straw like cattle;
> the infant shall play over the hole of the cobra,
> and the young child dance over the viper's nest. (Isa. 11:1-8)

That shoot of which Isaiah spoke is he of whom the angels sang in celebration of his birth: "Glory to God in highest heaven, and on earth his *peace* for men on whom his favor rests" (Luke 2:24). He is the one of whom the priest Zechariah said that he "will guide our feet into the way of *peace*" (Luke 1:79). He is the one of whom Simeon said, "This day, Master, thou givest thy servant his discharge in *peace*; now thy promise is fulfilled" (Luke 2:29). He is the one of whom Peter said that it was by him that God preached "good news of *peace*" to Israel (Acts 10:36). He is the one of whom Paul, speaking as a Jew to the Gentiles, said that "he came and preached *peace* to you who were far off and *peace* to those who were near" (Eph. 2:17). He is in fact Jesus Christ, whom Isaiah called the "prince of *peace*" (Isa. 9:6).

I suggest that if the activities of the scholar are to be justified, that justification must be found ultimately in the contribution of scholarship to the cause of justice-in-shalom. The vocation of the scholar, like the vocation of everyone else, is to serve that end.

The debate which one immediately enters, when considering how the scholar should go about determining the direction of his inquiries, is the debate between the defenders of pure theory and the defenders of praxis-oriented theory. Probably everyone in the contemporary world holds that some praxis-oriented theory is legitimate. The debate, then, is between those who go all the way to hold that only praxis-oriented theory is permissible, and those who, though allowing for the legitimacy of some praxis-oriented theory, are yet persuaded that it is important to have a significant number of scholars engaging in pure theory. (Many of these latter would go on to emphasize what they see as the danger of allowing into the academy those engaged in praxis-oriented theory.)

But what is pure theory? And what, correspondingly, is praxis-oriented theory? In his now well-known Inaugural Address at Frankfurt (1964), Jürgen Habermas remarked that:

> The word "theory" has religious origins. The *theoros* was the representative sent by Greek cities to public celebrations. Through *theoria*, that is through looking on, he abandoned himself to the sacred events. In philosophical language, *theoria* was transferred to contemplation of the cosmos. In this form, theory already presupposed the demarcation between Being and time that is the foundation of ontology. This separation is first found in the poem of Parmenides and returns in Plato's *Timaeus*. It reserves to *logos* a realm of being purged of inconstancy and uncertainty and leaves to *doxa* the realm of the mutable and perishable. When the philosopher views the immortal order, he cannot help bringing himself into accord with the proportions of the cosmos and reproducing them internally. He manifests these proportions, which he sees in the motions of nature and the harmonic series of music, within himself; he forms himself through mimesis. Through the soul's likening itself to the motion of the cosmos, theory enters the conduct of life.[3]

To the best of my knowledge, it was among the Pythagoreans that the conviction first emerged that the attainment of theoretical knowledge inherently has the effect of improving the character of the theorizer, and that, accordingly, this is justification for engaging in the pursuit of such knowledge. We may accordingly give the title of Pythagorean justification to the justification of theoretical inquiry by reference to the self-improvement that inherently results from gaining theoretical knowledge.[4]

A variant of the Pythagorean justification has its proponents yet today. Few persons any longer hold that the business of the theorizer is to contemplate the eternal order of the cosmos, thereby to have his soul ordered in imitation of the order contemplated. One does hear it said, though, that scholarship, by virtue of its methodology if not its results, frees its practitioners from prejudice, makes them more tolerant human beings, and gives them a "scientific" cast of mind. And quite clearly this can be regarded as a variant on the Pythagorean justification. According to this variant, it matters not at all whether any theoretical knowledge is actually attained. What counts is the pursuit. The process, not the product, produces self-improvement—inherently so.

In his Inaugural Address, Habermas suggests strongly that only the Pythagorean justification for theoretical inquiry is to be found in the pre-modern history of the West. And since he himself holds that learning is to be justified solely by the utility of its results for achieving various ends other than states of knowledge, he uses his telling of the history to suggest that his own position is faithful to the grand tradition of the West, whereas those who defend "pure theory" have departed from it. In my judgment this is a highly selective reading of the history. There is another tradition in the West, equally massive, which holds that some learning at least is justified by the inherent worth of the cognitive states which result and not merely by the worth of the effects flowing from them. To cite but two examples, this was the view of Augustine and of Thomas Aquinas. Let me call it, for the sake of convenience, the Aquinian justification. This is the justification of theoretical inquiry by reference to the inherent worth of the cognitive states achieved.

It is important to note that a person who holds that certain cognitive states of consciousness are of inherent worth need not hold that all such states are of equal worth. Some may be of more value than others. Clearly that was also the view of Augustine and Aquinas. Both held that knowing the eternal is of more worth than knowing the temporal. Augustine remarks that "if therefore this is the right distinction between wisdom and knowledge, that the intellectual cognition of eternal things pertains to wisdom, but the rational cognition of temporal things to knowledge, it is not difficult to judge which is to be esteemed more and which is less . . . . The former is to be preferred to the latter."[5] And Aquinas confirms his adherence to this line of thought when he says, "The greatness of a virtue, as to its species, is taken from its object. Now the object of wisdom surpasses the objects of all the intellectual virtues: because wisdom considers the Supreme Cause, which is God."[6]

On this matter of the relative worth of cognitive states of consciousness Immanuel Kant offered what has become an influential version of the Aquinian justification. Quite clearly Kant sided with Aquinas in regarding the pursuit of at least some theoretical knowledge as justified by the inherent worth of the knowledge attained. Likewise he held that within the body of knowledge which is of inherent worth, some is more worth knowing than other. But he did not locate the superiority in the object of knowledge, in the thing known. And in particular, he did not hold that knowledge of God is superior to knowledge of what is not God, nor that knowledge of the transcendent eternal in general is superior to knowledge of the temporal. For he held that we can have no knowledge of God, nor any of the transcendent eternal.

On Kant's view, the superiority of certain forms of knowledge is to be located in the formal characteristics of that knowledge. It is completeness of explanation and systemic unity that are the great desiderata in knowledge. Characteristic of human nature is an impulse toward the pursuit of ever greater completeness of explanation, and ever greater systematic unity, in the body of our collective knowledge. And this impulse, Kant obviously believes, is beneficent; the more complete and unified a body of knowledge, so much the better. To suppose, though, that there actually be a body of knowledge in which there are no remnants of incompleteness and disunity would be to suffer from illusion. There is no harm, perhaps even there is some benefit, in holding out before us as a luring vision the prospect of such a body of knowledge. But in fact we will never be in any other situation than that of striving for something more complex and more unified than what we have. Our lot is cast inevitably with the comparative. The superlative is forever beyond us.

This Kantian version of the Aquinian justification has gripped the conviction of many if not most scholars in the Western world. The perennial pursuit by mankind of a body of theory more complete and more unified than that which at the moment we possess is seen as justified by the inherent worth of the knowledge attained. It is not necessary, for the pursuit to be justified, that the knowledge attained prove useful.

I have classified this Kantian vision of the place of theorizing in human life as a version of the Aquinian justification, on the ground that it affirms the inherent worth of knowledge. At the same time, I have emphasized the radical difference between this version and Aquinas's own. No object is given preferential status in knowledge. Instead, preferential status is given to knowledge possessing certain formal characteristics. There is yet another difference worth noting. The ultimate goal of the scholar, says Aquinas, is that the scholar will have knowledge of God. No doubt the scholar, out of charity for his fellows, will seek to share his knowledge. But the picture Aquinas has in mind is not that each scholar will make his contribution to a body of human knowledge, and that this will include the knowledge by somebody or other of God. The goal of each scholar is that he himself will attain to knowledge of God. Kant's picture is profoundly different. Here the goal is that each of us will contribute to a body of human knowledge which is an advance, with respect to completeness and unity, on what we have presently. But in fact no single person will ever have that better body of knowledge. It will be parceled out across the community of scholars. The body of knowledge that any given scholar has will always be radically incomplete and lacking full coherence with knowledge possessed by the other scholars. There now exists a body of propositions each known by someone or other; and the goal of the scholar is to contribute to the formation of a new body of propositions, each known by someone or other, and such that the totality has greater completeness and unity than the present totality. But no one scholar will ever survey the whole of this edifice that together the community of scholars is building. All together are perennially engaged in building an edifice of which no one will ever see more than a tiny corner. And it may just be that the corner on which a given scholar works and which he surveys shows, during his lifetime, no increase in completeness and unity. The cognitive states he does have may nonetheless be of intrinsic worth to him. But they will be inferior to those he aimed to have, and to those which others will some day have, perhaps as the result of his contributions.

The English Renaissance writer Francis Bacon gave expression to yet a third influential line of thought concerning the justification of theorizing. "Knowledge is power," said Bacon. And clearly he thought that, for much knowledge, its value lies in power. The justification of the pursuit of theoretical knowledge lies in the power placed in our hands by the cognitive states attained.

The power Bacon had in mind was power over one's circumstances. The cognitive results of scholarship are of use in altering one's circumstances to conform to one's desires. The model of action which Bacon probably had in mind was this: Having it as my goal to bring about B, and believing that by doing A I will bring about B, I do A. And probably it was his view that scholarship can both provide the beliefs on the basis of which we act, and suggest new goals for which to act.

The Baconian justification is like the Pythagorean in citing, as justification for the pursuit of theoretical knowledge, the utility of such knowledge for achieving various non-cognitive benefits. It differs, though, in its identification of the relevant benefits. On the Pythagorean justification, the benefit which the attainment of theoretical knowledge yields is the moral benefit of altering the theorist's character for the better. And it was the conviction of the Pythagorean tradition that the practice of (the appropriate kind of) learning inherently yields this moral benefit. On the Baconian justification, the relevant benefit which the attainment of theoretical knowledge yields is the benefit of enabling us to alter our circumstances–the attainment of power. But this power is not thought of as inherently some good thing. Rather, the power in turn gets its justification by actually being used to alter one's circumstances in one way or another. The satisfaction of the Baconian justification requires that the results of learning be embedded within informed action. Learning is for action—action extrinsic to the action of learning. If learning is to be justified its results must be used in technology. And whether they are so used is a matter lying outside the hands of the scholar *qua* scholar.

The Baconian justification has of course so firmly gripped the conviction of Western man that today it has expanded far beyond what Bacon himself ever envisaged. It was principally alterations in our physical circumstances that Bacon had in mind when he suggested that the pursuit of knowledge is justified by the utility of its results for power. The pursuit of what might be called technical knowledge is what he urged. We in the twentieth century, having become aware of laws pertaining to human behavior and action, have seen the prospect of behavioral knowledge opening up before us, that is, of knowledge put to use in altering the actions of our fellow human beings in accord with our goals. Where previously an alliance existed between the researcher and the technologist of nature, now there also exists an alliance between the researcher and the technologist of society.[7]

In summary, in the West one finds a long history of those who affirm that scholarship is justified by the value of the non-cognitive effects and utility of the knowledge attained; but also one finds a long history of those who hold that some of it at least is justified simply by the inherent value of the cognitive states of consciousness it yields. Of course these positions are not incompatible. Not only may one branch of inquiry be justified by reference to one of such justifications and another, by reference to another; but even a single branch of inquiry may be justified in both ways. Some matters of knowledge may be worth having both for their intrinsic worth, and for the sake of their inherent effects or utility.

Now it seems to me obvious—too obvious to need arguing—that for lifting the burdens of deprivation and oppression and advancing the cause of shalom, theoretical knowledge is useful. It is, in fact, necessary. The Christian understanding of the scholar's vocation clearly leads to the conclusion that the pursuit of at least some theoretical knowledge is justified by its results and its utility.

The interesting question, though, is whether that is the whole of the matter. Is the acquisition of theoretical knowledge to be justified solely by reference to the effects and utility of knowledge? Or could it be that the having and the acquisition of knowledge is itself a good thing? Could it be that it is itself a dimension of shalom, a component in human fulfillment?

Man's shalom, according to the witness of the Old Testament prophets, includes justice for the widow and the orphan. It includes as well the love between parents and children, and delight in green pastures and flowing brooks. Does it also include theoretical knowledge—the understanding of man, the universe, and God that scholarship can give us?

I find it impossible to answer no to this question. To me it seems evident that understanding, comprehension, and knowledge constitutes a fulfillment of our created nature. To me it seems evident that human fulfillment is less than God meant it to be insofar as there is ignorance in place of understanding, bewilderment in place of comprehension. Of course human fulfillment does not consist exclusively of knowledge. And of course there is more to comprehension and understanding than the theorist provides us with. Further, over and over we discover that the rich interconnections of creation are such that knowledge has non-cognitive benefits and uses. Yet I want to say that a theoretical comprehension of ourselves and of the reality in the midst of which we live—of its unifying structure and its explanatory principles—is a component in the shalom God meant for us. Where knowledge is absent, life is withered.

Knowledge—some knowledge, anyway—is of inherent worth, in that it constitutes a component in our God-appointed fulfillment. The Aquinian justification joins to something real. Man is created a wondering creature, unfulfilled until his wonder finds fulfillment in knowledge.

Our goal has been to get at the root of pure theory/praxis-oriented theory debate. We are not yet there. For that debate, though it has a good deal to do with the issue of justification, is not directly about the proper justification of theorizing. Justification of theorizing operates, as it were, on a "second level." The person who offers such a justification first surveys the field of theorizing, and then gives an account of its benefits. But the pure theory/praxis-oriented theory debate pertains to scholars operating on the first level. It pertains to the principles on which they should choose the direction of their investigations–to what I shall call their "choice-principles."

If we are to formulate with clarity the issues here, we must keep in mind these two different levels: the primary level of choice-principle, and the secondary level of justification. But of course, what one believes concerning justification has bearing on what one recommends concerning choice-principles.

The person who adopts the Aquinian justification holds that certain cognitive states of consciousness are of inherent worth. Thereby he has available to him a choice-principle for determining the direction of his inquiries, a cognitive choice-principle: choose those directions of inquiry which hold the greatest promise of yielding cognitive states of intrinsic worth. And if he also holds that intrinsically worthwhile states of knowledge differ among themselves with respect to their worth, then in turn he has available to him a cognitive choice-principle for choosing *among* such states: choose those directions of inquiry which hold the greatest promise of yielding knowledge of greatest inherent worth for the greatest number of people.[8]

And now I can introduce the notion of pure theory. When the direction of inquiry that a scholar follows has been chosen by him for the reason that he judged it held promise of yielding knowledge of inherent worth, let us say that he is then engaged in pure theory. I think that very often what people mean when they speak of someone as engaging in pure theory is exactly this. By contrast, when the direction of inquiry that a scholar follows has been chosen by him for the reason that he judged it held promise of yielding knowledge resulting in, or useful for, something other than cognitive states, let us say that he is engaged in praxis-oriented theory.[9]

However, not all whom affirm the importance of pure theory mean by "pure theory" what I have just suggested. For some of these deny that cognitive states of consciousness have any inherent worth. If asked to give a justification for theoretical inquiry they might offer a Baconian theory, but certainly not an Aquinian one. Yet they affirm the importance of theorizing which is not praxis-oriented.

On first hearing, that is simply bewildering. How can someone hold that scholarship is justified exclusively by its utility in altering our circumstances in desirable ways, and at the same time recommend theorizing which is not praxis-oriented? What the Baconian justification straightforwardly yields is some such (non-cognitive) choice-principle as this: choose those directions of inquiry which hold the greatest promise of yielding knowledge useful in altering our human circumstances in the most desirable ways. But if one does in fact choose a direction of inquiry solely on this principle, then one is engaged in praxis-oriented theory. So how can one combine the Baconian justification for learning with insistence on the importance of theorizing which is not praxis-oriented?[10]

In the following way: by claiming that more technologically beneficial knowledge is likely to result if there are a number of researchers who direct their investigations with no regard to technological benefit. It is argued that if everyone directed his research along lines that he judged beneficial to the Department of Defense, the National Park Service, the Department of Health, Education and Welfare, etc., the long-range technological interests of mankind would be poorly served. In short, there is abroad in the contemporary world a confidence in the existence of a pre-established harmony between results that emerge from theory which is not praxis-oriented and those that in the long run are the most technologically beneficial.

But how then does such a person recommend that the scholar determine the direction of his inquiry—a person, that is, who holds that the worth of knowledge lies exclusively in its non-cognitive benefits, while yet believing that some researchers should avoid engaging in praxis-oriented theorizing? What choice-principle does he advocate? For choice there must be.

I think that most of those who think along the lines suggested would say this: the best way to serve the technological interests of mankind is to allow a sizeable body of researchers to pursue whatever matters they find of greatest intellectual interest to themselves. And theorizing thus pursued is what some have in mind by "pure theory."

So I suggest that two rather different understandings of "pure theory" are present in the contemporary world. Some mean by "pure theory" theorizing whose direction was chosen for the reason that the researcher judged it would yield knowledge of inherent worth. That is how I defined "pure theory" a few pages back. Call it, now, objective pure theory. Others mean by "pure theory" theorizing whose direction was chosen for the reason that the researcher judged it would prove intellectually interesting to himself. Subjective pure theory, we might call this.[11]

And now what does the Christian, who holds that it is the calling of the scholar to serve God's cause of justice-in-shalom, have to say about the pure theory/praxis-oriented theory debate? What does he recommend for the scholar's choice-principle?

He will not say that in principle only praxis-oriented theory is legitimate. Accordingly, he cannot simply adopt the principle: choose whichever direction of inquiry holds the greatest promise of yielding results or utility of greatest worth to the greatest number of people. For he holds, as I have argued, that at least *some* knowledge is of intrinsic worth. And that conviction will enter into his calculations as to which line of investigation to pursue.[12]

So how about the other way around: can he hold that in principle only pure theory is legitimate? Well, earlier I remarked on the necessity of theoretical knowledge for informed praxis. So if one held, nevertheless, that the theorist in determining the direction of his inquiries should never have his eye on practice, should always engage exclusively in pure theory, that position would have to be defended by holding to the pre-established harmony notion that always the best way for the theorist to serve the interest of praxis is to engage in pure theory.[13]

Now it is true, of course, that over and over knowledge acquired in the course of pure theory has in fact turned out to have some important practical applications. And sometimes it looks unlikely that the knowledge would have emerged if all scholars had been engaged only in praxis-oriented theory. But at the same time, what also turns out over and over is that the theoretical knowledge we need to accomplish some practical goal proves to be missing. Accordingly, we find that we have to acquire it in service of that goal. We have to engage in praxis-oriented theory. The point is so crucial as to merit repetition: *repeatedly the knowledge we need for our non-cognitive goals proves not to have emerged from pure theory.* As thinkers from the Third World have recently suggested, First World theorizing has contributed no significant intellectual resources to their goals of social reform, suggesting thereby that our Western "pure theory" is in fact not very pure, but is far more oriented to preserving our own social order than we like to think. In any case, I think it decisively clear that in principle, praxis-oriented theory is legitimate. We cannot assume that always the best way to serve praxis is to engage in pure theory.

So where does that leave us? It leaves us in the position of saying to the scholar that since both the intrinsic worth of knowledge and the beneficial results and utility of knowledge have legitimate claims on him, he will have to assess the priority of the one over against the other. He cannot engage in praxis-oriented theory without first considering the claims of knowledge which is of intrinsic worth; and he cannot engage in pure theory without first considering the claims of the inherent results and utility of knowledge. The scholar cannot operate exclusively with the choice-principle of selecting whatever direction of inquiry holds most promise of yielding knowledge of greatest inherent worth. But neither can he operate exclusively with the choice-principle of selecting whatever direction holds most promise of yielding knowledge of use for the non-cognitive concerns of greatest worth. Always he must engage in the difficult and complex task of weighing the one against the other, pure theory against praxis-oriented theory, deciding which holds most promise of contributing most substantially to the cause of justice-in-shalom.

And always he must do so in the light of his own concrete historical and cultural situation, and in the light of his own capacities. He cannot give an abstract, once-for-all-answer. The needs of mankind for knowledge are different in one place and time from what they are in another. They are different in South America from what they are in North America. Responsible scholarship always bears the marks of its time and place of birth.

Thus I find I cannot agree with the South American scholar Hugo Assmann, whom Miguez-Bonino quotes as rejecting "any *logos* which is not the logos of a *praxis*."[14] But equally I cannot give my approval to those scholars in the Western world who simply assume without question that they are justified in pursuing a logos which is not the logos of any praxis. If the scholar is to act responsibly, he cannot evade the difficult task of ascertaining priorities in his concrete situation. Yet Assmann's words have their point. For the scholar in the West is more often found to be irresponsibly ignoring the claims of praxis-oriented theory than he is found to be irresponsibly ignoring the claims of pure theory. So, for example, in the midst of the existential bewilderment of Americans as to the criteria for a just war, most of our scholars continued their pursuit of pure theory.

One thing more must be said here. A few pages back I distinguished between objective pure theory and subjective pure theory—that is, between theorizing pursued for the intrinsic worth of the knowledge it promise to yield, and theorizing pursued for the intellectual interest it promises to the researcher. Now the responsible scholar, I am persuaded, can never be content to pursue a line of investigation simply because it promises to be interesting to him. Of course he hopes that it will prove interesting. And he acknowledges that part at least of what gives worth to knowledge is that it proves of interest to human beings. But that some line of inquiry promises to be interesting, whether or not it is important, and then interesting just to him, perhaps to no one else, cannot all by itself ever be his decisive reason for pursuing it. He cannot put out of mind considerations of worth—and more specifically, considerations pertaining to what is of worth for his fellow human beings generally, not just to himself.

Augustine and Aquinas did not hold merely that knowledge of the eternal God is that form of knowledge which is of greatest inherent worth. They held that knowledge of the eternal God is the noblest of all such inherently worthwhile ends—not merely the noblest of all forms of knowledge but the noblest of all human ends. Further, it was their view that knowledge of God can, in part, be gained by way of theoretical reflection.[15]

On their view, accordingly, the pursuit of knowledge of the eternal God is the noblest activity available to a human being.[16]

Let us see briefly how this position is worked out by Aquinas. The true end (goal) of man, says Aquinas, is happiness. And "man's happiness consists essentially in his being united to the Uncreated Good . . . ."[17] Thus "the ultimate and principle good of man is the enjoyment of God . . . ."[18]

Now the essence of this union with God which constitutes man's ultimate happiness "consists in an act of the intellect . . . ."[19] Specifically, man's ultimate happiness consists in the intellectual act of knowing God in his essence.[20] The goal of achieving that happiness does, or should, govern our will; so one might say that "the delight that results from happiness pertains to the will."[21] But nonetheless the goal consists in an act of the intellect.

But why should it be supposed that knowing God—and incidentally, we may give the title of wisdom to such knowledge—why should it be supposed that knowing God is man's ultimate end? Why should it be thought that in wisdom lies man's ultimate beatitude? Because

> if man's happiness is an operation, it must needs be man's highest operation. Now man's highest operation is that of his highest power in respect of its highest object: and his highest power is the intellect, whose highest object is the Divine Good, which is the object, not of the practical, but of the speculative intellect. Consequently happiness consists principally in such an operation, viz., in the contemplation of Divine things. . . . Therefore the last and perfect happiness which we await in the life to come, consists entirely in contemplation. But imperfect happiness, such as can be had here, consists first and principally in contemplation, but secondarily, in an operation of the practical intellect directing human actions and passions.[22]

"Perfection and true happiness cannot be had in this life . . . ." Nonetheless, "a certain participation of Happiness can be had in this life."[23] "In so far as a man gives himself to the pursuit of wisdom, so far does he even now have some share in true beatitude."[24]

If wisdom constitutes the essence of man's ultimate happiness, how then does the "theological virtue" of charity fit into the picture? Well, charity may be defined as "the friendship of man for God,"[25] and the actualization of this virtue is then man's love for God. It may be said about charity that "since charity attains God, it unites us to God."[26] Now "likeness causes love."[27] And it is through the pursuit of wisdom that man "especially approaches to a likeness to God who 'made all things in wisdom.' And since likeness is the cause of love, the pursuit of wisdom especially joins man to God in friendship."[28] So it may be concluded that charity is an inherent result of that unity with God established by wisdom–that is, by knowing God.

But if the essence of human happiness consists just in an intellectual contemplation of God, is there then no need for human companionship in man's ultimate end? And is there no need for delight in nature? Is the existence of a just and happy community dwelling in harmony with nature just irrelevant to man's ultimate happiness?

Not perhaps irrelevant. But certainly unnecessary. Here in this life the happy man needs friends, and needs what will sustain the body.[29] But not so when he has attained perfect happiness. In the intellectual contemplation of God there will be no lack whatsoever. "If we speak of perfect Happiness, which will be in our heavenly Fatherland, the fellowship of friends is not essential to Happiness, since man has the entire fullness of his perfection in God."[30] Should we find ourselves in the presence of other human beings, love for them will result from love for God. Then friendship will be, "as it were, concomitant with perfect Happiness."[31] But the absence of human companionship will mean no deficiency in fulfillment. Likewise, the person who when disembodied has knowledge of God experiences no deficiency. "Since man's perfect Happiness consists in the vision of the Divine Essence, it does not depend on the body. Consequently, without the body the soul can be happy."[32] The person who knows and loves God will eventually receive a new body at the resurrection. He will then experience an increase in the extent of his happiness. However, he will experience no increase in its intensity.[33] And even then it should be added that the body to which his soul will be united will be "no longer animal but spiritual. Consequently [the] external goods [of our present bodies] are nowise necessary for that Happiness, since they are ordained to the animal life."[34]

Obviously this is a profoundly different perspective from that which I have outlined, yielding a view as to the proper relation of theorizing to human life generally which differs on very many points indeed. Let me call attention to just one difference, a difference which does not spring at once to view. Not every human being can be a scholar, be it for lack of time, of ability, or of inclination. Accordingly, what follows immediately from the Thomistic view is intellectual elitism. Learning in its highest form is for the benefit of the scholars themselves, lifting them up to a state of being higher than that of their fellows. The others remain outside, looking in, deriving at best vicarious benefit. To enter the world of theory is to leave behind what is inferior in end and action. It is to be freed, to be liberated, from the flickering gloom of the cave for the bright light of the sun. And only some can be freed. By contrast, in the position which I developed, scholarship is placed directly in the service of mankind.

A thoroughly non-elitist view of scholarship was espoused in an alternative view on the relation of learning to life—what might be called the traditional Protestant view. Reading their Old Testaments, the Protestants, and particularly the Calvinist Protestants, were struck by the "dominion" passages: subdue the earth and have dominion. They heard in these the message that humanity has a mandate from God–a "cultural mandate," as it came eventually to be called. Perhaps a plausible surface reading of the "dominion" words of the Old Testament is that man is there enjoined to engage in what Marx eventually called "productive labor." But that is not the way the Protestant tradition characteristically understood them. It understood them as enjoining not only productive labor but the whole formation of culture. And it understood the development of scholarship as an essential component in cultural formation—not just as an instrument for self-improvement, and not just as an instrument for beneficial alteration of one's circumstances, but as something good in its own right. God has declared it such, and enjoined its pursuit, so that it is part of man's obedient response to the cultural mandate.

But naturally it constitutes only one phase of man's total response. And the reformers saw no reason whatsoever for thinking it the noblest. Every occupation is to be a vocation before the face of God, each equal in nobility, if not in strategic importance, with the other. In God's sight, learning is no more noble than farming, theorizing no more noble than cabinetmaking, scholarship than politics. All legitimate occupations have the same status before God of being obedient responses to the cultural mandate. Elitism has been struck dead.

Yet some essential emphases are curiously missing here. What is emphasized is our calling to humanize the world. What is missing is the insistence that such humanizing is never to be done merely to place the print of our hands and minds upon nature, but always for human benefit. What is missing is the note that each person is to work for the benefit of his fellow human beings. That the scholar must consider the needs of his fellow human beings in directing his scholarship is never recognized.

What is also curiously missing is the theme of fall and renewal. The stress is all on man's creaturely calling to humanize the world. To that particular reorientation in our responsibilities which occurred when man fell and God set about to work for renewal, no attention is given. And thus that particular mode of the scholar's service to his fellow human beings which consists in his aiding in the cause of lifting the burdens of deprivation and oppression imposed by his fellow human beings goes unnoticed. What I have argued by contrast is that a scholar's inquiries must take their course in the light of the fallen condition of our actual society. Intellectual culture is never to be severed from the deprivations and oppressions to be found in our actual social condition. One cannot proceed as if we lived within a society which is pristine and unfallen, whose only deficiency is that it is not yet fully developed.

Further, there is a curious abstractness, a curious ahistorical quality, to the Protestant view. There is no sense of the seesaw battle taking place in history between forces that advance and forces that retard the coming of shalom, with the consequent necessity for the scholar to choose his strategic point of entry. In lordly fashion the scholar remains above the strife, "developing culture," writing his books while the Reichstag burns.

I think it must be said that the Protestant view, by virtue of ignoring these factors, has all too often encouraged the irresponsible pursuit of pure theory when praxis-oriented theory was called for. Thinking himself fully justified by the cultural mandate, the Protestant scholar all too often ignored the priorities of God's cause of renewal, and simply pursued whatever knowledge he thought worth acquiring for its own sake. True, he did not think that thereby he was doing something better than his fellows who were not scholars. But also he did not ask how he could enable them better to do what they were doing. And in particular, he acted as if cultural fulfillment could be attained without intermingling the struggle for fulfillment with the struggle for lifting the bonds of deprivation and oppression. Culture was removed from history and from society, and treated as a "world" of its own.

Objections to what I have said arise from all sides. Prominent among them is the claim that the existence of pure theory is an illusion. No one ever does engage in pure theory. Perhaps no one can. We delude ourselves in thinking that we do. All theory is in fact praxis-oriented. So it is said.

From the variety of reasons offered in support of this position, among the most common is one which makes use of Marx's thought. Those two great modern masters in the art of suspecting,[35] Marx and Freud, have taught us all to distinguish, on both the individual and the social level, between the genuine reasons for our actions, and what we offer as reasons but which are in fact rationalizations for the genuine reasons. We conceal from ourselves and others our genuine reasons by throwing up smoke screens of rationalizations. The claim, then, is that if we scrutinize those scholars who claim to be following some direction of inquiry for the reason that they judge it likely to lead to knowledge of inherent worth, we will see that they are offering rationalizations for their genuine reasons and not the genuine reasons themselves. In fact, so it is said, the true reason for their choice is their belief that that line of inquiry will advance their own self-interest by perpetuating the position of privilege and power enjoyed by themselves and their class.

Unfortunately I do not here have the space to give this claim the full consideration it deserves. I must content myself with saying that I am not persuaded that this cynical reading of human motivation is invariably the correct one. Immediately I must go on to observe, however, that very often it is correct. The human heart is deeply deceitful; and to their great credit Marx and Freud have taught us much about its devious paths. Often it is true that the scholar who says and even believes that he is engaged in pure theory is in fact working to shore up a society in which he occupies a position of privilege and power. He enjoys his position by producing scholarship whose secret motivation is to perpetuate that position. (And even when that is not his genuine reason, it may nonetheless be the consequences of his choices.) Accordingly, a responsible decision by the scholar on the priority of pure theory vs. praxis-oriented theory requires that he become "self-conscious." And as to the path of self-consciousness, there is none better than that of listening attentively to the message of the Bible, that great unmasker of deceit, while at the same time listening attentively to the cries of those who make the claim of deprivation and oppression—Gentiles listening to Jews, Jews to Arabs, men to women, rich to poor, South African whites to South African blacks, Dutchmen to Moluccans, North Americans to South Americans, the First World to the Third. The person who turns one of his ears to the prophetic unmasking word of the gospel and the other to the cries of those who suffer deprivation and oppression is not likely to suffer from the illusion that he is engaged in pure theory when in fact he is working to shore up his own position of privilege.

Notes

1. José Miguez-Bonino, *Doing Theology in a Revolutionary Situation* (Philadelphia: Fortress Press, 1975), 35.
2. This essay first appeared in *CSR* 9.4 (Summer 1980): 317-34.
3. Jürgen Habermas, *Knowledge and Human Interests* (Boston: Beacon Press, 1971), 301f.
4. Some might question whether this justification can in fact be ascribed to the Pythagoreans. Not being a specialist in the intricacies of Pythagorean scholarship, the best I can do is cite authority. To the best of my knowledge, there is no fragment from the Pythagoreans which decisively offers the justification cited. Here, though, is what Kirk and Raven say in their interpretation of some of the fragments pertaining to Pythagoras: "The central notions, which held together the two strands that were later to fall apart, seem to have been those of θεωρία (contemplation), κόσμος (an orderliness found in the arrangement of the universe), and κάθαρσις (purification). By contemplating the principle of order revealed in the universe—and especially in the regular movements of the heavenly bodies—and by assimilating himself to that orderliness, man himself was progressively purified until he eventually escaped from the cycle of birth and attained immortality." G. S. Kirk & J. E. Raven, *The Presocratic Philosophers* (Cambridge: Cambridge University Press, 1963), 288.
5. Augustine, *On the Trinity*, XII, 15.
6. Thomas Aquinas, *Summa Theologica*, IIa, Q. 66, Art. 5, *resp.* Hereafter, *ST*.
7. In recent years we have even seen a curious absorption of the Pythagorean tradition by the Baconian. The confidence was worn thin in our century that scholarship naturally tends toward self-improvement. To us it no longer seems that it tends naturally to improve our character. At the same time, however, our psychologists claim to have discovered laws concerning psychological self-alteration. And this has opened up the possibility of technologies for psychological self-improvement. Our technologists of self propose, for example, to teach us how to express our anger rather than suppress it. For it has been discovered, so they claim, that if one expresses one's anger, one will be a happier person.
8. There are other similar principles in the region here; for example: choose those directions of inquiry which hold the greatest promise of yielding knowledge of greatest intrinsic worth to oneself. It would overburden the text to canvass the various possibilities. What should also be observed is that the scholar operating with the principle in the text may find that he is confronted with great promise of gaining knowledge of moderate intrinsic worth and small promise of gaining knowledge of great intrinsic worth. Then he must weigh off the potential benefits of each option by a decision procedure. So too the scholar may be forced to choose between knowledge of lesser worth attainable by more people, and knowledge of greater worth attainable by fewer. Down through the ages, scholars have defended the latter choice by various notions of some vicarious benefit that mankind in general derives from the presence of the scholar in its midst.
9. In principle a scholar may have reasons of both sorts for following certain directions of inquiry. In such cases of coincidence, he will be engaged in both pure and praxis-oriented theory. Also, in following a given line of inquiry the scholar may be engaged in a mixture of pure and praxis-oriented theory.
10. The looseness to which I call attention between the justification offered for theory and the choice-principle used in determining the direction of one's theory is perhaps even more clear in the case of the Pythagorean justification. Neither on the ancient version of the Pythagorean tradition which Habermas describes, nor on the modern variant to which I alluded, does the interest which undergirds learning give the scholar any guidance in his decision as to which line of inquiry to pursue. It makes no difference whatsoever which facet of the cosmos' eternal order one contemplates; one's soul will be ordered nonetheless. It makes no difference whatsoever on which matters of inquiry one uses the scientific methodology; one's character will be purged. Yet the theorist must choose his direction of inquiry.
On the issue, the Renaissance humanists constituted an interestingly different version of the Pythagorean tradition from the ancients. At the heart of their program was a new vision of learning. In place of the formulation of theories characteristic of the schoolman, the humanist proposed the reading of classical texts and the study of classical history. He did not propose such hermeneutic/historical studies for the sake of the knowledge which would result. He proposed them for the sake of the results anticipated in the character of the scholar. Such studies, he thought, would make the scholar himself a cultured human being. And that was his ideal: the cultured man. Learning was for self-improvement. But the humanist was far indeed from thinking that every form of scholarly inquiry would produce the kind of self-improvement that he had in mind. He insisted that the theorizing of the schoolmen would not. Thus that particular justification which the humanists offered for learning yielded a principle of choice: hermeneutic/historical studies will be chosen over scholastic theorizing. Whether this justification also yields a principle for choosing within the area of hermeneutic/historical studies is much less clear.
11. Other justifications can be offered for engaging in subjective pure theory than that the knowledge which results will somehow satisfy the Baconian justification. Someone might argue, for example, that just the satisfaction of intellectual curiosity is one of the things which is of inherent worth for human beings. In this paper I do not at all try to state what, in general, makes some knowledge of greater inherent worth than other—though I assume that some is. Nor do I explore the connection between knowledge being of inherent worth, and the fact that someone or another finds that it's of intellectual interest. If satisfying one's intellectual interest is what gives knowledge inherent worth, then, given that intellectual interests vary, presumably which knowledge is of inherent worth also varies from one person to another. In any case, objective pure theory and subjective pure theory may not be such stark alternatives as the text above suggest. Still, we all sometimes have the experience of having an intense interest in acquiring some bit of knowledge which we judge unimportant and trivial—as in trying to solve some riddle or puzzle. Throughout our discussion we should also keep in mind the distinction between the state of *having* some item of knowledge and the experience of *acquiring* some item of knowledge. It seems to me that the contemporary scholar assigns relatively more weight to the latter than did the scholar in the tradition. Today we often prize the experience of acquiring knowledge more highly than the state of having it.

12. I am assuming that the principle *choose whichever holds the greatest promise of yielding results or utility of greatest worth to the greatest number of people*, will not necessarily coincide in its results with the principle: *choose whichever holds the greatest promise of yielding knowledge of greatest intrinsic worth to the greatest number of people*. For if it did, then of course the person who holds that some knowledge is of intrinsic worth could nonetheless use the principle formulated in the text. Likewise, I am assuming that the worth of the results or utility of knowledge will not always and necessarily outweigh the intrinsic worth of knowledge. For if it did, then again the person who holds that some knowledge is of intrinsic worth could nonetheless operate with the principle formulated by the text.

13. I am assuming that the intrinsic worth of knowledge will not always outweigh the worth of the inherent results or utility of knowledge. For if it did, then of course, the theorist would never go wrong if he engaged solely in pure theory.

14. José Miguez-Bonino, *Doing Theology in a Revolutionary Situation*, 88.

15. Though Augustine would add that it is only deepened knowledge which can come thus. The beginning lies in faith.

16. Compare these perceptive words of Miguez-Bonino: "The faith of Israel is consistently portrayed, not as a *gnosis*, but as a *way*, a particular way of acting, of relating inside and outside the nation, or ordering life at every conceivable level, which corresponds to God's own way with Israel. This background, so well attested in the Psalms, for instance, may explain Jesus' use of the word *way* to refer to himself. The motif, on the other hand, appears in paramedic contexts in Pauline literature. Faith is a 'walking.' It is unnecessary to point out that even the idea of knowledge and knowing has this active and participatory content." *Doing Theology*, p. 89.

17. *Summa Theologica*; Partial, Q. 3, Art.3, *resp.*
18. *ST,* Part IIB, Q. 23, Art. 8,*resp.*
19. *ST,* Part IIA, Q. 3, Art. 4, *resp.*
20. *ST,* Part IIA, Q. 3, Art. 8, *resp.*
21. *ST,* Part IIA, Q. 3, Art. 4, *resp.*
22. *ST,* Part IIA, Q. 3, Art. 5, *resp.*
23. *ST,* Part IIA, Q. 5, Art. 3, *resp.*
24. *Summa contra Gentiles*, I, 2.Hereafter, *SCG*.
25. *ST,* IIB, Q. 23, Art. 1, *resp.*
26. *ST,* IIB, Q. 23, Art. 3, *resp.*
27. *ST,* IIB, Q. 26, Art. 2, *obi.* 2.
28. *SCG,* I, 2.
29. *ST,* IIA, Q. 4, Art. 8; and *ST,* IIA, Q. 4, Art. 3.
30. *ST,* IIA, Q. 4, Art. 8, *resp.*
31. Ibid.
32. *ST,* IIA, Q. 4, Art. 3, *resp.*
33. Ibid.
34. *ST,* IIA, Q. 4, Art. 7, *resp.*
35. Miguez-Bonino's phrase in *Doing Theology,* p. 91.

4 The State of Evangelical Christian Scholarship (1988)

George Marsden

When talking about evangelical Christian scholarship, we should avoid lapsing into the kind of rhetoric that seems to presume that the traditions of Christian scholarship represented in our own communities are co-extensive with all of Christian scholarship.[1] We want to avoid the sort of parochialism suggested by a remark attributed to one of the promoters of Liberty University who said that one of Liberty's goals was someday to show that a Christian university could have as good a football team as Notre Dame's.

I am not the person best qualified here to comment on Notre Dame as a Christian university, but I have seen their football team play and I can say that they are indeed downright un-Christian. They are almost always selfish, mean and uncaring, not to mention brutal—which I did just mention. It will be interesting to see if the more rigorous Christian perspective at Liberty University will produce an alternative. I can warn them, however, that the last time there was a real attempt to have a Christian football team was at my alma mater, Haverford College. Haverford is a Quaker school and for years the Haverford football team practiced passive resistance. They had great practices; but it never got them anywhere. As Woody Allen once said of his experience at an inter-faith camp, he got beaten up by boys of every race, creed, and color. So with Haverford on Saturday afternoons in the fall. And so they abandoned their football program entirely.

We do not want, then, to claim too much when we talk about "Christian" this or that and we do not want to claim that evangelical scholarship and Christian scholarship are co-extensive.

When we talk about evangelical scholarship, we are talking about an international movement that, to the extent that it has been organized, has had largely American and British leadership. Moreover, in America, evangelicalism is a complex transdenominational movement that cannot be reduced to any of its subtypes. Nonetheless, to the extent there have been efforts to mobilize transdenominational evangelical scholarship, the leadership has been drawn disproportionately from the Reformed side of the American fundamentalist-evangelical movement. This is not to say that other evangelical traditions, holiness, pentecostal, anabaptist, black, Lutheran, Southern Baptist, and so forth, have not produced significant scholars. It is only to say that those Americans who have attempted to build evangelical scholarship into a movement have come mainly from the Reformed side of American evangelicalism (usually with British allies).

One of the striking features of the state of Christian scholarship today is that this relatively small community of mostly North American and British scholars is one of the few groups in the world who would sponsor a conference on this topic. There must be some Catholic counterparts; but in this country at least I think there is considerably less talk about Catholic scholarship than there was a generation ago. Essentially the same is true of old-line Protestant groups. If they were to talk about Christian scholarship, they would be talking about theological disciplines only. Their scholarship is pretty well confined today to theological seminaries. I think that there are not many communities today where one would find interests such as suggested on the present program, in the relationships of Christianity to the sciences, the arts, and the liberal arts.

Since most of the Christian scholarship of previous generations has died out or been secularized, perhaps the principal question we should ask concerning evangelical Christian scholarship today is whether it represents simply a transitional stage in the secularization of our community. Are evangelical academics today simply introducing secular standards to our community, but doing so by giving them the gloss of Christian education? Or is what we are seeing the emergence of an evangelical Christian Renaissance?

Perhaps we can illuminate this issue by considering where we have been. (There must be some reason why an historian was asked to speak on this topic.) How much has the enterprise of evangelical scholarship in this community changed in the past generation? We can go back forty years and see where we were then so as to get a better gauge of where we are now.

I pick forty years because it is a convenient round generational number and also because I have recently completed work on the origins of Fuller Theological Seminary, which was founded in 1947. The early Fuller is as good a place as any to look for the state of evangelical scholarship a generation ago. It is also appropriate because Carl Henry, one of the founders, is with us. Moreover, the same movement that produced Fuller eventually produced IFACS. So there is direct continuity.

What did this tradition of evangelical scholarship in America look like in the spring of 1947? To answer that question we have to rephrase it: What did fundamentalist scholarship look like in 1947? Forty years ago the movement we now call evangelicalism was not yet distinguished from fundamentalism. (Each of these terms, as I am using them, refers to those whom I call card-carriers, those who would apply the term to themselves; that is, one of their major ways of identifying themselves would be as part of a transdenominational fundamentalist or evangelical movement.) In 1947 this transdenominational movement was known primarily as fundamentalist; although since that term could be embarrassing, it was sometimes called evangelical, as in the National Association of Evangelicals (NAE), founded in 1942. When Carl Henry published his famous critique of this movement in 1947, however, he titled it "The Uneasy Conscience of Modern

Fundamentalism" [italics added]. Wheaton College, which recently had trained a remarkable generation of leaders who would soon take over such evangelicalism, was still unquestionably a fundamentalist college. Or to illustrate the point another way, in the 1940s Bob Jones, Sr., and John R. Rice were associated with the National Association of Evangelicals.

One of the manifestations of the alliances possible within this transdenominational fundamentalist movement was the agreement early in 1947 between Harold Ockenga and Charles Fuller in planning a new seminary. They might have seemed an unlikely pair. Ockenga, the dominant force in the NAE, was an intellectual pastor with a Ph.D. Fuller was the most popular evangelist of the radio era. His broadcasts were as popular as anything on the air; but he was never taken seriously by the nation's intellectual elite. Fuller had originally wanted his school to be a popular training center, especially for missionaries; but he was convinced by Ockenga that an even more urgent need was for a school that would also be a "center for scholarship." Fuller Seminary was thus designed to be one of the rare havens in the fundamentalist community where the theoretical would not be overwhelmed by the practical.

Fundamentalist scholarship was close to its nadir. Forty years before that, in 1907, conservative evangelicals could still have thought of themselves as having solid representation in the American academic establishment. Now they had virtually none.

We can get a pretty fair measure of the state things had reached, even in theology, if we look at the lineup of people whom Ockenga hoped to enlist for his new center for scholarship. Carl Henry was on the first list and was one of the bright spots. Perhaps more revealing, though, of the state of fundamentalist scholarship was that the centerpiece of the new faculty was to be Wilbur M. Smith. Smith was famous as a Bible teacher and a prolific writer of popular articles, Sunday school notes, books and pamphlets. He was also a bibliophile and often wrote about the urgency of producing evangelical scholarly literature. This was an important service for the fundamentalism of the time. It also gave Smith a popular reputation as a scholar. He had no degrees, however, and it would be fair to say he was primarily a popularizer of scholarship. His most formidable volume was a lengthy study of apologetics called *Therefore Stand* (1945). It was largely a compilation of quotations and in the later more sophisticated days at Fuller was known by the students as "Therefore Quote." Smith had no earned degrees, not even from high school. That he was so learned was a tribute to his native brilliance. He was not a scholar in the usual sense; but in the fundamentalist community of forty years ago, he was one of the very best available. Ockenga and Fuller agreed that Smith's support would be a "fleece" to test whether they should go ahead with the seminary project.

There simply were few accomplished senior scholars in the fundamentalist community and most of these few were already committed to highly partisan sub-movements, such as those represented by such theological seminaries as Westminister, Faith, and Dallas. Although Ockenga in his first search attempted to dislodge some from each of these schools, he succeeded only in getting Everett Harrison in New Testament from Dallas. Another symptom of how limited the pickings were was that one of Ockenga's very first choices, who did eventually come to Fuller, was Charles J. Woodbridge. Woodbridge, unlike Smith, had credentials. He had even studied abroad. But he too was primarily a popular Bible conference teacher. He also was an ardently separatist fundamentalist who, after a few years at Fuller, shook the dust off his feet and spent the rest of his career condemning such non-separatist "neo-evangelical" enterprises.[2]

If this list of most of the first round picks for Fuller Seminary was indicative of the state of fundamentalist-evangelical scholarship in the theological disciplines, the situation was worse in the non-theological fields. There were a few conservative evangelicals who were recognized scholars in their fields, but most of these would not identify themselves with fundamentalist-evangelicalism. Kenneth Scott Latourette, for instance, became president of the American Historical Association in 1947; but despite his conservative theological views, his loyalties were with ecumenical Christianity. No doubt there were others. In philosophy there was the Christian Reformed philosopher, William Harry Jellema, at the University of Indiana, and Gordon H. Clark, who identified unreservedly with the fundamentalist cause, was at Butler University in Indiana. Also at some fundamentalist and at some conservative denominational colleges there were some capable academics, but almost none had the leisure for independent scholarship. In 1947 a number of fundamentalist-evangelicals were saying that scholarship was essential to the cause, but for the time being, fundamentalism and scholarship were almost completely separated from each other.

Oddly, the connections with conservative evangelical British scholarship were at their nadir then also. In 1947 Ockenga had no Britishers on his slate of candidates, a situation that would have been unlikely for fundamentalist or evangelical seminaries in most decades either before or since. On the other hand, conservative Christians were considerably better represented in British scholarship and letters than in America. But American fundamentalist determination to make everyone choose sides had temporarily cut them off even from that source of allies. Not many American evangelicals had even yet discovered C. S. Lewis. This was a dark age.

In America the fundamentalist heritage set the agenda for whatever scholarship there would be in the sub-community. Fundamentalism was primarily an opposition movement. It was defined, first, by its opposition to certain recent secular beliefs and practices; second, by its opposition to liberal theologies that changed the Gospel to accommodate these secularizing changes; and, third, by opposition to the sort of ecumenical spirit in mainline denominations that was unalarmed by such changes.

The central strategic question facing the fundamentalist-evangelical community in 1947 was that of what form this opposition should take. Conflicting answers to this question were already beginning to divide the community into strict ecclesiastical separatists (like Woodbridge) who would take over the exclusive title "fundamentalist," and semi-separatists who would call themselves "neo-evangelicals" or evangelicals. Although some strict fundamentalists advocated simply withdrawing from much of the culture, giving up intellectual life, and preaching to save souls until Jesus returned, a more prominent theme in both the fundamentalist and evangelical wings of the party was that their ultimate goal was a new Reformation. They did not concede that the battle to make America a Protestant nation had been lost. Carl McIntire, the loudest spokesman for the separatists, described his movement as a "twentieth-century Reformation" and emphasized anti-Catholic and anti-communist political themes. Like Luther, he would take a strong "Here I Stand," and so he hoped to reverse the tide of Western civilization.

The emerging neo-evangelicals or the semi-separatists, who are our own principal progenitors, had similar goals, but a somewhat less strident strategy. Carl Henry spoke in his major volume of 1946 of "remaking the modern mind" and Harold Ockenga at the opening convocation of Fuller Seminary characteristically proclaimed the urgency of "rethinking and restating of the fundamental thesis of western culture."[3] Commenting on the widely perceived cultural crisis in the West following World War II, Ockenga emphasized that the only hope was a return to Christian principles for civilization. The only hope for the survival of true Christianity, moreover, was a return to evangelicalism. Hence the building of centers for evangelical scholarship was literally crucial to the future of civilization.

As Ockenga and Henry saw it, the crisis in Western civilization could be understood as the outgrowth of a disastrous turn of the Western mind, or the controlling assumptions of the age. These, they pointed out, had been secularized and relativized by totally replacing references to God and the Bible with human ideals and authority. What was needed then was a scholarly challenge to the controlling presuppositions of the secular mind and a clearer articulation of a Christian "world and life view."[4] This way of stating the issue reflected some early influences of Dutch thought on American evangelicalism. The school of Abraham Kuyper had developed the principle of the antithesis in first principles between the Christian mind and the secular mind. Kuyper went so far as to say that there were two kinds of people, regenerate and non-regenerate, and hence "two kinds of science."[5] American evangelicals had inherited the common sense, Baconian philosophical tradition that cherished the ideal of one compelling science for the whole race. So they were not inclined to carry this antithetic Kuyperianism as far as did some of the Dutch Americans, notably Cornelius Van Til of Westminster Theological Seminary. Nonetheless, Kuyperianism had an impact. Henry, for instance, dedicated *Remaking the Modern Mind* to "three men of Athens," Gordon H. Clark, William Harry Jellema, and Cornelius Van Til, all of whom had been influenced to one degree or another by the Dutch principles of presuppositional analysis of competing worldviews.[6]

The philosophical tensions in the beginnings of the move from common sense philosophy to modified Kuyperianism were paralleled by the struggle of the new evangelical community to develop a clear general strategy toward American churches and culture. The problem that conservative evangelicals faced was that only a generation before they had held a place in the academic establishment, but now they had lost that place. They were just beginning to realize that they would have to build their own institutions, starting almost from scratch. The question was whether they would become a sect, as were some of the strict fundamentalists, or whether they would be a reforming party on the edges of the mainline denominations. Those who became known as the new evangelicals adopted this latter strategy. One fundamentalist critic has aptly described it as "infiltration."[7] Their primary intellectual task would be apologetic, attempting to build an effective philosophical critique of other parties in contemporary thought. Thus they hoped to be a party for reform in American Protestantism and through that reform to regain the possibility of reshaping the dominant mind of Western civilization.

How well has this strategy succeeded, and where do things stand forty years later? There are some moderately encouraging signs. Today evangelicalism (broadly defined) is a recognized, even if fragmented and not always welcomed, force in American Protestantism. Evangelicalism even has some basis for claiming to be the wave of the future. Evangelicalism's strength in scholarship, however, is much less than its strength in other areas. Nevertheless, it is much stronger than it was forty years ago, and it is strong relative to most other Christian groups. A non-evangelical friend tells me that when he lectures in his American religious history survey on neo-evangelicalism he always points out that this is the most literate group of American Christians, writing and selling relatively more serious Christian books than any other major American Christian group. Such serious Christian literature still tends to come disproportionately, though far from exclusively, from more-or-less Reformed evangelicals, both British and American. In America today there are also scores of evangelical colleges, representing the scores of evangelical sub-traditions. These colleges include some with fine faculties and some can be classed in the better ranks of American liberal arts institutions. The discouraging dimension is that the total enrollments of all evangelical colleges is the equivalent of that of only about two major universities, so that evangelical Christian higher education makes up only a tiny proportion of American higher education today. There are also some self-consciously evangelical scholars in university positions, but they make up a tiny fraction of the whole.

In theological education, the situation is more encouraging. There, the largest and perhaps the best American seminaries are evangelical, a vast revolution from forty years ago. Another encouraging sign is in numbers of young evangelicals seeking graduate education. At least at a place like Duke, a disproportionate number of the degree candidates and applicants in the field of religion (at least half) are distinctly evangelical. People raised in strongly religious environments are more likely to think that beliefs are important and hence may become overrepresented in disciplines that still take ideas seriously, especially philosophy, religion, and intellectual history. In the long run this could have an important impact. It is too bad that we have hardly any graduate institutions for training these young people. This problem is difficult to resolve since at present it is still almost necessary for gaining credibility to get credentials from a leading secular institution. I think two parallel strategies are important. Evangelical scholars should continue to be involved in university higher education and at the same time evangelical educators should be building their own institutions with such standards of academic excellence that eventually they will gain wide academic recognition. I think this has already happened at the liberal arts level and there is no reason it cannot happen at university levels.

These mostly promising signs in evangelical scholarship are, of course, part of a larger picture of evangelical growth. This growth, we should keep in mind, is a mixed blessing. Religious movements flourish for a combination of reasons that include the disturbing along with the admirable. In the case of the growth of evangelical scholarship, for instance, one of the trends it reflects is the growing suburbanization and affluence of our communities. More and more evangelicals, like others in their social classes, are interested in higher education and so our academic enterprises have grown.

If we describe what is happening from this perspective, we are driven back to our central question. Is the growing interest in higher education among evangelicals a step on the way to the secularization of the movement? The growth of evangelical wealth and the rise in status among many white evangelicals have been important contributors to the rise of evangelical scholarship and educational institutions. Clearly we need that wealth for evangelical scholarship to flourish; but we do face the danger that the growing affluence of our communities could do us in. This is especially true, if we do not take a prophetic stance toward usual American attitudes toward wealth.

This social-economic factor is related to the larger issue of whether our community is simply secularizing. A number of observers from all sides recently have made the point that progressive evangelicalism, such as that which dominates our higher education, is at about the point where mainline Protestants were about a century ago. William Hutchison of Harvard has made this point. So has Leonard Sweet from a neo-orthodox viewpoint. Critics to the right make similar points. So does James Hunter in his survey of *American Evangelicalism: The Coming Generation* which documents moderate changes in some traditional beliefs among a minority of students at evangelical colleges and seminaries and emphasizes the secularization theme.[8] Are the changes taking place signs of a healthy tolerance for diversity and recovery of balance or are they symptoms of decline?

So here is the important question for us today. Evangelical scholarship has so far grown to only modest proportions, but these are substantial when the present is compared with forty years ago. The movement may be poised for continued geometric growth in the next forty years. But is this growth we are experiencing the sign of the emergence of a new major movement or is it a step toward secularization?

This is a serious and crucial question. Critics correctly point out that ever since Harvard went liberal in the eighteenth century American evangelical institutions have tended to drift to the left until their evangelical roots become unrecognizable. Is there anything in our movement to serve as a counterweight to such a trend? Specifically, is there anything to keep us from repeating the pattern of Protestant liberalism of a century ago? I see two major counterforces. First, I think it is immensely important that we are now living in a post-liberal age. The intellectual atmosphere is very different from forty years ago. Protestant liberalism has flowered and seems to be dying on the vine. It is difficult to see it as the exciting promise for the future. We can hope that we have learned enough from the fundamentalist-modernist era to retain our resolve to stay on the distinctly evangelical side, even if we reject the overstated emphases of fundamentalists in defending that side. We have perhaps an opportunity to exercise intellectual maturity, not being swept away by the pressures from either fundamentalism or liberalism. An essential component of being on the evangelical side is that, unlike modernism which attempted to wed Christianity to the prestige of modern scholarship, we design our scholarship to provide critical alternatives to the prevailing intellectual trends of the day.

The other counterbalancing hope I see comes from within our intellectual life itself. That is in the triumph—or nearly so—of what may be loosely called Kuyperian presuppositionalism in our community. Perhaps we could call this, more broadly, "Augustinianism," if that does not conjure up too many specifics. In any case I refer to a style of Christian thought that emphasizes that crucial to the differences that separate Christian worldviews from non-Christian ones are disagreements about pre-theoretical first principles, presuppositions, first commitments, or basic beliefs. Thus, without denying the value of human rationality, it denies the autonomy or competence of reason alone to adjudicate some of the decisive questions concerning the context within which rationality itself will operate.[9] This viewpoint can be contrasted with the older common sense, Baconian tradition that once dominated American evangelical thought. That tradition assumed that there was only one objective science for all people and hence that ultimately there should be no real distinction between Christian thinking and clear thinking. Christianity, they thought, should therefore be able to win its case on rational or scientific grounds.

The prevailing view now emphasizes that Christian thought and non-Christian thought, being founded on some opposed first principles, reflect wide differences in total worldviews. So those who presuppose that the universe was created by the God of Scripture are going to have many differences in viewpoint from those who suppose we have a chance universe. Since Christian principles will thus relate to all of thought and life (though not to all in the same degree) an important activity for such scholars is to define a Christian worldview or worldviews in contrast to the prevailing outlooks of our day. Though such emphases are not the only ones found among evangelical scholars today, they describe what I think is the dominant outlook.

One of the encouraging dimensions of the present state of evangelical scholarship is that this approach, which grew largely out of Dutch Protestant thought of a century ago, is so well suited to the intellectual style of our day. In the era since Thomas Kuhn and the rise of anti-foundationalism in philosophy, few claim today that there is just one worldview that can be demonstrated as superior on rational grounds alone. Even in the hard sciences, it is now widely recognized that the prevailing assumptions of communities play a role in what they count as true science. Evangelical Christians, of course, should not accept such trends uncritically. Typically, for instance, Kuyperians will qualify them with a chastened realism that is essential both to traditional Christian belief and to day-to-day human behavior.[10]

Early in this century most American intellectuals seemed to believe that ultimately one enlightened and scientific view would triumph for all educated humankind. Liberal Protestants shared in this view and so generally believed that eventually all Christians would have to be convinced of their views of religion and of Scripture. Almost all conservative Protestants held to the same principle, expecting that a triumph of rationality would lead to the universal vindication of their views. In both cases their outlooks reflected the combination of certain Enlightenment assumptions about rationality and Protestantism's long habit in America of thinking of itself as the cultural establishment whose views ought ultimately to prevail for all properly assimilated Americans and ultimately for the whole world.

Today's intellectual environment is far more pluralistic and we are fortunate to have available a developed intellectual tradition that is suited to taking account of the implications of that pluralism. Today I think it is much clearer than it was forty years ago that evangelicals do not have to take over the old Protestant agenda of dominating Western civilization or world civilization. Although we have benefited immensely from those who introduced this community to various versions of this Kuyperianism, I think it is clear that we no longer have to talk of remaking the mind of Western civilization. Rather, we should give up our vestigial establishmentarianism and accept our status as one community (or coalition of communities) within civilization. This is, I think, a healthier position for the church anyway.

For us as scholars this means that our agenda ought to be directed toward building for our community as solid a place in the pluralistic intellectual life of our civilization as is consistent with our principles. Helping to establish the intellectual viability of our world view and pointing out the shortcomings of alternatives can be an important service to our community and important dimension of our witness to the world. To perform this task properly requires a delicate combination of modesty and assertiveness. Our intellectual life must display the Christian qualities of self-criticism and generosity to others. Richard Neuhaus puts it well when he says we should have "reverence for those with whom we disagree"[11] while at the same time we properly attempt to establish for others the attractiveness of our worldview.

Establishing the attractiveness of a worldview, however, is not strictly or even primarily an intellectual enterprise. Rather we should hope that evangelical Christians will demonstrate the attractiveness of our world view by the way our communities address the whole range of human experience. This involves the way we live and not just the way we think. As Nicholas Wolterstorff has reminded us, action is the goal of Christian intellectual life. This does not mean that action is identical with intellectual life or can be substituted for it. These are important provisos in our pragmatically inclined communities where, as Mark Noll has observed, "to urge activist evangelicals to get more active is like pointing an addict toward dope."[12] Unfortunately, there is considerably more danger today of having intellectual and artistic life overwhelmed by various kinds of activism than there is danger of the reverse. Nonetheless, our goal is ultimately not primarily intellectual. As scholars our role is to play one modest part in building and enriching communities that are models of a balance of piety, worship, intellect, art, charity, and social concern.

Finally let me ask this question: what are the major challenges that we face today? I see three, two of which I shall mention just briefly. First, is that of politicization of the scholarly enterprise. Politics, broadly conceived, constitutes one of the operative religions for most people today. It is also the operative religion for many evangelicals. Sheer political partisanship could easily take over our scholarship, so that we could become fragmented into competing ideological camps. One antidote to this trend is to emphasize that Christian scholarship should always be self-critical scholarship, even though inevitably partisan to some extent.

A second challenge is simply that of maintaining our momentum in defining the distinctives of evangelical Christian scholarship. As I observed at the outset, one of the most striking features about Christian scholarship today is that so few communities are enthusiastic about promoting it. So one of our most important challenges is simply that of vindicating, for secular audiences but especially for Christian communities, the significance of our enterprise itself. Our communities must gain a vision of the primary importance of critically assessing the prevailing worldviews of our day and intelligently defining the distinctive characteristics of Christian views of reality.

The third of the challenges will perhaps be the most difficult to meet. Though we are in a far stronger position than forty years ago for dealing with pluralism in the larger scholarly community, the corollary is that we have to deal with more pluralism from within. In one sense this is a strength. Today there is wide recognition that "evangelicalism" is not a simple entity, but a loose coalition of sub-groups who share similar traits and traditions. Our presuppositionalism helps us to deal with such internal pluralism, to be less dogmatic than has been traditional in insisting that there is only one "evangelical" view of an issue. But how do we keep that recognition from drifting into a relativism? This has always been the problem for Protestantism, as their Catholic critics were quick to point out. Typically Protestants have responded with assertions that we have rational and scientific procedures for determining the one definitive meaning for Scripture. So Baptists thought they could rationally demonstrate that adult baptism was a requisite church ordinance, and non-Baptists thought they could demonstrate just as certainly that infant baptism was permissible as well. Today, with a clearer recognition of the limits of science and rationality, we should be in a position better to tolerate differing readings of the same texts.

But what if such disputes concern more central issues? In some cases, I think we can say that certain views go beyond the bounds of evangelicalism into something else. So I do not think you could have an evangelical who denied the bodily resurrection of Christ, or the atonement, or the necessity of regeneration, or that the Bible was uniquely inspired among religious books, or a number of other traditional evangelical emphases. But how do we set such boundaries for evangelicalism?

Finding the answer to such questions is especially perplexing for communities that have so little regard for the visible church or churches. Nonetheless, I see two steps in the right direction. First, whatever presuppositionalism we might have should not entail entirely abandoning traditional categories of common sense rationality in adjudicating disputes. Contrary to some twentieth-century mythology, some interpretations of texts are more reliable than others. And I see no reason to suppose that God has created us without the ability often to tell the difference between the relatively better interpretation and the relatively worse.

But let me put the point in broader terms. As I have argued here on an earlier occasion, I think that a central starting point of evangelical thought must be the incarnation. A starting premise in any coherent evangelical worldview is that we can know Jesus, the Jesus of history. We affirm that God has entered into real history and that we creatures can know something about God through this revelation in history. Moreover, this implies that we affirm that God has created us with sufficiently reliable mechanisms for knowing about reality, even on the basis of testimony of others, so that we can know what we need to of the historical Jesus through the revelation as it has come to us through Scripture. So a knowledge of the incarnate Christ among our fundamental principles excludes much of the historical and hermeneutical relativism of our day.[13]

The other step in the right direction I would propose is that we American Protestants, lacking much sense of the authority of any church, attempt to recover some sense of the value of tradition. This will always be an imperfect and not wholly reliable authority, but it could provide an important confirmatory test of our beliefs. Our sense of being part of a community of faith should involve a sense of being part of an historical community of faith. Our church is the church through the ages, not just churches today or all the evangelical churches we happen to like today. So one way critically to review our beliefs is to see which of our beliefs have stood the test of history. Which have been fundamental beliefs of churches in many times and cultures, not just the product of one era or social, political, or intellectual setting? This should not be the only way we arrive at which beliefs in the Christian tradition to emphasize, but it may be a helpful test for sorting out the extraneous from the fundamental.

This, for instance, seems to me to have been one of the principal failings of the fundamentalist movement in America. While proclaiming itself to be simply preserving the fundamentals of the faith, it mixed that enterprise with defense of a number of recent doctrinal inventions, emphases, and intellectual and cultural assumptions. One of the jobs of the historian, as I see it, is to help sort out those aspects of the tradition that represent responsible interpretations of Scripture over time from those which are principally expressions of the biases of one time and place.

Twentieth-century intellectual life has the peculiar bias that the newer an idea is the better it is supposed to be. When you think about it, this is an astounding bias, especially in an age when we are unusually conscious of the social-cultural origins of ideas. This bias for the latest idea seemed to make sense in the eighteenth century when it first became common. Then the faith in one universal science supported a faith in simple intellectual progress. But today, with the wide abandonment of the myth of a single science for humanity and with a high awareness of the importance of the sociology of knowledge, one would think that twentieth-century thinkers should be especially suspicious of new ideas (including strong emphases on the sociology of knowledge). Just to the contrary, however, today's scholars rush after the latest fads in much the same way that as children they rushed out to get Davey Crockett hats or hoola hoops. (I use these examples since the world is being taken over by baby boomers.) Evangelical scholars, by contrast, should benefit from the wisdom of many times and cultures. Though the ancientness of a belief is far from decisive evidence of its truth, it may provide reason to give that belief preferential consideration, especially if that belief has been long held by the communities we consider to well represent the church through the ages.

Not having a ringing, keynote-type ending, let me close rather with a very brief summary. It is arguable that we are witnessing the beginnings of a renaissance of evangelical scholarship. Even if so, evangelical scholarship has a long way to go. Compared with forty years ago, we seem to have made great strides. Compared with the wider intellectual community, we still represent a tiny minority enterprise. Assuming we do not lose sight of our primary task of building a strong sustaining community that witnesses to the Gospel by action as well as belief, it seems to me that we could sustain a healthy geometric growth in our enterprise if we maintained these three emphases: (1) a willingness not only to assert the superiority of our traditions, but to be self-critical and generous as well, (2) a continued emphasis on building critical analyses of the presuppositions dividing our thought from that of other worldviews, and (3) a healthy respect for the mainstreams of the Christian tradition as an antidote to the parochialisms both of our sub-communities and of our century. If we can maintain at least these three emphases, in addition to the fundamentals that define evangelicalism, then evangelical scholarship should not quickly drift into either a liberal Christianity or into the merely secular. Truly evangelical scholarship can flourish.

Notes

1. This essay first appeared in *CSR* 17.4 (June 1988): 347-60. This essay is a revision of Marsden's keynote address at the Institute for Advanced Christian Studies and the Institute for the Study of American Evangelicals in June 1987.

2. One of the best stories in the founding of Fuller is Ockenga's almost successful attempt to enlist another ardent separatist, Alan MacRae from Faith Theological Seminary, dominated by Ockenga's arch-rival Carl McIntire. This and other aspects of the account of the founding of Fuller are found in George Marsden, *Reforming Fundamentalism: Fuller Seminary and the New Evangelicalism* (Grand Rapids, Mich.: Eerdmans, 1987).

3. "The Challenge to the Christian Culture of the West," Convocation Address, Fuller Theological Seminary, October 1, 1947, *Fuller Theological Seminary Bulletin* 1:1 (1947).

4. Carl F. H. Henry, *The Uneasy Conscience of Modern Fundamentalism* (Grand Rapids, Mich.: Eerdmans, 1947), 14 & *passim;* Harold J. Ockenga, "Introduction," to *Uneasy Conscience*, 10.

5. Abraham Kuyper, *Principles of Sacred Theology*, trans. J. Hendrik DeVries (Grand Rapids, Mich.: Baker Book House, 1980 [1898]), 150-159.

6. Carl F. H. Henry, *Remaking the Modern Mind* (Grand Rapids, Mich.: Eerdmans, 1946).

7. This description was suggested to me by Edward Dobson.

8. James Hunter, *American Evangelicalism: The Coming Generation* (Chicago: University of Chicago Press, 1987).

9. One of the places where this view is discussed is in Alvin Plantinga and Nicholas Wolterstorff, eds., *Faith and Rationality: Reason and Belief in God* (Notre Dame, Ind.: University of Notre Dame Press, 1983).

10. A good example of such an alternative is found in Roger Lundin, Anthony C. Thiselton, and Clarence Walhout, *The Responsibility of Hermeneutics* (Grand Rapids, Mich.: Eerdmans, 1985).

11. Richard Neuhaus, ed., *Unsecular America* (Grand Rapids, Mich.: Eerdmans, 1986), 92.

12. Mark Noll, comment on earlier version of this paper.

13. "Evangelicals, History, and Modernity," in *Evangelicalism and Modern America*, George Marsden, ed. (Grand Rapids, Mich.: Eerdmans, 1984), 94-102.

5 On Developing Hopeful Virtues (1988)

Stanley Hauerwas

Therefore, since we are justified by faith, we have peace with God through our Lord Jesus Christ. Through him we have obtained access to this grace in which we stand, and we rejoice in our hope of sharing the glory of God. More than that, we rejoice in our sufferings, knowing that suffering produces endurance, and endurance produces character, and character produces hope, and hope does not disappoint us, because God's love has been poured into our hearts through the Holy Spirit which has been given to us. (Rom. 5:1-5)

What follows is meant to be an extended meditation on this text. I am adopting this strategy because I think this text provides us with some helpful suggestions about the nature, kind, and significance of the virtues for the Christian life.[1] At least on the surface the text seems to be about virtue. Suffering is not, of course, a virtue in itself. Endurance, character, and hope, however, seem to name dispositional characteristics that suggest virtue language is not foreign to the New Testament. Yet it is by no means clear why endurance, character, and hope are given particular status for illuminating the Christian life and/or why Paul seems to think them so closely interrelated. I call this a meditation because I hope to show how close attention to Scripture is compatible with and indeed requires critical reflection meant to help us lead better lives.

I think it important to dwell over these issues in order to test the current enthusiasm by many for the rediscovery of the significance of virtue for constructing the Christian life. I have obviously been among those attempting to rehabilitate virtue language for Christian ethics. That seems natural enough since not only in the New Testament are there lists that seem to name virtues (Gal. 5:22), but the Christian life, for all its variety in the New Testament, suggests that the Christian is characterized by certain enduring dispositional skills that should not be easily lost.

However, things are not quite that easy. I can illustrate this by telling you about two encounters. The first was with John Howard Yoder. During a lecture at Duke, Yoder used the phrase "dignity of the person" to suggest the kind of regard Christians should have for all people. I thought I had finally caught Yoder smuggling into his discourse an element foreign to the Scripture; an element, moreover, that comes from liberal ideology. Responding to my challenge whether such usage was consistent with his biblical realism, Yoder argued that "dignity of the person" was no more foreign to the Gospels than the language of virtue. Moreover, he suggested the New Testament at least seems to speak more about what we can and cannot do than it does about the virtues we ought to have. Thus in Galatians 5 just before we get the list of what appear to be virtues in verse 22—that is, love, joy, peace, patience, kindness, goodness, faithfulness, gentleness and self-control—we are forbidden in verse 19 to do the works of the flesh—immorality, impurity, licentiousness, idolatry, sorcery, enmity, strife, jealousy, anger, selfishness, dissension, party spirit, envy, drunkenness, carousing, and the like. Given such a list and what it implies about the human condition, maybe we ought to return to rules and law.

The second encounter occurred at a conference on the church and the university at Bethel College in North Newton, Kansas. I had written a paper called "How the Christian University Contributes to the Corruption of the Youth." I had used an argument by Martha Nussbaum that defended Aristophanes' critique of Socrates in *The Clouds* for engaging in dialectics indiscriminately—namely, it does no good to invite some to examine their lives prior to their being trained in virtue. When that is done the result is only moral cynicism, not virtue. I suggested that is exactly what the university does today, since we do not think it possible to expect our students to be virtuous or for the university to enhance or develop the virtues they have. After the paper, I was confronted by a young woman undergraduate who noted the Gospels seemed quite unconcerned with virtue. Rather the issue is one of discipleship. When the virtues are made central, Christians lose that which makes their morality intelligible—namely our lives as Christians are to be determined by our loyalty to a concrete person, not a set of abstract dispositions.

By reflection on this Pauline text, I hope to respond to these challenges. Of course, I cannot pretend to resolve all the disquiet many feel about the language of virtue, but I at least hope I will be able to suggest why the virtues help us express central aspects of the Christian life. Along the way I will also make some suggestions concerning the troubling issues about how the virtues are individuated as well as interrelated. This will provide the opportunity to explore why some claim that the virtues entail a narrative. Discussion of this, moreover, will force me to at least glance at the issue of whether, how, and what kind of an account of human nature is required in the attempt to construe the Christian life in terms of the virtues. This may seem a lot to hang on this text, but like most preachers I am confident the text is up to the task.

Yet I am going to ask even more of the text. For the text begins with the claim that we have been justified by faith. This emphasis on justification has often been one of the reasons many in the Christian tradition have thought the language of virtue suspect for displaying the nature of the Christian life. There are several ways in which this tension has been understood. In particular, justification suggests that our lives are given to us as a gift, whereas the virtues seem to imply that the moral life should be construed as an achievement. Moreover, the language of forgiveness that is so crucial for understanding justification seems to strike at the very heart of an ethic of virtue. The virtuous man or woman's whole purpose is to live in a manner such that they will never have to be forgiven for anything. Aristotle even suggests the virtuous person should avoid receiving favors, as such receptivity makes us vulnerable to fate, thus robbing us of the strength of character necessary to acquire the virtues in the right manner—that is, so that they cannot be lost or distorted.

Moreover, the emphasis on justification seems to make any developmental account of the moral life suspect. In contrast, an account of the virtues requires us to provide a sense of how growth in virtue is an intrinsic part of the moral life. From the perspective of justification the virtues cannot help but appear as attempts at self-justification; any attempt to acquire the virtues invites men and women to believe they can achieve rather than be given righteousness. Therefore questions of the nature and status of the virtues for displaying the Christian life must be set in the context of how best to understand moral development.

As usual, Karl Barth in *Church Dogmatics* puts the issue in its starkest form: "The relation between God and man is not that of a parallelism and harmony of the divine and human wills, but of an explosive encounter, contradiction and reconciliation, in which it is the part of the divine will to precede and the human to follow, of the former to control and the latter to submit. Neither as a whole nor in detail can our action mean our justification before God."[2] It might be thought that this is a theme peculiar to justification, but following this passage Barth says: "Our sanctification is God's work, not our own. It is very necessary, therefore, that there should be the encounter, the confrontation of our existence with the command of God."[3]

That Barth uses the language of command as primary is not, I think, accidental, given his emphasis on justification. From such a perspective the Christian life appears as a continuing series of responses to particular commands, but there is no continuing effect in those subject to those commands. There is continuity between the commands, but it is the continuity of the commander, not of those subject to the commands. For Barth, therefore, the fundamental image for the Christian life is not growth, but repetition. Only God's command is capable of such repetition for the

> repetition and confirmation of all other commands is limited: partly because, so far as content is concerned, they aim only at individual, temporally limited achievements; partly because they aim at attitudes and therefore at usages which once they are established need no new decision. But the necessity as well as the possibility of repetition and confirmation of the command of God is without limit. Even if it aims at the definite achievements and attitudes and actions and usages it always aims beyond them at our decision for Jesus, and just in this substance the decision demanded by God's command is of such a kind that it can and must be repeated and confirmed.[4]

Gilbert Meilaender has observed that this manner of construing the Christian life conceives of our existence primarily in terms of a dialogue. The Christian life has a distinctive nature, but that distinctiveness cannot be characterized by any progression. Rather, the Christian life is a "going back and forth, back and forth. That is to say, the Christian is simply caught within the dialogue between the two voices with which God speaks: the accusing voice of the law and the accepting voice of the gospel. Hearing the law, he flees to the gospel. Life is experienced as a dialogue between these two divine verdicts, and within human history one cannot escape that dialogue or process beyond it."[5]

This perspective, which has dominated Protestant theological ethic, assumes that texts like Romans 5:1-5 are supportive of this view of the Christian life—we are justified by faith. It is only the external action of God through Jesus Christ that has given us an access to this grace. Yet the second half of the text is less open to being so construed. We begin in hope made possible by our sharing in the glory of God, but "even more than that" we rejoice in our sufferings, as suffering produces endurance, and endurance produces character, and character produces hope—a movement of hope to hope. But the crucial question is whether this movement is getting us anywhere.

Most accounts of the Christian life have certainly thought such movement entails a sense of growth and development. The Christian life is not seen so much as a dialogue but rather as a journey through which people are gradually and graciously transformed by the very pilgrimage to which they have been called.

> Righteousness here is substantive rather than relational. It consists not in right relation with God but in becoming (throughout the whole of one's character) the sort of person God wills us to be and commits himself to making of us. Picturing the Christian life as such a journey, we can confess our sin without thinking that the standard of which we fell short, in its accusation of us, must lead us to doubt the gracious acceptance by which God empowers us to journey toward his goal for our lives.[6]

The battle lines between these two approaches are so well entrenched that one despairs of finding any way to resolve this dispute. My emphasis on the importance of character and virtue in the moral life has clearly put me on the side of those who think in terms of a journey. Yet I certainly do not think that this "developmental" view of the Christian life "unfolds" what was already there as potential. Growth in virtue either as individuals and/or as communities is not an inevitable movement to the higher and better. Our "nature" does not in and of itself provide all that is needed for growth in virtue. The virtues are not the result of the development of a teleology intrinsic to human nature.

I do not wish to deny that the virtues have something to do with our "nature" nor that the kind of persons we are should in some way inform how the individual virtues are determined. Yet I think Edmund Pincoffs is wrong to suggest "a just man is a just man. He needs no imprimatur to show forth what he is. Courage is no more a Catholic than it is a Buddhist virtue; honesty commends itself to Presbyterian and Coptic Christians alike."[7] Just as a Calvinist unbeliever is different from a Catholic unbeliever, the courage of a Christian is not the same as that of a Buddhist. No appeal to human nature is sufficient to insure such commonality. In this respect I think MacIntyre is right to argue that any account of the virtues requires a teleological understanding of human existence articulated through a community's narrative.

That, of course, is exactly what I want to suggest Paul's appeal to justification by faith is about. It would take us too far afield to discuss recent changes in the interpretation of Paul. Suffice it to say Paul has finally been rescued from the Lutherans by a recovery of the centrality of apocalyptic eschatology in his theology. As J. Christian Beker notes:

> Paul's proclamation of Jesus Christ (= the Messiah) is centered in a specific view of God and in a salvation-historical scheme. What does this mean? It expresses the conviction that, in the death and resurrection of Jesus Christ, the Covenant-God of Israel has confirmed and renewed his promises of salvation of Israel and to the nations as first recorded in the Hebrew Bible. These promises pertain to the expectation of the public manifestation of the reign of God, the visible presence of God among his people, the defeat of all his enemies and the vindication of Israel in the gospel. In other words, the death and resurrection of Jesus Christ manifests the inauguration of the righteousness of God.[8]

It is only against this background that we can understand why Paul conceives of the Christian life as a movement from hope to hope or why it is that hope is singled out as the virtue that frames the Christian life. For the hope we have been given is that which makes possible the locating of our lives in a new history, a new journey, that was not possible without the life, death, and resurrection of Jesus Christ.

It is a neat, important, and largely unexplored question what the relation may be between this eschatological understanding of the moral life of Christians and the teleological account MacIntyre, following Aristotle, says is needed for an ethic of virtue. While I think there is no necessary incompatibility between the eschatological and teleological—indeed for theological reasons I would argue a necessary compatibility—it is by no means clear what substantial and material terms best display that relation. I suspect such a discussion—which put abstractly is about the relation of nature (teleological) and history (eschatology)—will involve an account of the nature of happiness and its relation to suffering. When put in those terms the primary difference between Christian thought on these matters and someone like Aristotle is that for the former happiness can finally only be understood in terms of the life of a community—eschatologically, the communion of saints. That, of course, will make a great difference for how the virtues are understood.

I do not mean to suggest that my emphasis on the eschatological context for understanding the virtues of Christians makes impossible any comparison of Christian virtues with those of other communities. In fact, I suspect we share enough as humans—we all must die—that provides some basis for comparison if not commonality. Indeed, I find Robert Roberts' suggestion that virtues have a grammar—that is, a set of rules embodies a system of relation—that makes comparisons possible very suggestive. Thus gratitude has a structure, involving the reception of a non-obligatory good from another person, that has a kind of universality—that is, it is true of gratitude as a virtue wherever we find it.[9] It is unclear to what extent the grammars of the different virtues can be said to be grounded in our nature. However, I have no doubt that Roberts' suggestion allows for some formal parallel to be drawn across various virtue traditions.

Yet as Roberts suggests, appeals to nature are tricky indeed, especially in the Christian context. From the perspective of the Gospel the deepest truth about us is not that we share a common nature—even weak, needy, or fallible nature—but that we are forgiven sinners for whom Christ died. What we have in common is a common predicament that depends on the belief that a historically contingent life has determined the eschatological destiny of the universe. Roberts notes that it seems improbable that such a historical belief could form part of the grammar of any virtue. For "grammar" is a form of an informal sort of logic and logic makes no reference to historical events. Yet Roberts rightly argues

> the doctrine of righteousness through Christ's atoning death for sinners is the hub of the Christian view of the world, the axis upon which everything else turns. And the virtue of forgiveness is especially close to the hub. So in this case, like it or not, a particular historical belief is essential to the grammar of a virtue, and every exposition of Christian forgiveness must give a central place to this belief, just as every instance of distinctively Christian forgiveness involves envisioning the offender in the light of the cross. To put this in the terms of the Christian virtues-system, the historical fact that Christ died for sinners became an essential feature of human nature.[10]

Put it in terms of Romans 5, our nature is grounded in hope. That hope is embodied in our most basic needs and wants–to survive, to eat, to love—but such hope leads us to hope finally in God. Thus the movement is from hope to hope as we discover we can hope only because, as Paul says, we discover we stand in grace. More exactly, we do not begin in hope, but we rejoice in our hope as we learn that our hope is possible only as we learn to acknowledge it as a gift.

Yet Paul says we not only rejoice in our hope, but also in our sufferings. For suffering is also something we receive rather than do. Hope and suffering it seems are equally matters for rejoicing insofar as they make possible our hope of sharing in God's glory. In order to understand this aright, however, it is crucial that the story of Israel and Jesus Paul assumes not be forgotten. Otherwise the suffering in which we are told to rejoice might well be but a masochistic delight. Christians are not to suffer as an end in itself, any more than the self is to be sacrificed in and of itself. Rather suffering, as well as self-sacrifice, gain their theological intelligibility only as they are formed after Christ's likeness.

Not all suffering is to be the occasion for rejoicing, but only that which is correlative to the grace in which we stand. We can suffer from illness or tragic loss of a friend but such a suffering is not in itself to be the occasion for rejoicing. That is only possible when such suffering is given a *telos* through the suffering that comes from the faith that has been made ours through Jesus Christ.

Only that suffering is capable of producing endurance. For what is endurance but steadfast faithfulness to the cause of Jesus Christ? This can easily be misunderstood, as endurance can be associated with passive acceptance of evil. But the kind of endurance that Paul calls for us to embrace is that which is capable of turning our fate into destiny—that is, we are given the means to turn our past, which is a history of sin, into love capable of being of service to the neighbor. Endurance in this sense is closely associated with courage, since both involve essential stances toward death. Moreover, each gains its intelligibility by the kind of patience required to live in the presence of the hope of the kingdom.

Christians can endure because through Christ they have been given power over death and all forms of victimization that trade on the power of death. The ultimate power of Christ is the victory over death that makes possible the endurance derived from our confidence that though our enemies may kill us they cannot determine the meaning of our death. The power Christians have been given allows us to endure in the face of oppression exactly because we refuse to let our oppressors define us as victims. We endure because no matter what may be done to us we know that those who would determine the meaning of our life by threatening our death have already decisively lost.

Moreover, that is why it is "we" that rejoice in our sufferings that produces endurance, since this is not some individual achievement. The endurance required of Christians is possible only because it is the endurance of a whole people who are committed to remember the saints. For it is from the saints we learn how to be steadfast in the face of adversity. By remembering them we literally become members of a community and history that gives us the power to prevail.

The saints, of course, make no sense apart from the life and death of Jesus of Nazareth. The memory of the saints, therefore, derives its power from the memory of Him who is celebrated in a meal through which we are given the opportunity to share in His destiny. Death on a cross could not blot out Jesus' life, for by his resurrection a people is created capable of sustaining the virtues necessary to be a community of memory. Because of that memory we as Christians have the power to make our deaths our own by learning to endure.

Yet endurance, like suffering, is not an end in itself, since it produces character. This is not a means/ends relationship. We do not suffer so that we will endure and we do not endure in order to have character. Rather, the kind of suffering we take up endures and our endurance has character. For what is character but the naming of that history that we have been given through our endurance? That is why our character is an achievement, but it is an achievement that comes as a gift. (I am indebted to Alasdair MacIntyre for the way of putting the matter.) It comes not by constant effort to realize an ideal, but rather character is our discovery that we can look back on our lives and, by God's forgiveness, claim them as our own. Character, in other words, is that continuity of self that makes possible retrospective acknowledgements that our lives have been made more than we could acknowledge at any one time.

That is why Christian ethics is in such profound tension with accounts of the moral life that assume ethical reflection and behavior is primarily a matter of prospective judgments about this or that kind of decision. Such ethics are built on rationalistic self-deceptions that assume each individual has the power to determine her "choices." In contrast Christian ethics, at least the kind I am willing to defend, is not so concerned with decisions and choices, but rather with the kind of person that is prior to all choices.

Of course, it can still be asked if hope, endurance, and character are virtues. Are they habits or dispositions that form us to be what otherwise we have no capacity to be? I am obviously convinced that the language of virtue does help us see better what Paul is about in Romans 5. At the very least it is clear Paul does not begin with the question "what ought to be done?" The question of "what ought we to do" is nonsense if it is asked prior to the question of the kind of character we should have. We can only act in a world we can see and we can only learn to see by having one kind of character rather than another. As Wittgenstein reminds us, the world of the happy person is not the same as the world of the unhappy. This is not a psychological point, but an ontological claim about the way we are in the world. The character of Christians is only possible if Jesus has in fact risen from the dead.

For Christians the question of being is prior to the question of doing. Virtue is prior to act. Even more strongly put, we cannot even know what an action is until we are able to fit it into an agent's history. This is but to say that there is a strong and inherent relation between the intentional, the social, and the historical. Alasdair MacIntyre suggests we

> place the agent's intentions in causal and temporal order with reference to their role in his or her history; and we also place them with reference to their role in his or her history; and we also place them with reference to their role in the history of the setting or settings to which they belong. In doing this, in determining what causal efficacy the agent's intentions had in one or more directions, and how his short-term intentions succeeded or failed to be constitutive of long-term intentions, we ourselves write a further part of these histories. Narrative history of a certain kind turns out to be the basic and essential genre for the characterization of human actions.[11]

I think this is essential if we are to understand the relation that Paul has developed between hope, suffering, endurance, and character. For as I have tried to show, the interrelation between these reflects the assumption that in God's action in Jesus Christ we have been made part of an enacted narrative. The kind of hope, the kind of suffering, the kind of endurance, and the kind of character we are to have are but reflections of the story of what God has done in and through Jesus Christ. Hope, endurance, and character are those qualities of self that make possible our participation in that story. The virtues, the unity of self embodied in our character, give us direction by making our past intelligible. We develop by looking back.

That, moreover, is why the movement is ultimately circular—that is, from hope to hope. By being put on the way by hope we discover hope that does not disappoint. Aristotle suggested in the *Nicomachean Ethics* that the virtues are like a "second nature" because they are not implanted in us by nature nor contrary to nature, but rather "we are by nature equipped with the ability to receive them, and habit brings this ability to completion and fulfillment" (1103a 23–25). In like manner I think Paul is suggesting that through enduring suffering we discover that God has given us a character capable of sustaining a hope that does not disappoint. It is not as if the hope with which we began is deficient, but rather that very hope has put us on a journey that we could hardly anticipate when we began. By nature we cannot help but hope, but our nature is not sufficient to sustain that hope except as we are led by that hope to hope in God.

But why does character produce hope? It does so because as we learn to inhabit the narrative of God's work in Jesus Christ we learn to see all existence as trustworthy. It is not trustworthy in itself but because every part is related to hope by expanding our "nature" as we are taught to ask more and more of God's creation. In the language of the scholastics, God's grace rewards itself by increasing in us the ability to enjoy God forever.

The scholastics, of course, called this process "merit." No doubt that was an unfortunate choice of words, as it invites the assumption that men and women might be able to place God's grace under necessity. Yet Aquinas insists "Man is justified by faith not as though man, by believing, were to merit justification, but that he believes whilst he is being justified" (ST, I-II, 114, 6 Reply Obj, 1). We are ordained by God to an eternal life, of friendship with God, not by our own strength but by the help of grace (ST, I-II, 114, 2 Reply Obj, 1). Therefore merit but names the process by which God's grace becomes ours because of God's unwillingness to leave us alone. We can, perhaps, give up the word "merit" but I am convinced we cannot give up what it is meant to signify if we are to be faithful to Paul's insistence that the hope that is produced by our character will not disappoint us.

For what is merit but the love that has been poured out into our hearts by the Holy Spirit? So it is love that is at the beginning generating hope, and it is love at the end rejoicing in what it has created. That is why the language of development or growth cannot be avoided in any account of the Christian life; otherwise we deny the power of God's grace. We are destined to enjoy friendship with God, which is the only form of peace worth having, since it is activity in its purest form lacking or needing nothing.

I think it is only against this background that we can appreciate why Aquinas was ultimately driven to the extremely odd category of "infused moral virtues" (S.T.I.II. q.65, article 2; q. 63, art. 3). It is often times overlooked that Aquinas' familiar distinction between natural and theological virtues was qualified by his further contention that with charity all the moral virtues are infused—thus infused fortitude, infused temperance, infused justice, and infused prudence. These virtues are different "in species" than the natural virtues as they make it possible for us to act in relation with our life with God. As Robert Sokolowski suggests

> we seem to have not only a contrast between moral and theological virtues but also a contrast between two levels of moral virtues, the natural and the infused. In what sense does one remain a single agent in such differences? And how are the infused moral virtues to be compared with the acquired moral virtues? For

example, could a person who is weak in self-control as regards natural virtue be, at the same time, temperate and courageous through his infused virtue? Does he acquire such temperance and courage simply by infusion, without actual performance?[12]

Indeed Aquinas even goes so far, as Sokolowski notes, to say with Augustine that "where there is no recognition of the truth, virtue is false, even in good habits" (S.T.I.II.q.65, art. 2).

While I have no stake in underwriting the language of "infusion," I think that Aquinas is right to emphasize that the virtues that come from God's love are of a different kind than the "so-called" natural virtues. This does not mean that there is no continuity between natural and infused courage, but rather such continuity cannot be assumed by assertions about there being no disharmony between God's created and redeemed orders. Yet Sokolowski fears that Aquinas' distinction between natural and infused virtues might give the impression that the single human agent is split into two performers with two different contexts of action. He resolves this by suggesting that finally there is no difference between what the good person and the Christian is meant to do in the concrete—that is, to tell the truth, to be honest, to be temperate and courageous, to defend one's home and country.[13]

But surely this is to solve the problem far too easily, especially when we remember that the life of virtue is also a matter of perception. What Aquinas is rightly struggling with is the fact that the person whose life is lived in love and peace with God simply does not live in the same world as the person who does not. To use the language I have employed, they inhabit different narrative contexts. Yet we know the situation to be still more complex, since we know that as long as we are wayfarers, our selves are constituted by both of those narratives.

Which, of course, brings me finally to the problem of sin. It is sin, after all, that renders all talk of growth or development problematic. Just to the extent we think we are getting somewhere, that we are making progress, we in fact are only regressing as we attribute to ourselves what only God can do. Because of the undeniable power of sin perhaps it would be better to avoid all talk of development in the Christian life. Such talk is only an invitation to underwrite further our self-deceptive claim that we want to know the truth about ourselves. Moreover, it is the common testimony of the saints that the closer they get to God, the more their sin becomes an overwhelming reality.

Yet that is surely the reason why we cannot let the reality of sin determine our growth in hope. No sin is more damning than to fail to hope in the power of God's love to release us from our sin. Our growth in grace is not a denial of our sin. Without God's grace we cannot even know we are sinners. But because God has invited us to be part of his kingdom, the truth of our sin can be known and confessed without that knowledge destroying.

Forgiveness, therefore, is the hallmark of our growth in grace. This forgiveness is not our forgiving, which too often simply invites our attempt to dominate others. Rather we must be willing to accept forgiveness. Such acceptance is the means by which our souls are expanded so that hope is made possible, and through hope we learn to endure suffering, confident that God has given us character sufficient for such work. In short, God has given us all we need to finally be of one mind to live in God's story so that our virtues might finally be unified–that is why all virtues for Christians cannot help but be hopeful.

Notes

1. This essay first appeared in *CSR* 18.2 (December 1988): 107-117.
2. Karl Barth, *Church Dogmatics*. Vol. 2 Part 2, tr. G. W. Bromley et.al. (Edinburgh: T. and T. Clark, 1957), 644.
3. Ibid., 645.
4. Ibid., 612.
5. "The Place of Ethics in the Theological Task," *Currents in Theology and Mission,* 6 (1979): 199.
6. Ibid., 199.
7. Edmond Pincoffs, *Quandaries and Virtues: Against Reductionism in Ethics* (Lawrence, Kan.: University of Kansas Press, 1982), 162.
8. J. Christian Beker, *Paul's Apocalyptic Gospel: The Coming Triumph of God* (Philadelphia: Fortress Press, 1982), 30.
9. Robert Roberts, "Virtues and Rules," 13-14 (unpublished).
10. "Therapies and the Grammar of a Virtue," in *The Grammar of the Heart: New Essays in Moral Philosophy and Theology* (San Francisco: Harper and Row, 1988) 14-15.
11. *After Virtue* (Notre Dame, Ind.: University of Notre Dame, 1984), 208.
12. *The God of Faith and Reason* (Notre Dame, Ind.: University of Notre Dame Press, 1982), 78.
13. Ibid., 82.

6 When Faith and Reason Clash
Evolution and the Bible (1991)

ALVIN PLANTINGA

My question is simple: How shall we Christians deal with apparent conflicts between faith and reason, between what we know as Christians and what we know in other ways, between teaching of the Bible and the teachings of science?[1] As a special case, how shall we deal with apparent conflicts between what the Bible initially seems to tell us about the origin and development of life, and what contemporary science seems to tell us about it? Taken at face value, the Bible seems to teach that God created the world relatively recently, that he created life by way of several separate acts of creation, that in another separate act of creation he created an original human pair, Adam and Eve, and that these our original parents disobeyed God, thereby bringing ruinous calamity on themselves, their posterity, and the rest of creation.

According to contemporary science, on the other hand, the universe is exceedingly old—some fifteen or sixteen billion years or so, give or take a billion or two. The earth is much younger, maybe four and a half billion years old, but still hardly a spring chicken. Primitive life arose on earth perhaps three and a half billion years ago, by virtue of processes that are completely natural if so far not well understood; and subsequent forms of life developed from these aboriginal forms by way of natural processes, the most popular candidates being perhaps random genetic mutation and natural selection.

Now we Reformed Christians are wholly in earnest about the Bible. We are people of the Word; *Sola Scriptura* is our cry; we take Scripture to be a special revelation from God himself, demanding our absolute trust and allegiance. But we are equally enthusiastic about reason, a God-given power by virtue of which we have knowledge of ourselves, our world, our past, logic and mathematics, right and wrong, and God himself; reason is one of the chief features of the image of God in us. And if we are enthusiastic about reason, we must also be enthusiastic about contemporary natural science, which is a powerful and vastly impressive manifestation of reason. So this is my question: given our Reformed proclivities and this apparent conflict, what are we to do? How shall we think about this matter?

If the question is simple, the answer is enormously difficult. To think about it properly, one must obviously know a great deal of science. On the other hand, the question crucially involves both philosophy and theology: one must have a serious and penetrating grasp of the relevant theological and philosophical issues. And who among us can fill a bill like that? Certainly I cannot. (And that, as my colleague Ralph McInerny once said in another connection, is no idle boast.) The scientists among us do not ordinarily have a sufficient grasp of the relevant philosophy and theology; the philosophers and theologians do not know enough science; consequently, hardly anyone is qualified to speak here with real authority. This must be one of those areas where fools rush in and angels fear to tread. Whether or not it is an area where angels fear to tread, it is obviously an area where fools rush in. I hope this essay is not just one more confirmation of that dismal fact.

But first, a quick gesture towards the history of our problem. Our specific problem—faith and evolution—has of course been with the church since Darwinian evolution started to achieve wide acceptance, a little more than a hundred years ago. And this question is only a special case of two more general questions, questions that the Christian Church has faced since its beginnings nearly two millennia ago: first, what shall we do when there appears to be a conflict between the deliverances of faith and the deliverances of reason? And another question, related but distinct: how shall we evaluate and react to the dominant teachings, the dominant intellectual motifs, the dominant commitments of the society in which we find ourselves? These two questions, not always clearly distinguished, dominate the writings of the early church fathers from the second century on.

Naturally enough, there have been a variety of responses. There is a temptation, first of all, to declare that there really cannot be any conflict between faith and reason. The no conflict view comes in two quite different versions. According to the first, there is no such thing as truth *simpliciter*, truth just as such: there is only truth from one or another perspective. An extreme version of this view is the medieval two-truth theory associated with Averroes and some of his followers; some of these thinkers apparently held that the same proposition can be true according to philosophy or reason, but false according to theology or faith, true as science but false as theology. Thinking hard about this view can easily induce vertigo; the idea, apparently, is that one ought to affirm and believe the proposition as science, but deny it as theology. How you are supposed to do that is not clear. But the main problem is simply that truth is not merely truth with respect to some standpoint. Indeed, any attempt to explain what truth from a standpoint might mean inevitably involves the notion of truth *simpliciter*.

A more contemporary version of this way of thinking—the truth-from-a-standpoint way of thinking—takes its inspiration from contemporary physics. To oversimplify shamelessly, there is a problem: light seems to display both the properties of a wave in a medium and also the properties of something that comes in particles. And of course the problem is that these properties are not like, say, being green and being square, which can easily be exemplified by the same object; the problem is that it looks for all the world as if light cannot be both a particle and a wave. According to Nils Bohr, the father of the Copenhagen interpretation of quantum mechanics, the solution is to be found in the idea of complementarity. We must recognize that there can be descriptions of the same object or phenomenon which are both true, and relevantly complete, but nonetheless such that we cannot see how they could both hold. From one point of view light displays the particle set of properties; from another point of view, it displays the wave properties. We cannot see how both these descriptions can be true, but in fact they are. Of course the theological application is obvious: there is the broadly scientific view of things, and the broadly religious view of things; both are perfectly acceptable, perfectly correct, even though they appear to contradict one another.[2] And the point of the doctrine is that we must learn to live with and love this situation.

But this view itself is not easy to learn to love. Is the idea that the properties in question really are inconsistent with each other, so that it is not possible that the same thing have both sets of properties? Then clearly enough they cannot both be correct descriptions of the matter, and the view is simply false. Is the idea instead that while the properties are apparently inconsistent, they are not really inconsistent? Then the view might be correct, but would not be much by way of a *view,* being instead nothing but a redescription of the problem.

Perhaps a more promising approach is by way of territorial division, like that until recently between East and West Germany, for instance. We assign some of the conceptual territory to faith and Scripture, and some of it to reason and science. Some questions fall within the jurisdiction of faith and Scripture; others within that of reason and science, but none within both. These questions, furthermore, are such that their answers cannot conflict; they simply concern different aspects of the cosmos. Hence, so long as there is no illegal territorial encroachment, there will be no possibility of contradiction or incompatibility between the teachings of faith and those of science. Conflict arises only when there is trespass, violation of territorial integrity, by one side or the other. A limited version of this approach is espoused by our colleague Howard van Till in *The Fourth Day.* Science, he says, properly deals only with matters *internal* to the universe. It deals with the properties, behavior and history of the cosmos and the objects to be found therein; but it can tell us nothing about the *purpose* of the universe, or about its *significance,* or its *governance,* or its *status;* that territory has been reserved for Scripture. The Bible addresses itself only to questions of external relationships, relationships of the cosmos or the things it contains to things beyond it, such as God. Scripture deals with the status, origin, value, governance, and purpose of the cosmos and the things it contains, but says nothing of their, properties, behavior, or history.

Now van Till means to limit these claims to the prehistory (i.e., history prior to the appearance of human beings) of the cosmos; he does not hold that science and Scripture cannot both speak on matter of human history, for example.[3] This means that his view does not give us a general approach to *prima facie* conflicts between science and Scripture; for it says nothing about such apparent conflicts that pertain to matters of human history, or to matters concerning how things have gone in the cosmos since the appearance of human beings. Van Till limits his approval of this approach for very good reason; taken as a general claim, the contention that Scripture and science never speak on the same topic is obviously much too simple. First, there are many questions such that both science (taken broadly) and the Bible purport to answer them: for example, Was there such a person as Abraham? Was Jesus Christ crucified? Has anyone ever caught fish in the Sea of Galilee? Do ax heads ever float? Indeed, even if we restrict or limit the claim, in van Till's way, to the prehistory of the cosmos, we still find questions that both Scripture and science seem to answer: for example, Has the cosmos existed for an infinite stretch of time?

Further, it is of the first importance to see that when we remove that limitation (and here, of course, van Till would agree), then it is not true at all that the Bible tells only about status, value, purpose, origin, and the like. It tells us about Abraham, for example, and not only about his status and purpose; it tells us he lived in a certain place, made the long journey from Ur to Canaan, had a wife Sarah who had a son when she was really much too old, proposed at one time to sacrifice Isaac in obedience to the Lord, and so on. Even more important, the Bible tells us about Jesus Christ, and not simply about his origin and significance. It does tell us about those things, and of course they are of absolutely crucial importance to its central message; but it also tells us much else about Christ. We learn what he did: he preached and taught, drew large crowds, performed miracles. It tells us that he was crucified, that he died, and that he rose from the dead. Some of the teachings most central to Scripture and to the Christian faith tell us of concrete historical events; they therefore tell us of the history and properties of things within the cosmos. Christ died and then rose again; this tells us much about some of the entities within the cosmos. It tells us something about the history, properties, and behavior of his body, for example, namely, that it was dead and then later on alive. It thus tells us that some of the things in the cosmos behaved very differently on this occasion from the way in which they ordinarily behave. The same goes, of course, for the ascension of Christ, and for the many other miracles reported in Scripture.

So we cannot start, I think, by declaring that the teachings of contemporary science cannot conflict with the deliverances of the faith; obviously they can. We cannot sensibly decide in advance what topics Scripture can or does speak on; instead we must look and see. And in fact it speaks on an enormous variety of topics and questions—some having to do with origin, governance, status, and the like, but many more having to do with what happened within the cosmos at a particular place and time, and hence with what also falls within the province of science. It speaks of history, of miracles, of communications from the Lord, of what people did and did not do, of battles, healings, deaths, resurrections, and a thousand other things.

Let's look a little deeper. As everyone knows, there are various intellectual or cognitive powers, belief-producing mechanisms or powers, various sources of belief and knowledge. For example, there are perception, memory, induction, and testimony, or what we learn from others. There is also reason, taken narrowly as the source of logic and mathematics, and reason taken more broadly as including perception, testimony, and both inductive and deductive processes; it is reason taken this broader way that is the source of science. But the serious Christian will also take our grasp of Scripture to be a proper source of knowledge and justified belief. Just how does Scripture work as a source of proper belief? An answer as good as any I know was given by John Calvin and endorsed by the Belgic Confession—Calvin's doctrine of the internal testimony of the Holy Spirit. This is a fascinating and important contribution that does not get nearly the attention it deserves; but here I do not have time to go into the matter. Whatever the mechanism, the Lord speaks to us in Scripture.

And of course what the Lord proposes for our belief is indeed what we should believe. Here there will be enthusiastic agreement on all sides. Some conclude, however, that when there is a conflict between Scripture (or our grasp of it) and science, we must reject science; such conflict automatically shows science to be wrong, at least on the point in question. In the immortal words of the inspired Scottish bard William E. McGonagall, poet and tragedian, "When faith and reason clash, Let reason go to smash." But clearly this conclusion does not follow. The Lord cannot make a mistake, fair enough; but we can. Our grasp of what the Lord proposes to teach us can be faulty and flawed in a thousand ways. This is obvious, if only because of the widespread disagreement among serious Christians as to just what it is the Lord does propose for our belief in one or another portion of Scripture. Scripture is indeed perspicuous; what it teaches with respect to the way of salvation is indeed such that she who runs may read. It is also clear, however, that serious, well-intentioned Christians can disagree as to what the teaching of Scripture, at one point or another, really is. Scripture is inerrant: the Lord makes no mistakes; what he proposes for our belief is what we ought to believe. Sadly enough, however, our grasp of what he proposes to teach is fallible. Hence we cannot simply identify the teaching of Scripture with our grasp of that teaching; we must ruefully bear in mind the possibility that we are mistaken. "He sets the earth on its foundations; it can never be moved," says the Psalmist (Ps. 104:5). Some sixteenth-century Christians took the Lord to be teaching here that the earth neither rotates on its axis nor goes around the sun; and they were mistaken.

So we cannot identify our understanding or grasp of the teaching of Scripture with the teaching of Scripture; hence we cannot automatically assume that conflict between what we see as the teaching of Scripture, and what we seem to have learned in some other way must always be resolved in favor of the former. Sadly enough, we have no guarantee that on every point our grasp of what Scripture teaches is correct; hence it is possible that our grasp of the teaching of Scripture be corrected or improved by what we learn in some other way—by way of science, for example.

But neither, of course, can we identify either the current deliverances of reason or our best contemporary science (or philosophy, or history, or literary criticism, or intellectual efforts of any kind) with the truth. No doubt what reason, taken broadly, teaches is by and large reliable; this is, I should think, a consequence of the fact that we have been created in the image of God. Of course, we must reckon with the fall and its noetic effects; but the sensible view here, overall, is that the deliverances of reason are for the most part reliable. Perhaps they are most reliable with respect to such common everyday judgments as that there are people here, that it is cold outside, that the pointer points to four, that I had breakfast this morning, that 2+1=3, and so on; perhaps they are less reliable when it comes to matters near the limits of our abilities, as with certain questions in set theory, or in areas for which our faculties do not seem to be primarily designed, as perhaps in the world of quantum mechanics. By and large, however, and over enormous swatches of cognitive territory, reason is reliable.

Still, we cannot simply embrace current science (or current anything else either) as the truth. We cannot identify the teaching of Scripture with our grasp of it because serious and sensible Christians disagree as to what Scripture teaches; we cannot identify the current teachings of science with truth, because the current teachings of science change. And they do not change just by the accumulation of new facts. A few years back, the dominant view among astronomers and cosmologists was that the universe is infinitely old; at present the prevailing opinion is that the universe began some sixteen billion years ago; but now there are straws in the wind suggesting a step back towards the idea that there was no beginning.[4] Or think of the enormous changes from nineteenth- to twentieth-century physics. A prevailing attitude at the end of the nineteenth century was that physics was pretty well accomplished; there were a few loose ends here and there to tie up and a few mopping up operations left to do, but the fundamental lineaments and characteristics of physical reality had been described. And we all know what happened next.

As I said above, we cannot automatically assume that when there is a conflict between science and our grasp of the teaching of Scripture, it is science that is wrong and must give way. But the same holds vice versa; when there is a conflict between our grasp of the teaching of Scripture and current science, we cannot assume that it is our interpretation of Scripture that is at fault. It could be that, but it does not have to be; it could be because of some mistake or flaw in current science. The attitude I mean to reject was expressed by a group of serious Christians, as far back as 1832, when deep time was first being discovered: "If sound science appears to contradict the Bible," they said, "we may be sure that it is our interpretation of the Bible that is at fault."[5] To return to the poet McGonagall, "When faith and reason clash, 'Tis faith must go to smash."

This attitude—the belief that when there is a conflict, the problem must inevitably lie with our interpretation of Scripture, so that the correct course is always to modify that understanding in such a way as to accommodate current science—is every bit as deplorable as the opposite error. No doubt science can correct our grasp of Scripture; but Scripture can also correct current science. If, for example, current science were to return to the view that the world has no beginning, and is infinitely old, then current science would be wrong.

So what, precisely, must we do in such a situation? Which do we go with: faith or reason? More exactly, which do we go with, our grasp of Scripture or current science? I do not know of any infallible rule, or even any pretty reliable general recipe. All we can do is weigh and evaluate the relative warrant, the relative backing or strength, of the conflicting teachings. We must do our best to apprehend both the teachings of Scripture and the deliverances of reason; in either case we will have much more warrant for some apparent teachings than for others. It may be hard to see just what the Lord proposes to teach us in the Song of Solomon or Old Testament genealogies; it is vastly easier to see what he proposes to teach us in the Gospel accounts of Christ's resurrection from the dead. On the other side, it is clear that among the deliverances of reason is the proposition that the earth is round rather than flat; it is enormously harder to be sure, however, that contemporary quantum mechanics, taken realistically, has things right.[6] We must make as careful an estimate as we can of the degrees of warrant of the conflicting doctrines; we may then make a judgment as to where the balance of probability lies, or alternatively, we may suspend judgment. After all, we do not have to have a view on all these matters.

Let me illustrate from the topic under discussion. Consider that list of apparent teachings of Genesis—that God has created the world, that the earth is young, that human beings and many different kinds of plants and animals were separately created, and that there was an original human pair whose sin has afflicted both human nature and some of the rest of the world. At least one of these claims—the claim that the universe is young—is very hard to square with a variety of types of scientific evidence: geological, paleontological, cosmological and so on. Nonetheless a sensible person might be convinced, after careful and prayerful study of the Scriptures, that what the Lord teaches there implies that this evidence is misleading and that as a matter of fact the earth really is very young. So far as I can see, there is nothing to rule this out as automatically pathological or irrational or irresponsible or stupid.

And of course this sort of view can be developed in more subtle and nuanced detail. For example, the above teachings may be graded with respect to the probability that they really are what the Lord intends us to learn from early Genesis. Most clear, perhaps, is that God created the world, so that it and everything in it depends upon him and neither it nor anything in it has existed for an infinite stretch of time. Next clearest, perhaps, is that there was an original human pair who sinned and through whose sinning disaster befell both man and nature; for this is attested to not only here but in many other places in Scripture. That humankind was separately created is perhaps less clearly taught; that many other kinds of living beings were separately created might be still less clearly taught; that the earth is young, still less clearly taught. One who accepted all of these theses ought to be much more confident of some than of others—both because of the scientific evidence against some of them, and because some are much more clearly the teachings of Scripture than others. I do not mean to endorse the view that all of these propositions are true; but it is not just silly or irrational to do so. One need not be a fanatic, or a Flat Earther, or an ignorant Fundamentalist in order to hold it. In my judgment the view is mistaken, because I take the evidence for an old earth to be strong and the warrant for the view that the Lord teaches that the earth is young to be relatively weak. But these judgments are not simply obvious, or inevitable, or such that anyone with any sense will automatically be obliged to agree.

So I can properly correct my view as to what reason teaches by appealing to my understanding of Scripture; and I can properly correct my understanding of Scripture by appealing to the teachings of reason. It is of the first importance, however, that we correctly identify the relevant teachings of reason. Here I want to turn directly to the present problem, the apparent disparity between what Scripture and science teach us about the origin and development of life. Like any good Christian Reformed preacher, I have three points here. First, I shall argue that the theory of evolution is by no means religiously or theologically neutral. Second, I want to ask how we Christians should in fact think about evolution; how probable is it, all things considered, that the Grand Evolutionary Hypothesis is true? And third, I want to make a remark about how, as I see it, our intellectuals and academics should serve us, the Christian community, in this area.

According to a popular contemporary myth, science is a cool, reasoned, wholly dispassionate attempt to figure out the truth about ourselves and our world, entirely independent of religion, or ideology, or moral convictions, or theological commitments. I believe this is deeply mistaken. Following Augustine (and Abraham Kuyper, Herman Dooyeweerd, Harry Jellema, Henry Stob, and other Reformed thinkers), I believe that there is conflict, a battle between the *Civitas Dei,* the City of God, and the City of the World. As a matter of fact, what we have, I think, is a three-way battle. On the one hand there is Perennial Naturalism, a view going back to the ancient world, a view according to which there is no God, nature is all there is, and mankind is to be understood as a part of nature. Second, there is what I shall call Enlightenment Humanism; we could also call it Enlightenment Subjectivism or Enlightenment Antirealism: this way of thinking goes back substantially to the great eighteenth-century enlightenment philosopher Immanuel Kant. According to its central tenet, it is really we human beings, we men and women, who structure the world, who are responsible for its fundamental outline and lineaments. Naturally enough, a view as startling as this comes in several forms. According to Jean Paul Sartre and his existentialist friends, we do this world-structuring freely and individually; according to Ludwig Wittgenstein and his followers, we do it communally and by way of language; according to Kant himself it is done by the transcendental ego which, oddly enough, is neither one nor many, being itself the source of the one-many structure of the world. So two of the parties to this three-way contest are Perennial Naturalism and Enlightenment Humanism; the third party, of course, is Christian theism. Of course, there are many unthinking and ill-conceived combinations, much blurring of lines, many cross currents and eddies, many halfway houses, much halting between two opinions. Nevertheless, I think these are the three basic contemporary Western ways of looking at reality, three basically religious ways of viewing ourselves and the world. The conflict is real and of profound importance. The stakes, furthermore, are high; this is a battle for the souls of humankind.

Now it would be excessively naive to think that contemporary science is religiously and theologically neutral, standing serenely above this battle and wholly irrelevant to it. Perhaps parts of science are like that: mathematics, for example, and perhaps physics, or parts of physics—although even in these areas there are connections.[7] Other parts are obviously and deeply involved in this battle; and the closer the science in question is to what is distinctively human, the deeper the involvement.

To turn to the bit of science in question, the theory of evolution plays a fascinating and crucial role in contemporary Western culture. The enormous controversy about it is what is most striking, a controversy that goes back to Darwin and continues full force today. Evolution is the regular subject of courtroom drama; one such trial—the spectacular Scopes trial of 1925—has been made the subject of an extremely popular film. Fundamentalists regard evolution as the work of the Devil. In academia, on the other hand, it is an idol of the contemporary tribe; it serves as a shibboleth, a litmus test distinguishing the ignorant and bigoted fundamentalist goats from the properly acculturated and scientifically receptive sheep. Apparently this litmus test extends far beyond the confines of this terrestrial globe; according to the Oxford biologist Richard Dawkins, "If superior creatures from space ever visit earth, the first question they will ask, in order to assess the level of our civilization, is: 'Have they discovered evolution yet?'" Indeed many of the experts—for example, Dawkins, William Provine, Stephen Gould—display a sort of revulsion at the very idea of special creation by God, as if this idea is not merely not good science, but somehow a bit obscene, or at least unseemly; it borders on the immoral; it is worthy of disdain and contempt. In some circles, confessing to finding evolution attractive will get you disapproval and ostracism and may lose you your job; in others, confessing doubts about evolution will have the same doleful effect. In Darwin's day, some suggested that it was all well and good to discuss evolution in the universities and among the *cognoscenti;* they thought public discussion unwise, however; for it would be a shame if the lower classes found out about it. Now, ironically enough, the shoe is sometimes on the other foot; it is the devotees of evolution who sometimes express the fear that public discussion of doubts and difficulties with evolution could have harmful political effects.[8]

So why all the furor? The answer is obvious: evolution has deep religious connections, deep connections with how we understand ourselves at the most fundamental level. Many evangelicals and fundamentalists see in it a threat to the faith; they do not want it taught to their children, at any rate as scientifically established fact, and they see acceptance of it as corroding proper acceptance of the Bible. On the other side, among the secularists, evolution functions as a myth, in a technical sense of that term—a shared way of understanding ourselves at the deep level of religion, a deep interpretation of ourselves to ourselves, a way of telling us why we are here, where we come from, and where we are going. It was serving in this capacity when Richard Dawkins (according to Peter Medawar, "one of the most brilliant of the rising generation of biologists") leaned over and remarked to A. J. Ayer at one of those elegant, candle-lit, bibulous Oxford dinners that he could not imagine being an atheist before 1859 (the year Darwin's *Origin of Species was* published): "Although atheism might have been logically tenable before Darwin," said he, "Darwin made it possible to be an intellectually fulfilled atheist."[9] (Let me recommend Dawkins' book to you: it is brilliantly written, unfailingly fascinating, and utterly wrongheaded. It was second on the British best-seller list for some considerable time, second only to Mamie Jenkins' *Hip and Thigh Diet.)* Dawkins goes on:

> All appearances to the contrary, the only watchmaker in nature is the blind forces of physics, albeit deployed in a very special way. A true watchmaker has

foresight: he designs his cogs and springs, and plans their interconnections, with a future purpose in his mind's eye. Natural selection, the blind, unconscious automatic process which Darwin discovered, and which we now know is the explanation for the existence and apparently purposeful form of all life, has no purpose in mind. It has no mind and no mind's eye. It does not plan for the future. It has no vision, no foresight, no sight at all. If it can be said to play the role of watchmaker in nature, it is the blind watchmaker.[10]

Evolution was functioning in that same mythic capacity in the remark of the famous zoologist G. G. Simpson; after posing the question "What is man?" he answers: "The point I want to make now is that all attempts to answer that question before 1859 are worthless and that we will be better off if we ignore them completely."[11] Of course, it also functions in that capacity in serving as a litmus test to distinguish the ignorant fundamentalists from the properly enlightened *cognoscenti;* it functions in the same way in many of the debates, in and out of the courts, as to whether it should be taught in the schools, whether other views should be given equal time, and the like. Thus Michael Ruse: "The fight against creationism is a fight for all knowledge, and that battle can be won if we all work to see that Darwinism, which has had a great past, has an even greater future."[12]

The essential point here is really Dawkins' point: Darwinism, the Grand Evolutionary Story, makes it possible to be an intellectually fulfilled atheist. What he means is simple enough. If you are Christian, or a theist of some other kind, you have a ready answer to the question, how did it all happen? How is it that there are all the kinds of floras and faunas we behold; how did they all get here? The answer, of course, is that they have been created by the Lord. But if you are not a believer in God, things are enormously more difficult. How did all these things get here? How did life get started and how did it come to assume its present multifarious forms? It seems monumentally implausible to think these forms just popped into existence; that goes contrary to all our experience. So how did it happen? Atheism and Secularism need an answer to this question. And the Grand Evolutionary Story gives the answer: somehow life arose from nonliving matter by way of purely natural means and in accord with the fundamental laws of physics; and once life started, all the vast profusion of contemporary plant and animal life arose from those early ancestors by way of common descent, driven by random variation and natural selection. I said earlier that we cannot automatically identify the deliverances of reason with the teaching of current science because the teaching of current science keeps changing. Here we have another reason for resisting that identification: a good deal more than reason goes into the acceptance of such a theory as the Grand Evolutionary Story. For the nontheist, evolution is the only game in town; it is an essential part of any reasonably complete nontheistic way of thinking; hence the devotion to it, the suggestions that it should not be discussed in public, and the venom, the theological odium with which dissent is greeted.

Of course the fact that evolution makes it possible to be a fulfilled atheist does not show either that the theory is not true or that there is not powerful evidence for it. Well then, how likely is it that this theory is true? Suppose we think about the question from an explicitly theistic and Christian perspective; but suppose we temporarily set to one side the evidence, whatever exactly it is, from early Genesis. From this perspective, how good is the evidence for the theory of evolution?

The first thing to see is that a number of different large-scale claims fall under this general rubric of evolution. First, there is the claim that the earth is very old, perhaps some four and a half billion years old: the *Ancient Earth Thesis*, as we may call it. Second, there is the claim that life has progressed from relatively simple to relatively complex forms of life. In the beginning there was relatively simple unicellular life, perhaps of the sort represented by bacteria and blue green algae, or perhaps still simpler unknown forms of life. (Although bacteria are simple compared to some other living beings, they are in fact enormously complex creatures.) Then more complex unicellular life, then relatively simple multicellular life such as seagoing worms, coral, and jelly fish, then fish, then amphibia, then reptiles, birds, mammals, and finally, as the culmination of the whole process, human beings: the *Progress Thesis*, as we humans may like to call it (jelly fish might have a different view as to where the whole process culminates). Third, there is the *Common Ancestry Thesis:* that life originated at only one place on earth, all subsequent life being related by descent to those original living creatures—the claim that, as Stephen Gould puts it, there is a "tree of evolutionary descent linking all organisms by ties of genealogy."[13] According to the Common Ancestry Thesis, we are literally cousins of all living things—horses, oak trees, and even poison ivy—distant cousins, no doubt, but still cousins. (This is much easier to imagine for some of us than for others.) Fourth, there is the claim that there is a (naturalistic) *explanation* of this development of life from simple to complex forms; call this thesis *Darwinism,* because according to the most popular and well-known suggestions, the evolutionary mechanism would be natural selection operating on random genetic mutation (due to copy error or ultra violet radiation or other causes); and this is similar to Darwin's proposals. Finally, there is the claim that life itself developed from non-living matter without any special creative activity of God but just by virtue of the ordinary laws of physics and chemistry: call this the *Naturalistic Origins Thesis.* These five theses are of course importantly different from each other. They are also logically independent in pairs, except for the third and fourth theses: the fourth entails the third, in that you cannot sensibly propose a mechanism or an explanation for evolution without agreeing that evolution has indeed occurred. The combination of all five of these theses is what I have been calling "The Grand Evolutionary Story"; the Common Ancestry Thesis together with Darwinism (remember, Darwinism is not the view that the mechanism driving evolution is just what Darwin says it is) is what one most naturally thinks of as the Theory of Evolution.

So how shall we think of these five theses? First, let me remind you once more that I am no expert in this area. And second, let me say that, as I see it, the empirical or scientific evidence for these five different claims differs enormously in quality and quantity. There is excellent evidence for an ancient earth—a whole series of interlocking different kinds of evidence, some of which is marshaled by Howard van Till in *The Fourth Day.* Given the strength of this evidence, one would need powerful evidence on the other side—from Scriptural considerations, say—in order to hold sensibly that the earth is young. There is less evidence, but still good evidence in the fossil record for the Progress Thesis, the claim that there were bacteria before fish, fish before reptiles, reptiles before mammals, and mice before men (or wombats before women, for the feminists in the crowd). The third and fourth theses, the Common Ancestry and Darwinian Theses, are what is commonly and popularly identified with evolution; I shall return to them in a moment. The fourth thesis, of course, is no more likely than the third, since it includes the third and proposes a mechanism to account for it. Finally, there is the fifth thesis, the Naturalistic Origins Thesis, the claim that life arose by naturalistic means. This seems to me to be for the most part mere arrogant bluster; given our present state of knowledge, I believe it is vastly less probable, on our present evidence, than is its denial. Darwin thought this claim very chancy; discoveries since Darwin and in particular recent discoveries in molecular biology make it much less likely than it was in Darwin's day. I cannot summarize the evidence and the difficulties here.[14]

Now return to evolution more narrowly so-called—the Common Ancestry Thesis and the Darwinian Thesis. Contemporary intellectual orthodoxy is summarized by the 1979 edition of the *New Encyclopedia Britannica,* according to which "evolution is accepted by all biologists and natural selection is recognized as its cause.... Objections... have come from theological and, for a time, from political standpoints" (Vol. 7). It goes on to add that "Darwin did two things; he showed that evolution was in fact contradicting Scriptural legends of creation and that its cause, natural selection, was automatic, with no room for divine guidance or design." According to most of the experts, furthermore, evolution, taken as the Thesis of Common Ancestry, is not something about which there can be sensible difference of opinion. Here is a random selection of claims of certainty on the part of the experts. Evolution is certain, says Francisco J. Ayala, as certain as "the roundness of the earth, the motions of the planets, and the molecular constitution of matter."[15] According to Stephen J. Gould, evolution is an established fact, not a mere theory; and no sensible person who was acquainted with the evidence could demur.[16] According to Richard Dawkins, the theory of evolution is as certainly true as that the earth goes around the sun. This comparison with Copernicus apparently suggests itself to many; according to Philip Spieth: "A century and a quarter after the publication of the Origin of Species, biologists can say with confidence that universal genealogical relatedness is a conclusion of science that is as firmly established as the revolution of the earth about the sun."[17] Michael Ruse, trumpets, or perhaps screams, that "evolution is Fact, FACT, FACT!" If you venture to suggest doubts about evolution, you are likely to be called ignorant or stupid or worse. In fact this is not merely likely; you have already been so-called: in a recent review in the *New York Times*, Richard Dawkins claims that "it is absolutely safe to say that if you meet someone who claims not to believe in evolution, that person is ignorant, stupid or insane (or wicked, but I'd rather not consider that)." (Dawkins indulgently adds that "You are probably not stupid, insane or wicked, and ignorance is not a crime").

Well then, how should a serious Christian think about the Common Ancestry and Darwinian Theses? The first and most obvious thing, of course, is that a Christian holds that all plants and animals, past as well as present, have been created by the Lord. Now suppose we set to one side what we take to be the best understanding of early Genesis. Then the next thing to see is that God could have accomplished this creating in a thousand different ways. It was entirely within his power to create life in a way corresponding to the Grand Evolutionary scenario: it was within his power to create matter and energy, as in the Big Bang, together with laws for its behavior, in such a way that the outcome would be first, life's coming into existence three or four billion years ago, and then the various higher forms of life, culminating, as we like to think, in humankind. This is a semideistic view of God and his workings: he starts everything off and sits back to watch it develop. (One who held this view could also hold that God constantly sustains the world in existence—hence the view is only semideistic—and even that any given causal transaction in the universe requires specific divine concurrent activity.)[18] On the other hand, of course, God could have done things very differently. He has created matter and energy with their tendencies to behave in certain ways—ways summed up in the laws of physics—but perhaps these laws are not such that given enough time, life would automatically arise. Perhaps he did something different and special in the creation of life. Perhaps he did something different and special in creating the various kinds of animals and plants. Perhaps he did something different and special in the creation of human beings. Perhaps in these cases his action with respect to what he has created was different from the ways in which he ordinarily treats them.

How shall we decide which of these is initially the more likely? That is not an easy question. It is important to remember, however, that the Lord has not merely left the cosmos to develop according to an initial creation and an initial set of physical laws. According to Scripture, he has often intervened in the working of his cosmos. This is not a good way of putting the matter (because of its deistic suggestions); it is better to say that he has often treated what he has created in a way different from the way in which he ordinarily treats it. There are miracles reported in Scripture, for example; and, towering above all, there is the unthinkable gift of salvation for humankind by way of the life, death, and resurrection of Jesus Christ, his son. According to Scripture, God has often treated what he has made in a way different from the way in which he ordinarily treats it; there is therefore no initial edge to the idea that he would be more likely to have created life in all its variety in the broadly deistic way. In fact, it looks to me as if there is an initial probability on the other side; it is a bit more probable, before we look at the scientific evidence, that the Lord created life and some of its forms—in particular, human life—specially.

From this perspective, then, how shall we evaluate the evidence for evolution? Despite the claims of Ayala, Dawkins, Gould, Simpson, and the other experts, I think the evidence here has to be rated as ambiguous and inconclusive. The two hypotheses to be compared are (1) the claim that God has created us in such a way that (a) all of contemporary plants and animals are related by common ancestry, and (b) the mechanism driving evolution is natural selection working on random genetic variation, and (2) the claim that God created mankind as well as many kinds of plants and animals separately and specially, in such a way that the thesis of common ancestry is false. Which of these is the more probable, given the empirical evidence and the theistic context? I think the second, the special creation thesis, is somewhat more probable with respect to the evidence (given theism) than the first.

There is not the space here for more than the merest hand waving with respect to marshalling and evaluating the evidence. But according to Stephen Jay Gould, certainly a leading contemporary spokesman, "our confidence that evolution occurred centers upon three general arguments. First, we have abundant, direct observational evidence of evolution in action, from both field and laboratory. This evidence ranges from countless experiments on change in nearly everything about fruit flies subjected to artificial selection in the laboratory to the famous populations of British moths that became black when industrial soot darkened the trees upon which the moths rest."[19] Second, Gould mentions homologies: "Why should a rat run, a bat fly, a porpoise swim, and I type this essay with structures built of the same bones," he asks, "unless we all inherited them from a common ancestor?" Third, he says, there is the fossil record:

> Transitions are often found in the fossil record. Preserved transitions are not common, ... but they are not entirely wanting.... For that matter, what better transitional form could we expect to find than the oldest human, *Australopithecus afrarensis*, with its apelike palate, its human upright stance, and a cranial capacity larger than any ape's of the same body size but a full 1,000 cubic centimeters below ours? If God made each of the half-dozen human species discovered in ancient rocks, why did he create in an unbroken temporal sequence of progressively more modern features, increasing cranial capacity, reduced face and teeth, larger body size? Did he create to mimic evolution and test our faith thereby?[20]

Here we could add a couple of other commonly cited kinds of evidence: (a) We along with other animals display vestigial organs (appendix, coccyx, muscles that move ears and nose); it is suggested that the best explanation is evolution. (b) There is alleged evidence from biochemistry; according to the authors of a popular college textbook, "all organisms ... employ DNA, and most use the citric acid cycle, cytochromes, and so forth. It seems inconceivable that the biochemistry of living things would be so similar if all life did not develop from a single common ancestral group."[21] There is also (c) the fact that human embryos during their development display some of the characteristics of simpler forms of life (for example, at a certain stage they display gill-like structures). Finally, (d) there is the fact that certain patterns of geographical distribution—that there are orchids and alligators only in the American south and in China, for example—are susceptible to a nice evolutionary explanation.

Suppose we briefly consider the last four first. The arguments from vestigial organs, geographical distribution, and embryology are suggestive, but of course nowhere near conclusive. As for the similarity in biochemistry of all life, this is reasonably probable on the hypothesis of special creation, hence not much by way of evidence against it, hence not much by way of evidence for evolution.

Turning to the evidence Gould develops, it too is suggestive, but far from conclusive; some of it, furthermore, is seriously flawed. First, those famous British moths did not produce a new species; there were both dark and light moths around, before, the dark ones coming to predominate when the industrial revolution deposited a layer of soot on trees, making the light moths more visible to predators. More broadly, while there is wide agreement that there is such a thing as microevolution, the question is whether we can extrapolate to macroevolution, with the claim that enough microevolution can account for the enormous differences between, say, bacteria and human beings. There is some experiential reason to think not; there seems to be a sort of envelope of limited variability surrounding a species and its near relatives. Artificial selection can produce several different kinds of fruit flies and several different kinds of dogs, but, starting with fruit flies, what it produces is only more fruit flies. As plants or animals are bred in certain direction, a sort of barrier is encountered; further selective breeding brings about sterility or a reversion to earlier forms. Partisans of evolution suggest that, in nature, genetic mutation of one sort or another can appropriately augment the reservoir of genetic variation. That it can do so sufficiently, however, is not known; and the assertion that it does is a sort of Ptolemaic epicycle attaching to the theory.

Next, there is the argument from the fossil record; but as Gould himself points out, the fossil record shows very few transitional forms. "The extreme rarity of transitional forms in the fossil record," he says, "persists as the trade secret of paleontology. The evolutionary trees that adorn our textbooks have data only at the tips and nodes of their branches; the rest is inference, however reasonable, not the evidence of fossils."[22] Nearly all species appear for the first time in the fossil record fully formed, without the vast chains of intermediary forms evolution would suggest. Gradualistic evolutionists claim that the fossil record is woefully incomplete. Gould, Eldredge, and others have a different response to this difficulty: punctuated equilibriumism, according to which long periods of evolutionary stasis are interrupted by relatively brief periods of very rapid evolution. This response helps the theory accommodate some of the fossil data, but at the cost of another Ptolemaic epicycle.[23] And still more epicycles are required to account for puzzling discoveries in molecular biology during the last twenty years.[24] And as for the argument from homologies, this too is suggestive, but far from decisive. First, there are of course many examples of architectural similarity that are not attributed to common ancestry, as in the case of the Tasmanian wolf and the European wolf; the anatomical givens are by no means conclusive proof of common ancestry. And secondly, God created several different kinds of animals; what would prevent him from using similar structures?

But perhaps the most important difficulty lies in a slightly different direction. Consider the mammalian eye: a marvelous and highly complex instrument, resembling a telescope of the highest quality, with a lens, an adjustable focus, a variable diaphragm for controlling the amount of light, and optical corrections for spherical and chromatic aberration. And here is the problem: how does the lens, for example, get developed by the proposed means—random genetic variation and natural selection—when at the same time there has to be development of the optic nerve, the relevant muscles, the retina, the rods and cones, and many other delicate and complicated structures, all of which have to be adjusted to each other in such a way that they can work together? Indeed, what is involved is not, of course, just the eye; it is the whole visual system, including the relevant parts of the brain. Many different organs and suborgans have to be developed together, and it is hard to envisage a series of mutations which is such that each member of the series has adaptive value, is also a step on the way to the eye, and is such that the last member is an animal with such an eye.

We can consider the problem a bit more abstractly. Think of a sort of space, in which the points are organic forms (possible organisms) and in which neighboring forms are so related that one could have originated from the other with some minimum probability by way of random genetic mutation. Imagine starting with a population of animals without eyes, and trace through the space in question all the paths that lead from this form to forms with eyes. The chief problem is that the vast majority of these paths contain long sections with adjacent points such that there would be no adaptive advantage in going from one point to the next, so that, on Darwinian assumptions, none of them could be the path in fact taken. How could the eye have evolved in this way, so that each point on its path through that space would be adaptive and a step on the way to the eye? (Perhaps it is possible that some of these sections could be traversed by way of steps that were not adaptive and were fixed by genetic drift; but the probability of the population's crossing such stretches will be much less than that of its crossing a similar stretch where natural selection is operative.) Darwin himself wrote, "To suppose that the eye, with all its inimitable contrivances . . . could have been formed by natural selection seems absurd in the highest degree." "When I think of the eye, I shudder," he said. And the complexity of the eye is enormously greater than was known in Darwin's time.

We are never, of course, given the actual explanation of the evolution of the eye, the actual evolutionary history of the eye (or brain or hand or whatever). That would take the form: in that original population of eyeless life forms, genes A_1-A_n mutated (due to some perhaps unspecified cause), leading to some structural and functional change which was adaptively beneficial; the bearers of A_1-A_n thus had, an advantage and came to dominate the population. Then genes B_1-B_n mutated in an individual or two, and the same thing happened again; then gene C_1-C_n, etc. Nor are we even given any possibilities of these sorts. (We could not be, since, for most genes, we do not know enough about their functions.) We are instead treated to broad brush scenarios at the macroscopic level: perhaps reptiles gradually developed feathers, and wings, and warm-bloodedness, and the other features of birds. We are given possible evolutionary histories, not of the detailed genetic sort mentioned above, but broad macroscopic scenarios—what Gould calls "just-so stories."

And the real problem is that we do not know how to evaluate these suggestions. To know how to do that (in the case of the eye, say), we should have to start with some population of animals without eyes; and then we should have to know the rate at which mutations occur for that population; the proportion of those mutations that are on one of those paths through that space to the condition of having eyes; the proportion of those that are adaptive, and, at each stage, given the sort of environment enjoyed by the organisms at that stage, the rate at which such adaptive modifications would have spread through the population in question. Then we would have to compare our results with the time available to evaluate the probability of the suggestion in question. But we do not know what these rates and proportions are. No doubt we cannot know what they are, given the scarcity of operable time-machines; still, the fact is we do not know them. And hence we do not really know whether evolution is so much as biologically possible: maybe there is no path through that space. It is epistemically possible that evolution has occurred: that is, we do not know that it has not; for all we know, it has. But it does not follow that it is biologically possible. (Whether every even number is the sum of two primes is an open question; hence it is epistemically possible that every even number is the sum of two primes, and also epistemically possible that some even numbers are not the sum of two primes; but one or the other of those epistemic possibilities is in fact mathematically impossible.) Assuming that it is biologically possible, furthermore, we do not know that it is not prohibitively improbable (in the statistical sense), given the time available. But then (given the Christian faith and leaving to one side our evaluation of the evidence from early Genesis) the right attitude towards the claim of universal common descent is, I think, one of a certain interested but wary skepticism. It is possible (epistemically possible) that this is how things happened; God could have done it that way; but the evidence is ambiguous. That it is *possible* is clear; that it *happened* is doubtful; that it is *certain*, however, is ridiculous.

But then what about all those exuberant cries of certainty from Gould, Ayala, Dawkins, Simpson, and the other experts? What about those claims that evolution, universal common ancestry, is a rock-ribbed certainty, to be compared with the fact that the earth is round and goes around the sun? What we have here is at best enormous exaggeration. But then what accounts for the fact that these claims are made by such intelligent luminaries as the above? There are at least two reasons. First, there is the cultural and religious, the mythic function of the doctrine; evolution helps make it possible to be an intellectually fulfilled atheist. From a naturalistic point of view, this is the only answer in sight to the question "How did it all happen? How did all this amazing profusion of life get here?" From a nontheistic point of view, the evolutionary hypothesis is the only game in town. According to the thesis of universal common descent, life arose in just one place; then there was constant development by way of evolutionary mechanisms from that time to the present, this resulting in the profusion of life we presently see. On the alternative hypothesis, different forms of life arose independently of each other; on that suggestion there would be many different genetic trees, the creatures adorning one of these trees genetically unrelated to those on another. From a nontheistic perspective, the first hypothesis will be by far the more probable, if only because of the extraordinary difficulty in seeing how life could arise even once by any ordinary mechanisms which operate today. That it should arise many different times and at different levels of complexity in this way is quite incredible,

From a naturalist perspective, furthermore, many of the arguments for evolution are much more powerful than from a theistic perspective. (For example, given that life arose naturalistically, it is indeed significant that all life employs the same genetic code.) So from a naturalistic, nontheistic perspective the evolutionary hypothesis will be vastly more probable than alternatives. Many leaders in the field of evolutionary biologists, of course, are naturalists—Gould, Dawkins, and Stebbins, for example; and according to William Provine, "very few truly religious evolutionary biologists remain. Most are atheists, and many have been driven there by their understanding of the evolutionary process and other science."[25] If Provine is right or nearly right, it becomes easier to see why we hear this insistence that the evolutionary hypothesis is certain. It is also easy to see how this attitude is passed on to graduate students, and, indeed, how accepting the view that evolution is certain is itself adaptive for life in graduate school and academia generally.

There is a second and related circumstance at work here. We are sometimes told that natural science is *natural* science. So far it is hard to object: but how shall we take the term "natural" here? It could mean that natural science is science devoted to the study of nature. Fair enough. But it is also taken to mean that natural science involves a methodological naturalism or provisional atheism: no hypothesis according to which God has done this or that can qualify as a scientific hypothesis.[26] It would be interesting to look into this matter: is there really a compelling or even decent reason for thus restricting our study of nature? But suppose we irenically concede, for the moment, that natural science does not or should not invoke hypotheses essentially involving God. Suppose we restrict our explanatory materials to the ordinary laws of physics and chemistry; suppose we reject divine special creation or other hypotheses about God as *scientific* hypotheses. Perhaps indeed the Lord has engaged in special creation, so we say, but that he has (if he has) is not something with which natural science can deal. So far as natural science goes, therefore, an acceptable hypothesis must appeal only to the laws that govern the ordinary, day-to-day working of the cosmos. As natural scientists we must eschew the supernatural—although, of course, we do not mean for a moment to embrace naturalism.

Well, suppose we adopt this attitude. Then perhaps it looks as if by far the most probable of all the properly scientific hypotheses is that of evolution by common ancestry: it is hard to think of any other real possibility. The only alternatives, apparently, would be creatures popping into existence fully formed; and that is wholly contrary to our experience. Of all the scientifically acceptable explanatory hypotheses, therefore, evolution seems by far the most probable. But if this hypothesis is vastly more probable than any of its rivals, then it must be certain, or nearly so.

But to reason this way is to fall into confusion compounded. In the first place, we are not just given that one or another of these hypotheses is in fact correct. Granted: if we knew that one or another of those scientifically acceptable hypotheses were in fact correct, then perhaps this one would be certain; but of course we do not know that. One real possibility is that we do not have a very good idea how it all happened, just as we may not have a very good idea as to what terrorist organization has perpetrated a particular bombing. And secondly, this reasoning involves a confusion between the claim that of all of those scientifically acceptable hypotheses, that of common ancestry is by far the most plausible, with the vastly more contentious claim that of all the acceptable hypotheses whatever (now placing no restrictions on their kind) this hypothesis is by far the most probable. Christians in particular ought to be alive to the vast difference between these claims; confounding them leads to nothing but confusion.

From a Christian perspective, it is dubious, with respect to our present evidence, that the Common Ancestry Thesis is true. No doubt there has been much by way of micro evolution: Ridley's gulls are an interesting and dramatic case in point. But it is not particularly likely, given the Christian faith and the biological evidence, that God created all the flora and fauna by way of some mechanism involving common ancestry. My main point, however, is that Ayala, Gould, Simpson, Stebbins, and their coterie are wildly mistaken in claiming that the Grand Evolutionary Hypothesis is certain. And hence the source of this claim has to be looked for elsewhere than in sober scientific evidence.

So it could be that the best scientific hypothesis was evolution by common descent—i.e., of all the hypotheses that conform to methodological naturalism, it is the best. But of course what we really want to know is not which hypothesis is the best from some artificially adopted standpoint of naturalism, but what the best hypothesis is overall. We want to know what the best hypothesis is, not which of some limited class is best—particularly if the class in question specifically excludes what we hold to be the basic truth of the matter. It could be that the best scientific hypothesis (again supposing that a scientific hypothesis must be naturalistic in the above sense) is not even a strong competitor in that derby.

Judgments here, of course, may differ widely between believers in God and non-believers in God. What for the former is at best a methodological restriction is for the latter the sober metaphysical truth; her naturalism is not merely provisional and methodological, but, as she sees it, settled and fundamental. But believers in God can see the matter differently. The believer in God, unlike her naturalistic counterpart, is free to look at the evidence for the Grand Evolutionary Scheme, and follow it where it leads, rejecting that scheme if the evidence is insufficient. She has a freedom not available to the naturalist. The latter accepts the Grand Evolutionary scheme because from a naturalistic point of view this scheme is the only visible answer to the question, *What is the explanation of the presence of all these marvelously multifarious forms of life?* The Christian, on the other hand, knows that creation is the Lord's; and she is not blinkered by a priori dogmas as to how the Lord must have accomplished it. Perhaps it was by broadly evolutionary means, but then again perhaps not. At the moment, "perhaps not" seems the better answer.

Returning to methodological naturalism, if indeed natural science is essentially restricted in this way, if such a restriction is a part of the very essence of science, then what we need here, of course, is not natural science, but a broader inquiry that can include all that we know, including the truths that God has created life on earth and could have done it in many different ways. "Unnatural Science," "Creation Science," "Theistic Science"—call it what you will: what we need when we want to know how to think about the origin and development of contemporary life is what is most plausible from a Christian point of view. What we need is a scientific account of life that is not restricted by that methodological naturalism.

Alternatively, how can Christian intellectuals—scientists, philosophers, historians, literary and art critics, Christian thinkers of every sort—how can they best serve the Christian community in an area like this? How can they—and since we are they, how can we—best serve the Christian community, the Reformed community of which we are a part, and, more importantly, the broader general Christian community? One thing our experts can do for us is help us avoid rejecting evolution for stupid reasons. The early literature of Creation-Science, so called, is littered with arguments of that eminently rejectable sort. Here is such an argument. Considering the rate of human population growth over the last few centuries, the author points out that even on a most conservative estimate the human population of the earth doubles at least every thousand years. Then if, as evolutionists claim, the first humans existed at least a million years ago, by now the human population would have doubled a thousand times. It seems hard to see how there could have been fewer than two original human beings, so at that rate, by the inexorable laws of mathematics, after only 60,000 years or so, there would have been something like 36 quintillion people, and by now there would have to be 2^{1000} human beings. 2^{1000} is a large number; it is more than 10^{300}, 1 with 300 zeros after it; if there were that many of us the whole universe would have to be packed solid with people. Since clearly it is not, human beings could not have existed for as long as a million years; so the evolutionists are wrong. This is clearly lousy argument; I leave as homework the problem of saying just where it goes wrong. There are many other bad arguments against evolution floating around, and it is worth our while to learn that these arguments are indeed bad. We should not reject contemporary science unless we have to, and we should not reject it for the wrong reasons. It is a good thing for our scientists to point out some of those wrong reasons.

But I would like to suggest, with all the diffidence I can muster, that there is something better to do here—or at any rate something that should be done in addition to this. And the essence of the matter is fairly simple, despite the daunting complexity that arises when we descend to the nitty-gritty level where the real work has to be done. The first thing to see, as I said before, is that Christianity is indeed engaged in a conflict, a battle. There is indeed a battle between the Christian community and the forces of unbelief. This contest or battle rages in many areas of contemporary culture—the courts, in the so-called media and the like—but perhaps most particularly in academia. And the second thing to see is that important cultural forces such as science are not neutral with respect to this conflict—though of course certain parts of contemporary science and many contemporary scientists might very well be. It is of the first importance that we discern in detail just how contemporary science—and contemporary philosophy, history, literary criticism, and so on—is involved in the struggle. This is a complicated, many-sided matter; it varies from discipline to discipline, and from area to area within a given discipline. One of our chief tasks, therefore, must be that of cultural criticism. We must test the spirits, not automatically welcome them in because of their great academic prestige. Academic prestige, wide, even nearly unanimous acceptance in academia, declarations of certainty by important scientists—none of these is a guarantee that what is proposed is true, or a genuine deliverance of reason, or plausible from a theistic point of view. Indeed, none is a guarantee that what is proposed is not animated by a spirit wholly antithetical to Christianity. We must discern the religious and ideological connections; we cannot automatically take the word of the experts, because their word might be dead wrong from a Christian standpoint.

Finally, in all the areas of academic endeavor, we Christians must think about the matter at hand from a Christian perspective; we need Theistic Science. Perhaps the discipline in question, as ordinarily practiced, involves a methodological naturalism; if so, then what we need, finally, is not answers to our questions from that perspective, valuable in some ways as it may be. What we really need are answers to our questions from the perspective of all that we know—what we know about God, and what we know by faith, by way of revelation, as well as what we know in other ways. In many areas, this means that Christians must rework, rethink the area in question from this perspective. This idea may be shocking, but it is not new. Reformed Christians have long recognized that science and scholarship are by no means religiously neutral. In a way this is our distinctive thread in the tapestry of Christianity, our instrument in the great symphony of Christianity. This recognition underlay the establishment of the Free University of Amsterdam in 1880; it also underlay the establishment of Calvin College. Our forebears recognized the need for the sort of work and inquiry I've been mentioning, and tried to do something about it. What we need from our scientists and other academics, then, is both cultural criticism and Christian science.

We must admit, however, that it is our lack of real progress that is striking. Of course there are good reasons for this. To carry out this task with the depth, the authority, the competence it requires is, first of all, enormously difficult. However, it is not just the difficulty of this enterprise that accounts for our lackluster performance. Just as important is a whole set of historical or sociological conditions. You may have noticed that at present the Western Christian community is located in the twentieth-century Western world. We Christians who go on to become professional scientists and scholars attend twentieth-century graduate schools and universities. And questions about the bearing of Christianity on these disciplines and the questions within them do not enjoy much by way of prestige and esteem in these universities. There are no courses at Harvard entitled "Molecular Biology and the Christian View of Man." At Oxford they do not teach a course called "Origins of Life from a Christian Perspective." One cannot write his Ph.D. thesis on these subjects. The National Science Foundation would not look favorably on them. Working on these questions is not a good way to get tenure at a typical university; and if you are job hunting you would be ill-advised to advertise yourself as proposing to specialize in them. The entire structure of contemporary university life is such as to discourage serious work on these questions.

This is therefore a matter of uncommon difficulty. So far as I know, however, no one in authority has promised us a rose garden; and it is also a matter of absolutely crucial importance to the health of the Christian community. It is worthy of the very best we can muster; it demands powerful, patient, unstinting and tireless effort. But its rewards match its demands; it is exciting, absorbing and crucially important. Most of all, however, it needs to be done. I therefore commend it to you.

Notes

1. This essay first appeared in *CSR* 21.1 (September 1991): 8-32.
2. Perhaps the shrewdest contemporary spokesman for this view is the late Donald MacKay in *The Clockwork Image: A Christian Perspective on Science* (London: InterVarsity Press, 1974) and "'Complementarity' in Scientific and Theological Thinking" in *Zygon*, September 1974, 225ff.
3. *The Fourth Day* (Grand Rapids, Mich.: Eerdmans, 1986), 195.
4. See Stephen Hawking, *A Brief History of Time* (New York: Bantam Books, 1988), 115 ff.
5. *Christian Observer* (1832), 437.
6. Here the work of Bas van Fraassen is particularly instructive.
7. As with intuitionist and constructivist mathematics, idealistic interpretations of quantum mechanics, and Bell theoretical questions about information transfer violating relativistic constraints on velocity.
8. Thus, according to Anthony Flew, to suggest that there is real doubt about evolution is to corrupt the youth.
9. Richard Dawkins, *The Blind Watchmaker* (London and New York: W. W. Norton, 1986), 6 and 7.
10. Ibid., 5
11. Quoted in Richard Dawkins, *The Selfish Gene* (Oxford: Oxford University Press, 1976), 1.
12. *Darwinism Defended*, 326-327.
13. "Evolution as Fact and Theory" in *Hen's Teeth and Horse's Toes* (New York: Norton, 1983).
14. Let me refer you to the following books: *The Mystery of Life's Origins* (New York: Philosophical Library, 1984) by Charles Thaxton, Walter Bradley, and Roger Olsen; *Origins* (New York: Summit Books, 1986) by Robert Shapiro; *Evolution, Thermodynamics, and Information: Extending the Darwinian Program* (New York: Oxford University Press, 1987) by Jeffrey S. Wicken; *Seven Clues to the Origin of Life, Genetic Takeover and the Mineral Origins of Life* (Cambridge: Cambridge University Press, 1982) by A. G. Cairns-Smith; and *Origins of Life* (Cambridge: Cambridge University Press, 1985) by Freeman Dyson; see also the relevant chapters of Michael Denton, *Evolution: A Theory in Crisis* (Cambridge: Cambridge University Press, 1985).The authors of the first book believe that God created life specially; the authors of the others do not.
15. "The Theory of Evolution: Recent Successes and Challenges," in *Evolution and Creation*, ed. Ernan McMullin (Notre Dame, Ind.: University of Notre Dame Press, 1985), 60.
16. "Evolution as Fact and Theory" in *Hen's Teeth and Horse's Toes*, 254-55.
17. "Evolutionary Biology and the Study of Human Nature," presented at a consultation on Cosmology and Theology sponsored by the Presbyterian (USA) Church in December 1987.
18. The issues here are complicated and subtle and I cannot go into them; instead I should like to recommend my colleague Alfred Freddoso's powerful piece, "Medieval Aristotelianism and the Case Against Secondary Causation in Nature," in *Divine and Human Action*, edited by Thomas Morris (Ithaca, N.Y.: Cornell University Press, 1988).
19. "Evolution as Fact and Theory," 257.
20. Ibid., 258-59.
21. Claude A. Villee, Eldra Pearl Solomon, P. William Davis, *Biology* (Saunders College Publishing, 1985), 1012. Similarly, Mark Ridley in *The Problems of Evolution* (Oxford: Oxford University Press, 1985) takes the fact that the genetic code is universal across all forms of life as proof that life originated only once; it would be extremely improbable that life should have stumbled upon the same code more than once.
22. *The Panda's Thumb* (New York: 1980), 181. According to George Gaylord Simpson (1953): "Nearly all categories above the level of families appear in the record suddenly and are not led up to by known, gradual, completely continuous transitional sequences."
23. And even so it helps much less than you might think. It does offer an explanation of the absence of fossil forms intermediate with respect to closely related or adjoining species; the real problem, though, is what Simpson refers to in the quote in the previous footnote: the fact that nearly all categories above the level of families appear in the record suddenly, without the gradual and continuous sequences we should expect. Punctuated equilibriumism does nothing to explain the nearly complete absence, in the fossil record, of intermediates between such major divisions as, say, reptiles and birds, or fish and reptiles, or reptiles and mammals.
24. Here see Michael Denton, *Evolution: A Theory in Crisis* (London: Burnet Books, 1985), chapter 12.
25. "Evolution as Fact and Theory," 28.
26. "Science must be provisionally atheistic or cease to be itself." Basil Whilley "Darwin's Place in the History of Thought," in M. Banton, ed., *Darwinism and the Study of Society* (Chicago: Quadrangle Books, 1961).

7 Faith-Learning Integration
An Overview (1992)

WILLIAM HASKER

There is a gap in the literature on faith-learning integration.[1] On the one hand, there are broad, general, "worldviewish" discussions, presenting in a global fashion the challenge of integration.[2] On the other hand, there are a great many studies featuring particular disciplines and smaller areas within those disciplines as exemplified by many articles published in the *Christian Scholar's Review*. What is lacking, however, is a systematic mapping of the area in between of the general ways in which the worldview issues connect with the particular concerns of various disciplines. It is as though your neighborhood map store had a selection of globes and also an assortment of street guides for various nearby cities, but nothing in between—no maps of the interstate highway system, for instance. This essay aims to map some of that intervening territory.

Is such a map needed? I suspect that a map of this kind may be found useful, perhaps especially by scholars who are beginning to wrestle with the question.[3] What does and should faith-learning integration mean for my discipline? What is offered here is a way of approaching that question which is more detailed, and therefore more readily applicable, than the worldview studies, yet broader and more general than articles limited to a particular discipline. We shall discuss in order the nature of integration, the necessity for integration, strategies for integration, and dimensions of integration.

Faith-learning integration may be briefly described as a scholarly project whose goal is to ascertain and to develop integral relationships which exist between the Christian faith and human knowledge, particularly as expressed in the various academic disciplines. Here the terms faith and knowledge are taken quite broadly; in speaking of "the Christian faith" we are focusing on the cognitive content of faith, without excluding or minimizing the all-important dimensions of trust and commitment. Integration is concerned with integral relationships between faith and knowledge, the relationships which inherently exist between the content of the faith and the subject-matter of this or that discipline; such connections do not have to be invented or manufactured. But they do need to be ascertained and developed; unless this is done faith and knowledge may appear to be, and for practical purposes may be in fact, alien and unrelated to each other. Finally, faith-learning integration is especially concerned with the disciplines into which our knowledge is organized; the same concerns of subject-matter and methodology which lead to the distinction of disciplines also dictate that, initially at least, faith-learning integration is best pursued at the level of particular academic disciplines.

Our understanding of what faith-learning integration is may be assisted by a recognition of what it is not. Faith-learning integration is not the cultivation of personal Christian living on the part of the faculty member. Few things are as important in determining a faculty member's influence upon students as her or his personal spiritual and ethical life. But of course, the importance of personal spiritual development is not limited or specific to Christian scholars and teachers; it should equally concern Christian executives, Christian housewives, and Christian bricklayers. Faith-learning integration, on the other hand, is a specifically scholarly task; it is a specific responsibility of Christians who are engaged in the work of teaching and scholarship, and if (as often happens) they fail to perform this task it will not be done at all.

Faith-learning integration does not mean using academic disciplines as a source of illustrations for spiritual truths. An example of such use is found in an article explaining how teaching in a Christian day school differs from teaching in the public schools: "Two and two is always four, and God is always the same; you can depend on Him."[4] We would not disagree with what is being said here, though we might wonder whether saying it in this way is an effective teaching strategy. But it is clear that this example does not involve an "integral relationship" between the Christian faith and the discipline of mathematics; it is not an example of faith-learning integration. (Nor is such integration achieved by using "Christian" examples in the story problems.) If we as faculty members are disposed to use our disciplines for illustrative purposes our efforts will undoubtedly be more sophisticated than this, and there is nothing to criticize in finding useful illustrations from whatever source. But the point remains: the illustrative use of disciplinary materials in this way is not faith-learning integration.

Faith-learning integration is not a public relations program designed to convince constituents of the Christian character of an institution. The commitment that a college and its faculty make to the integration of learning with the Christian faith is properly seen as part of the broader commitment to serve Christ in every aspect of life. But the desire to exploit faith-learning integration in order to gain recognition as a "truly Christian" college carries with it dangers and possible distortions. Heavy use of the rhetoric of faith-learning integration does not guarantee that such integration is actually occurring, nor does it ensure that a college or its members will exemplify the highest Christian ideals in other respects. And it does not provide a guarantee that views which are antecedently favored by constituents on various points of contention will be affirmed and supported by faculty as a result of faith-learning activities. Above all, faith-learning integration is not a "quick fix" which instantly transforms a college into a model Christian community and its students and faculty into ideal Christian individuals. The integration of faith and learning is hard scholarly work. Like other scholarly work, it takes much time and effort to produce significant achievement. Much of it involves basic research, and immediate, highly visible results cannot be guaranteed. The commitment to do and to support such work is, we believe, one mark of a college which seeks to be in earnest about its Christian profession. But if the commitment to faith-learning integration is dominated by the desire to "prove something" about the institution, the effort is likely to be distorted or undermined.

Why exactly is faith-learning integration necessary? As we explore this question, it will help us also to get a better grasp of the nature of the task. David Wolfe points out that some Christians object to the very word "integration," because it seems to "presuppose a denial that truth is already one."[5] In a certain sense, this objection is justified. It is not as though there are two completely distinct and unrelated aspects of reality—say, Christianity and biochemistry—and it is up to us to create or invent a relationship between them. There is rather a single reality, all of which is created by God and under his dominion, and all of which we as his children and image-bearers must seek to understand. And for the mature Christian scholar it is, ideally, not a question of having on the one hand one's Christian faith, and on the other one's scholarly discipline, and needing to set up some kind of connection between them. Rather, one's scholarly thinking should already be permeated by Christian attitudes and beliefs, by Christian ways of seeing God's world—and, conversely, one's Christian vision of God's world should be already informed with the best insights gleaned from scholarly activity. In such a situation, one is not confronted with the task of "integrating" two more or less separate and disjointed bodies of knowledge and belief; rather, there is a unitary vision of truth.

And yet there is ample justification for speaking of "integration." First of all, though there is a unity of truth there is nevertheless a diversity in our ways of knowing that makes the unity of truth a difficult and demanding achievement for us humans. The way of knowing in biochemistry is through experiment and theorizing, while in theology we know truth by grasping and responding to God's revelation. Corresponding to these diverse ways of knowing there is a diversity in the ways of speaking, of asking and answering questions; this diversity is sometimes expressed by saying that we have here different "language-games." This diversity in ways of knowing and speaking provides a perennial challenge for the Christian scholar, and sets many traps for the student who would ignore it; those who would know God by the methods of the natural sciences and those who would understand scientific matters through scriptural revelation share a common record of ill-success. So as a matter of fact we as human knowers are confronted by diverse and apparently unconnected bodies of knowledge achieved through different means; it is precisely and only by "integrating" such diverse bodies of knowledge that the vision of a unity of truth is gained.

Yet another reason why a process of integration is necessary is found in the actual situation in the various academic disciplines. It hardly needs pointing out that the leadership of the academic disciplines is not in the hands of those who share the vision that "all truth is God's truth." While many Christian colleges provide a good undergraduate education and some offer limited graduate study, leadership in the various academic fields is vested in "prestige" graduate programs at leading secular universities.[6] Christian faculty members, having been trained in such institutions, have typically received little or no guidance in relating their graduate training to their Christian faith. As they begin their professional careers, then, they are in fact confronted with two "separate and disjoint bodies of knowledge and belief," simply because the graduate program has not assisted, and may have actively discouraged, the establishment of connections between them. Under these circumstances, to object to talk of "integration" is simply to deny the realities of the situation.

The necessity for integrating faith and discipline is first of all theological; it stems from the very nature of Christian faith itself. The Christian prays, "Thy will be done, on earth as it is in heaven." There is not a secular world and a sacred world, but a single world created by God and a single, unitary, truth which is known to God. To compartmentalize one's faith in one part of one's mind, one's scholarly discipline in another part, and to put one's business and civic concerns in yet other compartments is in effect to deny God's lordship over all of life. To do this brings several very real dangers. At a minimum, the failure to integrate means that one will lack the enrichment of an overall, unifying perspective by which to connect, unify, and comprehend all of what is known and experienced. It is also likely to mean that, in various respects, one will accept without question positions, viewpoints, and methods which are in serious tension or outright conflict with one's faith. The divided thinking which results can be a source of considerable discomfort for a reflective individual, and in some cases may even undermine one's faith. It also contributes to the impression, which in our day is extremely widespread, that Christian faith is essentially a purely private matter which has no bearing on the day-to-day business of life. To love God with all our minds requires that we try to think in a single, unified pattern all the truth he has enabled us to grasp.

For the Christian college, faith-learning integration is not only a theological but an educational necessity. It is necessary for the reason that education cannot be carried out in the most effective way without some broad framework of common assumptions which structure and motivate the curriculum. Every educator must at some point confront the questions: What is most important to learn, and to what end is it learned? If there are no answers to this, the educational enterprise becomes pointless and ineffective.[7] To the extent that there are answers, and the answers are operative in the actual shaping of the educational program, coherent and successful education becomes more possible.

This does not imply that the most effective education is one which is controlled by rigid dogma, with alternative views excluded from consideration. Christian colleges generally recognize, both in theory and in practice, that good education occurs as students are challenged by a wide variety of conflicting views. It is arguable that a Christian college with a commitment to faith-learning integration is in an especially strong position to encourage vigorous inquiry among its students. Energetic discussion is most likely to occur when the issues really matter to students and faculty, and they are far more likely to matter to those who hold deep-rooted beliefs which can be challenged, opposed, or perhaps supported by materials covered in a course.[8]

Given that the task of integration is inescapable, how can it be carried out? In this section we shall consider various strategies for integration, strategies which differ in their assessment of the existing relationships between the disciplines and the Christian faith, and therefore also in their understanding of what must be done in order for a Christian scholar to pursue the disciplines with integrity. Following David L. Wolfe and Ronald R. Nelson, we shall term these the compatibilist, the transformationist, and the reconstructionist strategies.[9]

According to the compatibilist strategy, "the integrity of both faith and discipline are in large measure presupposed ... [and] [t]he scholar's task is one of showing how ... shared assumptions and concerns can be profitably linked."[10] As is evident from this, the compatibilist does not recognize any deep, fundamental tension between the assumptions and procedures of her discipline and the Christian faith. She feels comfortable and "at home" both in her faith and in her scholarship; her aim is to demonstrate and exhibit the unity between them which already exists, at least potentially. As she practices her discipline she may (or again she may not) direct her studies in ways that are motivated by specifically Christian concerns. But she feels no need to challenge the underlying assumptions on which the study of her discipline normally proceeds. Since her faith and her discipline are already compatible, her task is simply to exhibit, to exemplify in practice, and to enjoy the compatibility which already exists.

The scholar who follows the transformationist strategy finds the relationship between his faith and his discipline to be somewhat more problematic than does the compatibilist. He does, to be sure, find some basic validity and integrity in the discipline as it is currently constituted. But he also finds the discipline to be lacking in insights and perspectives which are vital to him as a Christian. The proper response, then, is to recognize that there is "some legitimate insight in the disciplinary assumptions to begin with," and to go on from there to "remake or *transform* his discipline into one with a Christian orientation."[11]

Finally, there is the reconstructionist strategy. The reconstructionist, even more than the transformationist, finds a fundamental tension between the assumptions and claims of the existing, secular disciplines and those of the Christian faith. Indeed, he finds that the existing disciplines are so deeply permeated with anti-Christian assumptions of secularism, rationalism, and naturalism he has no choice but to reject them and to begin at the beginning in a "radical *reconstruction* of the disciplines on ... fully biblical foundations."[12] The reconstructed disciplines may still be called biology, geology, psychology, or philosophy. But they are all the same new disciplines with their own, distinctively Christian foundations, methodologies, and communities of inquirers; they are quite distinct from the biology, geology, psychology, and philosophy practiced by secular scholars and also by Christian scholars of compatibilist or transformationist persuasion.[13]

Now that we have the three strategies before us, how shall we assess them? One point which should already be clear is that the thoroughgoing reconstructionist stands at a greater distance from both the compatibilist and the transformationist than they stand from each other. Wolfe, indeed, claims that reconstructionism is not really faith-learning integration, on the grounds that this strategy "collapses the two-sided nature of the integrative process into a one-sided collection of Christian insights without systematic relevance to an academic discipline."[14] But this seems mistaken; the reconstructionist, to be sure, is no longer collaborating with the practitioners of the existing secular academic discipline, but he still must contend with the plurality of ways of knowing as well as with the distinctive subject-matter of his reconstructed discipline.[15] Furthermore, it is hard to see how one could rule out in principle the possibility that a Christian scholar might find a particular discipline to be so thoroughly unsound and permeated with anti-Christian assumptions that there is no acceptable response other than total rejection. And as we know, some Christian scholars have in fact reached that conclusion. They may be mistaken, and it may be that their own efforts at creating alternative disciplines are not especially successful or impressive. But if this is so, it should be possible to demonstrate it by evidence and argument; there is no need to prejudge the matter by ruling out reconstructionism in advance.

It may prove illuminating to view these three integrative strategies as attempting to respond to different kinds of questions about the relationship between Christianity and scholarship. The compatibilist, for example, is responding to the question, "Why would a Christian want to get involved with that?" asked about a particular discipline. Such questions are in fact often asked by Christians who are suspicious of scholarship, and sometimes also by secular scholars who suspect that a Christian practicing their discipline will twist and distort it into something it is not. (One might say they suspect all Christian scholars of being reconstructionists!) To such questions the compatibilist replies by showing that there are excellent reasons for a Christian to practice, and not to twist or distort, the discipline, because of inherent commonalities between the discipline and the faith. To quote Wolfe: "Genuine integration occurs when an assumption or concern can be shown to be internally shared by (integral to) both the Judaeo-Christian vision and an academic discipline."[16]

The transformationist, as we have seen, approaches his discipline with a somewhat different perspective. Committed by choice, training and calling to a particular discipline, he nevertheless finds it seriously lacking in certain ways as viewed from a Christian perspective. His question is, "How can this discipline be changed so as to correct what I as a Christian find to be its errors, and to supplement what I find to be lacking in its vision of truth?" He need not deny the compatibilist's contention that there are genuine commonalities between the faith and the discipline, yet he sees the need for a transformation of the discipline in order to correct what he perceives as serious flaws. (The compatibilist, if she admits that there are flaws in her discipline, will typically see them as the product of a "partial viewpoint" on reality taken by the discipline; the need is for this partial viewpoint to be placed into the context of a fuller vision of Christian truth, not for the discipline itself to be transformed.)

The reconstructionist has yet another agenda. He has, to be sure, asked himself why a Christian would want to be involved with the existing, secular discipline, and his answer is: "For no good reason!" The existing discipline is beyond help. Yet, there is still the subject-matter of the discipline which cannot be ignored—subject-matter of which a Christian account is needed. So he asks himself, "How can one think

Christianly about politics (or geology, or economics)?" And the answer is found in the reconstructed discipline.

It may further be pointed out that the various strategies, while distinct in their basic assumptions, need not be sharply separated in practice. One might, for instance, undertake to "reform" certain assumptions or procedures in one's discipline which one takes to be disharmonious with Christian truth, without going as far in this direction as a thorough going transformationism would require. Or, one might conclude that a particular school or movement within one's discipline is to be thoroughly rejected (thus in effect agreeing with the reconstructionist about that school or movement), while regarding other schools either as compatible with one's faith or at least as affording insights which should be incorporated into a transformed discipline. (One might be a reconstructionist about behaviorism but a transformationist about cognitive psychology.) And even reconstructionists seldom manage to free themselves from dependence on all aspects of the secular disciplines they have rejected. (Creation Science advocates are still dependent on many aspects of standard biology, for example.) So the three strategies may better be viewed as three points on a continuum, than as three mutually exclusive alternatives. Nevertheless, these strategies can provide a valuable framework for the Christian scholar approaching a specific discipline with the objective of faith-learning integration.

It may be helpful to consider an example which illustrates these considerations. In several issues of the *Christian Scholar's Review* different scholars have addressed the deconstructionist movement in literary criticism and philosophy. This is a movement which in its principal representatives (e.g., Foucault, Derrida) is clearly non-Christian and even anti-Christian, yet it has drawn a considerable range of responses. The stance of David Lyle Jeffrey and Roger Lundin is one of almost complete rejection.[17] Patricia A. Ward, on the other hand, sees more possibilities for constructive dialogue between Christians and deconstructionists,[18] and more recently James H. Olthuis, Merold Westphal, Gary J. Percesepe, and John D. Caputo all view deconstruction as affording important resources for Christian scholars, including insights which elsewhere are either unavailable or suppressed.[19] I shall not presume to pronounce as to which is the "best" or "most correct" Christian response to this movement; that question is still unresolved. But the range of response does illustrate different "strategies" for approaching this important contemporary movement.[20]

Suppose that a Christian scholar is convinced of the necessity of faith-learning integration, and of the need to devote significant resources of time and energy to this aspect of the scholarly task. Suppose, also, that she has formed at least a general idea concerning the relationship between the Christian faith and her discipline as it presently exists, and along with this a conception of the integrative strategy to be followed. How then shall she proceed? What exactly is to be done, in order to make faith-learning integration a reality? In this section we chart some dimensions of integration—that is, some basic kinds of questions which the scholar concerned with faith-learning integration may need to address.[21]

At this point I believe it is important to affirm an explicit acceptance of integrative pluralism—of the view that there is not one mandatory pattern for integration but rather a variety of approaches each of which may yield valuable results when properly applied. As Wolfe says: "Perhaps some disciplines lend themselves to one approach better than another. Perhaps the personality of the investigator is an important factor in the particular insights that are generated. In any case it must not be thought that one and only one approach is possible."[22] As Wolfe suggests, there may be a number of factors which are relevant to determining the best approach for a particular scholar to use at a particular time. One quite significant factor would seem to be the distinction between theoretical and applied disciplines. Clearly there is such a distinction, though it is not absolutely clear-cut. Even the most "theoretical" disciplines typically claim that there is something of a practical nature (above and beyond the "doing"— e.g., of history or philosophy— involved in the discipline itself) that one can do better as a result of having studied the discipline. And on the other hand, if the "applied" subject does not have a body of theory on which practice is based it can hardly justify itself as a discipline within the college curriculum. But the distinction is clearly seen in the criteria by which students are evaluated. A history major, for example, is better able to do all manner of things as a result of having studied history—practice law, for example, or serve in government, or administer a college. (If you doubt this, just ask your favorite historian!) But a graduating history major is not evaluated by her ability to do any of these things, but rather by her knowledge of history. The voice performance major, on the other hand, is expected to know a good deal of theory and music history, but his program has been a failure if he knows all this but just can't sing at all well. One discipline aims primarily at teaching its students to know something, the other at teaching them to do something.

The reason this distinction is relevant here is that the typical issues for faith discipline integration tend to be different for theoretical and applied disciplines. The probing questions concerning epistemological and metaphysical "foundations" are less likely to seem pressing for the applied disciplines—and on the other hand, as we shall see, these disciplines typically raise questions of their own which are not present, or not as pressing, for the theoretical disciplines. Let us see how this is so.

In the theoretical disciplines four major dimensions of integration can be identified, as follows:

1. World-view Foundations: Here the question to be asked is, What fundamental insights and convictions, derivable from the Christian world-view, are relevant to the discipline? The "insights and convictions" which are pertinent here may be found in the Scriptures, in commentaries and books of theology, in books written specifically about the Christian world-view, and in other sources. The conviction that the earth, the heavens, and everything in them were created by God and pronounced good by him is surely relevant to the Christian's study of the natural sciences. The doctrine that man is created in the image of God, and the insight that humans are fallen, sinful creatures are both highly relevant to the human sciences. And so on.

2. Disciplinary Foundations: Here the scholar considers the foundational assumptions—methodological, epistemological, and ontological—which are stated or presupposed as the basis of his discipline, and asks whether any of them are particularly significant or problematic from the standpoint of the Christian faith. This significance may be either harmonious with the faith, as is the natural scientist's assumption that the physical world has an orderly structure which is mind-independent yet accessible to investigation, or in conflict with the faith, like the assumption made by some psychologists that human behavior is entirely the product of environmental conditioning. In either case, the scholar's task is first to identify the foundational belief, then to subject it to scrutiny and determine its relationship to the Christian world-view. If it turns out that a particular assumption is both fundamental to the discipline and inimical to Christian belief, the scholar may find himself impelled in the direction of disciplinary transformation. One difficulty in this dimension of the integrative task is that all disciplines are not equally explicit about their fundamental assumptions; sometimes a good deal of digging is required. Help in this task may be found in discussions of the methodology and the philosophy of the various disciplines, as well as in work done by other Christian scholars on faith-discipline integration.

3. Disciplinary Practice: Here we are concerned with issues which arise in the day-to-day practice of one's discipline—of "doing one's job" as an historian, physicist, philosopher, etc. The historian may ask himself what aspects of history are of special interest to Christians, and also whether those aspects have been treated adequately by others, or whether valuable knowledge and insights may emerge from his own fresh study of those topics. The philosopher considers which questions in his field are of concern specifically to Christians, and how the existing, available answers to those questions comport with his Christian faith. The physicist might reflect concerning the relationship between various cosmological theories and the doctrine of creation. And so on. Resources for this dimension of integration are found primarily within the discipline itself, as well as in one's own understanding of the Christian world-view and in the writings of other Christian scholars.

4. World-view Contribution: In this dimension of integration we ask, what specific contribution does this discipline make to the Christian vision of reality? How does it enable us to understand God, and his world, and our fellow human beings differently than if the insights of the discipline were not available? What insights, projects, and activities does the discipline make possible? In short, what difference does the discipline make for Christians who are not its students and practitioners? The resources for this dimension of integration are found in the discipline itself, as refined through the examination called for in the other three dimensions, as well as in the scholar's grasp on the overall scheme of things to which the discipline is asked to contribute.

This last dimension, world-view contribution, is the one which has been least emphasized in the literature on faith-learning integration, so it may be worthwhile saying a few things in defense of its inclusion. First of all, this dimension emphasizes that the ultimate aim of faith-learning integration is not merely to complete the integrative task within each separate discipline, but to enhance our overall vision of reality in the light of Christ. It is not enough if the sociologist, the biologist, the literary scholar and the economist each has worked out how things stand in relation to the faith with respect to her own discipline, but there is no broader integration of the results of these labors. Our aim must be integral Christian scholarship, not only within each discipline but reaching across disciplinary boundaries. The unity of God's truth demands no less. Second, this emphasizes that elaborating the overall Christian worldview is a common responsibility of the entire faculty. If this world-view is to play a significant role in the educational process, it must be communicated to students, and if it is to be communicated it must be shared among faculty as a common possession. For each of us simply to do her "own thing" in her own classroom with her own discipline, and leave the students to put the pieces together, will not get the job done. Thirdly, this dimension helps to demonstrate the relevance of integration even to disciplines which sometimes tend to be only minimally involved in other dimensions of integrative activities.

Consider, for example, mathematics. One will probably have some difficulty finding in the Scriptures principles which are specifically relevant to mathematical research. The mathematician can deny, with some plausibility, that his Christian faith makes or ought to make a substantive difference to the way he conducts his study of the field: there is no "Christian mathematics"; the problems and methodologies of mathematics are the same for believer and non-believer. There may be dispute as to whether or not Christians have a stake in some particular position on the foundations of mathematics. But the foundations of mathematics is a primary concern for only a rather small percentage of mathematicians and for virtually no undergraduate students, so that the topic would seem to have at best limited relevance. But when we turn to the theme of world-view contribution, the picture changes dramatically. What contribution does the discipline of mathematics make to our understanding of the nature of the world God has created? What is the significance of the fact that so many processes in the world can be given precise mathematical description? (Consider the differences in the way nature is viewed by those who have absorbed the lessons of the mathematical natural sciences, from the purely poetic and mystical view sometimes taken by those who are ignorant of those sciences.) What, on the other hand, is the significance of the fact that some events and processes seem to defy mathematical analysis? It is hard to believe that there is nothing to be said on these topics, or that Christian mathematicians will be unable to say it. These questions do not, to be sure, belong to the discipline of mathematics as narrowly defined. But that is just the point of the question of world-view contribution: not to remain confined within a narrow definition of the discipline, but to explore and exhibit its relevance to the broader understanding to which it contributes. This indeed would seem to be an inescapable concern for Christian liberal arts education, and indicates once again the close connection between the ideal of a comprehensive, unifying perspective on "the way things are" and the vision of reality which derives from faith.[23]

As we turn from the "theoretical" to the "applied" disciplines, it is well to remind ourselves once again that the various disciplines in the curriculum do not all fit neatly into one category or the other. Most disciplines have both theoretical and applied aspects, and so also with the integrative dimensions: A discipline which would be classified as "theoretical" may have practical applications which require the Christian scholar to give consideration to one or more of the integrative dimensions associated with the applied disciplines, or vice versa. But with this caution in mind, we now consider the dimensions of integration for the applied disciplines, of which again there are four:

1. Theory Applied to Practice: As has been noted already, each applied discipline has a basis of theory on which practice is based, whether that theory is internal to the discipline (such as music theory) or "borrowed" from one of the theoretical disciplines (as education uses psychology). In principle, then, all of the same sorts of questions can arise concerning the theoretical components of applied disciplines, as arise concerning the theoretical disciplines. These questions may, however, seem less urgent for the applied disciplines, in view of their primarily practical orientation. But there is another kind of question about theory which is specific to the applied disciplines: What are the implications and results when this theory is put into practice? Consider for example the behavioristic school in psychology. From a theoretical standpoint, questions are often raised about the foundational assumptions of this approach—its mechanistic view of man, its determinism, its implicit materialism, its denial of human freedom and dignity, and so on. The educator and applied psychologist, however, may feel that they can use behaviorism as a practical tool without getting into such questions; their concern is not with behaviorism as the "ultimate truth" about human beings, but simply with whether or not it works. But for them, a quite different question arises: What are the effects in practice of using behavior modification, for example, as one's primary method of discipline in the elementary classroom? And how do those effects coincide or conflict with one's ultimate objectives as a Christian educator? Whatever the answer to this is (and no answer is prejudged here), the question places the theory of behaviorism in a light which would be unavailable apart from its practical use in education.

2. Ethics and Values: Whenever one is concerned with practice, with action, then ethics and values must play a role. And so the Christian educator, the "trainer" in an applied discipline, must ask himself: What am I offering to my students by way of ethical guidance concerning the practice into which I am initiating them? The assumption, common in secular education, that one simply equips students with neutral tools or skills which are to be used purely according to their personal whims and desires, is just not acceptable in a Christian education. One can not guarantee that guidance will be accepted and followed, but it is irresponsible not to offer it. Such guidance will include "professional ethics," where relevant, but it will go well beyond these often rather narrowly defined codes of professional conduct to include consideration of the ultimate objectives for which certain things are done, as well as of the implications of various

ways of meeting those objectives. In economics, for example, it is necessary to reflect on what the purposes of the economic system ought to be, and on various ways of fulfilling those purposes—are the human needs of the poor, for instance, better met by encouraging private enterprise, or by creating public welfare programs, or by some mix of these strategies?

3. Attitudes: Whenever service is performed, especially service done directly for human beings, it makes a tremendous difference in what spirit or attitude the service is done. We have all experienced that one physician leaves us feeling calm and hopeful while another, perhaps equally skillful on a technical level, leaves us uneasy and anxious. Perhaps the two doctors are equally dedicated to providing the very best care for the patient's welfare. But one of them succeeded, as the other did not, in communicating that dedication to us through a manner and an attitude which assured us that our needs were understood and that everything was being done to restore us to health. We know, too, the difference which our own attitude and treatment of students makes to how things go in our classes. In applied subjects, then, we need to lead students to reflect on the attitudes with which they will serve; this is a concrete application of our concern with ethics and values. Of course, we also need to instill in them, by example and precept, the best Christian attitudes and spirit of service.

4. Contribution to the Kingdom of God. If the ultimate goal of Christian study and theorizing is the elaboration of the Christian world-view, the ultimate goal of Christian practice is to build the Kingdom of God, in order that "Thy will be done, on earth as it is in heaven." How does our "doing" in the applied disciplines contribute to this? In a sense this also is a continuation of the concern with ethics and values, but it places those questions in a larger arena, the arena of God's total purposes for us his creatures. We may ask, with Nicholas Wolterstorff, how a particular form of activity contributes to shalom, to the good and satisfying human life under God's rule which he intends and desires for us.[24] And the answer to this question is of vital concern as we seek to integrate these activities, and the disciplines which instruct us in them, with the faith and the love we know in Christ.

This then is the challenge and the task of faith-learning integration. It is a challenge to which we as Christian scholars and teachers have committed ourselves in virtue of our calling. It is an area in which we do not have prepackaged answers waiting to be taken up and proclaimed; rather we must find our own answers in collaboration with Christian scholars everywhere.

Notes

1. This essay first appeared in *CSR* 21.3 (March 1992): 234-48.
2. Representative works along this line include Harry Blamires, *The Christian Mind: How Should a Christian Think?* (Ann Arbor, Mich.: Servant Books, 1978); Arthur F. Holmes, *Contours of a World View* (Grand Rapids, Mich.: Eerdmans, 1983); Brian J. Walsh and J. Richard Middleton, *The Transforming Vision: Shaping a Christian World View*

(Downers Grove, Ill.: InterVarsity, 1984); and Nicholas Wolterstorff, *Reason Within the Bounds of Religion* (Grand Rapids, Mich.: Eerdmans, 1976).

3. I use "scholars" as a general term to include practitioners of all the academic disciplines, while recognizing that some Christian academics prefer to designate themselves as scientists or artists or in some other way.

4. Cited by David L. Wolfe, "The Line of Demarcation between Integration and PseudoIntegration" (hereafter cited as "Demarcation"), in Harold Heie and David L. Wolfe, eds., *The Reality of Christian Learning: Strategies for Faith-Discipline Integration* (hereafter, *Reality*) (Grand Rapids, Mich.: Christian University Press, 1987), 4.

5. "Demarcation," 4.

6. My remarks in this section suggested to one referee the image of "a small band of faithful Christians holding off the united hordes of heathen." Clearly such an image is a caricature; for one thing, neither among Christians nor among non-Christians is there the kind of unity it suggests. And some disciplines and sub-disciplines are fairly open to Christian insights, or at least to insights reflecting Christian concerns. (In philosophy, for instance, this is true of the philosophy of religion and, to a lesser extent, of ethics; the philosophy of mind, on the other hand, tends to be dominated by a doctrinaire materialism.) But this caricature, like all caricatures, does contain a grain of truth: as Nathan Hatch has remarked, "Among contemporary intellectuals, the sway of secularism reigns virtually unchallenged, and its attack against the Christian faith remains heavy and sustained" ("Evangelical Colleges and the Challenge of Christian Thinking" in Joel Carpenter and Kenneth Shipps, eds., *Making Higher Education Christian* [Grand Rapids, Mich.: Christian University Press, 1987], 158).

7. "When a youngster like Lincoln sought to educate himself, the immediately available obvious things for him to learn were the Bible, Shakespeare and Euclid. Was he really worse off than those who try to find their way through the technical smorgasbord of the current school system, with its utter inability to distinguish between important and unimportant in any way other than by the demands of the market?" (Allen Bloom, *The Closing of the American Mind* [New York: Simon and Schuster, 1987], 59.)

8. Bloom, "[R]elativism has extinguished the real motive of education, the search for a good life," 34.

9. In this section we are heavily indebted to Wolfe, "Demarcation," and to Ronald R. Nelson, "Faith-Discipline Integration: Compatibilist, Reconstructionalist and Transformationalist Strategies" (hereafter, "Strategies"), both in *Reality*. It would seem that Nelson originated this classification of integrative strategies.

10. "Strategies," 320.

11. Wolfe, "Demarcation," 7 (emphasis in original).

12. Nelson, "Strategies," 325 (emphasis added).

13. I am indebted to Arthur Holmes for raising the question of how the strategies for integration elaborated here correlate with H. Richard Niebuhr's typology of stances on the relationship of Christ and culture (see his *Christ and Culture* [New York: Harper, 1951]).

14. Wolfe, "Demarcation," 8.

15. If the reconstructionist were to draw the content of his discipline exclusively from biblical and theological sources, Wolfe's comment would be justified. But this they typically do not do.

16. Wolfe, "Demarcation, 5 (emphasis in original). This is Wolfe's general definition of faith-learning integration; it obviously has a strong compatibilist flavor, though Wolfe does count transformationism as genuine integration.

17. David Lyle Jeffrey, "Caveat Lector: Structuralism, Deconstruction, and Ideology," *CSR* 17.4 (June 1988): 436-448; Roger Lundin, "The Cult and Culture of Interpretation," *CSR* 19.4, (June 1990): 363-387. It should perhaps be said that neither of these scholars simply repudiates deconstruction because it is "un-Christian" or "un-biblical"; rather, they criticize deconstruction in the light of what they take to be an older, and deeper, hermeneutical tradition.

18. Patricia A. Ward, "Worldly Readers and Writerly Texts," *CSR* 17.4 (June 1988): 425-435.

19. James H. Olthuis, "A Cold and Comfortless Hermeneutic or a Warm and Trembling Hermeneutic: A Conversation with John D. Caputo," *CSR* 19.4 (June 1990): 345-362; Merold Westphal, "The Ostrich and the Boogeyman: Placing Postmodernism," *CSR* 20.2 (December 1990): 114-117; Gary J. Percesepe, "The Unbearable Lightness of Being Postmodern," *CSR* 20.2 (December 1990): 118-135; John D. Caputo, "Hermeneutics and Faith: A Response to Professor Olthuis," *CSR* 20.2 (December 1990): 164-170; James H. Olthuis, "Undecidability and the Im/Possibility of Faith: Continuing the Conversation with Professor Caputo," *CSR* 20.2 (December 1990): 171-173.

20. Additional examples may be found in *CSR*. Thus, the symposium on Central American Development in 20.3 (February 1991) contrasts the compatibilism of Howard Wiarda, who finds that he can carry out his Christian values and commitments through "mainstream" political science, with the transformationism of Roland Hoksbergen and (especially) James C. Dekker, both of whom wish for more specifically and overtly Christian solutions to the problems of Central America. And the symposium on evolution in 21.1 (September 1991) pits Alvin Plantinga's (and Pattle Pun's) strongly transformationist views against the compatibilist or mildly transformationist approaches of Howard Van Til and Ernan McMullin. In the light of these and other examples, it may not be too much to say that the question of compatibilism vs. transformationism is one of the most important general issues confronting Christian scholarship at the present time.

21. Although we have included reconstructionism as a possible strategy for integration, it will be evident that these questions are more suitable to the compatibilist and transformationist strategies. A reconstructionist would say that if we as Christian scholars ask these questions about the existing disciplines, the conclusion we should reach is that we should abandon those disciplines and join him in his project of radical reconstruction.

22. Wolfe, "Demarcation," 10.

23. According to Bloom, the very idea of a comprehensive world-view is in American culture dependent on the idea of the Bible as a "total book": "[W]ithout the book, even the idea of the order of the whole is lost." (58).

24. See Nicholas Wolterstorff, *Until Justice and Peace Embrace* (Grand Rapids, Mich.: Eerdmans, 1982).

8 Jesus the Logician (1999)

Dallas Willard

Few today will have seen the words "Jesus" and "logician" put together to form a phrase or sentence, unless it would be to deny any connection between them at all.[1] The phrase "Jesus the logician" is not ungrammatical, any more than is "Jesus the carpenter." But it "feels" upon first encounter to be something like a category mistake or error in logical type, such as "Purple is asleep," or "More people live in the winter than in cities," or "Do you walk to work or carry your lunch?"

There is in our culture an uneasy relation between Jesus and intelligence, and I have actually heard Christians respond to my statement that Jesus is the most intelligent man who ever lived by saying that it is an oxymoron. Today we automatically position him away from (or even in opposition to) the intellect and intellectual life. Almost no one would consider him to be a thinker, addressing the same issues as, say, Aristotle, Kant, Heidegger or Wittgenstein, and with the same logical method.

Now this fact has important implications for how we today view his relationship to our world and our life—especially if our work happens to be that of art, thought, research, or scholarship. How could he fit into such a line of work, and lead us in it, if he were logically obtuse? How could we be his disciples at our work, take him seriously as our teacher there, if when we enter our fields of technical or professional competence we must leave him at the door? Obviously some repositioning is in order, and it may be helped along simply by observing his use of logic and his obvious powers of logical thinking as manifested in the Gospels of the New Testament.

Now when we speak of "Jesus the logician" we do not, of course, mean that he developed theories of logic, as did, for example, Aristotle and Frege. No doubt he could have, if he is who Christians have taken him to be. He could have provided a *Begriffsschrift*, or a *Principia Mathematica*, or alternative axiomatizations of Modal Logic, or various completeness or incompleteness proofs for various "languages." (He is, presumably, responsible for the order that is represented through such efforts as these.)

He could have. Just as he could have handed Peter or John the formulas of Relativity Physics or the Plate Tectonic theory of the earth's crust, etc. He certainly could, that is, if he is indeed the one Christians have traditionally taken him to be. But he did not do it, and for reasons which are bound to seem pretty obvious to anyone who stops to think about it. But that, in any case, is not my subject here. When I speak of "Jesus the logician" I refer to his use of logical insights: to his mastery and employment of logical principles in his work as a teacher and public figure.

Now it is worth noting that those who do creative work or are experts in the field of logical theory are not necessarily more logical or more philosophically sound than those who do not. We might hope that they would be, but they may even be illogical in how they work out their own logical theories. For some reason great powers in theory do not seem to guarantee significantly greater accuracy in practice. Perhaps no person well informed about the history of thought will be surprised at this statement, but for most of us it needs to be emphasized. To have understanding of developed logical theory surely could help one to think logically, but it is not sufficient to guarantee logical thinking and except for certain rarified cases it is not even necessary. Logical insight rarely depends upon logical theory, though it does depend upon logical relations. The two primary logical relations are implication (logical entailment) and contradiction; and their role in standard forms of argument such as the Barbara Syllogism, Disjunctive Syllogism, Modus Ponens and Modus Tollens—and even in strategies such as *reductio ad absurdum*—can be fully appreciated, for practical purposes, without rising to the level of theoretical generalization at all.[2]

To be logical no doubt does require an understanding of what implication and contradiction are, as well as the ability to recognize their presence or absence in obvious cases. But it also requires the will to be logical, and then certain personal qualities that make it possible and actual: qualities such as freedom from distraction, focused attention on the meanings or ideas involved in talk and thought, devotion to truth, and willingness to follow the truth wherever it leads via logical relations. All of this in turn makes significant demands upon moral character. Not just on points such as resoluteness and courage, though those are required. A practicing hypocrite, for example, will not find a friend in logic, nor will liars, thieves, murderers and adulterers. They will be constantly alert to appearances and inferences that may logically implicate them in their wrong actions. Thus the literary and cinematic genre of mysteries is unthinkable without play on logical relations.

Those devoted to defending certain pet assumptions or practices come-what-may will also have to protect themselves from logic. All of this is, I believe, commonly recognized by thoughtful people. Less well understood is the fact that one can be logical only if one is committed to being logical as a fundamental value. One is not logical by chance, any more than one just happens to be moral. And, indeed, logical consistency is a significant factor in moral character. That is part of the reason why in an age that attacks morality, as ours does, the logical will also be demoted or set aside—as it now is.

Not only does Jesus not concentrate on logical theory, but he also does not spell out all the details of the logical structures he employs on particular occasions. His use of logic is always enthymemic, as is common to ordinary life and conversation. His points are, with respect to logical explicitness, understated and underdeveloped. The significance of the enthymeme is that it enlists the mind of the hearer or hearers from the inside, in a way that full and explicit statement of argument cannot do. Its rhetorical force is, accordingly, quite different from that of fully explicated argumentation, which tends to distance the hearer from the force of logic by locating it outside of his own mind.

Jesus's aim in utilizing logic is not to win battles, but to achieve understanding or insight in his hearers. This understanding only comes from the inside, from the understandings one already has. It seems to "well up from within" one. Thus he does not follow the logical method one often sees in Plato's dialogues, or the method that characterizes most teaching and writing today. That is, he does not try to make everything so explicit that the conclusion is forced down the throat of the hearer. Rather, he presents matters in such a way that those who wish to know can find their way to, can come to, the appropriate conclusion as something they have discovered—whether or not it is something they particularly care for.

"A man convinced against his will is of the same opinion still." Yes, and no doubt Jesus understood that. And so he typically aims at real inward change of view that would enable his hearers to become significantly different as people through the workings of their own intellect. They will have, unless they are strongly resistant to the point of blindness, the famous "eureka" experience, not the experience of being outdone or beaten down.

With these points in mind, let us look at some typical scenes from the Gospels—scenes that are of course quite familiar, but are now to be examined for the role that distinctively logical thinking plays in them.

(1). Consider Matthew 12:1-8. This contains a teaching about the ritual law: specifically about the regulations of the temple and the sabbath. Jesus and his disciples were walking through fields of grain—perhaps wheat or barley—on the sabbath, and they were stripping the grains from the stalks with their hands and eating them. The Pharisees accused them of breaking the law, of being wrongdoers. Jesus, in response, points out that there are conditions in which the ritual laws in question do not apply.

He brings up cases of this that the Pharisees already concede. One is the case (I Sam. 21:1-6) where David, running for his life, came to the place of worship and sacrifice supervised by Ahimelich the priest. He asked Ahimelich for food for himself and his companions, but the only food available was bread consecrated in the ritual of the offerings. This bread, as Jesus pointed out (Matt. 12:4), was forbidden to David by law, and was to be eaten (after the ritual) by priests alone. But Ahimelich gave it to David and his men to satisfy their hunger. Hunger as a human need, therefore, may justify doing what ritual law forbids.

Also, Jesus continues (second case), the priests every sabbath in their temple service do more work than sabbath regulations allow: "On the sabbath the priests in the temple profane the sabbath, and are innocent" (Matt. 12:5). It logically follows, then, that one is not automatically guilty of wrongdoing or disobedience when they do not keep the ritual observances as dictated, in case there is some greater need that must be met. This is something the Pharisees have, by implication, already admitted by accepting the rightness in the two cases Jesus referred to.

The still deeper issue here is the use of law to harm people, something that is not God's intention. Any time ritual and compassion (e.g., for hunger) come into conflict,

God, who gave the law, favors compassion. That is the kind of God he is. To think otherwise is to misunderstand God and to cast him in a bad light. Thus Jesus quotes the prophet Hosea: "But if you had known what this means, 'I desire compassion, and not sacrifice' [Hos. 6:6], you would not have condemned the innocent" (Matt. 12:7; cf. 9:13). Thus the use of logic here is not only to correct the judgment that the disciples (the "innocent" in this case) must be sinning in stripping the grain and eating it. It is used to draw a further implication about God: God is not the kind of person who condemns those who act to meet a significant need at the expense of a relative triviality in the law. Elsewhere he points out that the sabbath appointed by God was made to serve man, not man to serve the sabbath (Mark 2:27).

Now the case of sabbath keeping—or, more precisely, of the ritual laws developed by men for sabbath observance—is one that comes up over and over in the Gospels, and it is always approached by Jesus in terms of the logical inconsistency of those who claim to practice it in the manner officially prescribed at the time. (See for example Mark 3:1-3, Luke 13:15-17, John 9:14-16, etc.) They are forced to choose between hypocrisy and open inconsistency, and he does sometimes use the word "hypocrisy" of them (e.g., Luke 13:15), implying that they knew they were being inconsistent and accepted it. In fact, the very idea of hypocrisy implies logical inconsistency. "They say, and do not" what their saying implies (Matt. 23:2).

And legalism will always lead to inconsistency in life, if not hypocrisy, for it will eventuate in giving greater importance to rules than is compatible with the principles one espouses (to sacrifice, for example, than to compassion, in the case at hand), and also to an inconsistent practice of the rules themselves (e.g., leading one's donkey to water on the sabbath, but refusing to have a human being healed of an eighteen-year-long affliction, as in Luke 13:15-16).

(2). Another illustrative case is found in Luke 20:27-40. Here it is the Sadducees, not the Pharisees, who are challenging Jesus. They are famous for rejecting the resurrection (vs. 27), and accordingly they propose a situation that, they think, is a *reductio ad absurdum* of resurrection. (vss. 28-33) The law of Moses said that if a married man died without children, the next eldest brother should make the widow his wife, and any children they had would inherit in the line of the older brother. In the "thought experiment" of the Sadducees, the elder of seven sons died without children from his wife, the next eldest married her and also died without children from her, and the next eldest did the same, and so on through all seven brothers. Then the wife died (small wonder!). The presumed absurdity in the case was that in the resurrection she would be the wife of all of them, which was assumed to be an impossibility in the nature of marriage.

Jesus's reply is to point out that those resurrected will not have mortal bodies suited for sexual relations, marriage, and reproduction. They will have bodies like angels do now, bodies of undying stuff. The idea of resurrection must not be taken crudely. Thus he undermines the assumption of the Sadducees that any "resurrection" must involve the body and its life continuing exactly as it does now. So the supposed impossibility of the woman being in conjugal relations with all seven brothers is not required by resurrection.

Then he proceeds, once again, to develop a teaching about the nature of God—which was always his main concern. Taking a premise that the Sadducees accepted, he draws the conclusion that they did not want. That the dead are raised, he says, follows from God's self-description to Moses at the burning bush. God described himself in that incident as "the God of Abraham, the God of Isaac, and the God of Jacob" (Luke 20:35 [Exod. 3:6]). The Sadducees accepted this. But at the time of the burning bush incident, Abraham, Isaac and Jacob had been long "dead," as Jesus points out. But God is not the God of the dead. That is, a dead person cannot sustain a relation of devotion and service to God, nor can God keep covenant faith with one who no longer exists. In covenant relationship to God one lives (vs. 38). One cannot very well imagine the living God communing with a dead body or a non-existent person and keeping covenant faithfulness with them.

(Incidentally, those Christian thinkers who nowadays suggest that the Godly do not exist or are without conscious life, at least, from the time their body dies to the time it is resurrected, might want to provide us with an interpretation of this passage.)

(3). Yet another illustration of Jesus's obviously self-conscious use of logic follows upon the one just cited from Luke 20. He would occasionally set teaching puzzles that required the use of logic on the part of his hearers. After the discussion of the resurrection, the Sadducees and the other groups about him no longer had the courage to challenge his powerful thinking (vs. 40). He then sets them a puzzle designed to help them understand the Messiah—for which everyone was looking.

Drawing upon what all understood to be a messianic reference, in Psalm 110, Jesus points out an apparent contradiction: The Messiah is the son of David (admitted by all), and yet David calls the Messiah "Lord" (Luke 20:42-43). "How," he asks, "can the Messiah be David's son if David calls him Lord?" (vs. 44). The resolution intended by Jesus is that they should recognize that the Messiah is not simply the son of David, but also of One higher than David, and that he is therefore king in a more inclusive sense than political head of the Jewish nation (Rev. 1:5). The promises to David therefore reach far beyond David, incorporating him and much more. This reinterpretation of David and the Messiah was a lesson learned and used well by the apostles and early disciples (See Acts 2:25-36, Heb. 5:6, and Phil. 2:9-11).

(4). For a final illustration we turn to the use of logic in one of the more didactic occasions recorded in the Gospels. The parables and stories of Jesus often illustrate his use of logic, but we will look instead at a well-known passage from the Sermon on the Mount. In his teaching about adultery and the cultivation of sexual lust, Jesus makes the statement, "If your right eye makes you to stumble, tear it out, and throw it from you; for it is better for you that one of the parts of your body perish, than for your whole body to be thrown into hell," and similarly for your right hand (Matt. 5:29-30).

What, exactly, is Jesus doing here? One would certainly be mistaken in thinking that he is advising anyone to actually dismember himself as a way of escaping damnation. One must keep the context in mind. Jesus is exhibiting the righteousness that goes beyond "the righteousness of the scribes and pharisees." This latter was a righteousness that took as its goal to not do anything wrong. If not doing anything wrong is the goal that could be achieved by dismembering yourself and making actions impossible. What you cannot do you certainly will not do. Remove your eye, your hand, etc., therefore, and you will roll into heaven a mutilated stump. The price of dismemberment would be small compared to the reward of heaven. That is the logical conclusion for one who held the beliefs of the scribes and the pharisees. Jesus is urging them to be consistent with their principles and do in practice what their principles imply. He reduces their principle—that righteousness lies in not doing anything wrong—to the absurd, in the hope that they will forsake their principle and see and enter the righteousness that is "beyond the righteousness of the scribes and Pharisees"—beyond, where compassion or love and not sacrifice is the fundamental thing. Jesus, of course, knew that if you dismembered yourself you could still have a hateful heart, toward God and toward man. It would not really help toward righteousness at all. That is the basic thing he is teaching in this passage. Failure to appreciate the logic makes it impossible to get his point.

These illustrative scenes from the Gospels will already be familiar to any student of Scripture. But, as we know, familiarity has its disadvantages. My hope is to enable us to see Jesus in a new light: to see him as doing intellectual work with the appropriate tools of logic, to see him as one who is both at home in and the master of such work.

We need to understand that Jesus is a thinker, that this is not a dirty word but an essential work, and that his other attributes do not preclude thought, but only insure that he is certainly the greatest thinker of the human race: "The most intelligent person who ever lived on earth." He constantly uses the power of logical insight to enable people to come to the truth about themselves and about God from the inside of their own heart and mind. Quite certainly it also played a role in his own growth in "wisdom" (Luke 2:52).

Often, it seems to me, we see and hear his deeds and words, but we do not think of him as one who knew how to do what he did or who really had logical insight into the things he said. We do not automatically think of him as a very competent person. He multiplied the loaves and fishes and walked on water, for example—but, perhaps, he did not know how to do it, he just used mindless incantations or prayers. Or he taught on how to be a really good person, but he did not have moral insight and understanding. He just mindlessly rattled off words that were piped into him and through him. Really?

This approach to Jesus may be because we think that knowledge is human, while he was divine. Logic means works, while he is grace. Did we forget something there? Possibly that he also is human? Or that grace is not opposed to effort but to earning? But human thought is evil, we are told. How could he think human thought, have human knowledge? So we distance him from ourselves, perhaps intending to elevate him, and we elevate him right out of relevance to our actual lives—especially as they involve the use of our minds. That is why the idea of Jesus as logical, of Jesus the logician, is shocking. And of course that extends to Jesus the scientist, researcher, scholar, artist, literary person. He just does not "fit" in those areas. Today it is easier to think of Jesus as a "TV evangelist" than as an author, teacher, or artist in the contemporary context. But now really!—if he were divine, would he be dumb, logically challenged, uninformed in any area? Would he not instead be the greatest of artists or speakers? Paul was only being consistent when he told the Colossians "all the treasures of wisdom and knowledge are concealed in him" (2:3). Except for what?

There is in Christian educational circles today a great deal of talk about "integration of faith and learning." Usually it leads to little solid result. This is in part due to the fact that it is, at this point in time, an extremely difficult intellectual task, which cannot be accomplished by ritual language and the pooh-poohing of difficulties. But an even deeper cause of the difficulty is the way we automatically tend to think of Jesus himself. It is not just in what we say about him, but in how he comes before our minds: how we automatically position him in our world, and how in consequence we position ourselves. We automatically think of him as having nothing essentially to do with "profane" knowledge, with learning and logic, and therefore find ourselves "on our own" in such areas.

We should, I believe, understand that Jesus would be perfectly at home in any professional context where good work is being done today. He would, of course, be a constant rebuke to all the proud self-advancement and the contemptuous treatment of others that goes on in professional circles. In this as in other respects, our professions are aching for his presence. If we truly see him as the premier thinker of the human race—and who else would be that?— then we are also in position to honor him as the most knowledgeable person in our field, whatever that may be, and to ask his cooperation and assistance with everything we have to do.

Catherine Marshall somewhere tells of a time she was trying to create a certain design with some drapes for her windows. She was unable to get the proportions right to form the design she had in mind. She gave up in exasperation and, leaving the scene, began to mull the matter over in prayer. Soon ideas as to how the design could be achieved began to come to her and before long she had the complete solution. She learned that Jesus is maestro of interior decorating.

Such stories are familiar from many areas of human activity, but quite rare in the areas of art and intellect. For lack of an appropriate understanding of Jesus we come to do our work in intellectual, scholarly and artistic fields on our own. We do not have confidence (otherwise known as faith) that he can be our leader and teacher in matters we spend most of our time working on. Thus our efforts often fall far short of what they should accomplish, and may even have less effect than the efforts of the Godless, because we undertake them only with "the arm of the flesh." Our faith in Jesus Christ rises no higher than that. We do not see him as he really is, maestro of all good things.

Here I have only been suggestive of a dimension of Jesus that is commonly overlooked. This is no thorough study of that dimension, but it deserves such study. It is one of major importance for a healthy faith in him. Especially today, when the authoritative institutions of our culture, the universities and the professions, omit him as a matter of course. Once one knows what to look for in the Gospels, however, one will easily see the thorough, careful and creative employment of logic throughout his teaching activity. Indeed, this employment must be identified and appreciated if what he is saying is to be understood. Only then can his intellectual brilliance be appreciated and he be respected as he deserves.

An excellent way of teaching in Christian schools would therefore be to require all students to do extensive logical analyses of Jesus's discourses. This should go hand in hand with the other ways of studying his words, including devotional practices such as memorization or *lectio divina*, and the like. It would make a substantial contribution to the integration of faith and learning.

While such a concentration on logic may sound strange today, that is only a reflection on our current situation. It is quite at home in many of the liveliest ages of the church.

John Wesley speaks for the broader Christian church across time and space, I think, in his remarkable treatise, "An Address to the Clergy." There he discusses at length the qualifications of an effective minister for Christ. He speaks of the necessity of a good knowledge of Scripture, and then adds:

> Some knowledge of the sciences also, is, to say the least, equally expedient. Nay, may we not say, that the knowledge of one (whether art or science), although now quite unfashionable, is even necessary next, and in order to, the knowledge of Scripture itself? I mean logic. For what is this, if rightly understood, but the art of good sense? of apprehending things clearly, judging truly, and reasoning conclusively? What is it, viewed in another light, but the art of learning and teaching; whether by convincing or persuading? What is there, then, in the whole compass of science, to be desired in comparison of it?
>
> Is not some acquaintance with what has been termed the second part of logic (metaphysics), if not so necessary as this, yet highly expedient (1.) In order to clear our apprehension (without which it is impossible either to judge correctly, or to reason closely or conclusively), by ranging our ideas under general heads? And (2.) In order to understand many useful writers, who can very hardly be understood without it?[3]

Later in this same treatise Wesley deals with whether we are, as ministers, what we ought to be. "Am I," he asks,

> a tolerable master of the sciences? Have I gone through the very gate of them, logic? If not, I am not likely to go much farther when I stumble at the threshold. Do I understand it so as to be ever the better for it? To have it always ready for use; so as to apply every rule of it, when occasion is, almost as naturally as I turn my hand? Do I understand it at all? Are not even the moods and figures [of the syllogism] above my comprehension? Do not I poorly endeavour to cover my ignorance, by affecting to laugh at their barbarous names? Can I even reduce an indirect mood to a direct; an hypothetic to a categorical syllogism? Rather, have not my stupid indolence and laziness made me very ready to believe, what the little wits and pretty gentlemen affirm, 'that logic is good for nothing'? It is good for this at least (wherever it is understood), to make people talk less; by showing them both what is, and what is not, to the point; and how extremely hard it is to prove any thing. Do I understand metaphysics; if not the depths of

the Schoolmen, the subtleties of Scotus or Aquinas, yet the first rudiments, the general principles, of that useful science? Have I conquered so much of it, as to clear my apprehension and range my ideas under proper heads; so much as enables me to read with ease and pleasure, as well as profit, Dr. Henry Moore's *Works*, Malebranche's *Search after Truth*, and Dr. Clarke's *Demonstration of the Being and Attributes of God*?[4]

I suspect that such statements will be strange, shocking, even outrageous or ridiculous to leaders of ministerial education today. But readers of Wesley and other great ministers of the past, such as Jonathan Edwards or Charles Finney, will easily see, if they know what it is they are looking at, how much use those ministers made of careful logic. Similarly for the great Puritan writers of an earlier period, and for later effective Christians such as C. S. Lewis and Francis Schaeffer. They all make relentless use of logic, and to great good effect. With none of these great teachers is it a matter of trusting logic instead of relying upon the Holy Spirit. Rather, they well knew, it is simply a matter of meeting the conditions along with which the Holy Spirit chooses to work. In this connection it will be illuminating to carefully examine the logical structure and force of Peter's discourse on the day of Pentecost (Acts 2).

Today, by contrast, we commonly depend upon the emotional pull of stories and images to "move" people. We fail to understand that, in the very nature of the human mind, emotion does not reliably generate belief or faith, if it generates it at all. Not even "seeing" does, unless you know what you are seeing. It is understanding, insight, that generates belief. In vain do we try to change people's heart or character by "moving" them to do things in ways that bypass their understanding.

Some months ago one who is regarded as a great teacher of homiletics was emphasizing the importance of stories in preaching. It was on a radio program. He remarked that a leading minister in America had told him recently that he could preach the same series of sermons each year, and change the illustrations, and no one would notice it. This was supposed to point out, with some humor, the importance of stories to preaching. What it really pointed out, however, was that the cognitive content of the sermon was never heard—if there was any to be heard—and does not matter.

Paying careful attention to how Jesus made use of logical thinking can strengthen our confidence in Jesus as master of the centers of intellect and creativity, and can encourage us to accept him as master in all of the areas of intellectual life in which we may participate. In those areas we can, then, be his disciples, not disciples of the current movements and glittering personalities who happen to dominate our field in human terms. Proper regard for him can also encourage us to follow his example as teachers in Christian contexts. We can learn from him to use logical reasoning at its best, as he works with us. When we teach what he taught in the manner he taught it, we will see his kind of result in the lives of those to whom we minister.[5]

Notes

1. This essay first appeared in *CSR* 28.4 (Summer 1999): 605-14.
2. See my paper, "Degradation of Logical Form," *Axiomathes* 1.3 (1997): 1-22, especially 3-7.
3. Herbert Welch, ed., *Selections from the Writings of the Rev. John Wesley* (New York: Eaton & Mains, 1901), 186.
4. Ibid, 198.
5. For necessary elaboration of many themes touched on in this paper, see J. P. Moreland's crucial book, *Love God with All Your Mind* (Colorado Springs, Colo.: Navpress, 1997).

9 Education for Homelessness or Homemaking?
The Christian College in a Postmodern Culture (2003)

STEVEN BOUMA-PREDIGER AND BRIAN WALSH

> *I wonder if I'll end up like Bernie in his dream*
> *A displaced person in some foreign border town*
> *Waiting for a train part hope part myth*
> *While the station changes hands.*[1]

Agricultural reformer Wes Jackson once observed that undergraduate education in America today tends to be little more than "education for upward mobility."[2] Indeed, he suggests that this is the only "major" that modern institutions of higher education seem to offer. As a result, he argues that precious little attention "is paid to educating the young to return home, or go to some other place, and dig in."[3] Kentucky poet-farmer and essayist Wendell Berry echoes Jackson when he laments that education today often dislocates people from their native place to such a degree that it has created "a powerful class of itinerant professional vandals" who are "now pillaging the country and laying it waste."[4] And environmental studies pioneer David Orr makes a similar claim with respect to American higher education when he states that "the conventional wisdom holds that all education is good, and the more of it one has, the better .... The truth is that without significant precautions, education can equip people merely to be more effective vandals of the earth."[5]

In our judgment, these perceptive cultural critics are right. Colleges and universities—small or large, public or private, Christian or secular—tend to educate for upward mobility, to alienate people from their local habitation, and to encourage the vandalization of the earth. In short, education today is in many respects education for global homelessness. In this paper we intend (briefly) to explore these claims about contemporary education, to set forth an alternative vision of education, and to describe some of the practical implications of such a biblically informed vision. Our thesis is simple: We propose that Christian higher education ought explicitly to aim at homecoming and homemaking.

This is an experimental paper. Our question is: What happens if we allow "homecoming" to be the guiding metaphor for our educational praxis? Erazim Kohak has wisely noted that metaphors "shape the context of our experience as a meaningful whole, deciding in the process not only what is primary and what derivative, but also who we ought to be and how we ought to act." In this sense, "a metaphor is a mask that molds the wearer's face."[6] And Neil Postman demonstrates specifically how metaphors shape the educational task.[7] So, if the real metaphor of higher education in America is that of "upward mobility," and if it is this metaphor that shapes our view of the student as client, customer, resource, professional-in-training, and citizen, then what happens if we shift the metaphor? What happens if we abandon upward mobility as the homeless-making metaphor that it is, secede from this education for homelessness and choose instead to foster an education for homemaking? What would that look like? If biblical faith shapes an imagination in which this world is our creational home, homelessness is the result of misplaced faith and failed stewardship, and the hope of redemption is for nothing less than the homecoming of God to a restored earth, then "homemaking" is a good candidate for a guiding metaphor in Christian educational endeavors.[8]

To try and unpack something of what this might look like, we will first revisit Jackson, Berry, and Orr to understand better their complaint. Then we will follow the lead of Berry and Orr to suggest provisionally and imaginatively what such a homemaking vision might look like if it became formative of our educational practice.

Wes Jackson contends that much of college and university education is education for upward mobility. Rather than learning how to become native to one's place—to know the people and plants and animals and customs of a particular locale and thus to live sustainably in that place—we are socialized into a materialistic way of life that blinds us to both the cultural and the ecological realities of our community and our landscape. We assume we will (and should) move upward—up the socioeconomic ladder—and become more mobile, moving from place to place. And we assume that these are unalloyed goods—good by their very nature. We do not question that upward mobility might not be such a good thing. But such a socialization process, Jackson contends, leaves us ecologically illiterate.

To test the plausibility of Jackson's claim, we need only ask ourselves a few questions. How many of our students know the trees that line the sidewalks on which they walk to and from class? How many of our students know the watershed from which their drinking water comes? How many of our students know where "away" is when they "throw things away"? If our students have no such specific knowledge of their peculiar place and how it works, how will they know how to take care of it, and why would they want to?

But "education for upward mobility" doesn't just result in ecological illiteracy. Students who have no intention of staying anywhere too long also demonstrate a profound geo-political, historical, and aesthetic ignorance as well. Without any sense of commitment to place, one pays no attention to neighbors, cares little about the dynamics of local community politics, never comes to understand the stories that have shaped this place to be the place it is, and never hangs around long enough to appreciate the art, literature, poetry, and folk traditions that this place has fostered. One never becomes a homecomer or homemaker because one is lost in the homelessness of mobility. To borrow metaphors from Kohak, education for upward mobility is education for wayfaring nomads who know nothing of the virtues of dwelling, the importance of roots, and love for place.

What if, Jackson muses, colleges and universities were to "assume the awesome responsibility to both validate and educate those who want to be homecomers—not necessarily to go home but to go somewhere and dig in and begin the long search and experiment to become native?"[9] What if, in order to achieve the sort of sustainable way of life that we must achieve in a shrinking world of limits, we worked toward "becoming native to our places in a coherent community that is in turn embedded in the ecological realities of its surrounding landscape?"[10] What if, given that upward mobility is often just a cipher for a kind of rootlessness and homelessness seemingly pervasive in our postmodern culture, institutions of higher education offered a "homecoming major"?[11]

Wendell Berry takes Wes Jackson's insights a step further. The "powerful class of itinerant professional vandals" that are pillaging our world and "laying it to waste" are the products (the metaphor is intentional) of an educational system that is governed by the superstition that the proper place in society of an educated person is "up." "Up is the direction from small to big," Berry comments. "Education is the way up. The popular aim of education is to put everybody 'on top.'" Berry then wryly comments, "Well, I think that I hardly need to document the consequent pushing and tramping and kicking in the face" in order to get on top and stay there.[12] We need to ask ourselves, and Berry will force us to ask ourselves, what are Christians doing "on top" of such a pile? What are Christians doing playing the same game of competitive upward mobility as everyone else? And why on earth are Christian educational institutions in this game? Perhaps we need to muse, with Berry, that "up" is "the wrong direction."[13]

Berry supports his claim about rampaging professionals with two observations. First, such folk must be "'upwardly mobile' transients who will permit no stay or place to interrupt their personal advance." They "must have no local allegiances" for "in order to be able to desecrate, endanger, or destroy a place . . . one must be able to leave it and forget it."[14] Success requires a transient mobility, which necessarily results in homelessness. The kind of careerism taken for granted in much of American culture implies that "one must never be able to think of any place as one's home; one must never think of any place as anyone else's home."[15] In such a context, successfully educated people "cannot take any place seriously because they must be ready at any moment, by the terms of power and wealth in the modern world, to destroy any place."[16] Placelessness and perpetual homelessness lie at the root of ecological vandalism.

Berry's second observation is that higher education is complicit in this vandalizing of the earth. As usual he minces no words:

Many of these professionals have been educated, at considerable public expense, in colleges or universities that had originally a clear mandate to serve localities or regions—to receive the daughters and sons of their region, educate them, and send them home again to serve and strengthen their communities. The outcome shows, I think, that they have generally betrayed this mandate, having worked instead to uproot the best brains and talents, to direct them away from home into exploitative careers in one or another of the professions, and so to make them predators of communities and homelands, their own as well as other people's.[17]

Loyalty to profession supersedes loyalty to place, and in that supersession everything is superseded. Berry is worth citing again at length:

According to the new norm, the child's destiny is not to succeed the parents, but to outmode them; succession has given way to supersession. And this norm is institutionalized not in great communal stories, but in the education system. The schools are no longer oriented to a cultural inheritance that it is their duty to pass on unimpaired, but to the career, which is to say the future, of the child. ... The child is not educated to return home and be of use to the place and community; he or she is educated to leave home and earn money in a provisional future that has nothing to do with place or community.[18]

Mobility replaces mindfulness. Homelessness banishes homecoming. Not only is going to college the first step "away from home," the educational endeavor itself propels one even further from home, never to return.[19]

An educational system established to train producers and consumers for a global market and rooted in an absolutization of efficiency and profitability is only successful when it produces docile and numb citizens who conform "to a rootless and placeless monoculture of commercial expectations and products."[20] It is not surprising, therefore, that the literature of "Generation X" is suffused with such images of placeless numbness. Writing in *Life After God*, Douglas Coupland confesses, " . . . I have never really felt like I was 'from' anywhere; home to me . . . is a shared electronic dream of cartoon memories, half-hour sitcoms and national tragedies." As such, Coupland says that he speaks with no distinct accent, or more accurately, he speaks with "the accent of nowhere—the accent of a person who has no fixed home in their mind."[21] Wendell Berry would say that the system has succeeded perfectly in producing such a generation of homeless young people. And it is no wonder then that we have seen nothing less than the "unsettling of America."[22] The double entendre is quite intentional: the unsettling of America—its suburbanization, mallification, McDonaldification—is unsettling and disturbing to those who perceive what is being lost and why.[23]

Let us now turn from Wendell Berry to another prophet who rails against the homelessness of the modern consumer, David Orr. Here are Orr's telling questions: If we are the most educated people in history, then why is the world under such profound ecological threat? Why are such highly educated people so ecologically blind, stupid, and malevolent? Why does a rise in linguistic literacy seem to parallel a concomitant increase in ecological illiteracy? Might it be that it is precisely because of our education that we are so ignorant of how the world works?[24]

Orr's thesis is devastatingly simple. "Education," he says, "is no guarantee of decency, prudence, or wisdom. More of the same kind of education will only compound our problems."[25] Indeed, Orr insists that our current patterns of education will only foster more ecological illiteracy precisely because such educational practices are rooted in a series of debilitating falsehoods that all conspire to render us displaced persons. For example, we falsely believe that the earth can be satisfactorily managed with enough scientific and technological know-how and that where there is an increase in the accumulation of information there is a concomitant increase in wisdom and knowledge. Moreover, says Orr, higher education in the West is also directed by the technicistic belief that we can restore what we have dismantled. And all of this happens within the context of an arrogant metanarrative of cultural superiority that is the mythological foundation of the whole educational/cultural enterprise.[26] Such education, so the myth goes, will make us better people.[27]

Now Orr's problem with such an approach to education isn't simply its unabashed arrogance and hubris. Rather, like Jackson and Berry, he sees the devastating effect of this kind of education in socioecological life. An information-driven education which is directed to scientific and technological control of a world that is here for our dismantling and restoration, all driven by an economic imperative that is identified with the very direction of civilization and the moral progress of humanity, spells disaster for our relation to ecosystems broadly speaking and local places in particular.

In the end, Orr says, such an educational practice produces people who relate to their world as "residents" rather than "inhabitants." And a culture of residents is a culture of homelessness. In his book, *Ecological Literacy*, Orr explains this distinction at some length. "The resident," Orr explains, "is a temporary and rootless occupant who mostly needs to know where the banks and stores are in order to plug in." By contrast, the inhabitant cannot be separated from a particular habitat "without doing violence to both.... To reside is to live as a transient and as a stranger to one's place, and inevitably to some part of the self." The inhabitant and place, however, "mutually shape each other."[28]

Later he expands on this distinction: "A resident is a temporary occupant, putting down few roots and investing little, knowing little, and perhaps caring little for the immediate locale beyond its ability to gratify.... The inhabitant, by contrast, 'dwells,' as Illich puts it, in an intimate, organic, and mutually nurturing relationship with a place. Good inhabitance is an art requiring detailed knowledge of a place, the capacity for observation, and a sense of care and rootedness."[29] And so while residents require only "cash and a map," inhabitants "bear the marks of their places," and when uprooted get homesick. And this is so because for the inhabitant, there is a place of dwelling in which one finds identity and from which one derives meaning and apart from which one feels lost and lonely. In short, "the plain fact is that the planet does not need more successful people," more residents; rather, "it needs more people who live well in their places," more inhabitants.[30]

Jackson, Berry, and Orr would all agree that contemporary education, at all stages, but most decidedly at the university level, is a process of forming people who will be residents, not inhabitants. This is an education of upward mobility that results in a pedagogy of disconnection and an ethos of displacement. In the context of a global economy, higher education produces career-oriented consumers who have no intimate knowledge of, or sense of commitment to, any place. This is an education for homelessness.

It is no surprise, then, that the postmodern condition is so often described in terms of homelessness.[31] Postmodern a/theologian Mark Taylor describes the postmodern self as a "wanderer," a "drifter," "attached to no home," and "always suspicious of stopping, staying and dwelling."[32] Interestingly, such a postmodern homeless drifter bears more than a casual resemblance to the endlessly acquisitive ego of late modernity, consuming the products, and more importantly, the images, that global capitalism serves up.[33] The commodification of all of life, most fully realized in the imperial regime of global capitalism, renders us all restless and insatiable consumers, unable to settle, permanently exiled from home.[34] Elie Wiesel is right. Ours is the age of the expatriate, the refugee, and the wanderer. "Never before have so many fled from so many homes."[35] But this is no longer exclusively the sociocultural condition of the politically, ethnically, and economically oppressed. We are now all in exile, all displaced, all disconnected from any sense of place that could carry the full weight of the notion of home.[36] And education has been a coconspirator in producing this culture of homelessness.

Commenting on Wallace Stegner's contrast between "boomers" and "stickers"—which roughly parallels Orr's residents and inhabitants, or Kohak's wayfarers and dwellers—Wendell Berry writes, "if enough of us were to choose caring over not caring, staying over going, then the culture would change, the theme of exploitation would become subordinate to the theme of settlement, and then the choice to be a sticker would become easier."[37] Herein is Berry's hope and program—to encourage stickers, dwellers, and inhabitants who have a love of place. But, while "commercial education"[38] sees the school, especially the college and university, as an "economic resource"[39] in a competition for wealth and power, Berry calls for an education that is accountable to what he calls the "party of local community."[40]

The party of local community believes that "the neighborhood, the local community, is the proper place and frame of reference for responsible work."[41] Therefore, an education that would recognize that locality is the proper scale of human endeavor—of human stewardship—would be an education that helps students "acquire a competent knowledge of local geography, ecology, history, natural history and local songs and stories."[42] According to Berry, such an emphasis on locality is neither a matter of a romantic return to roots, nor merely an escape from the anonymity of urban life. Rather, the focus on locality is a matter of societal, ecological, and cultural preservation and sustainability. It is a matter of ending the ecological and economic vandalism of the highly educated professional class in a global culture of homelessness and fostering an alternative vision of homecoming. But such homecoming is impossible without a love, care, knowledge, and intimacy with place.

In an address at a recent conference, Richard Mouw cited Craig Dykstra's conviction that scholarship and education that is decidedly Christian must be a scholarship and education that "sees deeply into the reality of things and loves that reality."[43] Berry would profoundly concur. But he would add that such love and such seeing is never generic, it is never universal, it is always placed, timed and particular. Just as we cannot love our neighbor "in general," but must always love this neighbor, here in this neighborhood, so also can we never love things in general or the world in general, or even creation in general, apart from a love, intimacy, knowledge, and care for a particular place. Indeed, Berry insists that the love of learning cannot exist apart from the love of place and community. "Without this love, education is only the importation into the local community of centrally prescribed 'career preparation' designed to facilitate the export of young careerists."[44] And then we are back to homelessness all over again. If you love your community, Berry says, you must oppose such education with all of your might. So we need to ask not only the abstract question, "Christian education—for what?", but the more concrete and personal questions, "Christian education—for whom?" and "for where?"

Christian scholarship and education, we are arguing, must be for the shaping and formation of Christian community. This is, we acknowledge, a variation on themes that have been developed by people like Nicholas Wolterstorff, Thomas Groome, Craig Dykstra, and Parker Palmer. But the Berryian twist on these themes of character and community is to note that "if the word community is to mean or to amount to anything, it must refer to a place (in its natural integrity) and its people. It must refer to a placed people."[45] And concurrently, "persons of character are not public products" of mass education. Rather, "they are made by local cultures, local responsibilities."[46]

In the face of a culture of disconnected homelessness, however, such locality—such placedness—requires the fostering of a connected intimacy that runs counter to the abstract distance that characterizes modern education and technological society. Even terms like "ecology" and "ecosystems," says Berry, "come from the juiceless abstract intellectuality of the universities which was invented to disconnect, displace, and disembody the mind." An education for homemaking, however, would insist that "the real names of the environment are the names of rivers and river valleys; creeks, ridges, and mountains; towns and cities; lakes, woodlands, lanes, roads, creatures, and people."[47]

According to Berry, there are at least two things that are required if we are to shift the paradigm of education from homelessness to homemaking, from vandalism to care. The first is that our education must engender an ethos of intimacy and affection.[48] This would require, we think, an abandonment of both the aggressive realism of modernist epistemology and the equally anthropocentric (and usually equally aggressive) anti-realist constructivism of postmodernism. In its place we would propose a relational epistemology rooted in a relational ontology.[49] And since we confess that this relationship is rooted in God's extravagant creational love, knowing this world is always, at heart, a matter of love. N. T. Wright describes such an epistemology of love beautifully when he says, "The lover affirms the reality and the otherness of the beloved. Love does not seek to collapse the beloved in terms of itself." In such an epistemology, "'love' will mean 'attention': the readiness to let the other be the other, the willingness to grow and change in oneself in relation to the other."[50] Educational theorist Parker Palmer makes a similar point when he says that "the act of knowing is an act of love, the act of entering and embracing the reality of the other, of allowing the other to enter and embrace our own."[51] We suspect that Berry would agree.

But there is a second thing that Berry says is required if we are to reaffirm community and place in all of our praxis, not least in education. And that is that in the name of community, for the love of place, and, most profoundly, for the sake of Christian discipleship, we must secede from the empire that has rendered us homeless. We know that this is a rather sensitive time to be talking about empire, but if the forces of displacement, disconnectedness, and homelessness are imperially imposed, then we must speak of empire. And Berry does not mince his words about Christianity and empire:

> Despite its protests to the contrary, modern Christianity has become willy-nilly the religion of the state and the economic status quo. . . . It has, for the most part, stood silently by while a predatory economy has ravaged the world, destroyed its natural beauty and health, divided and plundered its communities and households. It has flown the flag and chanted the slogans of empire. It has assumed with the economists that "economic forces" automatically work for good and has assumed with the industrialists and militarists that technology determines history. It has assumed with almost everybody that "progress" is good, that it is good to be modern and up with the times. It has admired Caesar and comforted him in his degradations and faults. But in its de facto alliance with Caesar, Christianity connives directly in the murder of Creation.[52]

The degree to which this prophetic critique of the modern church is true is the degree to which it is also true of Christian higher education and scholarship. In response to this, Berry advocates "a quiet secession by which people find the practical means and the strength of spirit to remove themselves from the economy that is exploiting them and destroying their homeland."[53] In his poem "The Mad Farmer, Flying the Flag of Rough Branch, Secedes from the Union," Berry calls us to secede from the union of power and money, government and science, science and money, genius and war, and "from outer space and inner vacuity."[54] An education for homemaking joins in such a secessionist movement.[55]

David Orr is a member of this movement. Let us now consider his contribution to an education for homemaking. An education for homemaking is rooted in the belief that this earth is truly our home. This planet, created good by God and one day to be renovated by that same promise-keeping God, is our home. To be faithful homemakers, therefore, we must know something about our home planet. This implies that we must educate for increased ecological literacy. Just as we educate for numeracy, or the ability to calculate, and literacy, or the ability to read, so also we must educate for understanding how the world works. At the risk of running into Berry's critique of juiceless intellectualism, let's call this an education in "ecolacy."[56]

But what exactly is ecolacy? What does it mean to be ecologically literate? David Orr describes the essence of ecological literacy as "that quality of mind that seeks out connections."[57] In contrast to the narrow specialization that characterizes so much education today, an ecological frame of mind seeks to integrate, to bring together, to see things whole. "The ecologically literate person has the knowledge necessary to comprehend interrelatedness, and an attitude of care or stewardship," and this must be accompanied by "the practical competence required to act on the basis of knowledge and feeling." Hence "knowing, caring, and practical competence constitute the heart of ecological literacy."[58] We must not only know, we must care. And we must not only care, we must have the wherewithal to act responsibly.

But concretely what does this mean? Orr offers a list of five necessary components of seeing things whole. First, we need "a broad understanding of how people and societies relate to each other and to natural systems, and how they might do so sustainably."[59] This presumes knowledge of how the world as a physical system works—knowledge of keystone species and succession, entropy and energy flow, niches and food chains. Ecological literacy, in short, implies a modicum of knowledge about the interconnectedness of all creatures great and small. In biblical terms, this is wisdom.

Second, we need to know "something of the speed of the crisis that is upon us."[60] Hence, we need to know the vital signs of our home planet—the trends concerning population growth and climate change, soil loss and species extinction, deforestation and desertification, energy use and air pollution.[61] A prescription is only as good as the diagnosis on which it is based. Our attempts to achieve wellness must, therefore, be based on a sober assessment of the health of the earth. Biblically, this is the ability to read the signs of the times, the ability to have prophetic discernment.

Third, ecological literacy, according to Orr, "requires a comprehension of the dynamics of the modern world."[62] In other words, we need some understanding of the historical, political, economic, and religious forces that have molded the contemporary world. What ideas and social pressures have brought us to where we are today? Ecological literacy, then, requires a well-rounded interdisciplinary education.

Fourth, ecological literacy requires "broad familiarity with the development of ecological consciousness."[63] Of special importance here is explicit attention to ethics and the nature of nature. Are we humans, for example, "conqueror of the land-community" or "plain member and citizen of it?"[64] Is the natural world "red in tooth and claw" or some Edenic paradise of harmony? Or perhaps neither but something else? Such an issue is of great importance, for whether and how we "follow nature," depends in large part on our idea of what nature is and of who we are as humans.[65] If we are to be homecomers and to love and care for a place, then we need to know what our "place" is. Biblically speaking, this is the doctrine of creation.

Fifth and finally, Orr maintains that we need "alternative measures of wellbeing" and "a different approach to technology." For example, Herman Daly and John Cobb's

"Index of Sustainable Economic Welfare," in contrast to other indicators such as "Gross Domestic Product," includes the depletion of nonrenewable natural resources and the costs of water and air pollution in its calculation of overall welfare.[66] And the work of E. F. Schumacher, to mention only one well-known example, illustrates how technology can and must be appropriate to the scale and needs of a people and its culture.[67] Again, biblically this is a matter of wisdom.

Echoing one of the central tenets of the Christian tradition, Orr says that ecological literacy is "built on a view of ourselves as finite and fallible creatures living in a world limited by natural laws."[68] Ecological literacy, in other words, is founded upon the theological insight that we are creatures—limited and liable to error—living in a world not of our own making. Being ecologically literate is, simply, knowing the rules of the house, and ought to engender a humble and thoughtful keeping of this God's blue-green earth.

So what is an education for homemaking? It is at the very least an education directed to ecolacy, directed to precisely that kind of intimacy and knowledge of place that Wendell Berry has been calling for. But of course this is, in itself, not enough. An education for homemaking requires much more.

Earlier in this paper we talked briefly about the significance of metaphors for shaping educational praxis. And we have asked what an education that is shaped by the guiding metaphor of homemaking might be. A closely related metaphor to home is that of hospitality. Home without hospitality is more akin to a fortress of exclusion and self-protection than anything that would cut through our disconnected placelessness with a place-shaped community. In a post September 11, 2001 world, the last thing we need is that kind of stance in defense of the "homeland." Down that path there is only more homelessness. Rather, home in the face of the other—especially the homeless or oppressed other—can never be a fortress. On this point, Emmanuel Levinas taps deeper springs of biblical insight with his insistence on the priority of the other who "paralyzes possession" of the home in order to keep home open to hospitality.[69]

David I. Smith and Barbara Carvill have suggested that hospitality to the stranger can serve as "a metaphor for the way both teachers and students understand and interact with otherness."[70] And while their discussion of the implications of such a metaphor clearly bears fruit in the area of foreign language education, education as hospitality is also thoroughly congruent with the direction of our proposal for education as homemaking. Hospitality, within the ethos of the classroom, in response to legitimate plurality and as an epistemological stance vis-à-vis the world is, we think, deeply homemaking.

And, of course, there would be something profoundly perverse about a discussion of an education for homemaking without addressing the pressing problems of geopolitical and economic homelessness. If it is tragically ironic that an increase in literacy always seems to accompany an increase in ecological illiteracy, then it is doubly tragic that a culture of affluent, upwardly mobile nomads should also produce millions of people who literally have no roof over their heads. This is truly a culture of homelessness, and the people on our inner city streets, together with the international refugees lined up at our borders seeking economic, political, and ethnic refuge bear witness to the moral bankruptcy of our culture and the complicity of education in that bankruptcy. Precisely because an education for homemaking is an education rooted in hospitality, Christian scholarship is called to shape character, communities, economic and political structures, and churches that offer a place for the placeless, home for the homeless.

So Christian higher education—for whom? For the homeless in our midst. The homeless wanderers that we have all become. For the homemaking God who is coming. And Christian higher education—for where? For our neighborhoods, our streams, our forests. For God's good earth. And Christian higher education—for what? For homemaking in the Kingdom of God. For the restoration of the creational home. For repairing the breach and restoring streets to live in.[71]

Notes

1. From Bruce Cockburn,"How I Spent My Fall Vacation" on the album, *Humans*, Golden Mountain Music Corp., 1980. Brian Walsh has addressed the dynamics of home, homelessness, and homecoming in Bruce Cockburn's lyrics in "One Day I Shall Be Home," *Christianity and the Arts* 7.1 (Winter 2000): 28-32.
2. This essay first appeared in *CSR* 32.3 (Spring 2003): 281-96.
3. Wes Jackson, *Becoming Native to This Place* (Washington, D.C.: Counterpoint, 1996), 3.
4. Wendell Berry, *Home Economics* (New York: Northpoint, 1987), 50.
5. David Orr, *Earth in Mind: On Education, Environment and the Human Prospect* (Washington, D.C.: Island Press, 1994), 5.
6. Erazim Kohak, "Of Dwelling and Wayfaring: A Quest for Metaphors," in Leroy S. Rouner, ed., *The Longing for Home*, Boston University Studies in Philosophy and Religion, volume 17 (Notre Dame, Ind.: University of Notre Dame Press, 1996), 31.
7. Neil Postman, *The End of Education: Redefining the Value of School* (New York: Vintage, 1996), especially chapter 9.
8. We have discussed the shape of a biblical worldview at greater length in other places. For an exposition of a biblical worldview in terms of creation, fall, and redemption (here translated as home, homelessness, and homecoming), see Brian J. Walsh and J. Richard Middleton, *The Transforming Vision: Shaping a Christian World View* (Downers Grove, Ill.: InterVarsity Press, 1984), part two. For an application of such an understanding of Scripture to environmental issues and with more attention to themes of home, see Steven Bouma-Prediger, *For the Beauty of the Earth: A Christian Vision of Creation Care* (Grand Rapids, Mich.: Baker Academic, 2001), especially chapters 4, 5, and 8.
9. Jackson, 97.
10. Ibid., 3.
11. Ibid. On the rootlessness of postmodern life, see Paul Wachtel, *The Poverty of Affluence: A Psychological Portrait of the American Way of Life* (Philadelphia: New Society, 1989), and J. Richard Middleton and Brian J. Walsh, *Truth Is Stranger Than it Used to Be* (Downers Grove, Ill.: InterVarsity Press, 1995), especially chapter 7.
12. Wendell Berry, *What Are People For?* (New York: North Point Press, 1990), 25.
13. Ibid., 26. Reflecting on the necessity of downward mobility later in the book, Berry writes, "We must achieve the character and acquire the skills to live much poorer than we do. We must waste less. We must work more for ourselves and each other" (201). We can just see it now—a new campaign by a leading Christian college: "the school of downward mobility!"
14. Berry, *Home Economics*, 51.
15. Ibid.
16. Wendell Berry, *Sex, Economy, Freedom and Community* (New York and San Francisco: Pantheon, 1992), 22. On the connection between homelessness and ecological degradation, see John F. Haught, "Religious and Cosmic Homelessness: Some Environmental Implications," in Charles Birch, William Eakin, and Jay B. McDaniel, eds., *Liberating Life: Contemporary Approaches to Ecological Theology* (Maryknoll, N.Y.: Orbis, 1991), 159-181.
17. *Home Economics*, 51-52. Berry makes a similar point in *The Gift of Good Land* (New York: North Point Press, 1981), in which he argues that schools are "powerful agents of the 'United States economy.' They do not prepare young people to stay at home and make the most of the best local opportunities. They serve the idea that it is good to produce little and consume much" (73).
18. Berry, *What Are People For?* 162-163. Perhaps a small correction is necessary here. It would be naïve to suggest that any education, at any time, passed on a cultural inheritance "unimpaired." Teaching (like all of life) is an interpretive endeavor and therefore always "impairs" in one way or another.
19. It is not surprising, then, that when we think of a "homecoming" weekend, our minds do not go immediately to family and our community of origin, but to the college that became our (temporary) home away from home that then impelled us on into further homelessness.
20. Berry, *Sex, Economy*, 151.

21. Douglas Coupland, *Life After God* (New York: Pocket Books, 1995), 174. The Smashing Pumpkins echo these themes in their song, "jellybelly":
> welcome to nowhere fast
> nothing here ever lasts
> nothing but memories
> of what never was
> we're nowhere, we're nowhere, we're nowhere to be
> nowhere, we're nowhere, we're nowhere to see

And in another song on the same album, lead singer Billy Corgan sings:
> i'm never coming back
> i'm never giving in . . .
> i disconnect the act
> i disconnect the dots
> i disconnect the me in me

We live in a nowhere land of disconnection, and there seems to be no way back home, no possibility of reconnection. Both songs are on the double CD *Mellon Collie and the Infinite Sadness*, Virgin Records, 1995.

22. Wendell Berry, *The Unsettling of America: Culture and Agriculture* (San Francisco: Sierra Club Books, 1986).

23. See also William Leach, *Country of Exiles: Destruction of Place in American Life* (New York: Pantheon, 1999), and James Kunstler, *Geography of Nowhere: The Rise and Decline of America's Man-made Landscape* (New York: Simon & Schuster, 1993), and its sequel, *Home from Nowhere: Remaking our Everyday World for the 21st Century* (New York: Simon & Schuster, 1996).

24. Sadly, this is not a new question or a new suspicion about "modern" education. Pioneering environmentalist Aldo Leopold perceptively raised the same problems fifty years ago: "One of the requisites of an ecological comprehension of land is an understanding of ecology, and this is by no means co-extensive with 'education'; in fact, much higher education seems deliberately to avoid ecological concepts" (*Sand County Almanac* [New York: Ballantine, 1970], 262).

25. David Orr, *Earth in Mind*, 8.

26. Compare this with Bob Goudzwaard's classic discussion of the progress motif in Western culture, *Capitalism and Progress: A Diagnosis of Western Society*, translated by Josina Van Nuis Zylstra (Toronto and Grand Rapids: Wedge and Eerdmans, 1979).

27. Echoing similar sentiments, Wendell Berry says that one of the foundational assumptions of "commercial education" (by which he means pretty much all formal education in America) is that "educated people are better than other people because education improves people and makes them good" (*Sex, Economy*, xiii).

28. David Orr, *Ecological Literacy* (Albany, N.Y.: SUNY Press, 1992), 102.

29. Ibid., 130. The reference to Ivan Illich is to his essay, "Dwelling," in *Co-evolution Quarterly* 41 (Spring 1984).

30. Orr, *Earth in Mind*, 12.

31. We have addressed themes of postmodern homelessness at greater length in Brian J. Walsh, "Homemaking in Exile: Homelessness, Postmodernity and Theological Reflection," in Doug Blomberg and Ian Lambert, eds., *Renewing the Mind in Learning* (Sydney: Centre for the Study of Australian Christianity, 1998), and Steven Bouma-Prediger, "Yearning for Home: The Christian Doctrine of Creation in a Postmodern Age," in Merold Westphal, ed., *Postmodern Philosophy and Christian Thought* (Bloomington, Ind.: Indiana University Press, 1999.)

32. Mark C. Taylor, *Erring: A Postmodern A/Theology* (Chicago: University of Chicago Press, 1984), 150, 157, 156, 147. Following Richard Bernstein, it is fair to say that Jacques Derrida's deconstructive project is "always encouraging us to question the status of what we take to be our center, our native home, our arche." *The New Constellation: The Ethical-Political Horizons of Modernity/Postmodernity* (Cambridge, Mass.: MIT Press, 1992), 183.

33. We echo here Roger Lundin, who has suggested that, "The desiring and acquiring self of postmodern cultural theory bears more than a casual resemblance to the unit of consumption at the center of market economies and democratic societies" (*The Culture of Interpretation: Christian Faith and the Postmodern World* [Grand Rapids, Mich.: Eerdmans, 1994], 73-74).

34. On the connection between postmodernity and global capitalism, see Nicholas Boyle, *Who Are We Now? Christian Humanism and the Global Market from Hegel to Heaney* (Edinburgh: T&T Clark, 1998), and Stanley Hauerwas, "The Christian Difference: Or Surviving Postmodernism," in Susan and Gerald Biesecker-Mast, eds., *Anabaptists and Postmodernity* (Telford, Penn.: Pandora Press, 2000). We heard Jürgen Moltmann draw the relation of cultural restlessness and economic insatiability to homelessness in an address entitled "Homecoming for Abraham and Sarah's Children and Augustine's Lonely Soul" at the American Academy of Religion meetings in New Orleans, November 1996.

35. Elie Wiesel, "Longing for Home," in Leroy S. Rouner, *Longing for Home*, 19. Edward Said makes a similar observation, from the other side of the Jewish/Palestinian divide, when he says that "our age—with its modern warfare, imperialism and the quasi-theological ambitions of totalitarian rulers—is indeed the age of the refugee, the displaced migration, mass immigration." "Reflections on Exile," in *Out There: Marginalization and Contemporary Cultures*, R. Ferguson, M. Gever, Trinh T. Minh-ha, and Cornel West, eds. (New York: New Museum of Contemporary Art; Cambridge and London: MIT Press, 1990), 357.

36. Please don't misunderstand us to be saying that the condition of the jet-setting corporate executive is the same as that of refugees and the socioeconomic homeless. Our point is simply that they are both, in very important respects, homeless and displaced.

37. Wendell Berry, *Another Turn of the Crank* (Washington, D.C.: Counterpoint, 1995), 70.

38. Berry, *Sex, Economy*, xii-xiv.

39. Berry, *What Are People For?* 133.

40. Berry, *Another Turn*, 17.
41. Ibid.
42. Ibid., 40.
43. Richard Mouw, "Assessing Christian Scholarship: Where We've Been and Where We're Going," at the Christian Scholarship . . . For What? Conference, Calvin College, Sept. 2001.
44. Berry, *What Are People for?* 164.
45. Berry, *Sex, Economy*, 168.
46. Berry, *What Are People for?* 26.
47. Berry, *Sex, Economy*, 35. One can see here that Berry has clear affinities with the bioregionalism movement. For comparison, see the essays in *Home! A Bioregional Reader*, edited by Van Andruss, Christopher Plant, Judith Plant, and Eleanor Wright (Philadelphia, Gabriola Island, B.C., Santa Cruz, Calif.: New Society Publishers, 1990).
48. Ibid., 168.
49. Our student, Stephen Robertson, has developed these themes at some length in an evocative M.T.S. thesis, "The Paradigm of Relationship: Speaking the Scriptural Language of Covenantal Relationship to a Postmodern World" (unpub. mss.: Toronto: Wycliffe College, 2001).
50. N. T. Wright, *The New Testament and the People of God* (London and Minneapolis: SPCK and Fortress, 1992), 64.
51. Parker Palmer, *To Know as We Are Known: Education as Spiritual Journey* (San Francisco: Harper SanFrancisco, 1983), 8.
52. Berry, *Sex, Economy*, 114-115.
53. Ibid., 17-18.
54. From *The Selected Poems of Wendell Berry* (Washington, D.C.: Counterpoint, 1998), 162-163.
55. Such an ethic bears some resemblance to the neo-Anabaptist perspective of Stanley Hauerwas and William Willimon in *Resident Aliens: Life in the Christian Colony* (Nashville: Abingdon, 1989).
56. Garrett Hardin seems to have coined the term in *Filters Against Folly* (New York: Penguin, 1985), 24. And see all of chapter 7.
57. Orr, *Ecological Literacy*, 92.
58. Ibid.
59. Ibid.
60. Ibid., 93.
61. In addition to its well-known publication, *State of the World*, the Worldwatch Institute also publishes a very useful compendium on environmental trends called *Vital Signs*.
62. Orr, *Ecological Literacy*, 93.
63. Ibid., 94.
64. Leopold, *Sand County Almanac*, 240.
65. Holmes Rolston, III, *Environmental Ethics: Duties to and Values in the Natural World* (Philadelphia: Temple University Press, 1988), 32.
66. Herman Daly and John B. Cobb, Jr., *For the Common Good* (Boston: Beacon Press, 1989), 401ff.
67. E. F. Schumacher, *Small Is Beautiful* (New York: Harper and Row, 1973).
68. Orr, *Ecological Literacy*, 95.
69. Emmanuel Levinas, *Totality and Infinity: An Essay on Exteriority*, A. Lingis, trans. (Pittsburgh: Duquense University Press, 1969), 171.
70. *The Gift of the Stranger: Faith, Hospitality and Foreign Language Learning* (Grand Rapids, Mich.: Eerdmans, 2000). On the broader theme of hospitality in Christian faith and practice, see Christine D. Pohl, *Making Room: Recovering Hospitality as a Christian Tradition* (Grand Rapids, Mich.: Eerdmans, 1999).
71. Isaiah 58:12.

10 Hospitality and Christian Higher Education (2003)

Elizabeth Newman

What does it mean for an institution to identify itself as Baptist or Catholic or by some other religious affiliation?[1] This has been an ongoing debate for at least some fifty years now, and we have been subjected to a variety of different answers. In former days, to be Baptist or Catholic meant that students would be nurtured in a Baptist or Catholic environment. This usually meant students (as well as faculty and administrators) were required to attend chapel or mass and to live up to certain moral norms. These constraints, however, increasingly came to be seen as both quaint and coercive. More typical today is to locate Christian identity in the availability of certain extracurricular activities, such as service projects or events sponsored by campus ministry.

Being Baptist or Catholic also generally meant students were required to take religion courses usually taught by Baptists or Catholics. Whereas initially these courses were more specifically Protestant or Catholic, today that is not necessarily the case. So departments began to call themselves "Religious Studies" to reflect the fact that this study was not catechesis or indoctrination but the unbiased or "scientific" study of religion.[2] Thus, this location of religious identity became increasingly diffuse as religion departments moved away from being particularly Catholic or Baptist.

In responding to the question of Christian identity, the comments of Thomas Hearn, President of Wake Forest University, are typical of today's milieu. In addressing the question, "Is Wake Forest sacred or secular?" Hearn states (quoting Joseph Butler, bishop of Durham and eighteenth century philosopher), "'Everything is what it is, and is not another thing.' That principle of identity leads us to conclude that Wake Forest is what it is. We should never be tempted to turn from the unique and promising path which is ours alone. Wake Forest is what it is."[3] Arguing that "education is not evangelism," Hearn goes on to embrace Wake Forest as an "unorthodox" institution that cannot be easily categorized. Hearn's description of Wake Forest's religious identity exemplifies nicely how the language often used today to describe an institution's religious identity has become increasingly vague and ambiguous. Thus, it is difficult to "locate" or state more specifically why or how the institution embodies its Christian heritage. Hearn defends his particular definition by invoking that "special feature of the Baptist tradition," namely that "each person is spiritually competent before God without the guidance of any ecclesiastical organization or creed. Each person is a priest."[4] Hearn thus invokes the "priesthood of all believers" to underwrite the idea that education is not indoctrination. Others have used it as well to claim that Baptists in particular are in a position to welcome diversity and to stand against parochialism and exclusion.[5]

It is my contention that these various ways of talking about Christian identity have been woefully inadequate. As I will discuss more fully, such descriptions have not given us the ability to sustain the venture of Christian higher education into the future. As both George Marsden[6] and James T. Burtcheall[7] have narrated, numerous institutions that were established by specific denominations have increasingly lost their particular religious identity. The reasons for this are, of course, complex. Often institutions downplayed their religious identity in order to secure funding from foundations such as The Peabody Trust, the Andrew Carnegie Foundation, or the General Board of Education.[8] Even more, Christian institutions did not want to appear too "sectarian," but desired instead to emulate the "best models" of higher education such as Harvard.[9] I wish to suggest, however, that the overriding reason that Christian institutions have failed to embody their particular identity is due to a malformed theology. In this essay, I will, first, explain what I mean by this malformation, and second, offer an alternative that will center on Christian hospitality as a lens through which we might speak more richly and truthfully about Christian identity and higher education.

The tendencies both to locate Christian identity in the extracurricular sphere and to describe that identity in broad and vague terms share certain common assumptions. Most charitably, we can describe this commonality as resting in the conviction that faith ought not to be coerced. Indeed, the response of one Baylor faculty to a recent survey about Baptist identity and higher education represents this sentiment, shared by many: attempts to integrate faith and learning are "at best treacherous and often lead to dogma and intolerance."[10] From this perspective, faith is a personal—meaning private—choice and therefore is not something that belongs in the classroom in any substantive sense.

This assumption—that the integration of faith and learning is treacherous and most likely dogmatic—however, inevitably relies upon the conviction that faith and knowledge are separate entities or exist in separate spheres. From this perspective, religious identity fails to penetrate the heart of the institution, its intellectual life. If an institution's religious identity is not intellectually viable, then one might quite rightly wonder whether or not it even belongs in the university. Taken to its logical conclusion, this way of thinking leads to the conviction that a Christian university (as George Bernard Shaw famously said about a Catholic university) is a contradiction in terms. The "unfettered" quest for truth seems to be clearly at odds with the conviction that truth has been divinely revealed.

The dichotomy between faith and knowledge has, of course, been subject to criticism from a variety of quarters. The split is often traced back to the Enlightenment, with Immanuel Kant serving as an instantiation of this division. Kant set religion within the limits of reason and assumed that reason was located primarily in the autonomous individual, who could then extricate him- or herself from tradition to arrive at certain self-evident moral and religious truths, thus Kant's classic definition: "Enlightenment is man's release from his self-incurred tutelage."[11] By tutelage, Kant meant our inability to use our minds without guidance from another.[12] Thus, as is well known, Kant and the Enlightenment more broadly influenced such academic ideals as scientific objectivism and moral universalism.

For my purposes, it is important to note that Kant's epistemology itself is not theologically neutral. He was in fact deeply influenced by his own German pietism, which located religious faith primarily in the inner realm of feeling and experience. Important as the passions are for our theological thinking and being, pietism nonetheless tended to reduce religion to the sphere of the ahistorical subject.[13] Thus, the church, the tradition, and the communion of saints, even, were not seen as essential mediators of the Christian faith. What then became identified as universally true, or as the true foundation, was "the moral law within." This is reflected in Kant's well-known observation that there were two things that appeared to him to be self-evident: the starry skies above and the moral law within. Such pietism tended to move toward a kind of gnosticism in that the individual had unmediated access to the moral law, which indirectly reflected the existence of God. That is to say, such knowledge was not mediated through history and through specific bodies and traditions. In fact some particular religious traditions increasingly came to be seen as "hopelessly corrupt, ridden with superstition and inherently incredible because they were grounded in the belief that God [had] actually entered history . . . ."[14] Kant himself, of course, did not fully come to terms with how his own German pietism shaped his conception of religion and knowledge. My point here is not simply to criticize Kant, from whom we have no doubt learned much; it is rather to call attention to a kind of theology that underwrites the split between faith and knowledge. The conviction that knowledge is real insofar as it is freed from particularity and tradition, sustained in part by pietism, is primarily gnostic in impulse: human bondedness to the world is seen as bondage, and our place in God's creation is thought of primarily in terms of negative limitation from which we must escape.[15]

A malformed gnostic theology continues to shape many debates surrounding Christian identity and higher education. At the institution where I recently taught (Saint Mary's College, Notre Dame), we had an interesting and contentious exchange about our current mission statement. The Vice President for Mission, in consultation with some students, staff, and faculty, attempted to change our current statement, arguing that it needed to be shorter and reflect more fully the vision of the Holy Cross sisters who founded the institution. Many of the faculty strongly opposed her efforts. Their opposition, among other things, centered on the use of two phrases that were regarded as especially offensive: "Gospel values" and "justice" (interpreted to mean biblical justice).[16] Our original statement uses the terms "religious sensibility" and "social responsibility," which, it was argued, are phrases more conducive to openness and diversity. By invoking such pious phrases as "Gospel values," some faculty charged our V.P. for Mission with "dumbing down" our current statement and thus "disassociating Saint Mary's with well-respected liberal arts colleges."[17]

Whatever one thinks about the various merits of either of these mission statements, the terms in which many faculty voiced their concerns nicely exemplify a Kantian epistemology and theology. First, the idea that religious language contributes to a kind of "dumbing down" reflects a universalist rationalism, which maintains that true intellectual discourse requires the privatization, or even abandonment, of explicitly religious language. From this perspective, and secondly, any invocation of particular religious language will necessarily sound exclusive (not universal) and therefore hostile to diversity.[18]

This call for diversity, common in the academy today, is typically regarded as a move against Enlightenment rationalism. While this might be true for some understandings of diversity, there is nonetheless in the academy today a kind of "ideology of diversity," the advocates of which assume they have turned away from a monolithic and foundationalist account of rationality (and thus the malformed theology described above). In some ways, of course, this is true, as can be seen by the profusion of various kinds of postmodernism. While postmodernism is a term notoriously difficult to define,[19] Richard H. Roberts speaks for many postmodern thinkers when he states: "We are all *victims* of social construction."[20] Such a claim usually means, among other things, that language imprisons the self and that any talk of "truth" must be subordinated to the inevitability of power. John Milbank states that the postmodern challenge, in contrast to the modern challenge, "turns out not to be the challenge of knowledge that mirrors, but of knowledge that is power . . . is there anything but power? Is violence the master of us all?"[21] This difference aside, however, the kind of theology that informs much of modernity continues to shape many postmodern convictions as well. That is, postmodern thought tends to interpret our timeful, historical, and natural places in the world in terms of negative limitation from which we must escape, only now the way out is not through foundationalism and the so-called God's eye view of the unencumbered self. Rather, escape lies in the unmasking of power and the de-centering of the self, a self that inevitably becomes a mouthpiece of power. Thus, Michel Foucault can write that "it is not man who takes the place of God, but anonymous thinking, thinking without a subject."[22]

While modernity tended to denigrate the created world (and thus the creation of time and history) by reducing knowledge to the objective "knowing self" and faith to the subjective "inner self,"[23] postmodernity turns from the created world by seeing our places only in terms of domination and "construct." Both positions turn away from and even display a hostility to our historicity, our status as created beings in time. Nicholas Boyle describes how Heidegger represents this kind of hostility from a postmodern perspective. For Heidegger, "We make the continuity, and so the history, of our existence by choosing our hero, choosing a tradition and inheritance that we have in common with others. We create our past in the image of our future, of the projection of our existence forward to its limit in death."[24] Yet as Boyle profoundly notes, "The flaw in this account is its ignoring of the extent to which our 'destiny,' the historicity of our existence (and indeed of existence itself) is a gift from others . . . . Behind Heidegger's reluctance to see historicity as a gift, and not only a construct, lies a general—but, as his analysis of the presuppositions of selfhood shows, not necessarily fundamental—*hostility to givenness.*"[25]

It is precisely this hostility to givenness, rooted in a malformed and essentially gnostic theology, that has shaped both those modern and postmodern assumptions that would separate faith from truthful knowledge. Modernity, in its flight to the objective and subjective realms, has failed to see and thus embrace the givenness of all our knowing: that knowledge rooted in faith and trust is logically prior to knowledge rooted in doubt or suspicion. Not only is it misguided to place "faith" in the realm of the subject, but, even more, it is a mistake to assume that faith and knowledge can even be separated. As we saw with Kant, certain convictions "may resist direct scrutiny yet they clearly fuel the entire venture."[26] Postmodernity too fails to see that our historicity, before it can be regarded as domination and "construct," is first of all gift. Thus, as Joseph Dunne points out, postmodern thought that affirms the inevitability of power often disavows epistemological and moral implications that might seem to follow from this affirmation. "One such implication is that there is a regime-independent truth, after all, a recognition of which might suggest and justify resistance to the encompassing domination."[27] By failing to acknowledge the givenness or giftedness of our existence, of some larger truth outside our subjective choices, postmodernism has no way of suggesting how to overcome domination since any construct inevitably posits one self against another.

Given these assumptions, it is not surprising that we have been hesitant or unable to speak to the ultimate purpose of higher education. If there is no sense of rootedness in time and place, then such ahistoricity makes it difficult to discern direction or *telos*. Without an understanding of the giftedness of time and of our very selves as constituted by a past and a future not simply "our own," we inevitably lack the means to determine a *telos* other than one we arbitrarily choose. All too often, a kind of enervating pluralism and relativism prevails, that is, "public life in a pluralist culture cannot be based on an agreement about ultimate goals and purposes of human life without being fundamentally unfair."[28]

This inability to speak to ultimate ends is nicely exemplified in an exchange between John Westerhoff, professor at Duke Divinity School, and Alice Gallin, past president of the American Catholic Colleges and Universities, at a 1978 conference entitled, "The Church's Ministry in Higher Education."[29] In this exchange, Westerhoff stated that the justification for church-related colleges was "the intellectual love of God . . . . It is not enough to say that religion is taught, religious organizations supported, or religious services provided. Indeed, it is faith, and not religion, that is of primary concern for Christians." In her response, Gallin objected to this position, claiming that her "theological understanding of faith, and the obedience which is consequent upon it, is that it is a gift from the Lord which enables us to say 'I believe' . . . . I do not see how it can be the ground for the institution's existence. I think, on the contrary, that the only legitimate goal of a college or university is an 'educational' purpose, i.e., to empower students to develop habits of mind such as analysis, criticism, synthesis, disciplined thinking."[30] While these habits of mind are probably ones that most academics would embrace in a general sense, Gallin avoids addressing the larger question, "To what end?" or "Knowledge for what?" Gallin locates "faith" in the subject and thus assumes that prior and larger commitments and convictions in no way inform "habits of mind."

The question about ends is important, however, because it helps ground or historicize our understanding of the purpose of education. Thus, it enables us to gain some clarity on the kinds of commitments or convictions we hope to foster in our students. For example, do we want to graduate students who use their excellent habits of mind to make as much money as they possibly can? Would we then even call these "habits of mind" excellent? Do we want them to become good consumers in the marketplace of ideas and things? Or do we hold some other vision about the nature of the good life? These questions are intended to point to the fact that the "intellectual virtues," like the "moral virtues," are going to look different depending on what larger context they derive from. Even more, as Mark Schwehn reminds us, following the Platonic Academy, the moral and intellectual virtues are necessarily interdependent, and both of these, in order to be robust, must be anchored within larger communal practices.[31] Thus, Gallin's failure to give a more robust account of "habits of mind" is related to her inability to speak to the ultimate end of education; namely, she ignores the larger context or story that drives her assumptions.

In contrast to Gallin, Monica Helwig, who followed Gallin as executive director of the ACCU, makes this provocative claim about the *telos* of Christian higher education: "If we look at higher education in terms of Christianity, then the goal for students is not the moment of graduation but the moment they die. What have they done with their lives? The goal should be a lifetime engagement in search of the reign of God."[32] In a similar vein, Mark Schwehn argues that knowledge itself must be transformed and the students' loves rightly ordered. According to Schwehn, Christian institutions of higher education should desire to teach students how to love God with the mind.[33]

This is, of course, a complicated task, and as mentioned above, the fear of proselytism hovers in the background. However, as I hope has become obvious in my argument, the issue is not whether or not to proselytize, but rather what kind of proselytism is the institution already in fact supporting? In other words, we are always engaged, even if not explicitly, in "promoting" certain assumptions and convictions to our students about what knowledges to cherish, what convictions to hold, and what purposes of life to embrace. From this perspective, the question is not how to bring faith and knowledge together, but rather what faith, what traditions and practices, and which commitments are already informing our learning and knowing?

To invoke the Christian practice of hospitality, then, is to call attention to a complex tradition, a story, a concrete place even, from which we think, come to know, engage the other, and generally move forward in our intellectual pursuit of truth. Christian schooling, as Stanley Hauerwas reminds us, is "not simply a question of transforming knowledge but rather whether a Christian university is supported by a community with practices that force us to reshape our imagination and our knowledge."[34] Hauerwas goes on to say that such re-imagination might well make students "dysfunctional" for living in the world as we know it. "But if you are profoundly dysfunctional, then you might also be free of the necessities that dominate your lives and all our lives today."[35] In what follows, I hope to suggest how the practice of Christian hospitality can give us language, skills, and virtues that enable us to speak more truthfully about Christian higher education. To practice hospitality faithfully means not only that the relegation of faith to the extracurricular sphere is overcome, but more importantly, that we are empowered to acknowledge and even embrace the ultimate *telos* of all true learning.

Thus, it is important to note that hospitality, in contrast to the modern/postmodern thinking described above, does not rely upon a hostility to givenness. Rather, hospitality delights in and is even defined as the welcoming of the other as gift. To practice this kind of welcome, we must see our own condition as gift, as something we did not simply create or construct, nor as something essentially oppressive. Dorothy Day, one of the most faithful practitioners of Christian hospitality in the twentieth century, claims that this practice is fueled by the conviction that the other is Christ (not like Christ). This, of course, flows from the conviction that all humans are created in the image of God who is Trinity. And as is well known, Day led the Catholic Worker movement, which was responsible for opening Houses of Hospitality (places for people without homes or food) around the nation.

While we obviously admire such work with the poor and homeless, we also might think the practice of hospitality seems better suited for that kind of work rather than for academic institutions focused on learning and the intellectual life. Indeed, Christine Pohl, in doing research for her excellent book, *Making Room: Recovering Hospitality as a Christian Tradition*, visited eight Christian communities "for whom hospitality was a way of life." None of these was primarily an educational institution.[36] Yet as her visit to St. John's and St. Benedict's monasteries reminds us (in that these monasteries founded colleges), teaching has also been a time-honored apostolic work in the Christian tradition, and thus one in which the practice of hospitality should surely be relevant. How so?

First, when we claim the other is Christ, we are at the same time claiming that our ways of knowing are not "foundational" but historical and mediated. That is, we are only able to welcome the other as Christ by being trained in a tradition that interprets the body of Christ in specific ways. That is, as Christ's Body, we are called to welcome others because here too Christ is present (see, for example, the Parable of the Last Judgment, Matt. 25:31-46). Jewish theologian Michael Wyschogrod rightly describes how the practice of hospitality relies upon an acknowledgement of our knowing as mediated and contingent: "The deepest sign of the presence of God, the fundamental reason for the wonder that is evoked by all contact with the spirit, is the occurrence of the unexpected. Salvation comes from unexpected quarters, at unexpected times, and through unexpected agents."[37] Not only is Wyschogrod driving home the point that all knowing, including our knowledge of God, is mediated knowledge, but he is also making the additional point that such mediated knowledge is radically contingent and, in a sense, unpredictable. The opposite atmosphere that "a priori rejects anything that is new... is the atmosphere of death. Death freezes and transforms life into the static and unchanging. In death, the only change that is possible is decay."[38] Stated differently, we might say that since the very nature of our existence is gift, a gift contingently given—that is, God did not "have" to create us, but rather desired to do so—our reasoning must always account or allow space for contingency, for the arrival of the unexpected or new in the form of gift.

Such unpredictability and emphasis on contingency could be interpreted as sounding like some form of relativism; that is, because we are radically contingent beings, we have no way of judging or assessing the arrival of the unexpected. Stated in terms of hospitality, this perspective would say we simply must welcome the stranger and end it at that. We have no way then to discern or judge what it is the stranger is offering. Relativism of course wants to go even further and claim we are in no position to "judge" the stranger. From this perspective, "hospitality" then simply underwrites the "ideology" of pluralism and diversity referred to earlier, where we simply allow or tolerate different "points of view."[39]

However, as Wittgenstein says about language abstracted from context (and we might add, tradition and practices), such relativism reflects thinking "gone on holiday." Such thinking can only happen when we forget the "place" from which we offer hospitality. Indeed, all forms of hospitality issue from particular places, reflective of larger stories. As mentioned above, the place of Christian hospitality is not simply the place of my own choosing, a conviction more consistent with Gnosticism since it fails to embrace the giftedness of our lives and callings. Rather, the place of Christian hospitality is before Yahweh, standing where Israel stood and living out of the conviction that our lives are given to us by a faithful God. So radically is our human place affirmed that God took His own place in creation, revealing the essential giftedness of creation, in which the Giver of life defeated the powers of death.

From this place, then, Christian hospitality already "judges" the other as Christ, a judgment that is not arbitrary but entails necessity, a necessity we discover by reflecting on the larger context or tradition upon which we are relying. For Christians, this necessity entails faithfulness to both God and the stranger, in which we are called to be faithful to the stranger in the same way that God is faithful to us, a faithfulness revealed or made known through the people of Israel and the Body of Christ.[40]

To give a more robust account of hospitality, as Schwehn suggests, we need also describe more fully the kinds of virtues that would sustain such a practice, virtues that are at once both intellectual and moral. To do this, we need to consider more fully how God is faithful to us. Responses to this question will help us then to discern how best to be faithful to strangers, or stated differently, how to be good hosts as well as good guests. One of the things I think we can point to is the patience of God, the time God takes to allow us space to grow closer to the truth of who we are. Patience has been defined as the willingness to bear the imperfections of another. And good hospitality means a certain willingness to "bear with" our guests, even as we realize our own need for others to do the same with us. If we move to the category of "intellectual hospitality," this means that we bear with, we practice patience, in our conversations with our colleagues and students as we together grope towards the particular truths at hand.

But patience must be balanced by courage. It seems a bit odd to describe God as courageous; however, if we focus on the life of Jesus, we certainly see courage fully displayed. In fact, we could describe Jesus' own life as a kind of courageous hospitality. Others have pointed out how Jesus, in his practice of hospitality, was both guest and host, and the "roles" were continually being reversed throughout his life. For example, he was a guest in the home of Mary and Martha, and as is well known, Jesus lifts up Mary, the one who sits at his feet and listens, as the more exemplary host. Yet, clearly, Jesus is also host, most obviously at the Last Supper. We could go on. But for my purposes, I want to point out that Jesus' hospitality is courageous because, whether in his role as guest or host, he does not waiver from speaking and living the truth in love. A vivid example that comes to mind is Jesus' endorsement of the woman who pours perfume on Jesus' feet, to the chagrin of Jesus' host, Simon the Pharisee ("Does he not know who this woman is?") and the astonishment of those who were at table with him. Jesus welcomes this one who loves him so much (because much has been forgiven her), but he also "welcomes" the bystanders to see and absorb a deeper truth, namely about the nature of forgiveness. Such truth speaking, such willingness to speak as faithfully as possible, human vessels that we are, requires courage in face of rejection and fear.

Of course, hospitality is a practice rooted in charity; it is in fact an extension of God's extravagant charity and is thus necessarily rooted in the conviction that we are all guests of God. We are all first recipients of God's grace and love. Such a conviction subverts the temptation to place ourselves always in the role of host and never recipient. In fact, hospitality is practiced most faithfully when these roles easily reverse themselves and we think of ourselves as both guests and hosts.[41] This means the virtue of charity is closely linked to that of humility, the willingness to place ourselves under the authority or truth of another.[42]

This description of the virtues is meant to be suggestive and not exhaustive. My larger claim is that the practice of hospitality—by reflecting a larger tradition and thus the formation of specific virtues—creates a place (a space) for Christian identity to appear as a whole way of life. The practice forms our understanding of the intellectual life and even more our understanding of the final goal of higher education: love and faithfulness to God.

As the above argument indicates, making distinctions and separating ourselves in some sense from other convictions, from "the world," are crucial if hospitality is going to be a truly vibrant practice. Adalbert deVogue, in fact, describes hospitality in the Benedictine tradition as resting on a "two-fold theme of reception and separation." He explains that "separation and hospitality are therefore two manifestations of the same love: following Christ and receiving Christ. The following draws us out of the world, but there again he comes to us under the appearances of those who are in the world, and we receive him. Then the love which has provoked the separation is verified in hospitality."[43]

Yet, in actual practice, especially in higher education, how does this making distinctions and separating ourselves from the "world" actually work? Surely hospitality, by its very nature, is not a practice that leads a community to withdraw from the world. In welcoming the stranger, the practice calls us to engage the other, to welcome the other, to extend charity and likewise to be open to receive from the "stranger." How is it that "making distinctions" might work in actual face-to-face encounters? Wouldn't this run the risk of driving the guest away and making her feel as if she was herself being negatively judged? Even more, on what basis do we make judgments while at the same time acknowledging our own fallibility and limited vision, one of the key reasons hospitality seems to welcome the guest in the first place, that is, to broaden our understanding and grasp of the truth?

At this point, I think we need to remember that hospitality is a practice ultimately in service to God and to God's truth as we understand it, and because of this, a practice also in service to the world. So, for example, practitioners of hospitality are justified or are displaying faithfulness to this practice (and thus to God and the world) when they judge or make distinctions about those ideologies or practices that contradict or even negate hospitality.

Two such interrelated practices come to mind: consumerism and compartmentalization. Others have noted how increasingly consumeristic assumptions are shaping higher education. Mark Edmundson, of the University of Virginia, for example, argues that "university culture, like American culture writ large, is to put it crudely, ever more devoted to consumption and entertainment, to the using and using up of goods and images." As an example of this academic consumerism, Edmundson describes evaluation day at the end of each semester where the students are playing the informed consumer. Evaluation forms are "reminiscent of the sheets circulated after the TV pilot has just played to its sample audience in Burbank." While Edmundson admits to playing the entertaining professor with "off-the-wall questions and sidebar jokes," he is nonetheless disturbed with the idea emerging from student comments that his function is to divert and entertain: "I want some of [my students] to say that they've been changed by the course."[44]

This practice of consumerism underwrites and in fact informs the conviction, discussed above, that our private choices determine our values and our identity, an identity believed to be entirely self-generated: "I am what my choices have made me." As Alasdair MacIntyre observes, these choices reveal not character but identity, so that to criticize one's choices is to take a negative view of the individual making the choices. More often than not the typical response is a retreat into solidarity with those with whom one agrees.[45] Christian hospitality is distinct from consumerism in at least two ways. First, consumerism, because it emphasizes that identity rests in my personal choices, fails to see how our lives can be construed as gift from others. Secondly, consumerism only welcomes the other in the "aesthetic" mode. Like Don Juan, it might entertain the other, but only for personal gain or enjoyment. In contrast, to name our lives as gifts of God's grace means that we are also saying our lives are not simply ours to control or consume however we wish.

A second related practice distinct from, and even antithetical to, hospitality is "compartmentalization." If we simply choose or create our identity, then we might well choose to be different in various "compartments" of our life; no larger good orders either our being or knowing. As Alasdair MacIntyre again notes, the new virtue becomes adaptability, and the new vice, inflexibility.[46] MacIntyre describes how this compartmentalization impacts Catholic higher education: "What the Catholic faith confronts today in American higher education . . . is not primarily some range of alternative beliefs about the order of things, but rather a belief that there is no such thing as the order of things of which there could be a unified, if complex understanding, or even a movement towards such an understanding. There is on this contemporary view nothing to understanding except what is supplied by the specialized and professionalized disciplines and subdisciplines and subsubdisciplines."[47] Hospitality is distinct from, and if practiced faithfully, overcomes such compartmentalization not only by being ordered by a larger good—faithfulness to God—but also by forming its practitioners to be persons of consistent character, capable of practicing the virtues that sustain hospitality across the different disciplines and compartments of their lives.

With these examples in mind, then, we can see the necessity of making distinctions for the sake of maintaining a vibrant sense of Christian hospitality. Gerard Lohfink, in fact, goes so far as to call this inability to make distinctions a "sickened state *of the spirit* in which everything is the same, everything is equally valid, nothing makes any difference. Where distinctions are no longer made, the old gods return."[48] Lohfink's point is, of course, that we must learn to make discerning distinctions about the God or gods we are ultimately serving.

Such drawing of distinctions, or we might say truth speaking, rests in the realization that truth cannot be coerced, but remains vibrant by the power of persuasion and attraction. Inasmuch as hospitality genuinely acknowledges the other as both similar (a child of God) and other (and thus eschews a foundationalist account of rationality), then it is a practice that allows for genuine difference to appear and true engagement to take place. Here I think we can remind ourselves that "truthfulness is a skill to acquire"[49] (a virtue), one that can only be learned through practice and engagement with another. Such truth speaking, then, requires community, since truth is not the possession of the isolated individual but is practiced in the "Body of Christ." This image reminds us that we need the other to be fully God's truth in the world.

That such truth lives by the power of persuasion and even more, attraction, is nicely reflected in Lohfink's description of "how it is possible for [the reign of God] to find lovers in the world." In his reflections on Matthew 13:44-46, Lohfink writes:

> There are people who stumble over the reign of God purely by chance. They were preoccupied with something completely different, but then, one day, they are confronted with the treasure. Others, like the rich merchant, have sought and looked everywhere, and finally they find what they have long dreamed of. As in all the double parables, then, the starting points are different, and

therefore the thing that unites the two speaks all the more loudly: both these finders do not waste a minute. They are overcome by the sparkle of the treasure and the shimmer of the pearl. 'When that great joy, surpassing all measure, seizes a man, it carries him away, penetrates his inmost being, and subjugates his mind. All else seems valueless compared with that surpassing worth.' . . . How, then, does God's omnipotence reach its goal in the world? – only through people and their freedom. It happens only through the fact that people are drawn and moved by that which they can desire with their whole hearts and with their whole might. But apparently it is only possible for them to desire in freedom what God also desires if they see, vividly, the beauty of God's cause, so that they experience joy and even passionate desire for the thing that God wills to do in the world.[50]

Lohfink goes on to discuss that the reign of God does not simply exist in the human heart or somewhere beyond history, but it is tangible and visible and requires in fact a concrete people. Thus, he is not reducing truth to simply an aesthetic emotion. God's truth is mediated and embodied concretely in the world. Stanley Hauerwas likewise discusses how the "polity" of the Kingdom known through the story of Jesus "can only be based on that power which comes from trusting in the truth." He quotes Rauschenbusch to make the point that Jesus wielded

no sword but the truth. But mark well, that truth was a sword in his hands and not a yardstick. It cut into the very marrow of his generation . . . But the truth that can do such things is not an old woman wrapped in the spangled robes of earthly authority, bedizened with golden ornaments, the marks of honor given by injustice in turn for services rendered, and muttering dead formulas of the past. The truth that can serve God as the mightiest of his archangels is robed only in love, her weighty limbs unfettered by needless weight, calm-browed, her eyes terrible with beholding God . . . Jesus deliberately rejected force and chose truth.[51]

The kind of truth, then, to which the practice of hospitality witnesses is a concrete truth mediated through specific people, which evokes sometimes joy, as Lohfink describes, sometimes terror, as Rauschenbusch indicates, and sometimes indifference. We hope, of course, that the practice of hospitality is joyful as gifts are exchanged and as we come to understand more truthfully our lives, our times, and our world. We also have to acknowledge, however, that guests might decide to depart. God's freedom allows for these various responses, even as we trust that God is already at work in the lives of those who depart for whatever reasons. Christian hospitality, however, requires its practitioners to use their freedom as not "an end in itself, but the necessary condition for a community to come to a more truthful understanding of itself and the world."[52]

It is important to add, however, that making the kinds of distinctions I discussed above is different from drawing boundaries, which is ultimately God's prerogative or God's work.[53] Even more, we might say that the body politic formed by Christian assumptions "has a center but ultimately no boundary, since God has chosen to recapitulate all things in that center."[54] Thus, the community that sustains the practice of Christian hospitality "works on the assumption that it has something to say that is communicable beyond its present boundaries and is humanly attractive or compelling across these boundaries . . . The world we inhabit is the potential scope of the community that is created by relation to Jesus . . . it is the social fact of a community with no foreordained boundaries."[55] This means that engagement with other persons, cultures, ideas, disciplines, knowledges, etc., is the scope of intellectual hospitality in a Christian setting.

One might well ask, however, whether making distinctions might entail drawing at least some boundaries. For example, how might my focus on making distinctions rather than drawing boundaries pertain to something like the hiring of faculty? In hiring, I think Christian institutions are called to let the potential candidate know the kinds of hopes, expectations, and practices that sustain the pursuit of knowledge and wisdom at this particular place. They should let the candidate know that being Catholic or Baptist, or more broadly Christian, is not simply a "private choice" nor a box to check on an application but rather a way of being and thinking that pervades the life of the institution. The focus is not so much on drawing boundaries about which persons may or may not join the adventure, rather the focus is on discerning and making judgments about how to live faithfully as an educational community; whoever desires is welcome to join the challenge.

As noted above, however, many of our institutions have failed at this task. Recent attention and conversation about Christian identity often make some faculty nervous, as they might feel as if they are now being asked to join a conversation or challenge they did not choose. A colleague recently told me that he thinks Christian institutions that have failed to attend to the fullness of Christian identity as this relates to education ought to ask forgiveness of those they have hired. That is, if an institution desires to embody its Christian identity more fully and thus to practice hospitality more faithfully, it ought to seek forgiveness from those living in its midst who were not made more aware of such identity and practices. This should be followed by a commitment of faithfulness to that person, that is, "You are welcome and encouraged to stay. We will not require you to leave." This would be an example of making distinctions (Christian discernment) rather than drawing boundaries.

As indicated throughout this essay, to become a faithful practitioner of Christian hospitality requires immersion in the Christian tradition. Perhaps this sounds "insular." However, I wish to suggest that the more insular approach is to assume that to be "an intellectual" requires loosening the moorings that bind one to a particular tradition, that is, that genuine rationality requires "autonomy." Such an autonomous approach is insular because it fails to acknowledge the ways in which some tradition(s) is in fact always informing our intellectual lives. As Robert Wilken, among others, has observed, "In many fields of creative work, immersion in tradition is the presupposition for excellence and originality. Think, for example, of music. On Saturday mornings, I often listen to a jazz show on National Public Radio that features interviews with famous and not-so-famous jazz pianists, saxophonists, drummers, trumpeters, etc., and I am regularly struck at how they speak with such respect of teachers and masters."[56] Wilken's comments indicate not only that we know through immersion in tradition, but also that such immersion requires apprenticeship: learning the skills and wisdom of masters who have embodied the tradition in excellent ways.

Thus, hospitality within the disciplines might move in one of several directions. First, critical reflection on the Christian tradition and hospitality across the disciplines would be important in developing the skills of Christian hospitality. For example, what might the disciplines of psychology, economics, or history look like if they took seriously the conviction that we are creatures dependent on God's hospitality to us? While in economics this would not mean we teach only one particular economic theory, it would mean that our status as God's guests should enter into the conversation. Christians care about economics, which literally means "household," because as guests we also consider ourselves stewards of the gifts God has given. Certainly there's a debate about what such stewardship means; it is precisely this kind of debate that should enter into how we perceive what counts as knowledge in economics. For example, is the metaphor that drives our understanding of economics the rational profit-maximizing individual or is it hospitality and the well-being of the whole household where, as Wendell Berry argues, people matter?[57] The same kind of reflection and analysis applies—albeit in different ways—to other disciplines as well. Even in mathematics, we might ask, "Is mathematics understood as a way to gain god-like status over the physical universe, or is it integrated into a way of life that acknowledges our status as creatures in a created order?"

In addition to analysis of the Christian tradition across the disciplines, the practice of hospitality in an educational setting would also foster, as much as is possible, an interdisciplinary approach to learning. For example, courses in theology and science could not only move toward overcoming the deep compartmentalization that has traditionally separated these two disciplines, but could also examine how these disciplines have drawn insights from each other (and thus by their very nature display a kind of hospitality).

Third, hospitality at Christian institutions of higher education ought to include the study of other and different traditions and practices. As Wilken notes, "Christian thought has always been a critical and rational enterprise, and at its best has welcomed the wisdom of the world into the household of faith."[58] At the heart of the practice of this kind of hospitality, of welcoming the "outsider," lies the conviction that the Christian tradition is never closed off, that our communal readings and performances are "provisional."[59]

A final suggestion of how practically to incorporate hospitality in the intellectual life of a college or university would be to include a course on hospitality, where the rich tradition of Christian hospitality as well as hospitality in other traditions is examined. For example, compare Camus' *The Guest*, a kind of existentialist hospitality, with Flaubert's *The Legend of Saint Julian*, more reflective of Christian hospitality.[60]

In closing, I think it must be said that attention to the practice of Christian hospitality cannot be for the sake of maintaining Christian identity in higher education. By focusing on hospitality, we are not seeking to secure a position before God and others, but are seeking to be faithful to God. Our practices, our ethics, are "about manifestation . . . to display [or enact] a reality that will cause thanksgiving and delight, that will cause people to give glory to [God]."[61] The sole reason for practicing hospitality is to participate in what God is already doing so that our efforts will redound to the glory of God. Any preservation of Christian distinctiveness will be a byproduct.

Notes

1. This essay first appeared in *CSR* 33.1 (Fall 2003): 75-94.
2. For a fuller account of the discipline of "Religious Studies," see D. G. Hart, "American Learning and the Problem of Religious Studies," eds. George Marsden and Bradley Longfield, *The Secularization of the Academy* (New York: Oxford, 1992), 195-233.
3. Thomas Hearn, "To Dream with One Eye Open, A Ten-Year Report to the University: 1983- 1993," Wake Forest University (1993): 15.
4. Ibid., 8.
5. See, for example, Walter Shurden, *The Baptist Identity: Four Fragile Freedoms* (Macon, Ga.: Smyth & Helwys, 1995), where he describes diversity as constitutive and distinctive of Baptist identity. Some Catholics also describe diversity as distinctive of Catholic identity. See, for example, the writings of Richard McBrien on Catholic identity and higher education or John Shea, "Here Comes Everybody," *Commonweal* (September 14, 1990): 509-511. That both Baptists and Catholics are eager to claim diversity as distinctive of who they are suggests that something other than their particular theologies might be forming such assumptions. In any case, such claims often lack full theological display and tend instead to reflect modern/postmodern understandings of diversity. I return to this point later in the essay.
6. *The Soul of the American University: From Protestant Establishment to Established Nonbelief* (New York: Oxford, 1994).
7. *The Dying of the Light: The Disengagement of Colleges and Universities from their Christian Churches* (Grand Rapids, Mich.: Eerdmans, 1998).
8. Burtchaell narrates how James Kirkland, president of Vanderbilt in the early 1900s, moved away from speaking in sectarian, that is, Methodist, terms about the university in order to garner significant funding from external sources. See "The Alienation of Christian Higher Education in America: Diagnosis and Prognosis," in Stanley Hauerwas and John Westerhoff, eds., *Schooling Christians: "Holy Experiments" in American Education* (Grand Rapids, Mich.: Eerdmans, 1992), 129-183.
9. As David Riesman observed (in 1952), American higher education is like a "snake with the leading research universities, such as Harvard, at the head, and the other lesser institutions following as the tail." While tremendous differences existed among the institutions, nevertheless they "took their leads from the head and tried to emulate it, each attempting to move farther and farther up the tail toward a more prestigious place near the front of the procession" (quoted in Douglas Sloan, *Faith and Knowledge: Mainline Protestantism and American Higher Education* [Louisville: Westminster John Knox, 1994], 9).
10. As quoted by Michael Beaty, Todd Buras, and Larry Lyon, "Christian Higher Education: An Historical and Philosophical Perspective," *Perspectives in Religious Studies* 24.2 (Summer 1997): 163.
11. Immanuel Kant, "What Is Enlightenment?" in *Foundations for the Metaphysics of Moral and What Is Enlightenment?* (Indianapolis: Bobbs-Merrill Educational Publishing, 1959), 85.
12. Ibid.
13. Bernard Lohse notes that "quite frequently, though by no means always, Pietism had a disintegrating influence upon the authority of Scripture and of the confessions . . . Orthodoxy had succeeded only in holding to the formalized and historicized truth of Scripture, while Pietism was in danger of making subjective experience the criterion for the objective validity of the affirmations of faith," in *A Short History of Christian Doctrine: From the First Century to the Present* (Philadelphia: Fortress, 1978), 224-225.
14. William H. Poteat, personal correspondence.
15. For further discussion of the relation of pietism and rationalism, see Burtchaell, *The Dying of the Light*, 462-464 and 838-847.
16. The fuller revised sentence reads: "Through commitment to Gospel values, the College provides an environment that nurtures lives of faith, justice and service, challenging women to make a difference in the diverse world in which they live."
17. Minutes from faculty assembly, September 13, 2000.
18. While I think the phrase "Gospel values" is better than "religious sensibility," it is nonetheless important to note that this phrase also displays a kind of modern rationalist influence because it suggests the Gospel is primarily about values. This way of putting the matter, however, indirectly underwrites the fact/value dichotomy, another

version of the faith/knowledge split. The Gospel is not simply about values, but rather and more fundamentally, it narrates a whole other way of seeing and being in the world, one in which the fact/value distinction is alien.

19. As Barry Harvey notes, Zygmunt Bauman may well give us our best handle on the ambiguity of the term in stating that postmodernity is "modernity without illusions (the obverse of which is that modernity is postmodernity refusing to accept its own truth). The illusions in question boil down to the belief that the "messiness" of the human world is but a temporary and repairable state, sooner or later to be replaced by the orderly and systematic rule of reason. The truth in question is that the 'messiness' will stay whatever we do or know, that the little orders and 'systems' we carve out in the world are brittle, until-further-notice, and as arbitrary and in the end contingent as their alternatives," in *Another City: An Ecclesiological Primer for a Post-Christian World* (Harrisburg, Penn.: Trinity, 1999), 6.

20. Richard H. Roberts, "Theology and the Social Sciences," in David F. Ford, ed., *The Modern Theologians* (Cambridge, Mass.: Blackwell, 1997), 714, my emphasis.

21. John Milbank, *Theology and Social Theory: Beyond Secular Reason* (Cambridge, MA: Basil Blackwell, 1990), 276.

22. As quoted in Nancey Murphy, "Textual Relativism, Philosophy of Language, and the Baptist Vision," in Stanley Hauerwas, Nancey Murphy, and Mark Nation, *Theology without Foundations: Religious Practice and the Future of Theological Truth* (Nashville: Abingdon, 1994), 253.

23. Hannah Arendt describes this "journey" as follows: namely, that modern world alienation consisted in a "twofold flight from the earth into the universe [foundationalism] and from the world into the self [subjectivism]," in *The Human Condition* (Chicago: University of Chicago, 1958), 6.

24. Nicholas Boyle, *Who Are We Now? Christian Humanism and the Global Market from Hegel to Heaney* (Notre Dame, Ind.: University of Notre Dame, 1998), 223.

25. As quoted in Stanley Hauerwas, *A Better Hope: Resources for a Church Confronting Capitalism, Democracy, and Postmodernity* (Grand Rapids, Mich.: Brazos, 2000), 224-225, my emphasis.

26. David B. Burrell, "A Catholic University," in Theodore Hesburgh, ed., *The Challenge and Promise of a Catholic University* (Notre Dame, Ind.: University of Notre Dame, 1994), 37.

27. Joseph Dunne, "Beyond Sovereignty and Deconstruction: The Storied Self," *Philosophy and Social Criticism* 21 (1995): 142.

28. Michael Beaty, et al., "Christian Higher Education: An Historical and Philosophical Perspective," 163.

29. Burtchaell recounts this exchange in *The Dying of the Light*, 713.

30. Ibid., as quoted, 831-832.

31. Mark Schwehn, *Exiles from Eden: Religion and the Academic Vocation in America* (New York: Oxford, 1993), 47 and 57.

32. As quoted in "Proclaim Jubilee," *Saint Mary's College News & Events* (February 21, 2000): 1.

33. Mark Schwehn, Keynote Address, "Models for Christian Higher Education: Strategies in the Twenty-First Century," University of Notre Dame, Notre Dame, Ind., June 12-14, 1998.

34. Stanley Hauerwas, *Sanctify Them in the Truth: Holiness Exemplified* (Nashville: Abingdon, 1998), 225.

35. Ibid., 226.

36. Christine Pohl, *Making Room: Recovering Hospitality as a Christian Tradition* (Grand Rapids, Mich.: Eerdmans, 1999), 188. The eight communities she visited are L'Abri Fellowship; Annunciation House; L'Arche; The Catholic Worker; Good Works, Inc.; Jubilee Partners; The Open Door Community; and St. John's and St. Benedict's Monasteries.

37. Michael Wyschogrod, *The Body of Faith: God and the People Israel* (London: Jason Aronson, 1996), 231.

38. Ibid.

39. Carl Braaten and Robert Jenson, in describing how many mainline churches have at times denied the gospel and accepted neopaganism, note that "if these [Orthodox Christian] convictions are not denied outright they are mingled with 'alternatives' in the name of 'pluralism,' 'multiculturalism,' 'feminism,' and 'hospitality'," in Carl E. Braaten and Robert W. Jenson, eds., *Either/Or: The Gospel or Neopaganism* (Grand Rapids, Mich.: Eerdmans, 1995), 2.

40. Other kinds of hospitality will be equally rooted in place, though the stories and traditions that form these will of course be different.

41. On this point, see especially Christine Pohl, "Hospitality from the Margins," in *Making Room*, 104-124.

42. John Howard Yoder reminds us that the "love of the enemy must include love of the intellectual adversary, including intellectual respect for the holders of the positions one must in conscience reject." John H. Yoder, *The Royal Priesthood: Essays Ecclesiological and Ecumenical*, Michael G. Cartwright, ed. (Grand Rapids, Mich.: Eerdmans, 1994), 6.

43. As quoted in Pohl, 139.

44. Mark Edmundson, "On the Uses of Liberal Education, As Lite Entertainment for Bored College Students," *Harper's* (September 1997): 39 and 40.

45. Alasdair MacIntyre, Lecture, Culture of Death Conference, University of Notre Dame (October 13, 2000).

46. Ibid.

47. Alasdair MacIntrye, "Catholic Universities: Dangers, Hopes, Choices," Conference on Higher Learning and Catholic Traditions, University of Notre Dame (October 13-14, 1999): 6. MacIntyre adds that "The undergraduate major, when taught by those whose training has led them to presuppose this view—for it is very often taken for granted, rather than explicitly stated— becomes increasingly no more than a prologue to graduate school, even for those who will never go to graduate school. And graduate school becomes a place where narrowness of mind is inculcated as a condition for success within each particular discipline in terms defined by its senior practitioners" (Ibid).

48. Gerhard Lohfink, *Does God Need the Church? A Theology of the People of God* (Collegeville, Minn.: Liturgical Press, 1999), 88, my emphasis. Lohfink makes this comment in his discussion of ancient Israel and states that part of the miracle of "Israel's identity is its ability to make distinctions." He adds that the *ekklesia* "needs this constant distinguishing as urgently as the synagogue does."

49. James McClendon, *Systematic Theology: Ethics* (Nashville: Abingdon, 1986), 41.

50. Lohfink, 46. Rowan Williams also discusses the power of attraction in *On Christian Theology* (Oxford: Blackwell, 2000), 255: "Generosity, mercy and welcome are imperatives for the Christian because they are a participation in the divine activity: but they are also imperative because they show God's glory and invite or attract human beings to 'give glory' to God—that is to reflect back to God what God is."

51. As quoted in Stanley Hauerwas, *A Community of Character: Toward a Constructive Christian Social Ethic* (Notre Dame, Ind.: University of Notre Dame, 1981), 46, my emphasis.

52. Ibid., 62.

53. Indeed, this observation—that the drawing of boundaries is divine work—can be extended to any given community or politics. Rowan Williams notes that "for both Jew and Gentile, the setting of the boundaries of a community was divine work: for the Jew because Israel was a people gathered and defined by the summons of God in the covenant tradition; for the Gentile because gods provided the sanctions of law and custom in the Greek city, and a divine monarch sanctioned the unity and cohesion of the *imperium Romanum*" (*On Christian Theology*, 231). That is, "boundaries" for any given politics or community are ultimately "divinely drawn" because they are "set," so to speak, depending on what god or gods a given community is serving.

54. Barry Harvey, "Where, Then, Do We Stand? Negotiating the Authorial Void at the End of History," unpublished, 16.

55. Williams, *On Christian Theology*, 230-231.

56. Robert L. Wilken, *Remembering the Christian Past* (Grand Rapids, Mich.: Eerdmans, 1995), 171. For a fuller analysis of the necessity of immersion or "indwelling" a particular tradition in order to know, see Michael Polanyi, *Personal Knowledge: Towards a Post-Critical Philosophy* (Chicago: University of Chicago, 1962).

57. Berry discusses this question in a number of different essays. See, for example, "Christianity and the Survival of Creation," in *Sex, Economy, Freedom and Community* (New York: Pantheon), 93-116.

58. Wilken, *Remembering the Christian Past*, 170.

59. Stephen E. Fowl and L. Gregory Jones, *Reading in Communion: Scripture and Ethics in Christian Life* (Eugene, Ore.: Wipf and Stock Publishers, 1998), 129. Fowl and Jones also provide a helpful discussion of the different kinds of "outsiders": those who govern our common life, those in our midst, those bearing a family resemblance, and those who are complete strangers.

60. I am in debt to the faculty of Georgetown College, Georgetown, Kentucky, for this final suggestion as well as possible books to use in such a course.

61. Williams, *On Christian Theology*, 258.

11 Needed: A Few More Scholars/ Popularizers/Activists
Reflections on My Journey (2007)

RONALD J. SIDER

Church and society are often misled by people offering simplistic, one-sided answers to the big issues of their time.[1] They pretend to know what they are talking about even though they lack the necessary expertise. Evangelicalism, especially, with its strong anti-intellectual strain, has often–whether one thinks of eschatology, science, family life or politics–been badly served by popularizers and activists with simplistic ideas and superficial solutions. Nor will that change unless more people with good scholarly training become effective popularizers and successful activists.

I am a scholar who spent several years of my life completing a Ph.D. at Yale to become a specialist in the sixteenth-century Reformation in Europe, but ended up teaching only one course in my whole career in my area of academic specialization. I did publish two scholarly books and a few technical articles in the area of my dissertation. But when people come up and thank me for "my book," I assume they mean *Rich Christians in an Age of Hunger*, not my scholarly book on the sixteenth-century reformer Andreas Bodenstein van Karlstadt.[2] For better or worse, I am best known as a popularizer. In fact, my problem, if it is a problem, runs even deeper. I have tried not only to combine popularizing with scholarly work, but have also been an activist and organizer.

Trying to do what I have done, however, is inevitably problematic for several reasons. First, good popular writing almost inevitably requires an interdisciplinary understanding that no single scholar possesses. The general public has little interest in simply that aspect of world hunger, for example, discussed in technical detail with professional expertise by the professor of business or the professor of economic history or the professor of small business development or the professor of Christian Ethics or Old Testament or New Testament . . . the list goes on and on. But all those specialties and more relate directly to the question: What is a faithful Christian response to world hunger today? The typical Christian layperson wants to read a coherent, reliable response to that broad question, not some specialized, technical paper that deals with one small aspect of the problem.

Unfortunately, no scholar, however brilliant, is familiar with all those fields. Hence, every popularizing scholar knows she is doing what in a sense she has no business doing.

Second, because of the complexity just noted, there is never enough time to read even half of the relevant literature. Anybody who has done a Ph.D. knows how to do exhaustive research and has strong inner inhibitions against starting to write before he has read most of the relevant literature. For the interdisciplinary popularizer, that is not possible.

Third, popularization requires simplification. That is not to say that simplistic distortion is inevitable. But good popularizing demands that one set aside many complexities in order to offer a clear, coherent statement of the central issues. That easily frustrates the popularizer who is also a scholar—not to mention the scholarly critics who are not popularizers!

Fourth, the popularizer runs the danger of losing touch with his or her field of scholarly expertise. This is not inevitable. It depends on the relative amounts of time one puts into the two areas and also on how closely connected one's scholarship and popular writing are. In my case, as a Reformation historian there was little direct connection. In the early years after grad school, I managed to publish two scholarly books and a few articles on the Reformation. But ten years later, when asked to write an encyclopedia article on Karlstadt, it took only about ten minutes to conclude that I had neither the time nor the interest in spending the month or two of research needed to catch up on the scholarship enough to accept the invitation. I declined, with a twinge of regret, realizing that was the end of my work in an area to which I had devoted at least five years of my life.

My activist, organizing work began in 1972. In late summer, I returned to the U.S. from several weeks of academic labor finalizing the sixteenth-century Latin and German footnotes so my doctoral dissertation would be published in the scholarly series, "Studies in Medieval and Reformation Thought," edited by Professor Heiko Oberman of Tübingen (and earlier Harvard) University. In the huge pile of mail I encountered on my return, I discovered an appeal sent to evangelicals across the country to donate funds to support evangelical Republican Senator Mark Hatfield's reelection campaign. I made a small contribution and then quickly organized a small evangelical political effort that resulted in a story in *Newsweek*. A follow-up letter to our donors led to a spring meeting at the first Calvin College Conference on Christian Faith and Politics. Thanksgiving of 1973 brought the Chicago Declaration on Evangelical Social Concern, and the founding of Evangelicals for Social Action (ESA) in 1974, which I have led for all but one year since. Even though I have had a full-time academic appointment for almost all of the years since 1968, I have invested vast amounts of time and energy in organizational and activist work on social issues.

During my career I have tried to combine the roles of scholar, popularizer, and activist. In this essay I first will describe five different "models" or approaches (three earlier efforts and then two more recent ones) in my attempt to combine scholarship, popularization, and activism. Especially in the last two, I can see an approach or model that may have applicability beyond my personal history.

In early 1996, I opened a packed press conference at the National Press Club in Washington with a prayer and then a statement declaring that this was God's creation, and therefore evangelical Christians were concerned about endangered species. There were two reasons for the Washington journalists' interest and the flood of resulting news stories on national TV that night and in scores of newspapers across the country in the next few days: first, a live cougar at the press conference representing endangered species; and second, the fact that this dramatic public stand by ESA and the Evangelical Environmental Network, or EEN, contradicted the widespread belief that all evangelical Christians were in the pocket of the new conservative Republican majority in the Congress which, in the view of many, was seeking to weaken drastically the Endangered Species Act.

It was my activist side that carried me into the environmental movement. I was generally concerned but had not written any popularizing, much less any scholarly, things on the topic when, in the early '90s, a caller from New York informed me that someone had told him I was an evangelical who cared about the environment. Would I help gather evangelical leaders to a meeting in New York City? I agreed and that led eventually to the very successful inter-religious coalition called the National Religious Partnership for the Environment. EEN, which I put together in the early years with the help of people like Bob Seiple of World Vision and University of Wisconsin scholar Calvin DeWitt, became the evangelical partner along with the United States Catholic Conference, the National Council of Churches, and the Coalition on the Environment and Jewish Life.

With no scholarly preparation on the topic, I have relied on scholars like Calvin DeWitt, Loren Wilkinson, and many others to try to make sure I get my facts straight. All my writing on the topic has been shorter popularizing pieces.

The second effort focused on the issue of Jesus' resurrection. In this case, I have combined scholarly and popularizing articles. My interest goes back to a period of vigorous intellectual doubt during my second year of college and then the appointment of evangelical historian John Warwick Montgomery as the new chairman of my history department for my junior and senior years as an undergraduate history major at Waterloo College in Canada. I embraced Montgomery's passion for scholarship and apologetics based on an historical argument for Jesus' resurrection. A couple of years later, when I was a leader of the InterVarsity-related Yale Graduate Fellowship and a doctoral student in history, it was almost inevitable that I would lecture to the group on the historical evidence for Jesus' resurrection.

That lecture—which I still give in much revised form—has gone through a lot of permutations and been published in at least a dozen different forms. My thinking has also benefited from considerable further study and writing. My sense of call at the time I first gave this lecture as a graduate student was to be a good Renaissance-Reformation scholar teaching in a secular university, where I would offer a low-key intellectual apologetic for historic Christianity. In order to deepen both my biblical and theological preparation for that task and to experience more of the full force of the modern challenge to orthodox Christianity, I decided to interrupt my doctoral program in history after I completed my comprehensive exams and spend three years at Yale Divinity School.

While there, I wrote a long paper on I Corinthians 15 for a class with New Testament Professor Nils Dahl that eventually appeared as two separate articles in two scholarly New Testament journals: *New Testament Studies* and *Novum Testamentum*. A somewhat technical article on historical methodology published in the *Scottish Journal of Theology* in 1972 added depth to my analysis. It also led to a fellowship in 1976 and many months of study preparing to write a scholarly book on historical methodology and the miraculous (which was never completed).

The third illustration—*Rich Christians in an Age of Hunger* and related publications and organizing efforts—is much more widely known than the previous two. With sales over 400,000 copies in seven languages, *Rich Christians* is my most successful effort at popularization. Had I known what I now do, I would have made quite different choices as a student to prepare for writing about world hunger and economic justice. I have only taken one—and that an introductory undergraduate—course in economics in my life. I did not take any courses in social ethics in my three years at Yale Divinity School in the '60s! I was simply not prepared either in economics or social ethics to write *Rich Christians*. Probably my best scholarly preparation for *Rich Christians* came from a number of courses in biblical studies at Yale Divinity School, and it may be significant that the best part of *Rich Christians*, and the part that has changed the least in the four revisions, is Part II on a biblical perspective.

The whole project started quite unintentionally as a sermon on world hunger for a tiny church in 1967. As I completed my sermon that Saturday afternoon, I felt that I should add some practical application to the two sections on the facts about world hunger and a biblical framework. The idea of a graduated tithe came to me, so I included it in the sermon and my wife Arbutus and I began to practice it. A few years later, IVCF's *His* magazine published a short article titled "The Graduated Tithe." Then InterVarsity Press gave me a contract to do a short book with the same name, but it grew like Topsy as I wrote it and for almost the only time in my career as an author, the publisher never argued even once with the title I suggested: *Rich Christians in an Age of Hunger*.

Knowing my lack of preparation in economics, I asked a number of friends who were economists to read the early drafts. I did not always take their advice, but they certainly helped me avoid some mistakes. A Calvin grad and doctoral student in economics, Roland Hoksbergen, greatly improved the economic analysis in the second edition in 1984. A couple years later, I joined Vinay Samuel in organizing a nine-year process called The Oxford Conference on Christian Faith and Economics which brought together a wonderfully diverse circle of scholars (economists, business professors, biblical scholars and ethicists) as well as business leaders and activists from around the world. That, too, deepened my scholarly analysis and strengthened subsequent editions.

Activism and organizing have also been a central part of my work in this third area: organizing international conferences on simple lifestyle and development; leading more than two decades of activity in ESA on the topic; founding and co-editing the semi-popular, semi-scholarly international journal *Transformation*; giving hundreds of speeches and writing dozens of short articles on world hunger; and, after I wrote the first edition, seeing poverty firsthand in my travels in Africa, Asia, and Latin America.

A fourth experience, which started in about 1995, has more of the right components for combining scholarship, popularization, and activism than any earlier efforts. ESA received a substantial grant to work on the question: "If the United States truly wanted to reduce domestic poverty dramatically, what would be the full range of things that government and other sectors in society would need to do simultaneously?" From the beginning, we set up the two-year-plus process as an interdisciplinary scholarly effort. We sought out the best evangelical scholars in all of the major areas that we knew needed simultaneous attention because they were all interlocked. Several scholars agreed to write foundational pieces dealing with underlying philosophical or biblical-theological issues to provide a conceptual framework. Others worked on specific aspects including health care, education, and income.

All the authors met together at regular intervals to discuss each other's developing drafts, argue about competing interpretations, and suggest improvements. Initially, we planned simply to publish this collection of scholarly essays (which Baker did, in a book called *Toward a Just and Caring Society*, edited by David Gushee). Partway through the process, however, it dawned on me that in addition to coauthoring one of the chapters of the scholarly volume, I should consider writing a shorter, more popular book drawing on the careful chapters being written for the scholarly volume. Everyone seemed to agree, so I set to work carefully rereading all the scholars' chapters, but also delving on my own into some of the most significant scholarship and data on the issues that I chose to highlight. I benefited enormously from the work done by the contributors to the scholarly volume. Several of them also agreed to read my first draft and virtually everyone reviewed any section related to their special expertise. *Just Generosity: A New Vision for Overcoming Poverty in America* was the result. Since the book had the good fortune of appearing just as American society was taking a vigorous new look at the role of faith-based programs, I was able, thanks in part to ESA and its members, to use the results of this process in a variety of activist ways including publishing several editorials in major newspapers, lobbying, speaking, writing short popular articles, and consulting in Washington.

I think this is a promising model for Christian scholars who seek to contribute to the public policy debate. The broad interdisciplinary approach of this process enabled us to look, if not at the whole picture, then at least at a large part of it, and to develop a comprehensive response to poverty based on solid scholarship. Few people, however, read collections of scholarly essays by a group of different scholars, and publishers are reluctant to publish them. They are simply too technical and often lack a tightly integrated argument. *Just Generosity* tried to state the comprehensive vision in a much briefer, more readable, integrated argument.[3] If I had been a more powerful writer and if ESA had had more organizing capacity, the results could have been much greater. This model—combining scholarship, popularization and activism—could be used effectively on a wide range of public policy issues.

The last, and most recent, approach also combines scholarship, popularization, and activism as I have dealt with the interrelationship between evangelism and social action in faith-based ministries. In this case, however, it was a brilliant graduate assistant, rather than academic colleagues, who provided the interdisciplinary help.

Sometime in 1994, I had requested a grant from the Lilly Endowment to study what difference it made when congregations running social ministries also included a strong evangelistic component. They were interested but wanted the proposal to interact in more detail with the considerable body of research on congregations that they had supported over several decades. I simply did not have the immediate time to study all of that literature carefully, so I asked Heidi Rolland, a very bright Wheaton sociology graduate who was then studying with me at Eastern Baptist Theological Seminary, to do an independent study with me, analyze that literature, and help refine the grant proposal. When we received the grant, she became the associate director of what became a five-year project studying the diverse ways that evangelism and social ministry interact in fifteen different congregations.

In early 2002, Baker published a popular book, *Congregations That Make a Difference*, drawing on this research, but aimed at local congregational leaders, written by Heidi, Phil Olson, and myself. Heidi and I have also completed a scholarly volume, *Saving Souls, Serving Society: Understanding the Faith Factor in Church-Based Social Ministry*, published by Oxford University Press in 2005, reporting on the same research for the scholarly and public policy communities. In this process, Heidi and I also drew on the scholarly expertise of others in several ways. Grant funds enabled us to use scholarly consultants. As I have in most of my interdisciplinary work, we also asked friends who were specialists in specific areas to review early drafts.

This research had the good fortune of occurring at the same time that scholars like John DiIulio, the secular media, public policy elites and the political world discovered that faith-based organizations were sometimes highly successful in desperately broken communities where almost everything else had failed. We were unusually well-prepared to participate in the national debate about Charitable Choice and faith-based organizations when it hit the front pages of our newspapers in 2000 and 2001. As a result, Heidi and I have given papers and participated in panels and study projects in Washington and elsewhere at a level beyond anything I had done in the past. We have published shorter articles based on this research in everything from the *Brookings Review* (and a Brookings book edited by John DiIulio and E. J. Dionne) to *Christianity Today* and several major newspapers. This model, combining scholarship, popularization, and activism, worked well because of several factors: 1) major foundation grants; 2) a gifted graduate student with training in a crucial discipline (sociology) where I had no expertise; 3) ESA's long track record on holistic ministry; 4) good connections to important public policy conversations through my friendship with John DiIulio; and 5) the good fortune to be completing significant research on an issue just as it became one of the hottest topics in national political debate.

What generalizations and conclusions do I draw from this brief sketch of my personal pilgrimage in combining scholarship, popularizing and activism? First, as much as possible, I think it is desirable to do research and write a scholarly piece on a topic before you publish a popular piece. (I formulated that as a personal guideline some years ago, but I have not been able, or at least have not taken the time, to do it consistently.) Second, since popularizing usually requires interdisciplinary knowledge, I have found it very helpful to develop friends who are experts in the relevant fields. I try to listen carefully to their advice without being intimidated by them. Third, I have sought to find expert, interdisciplinary help whenever I could whether via grants, a graduate assistant, a collaborative scholarly project, or friends who are expert in other disciplines. Fourth, I have tried to accept the fact that I cannot read all the relevant literature, but I carefully study a short selection of the best publications—and make sure I read authors from all the major competing approaches to the topic. Fifth, I seek to make modest claims, acknowledge my weaknesses, and remain ready to modify my position when further data warrants it.

Now I offer a few conclusions. First, good popularizing requires special skills: an ability to develop a broad synoptic vision; an instinct for quickly discerning the most crucial issues; a personality and mind that enjoys moving quickly from one issue to another; and the ability to write clearly and powerfully. Second, one must recognize that the kinds of choices I have made have consequences. While there are a few exceptions, like Martin Marty, most people cannot attempt the level of popularizing and activism I have sought and also become a widely recognized scholar. Third, I would discourage anyone from trying to do it unless you feel called, and both experience and friends confirm that you have the necessary gifts and thereby confirm that call. Not many people should do it! I do not mean for a moment to urge most scholars to abandon a life of extended, focused scholarly research in their specific area of professional expertise. What I have tried is not for everyone. Finally, some scholars must do it. Plato said that if the wise disdain the task of politics, then they must suffer being governed by fools. Somebody will write popularizing books for "the average person." If those with scholarly training will not do it, they should not complain when those with little expertise do it badly, embarrass the church, and mislead laypeople with one-sided, simplistic nonsense.

I hope that a few in each generation of Christian scholars will pray for the gifts, develop the skills, and pay the price of becoming far better popularizers and more effective activists than I have managed to be.

Notes

1. This essay first appeared in *CSR* 36.2 (Winter 2007): 159-66.
2. Ronald J. Sider, *Rich Christians in an Age of Hunger: Moving from Affluence to Generosity*, 5th ed. (Nashville: W Publishing Group, 2005); Sider, *Andreas Bodenstein von Karlstadt: The Development of His Thought 1517-1525* (Leiden: E. J. Brill, 1974).
3. Somewhat similar to the approach in this fourth "model" is the process that led to the National Association of Evangelicals' declaration, "For the Health of the Nation: An Evangelical Call to Civic Responsibility," unanimously adopted by the NAE board in October, 2004. Diane Knippers and I co-chaired a several-year process that brought together a broad range of evangelical scholars with expertise in a variety of areas needed to develop the beginnings of an evangelical political philosophy. In the course of several meetings, we reviewed and refined each other's essays which Baker published in 2005 in *Toward an Evangelical Public Policy: Political Strategies for the Health of the Nation* (co-edited by Diane Knippers and myself). The draft of the brief, popular document, "For the Health of the Nation," emerged out of the more scholarly essays. Again, the book appeared at an unusually propitious moment—soon after the 2004 elections when the secular media focused enormous attention on the political views of evangelical voters. The result was numerous stories in major national newspapers.

II. DISCIPLINARY AND INTERDISCIPLINARY INTEGRATION

12 The Concept of Natural Law (1972)

Arthur F. Holmes

> *Law is the brightest reason (ratio summa), implanted in Nature, which commands what ought to be done and forbids the opposite. . . . [Man] has been given a certain distinguished status by the supreme God who created him; for he is the only one among so many different kinds and varieties of living beings who has a share in reason and thought. . . . And since right reason is Law, we must believe that men have Law also in common with the gods. Further, those who share Law must also share Justice; and those who share these are to be regarded as members of the same commonwealth (civitas).*[1]

This is Cicero's classic statement about natural law as the ideal basis for civil society.[2] It is admittedly shaped by his Stoic view of nature and cosmic reason, but for centuries it has represented the claim in ethical, legal and political theory that there is an unchanging ideal law which may or may not exist in positive historical law, "an objective and universal justice which transcends men's particular expressions of justice."[3] This law is both rooted in the nature of man and accessible to him as a rational being.

The natural law tradition is quite diversified. It has been traced to Plato's development of his theory of forms in response to the ethical relativism and legal positivism of the Sophists. It has roots in Aristotle's constant appeal to what is "according to nature." It has been related to the biblical concept of the law of God written in human hearts (Rom. 1). Augustine speaks in this fashion, subjecting both civil law and rulers to the judgment of an inner, eternal law, and Calvin makes similar suggestions. Aquinas in his time combined Stoic, Aristotelian and biblical ideas, while the Renaissance and Enlightenment revival of natural law commingled Richard Hooker's Thomism with Cambridge Platonism and Grotius' use of the Stoic Cicero. Natural law theory still echoes in Thomas Jefferson's appeal to "the laws of Nature and of Nature's God" in the Declaration of independence.

Today it lives on in phenomenologically oriented Thomists like Yves Simon, while ordinary language analysts like H. L. A. Hart and Ian Ramsey are at pains to salvage from it what they can.[4] My own concern is to explore the resources of this tradition for contemporary Christian thought.

Several generalizations may be made about this diversified tradition. (1) It opts for a rationalist rather than a voluntarist view of ethical and political obligation, whether the voluntarism be Occam's appeal to God's will (as distinct from his eternal reason) or Hobbes' appeal to the ruler's will, or Rousseau's appeal to the people's will. (2) It stands in contrast, indeed in conscious opposition, to the legal positivism of the Sophists, of Carneades the skeptic, of Thomas Hobbes, of Hume, Mill and the utilitarians, and of Marcuse and the Marxists. Legal positivism regards all laws (moral as well as civil) as man-made regulations dependent on custom, utility or power rather than on laws of nature, whereas Cicero declared that ideally law is not derived from the decrees of peoples, the edicts of princes, or the decisions of judges. And John Locke rejected Hobbes' political absolutism in favor of the consent of the governed and the right of revolution, because he regarded civil law as an extension of natural law rather than its replacement; in his early essays on natural law and in *The Reasonableness of Christianity*, he held explicitly that rightness does not depend on utility.[5] (3) Natural law stresses the deontological element in ethics rather than accepting a purely teleological or utilitarian theory, for it judges laws and actions not so much by their effects (as did Hobbes and Mill) as by universal principles and unchanging moral ends. It has therefore an understandable appeal to the Christian mind. (4) Natural law has a minimal content identified by William Frankena in such ethical principles as "we ought to love our fellowmen" (benevolence), "all men ought to be treated equally" (distributive justice), and "everyone has the right to life, liberty and security of person."[6] Frankena adds that we are rationally justified [see (1) above] in accepting these principles, that they ascribe rights and obligations to all men as men, independently of office, agreement, civil law, or whatever [see (2) above], and that they judge all human institutions, rules and actions [see (3) above]. Such is the natural law theory, in general terms that tie it to no one philosophical formulation.

Parenthetically, the just war theory shares the same historical roots (Cicero, Augustine, Aquinas, Grotius, Locke, etc.) for it judges war by natural law, and attempts to bring the causes and conduct of war under moral and legal controls derived from natural law. Legal positivism and ethical utilitarianism, as is evident in current discussions of the subject, can only judge war by its effects. On the other hand Christian pacifism, at least in some of its expressions, seems to depend either on a view of political obligation that is independent of the natural law theory, or else on a voluntaristic ethic that justifies Old Testament wars as explicitly willed by God and regards the new commandment to love as exempting Christians from military service.

Within this complex of ideas and arguments, I want to focus on three ingredients of John Locke's version of the natural law theory: (I) its rationalistic method, (II) the "rule of reason," (III) its individualism. I shall examine objections raised by David Hume (in his *Treatise on Human Nature*, book III, part I, section i) to each of these ingredients, objections which are themselves of interest to the Christian philosopher and which are especially crucial today. My conclusion (which is neither fully developed nor adequately defended) is that we must modify Locke's view of law by moderating the rationalism evident in (I) and (II), and replacing the atomistic model underlying (III). Yet these suggestions retain the natural law opposition to (1) a pure voluntarism, (2) legal positivism, and (3) a purely teleological ethic. In other words, I want to remain within the natural law tradition as I have defined it above.

Cicero's classic statement plainly assumes that right reason can ascertain the minimal content of natural law and apply it to civil society; he seems to take for granted the Stoic epistemology that appealed to irresistible ideas—which the Enlightenment called "self-evident." Scholastic natural law, on the other hand, depends on Thomistic epistemology: the content of natural law is inferred from our abstract ideas of real essences. Now while Locke frequently cites the Thomist Richard Hooker, he also quotes Cicero and recommends Stoic-influenced writers like Hugo Grotius.[7]

Grotius was confronted by the breakdown of Christian unity in the religious wars that followed the Reformation. He could not appeal to religious sanctions for law in either war or peace but had to find some other basis, admittedly established by God, which would be binding on men regardless of what, if any, was their religious persuasion. He could resort neither like the Catholics to a scholastic legal philosophy nor like the Calvinists to the decrees of a sovereign God. Grotius accordingly turned to the older pre-Christian tradition of natural law. The setting of his Prolegomena to *The Law of War and Peace* is the argument between Carneades' legal positivism and Cicero's doctrine. Grotius agrees with Cicero, and like Cicero he appeals to universally self-evident truths, but in addition he seeks formal arguments for deriving just laws. In contrast to Carneades' skepticism about all knowledge, he shares the seventeenth century hope for mathematical-type demonstrations in every area of inquiry. Leibniz, it may be noted, once offered formal proof that Stanislaus Letizinsky had the rightful claim to the Polish throne,[8] as if deductive logic is determinative for politics and history as well as morality and law.

That John Locke too was aware of the dangers inherent in the religious divisions of his day is evidenced by his *Letter Concerning Toleration*. Like Grotius, he claimed that our moral duties are as logically demonstrable as mathematical truths.

> The idea of a supreme Being, infinite in power, goodness, and wisdom, whose workmanship we are, and on whom we depend; and the idea of ourselves, as understanding rational beings; being such as are clear in us, would, I suppose if duly considered and pursued, afford such foundations of our duty and rules of action as might place morality among the sciences capable of demonstration; wherein I doubt not but from self-evident propositions by necessary consequences, as incontestable as those in mathematics, the measures of right and wrong might be made out to anyone that will apply himself with the same indifferency and attention to the one as he does to the other of these sciences.[9]

Careful definitions, clarity and distinctness of thought, and an unbroken logical continuity in our chains of reasoning—these are the ideals he and his contemporaries derive from mathematics. But Locke differs from Grotius over where the demonstration is to start. He rejects not only innate moral ideas (to which Plato and Augustine appealed) but also real essences (to which Thomists appealed) and the appeal from universal consent (to which Cicero and Grotius appealed), for "all men of good will" manifestly do not agree. Neither moral knowledge nor any other kind of knowledge is based on universally accepted maxims. The deduction must start elsewhere.

Locke rejects real essences but not abstract ideas. He is a conceptualist with ideas of the self and of God, not a nominalist. Moral deductions start, then, with our knowledge of the self which, as Locke learned from Descartes, is intuitive, and our knowledge of God which, as Descartes again argued, is demonstrative. In other words, our ideas of man and God logically determine our moral principles. In many other regards Locke is an empiricist, but when it comes to moral matters, experience with its pleasures and pains serves only as a God-given tutor; for inferences from experience produce probability, not the mathematical demonstrability that Locke and his contemporaries seek for our moral and political obligations.

David Hume objects that moral principles are not derived from reason. Morality is not like the truth of analytic judgments, "discerned by the juxtaposition and comparison of ideas." "There has been an opinion very industriously propagated by certain philosophers, that morality is susceptible of demonstration; and though no one has ever been able to advance single step in these demonstrations, yet it is taken for granted that this science may be brought to an equal certainty with geometry or algebra."[10] Hume then cites the four kinds of relation of ideas which he established earlier in his *Treatise* (resemblance, contrariety, degrees in quality, and proportions in quantity and number), none of which applies to morality.

Yet he does not address Locke's claim that moral principles are deducible from our ideas of God and man. I suggest this is for two reasons. First, he has previously argued that we have neither an intuitive knowledge of the self nor a demonstrative knowledge of God. In this, he parts company with Descartes, Locke, and Berkeley. How then can ethical principles be deduced? Second, he does not accept the rationalist's definition of ourselves as, in Locke's words, "understanding rational beings." Man is rather a practical than a purely speculative being. In the opening paragraph of Book III of his *Treatise*, for instance, he distinguishes abstruse from practical philosophy as in the *Enquiry Concerning Human Understanding*. He makes his position clear by resorting to psychological as against purely logical grounds of belief in the *Enquiry*, and by showing the practical basis of religion in his *Natural History of Religion* in contrast to religion's lack of logical basis in his *Dialogues Concerning Natural Religion*. In morals and politics, as with religious and other beliefs, man decides and acts for practical rather than purely logical reasons. Now if man is not primarily a rational being, how can we deduce moral principles purely from his rational nature? And even if he were primarily rational, what moral principles could we deduce? Locke offers no specific deductions.

Let us grant two things to Hume: (1) The non-mathematical nature of moral arguments: Locke and his contemporaries were, I believe, far too ambitious for completely demonstrative proofs. (2) The poverty of Locke's view of man. Do these concessions commit us to Hume's conclusions? I think not. Hume's mistake is to assume that all rational judgments are of two sorts only: analytic (relations of ideas) and empirical (inferences from matters of fact). If there is another kind of reasoning that applies to morality, that is to say if the metaphysical presuppositions of ethics are neither intuitive truths nor empirical statements, then we can avoid Hume's objection and retain some notion of natural law.

Let me put it another way. The crucial epistemological difference between Hume and Locke is that while Hume is a pure empiricist and a nominalist, Locke exempts our knowledge of the self and of God from empirical argument and is a conceptualist. For Locke with his abstract ideas, ethical principles relate rationally to metaphysical conceptions. The relationship may not be deductive, for not all philosophical systems are of that sort. Locke's own thinking is systematic but the relationship between his mechanistic physics, his atomistic theory of perception, his associationist psychology, and his political individualism is not deductive; it is all rather built on the same analogy, using a model drawn from mechanistic science of independent particles ordered by fixed natural laws. This kind of interrelation is more that of a symphony in which the same theme is played in every movement, than a deductive system.[11] But if not all rational systems are completely deductive, Locke's included, then Locke may well be wrong in his rationalistic hopes. Yet conceding this much to Hume does not allow him to deny that morality has a rational basis. The same response, I suggest, may be made to G. E. Moore's form of the naturalistic fallacy: fact and value are related not by direct logical implication but by the more complex relations of a larger metaphysical scheme.

Our metaphysical presuppositions shape our ethics, even though moral rules are not always logically entailed by empirical generalizations. Metaphysical presuppositions are not empirical statements in the empiricist sense of Hume and Moore. Nor are they analytic judgments, in the sense of logically necessary relations of empirical ideas. They are synthetic judgments, held for their value in systematic understanding as well as on more personal grounds, yet they function as a priori principles which give perspective on moral matters and so shape ethical and political thought.

For any metaphysic in which being has intrinsic value, this should be obvious. The idealist therefore has less difficulty with the relation of nature to value than the naturalist, and the theist's basic affirmation of God as creator of heaven and earth suggests that value is an inherent potential in nature by virtue of its created order and purpose.[12] To this extent Locke is justified in claiming that our ideas of God and man provide a rational basis for morality. That a complete set of moral rules or even principles can be logically deduced with mathematical conclusiveness is a further claim I am not prepared to defend. Nor do we need to do so to avoid Hume's objection.

There is another ingredient of the natural law theory to which Hume objects, and it too comes from Cicero. As reason controls and subdues the animal in man, so law commands the wayward elements in a state, uniting them around common interests in a fair and reasonable harmony.[13] Justice, for Cicero as for Plato, requires a harmonious balance of the constituent parts: hence law and that kind of order.

John Locke echoes Cicero's claim. In the state of nature, according to Locke, individual interests prevail and each man independently pursues and protects his individual rights to life, liberty and property. But in that state of nature men are not ruled by reason as fully as they should be. A civil society is therefore established for the common interest, to preserve and extend individual rights by rational means. Natural law thereby becomes the source of civil law and judges all positive legislation. In a civil society, the rule of reason can be fully realized; it can be enforced on those who are not sufficiently rational of themselves.

But David Hume objects. Morality has to do with the passions and will: these are the springs of human action rather than reason of itself. Reason alone is inert, impotent in controlling the passions and will. Consequently no logical argument that derives moral duties can enforce those duties, unless it also (a) relates passions and volitions to their objects, and (b) proves a priori the necessary connection that obligates the will to the moral ideas in question.[14] Law derives its authority as morality derives its influence, not from reason but from self-interested feelings. Hume is accordingly a legal positivist.

He is not alone in these misgivings. Rousseau also had his doubts. In the state of nature instinct prevails. But in the civil state justice replaces instinct and confers upon man's actions "a moral significance that they hitherto lacked." We cannot derive adequate ideas of justice either from God or from pure reason. The laws of justice have no sanction in nature. "Laws are nothing more nor less than the terms of association of civil society." Rousseau too is a legal positivist.[15]

This rejection of the rule of reason in favor of the passions or feelings has found a contemporary voice in Herbert Marcuse. In his early essay "On Hedonism," he attacks the disjunction of reason and sensuality in idealist philosophy, and both *One-Dimensional Man* and *An Essay on Liberation* take issue with the Enlightenment conception of reason. But Marcuse adds another related dimension. Man is a historical being without an eternally fixed rational essence. In place of Locke's simple transition from the not-yet rational state of nature to the more fully rational civil state, therefore, Marcuse insists that man is still not-yet rational. Instead he sees a dialectical evolution of rationality that can now be completed. It is only hindered by blindly supposing that man and society are already fully rational. The Enlightenment rule of reason thereby represses the free development of rational man and society. Man is not-yet rational. Reason does not yet rule.

Hume, Rousseau, and Marcuse all question Locke's intuition that man is a thoroughly rational being, such that if reason rules society is just and free. If reason of itself cannot govern a man, how can it rule society? This question also arises from a very different vantage point.

Daniel Defoe is sometimes regarded as a popularizer of the natural law theory and of Locke in particular. He writes of the sovereignty of reason over all the actions of men and continually appeals to natural law. He sets Robinson Crusoe in a state of nature, introduces Friday and his countrymen, then the Spaniards and the English sailors, until a civil society has emerged. Crusoe's property rights derive from his work, so he contracts with the others to preserve his rights as well as theirs: he establishes a rule of reason for the common good. But Crusoe is uneasy: he fears men's passions and the trouble that ensues must be controlled. In his theoretical writings Defoe expresses doubts that the rule of reason is strong enough to guide a man to virtue.[16]

Robinson Crusoe reminds me of St. Augustine. In Book XIX of *The City of God* he has similar things to say about Cicero's ideal state. If a republic is defined as the rule of reason based on man's common acknowledgement of justice, then no such republic exists. In the first place justice is said to consist in giving to everyone what is his own; as long as men do not give God his due, justice does not exist. To this Cicero could well reply that natural law and justice are ideals which may not exist in political practice but must still be recognized as ideals. But Augustine claims, in the second place, that men do not naturally acknowledge justice: virtue has to be taught. For men are ruled not by reason alone but by what they love. A republic is better defined as an assemblage of reasonable beings bound together by a common agreement as to the objects of their love. It is this which distinguishes the City of God from all our Babylons and Romes. The latter, Augustine suggests, often resemble large robber bands more than a just and reasonable society.[17]

Can virtue be taught? As Plato pointed out it only can if it is a kind of knowledge, a purely rational idea. Cicero seems to assume that justice is precisely such a universally self-evident rational object and man is such a rational being that we can implement a just society. Augustine on the contrary presents man's attitude to God and his robber-like political behavior as evidence that virtue cannot readily be taught, that man is not purely rational, and that right understanding does not make a man just unless he can also be taught to love justice. Man is not yet as fully rational as he could be, nor is civil society.

Augustine of course would not buy the modern ways out. Neither cultured feelings (Hume and Rousseau) nor the play of imagination and a social revolution (Marcuse) can produce a just and rational society. For while imagination can sense new possibilities and the feelings can stir the will, they offer too variable and fickle a foundation. It is neither love of itself nor reason in itself, but the object of our love that makes the difference. Imaginative possibilities must be evaluated and cultured feelings must be guided by the object of our love if we are to avoid a bungling relativism whose laws turn out to be only the inner harmony of repressive "robber-bands." But the divine object Augustine finds worthy of man's love can meet even David Hume's stipulations. Love for God does relate the passions to their object, and it does obligate the will to moral law: love freely fulfils the law. The deontological emphasis is preserved, but with a more holistic view of man than the reason-emotion dichotomy of the Enlightenment could allow.

As ethics is shaped by metaphysical presuppositions, so Locke's rationalistic method and his notion of the rule of reason are fashioned by his idea of man. There is another ingredient of that idea to be considered, however, his individualism, which as we have noted is part of a larger conceptual scheme suggested and unified by a model drawn from the mechanistic science of his day. It is the atomistic model: particles of matter moving according to fixed laws of motion. It had proved fruitful in astronomy and physics, and seventeenth and eighteenth century philosophers used it in other areas of inquiry.

Thomas Hobbes, for example, extended it to his philosophy of language: words are the isolated atomic constituents of speech, organized by the laws of grammar and syntax. Particles of speech are like particles of matter, and the rules of language are like the laws of motion. Similarly in social theory, Hobbes pictured isolated individuals drawn into a society that is ordered by fixed laws which the monarch imposes.

Locke uses the same model. He analyzes experience into simple ideas, which are atomic particles of experience drawn together by laws of psychological and logical association. He pictures society as composed of isolated individuals, each with an intuition of himself, but without immediate knowledge of other selves. Each individual is an island; in the state of nature each is free to act as he thinks fit, without asking leave or depending on the will of any other man; each has his rights; yet they unite into a civil society under the rule of reason. For Hobbes, civil law suspends and changes individual rights, but for Locke it preserves them.[18]

Let me call this the "Crusoe Theory." In the state of nature, I am a Robinson Crusoe, a solitary individual on an island of my own, self-contained and sufficiently equipped by a rational providence to create a life by myself, a society of goats and things ruled by reason. But you, Friday, intrude into my natural state and you too have the right to life and liberty, even to clothing and other property. So do the Spaniards and the English sailors. So we contract together to be ruled by law for the common good. The common good is simply enlightened self-interest, without which our island-state has no purpose. Love and law alike are posterior to self-interest and arise from other needs than those essential in my original Crusoe-like isolation.[19]

The Crusoe theory is a distinctly modern adventure that the Roman Stoics did not attempt. For them as for Aristotle, men are by nature social beings. We all participate in the cosmic Logos, so that even in the state of nature we form an interrelated unity rather than being a disorganized hodgepodge of individual interests.

It is not surprising therefore that Hume objects. His problems with the relationship of fact and value are only aggravated by Locke's individualism, just as his problems with necessary causation are aggravated by Locke's atomistic theory of ideas. For Locke, social values are as artificial in comparison with the state of nature, as is the civil society which gives them birth. How can social values be logically derived from natural law if man by nature is such an individualist? How can the ideas of isolated rational beings cement their wills together and produce social action? As anybody who has lived knows, moral motivation is a *social* matter—a matter of peer pressure and identification with others at least as much as it relates to rational analysis.

Hume speaks of "approbation." He proposes that our regard for the public interest stems not from rational self-interest alone but from the passions. Positive legislation and particular moral obligations are a matter of convention, but social values like justice are rooted in a natural sympathy.

I do not wish to defend Hume's specific viewpoint or to attack it. My point is only that he rejects the individualism of the Crusoe theory because he believes that man is *naturally* a social being, that love and even law come *naturally*, and he believes this because man is not only rational but also an emotive being. In these basic regards, I am forced to agree.

We may observe in passing that this recognition could help resolve both Locke's and Hume's difficulties regarding our knowledge of other selves. For as phenomenologists have pointed out we feel and therefore think differently about persons than about other possible objects of knowledge. My knowledge of other selves is not limited to a desperate attempt to infer from the purely cognitive content of my private ideas that other minds exist. That is a pseudo-problem created by a faulty atomistic model, rather than a factual account of how indeed we do know other selves. Phenomenologically, interpersonal knowledge seems to ride piggy-back on the intentional character of interpersonal feelings like love and hate, sympathy and empathy, distance and rapport.[20]

The relation of individuals to the whole civil society and of positive law to natural law presents itself as one case of the relations of particulars to universals. This is evident in the effect Aristotelian realism had on the Thomistic view of both church and state, and in the relation of Hobbes' nominalism to his use of the atomistic model and the radical individualism of his "state of nature." But Locke is neither a realist nor a nominalist, but a conceptualist. In contrast to Hobbes the nominalist, he has a theory of abstract ideas. But in contrast to Aquinas the realist, his world includes only particular things and people and God, about whom we form general and abstract ideas. Consequently Locke conceives the state as a man-made abstraction; in reality it has no essence or ends of its own but is simply an association of individuals for ends which they as individuals share.

It may be objected that if Hume is a nominalist he should accept rather than challenge the individualism of Hobbes or Locke. Two responses may be offered. First, while nominalism is indeed the theoretical position with which Hume begins, his skeptical argument shows that position to be philosophically sterile. He proposes instead that belief and the human passions are the basis for action, without reopening the problem of universals. If he had reopened it, he would not have been led back to nominalism but on to some other conception of individuality. Second, his theory of belief, the human passions, and social values imply both that no man is an island, and that civil society is not an independent and universal reality in which people somehow participate. A civil society is rather an individual, dependent, historical thing—not a fixed but a developing society. If he fed this into the problem of universals, it would suggest a concept of law and civil society that rests on neither a nominalist (or conceptualist) individualism nor a realist statism, but on a recognition of the inherent value of *historical* individuality. In other words, he needs a historicized theory of universals, if he is to avoid Locke's individualism, seeing the state as neither the real universal that shapes individual destiny nor a merely human artifice of a particular sort.

Marcuse speaks to the point. He recognizes the historical, developing nature of both man and civil society. But he finds no basis for natural law: historical becoming has no universal essence. Marcuse's historicism makes him a sort of legal positivist. On the other hand, what we need, if the natural law theory is to be sustained in the historical perspective that sees man and society as not yet fully rational, is to see their changing historical nature as having real value within the unchanging potentiality of the whole created order.

I shall try to state this phenomenologically rather than abstractly.

1. No man is an island. He does not participate in an ocean of remote universal objects that wash up on his shores, nor need he surrender his rights in order to create order in a nominalistic world. From birth he is both dependent and independent, a social being, an individual embodiment of historical possibilities and natural laws. As Buber put it, "I-Thou" is the primary word, not "I" or "Thou" alone.

2. The state likewise is not just a conglomeration of particulars; it is an historically individual thing. Civil societies like individual persons are individual embodiments of unchanging possibilities in the created order. As such they have value in themselves; they have legitimate ends that may not be reduced to the ends of individual self-interest. Civil society and the civil law that orders the pursuit of its ends are therefore the "powers that be" ordained by God in a sense that particular rulers and particular legislation is not. The state has functions in the created order that no individual man *per se* can either assume or ignore.

Every individual thing in creation, whether a person or the civil society to which he belongs or a piece of positive legislation, is a historical development, not immutable but in some regards changing. Individual things are not fixed atoms of existence isolated from time by space, nor is their destiny determined by participation in and privation of fixed forms. Individuality has more meaning than that allows, and more positive importance to the whole. But how we value individual persons and civil societies and positive legislation depends on how we value our history, and on what meaning we find in the temporal character of all created existence. Individual persons both shape and are shaped by the civil society of which they are part. Individual persons and individual civil societies shape and are shaped by the movement of history and the purposes of time. But civil societies, like individual persons, are not yet fully rational or fully just. A man can honestly value his national heritage, and still be as incisive about social evils as an Old Testament prophet and as reform-minded as a morally principled liberal.

What I am suggesting is that natural law rests on the value and purposes invested by God in the created order, but without the myth of a disorganized state of nature preceding an ideally rational society now on earth. The created order is a historical process in which positive law should become a concrete approximation, appropriate to the requirements of history, of universal possibilities that are basic to the nature of things. The ideal of natural law is rooted in the potentialities of the created order. As an ideal it is capable of different embodiments in positive law at different times—which is, of course, what the natural law theory has often in principle claimed.[21]

We have parted company with Locke's individualism on two grounds: his account is phenomenologically inadequate, and his conceptualism allows a civil society no concrete reality or value of its own in the created order. But a historicized view of civil society and individuality also helps our modification of Locke's rationalistic method. The positive laws of a historical society are no more deduced from universally necessary principles than are the positive practices adopted by a free person for his individual ends; both are in measure free to choose. For Hegel a civil society and its choices are determined by the historical dialectic that works through and beyond the antitheses of the past to some synthesis that is not-yet. It seems to me that while the process may not be strictly dialectical, it is plainly the case that a civil society and its laws are shaped by working through and beyond the historical conditions which help define its possibilities. The rational method involved is neither entirely deductive nor strictly dialectical but rather dialogical—thinking "though and beyond" existing situations and existing laws in the light of those unchanging values for man as a creature of God which have been called "natural law." David Hume, for all his protestations, leads us in this direction, which is itself what a historicized theistic natural law proposal might lead us to expect: that a world-historical individual like Hume can open up a hopeful philosophical direction.

Notes

1. Cicero, *De Legibus* I. v. 18-19, 22-23, trans. by C. W. Keyes in the Loeb Classical Library.
2. This essay first appeared in *CSR* 2.3 (Spring 1972): 195-208.
3. John H. Hallowell, Foreword to Yves R. Simon, *The Tradition of Natural Law* (New York: Fordham University Press, 1965), viii.
4. For general treatments see H. Cairns, *Legal Philosophy from Plato to Hegel* (Baltimore: John Hopkins Press, 1949); A. P. D'Entrèves, *Natural Law: An Introduction to Legal Philosophy* (London: Hutchinson University Library, 1951); Carl J. Friedrich, *The Philosophy of Law in Historical Perspective*, 2nd ed. (Chicago: Phoenix Books, 1963) and *Transcendent Justice* (Durham, N.C.: Duke University Press, 1964). In more partisan fashion is John Wild, *Plato's Modern Enemies and the Theory of Natural Law* (Chicago: University of Chicago Press, 1953). Of current interest is H. L. A. Hart, The *Concept of Law* (New York: Oxford University Press, 1961), and Ian Ramsey, "Towards a Rehabilitation of Natural Law," in *Christian Ethics and Contemporary Philosophy* (London: S.C.M. Press, 1966), p. 382. Some similarities appear in Herman Dooyeweerd's view of the state as a "law sphere" whose unchanging ends are determined by the Creator, but this offers a more voluntaristic basis for law than in the natural law tradition generally. See *The Christian Idea of the State* (Nutley, N. J.: Craig Press, 1968), and *A New Critique of Theoretical Thought*, vol. III (Nutley, N.J.: Presbyterian and Reformed, 1957).
5. See Cicero's De *Legibus* I. xvi., and Locke's *Essays on the Law of Nature*, ed. W. von Leyden (New York: Oxford University Press, 1954). Also J. W. Gough, *John Locke's Political Philosophy* (New York: Oxford University Press, 1968), 16.
6. "On Defining and Defending Natural Law," in *Law and Philosophy*, ed. Sidney Hook (New York: New York University Press, 1964), 200-209. Also H. L. A. Hart, 189-195.
7. See S.P. Lamprecht, *The Moral and Political Philosophy of John Locke* (London: Russell and Russell, 1962), ch I, and in particular Locke's *Some Thoughts Concerning Education*, 184-189. Ernst Cassirer points out that Thomas Jefferson too spoke Stoic language, in *The Myth of the State* (New Haven: Yale University Press, 1946), 167. The principal source for Locke's political theory is of course his *Second Treatise on Civil Government*. See also J .W. Yolton, "Locke on the Law of Nature," *Philosophic Review*, LXVII, 477-498, and Leo Strauss, "Locke's Doctrine of Natural Law," *American Political Science Review*, LII. 490-501.
8. See Cassirer, Chapter XIII; D'Entrèves, 49-55.
9. *Essay Concerning Human Understanding*, IV. iii. 18, cf. IV. xii. 8. Cf. Locke's *Second Treatise of Civil Government* (Chapter ii): natural law is as intelligible to reason as the positive laws of a commonwealth, perhaps more so since it is less intricate.
10. *A Treatise of Human Nature*, III. i. 1 (Everyman Edition, vol. II, 172).
11. See Arthur F. Holmes. *Christian Philosophy in the Twentieth Century* (Nutley, N.J.: Craig Press, 1969), Chapter V.
12. On the nature of our moral knowledge, see further A. F. Holmes, *Faith Seeks Understanding* (Grand Rapids, Mich.: Eerdmans, 1971), Chapter IV. On the philosophical consequences of theism, Langdon Gilkey's *Maker of Heaven and Earth* (New York: Doubleday, 1959) is highly suggestive.
13. See the opening quotation of this essay. Also *De Re Publica*, II. xl, III. xxxiii-xxxv (Loeb Classical Library Edition, 181, 221-227).
14. *Treatise*, III. i. 1 (Everyman Ed., 167-169, 173-175).
15. *The Social Contract*, Book One, Chapter VIII and Book Two, Chapter VI. The quotations are from Willmoore Kendall's translation (Gateway Edition, 1954), 25-26, 55.
16. See M. E. Novak, *Defoe and the Nature of Man* (New York: Oxford University Press, 1963).
17. See also *City of God*, IV. Helpful discussions of Augustine's contributions to natural law theory may be found in Ernst Troeltsch, *The Social Teaching of the Christian Churches* (London: Macmillan, 1931), vol. I, 156f; and more fully in Herbert A. Deane, *The Political and Social Ideas of St. Augustine* (New York: Columbia University Press, 1963).

18. This contrast is developed by A. P. D'Entrèves, Chapter III and Yves Simon, *The Tradition of Natural Law* (New York: Fordham University Press, 1965), Chapter 4.

19. Locke's view of marriage suffers proportionately. See *On Civil Government*, Second Treatise, Chapter vii.

20. I develop this claim more fully in *Faith Seeks Understanding*, Chapter V, in relation to specific differences between the atomistic model and one that is more adequate phenomenologically. On the "Crusoe Theory" and the nature of individuality, see also my "Crusoe, Friday and God," *The Philosophy Forum* X, 307-327. Specifically on Locke, see W. M. Simon, "John Locke: Philosophical and Political Theory," *American Political Science Review*, XLV, 386-399.

21. I disagree with Jacques Ellul's claim that no law is inherent in human nature since God alone creates law. He seems to assume that God had no unchanging purpose in creation to which grace restores mankind, that God's law is therefore known only by revelation and not at all by reason, and that the natural law theory is a necessary bedfellow of natural theology which is a form of Gnosticism. He does not come to grips with the philosophical problems, least of all the problem of universals, yet he inclines towards a voluntaristic and teleological ethic. See *The Theological Foundations of Law* (Evanston, Ill.: Seabury Press, 1969).

13 Naturalism in the Natural Sciences
A Christian Perspective (1986)

PAUL DE VRIES

What is the business of natural scientists?[1] It is the discovery of explanations of natural phenomena. Natural scientists do not merely describe events; they seek to place events in the explanatory context of physical principles, laws, fields. However, only certain kinds of explanations make for acceptable natural science. Within the natural sciences, explanations refer only to natural objects and events. The personal choices and actions of human and divine beings are thereby excluded.

Initially, this exclusiveness of the natural sciences could well disturb a Christian scholar who has been taught to believe that our relationships to God should be integral to every aspect of our lives—including work in the natural sciences. Praise to God should always be on our lips, no matter what activity. But if we cannot talk about God within the enterprises of the natural sciences, then our scientific work seems hardly Christian. Christian scholars can find themselves on the horns of a dilemma—if we incorporate God-talk in efforts within the natural sciences, our work is no longer scientific.

Must a Christian who is a natural scientist live a double life? Must she be torn between the scriptural demand to glorify God in all things and the professional demand to be silent about God in matters scientific? I think not. The purpose of my philosophical musings here is to defend the claim that Christians should be quite comfortable with a specific kind of naturalism within the natural sciences.

The goal of inquiry in the natural sciences is to establish explanations of contingent natural phenomena strictly in terms of other contingent natural things—laws, fields, probabilities. Any explanations that make reference to supernatural beings or powers are certainly excluded from natural science. Apart from mathematical terms and truths of logic, things to which our theories in natural science refer are always contingent; each of them remains dependent on other things. I let go of my pencil and it immediately falls to the floor. Why? It would not be scientifically enlightening to say, "God made it that way." Similarly, scientists would not explain a particular rainstorm in terms of an

Indian's rain dance or a farmer's prayers. Rainstorms are explained in terms of natural factors, such as air pressure and temperature—factors that themselves depend on other natural factors.

In brief, explanations in the natural sciences are given in terms of contingent, non-personal factors within the creation. If I put two charged electrodes in water, the hydrogen and oxygen will begin to separate. If I were writing a lab report (even at a Christian college!), it would be unacceptable to write that God stepped in and made these elements separate. A "God hypothesis" is both unnecessary and out of place within natural scientific explanations.

The naturalistic focus of the natural sciences is simply a matter of disciplinary method. It is certainly not that some scientists have discovered that God did not make phenomena occur the way they do. The original causes or ultimate sources of the patterns of nature are not proper concerns within any of the natural sciences—though they remain a wholesome and legitimate concern of many natural scientists. The natural sciences are limited by method to naturalistic foci. By method they must seek answers to their questions within nature, within the non-personal and contingent created order, and not anywhere else. Thus, the natural sciences are guided by what I call methodological naturalism.

Methodological naturalism is quite different from metaphysical naturalism. Metaphysical naturalism is a philosophical perspective that denies the existence of a transcendent God. Methodological naturalism does not deny the existence of God because this scientific methodology does not even raise the question of God's existence. Unfortunately, these two kinds of naturalism have often been confused. As a result, it has seemed to the philosophically careless as if the natural sciences under the guidance of methodological naturalism have provided evidence for metaphysical naturalism. This confusion is regrettable and certainly inexcusable.

The natural sciences are committed to the systematic analysis of matter and energy within the context of methodological naturalism. As a result, if a natural scientist believes that there is no God and that only matter and energy exist and that only explanations within natural science are valid, then she cannot defend her opinions on the basis of any natural science because all these claims go far beyond the well-accepted methodological capacity of the natural scientific enterprise. Moreover, for the very reason that the scientific enterprise is limited to naturalistic explanations, we should all at least be honestly open to other types of explanations when we are not working in our laboratories or writing our natural scientific theories.

An example might make this methodological limitation on the natural sciences a bit clearer. If you ask me after a club meeting to explain why I raised my hand at a particular vote, I might give you a detailed account of the physicochemical brain states, the electrical charges traveling through neurons, the contractions of triceps and pectoral muscles, the movements of bones and cartilage, etc. That is, I could detail a true biological explanation of the event. But such a display of scientific precision would more likely irritate you than answer your question. In asking me to explain my vote, you would be interested in concerns outside of the naturalistic foci of the natural sciences. You would be interested in knowing about my purposes and reasons—concerns properly avoided by, for example, a biological explanation. I can explain an event within the constraints of methodological naturalism, and that explanation could be true and complete, but could still fail to answer a legitimate questions. Many legitimate questions concerning events in our world fall outside the realms of the natural sciences.

It is fascinating that at the present time there are two notable groups of people that seek to violate the natural sciences: the devotees of evolutionistic scientism on one hand and the devotees of creationistic biblicism on the other—groups represented by Carl Sagan and Henry Morris, respectively. To suit their own purposes, these groups seek to lead natural science away from its methodological naturalism, away from its commitment to systematic analysis of matter and energy. If we respect the proper role of the natural sciences, we will protest both the biblicists' and evolutionists' proposals. Whether they are conscious of this or not, both of these groups are exploiting the good name of the natural sciences for their own ideological programs. In contrast, the success of methodological naturalism provides no threat to Christian truth.

Quite distinct from the perspectives of either evolutionistic scientism or creationistic biblicism, some of the work of the well-respected Christian philosopher Nicholas Wolterstorff seems incompatible with methodological naturalism in the natural sciences. In his *Reason within the Bounds of Religion*, Wolterstorff describes and defends certain roles for what he calls "control beliefs." According to him, control beliefs function in two ways: because we hold them we are led both to reject some theories and to devise other theories.[2] In general, we structure various theories in order that they will not be inconsistent with, but rather "comport well with" our particular control beliefs.[3] Moreover, Wolterstorff claims that the "religious beliefs of the Christian scholar ought to function as *control* beliefs within his devising and weighing of theories."[4]

Should Christian religious beliefs guide the actual professional work of Christian scholars within the natural sciences? Wolterstorff believes they should do so in order that conformism with respect to science may be avoided. After all, we should not assume, "from the standpoint of authentic Christian commitment," that science is, and always will be, just right as it is. That would make us spiritual "brothers" with the logical positivists[5]—even though logical positivists fortunately now form an endangered species! Wolterstorff wisely points out that "no theory ever stands alone," for every scholar "confronts the world with a whole web of theoretical and non-theoretical beliefs."[6] When a contradiction is found between an attractive theory and a scholar's present web of beliefs, either that theory or some present belief must be surrendered.[7]

Given his vision of how control beliefs should work, Wolterstorff bemoans the failure of Christian scholars to provide, from their religious commitments, formative direction within the sciences.[8] He thinks it is sad that a general commitment to God as Creator "suggests nothing at all by way of any research program *within* biology."[9] According to him, the causes of such failings are Christian scholars' lack of understanding of the role their control beliefs play, their failure to develop Christian patterns of thought, their lack of knowledge of Christian theology and Christian philosophy, and their weakness of imagination.[10]

Without a doubt, these deplorable conditions have been all too common among Christian scholars—both within and outside the natural sciences. Despite such an accurate assessment, Wolterstorff's own vision is beset by several flaws. Three serious weaknesses are endemic to his perspective, making the literal following of his attractive vision neither desirable nor possible. Let me very briefly explain why, before I myself use some Christian "control beliefs" to defend the use of methodological naturalism in the natural sciences.

First, Wolterstorff's stated commitment to avoid contradictions and to enforce coherence among all our various beliefs is certainly virtuous, but also immeasurably ambiguous. Because of the diversities of our "language-games," a proposition in one theory within one discipline may only seem to contradict a proposition in another theory within another discipline. The "contradiction" is often only apparent. Similarly, a claim within a scholarly theory may only seem to contradict a historic Christian doctrine. It would be easy to be seduced by the surface grammar, and mistakenly compare "apples with oranges"—or even with the color orange! For example, as a doctrine of physics we may well accept that the total amount of matter and energy is constant. For the discipline of physics this doctrine is true and reliable. Nevertheless, Christians, whether physicists or not, generally believe that God brought matter and energy into existence. So it seems that matter and energy have not always been constant. This religious claim does not contradict the aforementioned accepted doctrine of physics because these two beliefs never touch—they are found in markedly different contexts. The presumed authority of religious control beliefs over theoretical claims is largely hamstrung by legitimate disciplinary boundaries.

It is also important to note that in more recent writings Wolterstorff has significantly softened his commitment to coherence. For example, in "Can Belief in God Be Rational If It Has No Foundations?" he repeatedly downplays, as an expression of his present Reidian approach, the importance of logical coherence, reasoning, and rationality.[11] He is now more aware of some of the potential pitfalls of attempts to establish coherence.

Second, Wolterstorff himself only poorly demonstrates the authority of control beliefs over theory development and acceptance. Certainly his vision may still be right even if he provides no good example of how it should be followed, but the lack of any good example raises questions about how his claims should be either understood or applied.

On the one hand, he presents only two cases in which he claims Christian control beliefs should affect theory selection: Freudian and behaviorist psychological theories should be rejected.[12] Perhaps he is right, but his reasons are far from convincing. Even if these two schools of thought involved a denial of "human freedom and responsibility," that denial could be compatible with some Christians' control beliefs. More importantly, neither Freudian nor behaviorist psychology requires the denial of human freedom and responsibility. Of course, human behavior is not exempt from causal factors; yet Freudian psychoanalysis seeks to define for patients areas where they can gain control. Psychoanalysis seeks to extend the areas of rational freedom and responsibility through discovering the very "causes" that the patient can control.[13] Even behaviorism within psychology can be correctly understand as a way of analyzing "a person as a physical system"[14] without asserting that a person is only a physical system. Psychological behaviorism is an attempt to make a type of psychology a natural science, under the constraints of methodological naturalism, and this attempt has certainly produced some valuable discoveries. However, what Wolterstorff and I both object to are the careless philosophical and "religious" pronouncements of people like B. F. Skinner when they claim that the limited focus of this kind of psychology is the entire human self. Christians can well value behaviorist psychological theory while denouncing the misguided attempts to pervert such a psychological theory into an entire philosophical anthropology.

On the other hand, Wolterstorff refers at length to examples of how changes in various theories have correctly, he thinks, led to changes in Christians' control beliefs.[15] In these cases, of course, the so-called control beliefs are no longer in control! I do not want to take exception to any of his examples. Surely our general understanding of Christian faith can always be subject to improvement from any source of God's truth, including some natural scientific theories. What bothers me here is the continued use of the misleading term "control beliefs." A better term would be "basic beliefs," or better yet, "pre-understandings." We should reserve the term "control beliefs" for beliefs to which we are so deeply committed that alterations of them would be extraordinarily rare. These secure beliefs are generally basic to our worldviews. In contrast, when most of one's examples involve alteration of control beliefs rather than the use of control beliefs to discern scientific theories, as in Wolterstorff's work, then "control beliefs" are misnamed.

Third, by focusing merely on the discerning and devising of theories, Wolterstorff misses the major function of genuine Christian control beliefs in discerning and devising the foundations of the various disciplines, and of the natural sciences in particular. Historically, various "worldviewish" control beliefs have had dramatic effect on the selection of assumptions and methodologies appropriate to the various natural scientific disciplines.[16] Here, as with theories, surface inconsistencies with other deeply held beliefs need not lead to an alteration of either disciplinary assumptions or the other beliefs. Difference of language-games must be recognized. Nevertheless, the basic assumptions and methodologies of the disciplines are more subject to "worldviewish" evaluations than are particular theories within disciplines. The basic disciplinary assumptions and methodologies lie at the borders of the different disciplines; it is on the basis of these assumptions and methodologies that disciplines are divided and can be compared. It is at the line of these disciplinary assumptions and methodologies that the major issues are raised in the philosophy of science, including Christian philosophy of science.

When a theory actually contradicts our genuine control beliefs, beliefs to which we are very deeply committed, we have four options. First, we can seriously challenge the assumptions or methodologies of the alleged "science"—as with astrology—and argue that it is only a pseudoscience. Second, we can seek to alter some of the basic assumptions and methodologies of the discipline that engendered or permitted the objectionable theory. This is a process that has often led to new scientific discoveries and changes in theories—from Copernicus to the present. In fact, significant theory change has occurred only when scholars have successfully challenged implicit or explicit disciplinary assumptions or methodologies. Third, we can come to understand the theory's restricted disciplinary focus—as with behaviorist psychology—and thoughtfully argue against any "worldviewish" uses of it. Fourth, perhaps our own control beliefs may need reevaluation, though we would be wise to consider this only very carefully and over a period of time. Often what seems at first to be a contradiction can be shown to be noncontradictory or can be resolved in another way. In brief, we either uncover the discipline as a kind of pseudoscience, attempt to alter the disciplinary assumptions or methods, seek to restrain the theory to its legitimate disciplinary context, or we ourselves might change. In each of these responses, disciplinary assumptions and methods play an important role. With this in mind, I wish now to defend, on the basis of Christian theological and philosophical commitments, the methodological naturalism of the natural scientific disciplines.

How should Christians approach methodological naturalism? We should be enthusiastic supporters of the naturalistic methodology of the natural sciences for the following six reasons.

First, Christianity teaches that regularity and coherence are discoverable within natural phenomena. Naturalistic methodology in the natural sciences can, therefore, be embraced on the assumption of God's coherent ordering of the world. God's existence need not be brought up within the natural sciences because the belief in his existence is already part of the historical foundations of the modern natural sciences. Because of the power and dependability of the Creator-God, we can expect to discover regular patterns of causation and interaction within the created, natural order. These patterns are often more impressive when they are studied in isolation (with the help of methodological naturalism) as natural scientists persistently pursue analyses of every factual interrelationship. In natural scientific work there is no need to be sidetracked by theological or philosophical speculation or analysis. Nevertheless, when the natural scientific analysis is done within the limits of methodological naturalism, we can then praise the Creator from a position of great knowledge and deeper appreciation.

Second, methodological naturalism is correctly understood as a useful approach to natural scientific work without prejudging its usefulness in other areas of life. With a balanced understanding of both the values and limits of natural science, one can appreciate the genuine validity of non-naturalistic explanations of events outside of the foci of the natural sciences.

For example, a farmer may explain a rainstorm as an answer to prayer without questioning a meteorological explanation—he may see God at work in the complex causal interrelationships that affect our weather. He can praise God for answers to prayer and also praise God for the awesome regularity that he sees within nature. Similarly, a medical doctor may, with scientific accuracy, prescribe the correct medicine and still praise God for the healing that takes place. God's handiwork can be seen in our bodily processes without our imposing a God-hypothesis into our understanding of physiology.

Basically for the very reason that natural science is methodologically limited to naturalistic explanations, everyone should thoughtfully consider other explanations which are outside the limits of the scientific focus—prayer, purposes, creation *ex nihilo*, personal will. In fact, the very articulated nature of the world discoverable under the constraints of methodological naturalism justifies great praise to God. But the method that is so successful for natural science would be a disaster in other disciplines. Could we discuss morals without purpose or theology without God?

Third, because the natural scientific disciplines are guided by methodological naturalism, they cannot pretend to provide answers to the ultimate questions. At some point in every explanation of phenomena, the question "Why?" can no longer be answered within science—except to say that we have gone as far as our methods of natural science have taken us at this time. Whether this is the entire valid explanation of whether more ultimate steps of explanation are appropriate (e.g., "God made it that way" or "This is the way God does it") is a question that must be decided outside the natural sciences. Without the discipline of methodological naturalism, some might stop their scientific research too quickly and merely rest in the comfort of the ultimate explanations. Nevertheless, methodological naturalism in the natural sciences and the ultimate explanations available to Christians are quite compatible. Unfortunately, various ultimate explanations are often promoted under the guise of scientific results. Since we have no compelling reason to believe that all truth is scientific, and since the natural sciences are limited by their methodological naturalism, one *must* rely also on resources outside the natural sciences when resolving ultimate questions such as those involving worldviews and the basic meanings and values for our lives.

For example, an understanding of the roles of genetic mutation and natural selection throughout the existence of the human race is a matter for natural scientific inquiry, but the question of the actual origin of the human race is an ultimate question. It is a question beyond the scope of the natural sciences with their naturalistic methodology, because it concerns the basic meaning and purpose of our existence. This is a "worldviewish" question, not a question for a natural science. Studying such an ultimate question simply under the guidelines of methodological naturalism would harmfully prejudice our conclusions toward metaphysical naturalism. We need to sharpen our understanding of the distinguishing characteristics of ultimate questions and consistently avoid applying only prejudicial methods (such as methodological naturalism) in studying them.

Fourth, Christians should be comfortable with methodological naturalism in the natural sciences because God himself is sovereign over all of life. God's power over all aspects of our lives does not depend on our forcing God-talk into every discipline or circumstance, nor does it depend on the superiority of theology over other disciplines.

As Abraham Kuyper pointed out, because God is sovereign over all of life, he is sovereign over every part of life as well. The internal structure of the scientific enterprise is part of the Kingdom of God. Thus, any manipulation of a natural science to suit the purposes of theologians, churches, or governments is an expression of a lack of faith. Within the sovereign sphere of science, we are free to study the works of God without having to make explicit reference to the Person of God or even to his existence.[17] God's works are manifest and open to study even by those who do not know him.

Fifth, the Incarnation should liberate Christians from any fear of methodological naturalism in the natural sciences, for when the Word became flesh, he did not overpower the human condition, but respected its constraints. He came into the world as it was. He was a fetus for nine months in a woman's womb. He grew up in the natural surroundings of Nazareth. He suffered with us and died. He was not biologically different from you and me. Certainly his purpose was unique and in his resurrection he conquered death, but he was a man for man and a man for God. Consequently, it should not be beneath our dignity to incarnate our natural scientific thoughts into the capillaries, valences, and gluons of methodological naturalism.

Finally, a Christian doing scientific work should be completely at home with methodological naturalism in that work, because life is much more than the natural scientific disciplines. Natural scientific theories are necessarily incomplete because the world is more than matter and energy. While working in the laboratory or analyzing data at a scientific desk, we might well see the world in terms of just matter and energy. After all, this is the proper focus of the natural sciences. The tragicomedy begins when a natural scientist forgets his humanity and claims that his matter-and-energy picture of the world is literally complete. This may be the saddest of the "absent-minded professor" jokes. It seems frighteningly easy for natural scientists to become so absent-minded that they forget that the theories they invent apply to themselves. Where in the energy-and-matter picture of the world are the scientist's love for his wife, his dreams for his children, his hopes for other scientists' praise, his commitment to scientific truth? Must the scientist fail to see the forest for the trees; must he fail to see the person for the bones and flesh? Surely he looks in the mirror when he shaves! Where in his theories is his personal irritation with his lab assistant or his appreciation of the beauty and grace of the co-ed that draws his attention outside his window! Could he have lost his ability to notice? How sad.

By letting our science be freely guided by methodological naturalism, we will be freer to point out the legitimate limitations of the natural sciences. Many truths lie outside the scope of the natural sciences—truths concerning human nature and human needs, truths concerning wholesome values and the meaning of life, truths concerning where we came from and where we are going. Think about it: a biology book provides small help for selecting a mate, much as an auto mechanic's manual is no source for vacation ideas. (We could end up divorced and still be in the driveway!) If we are free to let the natural sciences be limited to their perspectives under the guidance of methodological naturalism, then other sources of truth will be more defensible. However, to insist that

God-talk be included in the natural sciences is to submit unwisely to the modern myth of scientism—the myth that all truth is scientific.

The methodological naturalism of natural science need not be offensive to Christians. (1) We certainly expect to find structure within the created order. Nevertheless, (2) the value of this limited naturalistic focus is unique to science; (3) questions outside of this focus must be approached through alternative methodologies. Also, (4) the fact that God is not mentioned in the natural sciences does not exclude the effect of his Presence. On the contrary, (5) his Incarnation affirms his capacity to be at home in the natural order. Finally, (6) we should not force theological talk into science because the natural sciences are necessarily incomplete. Our lives are much more than the natural scientific disciplines, but the natural sciences must live within the constraints of their naturalistic methodologies. And what, for that matter, could be more natural?

Notes

1. This essay first appeared in *CSR* 15.4 (Summer 1986): 388-96.
2. *Reason within the Bounds of Religion* (Grand Rapids, Mich.: Eerdmans, 1976), 64.
3. Ibid.
4. Ibid., 66, his emphasis.
5. Ibid., 20.
6. Ibid., 39.
7. Ibid.
8. Ibid., 101.
9. Ibid., my emphasis.
10. Ibid., 101-104.
11. This article is in *Faith and Rationality*, edited by Alvin Plantinga and Nicholas Wolterstorff (Notre Dame, Ind.: University of Notre Dame Press, 1983); see especially 172.
12. See *Reason*, 64f. and 73.
13. See also C. Stephen Evans, "Must Psychoanalysis Embrace Determinism?" in *Psychoanalysis and Contemporary Thought* (New York: International Universities Press, 1984), 339-365.
14. Skinner, quoted in Wolterstorff's *Reason*, 64f.
15. See repeated examples in *Reason*, 80-86.
16. See controversial discussions of this in Stanley L. Jaki, *The Road to Science and the Ways to God* (Chicago: University of Chicago Press, 1978), and R. Hooykaas, *Religion and the Rise of Modern Science* (Grand Rapids, Mich.: Eerdmans, 1972).
17. See especially Kuyper's *Lectures on Calvinism* (Grand Rapids, Mich.: Eerdmans, 1931), Lecture IV.

14 Christian Philosophy and Cultural Diversity (1987)

Richard J. Mouw

Theologians have been paying much attention in recent years to such things as ethnicity, race, gender, and political-economic condition.[1] New schools of theology have emerged out of these sorts of investigations: Black Theology, Feminist Theology, Liberation Theology, and so on.

Can similar developments be observed in philosophical discussion? If so, they certainly do not have the same visibility as the theological trends. Theologians have a more attentive public than philosophers do. Theological discussion has immediate ramifications for the life of the ecclesiastical community, thus people—ordinary lay people as well as journalists and ecclesiastical officials—pay closer attention to what theologians say than any comparable groups do to the discussions of professional philosophers, even Christian philosophers.

Nor is philosophical attention to such matters likely to be as intense as the interest shown among theologians. The close ties that academic theologians have to the Christian churches place theologians in rather direct contact with an identifiable international and cross-cultural network of institutions, communities, and individuals—a network which reinforces a concern with cultural differences in a manner not experienced in many other disciplines (with the exception, of course, of cultural anthropology).

Even though this kind of strong institutional reinforcement is not present among professional philosophers, the fact is that increasing attention has been given in recent years to the role of cultural[2] factors in philosophical investigation. The conviction is regularly expressed these days that philosophers have not always been critically self-conscious about the cultural factors which have influenced their deliberations and formulations. This conviction has come to be expressed in at least two different ways. Some philosophers have explicitly charged that the profession is guilty of reflecting and reinforcing significant cultural biases in the manner in which philosophical inquiry has been pursued. This case has been made in North America especially by feminist and black philosophers, who have argued at special conferences and professional caucuses, as well as in newsletters and journals devoted to such discussions, that significant gender and racial biases have been manifest in both the organization and the content of professional philosophical discussion. On these accounts, Western philosophical reflection has not only been shaped by, it has also served to reinforce, racist and patriarchal cultural patterns.

A second way in which the conviction has been expressed has not been by overt accusation, but by a shift of focus in many areas of philosophical discussion, a shift which seems to be based on an implicit acknowledgement that correctives are needed with regard to the cultural awareness of philosophers. For example, evidence of a shift of this sort can be observed—or so it seems to me—by comparing the way in which ethical issues were treated by philosophers twenty years ago with the way in which ethical discussion is conducted today. In the 1950s and '60s many Anglo-American moral philosophers were very interested in demonstrating the "objectivity" of moral standards. When discussing these theses associated with the doctrine of ethical relativism many philosophers slid rather quickly over the actual substance of ethical diversity. They would admit that such diversity exists, but they would move on rather rapidly to the insistence that whatever the intricacies of ethical diversity, and whatever the plurality of cultural patterns and institutions to which this ethical diversity is undoubtedly related, there is nothing in this area that compels us to conclude that moral standards must be viewed in terms of an ultimate ethical relativism.

The fact is, though, that when we now examine many of the major contributions of Anglo-American philosophers to the "meta-ethical" explorations of two decades or so ago, it seems quite obvious that people like Hare and Toulmin and Baier and Nowell-Smith were clearly committed to accounts which were essentially relativistic in nature. Yet those writers often seemed embarrassed about—or at least, eager to minimize the significance of—the relativistic implications of their theories; typically they insisted that while certain kinds of ethical disputes are, of course, ultimately irresolvable, we ought to consider such resistant cases to be on the periphery—the "fanatical" fringe—of ethical discussion.

Today the mood seems to have changed. For one thing, Anglo-American ethicists seem much more interested in the detailed comparative study of diverse ethical-cultural systems; for example, rather than simply tossing out unexamined references to cannibalism or polygamy, they seem to sense some obligation to describe the network of cultural practices and beliefs out of which the ethical endorsement of such activities arises. Furthermore, philosophers seem much less reluctant today to promulgate straightforwardly relativistic accounts in ethics. And even where there remains a commitment to viewing ethical disagreements as in principle decidable, there is a sensitivity to the cultural and cross-cultural contexts of those disagreements. For example, Alasdair MacIntyre, who has certainly made it clear that he believes that it is possible to adjudicate rationally between competing moral claims and systems, nonetheless insists—unlike the pretenders to "objectivity" of the 1950s and '60s—that each "moral philosophy has some particular sociology as its counterpart," so that we cannot assess a morality apart from the cultural practices in which it is embedded. Practices in turn, according to MacIntyre, have histories; people are moral only in the context of social roles and traditions.³ MacIntyre is suggesting, in effect, that the proper rational adjudication of competing moral systems will require a rational adjudication with regard to the cultures in which those moral systems of thought are embedded.

An interest in cross-cultural issues also shows up quite explicitly in the current practice of the philosophy of science. The Kuhnian discussion of different natural scientific paradigms within the Western tradition has evolved into a much broader post-Kuhnian discussion of what a "science" as such is and of how we are to understand the differences between disparate "sciences," for example, between Western and non-Western sciences.

Similar matters are being attended to in the philosophy of the social sciences. Peter Winch's 1958 book, *The Idea of a Social Science*, seems to have been a major stimulant for placing the data of cultural anthropology closer to center stage in the philosophy of the social sciences. In 1970 an important collection of essays was published, entitled *Rationality*, in which philosophers, sociologists, and anthropologists discussed matters relating to the question of whether claims regarding the existence of cross-culturally binding norms of rationality can be sustained in the light of a recognition of the actual facts of cultural diversity.⁴ This broad-ranging discussion has been continued by many of the same participants in a more recent collection, *Rationality and Relativism*.⁵ The essays in both of these volumes are heavily laced with the detailed references to such things as the religion of the Dinka, the political systems of the Burma highlands, and beliefs of cargo cults, Zande magic, and the like.

In all this attention to the facts of cultural diversity on the part of philosophers there are at least two general issues that are being raised. The first is the degree to which philosophers must attend to this cultural diversity if they are to do a more adequate job of accounting for the general subject matter which they are purporting to explain as philosophers. Some philosophers are asking whether they have been limited in the past in their ability to offer proper explanations of ethical decision-making, aesthetic pursuits, or religious convictions, or even the nature of knowledge and belief, by their failure to investigate the diverse cultural contexts in which these phenomena are rooted.

The second issue is the degree to which philosophers have been negatively affected, not only by inadequate attention to the cultural complexity of the phenomena which they study, but also by a blindness to the ways in which their own perspectives on these phenomena have been distorted by cultural bias. In short, people are asking whether there are ways in which philosophical explanations themselves have been products of, or strongly influenced by, the cultural situatedness of the philosophers who have offered those explanations.

I have already alluded to many more issues than I could possibly discuss adequately in this paper. But it is not my present concern to raise specific issues for the purpose of proposing philosophical solutions. I am more interested here in exhortation than I am in argumentation. My intention is to offer a homily of sorts about the business of thinking cross-culturally in a Christian philosophical context. Like most homilies, my efforts here will include little if anything that is new or startling. Instead I will point to some matters that are already on the agenda of Christian philosophical discussion with the aim of encouraging Christian philosophers to deal with these issues in more sensitive and creative ways.

The first of my three homiletical points has to do with the continuity between the discussion of cross-cultural matters and conversations to which Christian philosophers are already committed. There is a sense in which a conscious wrestling with the phenomenon of cultural differences is a legitimate extension of the philosophical dialogue. Philosophers have long been fascinated with the fact of human disagreement. This fascination is not the only force that impels philosophical investigation; some philosophers have been energized by a focus on practical moral commitments, others have been moved by a deep desire to get clear about ontology, and still others have begun their deliberations with a fascination with questions about human nature. But an interest in noetic disagreement has certainly been one of the important energizing forces. Many of the most ambitious philosophical programs can be legitimately viewed as sustained attempts to demonstrate how seemingly fundamental disagreements can be dissolved. Much philosophical energy has been spent formulating the ways in which ethical or aesthetic or religious or scientific, or even philosophical, differences can be ultimately adjudicated. To focus specifically on the cultural rootedness of various sorts of human disagreements is, in an important sense, more of the same.

It is also more of the same for Christian philosophers in particular. The fascination with seemingly basic human disagreement, and with the possibilities of adjudicating such matters, has certainly been a central impulse in the doing of Christian philosophy. In both the Roman Catholic and the Reformed communities—the two Western traditions in which the idea of a "Christian philosophy" has been most firmly rooted—the concern with what we might think of as the epistemology of conflicting belief-systems has been a very prominent theme.

Indeed, for Calvinistic philosophers the interest in this theme has been almost an obsession—and understandably so, since it brings into focus an unavoidable tension in Reformed thought. Calvinism offers a very stark portrayal of the human sinful condition; the Reformed soteriological emphasis on God's sovereign control over the whole process whereby human beings are graciously reconciled to God must be seen against the backdrop of Calvinism's insistence that depraved human creatures are totally incapable of initiating, or contributing anything interesting to, the basic salvific process.

Once Calvinism has gotten started with this kind of negative assessment of fallen human abilities, any hint in the direction of modifying this assessment, by attributing, say, some sort of positive cognitive or volitional abilities to depraved human beings, will need special explaining. And the fact is that Calvinists have regularly gone out of their way to provide such explanations. These efforts have been necessitated by the fact that there is a significant line of Calvinists who have refused to deny the positive contributions of non-Christian thought. Calvin himself stands first in this line: his gloomy portraits of the reprobate mind stand side-by-side with appreciative references to the pagan scholars from whom he had learned so much as a student of rhetoric. Calvin explicitly appeals to Cicero's authority, for example, dozens of times in the *Institutes*.

Roman Catholics, whose portrayal of the "natural mind" is less gloomy that the initial Calvinist depiction, have not had to work on these epistemological issues with the same sense of urgency that has attended Calvinist epistemology. But they have, nonetheless, devoted much attention to such matters. One of the ways in which this interest has appeared on the agenda of twentieth-century Catholic thought is in the discussion, especially intense a few decades ago, of the idea of a "perennial philosophy." Roman Catholic philosophers disagreed among themselves over what sorts of philosophical positions were supposed to be reconciled within the framework of such a philosophy. But in the course of spelling out their differences they managed to develop a number of useful suggestions—as James Collins showed in his landmark essay on this topic[6]—for dealing with the fact of philosophical plurality as it shows up both within the Christian community and between Christian and non-Christian systems of thought.

At least two prominent communities of Christian philosophers, then, Roman Catholic and Reformed, seem to share a consensus regarding the importance of investigating the sources of seemingly basic or foundational human disagreements—even if that consensus has often expressed itself in the form of a passionate debate over the various accounts given within these communities regarding the noetic effects of sin. Attention to the ways in which cultural factors can block efforts at reconciling noetic differences among human beings seems to be a legitimate extension of this long-standing Christian philosophical interest in the epistemology of conflicting belief-systems.

Christian epistemological discussion, at least in these Roman Catholic and Reformed manifestations, has never been very far removed from an interest in communicating the Gospel. This interest is barely concealed in the discussions of a possible "common ground" between believer and non-believer conducted by both Aquinas and Calvin, as well as by Maritain and Barth—and even by McInerny and Plantinga, for that matter. The need for addressing such issues, which have a direct bearing on the communication of the Gospel, with a conscious focus on cultural factors has become a very urgent one today. To begin doing so we need to expend virtually no effort in translating the terms of the discussion into philosophical categories. That is already being done by the non-philosophers. When the psychologist Carol Gilligan argues that women experience moral dilemmas differently than men, because women experience selfhood and interpersonal relationships in a very different way than their masculine counterparts,[7] the issues have already been formulated in overtly epistemological and metaphysical terms. Much the same holds for anthropological accounts of the differences between the Siberian shaman's understanding of causality and that of the MIT physicist.

Translation into philosophical terms has often taken place, then, even before the questions are handed over to philosophers. But translation into the terms of Christian philosophical discourse—whose terms are shaped by a desire to promote understanding between human beings who bear the same divine image and who share in a common rebellion before the face of the one true God—will sometimes require considerable effort. Nevertheless the task is worthwhile, even urgent. And it is, to repeat, a task that has links to a long tradition of Christian philosophical discussion.

My second point has to do with the expectations that we bring to our cross-cultural explorations. It seems to me that Christians must approach these matters with both a confidence that there will be some sort of final resolution of the puzzles posed by culturally-rooted differences and a willingness to live with the fact of seemingly incommensurate perspectives for the time being.

Something like the conjunction of attitudes I am prescribing here is advocated by Richard Bernstein in his book, *Beyond Objectivism and Relativism*. Bernstein's title captures the spirit of his project: he wants us to hold out for something that goes beyond the acceptance of relativism, but he also wants us to spurn an easy objectivism. At first glance it might seem that Bernstein is engaged here in a futile attempt to avoid an unavoidable choice. How can there be an alternative to both objectivism and relativism? Either there are objective standards with reference to which human disagreements can be ultimately decided or dissolved, or there are not. Can one avoid choosing?

The trick that Bernstein employs in order to avoid the choice is his somewhat eccentric definition of "objectivism," by which he means "the basic conviction that there is or must be some permanent, ahistorical matrix or framework to which we can ultimately appeal in determining the nature of rationality, knowledge, truth, goodness, or rightness."[8] The key words here are "permanent" and "ahistorical." Bernstein does seem to believe in the ultimate decidability of what now appears to be incommensurable claims or perspectives. But he also believes that the norms or processes which will make sure resolutions possible are not presently in our possession. Thus, if by "objectivism" one means that there are presently, say, supra-cultural norms which can aid us in deciding cross-cultural disputes, then Bernstein is not an objectivist. But neither is he willing to embrace a relativism that insists that we will never possess the means for rationally deciding such matters.

I want to suggest that Christians should have some sympathies with Bernstein in his attempt to look for an alternative to both objectivism and relativism, as he delineates those positions. But I also thing that we must reject the Hegelianism of Bernstein's proposed alternative.

Strictly speaking, Bernstein does not talk so much of norms or standards that will someday develop, for the purpose of adjudicating seemingly basic disagreements, as he does of the creation of "those forms of communal life in which dialogue, conversation, *phronesis*, practical discourse, and judgment are concretely embodied in our every day practices"[9]; pursuing hints that he finds in Gadamer, Habermas, Rorty, and Arendt, he sees forces at work in history which can eventually form "dialogical communities that embrace all of humanity"[10]—communities wherein presently undecidable issues will be capable of resolution. Indeed, while in one sense there is, Bernstein insists, no inevitability about the appearance of such communities—the whole business could be sidetracked, for example, by nuclear annihilation—these communities of rational solidarity constitute "a *telos* deeply rooted in our human project."[11]

Christian theists will, I think, want to operate with a somewhat different overall scheme. If there is a God who is not himself involved in any process of epistemic growth, then presumably there already is and always has been an existing point of view from which seemingly basic disagreements can be rationally adjudicated. It seems safe to assume that the Christian God can already decide between, say, the explanations of Western science and those of Zande witchcraft; or, if those explanatory schemes must somehow be synthesized, then God has already done the synthesizing.

But if we think in terms of human access to the sorts of resolutions which God presently knows about, then presumably our expectation—if not our substantive doctrines—will be something like Bernstein's. Human beings will eventually be able to decide together between what presently appear to be basic differences because God will guide people toward, or reveal to them, the correct solutions.

There are even Christian grounds for formulating the case, as does Bernstein, in terms of "dialogical communities that embrace all of humanity." Biblical writings such as the books of Isaiah and Revelation place a strong emphasis on the ultimate formations of an eschatological community that is drawn from every tribe, tongue, people, and nation, in which will be displayed the cultural "wealth" and "glory" of the peoples of the earth (cf. Isa. 2:2-4, 25:6-10, 60:1-14; Rev. 5:9-10, 21:22-26). The Bible gives us good reasons for thinking that the present age is a time when God is preparing the world—in a very central way by the formation of a multi-national, multi-ethnic church—for the eschatological "gathering in" of the cultural gifts which have been distributed among the nations. Participation in cultural dialogue, then, can rightly be viewed as a very important Christian calling, even if that dialogue is frustrated in the present by what seems to be basic and unresolvable misunderstandings.

Again, our expectations, and the confidence that we can manifest in the seemingly fruitless dialogues that often occur, will have some resemblance to those which Bernstein nurtures. But this does not mean that the final consensus which Christians hope for will display the same sort of mix required by a Hegelian synthesis.

Alasdair MacIntyre is correct when he criticizes Bernstein's Hegelian formulations by insisting that there is often an "either/or of incommensurability" among conflicting points of view—and this certainly seems to be so in the face-off between diverse cultural perspectives—which "stubbornly resists dissolution into Bernstein's synthetic both/and."[12] But this doesn't mean, MacIntyre insists, that dialogue between stubbornly resistant positions is completely futile. Each point of view will bring to the encounter a history of "bafflement in the face of its own problems—some greater or lesser degree of failure" at dealing with matters which fall within its explanatory compass.[13] If the argument is pushed far enough, "it may be that one of the contending bodies of theory will turn out to afford possibilities of understanding both of the achievements and the limitations of its rival(s)—achievements and limitations, that is, judged by the standards of that rival—which that rival body of theory cannot provide either concerning itself or concerning its theoretical opponents."[14] Such cases show, on MacIntyre's account, that it makes sense to call a theory "rationally superior" when it "supplies the resources for writing a more adequate history both of its rivals and of itself than those rivals can supply."[15] When this happens MacIntyre thinks that the party providing the more adequate narrative has been vindicated: "the either/or of conflict has not been replaced by the both/and of synthesis; the conflict has been resolved in the exclusive favor of the victor."[16]

There is much that is helpful here, even though MacIntyre need not push so hard for the attainment of "exclusive" victories. Certainly one can acknowledge the existence of a point of view from which such dialogues can be judged, and also refuse to see all resolutions of such conflicts as necessarily taking the form of "both/and synthesis," without thereby insisting on the need to declare one of the contenders the exclusive victor.

There seem to be good Christian reasons for being wary of demanding unconditional surrender in intellectual dialogue—perhaps especially in cross-cultural dialogue. Nevertheless, MacIntyre is right to counter Bernstein's dialecticism with a refusal to impose the "both/and synthesis" format on all acceptable dialogic resolutions. The truth is not to be found by searching for the proper blend of apparent opposites; it is gained by following the arguments where they lead. If it does turn out that there are, at most, very few exclusive victories, this will not be due to some sort of "logic" that is built into the historical dialectic but because of a rather even distribution of finitude and perversity among human creatures. It is the awareness of these facts of the human condition, along with the conviction that while we presently see through a glass darkly we will someday know even as we are known, that should motivate Christians to enter into cross-cultural dialogue with a hope tempered by both patience and humility.

This brings me to my third point, which has to do with the benefits that we can gain from philosophical attention to cross-cultural issues.

At the 1979 World Council of Churches' Conference on Faith, Science and the Future, the Brazilian theologian Rubem Alves began his response to a British scientist's account of the nature of science with this parable:

> Once upon a time a lamb, with a love for objective knowledge, decided to find out the truth about wolves. He had heard so many nasty stories about them. Were they true? He decided to get a first-hand report on the matter. So he wrote a letter to a philosopher-wolf with a simple and direct question: What are wolves? The philosopher-wolf wrote a letter back explaining what wolves were: shapes, sizes, colours, social habits, thought, etc. He thought, however, that it was irrelevant to speak about the wolves' eating habits since these habits, according to his own philosophy, did not belong to the essence of wolves. Well, the lamb was so delighted with the letter that he decided to pay a visit to his new friend, the wolf. And only then he learned that wolves are very fond of barbequed lamb.[17]

Alves uses this parable to illustrate his own contention that Western science likes to account for itself in terms which hide its own eating habits; in this sense the lambs of the Third World understand what science is better than those who get paid to define the task of science. Western science, Alves argues, serves the goals of "the scientific civilization" whose ultimate aim is "the final assimilation of all non-western, non-scientific cultures" into itself—thereby dismissing "as superstitious the beliefs of other peoples, considered primitive."[18]

There are several levels on which this parable can be interpreted. Given the context in which his remarks were presented, it seems obvious that Alves means to suggest that Third World peoples often experience Western science as an exploiting technology rather than as the value-free inquiry of its theorists' formulations. But he puts his case more generally: the scientific attitude is expressive of a larger "civilizing" force that is intent upon assimilating—and in effect destroying—the belief-systems of non-Western cultures.

It is interesting to note here that the issues that Alves is talking about are ones which do not fit easily into the accounts that are often presented of the nature of cross-cultural dialogue. Alves pits "the scientific civilization" against the alleged "superstition" of "primitive" cultures. But the fact is that this way of portraying the conflict is not the same as what is often viewed as the unadorned confrontation between the First World and Third World cultures. For one thing, Alves goes on to use his lamb-wolf distinction in such a way that it also applies within Third World cultural contexts. It is not simply the case that, say, North American based corporations represent the wolf-culture while third world societies represent the lambs. Rather, the ruling class of "primitive" societies can themselves serve as wolves that prey upon the lambs: "If you ask any dictatorial regime to describe itself, the answer will be a marvelous one: nothing more benevolent, nothing more democratic, nothing more committed to the welfare of the people. But if you go to the jails of political prisoners, and ask the same question, the answer will be totally different."[19] Alves is not thinking of Third World or "primitive" cultures as such as the lamb-cultures. Instead, he means to be pitting the wolf-like culture of "scientific civilization," along with its wolfish accomplices in the Third World, against those who participate in what he calls "the culture of oppression."

Alves's discussion is one case where what is presented as a conflict between very different cultural perspectives turns out to be not very different from conflicts that often occur within our cultural conversations. What is at stake is differing ways of assessing the role of science in human culture, and alternative evaluations of a larger notion of a scientific rationality that is so often viewed as a proper framework for living and thinking in a civilized manner.

The kind of Third World perspective which Alves points to can enrich our own understanding of the issues that are at stake when these matters are being debated within our own cultural context. By looking at familiar topics from the unfamiliar viewpoint of those who are immersed in the "culture of oppression" we can become more sensitive to the latent functions and hidden effects of many of our cultural enterprises. In that process, we can gain a better perspective on our own cultural pretensions. In this sense, we have much to learn from perspectives which we can rightly, even as Christians, characterize as "primitive."

There is a stage in early childhood, Piaget tells us, when children are fond of asking "why" questions about physical phenomena, even though they are incapable of grasping causal type explanations as answers to those questions.[20] Thus, when little children ask why trees grow leaves they will often not be satisfied with, or even comprehending of, answers which make reference to the process of photosynthesis or some such thing. Rather, they will be happy to be told that trees grow leaves because they want to look pretty.

Piaget refers to this pattern of explanation as "pre-causality." At a certain point in the development of a child's "egocentric" orientation, the child begins to distinguish between the inner and outer worlds. When that happens the child manifests a tendency toward what Piaget calls "animism"—the investing of inanimate objects with animate characteristics. In the case of the tree, then, the child is insisting on viewing the tree as possessing wants and purposes of a rather social sort. And since it is not appropriate to view trees in this manner, it is a good thing that children proceed to a later stage of cognitive development where, for example, they ascribe animate characteristics only to animate entities and inanimate characteristics only in inanimate things.

Suppose we were to transfer this kind of analysis to the "macro" level, noting that there are "pre-causal" animistic cultures, where the inanimate is invested with animate characteristics, and where cultural agents do not seem ready to understand and utilize the kinds of causal explanations appropriate to cognitively mature cultures. Persons in these cultures may insist, for example, on personifying such objects as stars and planets, trees and flowers, rocks and rills, and so on.

What would be gained philosophically by us if we were to engage in a serious effort to understand such a culture? Is there anything that we can be taught by those whose way of encountering the world is characterized by these animistic patterns?

One thing we might note, in formulating answers to these questions, is that these animistic patterns are not altogether foreign to cultural phenomena that we can observe rather close to home. The occult revival in the suburbs, nativistic movements on university campuses, the rights of animals movement, Star-trek type fascination with the possibility of human-like on other planets—all of these smack, whatever may be our specific epistemic relation to any one of these phenomena, of an approximation to the immersion in "precausal" perspectives as characterized by Piaget, a perspective in which the lines between physical causality and personal motivation are blurred.

But it would be wrong to use Piaget's categories simply to condemn all of these matters out of hand. The claim, for example, that the positions of stars and planets can have a kind of purposive effect on human decision and destiny need not simply be taken as a regression to "precausality." It will turn out to be so only if commitments to astrological beliefs are formed without first separating the diversity of possible answers to the various kinds of "why" questions which Piaget distinguishes.

Suppose the Committee on the Scientific Investigation of the Paranormal, as part of their debunking efforts, sets out to show that there are no recognizable correlations between, say, personality type and the stellar configuration at the time of a person's birth. But suppose, instead, the study turns up evidence for some kind of correlation. I have no vested interest in promoting the thought that his might be the case. Quite the contrary. But it does seem to me wrong to dismiss claims that seem out of place in a "high-tech" culture simply on the ground that they fit well with a highly "personified" view of the natural order.

It may be, then, that we can learn something from so-called "primitive" cultures by allowing them to suggest for our consideration ways of viewing reality which, considered simply as manifestations of a pre-causal orientation may be immature, but may nonetheless turn out to be worthy of, as it were, post-causal consideration on the part of those who have carefully sifted all the relevant factors. To consider these "primitive" proposals as being worthy of our adult consideration may indeed be an important philosophical service to our own culture.

My line of defense here may still seem a little too condescending toward the perspectives on whose behalf I am pleading. And that may be a legitimate impression. Basically, I am asking that "their" beliefs be subjected to "our" kind of sifting and weighing, which may still betray a strong bias in favor of the habits of thought that are so closely associated with Western "modernity."

If so, then perhaps a bias of this sort is nonetheless a healthy precaution. There are any number of perspectives being marketed today which advocate a return to the naiveté of the child as a means of salvation. When these proposals require that we achieve this perspective by a kind of individual or collective amnesia—by means of, say, either a micro- or a macro- "primal scream"—then they are, I think, worthy of our resistance. But there are other proposals according to which the cultivation of a perspective like that of a child, or of a sensitivity to those kinds of explanatory factors to which children are especially attuned, is to be achieved only by means of a great effort, an effort which presupposes in an important sense the characteristics of adult maturity. When this is what is being proposed, then the call is not so much to childishness as to childlikeness.

The distinction between childishness and childlikeness has a long and honorable history. It is written that we must put away childish things. But it is also written that if we are willing to become as little children, then we will see the kingdom of heaven. For those of us who take this latter promise to be an important piece of good news, the philosophical pursuit of cross-cultural dialogue—even dialogue with the most "primitive" of cultures—will be a matter of more than intellectual significance.

The issues just discussed reinforce an earlier point. Christian thinkers should be wary of the kind of ethnocentrism that assumes that in cross-cultural dialogue a specific cultural perspective will be systematically vindicated. In this sense, MacIntyre's linking of the requirements of rationality to the attempt to tell an adequate story about the bafflements and failures associated with one's own perspective in relation to rival perspectives is an extremely helpful notion—even though he does not fully develop its potential as an instrument of cultural self-examination.

Surely those of us whose job it is to think carefully about the claims to rationality in the Western philosophical tradition cannot fail to acknowledge, if we take an honest look, that those claims have often been intimately related to projects of cultural and spiritual vanity and self-deception—to say nothing of cross-cultural exploitation. As Christians we certainly should be ready to admit these things. And once we have done so, we will never be able to settle for any story of Western rationality that is not honest about our own cultural and philosophical unrighteousness. That story must include, after all, the letters we philosophers have written to lambs about what it means to be wolves. If for no other reason, then, we desperately need cross-cultural dialogue as a means of forcing a kind of philosophical "hermeneutics of suspicion" upon ourselves so that we can get ready for that long-awaited "dialogical community" that will indeed "embrace all of humanity" by attempting here and now to construct a truthful narrative of our own past and present philosophical endeavors.

Notes

1. This essay first appeared in *CSR* 17.2 (December 1987): 109-21.
2. I am using "cultural" here to refer to the beliefs, valuing, customs, rituals, and the like, with reference to which a group organizes and integrates its patterns of social interaction. Such things as race, gender, and political-economic status can function, then, as "cultural" factors; it makes sense, for example, to speak of cultural patterns that are racist or patriarchal or oligarchal.
3. *After Virtue: A Study in Moral Theory* (Notre Dame, Ind.: University of Notre Dame Press, 1981), ch.14; see also MacIntyre's "Bernstein's Distorting Mirrors: a Rejoinder," *Soundings* 67. 1 (Spring 1984): 30-41.
4. *Rationality*, edited by Bryan R. Wilson (Oxford: Basil Blackwell, 1970).
5. *Rationality and Relativism*, edited by Martin Hollis and Steven Lukes (Oxford: Basil Blackwell, 1982).
6. "The Problem of a Perennial Philosophy," in James Collins, *Three Paths in Philosophy* (Chicago: Henry Regnery Co., 1962), 255-279.
7. Carol Gilligan, *In a Different Voice: Psychological Theory and Women's Development* (Cambridge: Harvard University Press, 1982).
8. *Beyond Objectivism and Relativism: Science, Hermeneutics, and Praxis* (Philadelphia: University of Pennsylvania Press, 1983), 8.
9. Ibid., 229.
10. Ibid., 231.
11. Ibid.
12. "Bernstein's Distorting Mirrors," 32-33.
13. Ibid., 31.
14. Ibid., 31-32.
15. Ibid., 32.
16. Ibid.
17. "On the Eating Habits of Science: A Response," *Faith and Science in an Unjust World: Report of the World Council of Churches' Conference on Faith, Science and the Future*, Volume 1, edited by Roger L. Shinn (Philadelphia: Fortress Press, 1980), 41.
18. Ibid., 42.
19. Ibid., 43.
20. *The Child's Conception of the World* (Totowa, N.J.: Littlefield Adams and Co., 1965), 169-193.

15 Psychology's "Two Cultures"
A Christian Analysis (1988)

Mary Stewart Van Leeuwen

Psychologists in the Anglo-American tradition suffer from an ironic but seldom-admitted schizophrenia.[1] While claiming progressively greater success in exposing hidden influences on the behavior of their clients and subjects, most have assumed that their own theories and methods can in principle be laundered of any personal, social, or metaphysical agenda to which psychologists themselves might privately adhere.[2] There have been historical exceptions to this mentality, of course, the chief of which originated with Freud, who (whatever one may think of his biologically reductionist anthropology) understood only too well that the unanalyzed analyst was in danger of muddying, rather than clarifying the therapeutic waters by the operation of his or her own defense mechanisms when confronting patients whose problems struck too close to home. But in general, as a psychologist of Catholic background once put it, "the average psychologist seldom applies his technical knowledge to himself; ostensibly his is the only immaculate perception."[3]

Self-examination, then, has not been a strong point throughout most of psychology's century-long history as a formalized discipline. But even outside the clinical tradition there has been at least one forum in North America in which questions about paradigms, politics, and even (although more rarely) metaphysics have regularly surfaced. I refer to the pages of the *American Psychologist,* the official monthly organ of the American Psychological Association, now approaching a half-century of continuous publication. In addition to reports of an empirical or theoretical nature, the *American Psychologist* has a tradition of publishing articles of a "metapsychological" sort—ones in which the paradigmatic *status quo* is not simply taken for granted and elaborated, but examined critically. For this paper I have examined a number of articles of the metapsychological sort published in the *American Psychologist* over the past ten years. From these, and from related writings in psychology and its cognate disciplines, the following three points will be developed:

1) Both theoretically and methodologically, Anglo-American psychology is the uneasy home of two competing and progressively more evenly matched

"cultures," the first positivist and scientistic, the second post-positivist and humanistic. There are subcultural themes within each culture which vary across time and constituency, but the broad contours of each and the gulf that separates the two can be clearly documented, as can the strengths and weaknesses of each.

2) Christian psychologists can be found in both cultures, and in each case can give plausible reasons for maintaining that their preferred camp is where thoughtful Christians should cast their lot.

3) Christians now choosing sides in this debate should consider the possibility of a "third way," one in which their control beliefs enable them to steer a fine line between reductionism and self-deification in psychological anthropology, and between positivism and skepticism in psychological epistemology. Whether Christians have the wit or the will to develop such a position (let alone have it accepted by the discipline at large) is, or course, another story.

I begin with a pair of companion articles which appeared in the *American Psychologist* in 1984. The first, by one of American psychology's elder statesmen, Gregory Kimble of Duke University, was entitled "Psychology's Two Cultures."[4] The second, co-authored by Leonard Krasner and Arthur Houts (from state universities in New York and Tennessee respectively), was "A Study of the 'Value' Systems of Behavioral Scientists."[5] In recent years the *American Psychologist* has published several attempts to analyze competing value systems within its constituency,[6] but these two are unique in attempting systematically empirical, as opposed to anecdotal, accounts of these subcultures. That the journal chose to publish two such studies side by side may be seen as a reassertion of empiricist values on the part of the editors, a concession to the growing literature critical of value-free conceptions of science, or possibly both.[7]

Kimble takes his cue from C. P. Snow's 1959 lecture on "The Two Cultures and the Scientific Revolution," in which, as a practitioner of both the sciences and the humanities, Snow deplored the gap in methods, values, and conceptual language that increasingly seemed to be separating these two major branches of Western culture.[8] "In psychology," Kimble asserts, "these conflicting cultures exist within a single field, and those who hold opposing values are currently engaged in a bitter family feud."[9] Armed with past analyses of these value conflicts, Kimble developed what he called the "Epistemic Differential"—a scale in which each of twelve discipline-related value issues is represented in bipolar form. Respondents rank themselves, on a scale of 1 to 10, with regard to their position on each issue—for example, scientific vs. humanistic values as motivators of scholarship, belief in the determinism vs. indeterminism of behavior, nature vs. nurture as the predominant shaper of human behavior, and objectivity vs. empathy as the best means of understanding behavior.

Kimble's responding samples were of three kinds: first, a group of undergraduate students with no previous training in psychology; second, a sample of over half the officers of the various divisions of the American Psychological Association (A.P.A.),[10] and third, members of the A.P.A. who belonged to only one of four divisions of the Association: Division 3 (Experimental), Division 9 (The Society for the Psychological Study of Social Issues), Division 29 (Psychotherapy), or Division 32 (Humanistic). His scoring procedure allowed a total item score to be assigned to each respondent, from -12 (the most extreme "scientistic" position) to + 12 (the most extreme "humanistic").[11] Results for the first two groups (heterogeneous samples of pre-psychology students and A.P.A. officers) showed a roughly normal distribution of scores, with the means in each case very close to the center—that is, showing no clear evidence for the "two cultures" phenomenon.

But once psychologists have sorted themselves into specific A.P.A. interest groups, the picture changes dramatically. Factor analysis of these scores isolated six scale items that could be referred to as the "scientist-humanist cluster."[12] On everyone of these, members of A.P.A. Division 3 (Experimental) had mean scores in the most extreme scientistic direction. Differences among the other three divisions, while still significant, were generally less pronounced, but all three groups were clearly more committed to the humanistic end of the continuum, with average scores in the predicted order: Division 9 psychologists were the most moderate humanizers, and Division 32 the most extreme. The "two cultures" phenomenon in psychology, Kimble concludes, "comes about as the result of a birds-of-a feather phenomenon. People with biases in either the humanist or scientist direction find their way into organizations where these values are dominant. Once they are there a process of socialization takes over. The biases that made the organization attractive in the first place are nurtured and strengthened. In short, the dual processes of selection and emphasis . . . are the bases for psychology's two cultures."[13]

Kimble's data also show that there are very few psychologists totally committed to one extreme or the other. Nevertheless, he affirms the general existence of the "two cultures" in psychology, and notes that "in the very same debate, one group may speak vehemently on points that the other group takes as trivial, or they talk at cross purposes. None of this will come as news to anyone who has attended a session of the A.P.A. council of representatives, or participated in a departmental faculty meeting."[14]

The companion study by Krasner and Houts is simpler in its sampling strategy, but more complex in its measures of values. It compared a sample of psychologists strongly associated with the development of the behavior modification movement[15] with a sample of randomly selected psychologists not identified with that movement, and asked members of each group to complete not one, but three different "values" scales. The first of these, a "Theoretical Orientation Survey," originally developed and used elsewhere, was designed to assess disciplinary commitments according to dimensions quite similar to those used in Kimble's study. The other two scales, designed for this particular study, included an "Epistemological Style Questionnaire" to assess degree of adherence to each of three different scientific "styles"—empiricism, rationalism, and metaphorism—and a 67-item "Values Survey" to assess respondents' views on a wider variety of issues (e.g., degree of ethical constraint appropriate in science, of government involvement in the economy and social services, of science in the solution of environmental and social problems, degree of adherence to a social Darwinist vs. an altruistic social philosophy, and to a theistic vs. an atheistic worldview).[16]

On the first two scales (assessing discipline-related assumptions) the two groups showed, if anything, even clearer differences than occurred in the Kimble study. Compared to the group of randomly selected, non-behavioral psychologists, those associated with the behavior modification movement were more anti-theoretical, less convinced of the existence of free will, more tied to purely quantitative and behavioral (as opposed to qualitative and self-report) data, more physically reductionistic in their view of human beings, less accepting of the use of metaphor in theorizing, and more convinced that value-free induction was possible in the conduct of psychological research.

On the third, more wide-ranging, "Value Survey Scale" there were no significant differences between the two groups on any of the issues polled: on the average, behavioral and non-behavioral psychologists leaned equally towards the view that science should be about facts not values, yet mixed this with a strong sense of research ethics and a moderate sense of social responsibility regarding the application of research findings. Both groups leaned equally (although not militantly) towards atheism rather than theism as a worldview, shunned social Darwinism while sharing a moderately conservative political philosophy, and were moderately against environmentalist legislation even though they supported more government control of health care delivery.

This second study thus supports the "two cultures" hypothesis regarding discipline-specific values, but not the idea that these two cultures might be paralleled by ideological polarization in other areas. Nevertheless, when the authors pooled the data for both groups and looked for certain inter-item correlations among the various scales, some weak yet significant relationships emerged between discipline-specific and other values:

> Subjects [behavioral or non-behavioral] who endorsed freedom of inquiry as opposed to ethical constraints on research, and who favored social Darwinism as opposed to social altruism also favored behavioral as opposed to experiential content emphasis within psychology. Subjects who endorsed the view that science is value-neutral also favored physiological reductionism and quantitative as opposed to qualitative methods in psychology. In contrast, subjects who endorsed the view that science is value-laden favored an intuitive approach to science.[17]

To the Christian analyst, perhaps the most intriguing aspect of these studies is not so much what does differentiate the "two cultures" in psychology as the failure of the theism/atheism dimension to enter into the picture at all. According to the second of these studies, theism and atheism are no differently distributed among behavioral and non-behavioral psychologists and, moreover, there is no significant correlation between strength of theistic beliefs on the one hand and patterns of either disciplinary or social values on the other. To a consideration of this point I will return, but for the moment let us consider some reactions to this pair of "two cultures" studies from later issues of the *American Psychologist*. Interestingly, none of the published responses endorsed the positivistic status quo which dominates academic psychology—perhaps because that which is in ascendancy generates no sense of defensiveness in its adherents. Actual reactions ranged from pleas for methodological reform to those calling for the wholesale replacement of the traditionally positivist paradigm by a post-positivist one emphasizing the sociology—and even the politics—of psychological knowledge.

According to the latter, psychology is as much about values as it is about objective facts. Moreover, psychological theorizing reflects the disguised ideology of its creators in ways that these two studies barely began to tap. Social psychologist Rhoda Unger reported her own research indicating that both socioeconomic background and political allegiance are strongly correlated with psychologists' position on the nature/nurture controversy. More specifically, psychologists from economically privileged backgrounds and/or of conservative political views were much more apt to endorse statements such as "Science has underestimated the extent to which genes affect human behavior"; "Most sex differences have an evolutionary purpose"; "Biological sex, sex role, and sexual preference are highly related to each other in normal people"; and "A great deal can be learned about human behavior by studying animals."[18] The apparent connection between political conservatism and allegiance to a more biologically determinist theory of human nature is particularly worrisome to feminist psychologists, because, in Unger's words, "[it] may account for the consistent reappearance of biology in controversies involving the empowerment of formerly disenfranchised groups. The assumption of whether a racial or sexual entity is a biological or a social group is fundamental to both political and scientific paradigms. Thus, a shift from the biological position (the study of sex differences) to a social position (the examination of gender) was a necessary step in the development of a new psychology of women."[19]

But it is not only feminist social psychologists who advocate the politicization of psychology in a more leftist direction. In an earlier *American Psychologist* article titled "Cognitive Psychology as Ideology," Clark University's Edward Sampson argued that current cognitive theory, by emphasizing the mental structures and operations of the individual, "represents a set of values and interests that reproduce and reaffirm the existing nature of the social order."[20] Taking his cue from the Frankfurt critical theorists, Sampson asserted that cognitive psychologists such as Piaget take the existing object and social worlds as given, and concentrate only on how the individual person schematizes and performs mental operations on these. In doing so, they fail to see how the existing social order may actually influence what persons take to be "given" and "immutable."

Far from wanting to remedy this situation by reasserting objectivist ideals, Sampson recommended "a critical study of psychology *and* society, a study that is self-conscious about its context [and] its values ... In this we would no longer spend our time describing what is, thereby participating in its reproduction; our aims would be more transformative, designed to increase human welfare and freedom. Of necessity, this would require a transformation of society."[21] Thus to Sampson (as to Unger) the problem is not so much that psychology is politicized as the fact that a) it has a tradition of denying its political assumptions by dressing them up in "scientific" language, and b) the political assumptions it does have are hierarchical and privilege maintaining, rather than egalitarian, in their underlying intent. But while this position may be something of an improvement on the attempt to have one's positivist cake and eat it too, its adherents offer no clear reasons (other than phrases such as "It seems a worthy role for the field"[22]) as to why the implicitly rightist agenda in psychology should be replaced by an explicitly leftist one.

A more radical variation on this same theme is the movement social psychologist Kenneth Gergen labels "social constructionism."[23] Strong on the sociology of knowledge thesis, Gergen rejects the possibility of mapping social reality in a historically decontextualized manner and comes close to defining scientific "truth" purely in terms of professional consensus at a given point in time. He believes, with Unger and Sampson, that psychology should consciously espouse an advocacy role on the side of the weak and disenfranchised. To this end, he would abandon the attempt to establish transtemporal laws of social interaction using the hypothetico-deductive approach, concentrating instead on the development of bold, general theories whose persuasive value alone might provoke social reform. But as with Sampson, although one may approve of Gergen's concern to make the value-base of psychology more explicit, it is not clear how he can simultaneously promote epistemological relativism and a particular ethical agenda, however laudable the latter may seem.[24]

Moreover, those committed to the more traditional combination of positivist epistemology and evolutionist anthropology have not taken the post-positivist challenge lying down. While conceding that they may previously have overestimated the continuity between human and animal learning, underestimated the complexity of the human mind, and paid too little attention to the ethical aspects of their research, these traditionalists offer paradigms for psychology that remain unremittingly naturalistic and scientistic. For example, in a 1981 *American Psychologist* article, Arthur Staats proposed to unify psychological theory around a "social behaviorist" paradigm which acknowledges reciprocal causality between the person and the environment; in the end, however, the person is still reduced to a product of the environment (now both internal and external, immediate and historical) with the result that such attempts never get beyond a "soft determinist" view of personhood.[25]

Bolder still are attempts to combine a soft-determinist anthropology with an epistemology which views scientific accounts of persons, at least in principle, as both ultimate and complete—even to the point of providing a moral framework. Such attempts hearken back to B. F. Skinner's "experimental ethics,"[26] but with a new, physiologically reductionist twist about which Skinner could merely conjecture wistfully. For example, the well-known neuroscientist Roger Sperry published in the 1977 *American Psychologist* his "unifying view of mind and brain." This was based on his theory that the mind, while not a separate substance from the brain, emerges from the brain to function as a non-reducible, causally powerful entity which can then affect the natural world from which it originally evolved. It is not Sperry's emergentism per se that is troubling; indeed, at least one philosopher has argued that such a position on the mind-brain question is compatible with the anthropological dualism of traditional Christian theology.[27] But Sperry goes on to claim that since values are inevitably a part of this emergent-mind complex, and since scientists have expert knowledge about the evolution and functioning of the brain (or at least possess the best methods for knowing progressively more about these) it follows that scientists are in the best position to dictate ultimate human values. In language worthy of both Carl Sagan and pop Eastern mysticism, he concludes his paper as follows:

> In the eyes of science, to put it simply, man's creator becomes the vast interwoven fabric of all evolving nature, a tremendously complex concept that includes all the immutable and emergent forces of cosmic causation that control everything from high-energy subnuclear particles to galaxies, not forgetting the causal properties that govern brains and behavior at individual levels. For all of these, science has gradually become our accepted authority, offering a cosmic scheme that renders most others simplistic by comparison. . . . It follows accordingly on the above terms that what is good, right, or to be valued is defined very broadly to be that which accords with, sustains, and enhances the orderly design of evolving nature. . . . Although man, as part of evolving nature and at the peak of the evolutionary scale, remains the prime consideration, mankind does stand to lose some of the uniqueness and "measure of all things" status accorded in some previous systems. A sense of higher meaning is preserved with a meaningful relation to something deemed more important than the human species taken by itself.[28]

If the above summary reflects the current state of psychology, we may seem reduced to choosing between the epistemological *hubris* of positivists and the moral self-righteousness of post-positivists.[29] Faced with such a choice, Christian psychologists might be forgiven for invoking a plague upon both these houses and starting to build one afresh on their own terms, even as they continue to "plunder the Egyptians" for materials worth preserving from each of these competing structures. In point of fact, however, the emergence of such a "third way" has been very slow to develop, at least among confessing Protestants. Why is this the case, and how, in practice, do most of these psychologists deal with the two competing cultures?

Let us recall the earlier observation that psychologists' position on the theistic-atheistic dimension was unable to predict adherence to either of the two cultures; indeed, it could not predict responses to any single item from the three "values surveys" used in the second of the "two cultures" studies. On reflection, perhaps this is not so surprising. With regard to social values at least, Christians with an equally high view of biblical authority can be pacifists or just war theorists, proponents of minimal or extensive government regulation, free-enterprisers or welfare-statists, and separatist or non-separatist with regard to the larger society. Indeed, one study of self-identified evangelical congressmen in Washington isolated at least four different "religious belief packages," each of which was consistently related to voting patterns running the gamut from extreme political conservatism to extreme liberalism. To come even close to predicting an evangelical congressman's vote (the authors concluded) "you need to know how he interprets his religion, not merely how he labels it."[30]

What is true of Christians in politics is equally true of Christians in psychology. A minority (as in the political sphere) are thoroughgoing separatists, convinced that the Bible is the sufficient and only valid textbook of human behavior.[31] Most, however, have a higher view of common grace, and are prepared to accept theoretical insights which are compatible with Scripture regardless of their origin. Moreover, basic theological differences among evangelicals in psychology appear to be quite minimal, at least as regards the doctrine of persons. None embrace metaphysical determinism, with its total denial of human freedom and moral accountability. Nor do many appear to be "closet humanists" who overemphasize human autonomy to the extent of endorsing narcissistic self-indulgence and/or denying the reality and persistence of sin. (There has, however, been a spate of books—some by Christians with culturally separatist leanings—sounding warnings against other Christians judged to be overly invested in the theories and therapeutic techniques of humanistic psychology.[32])

What does seem to account for the apparently even distribution of Christians across psychology's "two cultures" are differences in theological emphasis combined with one or more other factors. Among applied psychologists, professional context appears to be one such factor. Thus, for example, those working with undersocialized persons (certain types of criminals and substance abusers, overly indulged adolescents from wealthy homes, etc.) may lean heavily on the doctrine of sin, espouse more traditional views of social authority, and make more use of behavioral techniques of a "top-down" variety (e.g., rewards contingent on progressive behavior change, often within a controlled environment). By contrast, those working with oversocialized clients (for example, from abusive, authoritarian, or legalistic homes) are more apt to emphasize the doctrine of grace, the dignity which is part of *imago Dei* and must be valued and cultivated in all persons, and the advocacy role Christians are called to exercise on behalf of socially marginal groups. Their techniques, predictably, are more likely to be drawn from humanistic psychologies, with Rogerian "active listening" and "unconditional positive regard" high on the list. Whether the theological emphases of each group lead to or result from their respective work settings (or both) is a question which merits further investigation.[33]

But among practicing Christians in academic settings, what seems to count is the interaction of theological emphasis with a preferred philosophy of science. By and large Christians seem to agree that worldview considerations do, and should, influence the conduct of psychological research; but they differ regarding the points of the research process at which they believe these considerations may operate. Many (perhaps still the majority among evangelicals) hold that religious convictions should operate only in theory—and hypothesis-construction at the beginning of the research process, and in the practical application of results at the end. With regard to the intermediate steps, however, they still adhere to the belief that the context of theory justification can be made—at least in principle—totally value-free. It is claimed that in psychology, as in other sciences, the best means to this end is the assiduous operationalization and quantification of all variables and, where possible, the design and execution of experiments. Crucial to such a stand is adherence to the "unity of science" thesis—the notion that there is only one method which all genuine sciences employ, and that method consists of giving causal, deterministic explanations which are empirically testable.[34]

How is such an approach justified theologically, especially given the earlier observation that no Christian psychologists appear to embrace metaphysical determinism, with its reduction of personhood to a complex of mechanical responses to internal and external, past and present stimuli? It is justified by publicly rejecting anthropological reductionism in principle while simultaneously adhering to the unity of science thesis—that is, by embracing methodological, but not metaphysical determinism. On this account, the traditional methods of science yield only one "perspective" on human behavior (a deterministic one) to which others (from the humanities, the arts, and religion) must be added to yield a more complete picture. At the same time, however, it is assumed that the mechanical metaphor is the only legitimate one for academic psychologists to use in the study of human behavior—that because psychology threw its lot in with the Newtonian-leaning natural sciences a century ago, there can be no compromising this allegiance today.

Perspectivalists readily concede that the elimination of "bias" (read: "values") in the context of theory justification is a more difficult process in the social than in the natural sciences, because of the complexities that result when human beings study other human beings; indeed, they admit, such methodological purity may never be achieved, and psychologists may perforce have to become more humble about what their efforts can produce in terms of general laws of human behavior. Nevertheless, such purity remains the ideal of all psychologists—Christian or otherwise—committed to the unity of science and the hypothetico-deductive approach. In fact, to at least one Christian perspectivalist adherence to this ideal is part and parcel of concretely visible sanctification. In Donald MacKay's words:

> If we publish results of our investigations, we must strive to "tell it like it is," knowing that the Author is at our elbow, a silent judge of the accuracy with which we claim to describe the world He has created.... If our limitations, both intellectual and moral, predictably limit our achievement of this goal, this is something not to be gloried in, but to be acknowledged in a spirit of repentance. Any idea that it could justify a dismissal of the ideal of value-free knowledge as a "myth" would be as irrational—and as irreligious—as to dismiss the ideal of righteousness as a "myth" on the grounds that we can never perfectly attain that ... [Christians must not] forget that, whatever their difficulties in gaining objective knowledge, they are supposed to be in the loving service of the One to whom Truth is sacred, and carelessness or deliberate bias in stating it is an affront.[35]

But according to some critics, the adherents of this "perspectivalist compromise"[36] are both schizophrenic and falsely modest: the former because they disavow reductionism in principle while preserving it in the practice of the discipline, the latter because they disguise academic imperialism in the cloak of epistemological humility. That is, the perspectivalist readily confesses the problems of using the hypothetico-deductive approach in psychology, while at the same time demanding loyalty to that approach of all who would call themselves true (yea, even properly Christian) psychologists. Moreover, critics add, perspectivalists' adherence to the unity of science thesis carries with it the assumption that explanation in natural science is always deterministic in character, an assumption belied by modern quantum physical theory.[37]

Christian critics of perspectivalism further assert that it sidesteps difficult questions about human nature which it is the responsibility of Christian psychologists to consider. What does it mean that persons are formed in the image of God in a way that accords all human beings the potential for creativity, dominion, and moral responsibility? What does it imply for theory and method in psychology that we are simultaneously "dust of the earth" and imagers of God in a way that separates us from the rest of creation? And why (other than for reasons of historical precedent) do perspectivalists hold that psychologists should try to separate these two aspects of human existence, in effect telling their research respondents to put their transcendent qualities on hold while they are subjected to methods of inquiry originally designed for the study of subhuman phenomena?[38] These are questions to which Christian perspectivalists have given no answers.

Perspectivalists do, however, invoke other theological justifications for a high view of natural science, traditionally conceived. One is the doctrine of creation as espoused by Christians who participated in the formalization of science itself. The Christian worldview of Pascal, Bacon, Newton, Boyle, and many founders of Britain's Royal Society helped make science possible as an independent form of knowledge not beholden to the institutional church, precisely because these men believed in the goodness and the uniformity of God's creation, and in humanity's creational mandate to exercise responsible dominion over the earth. A number of Christian perspectivalists claim to be continuing in this Reformation-based tradition. But at the same time they tend to gloss over the fact that their role-models predate the nineteenth-century emergence of the social sciences, and that the continuity of the latter with natural science is precisely the issue under debate.[39]

Finally, some perspectivalists appeal to another aspect of the doctrine of sanctification—the Christian mandate to serve one's neighbor—as justification for a positivist philosophy of science. Science has so often been the birthplace of technologies which promote human welfare (from split-brain techniques to therapies for traumatic stress) that it seems subject to a kind of "halo effect" in the eyes of Christians whose theology stresses a service-oriented activism. But such a view, however laudable its motive, implicitly reduces science to technology, and explanation to empirical prediction—a view of natural science that its most successful practitioners have routinely rejected.[40] Moreover, it tends to assume that questions of research ethics can be settled on utilitarian grounds alone: as long as one's research is aimed at the greatest good for the greatest number, questions about informed consent, the use of deception, and the infliction of stress are deemed to be secondary. These issues too are often glossed over by perspectivalists.[41]

Dissatisfactions with the perspectivalist compromise can be summarized as follows: perspectivalists not only adhere to the unity of science thesis, but implicitly demand the same adherence of all others who would call themselves social scientists. In doing so, they are not only clinging to an outdated and inaccurate model of how the natural sciences operate, but are additionally producing truncated theories of human functioning by their refusal to consider, at least within the context of their own discipline, any explanations of human behavior other than deterministic ones.

As this debate continues to heat up among Christian psychologists, a paper in the 1985 *American Psychologist* by Notre Dame's George S. Howard deserves mention.[42] Drawing on the work of philosopher of science Ernan McMullin, Howard begins by educating the periodical's readership about the function of epistemic values in the conduct of natural science. Epistemic values are those standards employed by scientists to choose among competing theoretical explanations. At least six such values seem to have been regularly operative in the history of science, including not only predictive accuracy, but simplicity, internal coherence, consistency with other theories, unifying power (the ability to bring together hitherto disparate areas of inquiry), and fruitfulness (the capacity to supply metaphorical resources which help to resolve anomalies and extend the knowledge base).[43] For psychologists still of a positivist bent, "the crucial point of the above analysis is that epistemic values function as values, not as strict rules, to guide the work of science. McMullin, Kuhn, and others demonstrated that theory development in the most mature natural sciences is influenced by the selective application of epistemic criteria. This is, of course, a different picture of the operation of science than a traditional logicist would have chosen to paint."[44]

So far, Howard merely seems to be reinforcing the conclusions of the empirical studies of psychology's "two cultures" described at the beginning of this paper: epistemic values do operate in the context of theory justification in psychology, just as they do in natural science, even though many psychologists (ironically, those who pride themselves in being most "scientific," such as behavioral and experimental psychologists) refuse to acknowledge this. But Howard goes a step beyond affirming psychology's continuity with the rest of science on the basis of its adherence to the same epistemic values. Specifically, he believes that these values may have to be augmented "to the degree necessary to accommodate our subject matter's unique characteristics."[45] Central among those characteristics, Howard points out, is reflexivity, the capacity of persons to "self-reflect," or deliberate about themselves in a given situation, and so gain a measure of autonomy over what might otherwise determine their behavior.

As Howard points out, in science traditionally conceived "the notion of rational objectivity . . . required a lack of reciprocal interaction between observer and object. The scientist was to observe nature, but nature was not to reflect upon itself being observed."[46] There is, of course, a recurrent theme in science fiction about the chemist who sits alone in his laboratory, brooding about what to do with a strange concoction he has produced, when suddenly it occurs to him that the strange concoction is sitting alone in the test-tube brooding about what do with him. But in reality, as far as we know, reflexivity is a privilege (or a problem, depending on one's viewpoint) reserved to human beings: "No quark ever wondered why a physicist wanted to know that. No protein ever changed an attitude or two to curry favor with a biochemist. And no beetle ever told an entomologist to bug off."[47]

To mainstream psychologists, human reflexivity is simply a methodological annoyance—and one which can in principle be overcome by tighter experimental controls: one can keep subjects naive, or even deceived, as to the real purposes of the study, or (tighter still) use such unobtrusive techniques that subjects do not even know that they are being studied. The goal here is to give subjects a handicap in the mutual-observation game, thereby (hopefully) reducing them temporarily to the same level as the "pre-reflexive" entities for which the methods of science were originally designed. Hence the social dynamic between the observer and the observed is implicitly adversarial. Moreover, there is a hermeneutic of suspicion operative: one cannot, according to this approach, ever simply ask respondents to give an account of themselves, because their behavior is actually the product of forces beyond their control and largely beyond their ken.[48]

For Howard, the reality of human reflexivity has first of all an extra-experimental significance: persons are not merely participants in psychological research; they are also consumers of psychological theories. As such, they can, and do, alter their behavior on the basis of what psychologists proclaim. For Howard, "possible examples include individuals who actively resist agreeing with others' opinions ... because of their knowledge of the results of conformity studies. Or perhaps simply informing depressed clients that depressed people tend to be more self-critical would make them more aware of their self-derogatory tendencies and aid them in actually reversing these tendencies."[49] But precisely because public access to the results of psychological research often leads people to "reconstruct" their behavior and self-image accordingly, Howard holds that psychologists have a responsibility not to limit themselves to impoverished models of humanness: by viewing people only as reinforcement maximizers or information processors (for example), psychologists risk becoming "unwitting contributors to a self-fulfilling prophecy wherein humans actually become more like the model."[50]

Thus it may be all very well to argue for the exclusion of non-epistemic values from natural scientific theorizing; but Howard argues that the reality of human reflexivity makes social scientific theorizing an inescapably moral endeavor: because psychological theories are important "mirrors" by means of which people in Western culture "groom" themselves, and because, moreover, such theories are always underdetermined by empirical data, they can be crafted and disseminated in ways that work to people's benefit or detriment. The dominant "man-as-machine" metaphor has been beneficial inasmuch as it has helped to temper justice with mercy in legal decisions regarding the reduced responsibility of brain-damaged persons, or those from an environment so abusive that they are driven to desperate measures to escape it. But the same metaphor has also contributed to a sense of fatalism, "learned helplessness," and a dulled sense of personal accountability in our highly psychologized society. Therefore, Howard concludes, the discipline badly needs innovative theories and methods which will at least supplement, if not replace those which have leaned so heavily on exemplars drawn from the pre-twentieth century natural sciences.

Such a conclusion seems to be a reasonable compromise between the outdated positivism of psychology's scientistic subculture and the epistemological skepticism *cum* political partisanship of much of the humanistic one.[51] It should, moreover, be a conclusion attractive to Christians who have found the perspectivalist compromise less than satisfying: not only does it allow for the development of "active agent" theories of social behavior (which are compatible with the biblical notion of accountable dominion as part of the *imago Dei*); it also allows for a research approach in which the deceptive and adversarial stance between researchers and respondents can be replaced by a more honest and collaborative one—an approach which assumes that at least sometimes a hermeneutic of trust can appropriately operate. People may not always know, or be able to say, what they are up to; as finite and sinful creatures, they are often prey to forces outside their present awareness and control. But sometimes they can give an intelligible account of their actions, one which requires no other explanation beyond itself. A major task (heretofore badly neglected) of psychology is the exploration of *both* types of behavior, as well as the ways in which they interact.

For Christians wishing to take up this challenge, some helpful groundwork has been laid by philosopher Stephen Evans. Recognizing the need to deal with anthropological and epistemological questions simultaneously, he also realizes that Christian psychologists must do even this on an interdisciplinary basis, acknowledging the role that philosophical and theological dimensions inevitably play in their theory-building. With regard to anthropology, Evans rejects perspectivalism on the grounds that it embraces only a "relational" anthropology, one which holds that there is nothing unique about human beings per se (substantially or essentially), but instead locates human significance only in how God has chosen to relate to persons in a covenantal fashion. There is a moment of truth in this idea; indeed, it was strongly pushed during the Reformation and beyond as an antidote to human pride: "Nothing in my hands I bring; simply to Thy cross I cling," goes the old pietist hymn. Relational anthropology also seems to allow the perspectivalist to get the best of two worlds: by acknowledging the importance of covenant theology they maintain a Christian identity; at the same time, by asserting that what (if anything) makes humans unique is a strictly empirical, not a revelational question, they spare themselves the embarrassment of seeming like religious fanatics in the eye of their secular colleagues.

But Evans rightly asserts that the value of relational anthropology to perspectivalists is also its weakness:

> If human dignity lies in the fact that God cares about us, or in the possibility of our knowing about him, rather than in some unique human quality, then the theologian [or psychologist] is saved from making any potentially embarrassing claims about the difference between human and other animals.... Nor must the theologian [or psychologist] affirm any non-material soul or spirit as a factor in understanding human behavior.... [But] the advantages of immunity from scientific refutation and a theological barrier to human pride... are purchased

at a price. The price of immunity from scientific refutation is the danger of lack of relevance to contemporary thought forms. What cannot be refuted by science also cannot be supported by science, and may be difficult to relate to science.[52]

Evans also recognizes that the desire of Christian perspectivalists not to be "embarrassed" by scientific "findings" about the continuity of human and nonhuman functioning rests on assumptions about the empirical neutrality of science and its independence of metaphysical, religious, and even epistemic values. By contrast, he points to postpositivist scientists and philosophers who hold that in all sciences—but especially the social sciences—metaphysical and religious commitments play not only an inevitable, but a positive role. If this is so, writes Evans, then "we ought to allow our Christian assumptions to interpenetrate our actual work as scientists . . . . The challenge is to go beyond rejection [of science] and conformism [to the current social science paradigm] to doing scientific work . . . within a consciously Christian frame of reference."[53] By this criterion, the relational anthropology of the perspectivalist could be unapologetically reunited with a substantial anthropology claiming certain biblical "givens" about human nature, such as accountable dominion, sociability, gender identity, the quest for meaning, and a stubborn resistance to truth about one's condition before God.

By this criterion, too, the empiricist, "objective" perspective on personhood could well be supplemented, if not replaced, by an interpretivist, or "hermeneutical" approach, in which observing and explaining human action is strongly analogous, not to the natural sciences, but to the interpretation of a literary text. In Evans' words, "recognizing a human action involves understanding its meaning; explaining action is inseparable from understanding the reasons for an action. Nor is this a value-free enterprise. Deciding whether a person's reasons are genuine reasons involves, among other things, reflecting on whether the reasons are good reasons. This is so because actions performed for good reasons in many circumstances require no further explanation, while manifestly inadequate reasons are suspected of being rationalizations."[54] There are, of course, hazards lurking in this approach too. Epistemologically, if persons are more like "texts" than like materials in an experiment, can there be any intersubjectively verifiable criteria by which we can judge our readings of them, and if not, can a hermeneutical psychology be "real" science?

Anthropologically, if persons are rule-makers and rule-followers whose being is constituted not by nature but by cultural and linguistic activity, as some versions of the hermeneutic approach hold, then is not such autonomy as they do have merely a collective "social construction" (recall Gergen here) which the individual cannot critically transcend to exercise freedom or moral responsibility? On such a view, how can there be any universal criteria for judging among competing systems of rule-governed behavior? There remains only a profound cultural and moral relativism.[55]

But these problems also afflict the deterministic approach, whether metaphysically or merely methodologically embraced: persons viewed as the products of nature are also "beyond freedom and dignity" (to borrow Skinner's phrase), and since values under such a paradigm are similarly determined, there is no way to rank-order the moral or cultural systems to which such persons belong. Moreover, the permeation of even natural science by values—metaphysical as well as epistemic—renders it a much more "hermeneutical" endeavor than previously believed; yet theory-adjudication is still possible despite—indeed, even because of—such values. So too in textual interpretation: "Reasoned argument and criticism do succeed in showing that some interpretations are warranted and some are not. To say that an enterprise is hermeneutical does not imply then that it is totally subjective and irrational."[56]

Christians can legitimately use a basic biblical anthropology to navigate such hazards—one which recognizes the impact of nature, culture, and human freedom, but places all of these in the context of creational norms, the reality of sin, and the promise of redemption. As they do so, they can (in Evans' words) "join the contemporary conversation and participate in scholarly work, but with a healthy irreverence and suspicion of the contemporary scholarly establishments. [They] need to clearly tell an increasingly secular world what Christians think about human beings, and show them the power of such a perspective."[57]

Notes

1. The author would like to acknowledge the help of colleagues in the Calvin College Philosophy Department, both regular and visiting, in criticizing earlier drafts of this paper and making suggestions for its improvement.

2. This essay first appeared in *CSR* 17.4 (June 1988): 406-24.

3. Michael J. Mahoney, *Cognition and Behavior Modification* (Cambridge, Mass.: Ballinger, 1974), 289-90.

4. Gregory A. Kimble, "Psychology's Two Cultures," *American Psychologist* 39.8 (August, 1984): 833-39.

5. Leonard Krassner and Arthur C. Houts, "A Study of the 'Value' Systems of Behavioral Scientists," *American Psychologist* 39.8 (August, 1984): 840-850.

6. The following is a sampling of such essays published in the *American Psychologist* over the past decade: George W. Albee, "The Protestant Ethic, Sex, and Psychotherapy" 32 (1977): 150-61; Richard C. Atkinson, "Reflections on Psychology's Past and Concerns about Its Future" 32 (1977): 205-10; D. L. Bazelton, "Veils, Values, and Social Responsibility" 37 (1982): 115-21; Jerome D. Frank, "Nature and Function of Belief Systems: Humanism and Transcendental Religion" 32 (1977): 555-59; Frederick H. Kanfer, "Personal Control, Social Control, and Altruism: Can Society Survive the Age of Individualism?" 34 (1979): 231-39; David C. McClelland, "Managing Motivation to Expand Human Freedom" 33 (1978): 201-10; S. B. Sarason, "An Asocial Psychology and a Misdirected Clinical Psychology" 36 (1981): 827-36; Roger W. Sperry, "Bridging Science and Values: A Unifying View of the Mind and Brain" 32 (1977): 237-45.

7. See for example Thomas Kuhn, *The Structure of Scientific Revolutions*, 2nd ed. (Chicago: University of Chicago Press, 1970); Imre Lakatos and A. Musgrave, eds., *Criticism and the Growth of Knowledge* (London: Cambridge University Press, 1970); Ian I. Mitroff, *The Subjective Side of Science* (New York: Elsevier, 1974); Michael Polanyi, *Personal Knowledge: Towards a Post-Critical Philosophy* (New York: Harper and Row, 1958); Frederick Suppe, *The Structure of Scientific Theories* (Urbana, Ill.: University of Illinois Press, 1974); Stephen Toulmin, *The Philosophy of Science* (London: Hutchinson, 1958).

8. Charles P. Snow, *The Two Cultures and a Second Look* (original essay, plus a retrospective commentary) (London: Cambridge University Press, 1964).

9. Kimble, 834.

10. As of 1987, the American Psychological Association had forty-seven different divisions representing a total membership of over 76,000.

11. Each of Kimble's twelve scale items was set out with the humanistic position described at the right, the scientistic position at the left, and the numbers 0-10 between the two. The respondent's score was thus the number of items on which he or she took a position to the *right* of 5, minus the number of items on which the respondent took a position to the *left* of 5, ignoring all responses of 5. Because there were 12 items on the test, these calculations place each subject on a 25-point scale, from -12 (the most extreme scientistic position) to +12 (the most extreme humanistic position).

12. These items included issues such as importance of scholarly vs. humane values, commitment to determinism vs. indeterminism of behavior, preference for observation vs. intuition as a source of knowledge, commitment to heredity vs. environment as the chief determinant of behavior, and a concept of organisms as primarily reactive or creative.

13. Kimble, 838.

14. Ibid.; compare Kuhn, 151-152.

15. The sampling strategy for inclusion in the behavioral group included the following criteria: a) self-identification of their work as behavior modification during the period 1946-76; b) citation of the respondent's work in publications on behavior modification in the period 1946-76; c) at least one publication or presentation (exclusive of dissertations) prior to 1956; d) professional contact with at least one other member of this group.

16. Krasner and Houts' Theoretical Orientation Survey was first designed and used by Richard W. Coan. See his *Psychologists: Personal and Theoretical Pathways* (New York: Irvington, 1979). The term "metaphorism" in their Epistemological Style Questionnaire refers to a preference for theorizing by reducing complex concepts to familiar metaphors—e.g., Freud's "hydraulic" metaphor explaining the interaction of the id, ego, and superego, or Piaget's "equilibrium/disequilibrium" metaphor to explain the way that cognitive development takes place in children.

17. Krasner and Houts, 846.

18. Rhoda K. Unger, "Epistemological Consistency and Its Scientific Implications," *American Psychologist* 40.12 (December, 1985): 1413-14.

19. Ibid., 1414. See also Suzanne J. Kessler and Wendy McKenna, *Gender: An Ethnomethodological Approach* (Chicago: University of Chicago Press, 1895) for an elaboration of this view.

20. Edward E. Sampson, "Cognitive Psychology as Ideology," *American Psychologist* 36.7 (July, 1981): 730-43. (Quotation from 730.) Related critiques can be found in Susan Buck-Morss, "Socioeconomic Bias in Piaget's Theory and Its Implications for Cross-Culture Studies." *Human Development* 18 (1975): 35-49, and in Kenneth J. Gergen, "Towards Generative Theory," *Journal of Personality and Social Psychology* 36 (1978): 1344-60.

21. Sampson, 741-42, my italics.

22. Ibid., 741. Note that when social scientists speak of the "politicizing" of their respective disciplines, they may mean a) that extra-disciplinary values do in fact play a role, b) that such values *should* play a role, c) that although a) may hold, b) should not; or d) that both a) and b) hold, but the content of the predominant extra-disciplinary values should change. A helpful analysis of this debate by a sociologist can be found in Richard Perkins, "Values, Alienation, and Christian Sociology," *Christian Scholar's Review* 15.1, (September 1985): 8-27, with a subsequent response by Stephen Evans in 15.3. See also David Braybrooke, *Philosophy of Social Science* (Englewood Cliffs, N.J.: Prentice-Hall, 1987).

23. See for example Kenneth J. Gergen, "Social Psychology as History," *Journal of Personality and Social Psychology* 26 (May 1973): 309-20; *Towards Transformation in Social Knowledge* (New York: Springer-Verlag, 1982); and "The Social Constructionist Movement in Modern Psychology," *American Psychologist* 30.3 (March 1985): 266-75. Note also the parallels with Paul K. Feyerabend's *Against Method* (New York: Humanities Press, 1976), and with Richard Rorty's *Philosophy and the Mirror of Nature* (Princeton, N.J.: Princeton University Press, 1979).

24. It is possible to be a skeptic about the ability of natural science to deliver ultimate truth and still remain anti-skeptical about morality, but Gergen does not make clear his basis for such a distinction. It is also the case that epistemological relativism can be combined with an ethical agenda—but to be consistent, the adherent of such a position has to concede that this agenda has no normative force outside the "language-game" community in which it originated.

25. Arthur W. Staats, "Paradigmatic Behaviorism, Unified Theory Construction Methods, and the Zeitgeist of Separatism," *American Psychologist* 36.3 (March, 1981): 239-56. For a summary of criticisms of "soft determinism," or "compatibilism" (the view that a "free" action is merely an "uncoerced" or "internally-produced" [but still necessarily determined] event), see Richard Taylor, *Metaphysics*, 2nd ed. (Englewood Cliffs, N.J.: Prentice-Hall, 1984), 48-57. See also C. Stephen Evans, *Preserving the Person: A Look at the Human Sciences* (Downers Grove, Ill.: InterVarsity Press, 1976) and Del Ratzsch, *Philosophy of Science: The Natural Sciences in Christian Perspective* (Downers Grove, Ill.: InterVarsity Press, 1987).

26. B. F. Skinner, *Walden Two* (New York: MacMillan, 1948); *Beyond Freedom and Dignity* (New York: Knopf, 1971); *About Behaviorism* (New York: Knopf, 1974).

27. William Hasker, "The Souls of Beasts and Men," *Religious Studies* 10 (1974): 265-67; "Emergentism," *Religious Studies*, 1983. See also Karl Popper and John Eccles, *The Self and Its Brain* (New York: Springer, 1977) and Wilder Penfield, *The Mystery of the Mind* (Princeton, N.J.: Princeton University Press, 1975).

28. Sperry, 243-44.

29. But it should be noted from the Sperry quotation that positivists are not lacking in moral self-righteousness either.

30. Peter L. Benson and Merton P. Strommen, "Religion on Capitol Hill: How Beliefs Affect Voting in the U.S. Congress," *Psychology Today* 15.3 (Dec. 1981): 46-57.

31. See for example Jay Adams, *Competent to Counsel* (Grand Rapids, Mich.: Baker, 1970), and Richard Grenz, "Nouthetic Counselling Defended," *Journal of Psychology and Theology* 4 (1976):193-205. For summary of a more inclusive kind of Christian separatism as embodied in the so-called "Christian Reconstructionst" movement, see Rodney Clapp, "Democracy as Heresy," *Christianity Today* 31.3 (February 20, 1987):17-23.

32. See for example David Hunt and T. A. McMahon, *The Seduction of Christianity* (Eugene, Ore.: Harvest House, 1985). More balanced is Paul C. Vitz' *Psychology as Religion: The Cult of Self-Worship* (Grand Rapids, Mich.: Eerdmans, 1977). For a secular critique of the "culture of narcissism" in psychology, see Michael A. Wallach and Lise Wallach, *Psychology's Sanctions for Selfishness* (San Francisco: W. H. Freeman, 1983).

33. The contrast suggested in this paragraph is based on anecdotal observation only. I know of no systematic study demonstrating these trends, and offer them merely as suggestive.

34. Examples of this "perspectivalist" approach include Rodger Bufford, *The Human Reflex: Behavioral Psychology in Biblical Perspective* (New York: Harper and Row, 1981); Malcolm A. Jeeves, *Psychology and Christianity: The View Both Ways* (Leicester, U.K.: InterVarsity Press, 1976); D. Gareth Jones, *Our Fragile Brains: A Christian Perspective on Brain Research* (Downers Grove, Ill.: InterVarsity Press, 1981); Donald M. McKay, *The Clockwork Image* (London: InterVarsity

Press, 1974); *Human Science and Human Dignity* (London: Hodder and Stoughton, 1979); and *Brains, Machines and Persons* (Grand Rapids, Mich.: Eerdmans, 1980); and David G. Myers, *The Human Puzzle: Psychological Research and Christian Belief* (San Francisco: Harper and Row, 1978).

35. Donald M. McKay, "Objectivity in Christian Perspective," *Journal of the American Scientific Affiliation* 36.4 (December, 1984): 235.

36. The term "perspectivalism," as used in this section of the paper, was coined by Stephen Evans. See his *Preserving the Person*, ch. 9.

37. See for example Rom Harre, ed., *Scientific Thought, 1900-1960* (Oxford: Clarendon Press, 1969), or Ernest Nagel, *The Structure of Science* (London: Routledge and Kegan Paul, 1961).

38. For an elaboration of these criticisms, see C. Stephen Evans, "Must Psychoanalysis Embrace Determinism?" *Psychoanalysis and Contemporary Thought* 7 (1984): 339-75. See also Evans "Healing Old Wounds and Recovering Old Insights: Towards a Christian View of the Person for Today," in Mark Noll and David Wells, eds., *Christian Faith and Practice in the Modem World: Theology from an Evangelical Point of View* (Grand Rapids, Mich.: Eerdmans, 1988) and his "Human Persons as Substantial Achievers" (Unpublished Manuscript, St. Olaf College, Northfield, Minn.). See also Stanton L. Jones, ed., *Psychology and the Christian Faith* (Grand Rapids, Mich.: Baker, 1986), especially the chapters by Jones and Hodges.

39. See for example Myers, *The Human Puzzle*, Chapter 1, and in particular his appeal to Reijer Hooykaas, *Religion and the Rise of Modern Science* (Grand Rapids, Mich.: Eerdmans, 1972) and to Robert K. Merton, *Science, Technology, and Society in Seventeenth Century England* (New York: Fertig, 1970).

40. Stephen Toulmin, *Foresight and Understanding* (Bloomington, Ind.: Indiana University Press, 1961).

41. This attitude is most apparent in Jones, *Our Fragile Brains*, but also implicit in the writings of Jeeves, McKay, and Myers.

42. George S. Howard, "The Role of Values in the Science of Psychology," *American Psychologist* 40.3 (March 1985): 255-65.

43. For an elaboration see Thomas Kuhn, *The Essential Tension* (Chicago: University of Chicago Press, 1977), and Ernan McMullin, "Values in Science," in P. D. Asquity and T. Nickles, eds., *Proceedings of the 1982 Philosophy of Science Association*, Vol. 2. (East Lansing, Mich.: Philosophy of Science Association, 1983). For an elaboration of the importance of epistemic values to a Christian critique of psychology, see Mary Stewart Van Leeuwen, "North American Evangelicalism and the Social Sciences: A Historical & Critical Appraisal," *Journal of the American Scientific Affiliation* 40.4 (December 1988): 194-203.

44. Howard, 259. His references to Kuhn and McMullin are those cited in note 42. See also McMullin's "Two Faces of Science," *Review of Metaphysics* 27 (June 1974): 655-76, and "The Ambiguity of Historicism," in *Current Research in Philosophy of Science* (Philosophy of Science Association, 1978), 58-83.

45. Ibid., 260.

46. Ibid.

47. Paul Bohannan, "The Mouse that Roars," *Science* 81 (May 1982): 25-26 (quotation from 25).

48. See also Van Leeuwen, *The Sorcerer's Apprentice*, Ch. 2 and 3, and also her "Reflexivity in North American Psychology: Historical Reflections on One Aspect of a Changing Paradigm," *Journal of the American Scientific Affiliation* 35 (September 1983): 162-67.

49. Howard, 261.

50. Ibid., 263-64. See also Gergen, "Social Psychology as History," and two works on the sociology of popular psychological knowledge by Sherri Turkle: *Psychoanalytic Politics: Freud's French Revolution* (New York: Basic Books, 1978), and *The Second Self: Computers and the Human Spirit* (New York: Simon and Schuster, 1984).

51. It could also be argued that, by taking human reflexivity into account, psychological theorists would merely be appealing to the epistemic value of empirical adequacy—i.e., acknowledging that this is an observed, unique, and therefore important characteristic of persons. On such an account, it is not that psychology is differently conducted than the natural sciences, but that psychologists fail to understand how epistemic values inform all the sciences, and should learn to unify their discipline around these values, rather than the outdated unity-of-science thesis.

52. Evans, "Healing Old Wounds and Recovering Old Insights," pp. 5-6.

53. Ibid., 15-16. See also Nicholas Wolterstorff, *Reason Within the Bounds of Religion* (Grand Rapids, Mich.: Eerdmans, 1976).

54. Evans, "Human Persons as Substantial Achievers," 6-7. Empirical outworkings of this approach in psychology are exemplified in Van Leeuwen, *The Sorcerer's Apprentice*, Chapter 3 and *The Person in Psychology*, Chapter 11. See also Ronald S. Valle and Mark King, *Existential and Phenomenological Alternatives for Psychology* (New York: Oxford University Press, 1978), Braybrooke,, Evans, *Psychology as a Human Science*, and George Howard, *Dare We Develop a Human Science?* (Notre Dame, Ind.: Academic Publications, 1986).

55. This is a position which seems to be strongly implied by Peter Winch in his "On Understanding a Primitive Society," in D. Z. Phillips, ed., *Religion and Understanding* (Oxford: Basil Blackwell, 1967).

56. Evans, "Must Psychoanalysis Embrace Determinism?" 362.

57. Evans, "Human Persons as Substantial Achievers," 16.

16 The Cult and Culture of Interpretation (1990)

Roger Lundin

When Bill Curry resigned as the head football coach at the University of Alabama early in 1990, his father openly spoke of his anger at those who had sought his son's dismissal.[1] W. A. Curry believed that his son had never been accepted by fans who looked back to the days of the legendary Alabama coach, Paul "Bear" Bryant. "The hardest thing for him [Bill] I think is to never really be accepted by the Alabama family, the influential alumni who never really got behind him," explained the elder Mr. Curry. The coach's father went in that interview on to blast the disloyal alumni in explicit biblical terms: "It is amazing how many Judases and turncoats there are in the world. Bill's learned a hard lesson about people, I think. But Jesus Christ's advice in the Bible when you aren't welcomed is to dust off your feet on the way out of town. Maybe that's what Bill needs to do."

Yet while Mr. Curry heard in the uproar over his son the echoes of biblical themes, a University trustee detected nothing more than a problem of perspective. That trustee, Aaron Aronov, admitted that Curry's support at Alabama had "been diluted," but he blamed this on the coach himself. In the words of the Associated Press story, Aronov charged that Curry had "created problems for himself with an inaccurate perception that he lacked support at Alabama." The story quoted the trustee as having said, "I think Coach Curry has been oversensitive to what he perceives as a lack of fan support."

This brief exchange provides a graphic illustration of the clash of two paradigms of interpretation. And in this conflict of interpretive models, we can trace the outline of critical changes which have taken place in modern theories of language and hermeneutics. The remarks of Bill Curry's father represent an understanding of language which has its roots in Christian tradition. For the father of the Alabama coach, personal conflicts are to be thought of as individual scenes in the vast drama of spiritual history. W. A. Curry envisions a world in which the ancient language of spiritual warfare corresponds, however roughly, to the very modern realities of vocational conflict and fame.

On the other hand, the University of Alabama trustee appears to hold to a postmodern understanding of the dilemmas faced by Bill Curry as a coach. For Aaron Aronov, the key to understanding Bill Curry's dilemma might be better supplied by the wisdom of William Blake than by the prophetic judgments of Jesus. "If the doors of perception were cleansed everything would appear to man as it is, infinite," the English romantic poet Blake proclaimed in 1793,[2] and in turning the dispute into a problem of perception, the Alabama trustee was demonstrating his unwitting indebtedness to the romantic revolution in epistemology and to the triumph of perspectivalism in contemporary theories of interpretation.

Whether it is in everyday discourse or in the rarified vocabularies of critical theory, the language of perspective occupies a privileged place in the contemporary West, having assumed its position of prominence as a result of a series of events in intellectual and cultural history. At a time when confidence in epistemology has eroded significantly, perspectivalism seems to many to afford an opportunity for the isolated self—which has occupied a privileged place in Western science, philosophy, and art for more than three centuries—to sustain its faith in its own powers. Even though we may no longer believe in the ability of the self to achieve moral perfection or to acquire indubitable knowledge, we are still able, through our contemporary theories of interpretation, to sustain faith in that self's ability to find satisfaction through the exercise of its creative powers. In postmodern America, we can observe this faith in "perspective" at work in everything from the self-help regimens promising easy wealth and psychic health to the fantastic visions of academic critics who see creative interpretation as a kind of explosive charge for blasting through the imprisoning walls of the metaphysical past.

In contemporary critical theory, two examples of the triumph of perspectivalism are represented in the pragmatism of Richard Rorty and the utopian radicalism of Frank Lentricchia. Rorty espouses an "edifying" understanding of interpretation, one which shows the unmistakable influence of the perspectivalism of Friedrich Nietzsche. According to Rorty, the contemporary study of hermeneutics has happily served to promote that distinctively postmodern intellectual "attitude [which is] interested not so much in what is out there in the world, or in what happened in history, as in what we can get out of nature and history for our own uses." To the "edifying" or therapeutic interpreter, "getting the facts right (about atoms and the void, or about the history of Europe) is merely propaedeutic to finding a new and more interesting way of expressing ourselves."[3]

Frank Lentricchia and many other contemporary students of the humanities complain that Rorty's vision of interpretation concedes too much to the oppressive capitalist orders of the West. According to the Marxist critics, Rorty and the other edifying philosophers seek in their use of language nothing more that a way of "coping" with all that is imponderable and oppressive in the human condition. "Rorty's vision of culture is the leisured vision of liberalism: the free pursuit of personal growth anchored in material security," complains Lentricchia.[4] This Marxist critic rejects the passive perspectival view of human understanding, and promotes instead an aggressive approach to matters of interpretation and justice: "Interpretation always makes a difference. The kind of activity that a Marxist literary intellectual . . . should engage in is the activity of interpretation, an activity which does not passively 'see,' but constructs a point of view in its engagement with textual events, and in so constructing produces an image of history as social struggle, of, say, class struggle."[5] As he extols the liberating virtues of interpretation—celebrating the powers of language to construct and transform the world—Lentricchia is voicing the ideological concerns of an entire class of people in today's humanities departments, those who are members of what Roger Kimball has called "a new academic establishment, the establishment of tenured radicals."[6]

In whatever form it takes, the contemporary fascination with perspective and interpretation in academic study is grounded in a deeply embedded Western faith in the power of the individual will and the power of human language. The most important recent source of this preoccupation with interpretation may be the work of Nietzsche, whose views on language have exercised an extraordinary influence in the contemporary academic world. In a fragment written in 1873, Nietzsche asked "What, then is truth?" It is, he answered himself, "a mobile army of metaphors, metonyms, and anthropomorphisms—in short, a sum of human relations, which have been enhanced, transposed, and embellished poetically and rhetorically, and which after long use seem firm, canonical, and obligatory to a people: truths are illusions about which one has forgotten that this is what they are; metaphors which are worn out and without sensuous power; coins which have lost their pictures and now matter only as metal, no longer as coins.... To be truthful means using the customary metaphors—in moral terms: the obligation to lie according to a fixed convention, to lie herd-like in a style obligatory for all."[7]

For Nietzsche and his ideological descendants, all knowledge is a matter of perspective—an issue of interpretation, that is—and all interpretations are lies. It would be impossible for matters to be otherwise, Nietzsche would argue, because the only relationship of language to reality, of words to things, is that which has been established by acts of violence and power and through the agencies of habit and convention. It follows that since all uses of language involve deception, one can do nothing more than seek to dissemble with power and effectiveness. One lies, Nietzsche argues, for the purpose of satisfying one's desires or deepest needs: "In this condition [of intoxication] one enriches everything out of one's own abundance: what one sees, what one desires, one sees swollen, pressing, strong, overladen with energy. The man in this condition transforms things until they mirror his power—until they are reflections of his perfection. This compulsion to transform into the perfect is—art.[8]

If Nietzsche is a recent source for contemporary theories of interpretation, we may track other influences back through several centuries. In this essay, we will begin with the seventeenth century. At that time the outlines of a general theory of hermeneutics began to emerge even as a skeptical but influential minority in the Western world began to lose its faith in classical theism. In one sense, the decline of theism made inevitable the rise of our modern "transcendental pretence" of the self.[9] In another sense, however, the promotion of the transcendental self was itself one of the most powerful forces which quickened the pace at which a theistic understanding of transcendence lost its power as a unifying cultural force.

To claim that our contemporary passion for hermeneutics started to develop in earnest only in the seventeenth and eighteenth centuries is not to argue, of course, that hermeneutics is in any way a new subject.[10] In Greek mythology, Hermes was the messenger who shuttled between the conclaves of the gods and the world of mortals, conveying word of the divine judgments on human affairs. In Jewish and Christian history, long before the name of Hermes ever became attached to a formal discipline (in the eighteenth century) hermeneutical activity flourished. In both the classical and the Christian worlds, hermeneutics as a practice involved the effort to translate what was taken to be a divine, authoritative word into language which would have power and relevance for a particular community.

As interpreters began to reflect self-consciously about their practices in the early modern era, however, this long established view of interpretation underwent a dramatic transformation. With established texts and beliefs being questioned in revolutionary ways at that time, interpreters could no longer assume the reliability or authority of the documents and doctrines they were trying to understand. One consequence of this was that by the time of the romantic movement, hermeneutics had come to be associated with the search for ways of making discredited texts relevant to skeptical readers, instead of with the task of explaining an authoritative word or command. Rather than assuming the authority of the text in question, the romantic interpreter had to prove that authority by demonstrating the text's power to provide coherence and meaning for the life of its audience. In one sense, romanticism in literature and theology was a dramatic effort to snatch the ethical, aesthetic, and emotional relics of the Christian faith from its metaphysical house which was being consumed by the flames of skepticism.

In Christian proclamation under the influence of romanticism, the new understanding of hermeneutics led to a preoccupation with the status of the audience to be addressed with the Gospel. Pressured to demonstrate the relevance of Christian faith to its "cultured despisers" (Schleiermacher's memorable phrase), many Christian interpreters in the Enlightenment and romanticism pared the biblical narrative into an appealing shape in their attempts to appeal to an educated and often cynical audience. Whether they were promoting a rational or romantic God, these early modern interpreters were often willing to spend the capital of Christian belief in exchange for earning high interest in the marketplace of intellectual currency.

The Cartesian revolution had prompted Western thinkers to believe that the isolated, unaided self had the power to discover truth through its own ratiocination. This Cartesian confidence in turn served to promote the utopian visions of human progress and happiness which would figure so prominently in eighteenth century thought. It was when this utopianism suffered dramatic setbacks at the hands of epistemological skepticism and the French Revolution that the romantic understanding of hermeneutics was born.[11]

In the intellectual world, the romantic age bequeathed to us a psychological and grammatical understanding of the hermeneutical process; and in the culture as a whole, romanticism has played a key role in establishing "the triumph of the therapeutic."[12]

A therapeutic culture seeks to promote the efforts of the autonomous self to discover fulfillment independent of the restraints of precedent and community. "Ours is the first cultural revolution fought to no other purpose than greater amplitude and richness of living itself," Philip Rieff argues.[13] In that cultural revolution, the theory of interpretation has come to serve as a most useful tool in therapeutic hands. If Rorty is right when he celebrates the complete triumph of romanticism in Western culture ("About two hundred years ago, the idea that truth was made rather than found began to take hold of the imagination of Europe"), then what goal might there be for thinking but to construct interpretations which help us live contentedly in a world in which there is "nothing at stake beyond a manipulable sense of well-being."[14]

In short, in the postmodern West, we have inherited from romanticism an inveterate belief in the power of human language to transform the world, or at least to alter radically our perspectives of that world. It is this legacy which has bequeathed to the contemporary academy its faith in what might be called verbal fiat—its faith in the power of the human word to "transform things until they mirror [human] power," as Nietzsche puts it. This essay will examine several key developments by means of which the epistemological revolutions of the seventeenth and eighteenth centuries gave rise to dramatic conceptions of the self's power; we will see, however, that by the end of the eighteenth century, the rationalism and empiricism which had done so much to build up the Enlightenment self had themselves succumbed to the pressures of skepticism. In the ensuing crisis, which served as the genesis of the romantic movement, epistemology was dethroned by hermeneutics and the" culture of interpretation." As Ernst Behler has correctly observed, with romanticism "we are on the threshold of that phase of modernity of which we are still the inheritors."[15]

As Rene Descartes sat down before a fire in a room in Germany in the winter of 1619, he was embarking upon the paradigmatic intellectual journey of modernity. Hoping to discover a secure foundation for intellectual endeavor in general, he could have had little idea of the extent to which his experience and discoveries would eventually shape Western thought about interpretation in particular.

Descartes began his most famous intellectual exercise in isolation: "The onset of winter held me up in quarters in which, finding no company to distract me, and having, fortunately, no cares or passions to disturb me, I spent the whole day shut up in a room heated by an enclosed stove, where I had complete leisure to meditate on my own thoughts."[16] He had long before noticed that in matters of conduct it was necessary to follow "opinions one knows to be very unsure." Yet though he was willing to submit to authority in matters of morality, in the search for truth, "I thought I ought to do just the opposite, and reject as being absolutely false everything in which I could suppose the slightest reason for doubt, in order to see if there did not remain after that anything in my belief which was entirely indubitable." Descartes sought to strip away all certainties—everything from the information provided by his senses and by the mathematical "reasonings I had hitherto accepted as proofs" to the most basic distinctions between waking and sleeping. Left with nothing but the thought "that everything was false,"

Descartes "immediately ... became aware that, while I decided thus to think that everything was false, it followed that I who thought thus must be something; and observing that this truth: *I think, therefore I am*, was so certain and so evident that all the most extravagant suppositions of the skeptics were not capable of shaking it" (*DM* 53-54).

By unearthing the foundational *Cogito, ergo sum*, Descartes believed he had provided humanity with the firm foundation needed for the construction of the great house of knowledge. As an implacable foe of Aristotelianism and Scholastic obscurantism, Descartes was looking for nothing less than a universal procedure for discovering truth. He sought to replace the messiness of tradition and authority with the cleanliness of method. "In place of a specific plurality of human sciences," Jacques Maritain says of the Cartesian heritage, "we have one single knowledge: science, Science with a capital 'S,' Science such as the modern world was to worship it; Science in the pure state, radiating from unique and unparalleled geometric clarity, and that Science is the human mind."[17]

Very soon after Descartes, Benedict de Spinoza would apply Cartesian principles to the study of the Bible. As a Jew whose parents had fled to Holland to avoid religious persecution, Spinoza was acutely sensitive to the power of interpretive disputes in human affairs: "As I marked the fierce controversies of philosophers raging in Church and State, the source of bitter hatred and dissension, the ready instruments of sedition and other ills innumerable, I determined to examine the Bible afresh in a careful, impartial, and unfettered spirit, making no assumptions concerning it, and attributing to it no doctrines, which I do not find clearly therein set down."[18]

After he had completed his thorough examination of the Bible, Spinoza could declare that "I found nothing taught expressly by Scripture, which does not agree with our understanding, or which is repugnant thereto" (*TPT* 9). "Thoroughly convinced" that "the Bible leaves reason absolutely free," he concluded that "Revelation and Philosophy stand on totally different footings" and "that Revelation has obedience for its sole object." Therefore, "in purpose no less than in foundation and method, [Revelation] stands entirely aloof from ordinary knowledge; each has its separate province, neither can be called the handmaid of the other" (*TPT* 9-10).

In the eighteenth century, the wedge driven by Spinoza would serve as a most useful tool to those who wished to widen the gap between faith and reason. They could follow Spinoza's lead and affirm that the Bible is irrelevant to natural history, because "the meaning of Scripture should be gathered from its own history, and not from the history of nature in general, which is the basis of philosophy."[19] Since "nothing taught expressly by Scripture" contradicts human understanding, then Scripture has no significant knowledge to impart (*TPT* 195). The claims made by the Bible do "not aim at explaining things by their natural causes, but only at narrating what appeals to the popular imagination," and they do "so in the manner best calculated to excite wonder, and consequently to impress the minds of the masses with devotion" (*TPT* 90). According to Spinoza and others who followed him in the Enlightenment, the Bible uses poetry and stories only to beguile into obedience the naive minds and pliant wills of the unenlightened masses. For the enlightened thinker, rational and mathematical rigor will suffice in the search for truth.[20]

Even though the scriptural text has no unique or exclusive knowledge to reveal, Spinoza argues that we should nevertheless study it with the same rigorous standards we use in exploring nature. That is, first, we must examine the "nature and properties" of biblical language; then, we are to arrange the disparate materials of the scriptural texts under specific topics, leaving a special place for passages which are "ambiguous or obscure"; and finally, we should attempt to become "acquainted with the life, the conduct, and the pursuits of [the biblical] author" and learn "what was the occasion, the time, the age, in which each book was written" (*TPT* 103).

As Robert M. Grant has observed, Spinoza's techniques closely resemble those espoused by modern handbooks to the study of the Bible. Celebrating clarity and rationality above all else, Spinoza's methods sidestep the thorny disputes of scriptural interpretation. According to Spinoza, such skirting of controversy is appropriate in matters in biblical interpretation, "for scripture has no authority over the interpreter's mind. It may govern his actions, but only if he is somewhat unintelligent. If he is truly rational, reason alone will guide his whole life."[21]

According to Spinoza, there was little chance that the right to absolute individual freedom would come to conflict with the need for civil order. "I conclude," Spinoza explains near the end of the preface to *Theologico-Political Treatise*, "that everyone should be free to choose for himself the foundations of his creed ... ; each would then obey God freely with his whole heart, while nothing would be publicly honoured save justice and charity" (*TPT* 10). Harboring no doubts that "the true aim of government is liberty," Spinoza was confident that rationality would rule over human affairs and bring humanity a degree of happiness it had never before experienced.

As intellectual histories commonly point out, the flowering of rationalism in the decades after Descartes and Spinoza coincided with a decline in the authority of Christian belief for an educated minority. On many fronts, orthodoxy seemed threatened: Newtonian physics made conventional notions of miracle look implausible; the sufficiency of reason made revelation appear superfluous; and faith in universal, rational truth made the historical particularity of the gospel offensive. A hundred years or so after Spinoza, for example, only vestiges of Trinitarian theism seem to remain in the enlightened deism espoused by Voltaire: "United in this principle [i.e. of divine Providence] with the rest of the universe he [the theist] embraces none of the sects which all contradict each other. His religion is the most ancient and the most widespread: for the simple adoration of a God has preceded all the systems of the world. He speaks a language which all peoples understand .... He believes that religion consists neither in the opinions of an unintelligible metaphysics, not in vain appearances, but in worship and justice. To do good, that is his cult; to submit to God, that is his doctrine."[22]

It is a paradox that in many instances in the eighteenth century, skepticism about Christian doctrine only served to strengthen the confidence which enlightened individuals placed in the rational or emotive self. As Immanuel Kant argued in a key essay of the Enlightenment, intellectual autonomy is the necessary catalyst in the unfolding drama of culture. By releasing the self from slavish deference to transcendent authority, skepticism has freed it to draw from the fathomless well of its own untapped potential. According to Kant, the free and critical thinker is the person best suited to tap mankind's natural powers and prerogatives. "Enlightenment is man's leaving his self-caused immaturity," he wrote in 1784. "Immaturity is the incapacity to use one's intelligence without the guidance of another .... *Sapere Aude*! Have the courage to use your own intelligence! is therefore the motto of the enlightenment."[23] A "man may postpone for himself" his inevitable enlightenment, but only for a short time. "To resign from such enlightenment altogether," however, is to "violate and to trample underfoot the sacred rights of mankind."[24]

The claims for liberty made by Spinoza, Kant, and others were a tributary feeding into the stream of protestant individualism, and the confluence of these sources produced a torrent of changes in Western views of interpretation. As Hans Frei explains: "Not very much of protestant orthodoxy passed over into rationalist religious thought, but this one thing surely did: the antitraditionalism in scriptural interpretation of the one bolstered the antiauthoritarian stance in matters of religious meaning and truth in the other."[25] In other words, as orthodox protestants fought to affirm the perspicuity of Scripture and the priesthood of all believers, they ironically found themselves allied with rationalists who decried the obscurity of allegorical interpretation.

Under the twin influences of protestantism and rationalism, "the direct reading of the 'plain text' " became the" common ground among all the differing hermeneutical schools" in the eighteenth century. "Indeed," according to Prei, "it was this common position that made general hermeneutics possible. No matter what the singular truth of the Bible, the meaning of the texts as such could be understood by following the rules of interpretation common to all written documents." In searching for a general hermeneutic, critics in the eighteenth century were hoping to discover methods of textual analysis which would yield the single, plain meaning of any work to which these methods were applied. The desire for a method of this kind became so strong that belief in multiple meanings for the same text—literal, figural, moral and spiritual—"virtually disappeared as a major force."[26]

Throughout the eighteenth century, rationalist interpreters searched for the univocal meaning of the biblical text; given the spirit of that age, it is hardly surprising that a number of these interpreters discovered, of all things, that the Bible was a primer of rationalism and common sense. John Toland, for example, interpreted the Bible in precisely this manner in *Christianity Not Mysterious*, published in 1702. In that work, Toland's argument is that the clarity of the Bible's meaning confirms its truthfulness, for the Gospel "affords the most illustrious Example of close and perspicuous Ratiocination conceivable. . . . What is revealed in Religion, as it is most useful and necessary, so it must and may be as easily comprehended, and found as consistent with our common Notions, as what we know of Wood or Stone, of Air, of Water, or the like."[27] We know the Bible is true, in other words, because its meaning is plain to the simplest reader.

In a similar vein, almost three quarters of a century after Toland, Hermann Samuel Reimarus was to argue that in the history of the Church neither miracles nor mysteries had been important in establishing the unique authority of Jesus. Instead, Jesus won the hearts of men and women by appealing purely to "a reason which operates and has operated at all times so naturally, that we need no miracle to make everything comprehensible and clear. This is the real mighty wind that so quickly wafted all the people together. This is the true original language that performs the miracles."[28]

The rational God of Toland and Reimarus relied upon innocent, benevolent humans to act as his earthly agents. With men and women proving to be such capable servants, God had little need of a sacrificial Jesus who would suffer unto death for the sins of mankind. Indeed, because the Christ of the cross was an embarrassment for the enlightened temperament, individuals such as Thomas Jefferson labored to disentangle the simple Jesus ("the greatest of all the reformers of the depraved religion of his own country") from the web of Jewish superstition and Greek sophistry which had held him fast for centuries. "Abstracting what is really his [Jesus's] from the rubbish in which it is buried, easily distinguished by its lustre from the dross of his biographers, and as separable from that as the diamond from the dunghill," wrote Jefferson, "we have the outlines of a system of the most sublime morality which has ever fallen from the lips of man." Jefferson's hope, even as he approached the end of his life, was that the plain and rational sense of Jesus would "in time . . . effect a quiet euthanasia of the heresies of bigotry and fanaticism which have so long triumphed over human reason" and have wickedly afflicted mankind. "But this work is to be begun by winnowing the grain from the chaff of the historians of his life."[29] To that end, on two occasions Jefferson attempted to snatch the diamond from the dunghill, by culling from the gospels only those sayings of Jesus which he took to be consistent with a rational and benevolent understanding of that first-century Nazarene.

Even as Jefferson was writing his letters lauding the rational self, the moral sense, and the harmless vestigial Christianity he embraced, some thinkers in Western Europe could feel the tremors beginning to shake the Enlightenment ground of confidence in the self. And to be sure, by the end of the eighteenth century, twin revolutions—the Kantian epistemological revolution and the French political revolution—had produced cracks in the pillars supporting the edifice of the imperial self.

From Kant and David Hume, the challenge to self-certainty came as an attack upon claims about the mind's ability to apprehend reality, the thing-in-itself, directly. The empiricists and rationalists had taken their understanding of nature and the human mind to constitute indubitable knowledge of the primary structures of reality. With Kant especially, however, that confidence was shaken. "The first Copernican revolution had denied the obvious—that the sun revolved while the earth stood still," writes Robert Solomon. "What Kant denied seemed even more obvious, that the world was 'out there' and independent of our experience of it."[30] *The Critique of Pure Reason* pressed the claim—which has in the years since Kant become a commonplace of intellectual life—that the self does not so much discover pre-existing order in the world as it projects order creatively upon the world: "Since . . . nature's conformity to law rests on the necessary linking of phenomena in experience, without which we could not know any object of the world of the senses, in other words, such conformity rests on the original laws of the intellect; it sounds strange at first, but it is none the less true when I say in respect of these laws of the intellect: The intellect does not derive its laws from nature but prescribes them to nature."[31]

Though it disabled the rationalism and empiricism of the eighteenth century, the Kantian revolution did not cripple the self which had moved under the power of Enlightenment philosophy and science. After Kant, that self would soar with new wings—those of the recently discovered faculty of the imagination. As Solomon observes, "At the heart of ... the dramatic shift in Western thinking" that begins with *The Critique of Pure Reason* "is an enormous expansion in the concept of the self, its scope, power, and richness. The primary change is a shift from the passive to the active mode."[32]

For Kant at least, this active, creative self was not an isolated I but the "transcendental ego" of humanity imposing its forms upon the random facts of experience. What is given to humanity is the senseless information of the senses; the transcendental ego must supply the ordered meaning missing in the facts. Although some of Kant's admirers took his thought in directions he would have found appalling, he had already cleared a path for them in his work. By placing the active, knowing self at the center of things, he paved the way for more radical views which proclaimed the individual will's unbounded capacity to impress reality with its desires. In the arts in particular, Kantianism led to the development of a dramatically new conception of the creative spirit. "It was not until Kant that the realm of aesthetics assumed its own right," Ernst Behler has observed. "Romanticism brought about a new appreciation of artistic creation—a glorification of creative imagination—and made of the artist a spokesman for the godhead, an orphic seer, and prophetic priest."[33]

If the work of Kant represented in the intellectual sphere both the culmination and transformation of the Enlightenment experience, then the French Revolution proved to have similar consequences in politics and morals. Writing more than two decades after the fact, an Englishman described the astonishment which had filled the hearts of many who watched the Revolution unfold: "Every faculty of the mind was awakened, every feeling raised to an intenseness of interest, every principle and passion called into superhuman exertions. At one moment, all was hope and joy and rapture; the corruption and iniquity of ages seemed to vanish like a dream; the unclouded heavens seemed once more to ring with exulting chorus of peace on earth and good-will to men; and the spirit of a mighty and puissant nation ... seemed rising in native majesty to draw new inspiration from the rejoicing heavens."[34] Simon Schama explains that many of those who were at the forefront of the Revolution "were fascinated by seismic violence, by the great primordial eruptions which geologists now said were not part of a single Creation, but which happened periodically in geological time." The events of the Revolution proved to be, to borrow from Burke, "both sublime and terrible."[35] Out of this sublime cataclysm, countless poets, philosophers, and political observers anticipated nothing less than the dramatic renewal of the human race. In the words of the poet Robert Southey, "Old things seemed passing away, and nothing was dreamt of but the regeneration of the human race."[36]

In spite of all these hopes, however, the relentless crush of events, from the unmitigated barbarity of the Reign of Terror to the crowning of Napoleon as Emperor in 1804, brought devastation and disillusionment to a generation of revolutionary observers. The poet William Wordsworth immortalized this despair in Books X and XI of *The Prelude*. Of the Reign of Terror, he wrote that

> Domestic carnage now filled the whole year
> With feast-days; the old man from the chimney-nook,
> The maiden from the bosom of her love,
> The mother from the cradle of her babe,
> The warrior from the field—all perished, all—
> Friends, enemies, of all parties, ages, ranks,
> Head after head, and never heads enough
> For those that bade them fall....
> Most melancholy at that time, O Friend!
> Were my day-thoughts, my dreams were miserable;
> Through months, through years, long after the last beat
> Of those atrocities,...
> I scarcely had one night of quiet sleep,
> Such ghastly visions had I of despair
> And tyranny, and implements of death.[37]

The terrors of the revolution led to the excesses of reaction until, with the crowning of Napoleon, the cycle of hope and despair was complete. Wordsworth could only recoil in disgust at this last event, calling it the "last opprobrium, when we see the dog/ Returning to his vomit."[38]

Thus the reign of the rational God—the God who only recently usurped the mysterious lord of the medieval metaphysicians—came to an end in the final years of the eighteenth century. The Enlightenment bond of self, nature, and God seemed to have dissolved in the solutions of revolution and reaction oppression. Vanished was the reasonable God who had formed the cosmos and planted within the human mind the power to discern his reasonable and everlasting order.

The dramatic transformations of politics and philosophy in eighteenth century Europe coincided with major changes in biblical interpretation. Indeed in many ways, radical seventeenth century hermeneutical practices did as much as anything to prepare the way for the romantic revolution in literature and philosophy. Long before Wordsworth, Blake, or Emerson began to tout the virtues of imaginative inwardness, protestant radicals had eagerly championed the Christ who dwelled exclusively within the human heart.

By emphasizing the allegorical significance of Christian language for the inner life, the radical interpreters of the seventeenth century in their own way helped to bring about what Frei has called "the great reversal" in hermeneutics as much as Spinoza did with his rationalist analysis of biblical truth. As the Puritan revolutionaries and Pietists were redefining the Bible as a primer of human inwardness, skeptical interpreters were following the earlier lead of Spinoza in abandoning their faith in the power of biblical narrative to comprehend human experience and to serve as "the adequate depiction of the common and inclusive world."[39] By the end of the eighteenth century, "the great reversal had taken place; interpretation [had become] a matter of fitting the biblical story into another world with another story rather than incorporating that world into the biblical story."[40]

In protestant England and New England, the typological interpretation of the Scriptures played a particularly crucial role in preparing the way for the "great reversal" and the romantic revolution. To be sure, the typological method of reading history was hardly new in the seventeenth century, for it was rooted in the very earliest practices of the Christian church. The Bible itself makes extensive use of typology in those Gospels and Epistles which view the Old Testament saints and the nation of Israel as prophetic forerunners of the God's full revelation in Christ. In the history of the Church, many types have been seen as pointers to Christ, the antitype who stands "at the center of history, casting His shadow forward to the end of time as well as backward across the Old Testament."[41]

What made the typological practices of certain seventeenth century protestants in England and the New World unusual was the degree to which those Christians read their own experiences as signs of eschatological fulfillment. That is, they saw their activities as climactic events in the history of salvation.[42] Typologies always involve the seeing of similarities—Oliver Cromwell is like Moses, John Winthrop like Nehemiah. But for some of the sectarian protestants, the analogies came to seem like identities; and once the two parties in an analogy become identical, the first party is rendered superfluous. If to be like Christ means to become a Christ, then the person of Jesus himself becomes redundant.

The career of the English Puritan radical Gerrard Winstanley illustrates well the radical implications of this kind of typological reading. As Christopher Hill explains, for Winstanley

> the Virgin Birth was an allegory; so was the resurrection. "Christ lying in his grave, like a corn of wheat buried under the clods of earth for a time, and Christ rising up from the powers of your flesh, above that corruption and above those clouds, treading the curse under his feet, is to be seen within." Winstanley appears to reject any other resurrection or ascension. The resurrection of the dead occurs during our lives on earth: the day of judgment has already begun and some are already living in the kingdom of heaven. The casting out of covetousness and the establishment of a classless society will be "a new heaven and a new earth." Even more remarkably, all the prophecies of the Old and New Testaments regarding the calling of the Jews and the restoration of Israel refer to "this work of making the earth a common treasure." Salvation is liberty and peace. The second coming is "the rising up of Christ in sons and daughters"; the worship of any other Christ but the Christ within man must then cease.[43]

Though only a small number of protestants may have engaged in such interpretive practices, this method of scriptural interpretation nevertheless provided a clear stimulus to romanticism in late eighteenth century England and early nineteenth century America.[44] Daring typological readings enabled interpreters of the Scriptures to appropriate spiritual satisfaction from the Bible without being obligated to regard seriously its historical and cosmological claims. When, for example, they claimed that the second coming was only "the rising up of Christ in sons and daughters" and that the only Christ worthy of worship was the Christ within, the revolutionary protestant interpreters were cutting their ties to orthodox belief and Christian tradition. For the radical typologist, the Bible was a storehouse of images with mystic or inspirational power, rather than a narrative comprising an "adequate depiction of the common and inclusive world." The story of human liberation became primary in this reading of the Scriptures, and the Bible was seen as fitting "into another world with another story rather than incorporating that world into the biblical story."[45] With their descriptive power and narrative authority significantly weakened, the Scriptures increasingly were left to feed the self's insatiable appetite for metaphors and meaning.

While these radical interpretive practices may have been unusual in the seventeenth and eighteenth centuries, with the advent of romanticism in the late eighteenth century they became the dogma of a new cultural orthodoxy. First expounded by such figures as the English poet William Wordsworth, the German theologian Friedrich Schleiermacher, and the American essayist Ralph Waldo Emerson, this romantic orthodoxy still governs as the central ideology of modernity in the West.

By reconstituting the self as an intuitive source of beauty and values, the romantics sought to sustain the inherited beliefs of their culture by providing them with a new source. In the words of M. H. Abrams, "the romantic enterprise was an attempt to sustain the inherited cultural order against what to many writers seemed the imminence of chaos; and the resolve to give up what one was convinced one had to give up of the dogmatic understructure of Christianity, yet to save what one could save of its experiential relevance and values" seems to Abrams to have been an act "of integrity and of courage."[46]

For theologians of the romantic period, the struggle to salvage Christianity while celebrating the self involved an effort to maintain the "principle of autonomy" and "at the same time to account for and justify the place of religion in human life . . . . The question for many was thus whether religion in any form, traditional or deistic, could meet the Promethean ambitions which in Western Europe were firing the imaginations of the educated young as they entered upon" the nineteenth century.[47] Those efforts to promote the cause of human autonomy while preserving some place for religion led the romantics to create a refuge for the religious impulse within the confines of the self.

Schleiermacher explored that refuge in his speeches to the "cultured despisers" of religion. In the first of those speeches, he acknowledged that in the "ornamented dwellings" of nineteenth century Europe, "the only sacred things to be met with are the sage maxims of our wise men, and the splendid compositions of our poets."[48] Over the course of the previous two centuries, the physical sciences, politics, and philosophy had shown religious belief to be unnecessary as an explanatory device. And now, at the end of Enlightenment, Schleiermacher has to admit that the culturally astute people of his own day do not even need religion to provide them with happiness. Their "suavity and sociability, art and science have so fully taken possession" of their minds that they have no room for thoughts of the "holy Being" (*OR* 1). "I know how well," Schleiermacher tells the cultured despisers, "you have succeeded in making your earthly life so rich and varied, that you no longer stand in need of an eternity" (*OR* 2).

Having expressed his deep sympathy with their enlightened disdain of the doctrinal "habitations and nurseries of the dead letter," Schleiermacher nevertheless urges his listeners to "turn from everything usually reckoned religion, and fix your regard on the inward emotions and dispositions, as all utterances and acts of inspired men direct" (*OR* 16, 18). Only by drifting inward to the fluid source of all frozen systems, may the enlightened soul be carried to the heart of religion and meet the source of all sublimity: "I maintain that in all better souls piety springs necessarily by itself; that a province of its own in the mind belongs to it, in which it has unlimited sway; that it is worthy to animate most profoundly the noblest and best and to be fully accepted and known by them" (*OR* 21).

In his later masterpiece, *The Christian Faith*, Schleiermacher endeavored to develop a systematic theology out of his insights concerning the nature of the unique inner life of religion. "All propositions which the system of Christian doctrine has to establish," he argued, "can be regarded either as descriptions of human states, or as conceptions of divine attributes and modes of action, or as utterances regarding the constitution of the world."[49] Yet in spite of the fact that he had just affirmed the essential doctrinal equality of descriptions of human states of mind, utterances regarding the constitution of the world, and "conceptions of divine modes of action," Schleiermacher went on in *The Christian Faith* to "declare the description of human states of mind to be the fundamental dogmatic form." Statements about the nature of the world and action of God, on the other hand, "are permissible only in so far as they can be developed out of propositions" stemming from the experience of inwardness.[50]

Schleiermacher's redefinition of the nature of faith profoundly influenced Christian doctrine and hermeneutics. Helmut Thielicke has observed that the effect of Schleiermacher's romantic reconstitution of religion was to conflate the separate disciplines of "anthropology (human conditions), theology (divine qualities and modes of action), and cosmology (the nature of the world)." Faced with the fact that Schleiermacher was willing to deny "theological rank" to any theological proposition which could not be translated into anthropological language "without any loss of value," Thielicke asks rhetorically, "Does not this pave the way for the normativity of the anthropological analysis of existence?"[51]

For the theory of interpretation, the anthropological revolution guaranteed that primacy would be given to human subjectivity and to the process of appropriation. For the romantic mind of Schleiermacher, the hermeneutical enterprise was no longer a search for ways of translating divine demands or imparting revelatory knowledge to an eager audience. Because ethics, physics, and biology tell us all what we need to know about the nature of human action and the created order, revelation could only be an ornament on the body of secular knowledge which had been discovered and developed by autonomous men and women.

As a result, the task left to the interpreter of Christian texts was to translate them into language which an enlightened individual could understand without having to take offense at any insult to his or her independent intelligence. In Schleiermacher's understanding of hermeneutics, writes Karl Barth, "nothing remained of the belief that the Word or statement is as such the bearer, bringer, and proclaimer of truth, that there might be such a thing as the Word of God." Schleiermacher's understanding of the kerygma is of a "kerygma that only depicts and does not bring, that only states or expresses and does not declare. Truth does not come in the spoken Word; it comes in speaking feeling."[52]

At the very time that Schleiermacher was concluding his brilliant and revolutionary career, the American Ralph Waldo Emerson was entering upon his vocation as a romantic poet and essayist. And while there is no evidence of the specific influence of Schleiermacher upon Emerson, there are remarkable similarities between their convictions about the nature of religious experience and human understanding. In a pivotal early work, "The Divinity School Address," Emerson gives full expression to his romantic conception of Christian truth. The true source of revelation, Emerson tells the students of the Harvard Divinity School in the summer of 1838, was not a transcendent God who spoke definitively in the life of an ancient race and a first-century carpenter. No, revelation has its source in the inspired self filled with the "sentiment of virtue." Jesus Christ is important for what he can tell us about that soul, not for what he might be able to impart to it: "Jesus Christ belonged to the true race of prophets. He saw with open eye the mystery of the soul . . . . He saw that God incarnates himself in man, and evermore goes forth anew to take possession of his world."[53]

Because truth "is an intuition" and "cannot be received at second hand," Emerson claims that the students he is addressing must go forth as "newborn bard[s] of the Holy Ghost," preaching "a faith like Christ's in the infinitude of man." Men and women may "have come to speak of the revelation as somewhat long ago given and done, as if God were dead," but the inspired self knows to heed the call of "new revelation . . . In the soul, then, let the redemption be sought. In one soul, in your soul, there are resources for the world. Whenever a man comes, there comes revolution" (*EM* 885).

It is important to recognize that for Emerson and other romantics, the truth discovered within the self was a mirror image of the truth hidden within nature. When we study nature and history, Emerson explains in "The American Scholar," we are simply classifying a multitude of facts. And "what is classification but the perceiving that these objects are not chaotic, and are not foreign, but have a law which is also a law of the human mind" (*EM* 55)? The mind finds itself "tyrannized by its own unifying instinct," and so it "goes on tying things together, diminishing anomalies, discovering roots running under ground, whereby contrary and remote things cohere, and flower out from one stem" (*EM* 55). The end of this process is the discovery that the same moral and spiritual laws are at work within nature as within the human mind: "And, in fine, the ancient precept, 'Know thyself,' and the modern precept, 'Study nature,' become at last one maxim" (*EM* 56).

By linking human consciousness to God and nature by means of human feeling, the romantics were able to sustain the Cartesian tradition's faith in the self's ability to discover the truth. For Emerson, Schleiermacher, and others of the age, what coheres within the self also corresponds in some way to the truth permeating nature and the divine consciousness. That truth within nature, however, is hidden in hieroglyphic form and is in desperate need of interpretation. Hence, the poet in romanticism takes the place of the preacher or the Pope in the hermeneutical process: "For, as it is dislocation and detachment from the life of God, that makes things ugly, the poet, who re-attaches things to nature and the Whole—re-attaching even artificial things, and violations of nature, to nature, by a deeper insight—disposes very easily of the most disagreeable facts" (*EM* 455).

In Emerson's world, all of us are potential poets capable of recognizing "in every work of genius . . . our own rejected thoughts" coming "back to us with a certain alienated majesty" (*EM* 259). What those rejected thoughts tell us is that each of us has the power to manipulate reality for our own well-being: "As the world was plastic and fluid in the hands of God, so it is ever to so much of his attributes as we bring to it . . . In proportion as a man has any thing in him divine, the firmament flows before him and takes his signet and form. Not he is great who can alter matter, but he who can alter my state of mind" (*EM* 65).

Emerson and Schleiermacher represent the triumph of inwardness in the development of the Western theory of interpretation. In their work and that of others of the romantic period, we witness the demise of efforts to find a correspondence between the biblical narrative and the book of nature or the events of history. In the world of romantic inwardness, hermeneutics became the art of reconciling the antiquated language of the Scriptures to the realities of the expansive, intuitive self. Writers such as Emerson effected that reconciliation by making the Bible an illustration of the saga of human inwardness. In what Hans Frei might consider the absolute "eclipse of biblical narrative," Emerson wrote in "Self-Reliance": "Time and space are but physiological colors which the eye maketh, but the soul is light; where it is, is day; where it was, is night; and history is an impertinence and injury, if it be anything more than a cheerful apologue or parable of my being and becoming" (*EM* 899).

To follow the course of romantic thought from the time of Emerson and Schleiermacher to the postmodern age would be the work of another essay. Such an essay would trace the complicated developments which led from the epistemological confidence of romanticism to the interpretive skepticism of postmodernism. That history would show that in the many shifts which have led from romanticism to the world of contemporary theory, a constant factor has been the steady erosion of belief in the correspondence of the self's spiritual and moral aspirations to the realities of nature and historical process. For the postmodernist, language may still cohere as a manifestation of human desire, but it does not correspond to any reality outside the self. As Rorty clearly puts it: "To say that truth is not out there is simply to say that where there are no sentences there is no truth, that sentences are elements of human languages, and that human languages are human creations."[54] Though it has lost its ancestors' faith in the correspondence of the self to nature, the ironic, therapeutic self of the postmodernists is nevertheless the direct spiritual descendant of the willful imaginative self of the romantics.

For the contemporary Christian student of the Bible and church history, the primacy of interpretation in contemporary theory poses important challenges. Perhaps most important is the one it presents to the proclamation of the truth. That is, romantic theories of interpretation undercut any reading of a text which claims to be anything more than the announcement of the discovery of a particular state of potential of the self. As we have already heard Thielicke argue, by focusing attention on "the adult self who is summoned to appropriate the message" of the Gospel, the tradition of Schleiermacher paves "the way for the normativity of the anthropological analysis of existence...The question is—and it is the crucial issue in modern theology—whether in a very lofty, profound, and unintentional way the kerygma is put under man's control, so that in the last analysis theology is reduced to a mere chapter in anthropology."[55]

To understand the consequences of the shift in interpretation represented by the revolutions of Enlightenment and romantic selfhood, we might consider briefly the case of the twentieth century theologian Reinhold Niebuhr, and specifically his understanding of the resurrection. Throughout his work, Niebuhr gave a central place to this doctrine; indeed, the whole of *Human Destiny* (Volume 2 of *The Nature and Destiny of Man*) relies upon the symbolic power of the resurrection to assure us that God redeems and fulfills the course of human history. As Niebuhr wrote to the Scottish philosopher Norman Kemp Smith in 1940, the wisdom of the resurrection was "the idea that the fulfillment of life does not mean the negation and destruction of historical reality (which is a unity of body-soul, freedom-necessity, time-eternity) but the completion of this unity." But as soon as he had written that defense of the relevance of the resurrection, Niebuhr added the following comment to assure Kemp Smith that he was not a supernaturalist: "I have not the slightest interest in the empty tomb or physical resurrection."[56]

Because of the prevailing scientific naturalism of this century, then, Niebuhr felt that he could not possibly believe in the resurrection as an "event" of any kind. As a symbol, the resurrection might have great power, but ultimately it can refer to nothing more than our human faith in the meaningfulness of life. The word does not correspond to any state of affairs or event in history, but is instead the most powerful expression we have of our belief in the coherence of meaning: "The Christian hope of the consummation of life and history . . . is an integral part of the total Biblical conception of the meaning of life."[57]

The example of Niebuhr is evidence of the fact that in the tradition of Schleiermacher and the Romantics, the desire to accommodate Christian doctrine to the reigning paradigms of science and epistemology is so strong that questions about the descriptive power of Christian symbols can only be dismissed as fruitless or irrelevant. If naturalism makes the possibility of a resurrected Christ seem to be an absurdity, then one must reinterpret the symbol, to season it for the tastes of the modern intellectual palate. If we must abandon belief in the empty tomb in order to maintain the magical power of all that the word resurrection conjures up, so be it.

That there are clear parallels between Niebuhr's theology and the broader cultural tradition of romanticism would seem confirmed by the following observation made by the recent British novelist Iris Murdoch:

> It is equally interesting that after a period of irreligion or relative atheism there have been signs of a kind of perceptible religious renewal in certain changes in theology.... In England one is experiencing a demythologization ... of theology which recognizes that many things normally or originally taken as dogmas must now be considered as myths. In this there is something which might have a profound impact on the future which, for the ordinary person, might return religion to the realm of the believable. T. S. Eliot said that Christianity has always adapted itself in order to be believable. Thus, if one defines art in religious terms, I believe its vocabulary is not outmoded and that one might even be able to establish a connection between the work of theology and that of art in their actual form.[58]

Granted, there is in the Christian life always a tension between the Scriptures in themselves and the need to apply them to the demands and patterns of present reality. But for Niebuhr, Murdoch, and innumerable others in the romantic interpretive tradition, the temptation is to make all human understanding a matter of accommodation and application. The Bible and Christian tradition, in this line of thinking, may console our spirits and help to organize the categories of our thought, but they have lost the power to reveal, to speak to us with a binding address. When all knowledge becomes application, eventually there may be nothing left to apply.[59]

Richard Rorty shows with remarkable clarity what the fate of Christian language is in the romantic and Nietzschean interpretive traditions. In "The Contingency of Language," the first chapter of *Contingency, Irony, and Solidarity*, Rorty writes that "the suggestion that truth ... is out there is a legacy of an age in which the world was seen as the creation of a being who had a language of his own."[60] For Rorty the revolutionaries and poets of the late eighteenth century "glimpsed" a truth which only perspectival postmodernism has come to see clearly—"that anything could be made to look good or bad, important or unimportant, useful or useless, by being redescribed" (*CIS* 7). The romantics had only a "dim sense" that those whose language changed "so that they no longer spoke of themselves as responsible to nonhuman powers would thereby become a new kind of human beings" (*CIS* 7). By the end of the twentieth century, however, the outline of that new human being has become evident for Rorty. The new human is the liberal ironist, the one who takes delight in the satisfactions of language without ever making the pretentious error of trying to assert that language reflects some kind of "truth as a deep matter." "An ideal liberal society is one which has no purpose except freedom.... It has no purpose except to make life easier for poets and revolutionaries while seeing to it that they make life harder for others only by words, and not deeds. It is a society whose hero is the strong poet and the revolutionary because it recognizes that it is what it is, has the morality it has, speaks the language it does, not because it approximates the will of God or the nature of man but because certain poets and revolutionaries of the past spoke as they did" (*CIS* 60-61).

Having entitled his Gifford Lectures *The Nature and Destiny of Man*, Niebuhr was expressing his confidence that he could affirm the centrality and truthfulness of Christian doctrine, even as he interpreted the Bible as a symbolic expression of human desire which was also somehow the revelation of the will of God. At a specific time when fascism and Stalinism appeared to make Christian views of sin more relevant than they had been for several centuries, Niebuhr's apologetic revivified classic doctrines. Ironically, however, it was precisely Niebuhr's exclusive emphasis upon the usefulness of those doctrines as philosophical and psychological interpretations which made them appear to many to be expendable once they had lost their timely explanatory power. In a perspectival, therapeutic culture, language can only be seen as an extension of human desire, and when one way of talking no longer seems useful—say the way dominated by words such as sin, forgiveness, grace, God, and judgment—then there is no reason at all not to drop that vocabulary and start speaking another one which might prove more efficient in the pursuit of human happiness: "'The nature of truth' is an unprofitable topic, resembling in this respect 'the nature of man' and 'the nature of God . . . 'But this claim about relative profitability, in turn, is just the recommendation that we in fact say little about these topics, and see how we get on" (*CIS* 8).

Rorty is confident that all of the languages of truth—whether they be those of Christian orthodoxy, Cartesianism rationalism, or Baconian empiricism—will inevitably grow so uninteresting as to become obsolete:

> Once upon a time we felt a need to worship something which lay beyond the visible world. Beginning in the seventeenth century we tried to substitute a love of truth for a love of God, treating the world described by science as a quasi divinity. Beginning at the end of the eighteenth century we tried to substitute a love of ourselves for a love of scientific truth, a worship of our own deep spiritual or poetic nature, treated as one more quasi divinity. The line of thought common to Blumenberg, Nietzsche, Freud, and Davidson suggests that we try to get to the point where we no longer worship anything, where we treat nothing as a quasi divinity, where we treat everything—our language, our conscience, our community—as a product of time and chance. (*CIS* 22)

In Rorty's radically contingent world, interpretation can never represent anything more than my effort to understand how the claims of other persons and texts can threaten or be useful to me; the power of interpretation can be nothing more than the power to shape the world to my own private ends, whatever they might be.

At the beginning of this essay, I referred to the conflict of interpretive paradigms surrounding the departure of Bill Curry from the University of Alabama coaching job. Curry's father found the biblical story to be a convincing and adequate description of the struggles of his son, while the university trustee relied upon a vocabulary of perspectivalism to assess the coach's dilemma. Rorty would undoubtedly understand the conflict between these two paradigms. After all, he writes in *Contingency, Irony, and Solidarity*, "interesting philosophy is, implicitly or explicitly, a contest between an entrenched vocabulary which has become a nuisance and a half-formed new vocabulary which vaguely promises great things" (*CIS* 9). In a culture enamored of efficiency and self-fulfillment, and committed to no ideal higher than that of indeterminate freedom, the biblical story is likely to seem little more than a nuisance, while perspectivalism indeed seems vaguely to promise "great things."

This essay has sought to argue that no matter how useful they find these new vocabularies of usefulness to be, Christian interpreters have something essential at stake in the "entrenched vocabulary" which the therapeutic model is seeking to supplant. The history of interpretation since Schleiermacher and the romantics has largely been an effort to carry on the epistemological revolution of Spinoza and Descartes by other means. The therapeutic and utopian selves of contemporary theory differ from these intellectual predecessors mainly in the degree to which they have exchanged a vocabulary of truth for languages of perspective and interpretation. As Christian interpreters grapple with the reigning paradigms of postmodernism, they need to be reminded, in the words of Helmut Thielicke, that "God's Word is not interpretative; it is creative. It brings forth being out of nothing. It thus transcends all analogies and all supposedly common planes.... Being an active rather than an interpretative... word, God's Word changes the self rather than disclosing it."[61]

To point to the dilemmas posed by the romantic self and romantic theories of interpretation is not, of course, the same thing as arguing that it would somehow be possible to move back to a time before the self became a pressing concern for theology in particular and Western culture in general. No, the goal of the Christian interpreter should not be to deny intellectual history, but to have the courage to address that history with authority when it has suppressed the truth. As Thielicke has argued, "we need to consider whether the elimination of the question of transcendence from the reflective consciousness is not perhaps due to Neronic suppression, to what Paul calls 'holding down the truth in unrighteousness' (Romans 1:18)."[62] In declaring that the only possible truth—the only transcendence, indeed—is lodged in the coherent patterns of the reigning paradigms of language, the perspectival or therapeutic view of knowledge involves nothing less than the massive suppression of an entire dimension of the truth. There is, after all, a profound difference between saying that we see the truth as through a glass, darkly, and claiming that all we can do with language is attempt to make nature mirror our own power. What the Christian looks for in Creation is something greater than the stunning reflection of his or her own desiring countenance. What the Christian listens for in the proclamation of the Word of God is more than the echo of his or her own clamoring voice. If this were not so, then we, of all people, would be "most to be pitied."

Notes

1. This essay first appeared in *CSR* 19.4 (June 1990): 363-87.
2. "The Marriage of Heaven and Hell," in *The Norton Anthology of English Literature*, Vol. 2, 5th ed., ed. M. H. Abrams et al (New York: W. W. Norton, 1986), 67.
3. *Philosophy and the Mirror of Nature* (Princeton, N.J.: Princeton University Press, 1979), 359.
4. *Criticism and Social Change* (Chicago: University of Chicago Press, 1985), 19.
5. Ibid., 11.
6. "The Humanities at Williams," *The New Criterion* 8 (Jan 1990): 43. What Wayne Booth said more than a decade ago about the proliferation of studies of metaphor might be applied equally to the contemporary study of interpretation: "Students of metaphor have positively pullulated . . . . I'll wager a good deal that the year 1977 produced more titles [on metaphor] than the entire history of thought before 1940. We shall soon no doubt have more metaphoricians than metaphysicians . . . I have in fact extrapolated with my pocket calculator to the year 2039; at that point there will be more students of metaphor than people." "Metaphor as Rhetoric: The Problem of Evaluation," in *On Metaphor*, ed. Sheldon Sacks (Chicago: University of Chicago Press, 1979), 47.
7. "On Truth and Lie in an Extra-Moral Sense," in *The Portable Nietzsche*, ed. and trans. Walter Kaufmann (New York: Penguin, 1976), 46-47.
8. *Twilight of the Idols*, trans. R. J. Hollingdale (London: Penguin, 1968), 72.
9. Robert C. Solomon, *Continental Philosophy since 1750: The Rise and Fall of the Self* (Oxford: Oxford University Press, 1988).
10. Rorty argues that hermeneutics is the rightful heir to the throne abdicated by epistemology in its failure: "Hermeneutics does not need a new epistemological paradigm, any more than liberal political thought requires a new paradigm of sovereignty. Hermeneutics, rather, is what we get when we are no longer epistemological." *Philosophy and the Mirror of Nature*, 325.
11. In the past few years, several significant books have attempted to trace the complex history of contemporary theories of the self and interpretation. Perhaps the most comprehensive and useful in Charles Taylor, *Sources of the Self: The Making of the Modern Identity* (Cambridge: Harvard University Press, 1989).
12. Philip Rieff, *The Triumph of the Therapeutic: Uses of Faith After Freud* (New York: Harper & Row, 1966). For further discussion of the therapeutic model, see also Rieff, *Fellow Teachers/of Culture and Its Second Death* (Chicago: University of Chicago Press, 1985); Alasdair MacIntyre, *After Virtue*, 2nd ed. (Notre Dame, Ind.: University of Notre Dame Press, 1984); Robert Bellah et al, *Habits of the Heart: Individualism and Commitment in American Life* (Berkeley: University of California Press, 1985).
13. *Triumph of the Therapeutic*, 240. Though my earlier citation of the examples of Rorty and Lentricchia might seem to indicate that the "utopian radicals" would be highly uncomfortable with a therapeutic culture, that is not often the case. The disagreements between the likes of Rorty and Lentricchia are differences of degree rather than kind; they are about tactics and strategies, not about ends.
14. Richard Rorty, *Contingency, Irony, and Solidarity* (Cambridge: Cambridge University Press, 1989), 3; Rieff, *Triumph of the Therapeutic*, 13.
15. "Foreword" to *German Romantic Criticism*, ed. A. Leslie Willson (New York: Continuum, 1982), xii.
16. *Discourse on Method and The Meditations*, trans. F. E. Sutcliffe (Harmondsworth: Penguin, 1968), 35. Hereafter cited as *DM*.
17. *The Dream of Descartes*, trans. Mabelle L. Andison (New York: Philosophical Library, 1944), 168. Paul Hazard and Stanley Jaki have expressed similar reservations about the implications of the Cartesian revolution. By Hazard, see *The European Mind: 1680-1715* (Cleveland: Meridian Books, 1963), 119-154; and by Jaki, see *Angels, Apes, and Men* (Peru, Illinois: Sherwood Sugden, 1984), 11-40.
18. *A Theologico-Political Treatise*, R. H. M. Elwes (New York: Dover, 1951), 8. Subsequent references in the text as *TPT*.
19. "The interpretation of nature, he says in the *Theologico-Political Treatise*, is to inspire a new hermeneutics ruled by the principle of the interpretation of Scripture by itself. This step of Spinoza's, which does not interest us here from the strictly biblical point of view, marks a curious rebound of the interpretation naturae upon the interpretation of Scripture: the former scriptural model is now called into question, and the new model is henceforward the interpretatio naturae." Quoted in Paul Ricoeur, *Freud and Philosophy: An Essay on Interpretation*, trans. Denis Savage (New Haven: Yale University Press, 1970), 25.
20. "Convinced, as Descartes was, that human controversies and confusions are, in essence, a matter of failed communication, of definitions not made or adhered to with sufficient rigor, Spinoza aimed at a grammar of truth. Where we define our terms closely, where we relate these terms in consistent propositions, we shall be able to put questions to which God—or his echoing aggregate which is the World—will give valid reply." Quoted in George Steiner, *Extraterritorial: Papers on Literature and The Language Revolution* (New York: Atheneum, 1976), 75-76.
21. Robert M. Grant, *A Short History of The Interpretation of the Bible*, rev. ed. (New York: Macmillan, 1963), 150.
22. As cited in Franklin L. Baumer, *Modern European Thought: Continuity and Change in Ideas, 1600-1950* (New York: Macmillan, 1977), 195. There is a voluminous literature on the fate of Christian belief in the eighteenth century. In addition to Baumer, 140-255, G. R. Cragg provides a judicious survey (of the Enlightenment and English Christianity) in *Reason and Authority in the Eighteenth Century* (Cambridge: Cambridge University Press, 1964).
23. "What is Enlightenment?" trans. Carl J. Friedrich, in *The Philosophy of Kant*, ed. Carl J. Friedrich (New York: Modem Library, 1949), 132.
24. *The Philosophy of Kant*, 137.
25. *The Eclipse of Biblical Narrative: A Study in Eighteenth and Nineteenth Century Hermeneutics* (New Haven: Yale University Press, 1974), 55.

26. *Eclipse*, 55, 56.
27. As cited in Basil Willey, *The Eighteenth Century Background: Studies on the Idea of Nature in the Thought of the Period* (Boston: Beacon, 1961), 9.
28. Hermann Samuel Reimarus, *Fragments*, trans. Ralph S. Fraser, ed. Charles H. Talbert (Philadelphia: Fortress Press, 1977), 269.
29. Jefferson to William Short, October 31, 1819, in *Thomas Jefferson: Writings*, ed. Merrill D. Peterson (New York: The Library of America, 1984), 1431.
30. *Continental Philosophy*, 28.
31. "Prolegomena to Every Future Metaphysics That May Be Presented as a Science," trans. Carl J. Friedrich, in *Philosophy of Kant*, 91.
32. *Continental Philosophy*, 26-27.
33. *German Romantic Criticism*, viii-ix.
34. As cited in M. H. Abrams, *Natural Supernaturalism: Tradition and Revolution in Romantic Literature* (New York: W. W. Norton, 1971), 330.
35. *Citizens: A Chronicle of the French Revolution* (New York: Alfred A. Knopf, 1989), 860-61.
36. As cited in Abrams, *Natural*, 330.
37. *The Prelude: A Parallel Text*, ed. J. C. Maxwell (London: Penguin, 1986), 418, 420. [Book X, 330-37; 369-72, 74-76. 1805 version.]
38. *The Prelude*, 454. [Book X 11. 936-37.]
39. *Eclipse*, 3.
40. Ibid., 130.
41. Sacvan Bercovitch, *The Puritan Origins of the American Self* (New Haven: Yale University Press, 1975), 36.
42. Perry Miller did pioneering work on this topic. See his *Errand into the Wilderness* (Cambridge: Harvard University Press, 1957). For a fuller examination of the revolutionary potential of scriptural reading in seventeenth century England, see Christopher Hill, *The World Turned Upside Down: Radical Ideas During the English Revolution* (Harmondsworth: Peregrine Books, 1984), and for early New England, see Bercovitch, *Puritan Origins*.
43. Hill, *World Turned*, 144-45.
44. For the influence of Puritan radicalism on English Romanticism, the classic study is Abrams's *Natural Supernaturalism*. See also Harold Bloom, *The Visionary Company: A Reading of English Romantic Poetry*, rev. ed. (Ithaca: Cornell University Press, 1971). The influence of Puritan typological interpretation on American Romanticism is documented in Bercovitch, *Puritan Origins*, 136-86. In the past several decades, many works have documented and analyzed the role of millennial interpretation in American political, religious, and social life. A particularly comprehensive account is given in Ernest Lee Tuveson, *Redeemer Nation: The Idea of America's Millennial Role* (Chicago: University of Chicago Press, 1968).
45. *Eclipse*, 130.
46. *Natural Supernaturalism*, 68.
47. Bernard M. G. Reardon, *Religion in the Age of Romanticism: Studies in Early Nineteenth Century Thought* (Cambridge: Cambridge University Press, 1985), 32, 33.
48. *On Religion: Speeches to its Cultured Despisers*, trans. John Oman (New York: Harper & Row, 1958), 1. Subsequent references in the text *OR*.
49. *Friedrich Schleiermacher: Pioneer of Modern Theology*, ed. Keith W. Clements (London: Collins, 1987), 140.
50. Ibid., 141.
51. *The Evangelical Faith*, Volume 1. Prolegomena: *The Relation of Theology to Modern Thought Forms*, trans. and ed. Geoffrey W. Bromiley (Grand Rapids, Mich.: Eerdmans, 1974), 45.
52. *The Theology of Schleiermacher*, trans. Geoffrey W. Bromiley, ed. Dietrich Ritschl (Grand Rapids, Mich.: Eerdmans, 1982), 210.
53. *Emerson: Essays and Lectures*, ed. Joel Porte (New York: The Library of America, 1983), 885. Subsequent references in the text as *EM*.
54. *Contingency, Irony, and Solidarity*, 5.
55. *Evangelical Faith*, vol. 1, 53.
56. As cited in Richard Wightman Fox, *Reinhold Niebuhr: A Biography* (New York: Pantheon Books, 1985), 213.
57. *The Nature and Destiny of Man*, Vol. II: *Human Destiny* (New York: Charles Scribner's Sons, 1949), 298.
58. As cited in Peter S. Hawkins, *The Language of Grace* (Cambridge, Mass.: Cowley Publications, 1983), 134-35.
59. "Inquiry into the act and possibility of faith hardly leaves time for the content of faith. Intensive preoccupation with the question of method blinds us to what methodologically purified perception should show us. 'They are continually sharpening knives and no longer have anything to cut' (Karl Rahner)." Quoted in Thielicke, *Evangelical Faith*, Vol 1, 52-53.
60. *Contingency, Irony, and Solidarity*, 5. Subsequent references in the text as *CIS*.
61. *Evangelical Faith*, Vol. 1, 156.
62. Ibid., 241.

17 Traditional Christianity and the Possibility of Historical Knowledge (1990)

Mark A. Noll

What can we know about the past?[1] About the shape and significance of the actions, thoughts, institutional creations, assumptions, and intentions of those who have lived before us?[2] And how should we think about efforts to describe and interpret the past? Given the nature of the human mind, given the character of the evidence linking our present existence with past lives, and given the relationship of human thought whether past or present to the conceptual frameworks provided by societies and cultures as a whole, what is possible and what is not possible to affirm about our knowledge of the past?

These are questions which historians, surprisingly, have only recently addressed, and then only in a desultory fashion. Historians are usually much more eager simply to set about their work than they are to theorize about it. In recent years, however, this casualness about the broader intellectual implications of the effort to recover the past has begun to change, and that for several reasons.

In the first instance, it has grown increasingly clear how "political" (in the broad sense of the term) historical writing is and always has been. The development of "professional history" in the universities over the last two centuries obscured the political character of historical writing for some time. Early leaders of academic history in Europe and in this country prided themselves on a detachment and an objectivity that they felt defined their advance over earlier, amateur, and much more obviously partisan historians of previous generations.[3] The simple act of self-reflection during several generations of professional historical work has made it clear, however, that history writing has always served political purposes, not just in what historians write but also in how they conceive the nature of their tasks. This same conclusion is also the point of compelling formal studies, of which Peter Novick's recent *That Noble Dream: The "Objectivity Question" and the American Historical Profession* is the most impressive.[4] In retrospect, it is evident that the first great professional historians in nineteenth-century Europe wrote to heighten the rising sense of nationalism among the European peoples. Just as clear in our own day is the way that political considerations (again, in the broad sense of the term) shape historical writing. This generalization has been most obviously true for works written by officially sponsored historians of communist countries and by dissidents within those countries. But it is just as true for Western chroniclers of the Cold War, where Leftist historians follow the evidence and assign substantial responsibility for the Cold War to the United States and Rightest historians follow the evidence and assign substantial responsibility for the Cold War to the Soviet Union. It is illustrated by historians of the Reconstruction period in American history, where an individual historian's degree of sympathy with the modern civil rights movement invariably has correlated with that historian's interpretative conclusions about the efforts of radical Reconstructionists to bring about a better life for blacks in the postbellum South. It is true for historians of homosexuality, where gay liberationists find widespread acceptance of homosexual practice in the past and defenders of traditional values find persistent opposition to homosexual practice in the past. Political intent is also manifestly apparent in the writing of church historians. An immense distance, for example, separates the tone of Roman Catholic histories of the Reformation written before the Second Vatican Council, which asked Catholics to exercise greater charity in evaluating other groups of Christians, and those histories of the Reformation written by Catholics after Vatican II. Recently, in short, even historians with their noses deeply buried in the archives have come to sense that more is at work in reporting their findings than simply letting the facts fall where they may.

A second modern condition that has heightened the visibility of philosophical questions about our knowledge of the past is the proliferation in almost all academic disciplines of voices questioning the once widely-shared ideal of detached, rational, scientific inquiry. The reasons for questioning that ideal are various: it is described as the tool of patriarchialist, capitalist, and racist oppressors; it is denounced as dehumanizing; it is depicted as intellectually incoherent. But in each case, the effect is to call into doubt the ability of researchers to move smoothly from a collection of facts to the presentation of universally valid truth.[5] In philosophy, a turn toward pragmatism, illustrated by revisionist works like Richard Rorty's *Philosophy and the Mirror of Nature* (1979), ridicules traditional quests for the truth about perception, being, and the good, and promotes in their place a picture of knowledge as the transient consensus of privileged intellectual communities. In literary theory, deconstruction a la Jacques Derrida or Stanley Fish denies the stable or systematic relationship between words and either the ones who write the words or the things the words are supposed to stand for. In cultural anthropology, the immensely influential work of Clifford Geertz is usually thought to undercut the notion of stable, universal conceptions of truth. In jurisprudence, proponents of Critical Legal Studies defend the multivalent nature of law and its interpretation, arguing, in the words of one such theorist, that "there are as many plausible readings of the United States Constitution as there are versions of *Hamlet*."[6] In psychology, a hermeneutical turn has called into question Freud's own pretentions about the scientific character of psychoanalysis. And in social theory, influential theorists from the Continent like Michel

Foucault and Jürgen Habermas define almost all cultural verities—whether about sexuality, mental health, diet, or the distribution of economic resources—as functions of shifting power relationships. Such voices, with their flat rejection of objective, value-neutral research, have become increasingly important among historians because of the trend that has been strengthening throughout the twentieth century for opening up historical work to the concepts, materials, and strategies of the various social sciences and humanities.

A third influence rousing historians from dogmatic slumbers has been even more unnerving. It is the conviction proposed most influentially by Thomas Kuhn in his 1962 essay, *The Structure of Scientific Revolutions,* that even natural science—the intellectual standard since Newton for hard, real, genuine knowledge—may itself be less fixed, less intellectually pristine, less value neutral than all of Western civilization once assumed.[7] Such a suggestion is significant for historians because the goal of most professional historians over the last century had been to justify their existence by demonstrating that they too were scientific, that they were shedding the burdens of value-laden, subjective, and partisan history.[8] But Kuhn's shocker, though disconcerting enough, was only an opening salvo. His focus was on the internal operations of science, and his intent was to mount a back-handed defense of "normal science" on a pragmatic foundation more in line with the lived realities of scientific experience instead of the self-gratifying myths of scientific heroism. Other, more radical historians of science went much beyond Kuhn. They argued that scientific knowledge was relative not only to intellectual shifts internal to the guild of professional scientists. It was also relative to the very same social, political, racial, sexual, and economic conventions of culture that seem to have shaped so decisively the social sciences and the humanities.[9] These historians of the external relations of science have made their most impressive cases studying the age of Newton and the rise of Darwinism in Britain, as well as the American commitment to conceptions of common-sense, Baconian empiricism in the early United States.[10] In these instances, along with many others, it has not been difficult to show that what scientists and awed non-scientists held to be the sanitized results of pristinely objective inquiry were in fact products, at least in large part, of religious or social pre-conceptions, competition for status, eagerness for warrants to justify influence, and still other factors having nothing directly to do with the study of nature as such. With the anchor of scientific objectivity drifting, if not lost altogether, aspirations to write history scientifically were cast adrift on a very choppy sea.

This combination of influences has shaken even some very imperturbable historians into sober reflection on the nature of their enterprise. The result is that for the last few years rumors of an "epistemological crisis" concerning the status of knowledge about the past have swept even the out-of-the way landscapes that historians inhabit.[11] Even they have awakened to the fact that the general chaos characterizing contemporary Western epistemology does not exempt the effort to understand the past.

This state of affairs presents a matter of pressing concern for all of us. The sense of who we are, what we are here for, and what we may hope for in the future are all dependent, to a greater rather than lesser degree, upon our understanding of where we have come from, on who and what has contributed to our development. Upon the least reflection, almost everyone will admit to the sense of having been shaped by a multitudinous inheritance—ideals, scandals, patience, struggle, death, celebration, worship, love, disillusionment, hope, selfishness, altruism, and so much more—all experienced before we arrived on the scene, all having left some record that (we hope) can guide and enrich our existence, and all worthy of passing on in some fashion to our children. And so, in these general terms, the debate over how we know the past is a debate on how we define ourselves.

But if the crisis in historical knowledge is important in general, it is even more important for the members of Christian communities, since Christianity hinges critically in at least two ways upon an ability to understand the past.

At stake, first, is the foundation of Christian faith. Christians, at least those in the broad stream of confessional Catholicism, Orthodoxy, and Protestantism, affirm that their very existence is defined by the meaning of purportedly historical events—an omnipotent deity who from nothing created the heavens and the earth, the same God who called Abraham to be the father of many nations, who threw the Egyptian horse and rider into the sea in order to preserve his purpose among a chosen people, and who showed himself and his loving intentions for humanity supremely in becoming a person himself. The historical record of Jesus, the incarnate Son of God, is for Christians even more foundational than the historical record of their own lives—that he was conceived by the Holy Spirit, born of the Virgin Mary, and lived a life of moral perfection; that he suffered under Pontius Pilate, was crucified, dead, and buried; that on the third day he rose again from the dead, ascended to heaven, and will come again to judge the living and the dead.

Implicit, moreover, in affirming these events in the history of salvation is a definite view of historical understanding. These events, Christians hold, may be known to be factual. In addition, there may be a reasonable degree of certainty and a reasonable degree of consensus among believers as to what these long-past events mean for our lives in the late twentieth century. Reliable records of these events, supremely in the Bible, present the story with a basic accuracy. The meaning of events described in the Bible has been handed down in lines of reliable tradition that show us (though at a distance of 2,000 years and more) the significance of those ancient events today. Finally, by understanding the nature of those events and acting on that understanding, people may be reconciled to God, may be brought to see the infinite worth of other humans, and may become agents of God's work in the world.

At stake is also, however, another range of issues besides those related narrowly to faith itself, for Christians have traditionally held that their picture of God and his works has far-ranging implications for more general knowledge. That is, the same sort of historical realism that undergirds Christian understanding of the gospel is matched by a general epistemological realism with respect to the creation. In a set of assumptions that may be found in different versions, Christians have usually assumed that because God is the creator of the material world and the institutions of civilization, because God has made human beings in his image, and because God wills for humans to subdue the earth, the possibility exists for human beings to come to know some things about the material world and the world of human institutions. This epistemological confidence in general knowledge about the world also entails definite assumptions about historical knowledge, for it is based precisely on what the historical records of Scripture and Christian tradition tell of God's actions and of his character, and on what we may assumed even in a post-modern world to draw reliably from those records.

These Christian assertions about historical knowledge have always been a challenge to searching minds. They were "foolishness" to "the Greeks" that the Apostle Paul described in his first epistle to the Corinthians. In the eighteenth century, their scandalous audacity offended Gotthold Ephraim Lessing who described instead an "ugly ditch" between particular historical assertions and general truths of reason.[12] They stimulated David Hume, Immanuel Kant, and a whole host of their successors to propose alternative conceptions of knowledge, truth, and the past. But they have become even more of a challenge as modern currents undercut ever more persistently the conventions that citizens of the West generally used to entertain about our ability to know and interpret the past.

What, then, may be said from a Christian point of view about the crisis in historical knowledge? At this point, the temptation is great to slide around the issue. Some very capable historians have taken this approach, most notably the distinguished scholar of early modern England, J. H. Hexter, who made a kind of career out of pooh-poohing thorny issues of philosophy and historiography by championing the ability of a sympathetic common sense to cut through the Gordian knots of historical uncertainty.[13] The temptation for believers to sweep the challenges under the rug, simply to preach louder, to ignore these issues in hopes that they will soon go away is not necessarily foolishness. The sort of people who most readily heed the Christian message seem also to have the fewest qualms about affirming that we can know quite a bit about the past. At the present moment, the temptation to treat hesitations about historical knowledge as a passing fancy is strengthened by events in Eastern Europe, where a host of common-sense historiographers have turned the world upside down in no small measure because they believe implicitly in the reliability of human knowledge about the past.

But we are not in Eastern Europe and American higher education is not the place where proletarian assumptions about historical knowledge are encouraged. So, while being aware of the complexity of the general problem, I would like to offer a Christian response to the issues posed by the crisis in historical knowledge, and to do so, moreover, in terms posed by those who have, with telling force, exposed the dimensions of that crisis.

The plan is, first, to describe briefly three wide-spread and influential twentieth-century attitudes toward knowledge of the past. These attitudes—which may be called the scientific, the ideological, and the relativistic—have predominated at different times over the last century. All of them are also defended today.

Second, an argument will be made that a Christian perspective on knowledge can provide not only a, but *the best* foundation for restoring confidence in the human ability to know the past reliably. By implication, this will also be an argument that the Christian faith provides a secure foundation for acquiring reliable knowledge about many other aspects of the material world and the world of human interactions.

Finally, the paper moves beyond a utilitarian recommendation of Christianity for its usefulness in recovering a certain degree of confidence in historical knowledge to suggesting that, even by the reasoning of relativistic theories of knowledge, Christianity should be regarded not just as historiographically useful, but also as true.

The first attitude was one promoted by the founders of professional history in the United States. It is the conviction that genuine knowledge of the past must be derived through verificationist procedures modeled directly on a strictly empirical conception of the physical sciences. This position may be called positivistic, scientistic, or with greater charity, scientific. It was the embodiment among historians of the Enlightenment ideal hailed by Alexander Pope in the eighteenth century: "Nature and nature's laws lay hid in night / God said, let Newton be, and all was light." If only those who wrote about the past could do so with the impartial objectivity of a Newton, the results would be as revolutionary in history as his had been in science. Among historians, this position enjoyed some vogue in England as early as the mid-nineteenth century, especially in the work of H. T. Buckle.[14] It flourished in America from the beginning of modern university study in the 1870s through the First World War as historians routinely promoted the idea that history should be a strictly empirical science. George Burton Adams summed up this general opinion in his presidential address before the American Historical Association in 1908. The job of historians, Adams argued, was "to ascertain as nearly as possible and to record exactly what happened." Questions concerning "the philosophy of history" were wisely left of "poets, philosophers and theologians." Historians knew, Adams went on, that "at the very beginning of all conquest of the unknown lies the fact, established and classified to the fullest extent possible." Others may yield to "the allurements of speculation," but "the field of the historian is, and must long remain, the discovery and recording of what actually happened."[15]

Conservative Protestants have a special reason for looking kindly upon this conception of scientific history, for over the last generation conservative Protestant historians have worked their way back into the ranks of university students of history by adopting objective standards. At least since the 1940s, a considerable number of British and American historians of confessional or evangelical Protestant conviction—among others, Herbert Butterfield, Patrick Collinson, and Margaret Spufford in Britain; Kenneth Scott Latourette, E. Harris Harbison, Arthur Link, Lewis Spitz, Timothy Smith, Martin Marty, and George Marsden in the United States—have won recognition in the academy for their work precisely by demonstrating their skill at writing objective history. To do so, these historians have abandoned—at least while working within university precincts—the church's long tradition of providential historiography that stretches back to Constantine's Eusebius. In theological terms, the historians have switched over to consider historical writing as situated in the sphere of creation rather than in the sphere of grace, as a manifestation of general rather than special revelation. Put differently, Christian historians in the modern academy have made the implicit confession that history is not theology. This confession means that they construct their accounts of the past from facts ascertained through documentary or material evidence and explained in terms of natural human relationships.

Christian historians may have exploited scientific history to reenter the academy, but the burden of Christian analysis also shows manifest shortcomings in the extreme statements of the scientific ideal. The perversion of scientific history lies not in its use of empirical methods, but in its shortsightedness about the process that culminates in written history. The agents of history—those who act and who witness actions, those who make and transmit records, those who attempt to reconstruct past actions on the basis of those records—are people with worldviews, biases, blindspots, and convictions. Moreover, the most important human actions—responsible choices with consequences—are the very ones most resistant to the kind of replication and control required for a strictly empirical science. In short, the positivist presupposition about historical knowledge arises out of a good thing, but a good thing carried recklessly beyond its own limits.

A second contemporary presupposition about historical knowledge is much more widely shared among both academics and non-academics. It is the assumption that historical writing exists in order to illustrate the truth of propositions known to be true before study of the past begins. This stance may be called the ideological presupposition. In the modern world it is almost certainly the most widely practiced form of history. It could also be called the "whig" view of history, defined over a half-century ago by Herbert Butterfield as the telling of "a story which is meant to reveal who is in the right."[16] In simplest terms, this assumption holds that written history exists to illustrate two things: first, how similar all of the past is to the present; and second, how clearly the past reveals the inevitable emergence of the present conditions which most concern the historian. Western Christians often think of Marxism as the major proponent of such an ideological view, and with some justice. In crass and not so crass forms, Marxist history has had to fit.[17]

Ideological history, however, was not invented by Karl Marx. It rather began with the ancient Greeks and Romans, and then received an especially strong boost from early Christian historians. With the spread of Christianity, the content of history changed, but the form remained the same. The most influential early church historians, Eusebius and Orosius, specified how developments in Greece, Rome, and the Middle East demonstrated God's designs for the universal spread of the church.[18] This ideological conception of history prevailed among Christians in the Middle Ages, and then in competing versions among Catholics and Protestants into the nineteenth century.[19] It is still probably the dominant perspective in many religious traditions to this day, Protestant evangelicals more than most.

In other venues, ideological history has provided the form for the national histories written during the modern period. Under the influence of various romantic movements, it flourished during the nineteenth century as an effort to find the distinctive *Geiste* of the individual European *Völker*. The approach has always been important in the self-conception of Americans. More recently, feminist and black perspectives have generated a great amount of work exploiting innovative historical research for substantially predetermined conclusions. And in recent years, a particularly active form of ideological history in the United States has drawn together national, Christian, and political elements. It is the view that history reveals how American democratic capitalism developed under the active providence of God.[20]

A third modern attitude toward historical knowledge, if not the most prevalent, is certainly the most articulate in the academy. It is the assumption that we cannot in any traditional sense really know the past, that all history is a creative reconstruction of how, for whatever reason, the historian would like things to have been. The theoretical denial of the objectivity of historical knowledge enjoys a robust life in the academy. We may call it the relativistic view, a position with important, even contradictory, manifestions.

In the world of Anglo-American history writing, an influential view of historical relativism was first expressed by Carl Becker and Charles Beard, two of America's most influential historians of the century's first decades. Becker provided the most famous exposition of these views when he addressed the American Historical Association as its president in 1931. In that address Becker gave full expression to the convictions that circumstantial predilections determine a vision of the past. History, he said, is "an imaginative creation, a personal possession which each one of us . . . fashions out of his individual experience, adapts to his practical or emotional needs, and adorns as well as may be to suit his aesthetic tastes."[21] Beard and Becker were recalled from solipsistic applications of their position by the events of World War II. Both were appalled by the thought that historical study, as they had earlier described it, could offer no principled reasons for favoring the Allies over the Axis Powers. Yet others soon arose to pursue the path they had prepared.

Over the last quarter century the number of serious proposals questioning the possibility of historical knowledge in anything like its traditional sense have increased dramatically. As noted above, these are now commonplace in philosophy, literary criticism, anthropology, jurisprudence, political theory, and psychology. Among historians one of the most visible proponents of the view is Hayden White, whose major study, *Metahistory*, argued in 1973 that "the historian performs an essentially poetic act, in which he prefigures the historical field and constitutes it as a domain upon which to bring to bear the specific theories he will use to explain 'what was really happening' in it."[22]

The central argument underlying this view is that present circumstances and present realities so thoroughly define the vision of a historian that our supposed knowledge of the past is actually an expression of the historian's own longings, self-interest, ideology, or psychology. No path exists to the past which is not a disguised tour of the present.

In extreme form, the relativistic conception is a triple offense to Christian faith. Christians hold that a realm of reality beyond the immediate sensory perception of this generation is the fundamental reality which makes possible the perception of all other realities. They believe, furthermore, that this more basic reality was manifest with unique force in events and circumstances of history. And they affirm that this reality is supernatural as well as natural, that it stems originally from God. It is hard to imagine a sharper antithesis than that between such Christian views and extreme statement of relativistic assumptions about historical knowledge.

At the same time, more modest statements of historical relativity turn out to comport surprisingly well with basic Christian teaching. In fact, insights from the relativistic and ideological approaches to history may be even more useful for a Christian effort to defend the reliability of historical knowledge than those associated with the notion of scientific history.

The Christian faith does, in fact, offer a conserving strategy to meet the epistemological crisis of historical knowledge. It holds out the assurance that there is a past, real in itself, which we may actually study and genuinely come to know. To put the matter in altogether utilitarian terms: come to Christ and regain your confidence that historical research can lead to at least a measure of genuine knowledge about the past. Faith in God, rather than confidence in the capabilities of humans as defined by Enlightenment visionaries, enables us to reach some of the goals advanced by defenders of scientific history.

To make this claim stick, we must begin by defining the kind of Christianity we are talking about. The sort of Christian faith that is best able to restore confidence in our ability to know the past is the full-blown theism of Augustine, the Catholic mystics, the Protestant reformers, and, closer to the Enlightenment itself, the French Catholic Nicolas Malebranche, the British Bishop George Berkeley, and the New England Congregationalist Jonathan Edwards. This sort of Christian faith affirms that God is not just the creator and passive sustainer of the world, but also that his energy is the source of the world's energy and his will the foundation of its existence.

There are different ways of describing this kind of Christian belief, but all of them stress the world's radical dependency upon God, the human mind's derivative relation to the divine mind, and the benevolent intention of God to share with humans an understanding of the reality he sustains. A summary of Malebranche's arguments, for example, speaks of his convictions concerning "man's dependence on God. It is God who creates us and conserves us from moment to moment and who alone acts on us and for us. Owing our existence and actions as well as our knowledge to God, we are truly united with him." Berkeley, J. O. Urmson summarizes, "certainly thinks that the metaphysical explanation of why some ideas have coherence, liveliness and independence of our wills is because God, the infinite spirit, causes them. Thus metaphysical reality is to be explained in terms of the activity of God." Jonathan Edwards put it perhaps most directly: "That which truly is the substance of all bodies is the infinitely exact and precise and perfectly stable idea in God's mind, together with his stable will that the same shall gradually be communicated to us, and to other minds, according to certain fixed and exact established methods and laws: or in somewhat different language, the infinitely exact and precise divine idea, together with an answerable, perfectly exact, precise and stable will with respect to correspondent communications to created minds, and effects on their minds."[23]

What these ideas of God and the world share is a rejection of the deistical notion that God made the world, established its laws, created humans with certain mental capabilities to understand the world, and then stepped back to see what would happen. Since the mid-eighteenth century, Christians, no less than nonbelievers, have been enamored of this Enlightenment view of God. It is a view which fueled a search for Arguments from Design to demonstrate the existence of God, which led to increasingly frenzied efforts at demonstrating the benevolence of God over against supposedly autonomous standards of justice, which heightened concern for the apologetic value of miracles as events where God intervenes in a world proceeding normally under its own inner compulsion, and which placed a great burden upon believers to justify their faith rationally with the procedures that the great scientists used to reason about nature. The historian James Turner has well described the burden this view placed on believers from the time of the Enlightenment onwards: "As Newton was deified, so the temptation was great to Newtonify the Deity. If science and rationalism had raised questions about God and unsettled belief, then, what more logical response than to shore up religion by remodeling it in the image of science and rationality? Accordingly, many spokesmen of the church—theologians, minister, lay writers—enthusiastically magnified the rationalizing tendencies already apparent within belief, increasingly conceived assurance of God as a matter of the intellect and the grounds of belief as rationally demonstrable."[24]

Against these Enlightenment conceptions of God, Christians like Malebranche, Berkeley, and Edwards postulated a deity who filled the universe he had created, who activated the minds he had made in his own image, and who brooded over the world with constant love as well as distant power. This is the sort of Christianity that can rescue historical knowledge. The rescue operation consists of several steps, each resting on central teachings of the Christian faith. Together, these steps recognize a substantial contribution from relativistic as well as from scientific ideas of history, but are not in the end necessarily dependent upon either, or upon the practices of ideological historians.

(1) First, this view of God affirms that the divine creation and sustaining of the world is the foundation for epistemological confidence of whatever sort. Humans may have hope in their efforts to understand the world, past or present, because the reality of the world external to ourselves depends ultimately upon God rather than upon ourselves. Humans may have a reasonable degree of confidence that their minds are able to grasp some elements of reality external to themselves because their minds have been made in the image of God who is responsible for that external reality. And humans may trust that there is some sort of meaningful correspondence between external reality and their own internal mental capacities because they themselves, along with external reality, all flow from a single coordinate act of divine creation and all share in the same providential maintenance.

The doctrine of creation also shows why the analogy between historical study and scientific research is a fruitful one, if the analogy is taken in a general sense. Because of creation, the historian's reliance upon the empirical data of research resembles the scientist's reliance upon empiricism. In both cases scientists and historians do their work assuming the contingency of events—that is, they believe that knowledge depends more upon an ability to perceive the event in its own development than upon deductive explanations brought to the event. Christians like Malebranche, Berkeley, and Edwards contended that researchers were able to believe in the independent reality of those events outside of themselves, and in their mind's ability to follow the course of external developments, only because they were trusting, implicitly or explicitly, in God. Malebranche, Berkeley, and Edwards affirmed comprehensive theism in part because they felt that only such a theism was capable of sustaining the unusually productive potential of science. Theirs was an idealism in service to science. Their view of God is equally reassuring for efforts to understand the past. Early modern scientists and defenders of scientific history both overstated the degree to which they could be free from pre-understandings. Yet they also displayed a laudable confidence in the world *extra nos* because God had made it, because God sustains it, and because God opens it to humans through mental abilities that also come from his gracious hand.[25]

(2) The analogy between scientific and historical research leads us to a second consideration. If a Christian doctrine of creation looks in the first instance like a warmed-over version of scientific history, it also points in a relativistic direction as well. If we say that humans may be confident about obtaining true knowledge in science or history because they may be confident in God's creating power, we are conceding one of the most important principles of the relativistic approach to history. This concession is that arguments about the meaning of particular historical events, conditions, or circumstances must also be arguments, however implicit, about "the nature of things" more generally. The same is true for science. For example, when scientists discuss the question of the nature of light, they must also discuss, at least implicitly, the reliability of human perception, the nature of probability, the meaning of human measurements, and many other metaempirical subjects. Similarly, for historians to argue about what "caused" the Civil War or the Cold War, or about why the relationships between men and women in Western civilization have changed over time, is also to argue about human nature, ideals of social order, the nature of evil, and whether there is a possibility for human progress. In other words, when we affirm that a belief in creation stands behind the possibility of objective knowledge, we are also confirming a major tenet of the relativists, that all knowledge, whether historical or scientific, is a function of some point of view, and in that sense ideological or relativistic.

And there are other ways in which Christian teaching points to the relativity of historical knowledge. The doctrine of the Fall and the resultant depravity of human nature suggest that the human moral condition obscures vision, presumably for historical as well as moral reasoning. The Scriptures are replete with warnings concerning the way that idolatry or willful disobedience of the divine law makes humans "blind" or "deaf" (e.g., Is. 6:9-10; 42:18-20; 43:8; Matt 15:14; 23:16ff; 2 Cor. 4:4; 2 Peter 1:9), and they describe how sinfulness "darkens understanding" (Eph. 4:18). Except in those Christian traditions that teach perfection for believers in this life, the skewing of perspective caused by the human bent toward self characterizes the vision of believers as well as for those who are not believers. An ability to understand the past objectively and without distortion, in other words, is not confirmed by Christian doctrine about the human condition.

There are, however, more positive Christian teachings that can also lead to the conviction that God intends historical understanding to be relative to specific times, places, and circumstances. These teachings have to do with the dignity of particularities, with the awareness that it is God who made humans in such a way that they could benefit from particular adaptation to particular cultural circumstances. The record in the first chapters of Genesis, that God assigned humans the stewardship of the earth, certainly implies divine sanction for the particular adaptation to different landscapes, climates, and cultures that such a stewardship requires. And whatever one makes of the historical or moral implications of the Tower of Babel, it is clear that God ordained the multiplicity of human languages, with the consequent particularities of cultural understanding that the diversity of tongues entails. Again, these teachings indicate that while we have come relatively late to consider the different perspectives created by differing cultural circumstances, it was God's determinate will that ordained those varying circumstances.

In addition, the Incarnation and the outworking of redemption in the particular culture of first-century Judaism suggests something—if only a dim shape within a mystery—about the dignity of human actions and perspective rooted in very specific historical circumstances. If God accomplished redemption for humanity "when Cyrenius was governor of Syria" and "under Pontius Pilate," is not God also telling us that he fully affirms the appropriateness of his saving action taking place within the context of one particular set of cultural circumstances? Christians traditionally have affirmed—and rightly so—the universal meaning for all people everywhere of those saving acts in first-century Judea under Roman rule on the edge of Hellenistic civilization. But could Christians not also confess that the cultural particularity of redemption affirms the appropriateness of cultural particularity? If so, the conclusion would have to follow that those who lived "when Ghengis Khan was governor of Mongolia" or "under President McKinley"—and who experienced the world from the particular cultural perspective of those times and places—would be fully justified in doing so because of the way that God himself had dignified the perspective of a singular cultural setting. On the basis of such reasoning, the writing of history from the point of view of a particular culture becomes not only inescapable, but also divinely ordained and good. Relativism, in other words, has a divine sanction.

(3) But, third, this kind of Christian relativism must not be mistaken for skepticism about historical knowledge or considered support for nihilistic conclusions about the possibility of knowing the past. To race incautiously from this kind of Christian relativism—and perhaps from other forms of modest relativism as well—to skeptical or radically historicist conclusions is unnecessary. If we admit that our knowledge about the past (or the world in general) is relative to our points of view, our characters, our particular perspectives, we are not necessarily saying that we are condemned to a merely imaginative grasp of the past. The Christian reason for this assertion includes doctrines concerning the unity of humanity and concerning humanity as the image-bearer of God.

The unity of human nature is built into the foundation of Christian teaching. In particular, it is the predicate of redemption: "As in Adam all die, so also in Christ shall all be made alive" (1 Cor. 15:22). For historiographical purposes, this Christian teaching means that all humans must be alike—not just in their moral nature, but also in their propensity to write about the past from within the perspective of their own particular cultures. That is, the relativity of historical understanding that arises from diverse perspectives, frameworks, and cultures is kept from historiographical solipsism by the fact that a common human nature underlies the production of different views of the past. Humans are going to conclude different things about the past, but the fact that all humans share Godgiven qualities of conscience, intellectual potential, and social capabilities means that differing views of the past will not differ absolutely. The differing conditions of human cultures mean that histories will never be the same; the commonalities of human nature mean that histories will never be absolutely antithetical.

As it happens, this extrapolation of Christian teaching fits fairly well with the logic of historical relativism. If all history is relative, due to the placement of the historian within the historian's own times, it must then follow that it is universally true that people write about the past in terms of their own present circumstances. And if this is true, then historical relativism yields one non-relative reality: viz., all people write history the same way. If we put this in different words, we are led by relativistic arguments themselves to consider a second Christian doctrine that brightens the picture of historical relativism. Relativist views of historical knowledge depend upon the positive assertion that all humans in every time and every place construe the past relative to their own circumstances—that is, that humans are active and creative in similar ways as they draw meaning from their examination of the past. This assertion about what humans do variously assumes something about what humans are uniformly, agents who imaginatively create a mental picture of the world that they inhabit.

Such reasoning leads naturally to the Christian doctrine that humans are made in the image of God. Many of the traits and attributes that characterize God also characterize human beings. Such teaching is a constant in all Christian traditions, as is also the qualification that the image of God in humans is limited by our finiteness and distorted by our sin. But the positive statement of the doctrine is that human actions and human states of mind bear a resemblance to divine actions and divine states of mind. With this doctrine, and observing the imaginative energy that humans display in describing the past, we may conclude, not that humans are *creative* in understanding the past, but that they are *re-creative*.

The suggestion that people are and should be active re-creators of the past fits especially well with the full-blown theism of the Christian philosophers mentioned above, Malebranche, Berkeley, and Edwards. Their view was that the world, with all its regularities of physical nature and human society, continues to exist because God thinks it into existence moment by moment. These Christian philosophers were idealists, or tended in an idealist direction. The world simply is an extension of the mind of God. From that perspective, the element of human creativity in describing and evaluating the past becomes a creativity that explicitly imitates the divine creativity in sustaining the world. The human activity of recreating the past images the divine activity that constantly engenders the world.

In trying to show how Christian doctrine supports confidence in our ability to know the past, but that it does so in ways closer in form to the principles of relativistic history than to scientific history, I have raced rapidly past far too many complicated and important questions. I have offered merely a sketch that has not even touched upon what we might call anomalies in the Christian paradigm, specifically the problem of evil and the nature of human free will. But even from such a superficial and incomplete outline, perhaps it may be clear why it is possible to say that, from a Christian angle of vision, we are able to reach the scientific goal of reliable knowledge about the past only by embracing principles from the relativist depiction of historical knowledge.[26]

Thus, from the perspective of the great Christian idealists of the eighteenth century, the correspondence theory of historical knowledge—the theory that the written product of research can correspond to the actual experience of what happened—is valid only because there is no material "out there" out there. Correspondence works, but the correspondence is between our minds and God's mind.

Next, we may progress in our understanding of the past, not if we are confident in human autonomy (as the great proponents of scientific history have been), but if we celebrate our dependence upon God.

Then, we may say we have objective knowledge about the past only because our knowledge is relative—relative to our circumstances, relative to our nature, and relative to God.

Finally, it is possible to conclude that we can reach toward a true picture of the past, not because we have abstracted ourselves from the influence of cultural bias, but because we embrace wholeheartedly the particularity of cultural situations.

(4) But, fourth and finally, we must return to Christian reasons for why our knowledge of the past will never be entirely correct, fully true, or completely satisfactory. We might think that if historical knowledge depends upon the person and work of God, we would have the highest confidence in obtaining a perfectly true picture of the past. All that is necessary is to seek the divine perspective. But it is precisely Christian revelation that describes the effort to obtain the divine perspective as grossest idolatry and the source of profoundest evil. The height of foolishness is to confuse the tasks of creator and creature (Rom. 1). Humans are creatures, not the creator. As such we will always be limited by our finitude from seeing the whole picture. We will always be predisposed by our fallenness to misconstrue the results of historical inquiry for our own idolatrous satisfaction. We will always be trading the advantages that come from living in the God-ordained particularities of our own cultures for the blindness that comes from being unable to see what is so obvious to those who gaze upon the past from other frames of reference.

Historian Bruce Kuklick once helpfully illuminated the question of historian's self-perception by arguing that many historians see themselves in the position of "ideal observers"—that is, individuals who through research make themselves nearly omniscient about particular historical events and who may then consider their evaluative reactions to be the normative reactions that all humans would experience if they too had carried out the investigation. However productive this self-depiction may be, Kuklick was quick to see its limits. As he put it, "Making an evaluation consists in part in *attempting* to put ourselves into a position of an ideal observer. Because this is ultimately impossible, however, there may be . . . disagreement about what is right or wrong . . . . [W]e have no guarantee that our reactions are similar to [others'] and thereby allow us to decide correctly . . . . [T]he conclusive answer to any evaluative question always eludes us and our evaluations will always be insecure. Men, in short, are only *like* God." But from his point of view as one examining the behavior of historians, Kuklick did not consider our inability to be God "a serious shortcoming."[27] There is still much of value to be discovered about the past through our efforts to act as though we could be ideal observers.

In Christian terms: we do see, but through a glass, darkly.

The historiographical conclusion, then, is that Christian teaching offers a solution to the crisis of historical knowledge, and indeed of scientific and other kinds of knowledge. The nature of the solution is to propose that we can have reliable knowledge and real understanding of the past, but that this knowledge and understanding must be modest. Christian teaching does not warrant the belief that we can obtain full and complete understanding, but it does provide reasons for a chastened realism about our grasp of history and indeed for other areas of research.

But this statement cannot really be the conclusion, for we must now ask, is Christianity in fact true? Christianity of the sort I have proposed may provide a theoretical defense for a modest realism, but that defense is of little consequence if Christianity itself is not true. Or at best such an argument might provide a bit of parochial reassurance for those already committed to faith, but mean absolutely nothing to those who consider Christianity passe, outmoded, or false.

But how, then, if we have acknowledged that Christianity does not support naively objectivist modes of demonstration, can we recommend Christianity as true? One answer is to assert that an apology for Christianity must begin where our knowledge of the past begins, with an understanding that is relative to our own perspectives. This strategy poses no difficulty for the religion of the Bible, since we read repeatedly in Scripture that the ability to rest in the truth of God depends upon a willingness to align our vision with the truth that is being proposed. In other words, the Scriptures talk of a faith confirmed by experiencing it: "Taste and see that the Lord is good! Happy is the one who takes refuge in him!" (Ps. 34:8) They are frankly perspectivalist: "Whoever would draw near to God must believe that he exists and that he rewards those who seek him." (Heb. 11:6) They stress that even the ability to believe rests upon God's actions in changing the orientation of perspectives. In the words of Jesus, only when God alters our framework of reference are we then eager to come to God: "All that the Father gives me will come to me; and him who comes to me I will not cast out." (John 6:37) There is, thus, no Christian reason for expecting a demonstration of Christianity that fits the Enlightenment ideal of objective, scientific proof.

To be sure, believers and non-believers continue to share a common humanity, and that common humanity allows for a great deal of argument and demonstration of the sort that the Apostle Paul pursued on his missionary journeys and that other apologists have also advanced effectively. Yet the larger reality is that Christianity itself seems to suggest that the day of value neutral persuasion is over, at least for now. Instead, the faith seems to teach that if a person's perspective is defined by fixation upon the self, that person simply will not see why it is good to turn to God.

But what then is left for a believer to say to a non-believer who might be willing to concede that a Christian frame of reference offers a response to crises of historical knowledge, at least if one is a Christian? As it turns out, quite a bit may be said.

In biblical terms, the recognition that it is God who brings about belief is the source, not of despair, but of hope. To recognize that my perspective is turned away from God, that I deny God, is to recognize that I am now numbered among those who are lost unless God draws them to himself. But this is not such a bad place to be in. So long as I think I have the capacity within myself to alter my own frame of reference by myself, I cannot be one whom God is changing to love and enjoy himself. When I come to see that only God can reorient my perspective away from lesser realities to supreme realities, then I am in a position to be drawn by God into his love. Only when I realize how bound I am by the particularities of my own experience, can I come to sense how the particularities of the Incarnation open up a way of truth and love.

An apology for Christianity can also use the language of relativism. Why become a Christian? Because of anomalies within other paradigms. To be sure, a person will not be able to experience the satisfactions of the Christian paradigm until that person undergoes a revolution, a gestalt shift from a paradigm defined by the centrality of the self to one defined by the centrality of God. But since all humans experience life within paradigmatic frameworks, we may confidently expect some common experiences to be present in all paradigms, however differently they are perceived. Within some paradigms the anomalies of historical knowledge when construed scientifically, relativistically, or ideologically may be enough to precipitate a personal revolution that leads to embracing a Christian paradigm and its confidence in reasonably secure knowledge of the past. But even for such ones who might find historiographical anomalies an occasion for embracing the Christian paradigm, there will be other anomalous experiences. Those anomalies will be shared by all humans who do not love and enjoy God, regardless of their interest in history. Of all such possible anomalies, the one that will recur with the greatest frequency and cause the greatest disquiet is the sense of beauty, truth, clarity, goodness, and holiness that is given to all men and women to glimpse, whatever their frames of reference, in the face of Jesus Christ.

Notes

1. A version of this paper was presented as the Timothy Dwight Lecture in Christian Thought for the InterVarsity chapter at the University of Pennsylvania, February l, 1990, at which time the response of those who attended helped clarify the argument. I am also grateful to George Marsden for encouragement in pursuing the subjects of this paper. Brief sections of what follows are adapted from Mark A. Noll, "Contemporary Historical Writing: Practice and Presuppositions," *Christianity and History Newsletter* (University and Colleges Christian Fellowship, Great Britain), Feb. 1988, pp. 15-32; and "Scientific History in America: A Centennial Observation from a Christian Point of View," *Fides et Historia* 14 (Fall/Winter 1981): 21-37.
2. This essay first appeared in *CSR* 19.4 (June 1990): 388-406.
3. On the scientific aspirations of early professional historians, see Ernst Breisach, *Historiography: Ancient, Medieval, and Modern* (Chicago: University of Chicago Press, 1983), 272-90; D. W. Bebbington, *Patterns* in *History: A Christian View* (Downers Grove, Ill.: InterVarsity Press, 1979), 68-91; and John Higham, with Leonard Krieger and Felix Gilibert, *History: The Development of Historical Studies in the United States* (Englewood Cliffs, N.J.: Prenctice-Hall, 1965), 92-103.
4. Peter Novick, *That Noble Dream: The "Objectivity Question" and the American Historical Profession* (New York: Cambridge University Press, 1988). For a spirited rejoinder to Novick that argues for a larger range of mediating positions between simplistic objectivism and trendy relativism, see James T. Kloppenberg, "Objectivity and Historicism: A Century of American Historical Writing," *American Historical Review* 94 (October 1989): 1011-30.
5. The rest of this paragraph depends on the summary in Novick, *That Noble Dream, 522-72;* and Quentin Skinner, ed., *The Return of Grand Theory in the Human Sciences* (New York: Cambridge University Press, 1985), especially the chapters on Gadamer, Foucault, Derrida, and Levi-Strauss.
6. Sanford Levinson, "Law as Literature," *Texas Law Review* 60 (1982): 391-92, as quoted in Novick, *That Noble Dream,* 555.
7. Thomas S. Kuhn, *The Structure of Scientific Revolutions,* 2nd ed. (Chicago: University of Chicago Press, 1970). A good survey of responses to Kuhn from various disciplines is Gary Gutting, ed., *Paradigms and Revolutions: Applications and Appraisals of Thomas Kuhn's Philosophy of Science* (Notre Dame: University of Notre Dame Press, 1980).
8. An excellent discussion of that scientific ideal is found in Henry Warner Bowden, *Church History in the Age of Science: Historiographical Patterns in the United States, 1876-1918* (Chapel Hill, N.C.: University of North Carolina Press, 1971).
9. For judicious commentary on these developments, see David N. Livingstone, "Farewell to Arms: Reflections on the Encounter Between Science and Faith," in *Christian Faith and Practice in the Modern World: Theology from an Evangelical Point of View,* eds. Mark A. Noll and David F. Wells (Grand Rapids: Eerdmans, 1988), 239-62.
10. For example, Margaret C. Jacob, *The Cultural Meaning of the Scientific Revolution* (Philadelphia: Temple University Press, 1988); James R. Moore, "Crisis Without Revolution: The Ideological Watershed in Victorian England," *Revue de Synthese* 107 (1986): 53-78; and Theodore Dwight Bozeman, *Protestants in an Age of Science: The Baconian Ideal and Antebellum American Religious Thought* (Chapel Hill: University of North Carolina Press, 1977).
11. For the phrase, "epistemological crisis," see Novick, *That Noble Dream,* 573; and Joyce Appleby, "One Good Turn Deserves Another: Moving Beyond the Linguistic; A Response to David Harlan," *American Historical Review* 94 (Dec. 1989): 1326, 1328. The broader issues involved are the subject of an extensive series of essays in the *American Historical Review* 94 (June 1989): 581-698; and in "A Round Table: What Has Changed and Not Changed in American Historical Practice?" *Journal of American History* 76 (September 1989): 393-478.
12. For sound Christian analysis, see Gordon E. Michalson, *Lessing's "Ugly Ditch": A Study of Theology and History* (University Park, Penn.: Penn State University Press, 1985).
13. J. H. Hexter, *Doing History* (Bloomington, Ind.: Indiana University Press, 1971); and *The History Primer* (New York: Basic Books, 1971).
14. Briesach, *Historiography,* 274-75.
15. George Burton Adams, "History and the Philosophy of History," *American Historical Review* 14 (1909): 223, 226.
16. Herbert Butterfield, *The Whig Interpretation of History* (New York: W. W. Norton, 1965 [orig. 1931]), 130. For an application of Butterfield's wisdom to the world of American evangelicals, see Nathan O. Hatch, "'The Clean Sea-Breeze of the Centuries': Learning to Think Historically," in Mark A. Noll, George M. Marsden, and Nathan O. Hatch, *The Search for Christian America,* new ed. (Colorado Springs: Helmers & Howard, 1989), 145-55. On history as the servant of ideology, see Arnaldo Momigliano, "History in an Age of Ideologies," *American Scholar* 51 (Autumn 1982): 495-507.
17. See Gordon A. Craig, "The Other Germany," *New York Review of Books,* September 25, 1986, 62-65.
18. Briesach, *Historiography,* 45-50, 63-69, 77-78; and Charles Norris Cochrane, *Christianity and Classical Culture* (New York: Oxford University Press, 1944), 183-86.
19. A fascinating discussion of that process is A. G. Dickens and John Tonkin, *The Reformation in Historical Thought* (Cambridge, Mass.: Harvard University Press, 1985).
20. That view, with examples, is examined in Noll, Marsden, and Hatch, *The Search for Christian America.*
21. Carl Becker, "Everyman/His Own Historian," *American Historical Review* 37 (1932): 228; and more generally, Cushing Strout, *The Pragmatic Revolt in American History: Carl Becker and Charles Beard* (Ithaca, N.Y.: Cornell University Press, 1958).
22. Hayden White, *Metahistory: The Historical Imagination in Nineteenth-Century Europe* (Baltimore: Johns Hopkins University Press, 1973), x.

23. Willis Doney, "Nicolas Malebranche," *The Encyclopedia of Philosophy*, 8 vols. (New York: Macmillan, 1967), 5:140; J. O. Urmson, *Berkeley* (Oxford: Oxford University Press, 1982), 37; and Jonathan Edwards, "The Mind," in *The Works of Jonathan Edwards: Scientific and Philosophical Writings*, ed. Wallace E. Anderson (New Haven: Yale University Press, 1980), 344.

24. James Turner, *Without God, Without Creed: The Origins of Unbelief in America* (Baltimore: Johns Hopkins University Press, 1985), 49.

25. This reading of early modem science is based on Michael B. Foster, "The Christian Doctrine of Creation and the Rise of Modem Natural Science," *Mind* 43 (1934): 446-68; Daniel O'Connor and Francis Oakley, eds., *Creation: The Impact of an Idea* (New York: Charles Scribner's Sons, 1969); Charles Webster, *The Great Instauration: Science, Medicine and Reform, 1626-1660* (New York: Holmes and Meier, 1976), 493-510; and Eugene M. Klaaren, *Religious Origins of Modern Science* (Grand Rapids, Mich.: Eerdmans, 1977), 185-91.

26. I use here and in the next four paragraphs an admirable arrangement of the goals of scientific history from Novick, *That Noble Dream*, 568.

27. Bruce Kuklick, "The Mind of the Historian," *History and Theory* 8 (1969): 329.

18 Christian Scholarship in Sociology
Twentieth Century Trends and
Twenty-First Century Opportunities (2000)

NANCY T. AMMERMAN

At the beginning of the twentieth century, few in the young field of sociology would have questioned the importance of studying religion.[1] Emile Durkheim devoted a major treatise to the subject and worried considerably that a society without the binding force of the sacred was impossible.[2] Max Weber's sweeping historical vision saw Protestant ideas and practices as the major engine that had driven the early stages of a capitalist economy that he worried was now soulless.[3] Writing from European countries where established churches had wielded considerable cultural and political power, these founding fathers knew that they had to understand the force of religion if they were to explain the workings of society.

Similarly, early twentieth-century Christian leaders knew that if they were to understand and direct the course of the church, they would have to harness the insights of sociology to the task. Social Gospel theologians had already plowed the ground by employing a social critique in their drive toward the Kingdom. In the early part of the twentieth century, a few seminaries began to employ sociologists to help their graduates understand the rural and urban contexts in which they would minister. And soon thereafter, the tradition of church-based research began, most notably exemplified by H. Paul Douglass.[4] Based in denominational offices, at the National Council of Churches, and in seminaries, researchers examined the demographic characteristics of churches and their contexts, helped plan new church starts, documented the prevalence of programs and problems, and tracked the careers of clergy. Sometimes they offered their employers a longer or broader view of the societal forces shaping those churches, clergy, and programs; but more commonly, this was "applied" not "basic" research. While most of these researchers were well-trained, well-read, and aware, the nature of their work kept the focus internal to the church. The trajectory of their knowledge and associations remained separate from the trajectory of the growing academic field of sociology, as much because sociology ignored them as because of the nature of their own work.

The academic field was indeed going in a very different direction, making it eventually quite distinct from anything recognizable as "Christian" scholarship. For most of this century, the best proxy we have for such "Christian scholarship" is research that takes religion as its subject. It is, of course, a poor proxy. Not all of the religion in question is even Christian, nor are the concerns of the researchers primarily with the nurture of the faith. Nevertheless, the presence of a scholarly agenda that places religious faith at the center of concern is the best proxy we have for religious trends in twentieth century sociology.

While early sociological theorists had been convinced that they had to understand religion, they did not believe religion would survive as a vital force in modern society; and that belief shaped the course of the field for the rest of the century. What evolved was a pervasive myth. The story goes something like this: "Once upon a time all of life was full of mysterious forces. Whatever could not be explained was chalked up to divine action. Sacred symbols and stories legitimated all social power. Eventually, all this sacred power was drawn together into offices and institutions that defined the moral, political, and social life of a people. Religious officials stood at the center of the society, either wielding governmental power directly or defining the boundaries within which others could wield such power. Whether or not any given ordinary individual had strong religious sensibilities didn't matter, because the whole culture carried the meanings and mores of religion."[5] But then the evil beast of modernity arrived. [Or, alternative reading: then the great white knight of enlightenment rode into view.] Slowly the sacred disappeared from view, taking refuge in the tiny crevices of the "private sphere." The authority of religious leaders was usurped by scientists, and might and right were defined by political leaders and technocrats. "Public" life was disenchanted, and despite periodic rumblings from the "private" sphere, religion was forever robbed of its power.

This is a compelling story. It is one we have told and retold, argued over and researched. It makes sense of a great deal of what we see. But like all such stories, it belongs to those who have the power to speak it. It has been crafted to make sense of the lives of those whose lives "count." Fundamentally, this is a story about the intellectual elites, mostly white and mostly male, in Europe and the U.S. It makes sense of the world they see and the life they lead, even if it could never be an adequate theory of social life here or anywhere else in the world. It is utterly lacking as a description of the actual social world as experienced by those outside that small elite circle.

Nevertheless, it is a story with great power to shape the behavior of those who believe it. Because most sociologists believed Weber, Durkheim, and Marx, they believed that an increasingly complex social world would separate the functions and mores of one institution from another, relegating religious institutions to a more constrained role. They believed that an increasingly rationalized world would shed its remnants of mystification, forcing even the remaining religious traditions to objectify and rationalize their beliefs. They believed that when the veils of class interest had been lifted, people would shun the mythic and moral legitimations that kept old social orders in place. And because they believed all those things, they saw no reason to study the elements of a dying social order. More importantly, because their own world was rationalized, specialized, and critical, the assumptions of the myth made perfect sense to them.

By the 1950s, the theories of Talcott Parsons were reigning supreme, and those who still thought they ought to pay some attention to religion took their cue from him. Where does religion go in this modern, differentiated, privatized world? It retreats into individual meaning systems or is diffused into generalized cultural values.[6] This emphasis on values coincided nicely with the available research technologies of the day. In those post-war years, sociologists were perfecting their use of survey research, asking thousands of individuals every year about their opinions, beliefs, attitudes, and behavior. With chi-square tables and correlations in hand, they tried to sort out grand cultural patterns based on the cognitive constructs that lurked in the minds of survey respondents. A decade later, Parsons was passé, and critical sociology seemed more attuned to the conflict-ridden Sixties. Attention to beliefs, values, and attitudes had passed from the scene, as well. No need to study religious attitudes; critical sociologists knew that behavior is really governed by situations and interests, not by cognitive constructs.

If sociologists were paying attention to religion at all, in those days a generation ago, they might have noticed the beginnings of membership declines in the mainstream Protestant churches. And if they did, they may have nodded in satisfaction to themselves, sure that this was further evidence that their basic assumptions about religion were right. No need to study religious institutions; they are dying. By the time I was picking a dissertation topic twenty years ago, the prevailing culture in the field was pervasively secular (even if the culture we were studying was not). When I announced that I wanted to do a dissertation on fundamentalism, my professors were not so much opposed as quizzical: "Religion. Hmm. How quaint. I suppose one could study that." Religion had simply passed off their radar screens as a subject of study.

Just what is the current intersection between the study of religion and the study of sociology? We have reason to worry about both of the branches that have borne these concerns in the past, that is, both church-based researchers and academy-based scholars. There are fewer and fewer Christian scholars who have put their skills to work as researchers for church bodies—not because individuals no longer wish to work in these settings, but because the church bodies that used to employ them can often no longer afford the luxury of a research staff. And, as we have seen, the culture and mythology of the field itself have moved away from the concerns about religion that were present in the founding generation.

But has religion indeed disappeared as a subject of study? Assuming that we might gain some indication of research activity from what is published in three of the leading journals in the field—*American Sociological Review, American Journal of Sociology*, and *Social Forces*—I took a look at all the issues from 1994 to 1998. While my counts may admittedly have missed a few articles in which attention was given to religion, it appears that over that period, these three journals have published about thirty articles in which religion was a major topic. That constitutes about 4% of the total number of articles published. Similarly, our disciplinary journal of book reviews, *Contemporary Sociology*, has published over 3,000 reviews during that time, about 4% of which were of books dealing primarily with religion.

While that is a relatively small percentage, I suspect that several other subfields might have done similar counts with similar results. There are simply too many subfields in this now highly specialized discipline for any one focus to gain dominance. The most numerous topics in journals and among published books are race, gender, stratification, economic development, national and global political institutions, family and work, demography and immigration, and the like. The study of religion, then, is a relatively small, but persistent, presence in the books and journals that gain attention in the discipline at large.

As with most sub-specialties, the study of religion in sociology is often isolated, rarely overlapping with other fields. That is, only rarely does an article or book explicitly on one of sociology's "hot" topics also address the role of religion—an exploration of gender roles or economic development that takes religion into account, for instance. The reverse, however, is not true: books and articles on religion do address many of the otherwise hot topics. A survey of recent titles catalogued by OCLC under "American religion" revealed that nearly one third of those books dealt with race, gender, and ethnicity as they affect American religion. Historians, religious studies scholars, theologians, and others are actively seeking to understand the relationship between religion and these other social realities, even when sociologists are not. That is, there is attention from religion to sociology, but not often in the other direction.

More commonly, sociology books and articles on religion address issues that at least on the surface appear to be only of relevance within the study of religion— changing attitudes among American Catholics, the takeover of the Southern Baptist Convention, ordination of women clergy, and such. The titles of many sociology of religion books do not automatically signal to others in the larger field that they are of relevance to people who study social movements, organizations, families, economic development, and the like. As in much of the rest of academe, we are often specialized in ways that fail to signal the overlapping significance of our work.

Another way to look at the status of the study of religion within sociology is to ask how and whether religion is being taught—especially to undergraduates—in university departments of sociology. To get a very rough answer to that question, I looked at the on-line 1998-99 course listings from ten universities, all with high status as places to study sociology. They were both public and private and scattered throughout the regions of the country. Two had no courses on religion or that mentioned any religious topics. Eight had at least one basic religion and society course. Of those eight, one had one additional course, two had two additional courses, and one had three, for a maximum of four courses on religion in any of these prestigious sociology departments. In several places, the description of the basic introduction to sociology course mentioned religion alongside the family, economy, stratification, and the like, as basic areas to be covered. But almost never was religion mentioned as a factor to be studied in courses on the family, social movements, organizations, political mobilization, race, gender, or any other aspect of society. That, of course, does not mean that professors do not touch on the significance of religion when teaching about other aspects of society. But it does mean that they do not generally list religion as a variable that is so fundamental to understanding their subject that it must be included in a basic description of the course.

And what about the study of religion in sociology graduate departments? Here my evidence is of a slightly different sort. In 1998, Stephen Warner and I conducted an informal poll to discover how often sociology graduate students writing dissertations on religion-related topics were seeking advisors and readers outside their own departments, in most cases because their own department did not have the faculty resources necessary to support their work. We concluded that at any given time about two dozen Ph.D. students who are doing work in sociology of religion reach outside their own university to find at least one of their advisors.

From the stories we heard back from our query, we think it is also a safe guess that a fair number of students who would like to write dissertations in sociology of religion are discouraged from doing so, either by active opposition from members of their department (we heard that reported from a couple of students) or because their department lacks a specialist on religion and discourages outside advisors.

In sum, then, religion is a small but persistent presence in the scholarly publishing in sociology. It is an even smaller and not always surviving presence in the curricula of sociology departments. The lingering relative absence of attention to religion in teaching and publishing in sociology reflects the current culture in the discipline, and it reflects the training and emphases of the last generation (or more) that has created that culture. When we look at what is being taught and published in the discipline as a whole, it would be easy to conclude that the study of religion is indeed marginalized and often excluded entirely from our professional efforts to understand today's society.

A quite different assessment of sociological interest in religion would come, however, from an examination of the professional associations of scholars who engage in research on religion. There are multiple professional societies for sociologists of religion, all of them thriving. The Society for the Scientific Study of Religion and the Religious Research Association are interdisciplinary, but comprise majorities of sociologists. Both publish moderately selective journals and host a joint meeting each fall that attracts five hundred or more participants and presenters. Articles from the *Journal for the Scientific Study of Religion* are now the eighth most frequently cited among journal articles in sociology. The Association for the Sociology of Religion has been meeting in tandem with the American Sociological Association (ASA) meetings for fifty years and allows for the presentation of well over one hundred papers each year, many of them by graduate students and younger scholars. In addition, formed less than five years ago, the Religion Section in the ASA has brought a focus on religion directly into the larger professional body. The section has grown rapidly, with over five hundred members (a third of them students), at last count.

What are we to conclude from this seeming disjuncture between active professional activity, especially among younger scholars, and a relative lack of penetration of the discipline's mainstream departments, journals, and reviews? Are there currents of change present in the discipline? While the evidence on publishing and teaching makes clear that much of the old culture is still in place, the evidence of lively interest in the study of religion among younger scholars offers a hint of different stories in the making.

Stephen Warner has pointed out to us many of the ways in which the old story of secularization—that "old paradigm," in his words—no longer makes good sense of much of the data we encounter when we study religion.[7] It also fails to make sense because it is not—and probably never was—the story of everyone, either in Europe or in the U.S. Similarly, the stories about religious decline in the U.S. have always been wrong,[8] a situation we might have noticed if we had also noticed the elite bias of the myth governing our field. If we had noticed that bias, we might have looked beyond membership numbers in the establishment institutions to practices outside those institutions. Instead of looking at the grand theories of theologians to see how they have accommodated the grand theories of scientists, we might have looked at the common sense and experience of everyday life. But that sort of critical, bottom-up theorizing would have to wait for appreciable numbers of women and people of color to enter the field.

Part of what is dislodging the old culture and its dominant myth of secularization is, in fact, the diversity of persons who now occupy the field—increasing numbers of women, people of color, and people from outside Europe and the U.S. But at least three major cultural events have challenged that old myth, as well. One is the growing global consciousness of our discipline and the erosion of "development" models that expected every society on earth to go through the same stages of change that Europe had experienced. As we have seen that societies from Iran to Indonesia and from Brazil to Bangladesh are moving in their own ways toward full participation in global markets and culture, we are also noticing that religion does not seem to be disappearing or retreating to the margins.

But we did not have to go half way around the world to notice that religion did not seem to want to die. The rise of the new Christian right in this country made abundantly clear that religious ideas and institutions have ample political, economic, and cultural power.[9] Similarly, the appearance of a variety of new religious movements, many of them appealing to the very intellectual elites who were supposed to be immune from religion, created additional doubt in the adequacy of secularization as an account of our society's history and future.

Throughout this essay, I have returned to the ways in which our conceptual schemes have failed us. Yes, this is a "new paradigm" I am trying to describe. But what I am suggesting is that the context for that new paradigm is nothing less than the decentering of modernism and secularization as the discipline's primary interpretive frame.[10] Modernist frames assumed functional differentiation, individualism, and rationalism as "the way things are." Modernist frames looked for a clear line between rational, this-worldly action and action guided by any other form of wisdom, relegating explicitly religious knowledge to the scrap heap of superstition. Modernist frames looked for the individualized "meaning system" that would be carved out of differentiation and pluralism, the "sacred umbrella" that could be carried when no sacred canopy existed.

I hesitate to invoke the word postmodern, given all its baggage, but it seems to me a useful concept here. In a number of ways, we are seeing a fundamental shift in perspective that is allowing sociologists to begin to see what they could not see before. New persons entering the field, new events that do not fit the old frameworks, and a new questioning of basic modernist presuppositions are combining to create new opportunities for the study of religion in sociology.

So where is this shift beginning to be evident? Where have we seen progress in sociology's ability to explain the obvious persistence of religious ideas and organizations?

- Attention to the experiences of previously marginalized groups is one of the ways in which the study of religion is being revived and re-framed.[11] When the subject is women, life in the southern hemisphere, immigrants, and the like, the role of religion is often unavoidable, even if many sociologists resolutely still try to do just that.
- There have also been significant changes in the study of voluntary organizations. There is now a much more widespread recognition that when one speaks of the voluntary sector, one simply must include religious organizations and religious motivations.[12] Particularly as the political climate has turned attention to the role of churches in the delivery of social services, sociologists are paying more attention to religious organizations as a field of study.
- Similarly, I think there is a growing recognition that religious ideas, rituals, and organizations are important players in many social movements. If one wishes to understand the dynamics of movement mobilization, attention to these religious dimensions is essential. At long last people are noticing that the role of religion in the civil rights movement, for instance, went beyond the fact that Martin Luther King, Jr. happened to be a preacher.[13]
- Curiously, the study of organizations of all kinds has taken what some describe as a "cultural" turn.[14] As a result, scholars are paying attention to the ways in which every organization has its myths and rituals.[15] Some have even gone so far as to describe the governing assumptions of some organizational sectors in terms of a salvation myth.[16] The discouraging thing about all of this talk about religion among organization theorists is that they do not seem to realize that anyone has ever actually studied such things as myths and rituals and might, therefore, be able to offer them some analytical assistance.
- In the realm of sociology's general theories, feminist and other radical critiques have created a space for the non-rational.[17] While many of these critiques see religious power and symbol as oppressive, they nevertheless know that they must take such elements seriously.

- Changes in our research technologies have helped, as well. During the last decade, many of the major survey research organizations have consulted with sociologists of religion and added questions on religion to the databases that still form the bedrock on which so much of our sociological knowledge is built. With data to analyze, we can anticipate more published results in the future.
- At the same time, there has also been increasing skepticism about survey research and the presumably universal theories built from it. In a turn from the universal to the particular, case studies of human association have gained some currency. And where better to find people associating than in religious groups?

The jury is still out. It is still possible that sociology's younger scholars and all those who are bringing new perspectives into the discipline may yet be forced to conform to the old culture. But it seems to me that the tide may be turning. First, there is now room for the recognition that all scholarship proceeds from the standpoint and interests of the scholar and a recognition that no study of society can proceed without the plural perspectives represented by all sorts of scholars. The discourse in the field is simply different today.

But second, the field itself is destined to be enhanced by the presence of younger scholars who are both determined that the study of religion is essential to an understanding of society and determined that they will study religion from squarely within the mainstream of the field, not from a separate ghetto. They are determined to remain in the conceptual and methodological conversation of the discipline, determined to be both borrowers and lenders in that exchange. They think that the study of religion has something to offer the discipline as a whole, and they have the necessary skills and institutional positions within mainstream departments to make that offering a reality.

This is an emerging conversation that promises to change the very myths that have shaped the field, and only as those myths are eroded will the field be able to fulfill its promise. Sociology will never be able to claim its birthright as a discipline until it takes off its Enlightenment blinders to pay attention to all the elements of the society it is supposed to be explaining. Christian scholars have important opportunities to participate in the re-framing that is now underway.[18]

Notes

1. This essay first appeared in *CSR* 29.4 (Summer 2000): 685-94.
2. Emile Durkheim, *The Elementary Forms of the Religious Life*, trans. Joseph Ward Swain (New York: Free Press, 1915).
3. Max Weber, *The Protestant Ethic and the Spirit of Capitalism*, trans. Talcott Parsons (Boston: Beacon, 1905 [1958]).
4. H. Paul Douglass and Edmund de Brunner, *The Protestant Church as a Social Institution* (New York: Harper and Row, 1935); H. Paul Douglass, *The Church in the Changing City* (New York: Doran, 1927); Jeffrey K. Hadden, "H. Paul Douglass: His Perspective and His Work," *Review of Religious Research* 22 (September 1980): 66-88.
5. It is important to note that this account is deliberately framed as a story and not as a careful theoretical argument. It draws on several theoretical arguments, but is not identical to any of them. This way of framing the

argument draws on Nancy T. Ammerman, "Telling Congregational Stories," *Review of Religious Research* 36:1 (June 1994).

6. Talcott Parsons, "Religion and Modern Industrial Society," in *Religion, Culture, and Society*, ed. Louis Schneider (New York: Wiley, 1964), 273-98.

7. R. Stephen Warner, "Work in Progress toward a New Paradigm for the Sociological Study of Religion in the United States," *American Journal of Sociology* 98:5 (March 1993): 1044-93.

8. Roger Finke and Rodney Stark, *The Churching of America* (New Brunswick, N.J.: Rutgers University Press, 1992).

9. For a discussion of the nature of religious cultural power, see N. J. Demerath, III and Rhys H. Williams, *A Bridging of Faiths: Religion and Politics in a New England City* (Princeton, N.J.: Princeton University Press, 1992); and Nancy T. Ammerman, "Review of *A Bridging of Faiths* by N. J. Demerath and Rhys H. Williams," *Society* 31:1 (November/December 1993): 91-93.

10. Here I draw on work I have elaborated in Nancy T. Ammerman, "Organized Religion in a Voluntaristic Society," *Sociology of Religion* 58:2 (Summer 1997).

11. See, for example, R. Stephen Warner and Judith Wittner, eds., *Gatherings in Diaspora* (Philadelphia: Temple University Press, 1998).

12. Wuthnow's work has been critical in this turn. For example, see Robert Wuthnow, *Acts of Compassion: Caring for Others and Helping Ourselves* (Princeton, N.J.: Princeton University Press, 1991).

13. Among the best studies is Aldon D. Morris, *The Origins of the Civil Rights Movement: Black Communities Organizing for Change* (New York: Free Press, 1984). But see also Mary Patillo-McCoy, "Church Culture as a Strategy of Action in the Black Community," *American Sociological Review* 63 (December 1998): 767-84.

14. Paul J. DiMaggio, "The Relevance of Organization Theory to the Study of Religion," in *Sacred Companies*, eds. N. J. Demerath, Peter Dobkin Hall, Terry Schmitt, and Rhys Williams (New York: Oxford University Press, 1998), 7-23; Roger Friedland and Robert R. Alford, "Bringing Society Back In: Symbols, Practices, and Institutional Contradictions," in *The New Institutionalism in Organizational Analysis*, eds. Walter Powell and Paul DiMaggio (Chicago: University of Chicago Press, 1991), 232-63.

15. John W. Meyer and Brian Rowan, "Institutionalized Organizations: Formal Structure as Myth and Ceremony," in *The New Institutionalism*, 41-62.

16. Jeffrey Alexander, "The Promise of a Cultural Sociology: Technological Discourse and the Sacred and Profane Information Machine," in *Theory of Culture*, eds. Richard Munch and Neil J. Smelser (Berkeley: University of California Press, 1992), 293-323.

17. Dorothy Smith, "A Sociology for Women," in *The Prism of Sex: Essays in the Sociology of Knowledge*, eds. J. Sherman and E. Beck (Madison, Wis.: University of Wisconsin Press, 1979), 135-87.

18. This essay is a revised version of a talk given at the Conference on Religion and Higher Education at Notre Dame University in March 1999.

19 Michelangelo's Mirrors (2002)

Luke Reinsma

At first it is difficult to locate St. Bartholomew, clutching his bloody rag of flesh, in what is the largest and one of the most important paintings in the history of Western art: Michelangelo's *Last Judgment*.[1] If it is hard to find him, his right hand wielding the knife that had skinned him alive in Armenia, it is because he is one of over three hundred figures swirling counterclockwise about an heroic Christ: skeletons, men, women, saints, the Virgin Mary, martyrs, demons, the mythic figures of Charon and Minos, the blessed and the damned hurled throughout eternity.[2] "In this work," wrote Ascanio Condivi, Michelangelo's fawning biographer, he "expressed all that the art of painting can do with the human figure."[3]

There on the west wall of the Sistine Chapel, just above the altar and to our left, the stunned and wondering dead extricate themselves from their tombs. Angels reach down to pull them into heaven, where Christ sits like a magnificent Hercules just above the center of the composition, his right arm sheltering the Madonna, his left casting aside the damned. In the two lunettes above, angels, wingless and muscular, struggle to bear away the cross on which Christ was crucified, the column on which He was flogged. Below Christ and to His left, there is a crouching sinner, his face partly covered with his palm, who has the look of someone who has failed a very important examination. To our right, web-footed devils drag his companions down to hell, where the ferryman Charon flails at the damned with his oar, driving them out of his craft. In the far right-hand corner, an ass-eared Minos, a serpent enveloping his waist, surveys this hellish company with grim satisfaction.

And there, in the midst of this furious melee, sits our bearded Bartholomew at the feet of Christ, his muscular torso twisted towards his savior, his raised knife demanding retribution. About him, his fellow martyrs brandish their own instruments of torture: St. Sebastian, his fatal arrows; St. Lawrence, the gridiron on which he was broiled; St. Catherine, the toothed wheel that tore her asunder. But it is in the middle of things, literally, that the bearded Bartholomew clutches his bloody skin, with its elongated arms, grizzled hair, hollow eyes, and broken nose. If we were to draw a line stretching from the cross in the upper left to Minos in the lower right — a line of fate, according to art historian Leo Steinberg — it would run through Christ.[4] And through the horrified sinner who has flunked his final. And through the distorted features of the flayed skin with its broken nose, its mouth sagging into a grimace of disbelief and despair.

When Michelangelo erected the scaffolding for the *Last Judgment* on the west wall of the Sistine Chapel in 1535, he was sixty years old. He would turn sixty-six before it was dismantled. It was Pope Clement VII who had commissioned the fresco, perhaps in response to the Protestant revolt that Luther had spawned when he posted his 95 theses in Wittenberg in 1517. Or perhaps Clement remembered how the soldiers and mercenaries of the Holy Roman Emperor Charles V had ransacked Rome a decade later, pillaging churches and monasteries, sacking even St. Peter's and the Vatican, holding the Pope himself for 100,000 ducats in ransom. Or perhaps it was because the King of England, Henry VIII, unable to gain papal permission to divorce himself from Catherine of Aragon, had wrested the Anglican Church free from Rome. By now, Denmark, Sweden, half of Germany, and part of Switzerland had likewise broken away from the Catholic Church. It must have seemed as if the world were falling apart, as if the final days were at hand.

No sooner had Michelangelo returned to Rome in response to the papal summons, however, than Clement died. Once again he was free to work on the tomb of Julius II, for which he had been carving a magnificent Moses, as well as companion pieces. Or so he thought. For the newly elected pope, Paul III, was just as eager as his predecessor to commemorate his rule with the work of Michelangelo, the celebrated creator of the *Pietà*, the *David*, the ceiling of the Sistine Chapel. The story goes that the Pope and eight of his cardinals went to visit Michelangelo in his house on the Macel' de' Corvi. Nosing about the sculptor's drawings and carvings, one of them exclaimed of the Moses, "This figure alone would suffice to honor the tomb of Julius!" Dismayed, Michelangelo protested that he was still under contract to the family of Pope Julius, the heirs of the Della Rovera estate. "I have waited thirty years to have you in my service," roared Pope Paul III. "Now that I am Pope, can't I satisfy this desire? Where is this contract? Let me tear it up!"[5]

It took a year to prepare the west wall. The altarpiece was removed. Two windows were bricked up. Several exquisite quattrocento frescoes by the fifteenth-century master Perugino, one of the *Finding of Moses* and another of the *Nativity*, were chiseled out. But then the two lunettes that Michelangelo had painted years before on either side of Jonah had to go as well, to allow for a homogeneous composition that would cover the entire wall. Giorgio Vasari, the earliest of Michelangelo's biographers, tells us that the entire wall was rebuilt of specially baked bricks to prevent moisture from seeping into the painting, and that the upper wall was projected out nearly a foot beyond its base, so as to discourage dust from settling on its surface (which only encouraged the centuries-long accumulation of soot and grease from the altar candles below). And then, after the surface of the wall was prepared for oil painting under the direction of Sebastiano del Piombo, Michelangelo spent another six months scraping clean the surface and replastering the wall in order to prepare it for a fresco, as he had painted the ceiling. Oil painting was good for lazy people like Sebastiano and for women, said Michelangelo, who despised the preeminent oil painter of his day, Leonardo da Vinci, and who never married. "I have only too much of a wife in this art of mine," he once told a priest who begrudged Michelangelo his solitude. And she "has always kept us in tribulation."[6]

All his life, he worked in solitude. In this respect, as in many others, he was the antithesis of Raphael, who lived in Rome like a prince, surrounded by disciples and sycophants; and of Leonardo da Vinci, whose aristocratic élan must have driven Michelangelo to distraction. At the age of sixty, he was a gnarled, crotchety old man, unexceptional in appearance in an age that celebrated appearance. He wore old clothes and lived like a beggar, eating whatever was at hand—a crust of bread, a scrap of dried fish—in order to continue his work. "He told me that often in his youth he slept in his clothes," writes Vasari, "being weary with labour and not caring to take them off only to have to put them on again."[7]

In the Accademia in Florence, there is a bronze bust of Michelangelo, cast shortly after his death by his devotee Daniele da Volterra, which gives us a sense of his character: his grizzled gray hair; his high, furrowed brow; his crushed nose; his haggard face, lined with pain. If we compare the paintings of Leonardo da Vinci to those of Michelangelo—Da Vinci's languorous *Virgin of the Rocks*, say, to Michelangelo's muscular Madonna in the *Doni Tondo*—we will see the difference between the two. It is the difference between one who has looked outward all of his life and who has seen everything—the tendrils of flowers, shawls and lace, fossils, embryos, the desiccated bodies of old men—and the other who has looked inward, who stripped his paintings of buildings and landscape, of decorative arabesque, until there is nothing left but foreground—nothing but human beings reclining, standing, falling, tumbling, collapsing in the presence of the Old Testament Yahweh. Until there is nothing left but himself, stripped bare, brooding and angry, haunted by how much had been left unfinished in the sixtieth year of his life—the Medici chapel, the tomb of Julius. As he had railed against the oil painter Sebastiano del Piombo, so he railed against the world. He would not permit his nephew Lionardo to visit him, lest his difficulties be increased. When he fell from the scaffold, he barricaded himself in his apartment, refusing to see the doctor dispatched by the Pope. On two occasions, shortly before his death, Vasari writes, he burned most of his drawings and preparatory cartoons "so that no one could see his efforts and the ways his genius expressed itself."[8] Not for nothing was he called, like the fearsome Pope Julius II himself, *terribilità*. He had spent a lifetime consumed with visions, with a passion that veered between inspiration and fury. It was as if he had spent a lifetime carving himself, from the inside out.

The *Last Judgment* was opened to the public on October 31, 1541—All-Hallows Day—twenty-nine years to the day after the unveiling of the ceiling. It was everything that the ceiling was not. While the one was about the creation of the earth, the other was about "the foundering of a civilization"—about a European civilization and a religious order that seemed in ruins.[9] While the one had celebrated the creation of Adam formed in the image of God, here the bodies seemed lumpish, massive, weighed down by their leaden flesh. While the one was about humanity, this was about us—about isolated human beings terrifyingly aware of their own fate. And while the one was balanced and symmetrical, each of its figures locked into place by an elaborate *trompe l'oeil* scheme of beams and rafters, the other was a violent swirl of activity set against the frameless backdrop of eternity. It is "not a contained system so much as an act of aggression, assaulting both mind and body," writes Steinberg in *Michelangelo's Last Paintings*: "It assaults the mind by flooding it in excess, by the urgency of the subject, even by the shocks of obscenity; and the body, by disturbing the sense of safety which one derives from abiding indoors. By its seeming obliteration of the altar wall, Michelangelo's frameless fresco converts the Chapel into a huge open shed, or hangar, its protective screen melted away to reveal the perpetual imminence of the Last Day."[10]

Little wonder that the painting shocked so many. For a start, there is the herculean Christ. There are the wingless angels, virtually indistinguishable from saints and sinners. There is the bearded St. Bartholomew, who bears little resemblance to the Bartholomews who had come before—and even less to the clean-shaven death mask he grasps in his hand. There is the ferryman Charon from out of Greek legend, who preempted the role of St. Michael, traditional weigher of souls. And everywhere there is indecorum, preposterous postures, the shamelessness of virgins. "And everywhere," as Steinberg puts it, "the publicity of private parts."[11] Even before the fresco was three-fourths completed, when Pope Paul went to inspect the work in the company of his Master of Ceremonies, Biago da Cesena, his attendant complained of so many naked figures in so sacred a place. It was a picture more fit for a *bagnio*, a bathhouse, he said, than for the chapel of a pope. Nettled by these remarks, Michelangelo is said to have planted the head of Biago upon the torso of Minos, judge of the damned. When the prelate complained of his plight, the Pope said that he could do nothing for him. "Had the painter sent you to Purgatory, I would have used my best efforts to get you released," he said, "but I exercise no influence in hell."[12] So affronted were the leaders of the so-called Counter Reformation, that a generation later, in January of 1564, the Council of Trent commissioned Daniele da Volterra to "reform" the *Last Judgment* by painting over its private parts—an unhappy task that would forever after earn him the contemptuous sobriquet *il Braghettone*, the britches maker.

But no one's complaint was more barbed and dangerous than that of the Venetian author and literary critic Pietro Aretino, who once boasted that his poison pen had extorted 25,000 gold crowns from the princes of Europe. In 1537 Aretino sent Michelangelo a letter describing his version of the *Last Judgment*: "I see Time sapless and trembling for his end has come, and he is seated on an arid throne." Informing his admirer (untruthfully) that he had already finished a large part of the fresco, Michelangelo apologized for being unable to "realize" Aretino's vision for the painting. The following January, however, the purpose of the correspondence became clear, for Aretino wanted his own Picasso, an original Michelangelo, "one of those drawings you toss carelessly in the fire." There was no reply. Outraged at such an affront, in 1545 Aretino poured out the acid of his pen in a flood of paragraphs excoriating the *Last Judgment* and its creator. Beginning with praise for the work of Raphael—a calculated insult—Aretino accused Michelangelo of "desecrating the major chapel of Christendom merely to gratify his art by painting figures 'more permissible on the walls of a voluptuous brothel than on the walls of a choir.'" ("'Better to displease the artist,' he added sanctimoniously, 'than to offend Christ by keeping silent.'") After implying that his drawings were not all that Michelangelo gave his handsome young friend Tomasso Cavalieri and after a spiteful dig at the unfinished state of the tomb of Julius, Aretino pointed out that all of this vitriol could have been avoided, had the artist but accepted his own design. Kings and princes reply to the letters of Pietro Aretino, he added in a huffy postscript.[13]

This is why the St. Bartholomew looks nothing like his predecessors, much less like the deflated visage he holds in his hands. It is not just that his muscular torso is not his, but that of the so-called *Torso Belvedere*, unearthed from Italian soil a century earlier and copied by Michelangelo a half-dozen times, most notably in his slave and captives.[14] As it turns out, neither the bust of St. Bartholomew nor his death mask is his either. For in a fit of pique and anger, Michelangelo cobbled together a martyr from out of the *Torso* that he loved and the critic whom he loathed. *Veritas odium parit* was Aretino's motto—"Truth begets hatred"[15] —and so it did, for on the *Torso Belvedere* Michelangelo planted the head of his least-favorite art critic, Aretino, who wields in his right hand his pen/knife and in his left the flayed skin of Michelangelo himself.[16]

The give-away, of course, is the broken nose, which permitted Francesco La Cava, an Italian physician, to identify the artist's self-portrait in 1925. The distinctive nose, writes Condivi, was flattened "not by nature but because when he was a boy a man called Torrigiano de' Torrigiani, a bestial and arrogant person, with a blow of his fist almost broke off the cartilage of Michelangelo's nose, so that he was carried home as if dead."[17] As Benvenuto Cellini tells the story in his *Autobiography*, the young apprentices Torrigiano and Michelangelo had been sent to the church of the Carmine to learn drawing from the paintings of Massacio. It was Michelangelo's habit to banter with his companion, and one day Michelangelo so annoyed him, as Torrigiano recalls it, that "I gave him such a blow on the nose that I felt bone and cartilage go down like biscuit beneath my knuckles."[18] For the record, Torrigiano would go on to carve the tomb of King Henry VIII's father in Westminster Abbey only to end his days in a prison cell in Seville, where he fell into the hands of the Inquisition.

So this broken nose, this rag of flesh, is Michelangelo's own. At first glance, then, the portrait would seem to offer a rueful commentary on what it is like to be flayed alive by the acid pen of a critic—a sentiment perhaps not unfamiliar to those of us who have been, likewise, flayed by the pens of our readers.

But that is to sell the self-portrait short. It is not enough to turn Michelangelo's death mask into a curiosity piece, an amusing anecdote for the art classes. On the contrary, I want to argue that this self-portrait is dead serious. And that it is located not just in the midst of the *Last Judgment*, but in the midst of Michelangelo's lifelong exploration of the Christ figure in his *Pietàs*—the one perfected in his youth, two more carved in the silence and solitude of the night in the final days before his death. For these *Pietàs*, I would argue, are not only about Christ but about himself. Like the death mask of St. Bartholomew, the *Pietà* was for Michelangelo another of his mirrors.

Michelangelo's earliest *Pietà*—the word is a play on the Italian words for "piety" and "pity"—is in St. Peter's in Rome. It needs little introduction, for the pyramidal composition of its sorrowful Virgin contemplating the dead Christ, who lies upon her lap, is one of the most perfect sculptures in the Western tradition. It was carved in 1499, nearly a half century earlier, when Michelangelo was 24 years old. Prophetically, Michelangelo's friend Jacopo Gallo, who secured the commission from the French Cardinal Jean de Villiers, promised that it would be "the finest work in marble which Rome to-day can show, and that no master of our days shall be able to produce a better."[19]

The *Pietà* is about youth and ideals, but most of all, it is about beauty. Chafing against the strictures of tradition, as he would all his life, Michelangelo removed from the scene Saint John and the Magdalen, who had traditionally helped the frail Madonna support the inert body of a grown man. So there is only the Virgin, her sumptuous draperies enveloping the calm beauty of an earth mother, offering her left hand to us in a sublime gesture of sorrow and compassion. Effortlessly—none of the contortions and suffering of the medieval *pietàs* here!—she cradles the lifeless body of her son.

She is very beautiful, and it is a beauty that is evoked by serenity. For an artist whose female figures were almost invariably modeled after males, the melancholy of her oval face, her eyes half-lidded in reflection, the perfect polish of her skin—all of this renders her even more remarkable. It is, in fact, Michelangelo's most finished sculpture, and it is the only one he ever signed. On a ribbon running across the Virgin's breast, the inscription reads: MICHAEL ANGELUS - BONAROTUS - FLORENT - FACIEBAT. Michelangelo Buonarotti of Florence made this.

So beautiful is she that the *Pietà* evidently scandalized its public. Fifty years later, the Florentine church of Santo Spirito installed a life-size marble replica of this masterwork, only to receive the anonymous complaint of one of its parishioners denouncing the cathedral's recent acquisitions, including certain "dirty and filthy marble figures," such as Bandinelli's nude *Adam and Eve*—and "that inventor of obscenities, Michelangelo Buonarroti, who is concerned only with art, not with piety." "All the modern painters and sculptors, pursuing Lutheran whims," the letter added, "now paint and carve nothing for our holy churches but figures that undermine faith and devotion."[20]

Even Pietro Aretino sharpened his quill on the *Pietà*, criticizing Michelangelo for his lack of judgment, complaining that the virgin was too young. It was a complaint that evidently stuck, writes Steinberg,[21] for Condivi asked Michelangelo to explain. "Don't you know that women who are chaste remain much fresher than those who are not?" replied the young sculptor. "How much more so a virgin who was never touched by even the slightest lascivious desire which might alter her body?"[22] But the argument smacks of sophistry, for there is, in fact, a sublime aesthetic quality to the sculpture that simultaneously complements and subverts its religious sensibility. To put a fine point on it, in a setting other than St. Peter's, the Virgin could pass for an Artemis; the supple body of Christ, for an Adonis. Which is to say that our anonymous parishioner truly did understand how much the young and idealistic Michelangelo was in love with the sensual beauty of youth—this mirror of his soul, this image of divine perfection.

The idea, of course, was that such physical beauty was not an end but a beginning. It was a distinctly Neoplatonic notion, ultimately derived from Plato's *Symposium*, which Michelangelo had picked up from the table of Lorenzo de' Medici in whose sculpture garden he had studied in his youth. The idea was, as the Neoplatonists would have it, that beauty was but a sign of the inner grace and goodness that God has bestowed upon us. The idea was that external beauty was but the rung of a ladder, the means by which the soul, seeking God, might ascend to higher degrees of knowledge and love until achieving communion with God. Nearly two centuries earlier, the Florentine poet Petrarch had written his sonnets of love governed by such a conception: that God's brilliant beauty, his divine love, has cast its beams on those about us. There is a kind of beauty "which is seen in the bodies and especially in the faces of men," writes Michelangelo's contemporary Baldassare Castiglione in *The Book of the Courtier*, and it "excites this ardent desire that we call love, —we will say that it is an effluence of divine goodness, and that . . . it is diffused like the sun's light upon all created things."[23] Dante took up the theme in his *Divine Comedy*, as did Michelangelo himself in his twenty-third sonnet:

> The pure ethereal soul surmounts that bar
> of flesh, and soars to where thy splendours glow,
> free through the eyes; while prisoned here below,
> though fired with fervent love, our bodies are.[24]

The Elizabethan poets Spenser, Sidney, and Shakespeare do the same by the end of the sixteenth century. It meant that one could have one's flesh and despise it, too: that one could find God not despite, but through the body. It meant, if one turned one's back upon "unbridled desire," as Castiglione writes,[25] that the beauty of the human figure might be not an obstacle, but a means of contemplating the face of God. But it is a tricky kind of balancing act, this celebration of beauty, this attempt to steer a middle path between pagan strength and Christian mysticism. Perhaps only Michelangelo's *David*, which he completed in 1504, five years after the *Pietà*, achieves this balance. If one veered too far one way, the figures would turn into idealized abstractions; too far the other, and they turn lumpish and leaden, tumbling out of the sky.

This is why, in passing, the serene and magnificent ceiling of the Sistine Chapel earned Michelangelo—the creator creating the Creator creating—the appellation "divine." Set in the mid-point of Michelangelo's career, between the naiveté of his youth and the melancholy despair of his old age, it achieves the perfect balance between the ignorance that it moves from and the revelation that it moves toward, between the drunkenness of Noah and God's separation of light from darkness, between earth and heaven, the material and the ideal, darkness and light.

Nearly a half century later—almost a decade after the completion of his *Last Judgment*—Michelangelo was supervising the reconstruction of the basilica of St. Peter's by day and working on yet another *pietà* by night. Technically, it was a deposition: the dead weight of Christ lowered from the cross, supported to his right by the Magdalene, to his left by the Madonna, from behind by a hooded figure, perhaps Joseph of Arimathea, probably Nicodemus.[26] But his contemporaries came to refer to it as the *Florentine Pietà*. Although he was now in his seventies, "his genius and strength could not live without creation," writes Vasari, who goes on to describe the fury with which he sought out his soul in this block of marble: "He said that work with a chisel kept him in health. He worked at night and slept very little, and had made himself a helmet of cardboard to hold a lighted candle on his head so that with both hands free he could light what he was doing. Even at that age he cut the marble with such impetuosity and vigour that it seemed to fly in pieces. He broke off in one blow great fragments four or five inches thick and left a line so pure that if he had gone a hair's-breadth further he would have risked ruining the whole."[27]

But Michelangelo did ruin it. According to Vasari, a flaw in the marble tested his patience, which he lost, and he smashed the sculpture into several pieces with his hammer—hence the shattered left arm of Christ and the missing leg, which had originally been slung over the thigh of the Virgin Mary. As the story goes, Michelangelo's servant Antonio begged for the remnants, only to sell them to a Florentine sculptor named Tiberio Calcagni, who asked Michelangelo's permission to finish it. Tiberio's mediocre efforts have marred the sculpture; his inexpressive Magdalene is too small to support Christ's weight, for instance. But the rest is all Michelangelo: the athletic, polished torso of Christ, twisting in a *serpentinata* pose, His head collapsed into the roughly blocked-out face of the Madonna. As is the towering figure of Nicodemus, an old man in a monk's cowl, stooped over with the weight of his burden, bent with sorrow, ravaged with age. He is, as Vasari recognized, Michelangelo himself.

It was to be his tombstone. As the earlier *Pietà* was to Michelangelo's youth, so is this brooding, half-finished *Florentine Pietà* to his age. While the one is supremely harmonious, a triumph of serenity over sorrow, a seemingly effortless erasure of weight and death, so angular and contorted is the other, that not even the three are capable of sustaining the physical burden of the dead Savior. While the one epitomizes the High Renaissance, the other points toward Mannerism, the Baroque. While the one is Michelangelo's most finished sculpture, painstakingly polished, the other is shattered, blocked out, and incomplete—as *non finito* as his slaves and captives, entombed in stone. It was as if "his passion for abstract pefection" made it increasingly "impossible for any work to be materially completed."[28]

If we study Michelangelo's self-portrait in the *Florentine Pietà*, half-hidden behind the high altar in the Duomo, the cathedral in Florence, half-buried in the shadows of a monk's cowl, we find a face pitted by the chisels of regret, fear, and longing. "Perhaps no other work of Michelangelo is so human or speaks so directly to the soul," writes Romaine Rolland.[29] Our first reaction is that Michelangelo ran out of time—that he had neither the strength nor the years to finish the sculpture, to polish the skin. But when we look again, when we set the *Florentine Pietà* against the trajectory of a lifetime of sculpture and painting, it is as if he had carved through the surface, as if he had sliced through the skin, through the beauty, *through* the externals, to get at the form beneath—to get at the essence of sorrow, the weight of death. "It is his whole soul laid bare," writes Rolland.[30] It is, in short, as if he had flayed his own self.

Six days before his death in February of 1564 and three weeks before his eighty-ninth birthday, Michelangelo was still at it, reports his friend the britches maker, carving his ultimate sculpture, the *Rondanini Pietà*. Here everything has been cut away. An inexplicable arm and the leg of a man, now the Virgin's, are all that remain of four original figures, so that now there is only a roughly blocked-out Madonna and Christ. Having cut away the upper portion of the Christ figure, Michelangelo tried to carve him again from out of the diminishing block of stone—his head from out of the Madonna's shoulder, his arm from out of her torso. From one point of view, the result is a record, as Linda Murray writes, of "the fumbling struggles of a very old man [trying] to force his trembling hand to follow the vision in his mind's eye."[31] From another point of view, however, it is all Michelangelo, so stripped of substance, of beauty, that it is all essence. "In the humility of his last years," writes Kenneth Clark, "Michelangelo has pared away everything that can suggest the pride of body, till he has reached the huddled roots of a Gothic wood carving.... the sacrifice of this form, which for over sixty years had been the means of his most intimate communications, gives to this shattered trunk an incomparable pathos."[32]

Sixty years before, there was only beauty. "He... loved not only human beauty but everything beautiful in general," writes Condivi, "a beautiful horse, a beautiful landscape ... admiring them all with marveling love and selecting beauty from nature as bees gather honey from flowers."[33] But in his seventies, it had turned to ashes. "Teach me to hate the world so little worth," he writes in Sonnet 66, "and all the lovely things I clasp and prize." By now the flesh was no longer a blessing but a curse, a goad, a leaden weight, a shroud that gripped his soul in a living death. Michelangelo's poems are haunted by this nightmarish theme: that his soul is trapped like a pith in its rind, that he longs to escape his skin as a serpent might slough off its own. "Man lives in a sack of leather," he said.[34]

Again and again in these final years, Michelangelo's drawings and sketches are haunted by these images of Christ—Christ crucified, Christ deposed, Christ resurrected, Christ in judgment—as if the repeated mantra of Christ's figure might finally rend apart the shroud of mortality. Even his art, which had seemed in his youth a means of touching God, has become an illusion, a "fantasy," as he puts it in Sonnet 65, written for Vasari in 1554, in the seventy-ninth year of his life:

> Already now my life has run its course,
> And, like a fragile boat on a rough sea,
> I reach the place where everyone must cross
> And give account of life's activity.
> Now I know well it was a fantasy
> That made me think art could be made into
> An idol or a king. Though all men do
> This, they do it half-unwillingly.

> The loving thoughts, so happy and so vain,
> Are finished now. A double death comes near—
> The one is sure, the other is a threat.
> Painting and sculpture cannot any more
> Quieten the soul that turns to God again,
> To God who, on the cross, for us was set.

This may explain why Michelangelo mutilated the *Florentine Pietà*. Vasari offers three explanations for the destruction, as if uncertain of which to choose: the marble was flawed; Michelangelo, a perfectionist, grew impatient with imperfection; his servant Urbino was constantly nagging him to complete the project. Art critics have offered another half-dozen hypotheses, ranging from the psychoanalytic to the iconographic.[35] Perhaps the most convincing explanation is that of Steinberg, who argues that Christ's left leg, once slung over the thigh of the Madonna, pushed the erotic implications of His spiritual union with the Madonna too far. Long a metaphor for love, the slung leg epitomized a sculpture that was unbearably and, finally, unacceptably physical. "His demolition then would be a renunciation," writes Steinberg.[36] But I think the explanation is at once more simple and more tragic than this: it is about the inability of the material to capture the immaterial world—the inability of body to capture spirit, of Michelangelo to find himself.

Thus the look of anguish and despair in the features of Michelangelo, dangling helplessly from the hand of St. Bartholomew/Aretino in the middle of the *Last Judgment*: what looks like a rueful joke—Michelangelo flayed alive by the pen of Aretino—turns out to be deadly serious. Sloughed off as if by a snake, Michelangelo's disembodied skin is all that is left of his mortality, all that he has to offer of himself. St. Bartholomew has his knife; St. Lawrence, his gridiron; St. Catherine, her wheel; but all Michelangelo has is this rag of flesh: this art, these paintings, these sculptures, these poems, this brief and unworthy life.

So it is no accident that this bloody remnant of Michelangelo is poised in the middle of things, literally—between the *Pietà* in Rome and the other in Florence, between heaven and hell, between Christ and the shame-faced sinner—for in the *Last Judgment* the fate of Michelangelo's very soul hangs in the balance.[37] In this painting it is not only humankind but also Michelangelo who is on trial, and not just once, clutched in the hands of St. Bartholomew, but again and again, for this moving painting provides us not with a self-portrait but with self-portraits of Michelangelo, with a multiplicity of mirrors in which he sees himself—as we see ourselves as well. For he is the dead man emerging in wonder from his tomb. It is he who is pulled up by the chain of his rosary into heaven. It is he who has failed his examination. And it is he who cowers beneath the flailing oar of Charon. "So near to death," writes Michelangelo in Sonnet 71, "so far from God, forlorn."

Notes

1. For Michelangelo's *Last Judgment*, see especially Charles de Tolnay, *Michelangelo: The Final Period* (Princeton: Princeton University Press, 1960), 19-50; Leo Steinberg, "Michelangelo's 'Last Judgment' as Merciful Heresy," *Art in America* 63 (November-December 1975): 49-63; Marcia B. Hall, "Michelangelo's *Last Judgment*: Resurrection and Predestination," *Art Bulletin* 58 (1976): 85-92; Leo Steinberg, "A Corner of the Last Judgment," *Daedalus* 109 (1980): 207-73; Jack M. Greenstein, "'How Glorious the Second Coming of Christ': Michelangelo's *Last Judgment* and the Transfiguration," *Artibus et Historiae* 20 (1989): 33-57; Valerie Shrimplin, "Hell in Michelangelo's *Last Judgment*," *Artibus et Historiae* 30 (1994): 83-107; Bernadine Barnes, "Metaphorical Painting: Michelangelo, Dante, and the *Last Judgment*," *Art Bulletin* 77 (1995): 64-81; and Beat Wyss, "The *Last Judgment* as Artistic Process: the Flaying of Marsyas in the Sistine Chapel," *Res* 28 (Autumn 1995): 62-77.
2. The essay first appeared in *CSR* 31.3 (Spring 2002): 287-300.
3. Ascanio Condivi, *The Life of Michelangelo*, trans. Alice Sedgwick Wohl (Baton Rouge: Louisiana State University Press, 1976), 83.
4. See Leo Steinberg, "The Line of Fate in Michelangelo's Painting," *Critical Inquiry* 6 (1980): 421-36.
5. See especially Howard Hibbard, *Michelangelo* (New York: Harper & Row, 1974), 239-40; and Charles H. Morgan, *The Life of Michelangelo* (New York: Reynal, 1960), 182.
6. Quoted in Giorgio Vasari, *Lives of the Most Eminent Painters, Sculptors, and Architects*, trans. Gaston Du C. Vere (New York: Harry N. Abrams, 1979), 1931.
7. Ibid., 1927.
8. Charles Sala, *Michelangelo: Sculptor, Painter, Architect* (Paris: Pierre Terrail Editions, 1996), 145.
9. Gilles Néret, *Michelangelo 1475-1564* (Köln: Taschen, 1998), 77.
10. Leo Steinberg, *Michelangelo's Last Paintings* (New York: Oxford University Press, 1975), 40.
11. Steinberg, "A Corner of the Last Judgment," 208.
12. Quoted in Vasari, *Lives*, 1883; cited in John A. Symonds, *The Life of Michelangelo Buonarroti* (New York: Modern Library, 1928), 337. Although Steinberg dismisses the anecdote as "silly" ("Corner" 215), Tolnay repeats Vasari's account (*Final Period* 46).
13. See ibid., 45-46; Morgan, *Michelangelo*, 189; and Linda Murray, *Michelangelo* (London: Thames and Hudson, 1980), 151. For a further account of Pietro Aretino's response, see also Bernadine Barnes, "Aretino, the Public, and the Censorship of Michelangelo's *Last Judgment*," in *Suspended License: Censorship and the Visual Arts*, ed. Elizabeth C. Childs (Seattle: University of Washington Press, 1997), 59-84.
14. Leonard Barkan, *Unearthing the Past: Archaeology and Aesthetics in the Making of Renaissance Culture* (New Haven: Yale University Press, 1999), 198.
15. Barnes, "Aretino," 61.
16. This is nothing new. According to Tolnay, Ricci first noted the resemblance of Bartholomew to Aretino in *Il Gionale d'Italia* (June 2, 1925); and Francesco La Cava identified Michelangelo's self-portrait in *Il Volto di Michelangelo Scoperto nel Giudizio Finale* (Bologna: Zanichelli, 1925), although Tolnay claims to have identified the portrait earlier, as had a contemporary of Vasari (for which, see Tolnay, *Final Period*, pp. 114, fn. 44, and 118, fn. 62, respectively).
17. Condivi, *The Life of Michelangelo*, 108.
18. Quoted in Benvenuto Cellini, *The Life of Benvenuto Cellini*, trans. John A. Symonds (New York: Charles Scribner's Sons, 1920), 20; cited in Condivi, ibid., 146.
19. Quoted in Symonds, *The Life of Michelangelo Buonarroti*, 44-45.
20. Leo Steinberg, "The Metaphors of Love and Birth in Michelangelo's *Pietàs*," in *Studies in Erotic Art*, eds. Theodore Bowie and Cornelia V. Christenson (New York: Basic Books, 1970), 231.
21. Ibid., 234.
22. Condivi, *The Life of Michelangelo*, 24.
23. Baldassare Castiglione, *The Book of the Courtier*, trans. Leonard E. Opdycke (New York: Horace Liveright, 1929), 286.
24. Michelangelo, *The Sonnets of Michelangelo*, trans. John A. Symonds (London: Vision Press, 1950).
25. Castiglione, *The Book of the Courtier*, 287.
26. On the identity of the hooded figure in the *Florentine Pietà*, see especially Barkan, *Unearthing the Past*, 407 fn. 49.
27. Vasari, *Lives*, 1927; cited in Romain Rolland, *Michelangelo*, trans. Frederick Street (New York: Duffield & Company, 1915), 125.
28. Barkan, *Unearthing the Past*, 337.
29. Rolland, *Michelangelo*, 127.
30. Ibid., 128.
31. Murray, *Michelangelo*, 202.
32. Kenneth Clark, *The Nude: A Study in Ideal Form* (New York: Pantheon Books, 1956), 259.
33. Condivi, *The Life of Michelangelo*, 105.
34. Cited in Steinberg, *Michelangelo's Last Paintings*, 39.
35. For which, see Moshe Arkin, "'One of the Marys . . .': An Interdisciplinary Analysis of Michelangelo's Florentine Pieta," *Art Bulletin* 79 (1997): 493-518.
36. Steinberg, "Metaphors of Love and Birth," 253.
37. Tolnay pushes this theme even further, identifying the woman in a widow's veil, peering out from behind St. Lawrence, as Vittoria Colonna, who pities the tragic descent into Hell of her friend Michelangelo (*Final Period*, 45).

20 Rejecting Neutrality, Respecting Diversity

From "Liberal Pluralism" to "Christian Pluralism" (2006)

JONATHAN CHAPLIN

Western liberal democracies which hitherto had considered themselves to be stable, confident, and tolerant are increasingly perplexed and disoriented by the presence within them of strong and articulate cultural, religious, and other minorities whose claims are disrupting that comfortable self-image.[1] Such minorities seem unappeased by the lofty assurances of impartial treatment promised by liberal elites and determined to press their claims for acknowledgement upon an ambivalent or hostile public. In a culture increasingly driven by what Charles Taylor calls the "politics of recognition," "misrecognition has now graduated to the rank of a harm that can be hard-headedly enumerated along with [inequality, exploitation, and injustice]."[2]

Christians in liberal democracies also experience this phenomenon as challenging and even bewildering, the more so if they regard their own liberal democracy as rooted in a culture formed significantly by Christian faith. Among the latter, for example, are the advocates of a "Christian nation" position.[3] Already fighting a rearguard action against the progressive secularization of public life and public institutions, they now find themselves even more anxious over the additional dilemmas provoked by issues such as the legal toleration of "deviant" lifestyles, the regulation of immigration, the advances of multiculturalism in education, and more broadly the politics of identities which they do not share.

For some, the USA—and increasingly Canada—is entering a period of "culture wars," as James Davison Hunter terms it, a struggle for the "soul" of the nation in which defenders of the Judeo-Christian tradition are confronted, as they see it, with a concerted secularist assault. In the USA, many of those who share this reading of the contemporary situation thus exhort us to revive an interest in the First Things upon which the American Republic was founded.[4] While "Fundamentalists" are blamed, sometimes unfairly, for stoking up such culture wars and fuelling the intolerance which blocks thoughtful resolutions, other Christian voices have offered a variety of careful responses (and I draw on some of them below).[5] Whatever their stance, however, many Christians north and south of the border recognize in Stephen Carter's analysis of *The Culture of Disbelief*[6] much evidence from their own experience of how "law and politics trivialize religious devotion" and so seem to corrode the cultural forms which they had for so long enjoyed as a blessing of divine providence.[7]

This essay argues for a "Christian pluralist" response to the dilemmas of the kinds of pluralism noted above. After introducing a typology of pluralisms in the first part, I examine in the second the various ways in which liberalism has typically dealt with pluralism, and then consider in the third part the ideas of one of the most pluralistically inclined and diversity sensitive liberals, namely William Galston, a prominent political philosopher and former adviser to President Clinton. The purpose of this review of liberalism is not only to provide information about what liberals are thinking but also to exploit such thinking in order to highlight a vitally important point about the kind of pluralism I think Christians should defend, a point often elided in Christian discussions. After critically assessing three possible Christian responses to pluralism in the fourth part, I shall suggest in the fifth that Christian political thinkers should openly embrace a conclusion they themselves frequently draw from their own critiques of liberalism: that there is no such thing as pluralism *simpliciter*—neutral pluralism—but rather a plurality of pluralisms, each expressing a definite political perspective. Specifically, I shall argue that just as liberals necessarily and legitimately seek to realize an authentically liberal pluralism, so Christians necessarily and legitimately seek an authentically Christian pluralism. "Christian pluralism" is not only not a contradiction in terms but is an essential aspiration for an authentically Christian political perspective. If Christians merely seek a neutral pluralism, they risk lapsing into the language—for them inauthentic—of secular liberalism.

Of course, not all liberal thought is "secular." Christian and liberal political thought have influenced each other through long and complex historical associations, and they share many substantive political commitments. By "liberalism" I am referring to the modern tradition of political philosophy which accords primacy to individual freedom, deriving other political principles—such as justice, rights, or community—from it. "Secular liberalism," then, is that strand of liberalism which construes individual freedom in secularist terms, that is, as rooted in the moral and spiritual autonomy of human beings. Not surprisingly, many Christian political thinkers, especially those adhering to "orthodox" or "traditional" convictions, find themselves at presuppositional variance with this strand of liberalism, and at odds with some of its major policy implications.[8]

A valuable typology of pluralities proposed by Richard Mouw and Sander Griffioen proves useful in assessing liberal views of pluralism and in sketching the contours of a Christian response.[9] These authors distinguish between three fundamental kinds of societal plurality: associational, contextual, and directional.[10] Associational plurality refers to the plurality of qualitatively distinct, functionally specific associations, institutions, or communities populating a modern society: familial and kinship, educational, economic, occupational, artistic, political, religious, and so on. Mouw and Griffioen propose that such associational plurality is not merely a contingent historical phenomenon (as historicism asserts), nor solely an outcome of the exercise of individual choice (as individualistic liberalism holds), but rather a reflection of enduring, deep-going structurations rooted in human social nature as created by God.[11] The multiple capacities, inclinations, and needs of human nature find their social expression today in multiple types of association, each focused primarily on channeling one of them.[12] The burgeoning literature on the institutions of "civil society" testifies to a growing appreciation of this type of plurality.[13]

I find it problematic, however, to refer to this type of plurality as "associational," since many of the social structures which it embraces—for example, kinship, political or religious structures—are not fundamentally associational (i.e. voluntary) in character but are better termed "institutions," "communities," or "corporations."[14] I therefore follow Skillen in referring to this type of plurality as "structural," leaving open the specific way in which each social structure is actually constituted. I also want to propose that structural plurality has ontological primacy, since it arises from the most fundamental and enduring imperatives of our created social nature, giving rise to what might be called the social analogue of "creational kinds." Defending structural plurality, then, is not to be reduced merely to defending freedom of association (although it certainly includes that).

Contextual plurality refers to the plurality of distinct cultural contexts existing across the world, increasingly within one and the same (multicultural) society, and arising from differences in language, ethnicity, custom, or historical tradition; I shall call it "cultural" plurality. Although particular cultures are not, like some social structures (such as families), "creational kinds" with a determinate normative structure, the fact of cultural plurality is equally expressive of the potential for human social diversity rooted in divinely created potentials.[15] Indeed, cultural plurality and structural plurality are inseparable: families and states, for example, inevitably bear the imprint of their cultural context. The plurality of particular cultures, each opening up a different facet of God's gifts of social intercourse, communal organization, linguistic and artistic expression, intellectual and technical exploration, and so on, is not something that should be resisted by Christians but rather joyfully celebrated.[16]

The third type, directional plurality—the focus of this paper—embraces the plurality of religions, worldviews, or other fundamental spiritual orientations or directions (the liberal political philosopher John Rawls calls them "comprehensive doctrines"[17]) existing in contemporary societies. These might be "religious" in the traditional sense, or secular, or pagan, but in each case the relevant point is not simply that these directions exist but that they direct: many dimensions of culture and society, including the diverse social structures within them, are powerfully molded by one or more of them. Certainly the fundamental political values of a society—such as, in liberal democracies, autonomy—are conditioned by such directional perspectives.[18] To make clear the inseparable link between this type of plurality and the other two, we might say that the plurality of directions reveals divergent spiritual responses—shalom-enhancing or shalom-denying—to the normative structural and cultural possibilities given by God in creation. Structural and cultural plurality are not only the theater of God's glory, but also the site of human spiritual contestation.

Thus, while structural and cultural plurality are divine gifts to be celebrated, this clearly cannot be said of directional plurality.[19] Deep differences of spiritual direction cannot, from a Christian viewpoint, be regarded as anything other than the bitter fruits of the Fall, the result of a cataclysmic splintering of the intended spiritual unity of humankind under God. From some directional standpoints—Hinduism or radical postmodernism, perhaps[20]—such radical spiritual differences may be a cause for rejoicing, but the Christian belief in sin as spiritual rebellion against the truth makes it a matter for profound lament.[21]

The three types of plurality are inseparably connected. Nowhere is there an example of a distinct social structure (the family, the school, etc.) which is not embedded within a particular cultural context, or which is immune from any directional influence. Nor do spiritual directions float freely above particular structural and cultural embodiments. Discussions of the three types of plurality go awry when they are conflated. This can occur when directional identity is collapsed into cultural identity—religion into ethnicity, for instance—the result of ignoring the independent reality and causal power of the former[22] (the predominant tendency of secular liberalism). Or it can occur by treating cultural communities and/or directional communities as social structures – nations as states, or religions as churches, for instance—and so attributing to the former rights, duties, projects, perhaps even intentions, which can only meaningfully be attributed to the latter. Thus, for example, a cultural community like a nation is not a social structure in the sense defined above—it is not even a political association – and should not be treated as one, though it will condition the structures which happen to populate the society in which it is dominant.[23]

The political relevance of this threefold typology becomes clear when we focus specifically on the state, the political association.[24] The state faces the extremely complex and demanding task of striving for a just adjudication among all the various manifestations of structural, cultural and directional plurality. Put differently, one example of structural plurality—the state—has the unique responsibility to establish a framework of just public laws and policies, sanctioned finally by the possibility of force, for the diverse cultural and directional communities domiciled within its territory.[25] It is because of the compulsory and coercive character of this responsibility that the dilemma of pluralism is so pressing. The prospect of the state coercively arbitrating among competing directional or cultural communities renders the dilemma particularly acute, not only for Christians but also for secular liberals, as we shall now see.

Contemporary liberal political theory finds itself increasingly exercised by vigorous assertions of cultural and directional particularity which earlier generations of liberal theorists had thought were adequately accommodated within liberalism's universal, abstract principles of justice. Liberalism didn't deny the reality of cultural and directional attachments, even their own, but often failed to register their political importance.[26] Unlike questions of economic inequality or democratic accountability, the assertion of claims arising from cultural or directional particularity was seen as insufficiently likely to force difficult distributive or adjudicative choices, and so not to warrant extensive philosophical reflection. Of course liberals, regarding at a distance those older and—to them—alien forms of culture or religion which they classified as "traditional," could recognize how their "primitive" and "irrational" dynamics, in polities in Africa, Asia, the Middle East, Latin America, or south-east Europe, could have been or could still be sources of profound political discord. But the long-term solution to such discord lay in "modernization," and eventually history would take care of the problem.

Modernization had, of course, taken care of the problem within western societies, or at least was well on the way to doing so. Ancient cultural and directional feuds had been dissolved in the acids of modernity and those pockets of resistance from traditional communities (the Irish in Britain, the Basques in Spain, the Quebecois in Canada, for instance) would in due course wither away.[27] Indeed, some liberals have claimed to be able to trace an even grander historical narrative taking place, heralding the "end of history," the atrophy of history's crabbed and reactionary ideologies, and the universal realization of liberal democracy and capitalism[28]—now amply aided and abetted, of course, by "globalization."

But what Taylor calls "the politics of recognition" has been stubbornly reasserting itself against this universalizing trend, giving rise to a much more challenging manifestation of cultural and directional plurality than had hitherto presented itself. In the face of a resurgence of multiple claims to the political recognition, or even the active promotion, of such particularity, liberals have fashioned a second line of response: not to deny the importance of such issues, but to invalidate their political legitimacy. Such claims are deemed to be illegitimate breaches of the liberal principle of state neutrality towards citizens' fundamental worldviews – what Rawls calls "particular conceptions of the good." Such claims, Rawlsian liberals hold, make demands going well beyond the basic resources, rights, and liberties—Rawls calls them "primary goods"—which a liberal state must secure for all its citizens. Such highly particular demands are located by liberals in (critics would say relegated to) what Rawls calls the "background culture" (civil society) and may not determine what constitutes the "domain of the political" (the state), nor may its promotion be a legitimate object of public policy.[29]

So for many modern and contemporary liberals, claims arising from cultural and directional particularity have been deemed either politically insignificant or normatively inadmissible. This is not to say that all of the specific goals pursued by proponents of such particularity have been ignored or dismissed by such liberals, but they have been justified in specifically liberal terms. Pierre Trudeau's bilingualism policies, for example, went some way towards meeting the cultural demands of French Canadians, but were legitimated not, as Taylor proposed, in terms of shared goods—such as the survival ("la survivance") of a cultural patrimony—but rather as extensions of the principle of equal individual rights, in this case, the right to be able to speak in the language of one's choice (anywhere in Canada).[30] And those American liberals who supported affirmative action programs generally did so on parallel grounds: for individuals who, by virtue of their inherited social locations, had experienced historically entrenched forms of discrimination (women, Blacks, Latinos, Asians), to enjoy the "equal protection of the laws" in a substantive and not just a formal legal sense mandated not identical but preferential treatment by public institutions.

Such responses arise from within the existing paradigm of liberal individualism: they merely give new recognition to a distinct feature of individuals—their cultural "preference"—which hitherto was unjustly excluded from the package of basic individual rights secured by a neutral liberal state.[31] But now the earth is moving under this individualist and neutralist paradigm. The "background culture" has thrust itself to the foreground and is invading the "domain of the political" with a vengeance. Feminists, deconstructionists, advocates of minority cultures and gay/lesbian rights, and of course religious believers, are now mounting frontal assaults on the edifice of abstract liberal universalism, charging that it necessarily suppresses what is most important about their identities. Liberals have thus been forced to revisit their most fundamental philosophical assumptions and political aspirations.

One response to such assaults among liberals has been to openly defend the clear moral superiority of what Rawls calls "comprehensive" liberalism and declare an intention to continue to shore up the liberal character of society or refashion it wherever liberalism is in retreat or has not yet prevailed. This will involve, these liberals announce, the refashioning of "illiberal" communities—notably religious ones—according to the secular liberal principles governing the larger society. Stephen Macedo, perhaps the most candid representative of this response, argues for a "transformative" liberalism which conceives of law not merely as classical-liberal boundary-setting but as the intentional formation of "liberal" citizens.[32] A liberal constitution should not merely protect individuals' negative freedom but "must shape the way that people use their freedom and shape people to help ensure that freedom is what they want.... it must constitute the private realm in its image and it must form citizens willing to observe its limits and able to pursue its aspirations."[33] "No one has a right to a level playing field."[34] The implication for religion is that, since liberal democracy "needs the right sort of civic culture," then "religious communities of the right sort are an important part of this culture."[35] Liberals must "recognize the supreme importance of constituting diversity for liberal ends."[36] Macedo is aware of the charge that his liberal transformationism could be construed as the "oppression" of minority religions finding themselves at odds with liberalism. He acknowledges that liberalism increases the psychological cost of holding such beliefs, but supposes that this involves only a "gentle" and wholly legitimate transformationist strategy.[37] His conclusion is that "[t]he extinction of many, if not all, of the communities that pose truly radical alternatives to liberal democratic political principles is to be welcomed."[38]

Macedo's monistic vision of liberalism implies a political system in which, as Galston puts it, "constitutional uniformity crushes social pluralism."[39] Liberal monism is gaining ground in part because of the fear that the violent consequences of political fragmentation in non-western societies might be reproduced at home. This fear, of course, was terrifyingly realized in the 9/11 terrorist attacks, which thrust some such liberals into a posture of aggressive defiance towards those perceived to be threatening western liberal culture. Others, however, had already been genuinely searching for new models to accommodate better cultural and directional diversity, not mainly for prudential reasons but out of a principled recognition of the need for greater toleration of directional and cultural diversity. It was a combination of both which motivated Rawls to make his far-reaching move a generation ago from "comprehensive" to "political" liberalism, a liberalism supposedly confining itself to seeking consensus only on core political principle of justice and remaining entirely agnostic on the directional foundations of such principles. Many have pointed out, however, that his well-intentioned aspiration to accommodate directional and cultural diversity nevertheless signally fails to achieve its objective.[40] Still others, with varying attachments to liberalism, have engaged in more searching reappraisals of the liberal paradigm in the light of the irruption of such diversity. Even those sympathetic to Rawls's overall stance have criticized the inadequacy of his analysis of cultural and directional diversity. Will Kymlicka, for example, has developed an influential liberal theory of cultural rights, intended to safeguard as much autonomy for minority communities as a liberal society can tolerate.[41] Christians espousing pluralism but critical of neutralist liberalism have many more potential dialogue partners than they did a generation ago. One of the most congenial is William Galston, to whom I now turn.

Galston is one of a growing chorus of liberal theorists rejecting the claim that liberalism should aspire to realize a state which is neutral with respect to particular conceptions of the human good. Liberalism, he affirms, is certainly committed to providing space within which many such conceptions can flourish. Indeed it is defined by a (rebuttable) presumption of the "expressive liberty" of individuals and groups, their right to live their lives "in accordance with their own understanding of what gives life meaning."[42] Yet liberalism nevertheless depends on a substantive theory of the good and a liberal state will be one which self-consciously advances that good, promotes liberal purposes, and nurtures liberal virtues.[43] Galston observes a deep but occluded tension within liberalism between its commitments to autonomy and to diversity, the former originating in the "Enlightenment Project," the latter in the "Reformation Project."[44] Contrary to its own aspirations, autonomy-liberalism fails to take deep diversity seriously enough, erroneously supposing that autonomy yields diversity and that diversity necessarily enhances autonomy. Yet by imposing a regime oriented to promoting autonomy-favoring ways of life it necessarily squeezes out deep diversity. "[T]he decision to throw state power behind the promotion of individual autonomy can weaken or undermine individuals and groups that do not and cannot organize their affairs in accordance with that principle without undermining the deepest sources of their identity. . . . [S]tate-supported commitment to autonomy tugs against specific kinds of lives that differ fundamentally, not just superficially, from many others whose disappearance would reduce social diversity."[45] Galston asserts instead that liberalism should privilege diversity over autonomy and proposes a liberal "Diversity State" to that end. Such a state will embody "public principles, institutions, and practices that afford maximum feasible space for the enactment of individual and group differences, constrained only by the requirements of liberal social unity."[46] He thus strongly endorses the principle of the "expressive freedom" of associations as enunciated over time by U.S. courts.[47] The principle reflects a "diversity model of free association," according to which "groups may be illiberal in their internal structure and practices as long as freedom of entrance and exit is zealously safeguarded by the state."[48] This stands in contrast to an "autonomy model" where associational freedom is "subject to the constraint that the internal structure and practices of all groups must conform to the requirements of individual autonomy."[49] Respecting such expressive associational freedom is vital if the inescapable "colonization effects" of a state on its sub-communities are to be mitigated. A diversity state should, wherever possible, seek to mitigate such effects.[50]

Admirably, Galston recognizes that a liberal diversity state will not emerge spontaneously from a tolerant society but will have to be deliberately constructed.[51] Indeed, "the more seriously we take diversity, the more seriously we must take the unitary public structure that both protects and circumscribes the enactments of diversity."[52] This is an acute observation: respecting diversity is not—contra Robert Nozick and other libertarians posing as champions of diversity[53]—a matter of rolling back the frontiers of the state. It is not secured by a policy of laissez-faire but only by a robust constitutional, legal, and public policy framework intentionally oriented to protecting diversity.[54] This, of course, will also involve framing its legal and political boundaries. Not just any expression of diversity will be tolerated by a liberal state: it will not peddle the illusion of being a neutral state capable of comprehensive "equal treatment" but will remain an avowedly liberal state, intentionally promoting the "requirements of liberal social unity." For a constitution is not a mere set of procedures but "represents an authoritative partial ordering of public values."[55] This qualification will inevitably place specific and possibly contentious limits around what it deems to be politically and legally acceptable. What, then, will be the public values rightly governing a liberal diversity state?[56]

Two examples seem non-controversial and would no doubt be affirmed by Christians (and others): the protection of human life ("no free exercise for Aztecs"), and the protection and promotion of physical security of the person (including, we might surmise, no sexual freedom for pedophiles, and no freedom of expression for homicidal anti-abortionists[57]). But Galston's diversity state will also promote the development of "social rationality"—"the kind of understanding needed to participate in the society, economy and polity."[58] The meaning of this is vague and likely more controversial, as is evident from its implementation in education. On the one hand, and in keeping with his diversity model of associations, Galston favors an "accommodationist" stance towards private schools.[59] Nor would a liberal diversity state require public or private schools to "require or strongly invite students to become skeptical or critical of their own ways of life."[60] On its face, it appears that religiously-based schools would flourish in such a state. Yet, unavoidably, "the scope of permissible diversity is constrained by the imperatives of citizenship."[61] For instance, a key element of a liberal diversity state's "basic structure" would be a requirement that all schools actively promote "tolerance."[62] Pursuant to the development of "social rationality," a liberal state may "intervene against forms of education that are systematically disenabling when judged against this norm."[63] This would include setting guidelines requiring schools to inform students of ways of life different from their own.[64] But depending on how broadly these were interpreted, such a requirement could lead to public regulation of a school's internal practices deemed quite intrusive by those running it. While state interventions like these seem nowhere near as invasive as those implied by Macedo's "transformative" model, they are nevertheless a consistent application of inherently contestable liberal political purposes.

This seems to be but one instance of what Galston calls the "regime effects" of a liberal diversity state upon its citizens and their associations: the "inevitable if informal consequences of public principles for private groups." What Galston says about them is revealing about his expectations regarding the distribution of directional or cultural power in a liberal diversity state: "Think of the social space constituted by liberal public principles as a rapidly flowing river. A few vessels may be strong enough to head upstream. Most, however, will be carried along by the current. But they can still choose where in the river to sail and where along the shore to moor. The mistake is to think of the liberal regime's public principles as constituting either a placid lake or an irresistible undertow. Moreover, the state may seek to mitigate the effect of its public current on the navigation of specific vessels whenever the costs of such corrective intervention are not excessive."[65] This reveals clearly that the sub-communities which a liberal diversity state aims to protect are expected to be countercultural minorities located on the margins of a dominant liberal community. Admittedly the members of these communities are still acknowledged as equal citizens enjoying full individual and associational rights. But they are evidently not envisaged as major public players: they are publicly accommodated, but not integrated into the public realm itself as active participants in shaping the destiny of the political community on a par with the leading directional or cultural communities. The image of isolated vessels struggling upstream against a powerful current is not likely to make minority communities feel maximally welcome and hardly seems consistent with Galston's "comprehensive opposition to all forms of cultural establishment."[66]

It is likely, then, that some Christians would want to dispute important details of where Galston draws the line between expressive associational freedom and the "requirements of liberal social unity."[67] But the main point I want to draw from Galston's account is that it discloses something inescapable about liberalism in general, namely that its advocates, whether self-proclaimed neutralists or not, are necessarily committed to a distinctively liberal constitution of diversity. Admittedly, Galston insists that a liberal political community does not embrace the whole of its citizens' lives; its conception of political order is not as suffocating as Macedo's.[68] Yet liberal pluralism, Galston rightly asserts, is a "regime," not a "suicide pact:" "Liberal pluralist institutions are not debarred from securing the conditions of their own perpetuation."[69] A liberal state adjudicating among diversities must necessarily place boundaries around the scope of permissible diversity which inescapably depends upon contested political principles: liberal principles. The kind of pluralism this diversity-sensitive liberal can offer remains, as he tells us, a species of liberal pluralism. (And this is bound to be problematic at certain points for adherents of orthodox Christianity, since while they will certainly value individual freedom, they will not typically regard it as the supreme or primary political value, nor will they construe it in secularist terms as many liberals will.)[70]

But I now want to suggest that this point is true because a deeper point about the general structure of all political communities is true: that the imperatives of the "unitary public structure" which constitute every such community and establish limits to what is regarded as acceptable directional diversity within it are never directionally neutral, but necessarily reflect the preponderant influence of one or more particular directionally-oriented political perspectives. This fact may be, but need not be, oppressive; but it is constitutive. Yet I want to claim further that this point is true because a yet deeper point is true: that the structural reality of the political community not only always constitutes limits to the public toleration of directional diversity but also, in the first instance, makes possible the political articulation of such diversity by constituting the very community in which it can come to expression. The structural, institutional imperatives of a political order constitute a political community in which diversity is simultaneously facilitated and circumscribed. I now elaborate this central claim by means of a critical assessment of three alternative Christian responses to directional plurality.

Liberal pluralism, then, is legitimately and necessarily committed to an authentically liberal model of a diversity state. In the final section I will suggest that Christian political thought (at least the strands upon which I draw) is also necessarily committed to an authentically "Christian diversity state," and that a Christian aspiration to shape our political communities further in the direction of such a state is entirely legitimate. I will argue that, since no neutral pluralism is possible, Christians should be unapologetic about the fact that the variety of pluralism they seek is not *mere pluralism*, but *Christian pluralism*. Christian advocates of pluralism may be guilty at best of incoherence, at worst of disingenuousness, if they attempt to deny or conceal this objective. I clarify my position by distinguishing it from three other possible Christian responses to the situation of radical directional plurality and pretended liberal hegemony: Christian monism, Christian agonism, and Christian establishment.

Christian monism involves the attempt to restore a comprehensive Christendom. In the face of liberal hegemony, this approach would aspire to seize (back) control from liberalism and work (democratically) towards a monopolistic "Christian state." Advocates of a "Christian nation" view urge a version of this strategy.[71] Rather than expounding upon this familiar position, however, I consider a more colorful formulation of monism at the pen of radical postmodern Stanley Fish, who has some unsolicited advice for Christian pluralists. Fish scornfully rejects attempts by Christians or other religious believers to seek merely to be included in the liberal neutralist game. In "Why We Can't All Just Get Along,"[72] he castigates what he sees as the inconsistency of Christian writers like Michael McConnell or Stephen Carter who seek to persuade liberalism to live up to its own principle of toleration and grant them the equal right to a seat at the table of liberal public debate. This strategy of persuasion, he charges, is not a challenge to but a straightforward accommodation to secular liberalism since it depends upon an acceptance of the terms of public debate set by secular liberalism, especially liberalism's illusory hope of discerning shared "principles" to which all can assent but which depend on no one's actual convictions.[73] But liberalism cannot, any more than any other political theory, come up with any coherent universalizable principle or practice of toleration. Decisions on who is allowed at the table cannot be impartially justified: "There can be no justification (apart from the act of power performed by those who determine the boundaries) and . . . therefore any regime of tolerance will be founded by an intolerant gesture of exclusion."[74] In the public realm, participants—whatever they think they are up to—are necessarily involved, not in a quest for shared ground, but in contending assertions of power. Indeed, "the specifying of common ground is itself a supremely political move."[75] His conclusion? "[A] person of religious conviction should not want to enter the marketplace of ideas but to shut it down. . . . The religious person should not seek an accommodation with liberalism; he should seek to rout it from the field, to extirpate it, root and branch."[76] Christians should play to win.[77]

Now it is true that the writings of the authors Fish critiques are not always adequately developed or internally consistent.[78] But Fish's unsolicited advice to Christians rests on an equally problematic understanding of the political realm as mere contestation. Democratic politics is just another site of the tribal power-struggle in which a "winner-takes-all" rule prevails: ". . . If the political is . . . the realm in which we live and move and have our being, conflict—the clash of opposing points of view—is not simply a dimension of it but the whole of it, and structures everything we do . . . ."[79] As Fish puts it, politics "goes all the way down."[80] However, while politics may indeed potentially touch on any sphere of social life (it is extensive), it does not and should not go all the way down when it touches any particular sphere (it is not intensive). Fish chides liberals for denying that "acts of exclusion and stigmatization are inevitable in any liberal regime that really wants to be a regime and not an endless philosophy seminar."[81] But his own conception of politics seems to oscillate between these two—between a brute power-struggle and a mere ongoing contest of intellectual viewpoints. I would argue, however, that in acknowledging the political community as a regime, we are not only or in the first place taking note of its coercive power, but are also identifying it as a particular kind of institution with specifiable—and not infinitely manipulable—structural features (legal authority, universal jurisdiction, coerciveness, publicity, etc.), and a structural purpose, i.e. promoting the public good (or some comparable definition). Political contest takes place—indeed is defined as political, rather than intellectual, ethical, or religious—within the framework of a set of given institutions structured to perform that particular function (however badly they do so). The fact that what "the public good" means is itself contested by political partisans does not remove the equally important fact that such partisans are necessarily operating within the structural constraints of a political regime, constraints differing in kind from those operative within other kinds of social structure (such as a family or a university) and which partisans cannot define (away) merely by asserting their own distinctive political perspective. Fish concentrates only on the potentially negative aspect of the structural nature of the political community (its power to coerce and exclude), ignoring its inherently positive aspect—the establishment of a community structured to promote the public good.

A second position is *Christian agonism*, represented by Ashley Woodiwiss.[82] Woodiwiss proposes a "postliberal Christian Democratic theory" drawing on secular theorists of "agonistic democracy" such as Chantal Mouffe and Nancy Fraser and political theologians such as John Milbank, Stanley Hauerwas, and Miroslav Volf.[83] Like Fish, his point of departure is the empirical state of affairs that there no longer exists a neutral, univocal, and universally accessible public discourse which can serve as a benchmark for legitimate public debate and decision. With Fish, too, he asserts that the liberal aspiration towards a stance of generally acknowledged neutrality, whether substantive or procedural, among political partisans is futile and potentially hegemonic. Rather, a pervasive multiculturalism and radical pluralism have generated today a multiplicity of contending "publics." Democracy can no longer posture as the forum for a quest for rational consensus but has now been transformed into an arena of "agonistic" contestation among radically different communities. There can be no "common good" in such a situation of radical difference.[84]

In such a context, Christians should renounce all vestiges of Christendom thinking, recognize themselves as a subordinated—"subaltern"—social group excluded from the centers of power, and enter the political sphere as one "subaltern counterpublic" among many. This will involve, not the classical project of articulating universal political principles, but the reaching of contingent judgments about how the Christian community should relate itself to other subaltern counterpublics with which it can find "neighborly affinity."[85] "Caught in an agonistic context, inextricably committed to public life yet possessing no sovereignty over it, the Christian community (or communities) must struggle to make sense of the requirements that this context dictates both for the preservation of its identity and for its relations with the other." The Christian citizen today is "neither ruler nor victim, but . . . diplomat, negotiating the what and whither of subaltern dialogues concerning identity and otherness."[86] The church, accordingly, will nurture Christian citizens in the practices of "peaceableness" and "self-restraint."

Woodiwiss is right to reject the hubristic and illusory claims of an imperialistic liberal universalism and to acknowledge the depth and inescapability of radical cultural and directional plurality. He is also right to observe that, increasingly, the Christian community, as many others, can only live authentically by placing itself in conscious confrontation with a pervasive secular liberal hegemony. I suggest, however, that his model of Christian agonism can at best serve as one component of an adequate Christian theory of democratic politics. It is deficient in two senses. First, as with Fish's model, it is parasitic upon the existence of a "regime," a democratic political community. It lacks an account of the nature and normative purpose of the state as the institutional context which alone makes political advocacy, whether agonistic or consensual, possible in the first place. This explains why characterizing the task of Christian citizenship today as involving mere subaltern diplomacy is an incomplete description of contemporary Christian political experience. The task of inter-communal negotiation among subaltern publics is an important one, and one to which Christian communities might be expected to make a distinctive contribution. But it is, first, often not a political task at all: it may not involve public authority, only civil society. And where it is political, it must tacitly assume the existence of relatively settled democratic constitutional procedures, which it then proposes to employ in the pursuit of its chosen (and worthy) objectives, but for which it seems disinclined to supply an adequate justification. As I have suggested, a political "constitution" does just that: it constitutes a political community and so establishes a common, public realm which defines the interactions of its members as political. And, crucially, in so doing, it also circumscribes the scope of the "difference" between them. All genuinely political demands—as opposed to private assertions or confessions—necessarily entail claims regarding the public good and the role of the state in promoting it, even if, as so often, they are voiced as or appear as (or are even intended as) mere sectional (or subaltern) claims. Christian agonism certainly might contribute to the nurturing of virtues of peaceableness and self-restraint in civil society, but it seems not to have adequate resources to generate a normative understanding of the constitutional democratic state which makes such action in civil society or democratic politics possible.[87]

Second, it is not clear that Christian agonism can produce a sufficiently robust principled argument for respecting directional (and cultural) plurality. It is true that a recognition of the radical plurality, contingency and fallibility of our political judgments, and of the propensity of states to exclude and oppress, lends additional support to a claim for such respect: since we or our states are likely to make mistakes when we draw the boundaries, as we must, around the expressive liberty of associations, for example, we had better make those judgments modestly. But even if we or our states had perfect political judgment, we would also need an account of the distinctive jurisdictions of state and other social structures (or cultural communities) in respect of directional matters. Without an account of what states are actually entitled to do in respect of directional plurality, even the most skilful subaltern diplomat will not have any clear criteria for deciding what kind of laws or policies it is appropriate to urge upon the state. Agonistic democratic activity may then tend to collapse into mere pragmatic negotiation (making it look too much like the discredited interest-group pluralism of the 1950s), or it will tacitly appeal to, while ostensibly eschewing, some unarticulated normative conception(s) of the jurisdiction of the state.

A third position is represented by Graham Walker. Like Woodiwiss, Walker eschews a monistic response to liberal hegemony, but instead espouses a restrained form of *Christian establishment*.[88] In a forceful rebuttal of Michael McConnell's argument for pluralism,[89] Walker joins in the charge that the supposedly inclusive pluralism McConnell advances is illusory and untenable, either collapsing inevitably into an oppressive liberal secularism or precipitating social fragmentation. McConnell is, Walker says, right to claim that secular liberal neutralism in fact amounts to the "covert and unacknowledged" establishment of secularism,[90] but wrong to respond to it by promoting the chimera of state neutrality towards (or "equal treatment" of) religion. In every political community, some form of establishment is "inexorable." This is not because of the deliberate intentions of officers of the state but because of what Galston calls "regime effects": as Walker puts it, "a political society's constitution of religion forms consciousness."[91] Not only is the pursuit of equal treatment chimerical, it is also unwittingly accommodationist towards secularism: "It is . . . merely secular neutralism writ large. Political authority is still secular and ostensibly neutral, only its neutrality extends to groups rather than to individuals . . . . It will either secularize and eviscerate (and thus homogenize) religious differences at only a slightly slower rate than secular neutralism, or, precisely insofar as it does not do that, it will ultimately pluralize society to an untenable degree."[92]

Exactly why would it homogenize religious differences? Because the demands of political unity would require that the state only include "those religions whose tenets demand benignity and benevolence, whose doctrines require minimal public validation, and whose view of religion is more individualistic than communal"—in short, religions looking like Protestantism.[93] If, on the contrary, it did strive to respect deep religious plurality, it would "careen toward Balkanization . . . . Authentic pluralism ushers in authentic war."[94]

Walker's solution is not a comprehensive religious establishment, but a partial, constitutionally limited one, a mixed constitution in which the state would overtly prefer one religion or a limited number of religions, "while constitutionally binding itself to protect the prerogatives of constitutionally subordinate religious orientations." Such a state would couple a "free exercise" clause with a positive "establishment" clause, thus promoting a religious orientation while not requiring it.[95] Crucially, under partial establishment the state would not merely offer symbolic endorsement of a religious orientation but would also look to it for guidance on a wide range of controversial legal and policy questions relating to issues such as ethnicity, language, sexual orientation, property, culture, and education.[96] The aim, however, would not be a thoroughgoing refashioning of society in the image of the dominant orientation, as with Macedo or Fish. In a mixed constitution, "even while it makes its official preferences plain [a state] can scrupulously remind citizens of their prerogatives of individual nonconformity."[97]

Walker's proposal is commendable both for its genuine attempt to accommodate directional diversity as well as for its insistence on public honesty in regards to the dominant directional orientation(s) guiding the constitutional framework required for such accommodation.[98] It is, however, problematic for almost exactly the opposite reason that Christian agonism is. Whereas Woodiwiss's conception of the political realm is too attenuated (too thin), Walker's is too capacious (too thick). While Walker is right to observe that all political communities require a common political identity based on the civic virtues necessary to sustain social cohesion, his estimate of the breadth of that cohesion is inflated. He tells us that "it simply cannot be, and nowhere has ever been the case, that citizens of a polity find their common identity in differing with one another over fundamental questions."[99] That is evidently true in the sense that a mere "agreement to disagree" cannot itself suffice as a basis of political order. One cannot found a polity on the mere principle of directional toleration alone. But a crucial ambiguity infects the following sonorous formulation of the point: "Man is a political animal, and if he is denied unity in the common affirmation of truth, he will find unity in the common denial of it."[100] That common denial is, of course, what he thinks supplies the social cohesion keeping secular liberal polities together. But what kind of "truth" is at stake here? Walker fails to make a vital distinction between directional truth—the ultimate truth about our existence—and political truth—the truth about the shape of a normative political order. While I in no way suggest that these two spheres of truth can or should be divorced, I think there is ample historical evidence that citizens can sometimes reach relatively enduring agreement on truth claims of the latter kind—on the broad design of a political constitution—without agreeing on truth claims of the former kind.[101] This, as Galston correctly observes, is an important legacy of "the Reformation project." Adherents to different directional visions evidently can reach some measure of consensus on the nature of a constitution notwithstanding their directional disagreements. Such agreement can be attained without the state officially favoring one or more religious orientations, and the evidence suggests that even partial establishment is likely to breed resentment from non-recognized groups and to produce a spiritually empty civil religion. Insisting on the distinction between religious and political truth-claims is not to embrace a neutral state, only a limited state. It is to identify correctly the boundaries of the different structural spheres—ecclesial and political—in which distinct (though not incoherent or incommensurable) kinds of truth claims are appropriately authoritative.[102]

There are, then, significant problems with neutrality, monopoly, agony, and establishment. My own position—Christian pluralism—has parallels with Galston's model of a liberal diversity state but acquires its distinctive orientation and priorities from what I hope is an authentically Christian conception of the state. (Obviously, I don't claim that this is the only authentically Christian conception.) The model of Christian pluralism I propose advocates a Christian diversity state which seeks to maximize respect for directional diversity subject to the inevitable constraints on diversity arising from a wider Christian conception of the nature and role of the state and other associations. Here I can only sketch the outlines of such a state, merely gesturing towards the sources on which I draw.[103] But some of its central features have already been anticipated, so let me summarize those first. A Christian diversity state would strongly affirm several specific institutional components of Galston's model. First, it would endorse the high value of personal freedom and the basic human rights and resources consonant with human dignity. Second, it would impose only moderate demands on citizenship and on patriotism, recognizing that religious citizens will recognize other prior and higher loyalties to faith, family, and other communities. Third, it would proceed from a (rebuttable) presumption in favor of expressive associational freedom. But it would enrich that notion with a wider conception of structural plurality (such as family, church, etc.); the freedom of non-state communities involves more complex legal and social space than

Galston acknowledges. Associational freedom is but one instance of the three types of plurality that, as we saw, are distinguished by Mouw and Griffioen. Thus, fourth, a Christian diversity state would be attentive to all three types, recognizing structural and cultural plurality as rooted in and deriving their own normative design from the inclinations of created order, and acknowledging directional plurality (itself a result of the fall) as deserving of just adjudication. But, fifth, and crucially, it would embrace all these things on the basis of a clear understanding of the normative content and limits of the purpose of the state itself. Galston certainly sheds important light on the state's limits. This follows from his strong affirmation of the "structural" type of plurality, the plurality of associations, communities and institutions populating a free society. Diversity liberalism affirms the principle of "political pluralism:" the state is "limited, not plenipotentiary," since there are "multiple, independent and sometimes competing sources of authority over our lives."[104] He also recognizes that deep cultural and directional diversity cannot be protected concretely without a vigorous, legally protected associational independence.

But it is not enough merely to observe that state authority is limited by other social authorities. The state, too, limits those other social authorities by its distinctive authority, and that authority exists to serve its unique normative purpose. Earlier I defined that purpose (loosely) as the promotion of the "public good." Other terms that might be used would include the Catholic notion of the "common good," or the neo-Calvinist notion of "public justice."[105] This is not the place to parse or elaborate such terms, or to adjudicate among competing versions of them.[106] I merely notice one point, namely that important Christian traditions have long accorded to the state the role of safeguarding and advancing a distinctively public dimension of society—in older language, the "commonweal"—and have recognized the state's special authority over persons and other associations and communities pursuant to that responsibility. Such a substantive notion of an inherently public good is absent from liberal formulations (especially secularist ones), which derive the purpose and limits of the state ultimately from the freedom of individuals.[107]

A Christian diversity state, then, would not merely seek to promote a neutral state which Christians happened to be able to endorse, i.e. one in which the scope of liberal neutral statecraft had been expanded sufficiently to satisfy Christian demands for inclusion. It would offer much more than a pluralist or communitarian gloss on individualistic liberal neutralism, but would aspire towards an authentically Christian model of a directionally tolerant constitutional democracy, incorporating and building on the features just noted.

Some Christian defenders of the protection of directional plurality either do not acknowledge this point or are too reticent on it. Michael McConnell, for instance, continues to invoke the unqualified language of neutrality,[108] asserting that the pluralist state "affirms the equality of all citizens by allowing all to participate in public affairs without privileging any particular ideology or mode of persuasion."[109] David Hollinger also describes his model of Christian engagement as "Christian influence within pluralism," yet without posing the question whether pluralism can be constituted neutrally with respect to the contending views of its participants.[110] Other Christian accounts are replete with such formulations.[111] What McConnell is referring to here is the equal right of all citizens, whatever their directional persuasion, to provide input into the democratic system. This is an obvious implication of the principle of free political speech, which a Christian diversity state would fully endorse. But there are two problems with such unqualified invocations of "neutrality" or "equal treatment." First, they do not acknowledge that the limits which every state needs to place on "acceptable" democratic inputs (laws against incitement to violence or hate speech, for example) will, however minimal, inevitably be controversial from someone's vantage point. Such limits will be particularly controversial when they restrict directionally-motivated speech. As Kent Greenawalt points out, defining what counts as acceptable religious political speech—indeed defining what counts as religion—can be a formidably difficult and controversial task from which even judges (perhaps especially judges) shy away.[112]

Second, McConnell is ambiguous on whether the output of such democratic activity—the substantive content of policies and laws—is equally reflective of the various directional standpoints in society. Many advocates of pluralism imply that the output of "equal treatment" of different directional visions can readily be recognized as such by all participants in democratic debate. But this expectation does not take the full measure of the radical directional differences with which contemporary states have to deal.

A similar lacuna emerges at one point in Mouw and Griffioen's discussion of the relation between directional and associational plurality. They rightly point out that it is necessary not simply to assert the existence of a plurality of associations (what I have called "social structures") but also to provide an account of the nature and coherence of such associations. An "integrative vision" of associational plurality is required, and this can only be supplied by a specific directional perspective. They then pose the question of whose directional perspective should provide the integrative vision, replying, quite rightly, that this should be allowed to emerge "out of the give-and-take of public debate, without granting any specific directional orientation a favored status in the discussion."[113] However, when the public debate occurs within the context of the state—when it is a debate over compulsory laws and public policies rather than, say, a university seminar or an inter-faith dialogue—it must reach a point of closure and issue in a political decision equally (and coercively) binding on adherents of all directional perspectives. Mouw and Griffioen do not raise the question whether it is reasonable to expect that such decisions, and indeed the constitutional norms which frame how they are made, will be perceivable and receivable by all citizens as respecting a norm of complete impartiality among all directional visions.

Elsewhere Griffioen rightly observes that the political community must act on the basis of definite "structural norms" (earlier I called them structural constraints) arising from its very nature and purpose. Such norms, he claims, must be commonly held since in the absence of at least minimal commonality on this purpose the political community will simply dissolve: these are indeed community-constituting norms, not mere (inter-) subjective viewpoints. Where they are entirely absent, a political community either does not exist or is close to collapse. "It is the normative structure of the political realm itself, rather than any substantive [i.e. subjective] consensus among the different religious-ideological persuasions, which provides the basis for the commonality."[114] The very existence of a minimally functioning political community, secured finally not by subjective human agreement but by the imperatives of created order, testifies to at least some area of political commonality. This crucial insight is often overlooked in both Christian and secular liberal discussions.

But while (as I proposed) such community-constituting norms partially circumscribe the limits of political difference, they obviously do not secure widespread political consensus on substantive constitutional or political issues. As soon as we seek to give an account of those community-constituting norms in terms of subjective political conceptions, directional divergences will quickly come into play. We should, of course, aspire towards whatever consensus is contingently attainable, especially on the constitutional principles which will frame the political community of which we are all members (however disaffected).[115] But there is less and less reason today to expect that an overlapping political consensus like this, even where attainable, will also include a common acknowledgement that its effects will be wholly impartial with respect to the plural directional visions sustaining citizens' commitments to it.[116]

The implication of rejecting liberal neutrality, then, needs to be confronted explicitly by Christians: in the course of shaping and reshaping the content of the overlapping political consensus on the constitutional lineaments of a state which seeks to accommodate directional plurality, the influence of one or more directional visions will, inescapably, be preponderantly (or at least disproportionately) felt, especially by those in directional communities with little public influence or with a history of exclusion. If this is so, then it will be misleading to imply that the desired result of Christians' (democratic) striving to realize a constitutional consensus more in keeping with Christian principles will be a political stance towards directional plurality conforming to some *direction-independent* criterion of impartiality. We should not seek a Christian establishment, however moderate and religiously tolerant. But just as liberals like Galston legitimately seek a liberal diversity state, we may legitimately—and will inevitably—seek a Christian diversity state.

Such a state will place certain directionally-motivated activities outside the realm of legally permitted directional toleration. It might exclude, not only "free exercise for Aztecs," but also, for example, things like the following: abortion on demand, unregulated capital exchanges or property development, destruction of rain forests, female genital mutilation, and same-sex marriage. All of these have been and will be advocated by some Christians as non-negotiable political demands, as among what Rawls terms "fundamental matters of justice."[117] Christian ecologists urging a radical repudiation of our consumerist lifestyles will not want public policies to accord equal status to claims arising from a rapacious industrial capitalist ideology premised on the limitless exploitation of nature; nor should they. It will not be persuasive in cases like these to claim that the state is implementing a directionally-impartial structural norm, since such stances can only appear to adherents of rival directional visions as partial, indeed to some as palpably "discriminatory." Such adherents will differ on what the purpose of the state itself is (what "the public good" requires) and on what the norms of other social structures are. Capitalist ideologues will necessarily perceive the policies of a Christian Ecology government as discriminatory and overweening, indeed as a direct assault on the essential "structural norm" of the business corporation, not as the impartial administration of public justice. Or, those arguing against the legal recognition of same-sex marriages will not get far merely by arguing that the "structural norm" of marriage, its unique associational identity, is being ignored by advocates of such recognition. It is that very identity, and as a result its supposed public entitlements, which is being contested by partisans of deeply divergent directional perspectives.[118]

On such questions, a political decision one way or the other (when it comes) has little prospect of being recognized by all sides as an example of equal treatment, and it seems increasingly inadvisable—perhaps disingenuous—to project it as such. Perhaps the best that can be hoped for in such deep conflicts is that, after careful and patient democratic dialogue, some partisans might reach the point of being able to concede: "Well, given the political principles emerging from your directional assumptions, including those about the structural norm of the state (family, corporation, etc.), I can see why you regard this policy as both right and fair; but from my vantage point, it is frankly oppressive." I am not suggesting that all or even most political debates will reveal conflicts as deep as these. Often directional divergences will not surface (or will not be present) and consensus will emerge without anyone experiencing directional exclusion. But a formulation of a Christian case for pluralism has to account not just for the easy cases but also for the most vexatious; indeed, especially for those.

My conclusion, then, is that a respectful treatment of directional plurality—one which, from a Christian perspective, genuinely aspires to be "impartial"—must be the aim of a Christian pluralism, but that no directionally neutral criterion of what counts as impartiality is available in a society characterized by deep directional diversity. If this is true, then it must follow that the state—at least some of the time, at least on fundamental issues of justice—cannot avoid bearing the impact of and so in effect favoring a particular spiritual direction, either in respect of democratic inputs or outputs or both. And, if so, the political objective Christians should set for themselves cannot be mere directional pluralism—not "freestanding" pluralism—but Christian pluralism: a political adjudication of directional and other types of plurality which openly allows Christian political principles to mould a constitutional consensus. Such a consensus, while intended to be as accommodating as possible to directional diversity, seeks to delineate the boundaries of legally permissible directionally-motivated activity in terms of a consciously Christian conception of the purpose of the state and other social structures (which I have merely sketched here). To put this even more pointedly: only such a Christian conception can generate an argument for directional toleration which Christians could consistently endorse, for we would not want our commitment to respecting directional plurality to depend upon a secularist political principle we cannot authentically own. Vigorously defending directional plurality and consciously shaping the state in a Christian direction are not only compatible, but—from a Christian directional standpoint—mutually implicative.[119] If this line of argument is correct, then the implication is that Christians should stand ready to declare honestly—and, where appropriate, publicly[120]—that they aspire to reshape the boundaries of legally accepted expressions of directional plurality in their societies in the light of a vision of state and society rooted in Christian faith. Such a declaration, it need hardly be added, is intended not to close off democratic debate but rather to reinvigorate and enrich it. And Christians can have faith in the possibility of such genuine interdirectional communication because their vision is not advanced as mere tribal confession but as an attempt to account for universal, creation-based conditions for just political order—conditions which all human beings experience and of which all must in some way render an account.[121]

Notes

1. This essay first appeared in *CSR* 35.2 (Winter 2006): 143-76.
2. Charles Taylor, "The Politics of Recognition," in *Multiculturalism: Examining the Politics of Recognition*, ed. Amy Gutmann (Princeton, N.J.: Princeton University Press, 1994), 64.
3. See, for example, *God and Politics: Four Views of the Reformation of Civil Government*, ed. Gary Scott Smith (Phillipsburg, N.J.: Presbyterian & Reformed Publishing Co., 1989), chs. 9 and 13.
4. This exhortation has not yet, however, extended to an interest in (what Canadians call) the "First Nations" coercively displaced by European Christian colonizers.
5. For a "separationist" perspective, different from my own, see Derek Davis, "Equal Treatment: A Christian Separationist Perspective," in *Equal Treatment of Religion in a Pluralistic Society*, eds. Stephen V. Monsma and J. Christopher Soper (Grand Rapids, Mich.: Eerdmans, 1998).
6. *The Culture of Disbelief: How American Politics and Law Trivialize Religious Devotion* (New York: Basic Books, 1993). See also his *God's Name in Vain: The Wrongs and Rights of Religion in Politics* (New York: Basic Books, 2000).
7. For arguments that, on the contrary, religion—especially Protestant Christianity—still enjoys a position of unhealthy dominance in American public life, see Gregg Ivers, "American Jews and the Equal Treatment Principle," in *Equal Treatment of Religion in a Pluralistic Society*, eds. Monsma & Soper. For a careful analysis of the influence of "secularism," see George Marsden, "Are Secularists the Threat? Is Religion the Solution?" in *Unsecular America*, ed. Richard J. Neuhaus (Grand Rapids, Mich.: Eerdmans, 1986). Nicholas Wolterstorff presents an illuminating analysis of the current condition of (secular) liberalism, and an argument in favor of pluralism, in "From Liberal to Plural," in *Christian Philosophy at the Close of the Twentieth Century*, eds. Sander Griffioen and Bert M. Balk (Kampen: Kok, 1995).
8. Theologically "liberal" Christians tend to find greater affinity with secular liberalism. Cf. Rogers M. Smith, "'Equal' Treatment: A Liberal Separationist View," in *Equal Treatment of Religion in a Pluralistic Society*, eds. Monsma & Soper.
9. *Pluralisms and Horizons: An Essay in Christian Public Philosophy* (Grand Rapids, Mich.: Eerdmans, 1994). The authors note that each of these types of plurality can in the first instance be viewed descriptively: we can simply observe that they exist, and then consider how to respond to their presence; or they can be viewed normatively, as states of affairs we should favor. Assuming that all types do indeed exist today in western societies in varying degrees of abundance, my interest is in the normative question.
10. Associational and directional plurality are referred to by James Skillen as "structural" and "confessional" pluralism respectively, in *Recharging the American Experiment: Principled Pluralism for Genuine Civic Community* (Grand Rapids, Mich.: Baker/CPJ, 1994). Mouw & Griffioen's introduction of a third variety, contextual pluralism, is a valuable complement to Skillen's distinction.
11. This reflects the influence of a distinctively Calvinian conception of society as rooted in the created order. There isn't space to defend that view here, but I shall appeal to it at various points. I'm aware, of course, that Barthians, Anabaptists, and others would raise objections to this conception.
12. Cf. *Pluralisms and Horizons*, 125ff. This implication of Mouw and Griffioen's notion of associational pluralism is inspired by the Kuyperian principle of the "sphere sovereignty" of social institutions, their God-given responsibility to fulfill a distinctive social calling in the service of human society. Cf. *Political Order and the Plural Structure of Society*, eds. Skillen & McCarthy, and *Religion, Pluralism and Public Life*, ed. Lugo.
13. Cf. *The Essential Civil Society Reader: Classic Essays in the American Civil Society Debate*, ed. Don E. Eberly (Lanham, Md.: Rowman & Littlefield, 2000); Jean L. Cohen & Andrew Arato, *Civil Society and Political Theory* (Cambridge, Mass.: MIT Press, 1992).
14. Mouw and Griffioen note in passing that the term "associational" is potentially misleading. *Pluralisms and Horizons*, 16.

15. Other Christian thinkers have viewed cultures similarly. In addition to the vast literature on cross-cultural missiology, see Miroslav Volf, "How Can You Be Croatian?," *Books & Culture* (Jan/Feb 2001), 28-31; *Exclusion and Embrace* (Nashville: Abingdon, 1996); and William Storrar, *Scottish Identity: A Christian Vision* (Edinburgh: Handsel Press, 1990).

16. Cultural difference can, of course, also become a potent source of misunderstanding and fear, but Christians of all people should be among those striving to drown out the anxious murmurs with the sound of celebration.

17. Rawls, *Political Liberalism* (New York: Columbia University Press, 1993, 1996), 58.

18. Political ideologies which aim to unite such values around a coherent and compelling vision can be seen as the political crystallizations of such directions. For a penetrating Christian analysis of modern political ideologies, see Koyzis, *Political Visions and Illusions*.

19. I am not referring here to the richly variegated manifestations of Christian faith as it comes to local expression within particular cultural or denominational forms: insofar as these serve as the contextual medium in which such faith is historically embodied, they too may be celebrated.

20. It is worth noting that one of the most significant recent statements of this view has come from the "postmodern" liberal pen of Rawls, for whom the "burdens of judgment" make the emergence of radically incompatible comprehensive doctrines a salutary witness to the free exercise of rationality. Cf. *Political Liberalism*, 48-66.

21. The biblical themes of idolatry and spiritual warfare seem to require such a stance, though of course this is compatible not only with mutual respect for different faiths but also with inter-faith dialogue (what Mouw & Griffioen term "dialogical theocentrism" [*Pluralisms and Horizons*, 101ff.]) and generous-spirited cooperation on matters of common concern.

22. Cf. George Vandervelde, "Native Self-Government: Between the Spiritual Fire and the Political Fire," in *Towards an Ethics of Community: Negotiations of Difference in a Pluralist Society*, ed. James H. Olthuis (Waterloo, Ont.: Wilfred Laurier University Press, 2000), 186-199.

23. Cf. Koyzis, *Political Visions and Illusions*, 117. I have here slipped in the term cultural and directional "communities," which invites explanation. Whereas cultures and spiritual directions are not social structures, it is meaningful to speak of them as generating identifiable "communities," so long as we do not read this term as implying organized structure, specific purpose, or the capacity for agency. Thus, indigenous peoples qualify as cultural communities, as do the French, English, or Japanese nations. Equally, we have a reasonably clear idea of what we mean by terms like "the Islamic community" in the USA or "the liberal humanist" academic community in the West. The boundaries of cultural and directional communities are hard to define and their borders are porous. The absence of the three properties listed above explains why these communities are not "social structures" in the sense that I am using this term.

24. On this point, Skillen's analysis in *Recharging the American Experiment* begins where Mouw and Griffioen's leaves off. Cf.. also Skillen & McCarthy, eds., *Political Order and the Plural Structure of Society*.

25. This does not exhaust its responsibilities: it also has responsibilities for the interests and rights of individuals (some of which will be cultural(e.g. language rights) or directional (e.g. freedom of conscience) in character); for other dimensions of the public good; and for just international relations. (For brief elaborations of this view of the state's role, see Jonathan Chaplin, *Faith in the State: the Peril and Promise of Christian Politics* [Toronto: Institute for Christian Studies, 1999]; Jonathan Chaplin, "Defining Public Justice in a Pluralist Society: Probing a Key Neo-Calvinist Insight," *Pro Rege* [March, 2004].)

26. Will Kymlicka correctly points out, however, that some earlier strands of liberalism were much more comfortable with negotiating the challenges of deep cultural diversity than were their twentieth-century successors. Cf. Will Kymlicka, *Liberalism, Community and Culture* (Oxford: Clarendon, 1989), ch.10; *Multicultural Citizenship* (Oxford: Clarendon, 1995), ch. 4.

27. Indeed in Canada, the Quiet Revolution in Quebec in the 1960s appeared to some to be the harbinger of precisely such a process (even though in the short term it actually stoked up separatist impulses), just as the current secularization of Irish public culture, the recent emphatic public repudiations of violent Basque separatists (ETA) in Spain, and the precarious advance of Iranian "modernizers" have also been taken to be doing.

28. Francis Fukuyama, *The End of History and the Last Man* (London: Penguin, 1997).

29. John Rawls, *Political Liberalism*, 14.

30. For a Christian critique of Trudeau's liberalism, see John Hiemstra, "Trudeau and the French Canadians," in *Political Theory and Christian Vision*, eds. Jonathan Chaplin & Paul Marshall (Lanham, Md.: University Press of America, 1994), 184-211.

31. Will Kymlicka calls these "polyethnic rights" in distinction from the collective rights claimed by cultural communities. Cf. *Multicultural Citizenship*, 30. They are, of course, in great demand, if often difficult to define, as ongoing American debates about "affirmative action" show. For a deconstructive assault on this idea, see Stanley Fish, *The Trouble with Principle* (Cambridge, Mass.: Harvard University Press, 1999), ch. 1.

32. Stephen Macedo, "Transformative Constitutionalism and the Case of Religion: Defending the Moderate Hegemony of Liberalism," *Political Theory* 26.1 (1998), 56-80. His argument is elaborated in *Diversity and Distrust: Civic Education in a Multicultural Democracy* (Cambridge, Mass.: Harvard University Press, 2000). Two things are striking about Macedo's formulations in this article: first, the complete absence of any arguments as to why liberalism monism might be thought to be superior to its rivals; second, his assumption throughout of the third person plural voice—he simply takes for granted his entitlement to speak for the dominant liberal establishment: "We have every right and plenty of reason, in the end, to aim at a 'moderate hegemony' of liberal public values" (Macedo, "Transformative Pluralism and the Case of Religion," 76). No accounts of who "we" are, or what that reason might be, are offered.

33. Ibid., 58.

34. Ibid., 70.

35. Ibid., 65. His position reflects what Nancy Rosenblum calls "the logic of congruence," one requiring the internal life of religious associations to mirror the public principles of liberal democracy, and which she resists. Nancy Rosenblum, "Amos: Religious Autonomy and the Moral Uses of Pluralism," in *Obligations of Citizenship and Demands of Faith: Religious Accommodation in Pluralist Democracies*, ed. Nancy Rosenblum (Princeton: Princeton University Press, 2000), 188.

36. Macedo, "Transformative Constitutionalism and the Case of Religion," 73.

37. Ibid., 70, 76.

38. Ibid., 75.

39. Galston, *Liberal Pluralism: The Implications of Value Pluralism for Political Theory and Practice* (New York: Cambridge University Press, 2002), 20.

40. For a sample of recent Christian critiques, cf: Christopher Eberle, *Religious Convictions in Liberal Politics* (Cambridge: Cambridge University Press, 2002); Wolterstorff's half of Robert Audi & Nicholas Wolterstorff, *Religion in the Public Square* (Lanham, Md.: Rowman & Littlefield, 1997); Ashley Woodiwiss, "Rawls, Religion, and Liberalism," in *The Re-Enchantment of Political Science: Christian Scholars Engage Their Discipline*, eds. Thomas W. Heilke and Ashley Woodiwiss (Lanham, Md.: Lexington Press, 2001), 65-83; Jonathan Chaplin, "Beyond Liberal Restraint: Defending Religiously-Based Arguments in Law and Public Policy," *University of British Columbia Law Review* 33 (2000) (Special Issue on Religion, Morality and Law), 617-646; Paul Brink, "Negotiating a Plural Politics: Public Liberty, Public Reason and the Duty of Civility," paper given at the Annual Meeting of the American Political Science Association, Atlanta, Ga., September 1995.

41. Kymlicka, *Liberalism, Community and Culture, and Multicultural Citizenship*. Nancy Rosenblum's work advocating wider accommodation for non-liberal religious communities moves in a similar direction. *Obligations of Citizenship and Demands of Faith*, ed. Nancy Rosenblum, Introduction and ch. 6; and *Membership and Morals: The Personal Uses of Pluralism* (Princeton: Princeton University Press, 1998), ch. 3. Communitarian liberals Charles Taylor, Michael Walzer and John Gray have advanced a variety of powerful arguments in favor of a recognition of cultural plurality by liberal societies. Cf: Taylor, "The Politics of Recognition"; Michael Walzer, *Spheres of Justice: A Defense of Pluralism and Equality* (Oxford: Blackwell, 1983) and *On Toleration* (New Haven: Yale University Press, 1997); John Gray, *Two Faces of Liberalism* (New York: Free Press, 2000). Cf. also James Tully, *Strange Multiplicity: Constitutionalism in an Age of Diversity* (Cambridge: Cambridge University Press, 1995).

42. Galston, *Liberal Pluralism*, 1; see 28, 101.

43. William Galston, *Liberal Purposes: Goods, Virtues and Diversity in the Liberal State* (Cambridge: Cambridge University, 1991).

44. William Galston, "Two Concepts of Liberalism," *Ethics* 105 (April 1995), 525-6. My exposition focuses on this article. Cf. also his "Expressive Liberty, Moral Pluralism, Political Pluralism: Three Sources of Liberal Theory," in *William and Mary Law Review* 40.3 (1999), 869-907.

45. Galston, "Two Concepts of Liberalism," 521. Further: "To place an ideal of autonomous choice—let alone cosmopolitan bricolage—at the core of liberalism is in fact to narrow the range of possibilities available within liberal societies. In the guise of protecting the capacity for diversity, the autonomy principle in fact represents a kind of uniformity that exerts pressure on ways of life that do not embrace autonomy" ("Two Concepts of Liberalism," 523). His point is not that autonomy is itself a questionable value, but that the dominant strand of modern liberalism has turned it into a hegemonic value at the expense of others such as community, tradition, or authority.

46. Ibid, 524. Cf. Galston, *Liberal Pluralism*, 20. Diversity liberalism will thus tolerate deep directional difference better than autonomy-liberalism. For example, autonomy-based Enlightenment liberals necessarily exclude those who cannot embrace the Enlightenment and its subordination of religion by reason, whereas diversity-liberals do not necessarily favor religion over reason but in fact make room for many religious and non-religious ways of life. A diversity-state will certainly protect autonomy, but only as one among many possible ways of life. Such a diversity state, he adds, stands a good chance of securing what Rawls calls an "overlapping consensus" ("Two Concepts of Liberalism," 526-7). However, Rawls himself exemplifies the autonomy-strand of liberalism. As Galston notes, Rawls's restrictive definition of "reasonable pluralism"—the only kind that can be tolerated within a liberal regime—excludes those who, for example, do not embrace the "essentials of democracy" or the "conclusions" of science (ibid., 518-520).

47. *Roberts v. U.S Jaycees* 468 U. S. 609 (1984) 622-23: "According protection to collective effort on behalf of shared goals is especially important in preserving political and cultural diversity and in shielding dissident expression from suppression by the majority." Indeed, commenting on Bob Jones University's notorious rule against interracial dating, he even ventures: "In many cases of conflict between First Amendment-protected associations and compelling state interests such as ending racial segregation, the flat prohibition of conduct judged obnoxious by public principles seems hard to square with the minimum requirements of free exercise" (Galston, "Two Concepts of Liberalism," 532). He rejects, however, offering any government support (e.g. federal tax exemption) to organizations internally flouting established constitutional principles like racial equality, a policy he calls "reverse exemption." Galston, *Liberal Pluralism*, 112.

48. "While value pluralism suggests that a wide range of family practices, including (say) arranged marriages, may be acceptable, cultural communities may not use their practices as instruments of imprisonment against members who have ceased to believe in them." Galston, *Liberal Pluralism*, 56.

49. Galston, "Two Concepts of Liberalism," 533.

50. Ibid., 530-1.

51. Its essential preconditions are threefold. First, the basic structure of a diversity state will display five features: cultural disestablishment ("comprehensive opposition to all forms of informal establishment"); a strong system of tolerance ("the principled refusal to use coercive state instruments to impose one's views on others"); a tolerance-promoting educational system; prohibitions against groups that recruit coercively or block exit; and a strong defence of the core elements of shared citizenship. This basic structure needs to be supplemented, second, by a range of

constitutional policies, including wide parental rights; a non-autonomy based system of public education supplemented by private education; wide associational rights, and "an accommodationist, pro-exemption understanding of religious exercise." A diversity state will, third, require of its citizens certain public strategies, such as removing as many contested issues as possible from the arena of national legislation and regulation, and respecting the difference between state permission for expressions of diversity (which is vital) and state support for such expressions (which is problematic). Galston, "Two Concepts of Liberalism," 528-530.

52. Ibid., 528-9.

53. Cf., for example, Nozick's "Framework for Utopia," which includes a case for associational freedom, in *Anarchy, State, and Utopia* (Oxford: Blackwell, 1974). For a critical discussion of Nozick, see Jonathan Chaplin, 'How Much Cultural and Religious Pluralism Can Liberalism Tolerate?' in *Liberalism, Multiculturalism and Toleration*, ed. John Horton (London: Routledge, 1994).

54. This point is forcefully made in Monsma, *Positive Neutrality*.

55. Galston, Liberal Pluralism, 66.

56. The promotion of "autonomy" is, commendably, absent from his list of such values, since autonomy is but one of the diverse lifestyles tolerated by the diversity state. "Freedom," however, is on this list. Cf. *Liberal Purposes*, 175.

57. Or, for that matter, for practitioners of an unrestrained "pro-choice" position.

58. Galston, "Two Concepts of Liberalism," 525.

59. He supports the court's exemption of Amish children from the requirements of high school attendance, denying that "a completed high school education [is] a precondition for full and effective citizenship." (This was secured in the landmark case *Wisconsin v. Yoder* 406 U.S. 205 (1972)). And he endorses the right of parents to withdraw children from elementary education, so long as a home-schooling alternative is provided. Ibid., 528 n29.

60. Ibid., 529.

61. Ibid., 528.

62. "The liberal state has a legitimate and compelling interest in ensuring that the convictions, competencies and virtues required for liberal citizenship are widely shared." Ibid., 529.

63. Ibid., 525. Emphasis added.

64. This requirement has teeth, involving four quite demanding conditions necessary to make it practically meaningful: knowledge conditions, capacity conditions, psychological conditions, and fitness conditions. Galston, *Liberal Pluralism*, 123.

65. Galston, "Two Concepts of Liberalism," 530.

66. Galston raises but does not pursue the possibility of granting certain minority communities a status intermediate between foreigner and full citizen—akin to the category of "resident alien"—and, accordingly, ceding them greater autonomy to govern their own internal affairs, offering them fewer public benefits, and burdening them with fewer liberal citizenship duties (*Liberal Pluralism*, 127-8).

67. For example, Galston writes: "If limited (even involuntary) participation in civil programs requires civil associations to govern the totality of their internal affairs in accordance with general public principles, then the zone of legitimate diversity is dangerously narrowed. A liberal pluralist jurisprudence consistent with the overall theory I am defending would limit the reach of public principles to those areas in which...[such] associations are participating directly and substantially in programs that confer public benefits on their members" (*Liberal Pluralism*, 114). This raises the question whether, for example, Galston would endorse the provisions of the "Charitable Choice" legislation, which are, for many pluralists, a minimum requirement of directional nondiscrimination.

68. Galston, "Expressive Liberty," 897; *Liberal Purposes*, 292.

69. Galston, *Liberal Pluralism*, 126.

70. See above, pp 3-4; and note 55.

71. For varying accounts of American versions, see David Hollinger, "Pluralism and Christian Ethics: Responding to the Options," *Christian Scholar's Review* 30.2 (Winter, 2000), 163-183; James Skillen, *The Scattered Voice: Christians At Odds in the Public Square* (Grand Rapids: Zondervan, 1990), esp. chs. 2, 8; Greg L. Bahnsen, "The Theonomic Position," Harold O. J. Brown, "The Christian America Position," and William Edgar, "The National Confessional Position," in *God and Politics*, ed. Gary Scott Smith. "Principled Pluralism," the closest to my position, is presented in Smith's volume by Gordon J. Spykman.

72. Stanley Fish, "Why Can't We All Just Get Along?" in *First Things*, February 1996, 18-26. For a more extended statement, see his "Mission Impossible: Settling the Just Bounds between Church and State," in *Law and Religion: A Critical Anthology*, ed. Stephen M. Feldman (New York: New York University Press, 2000), 383-410. Versions of both articles reappear in *The Trouble with Principle*.

73. For his full argument against supposedly impartial liberal "principles," see *The Trouble with Principle*.

74. Fish, "Mission Impossible," 387.

75. Ibid., 389. And: "Whatever 'principle' we might offer as a device for managing the political process will itself be politically informed . . . ." (400).

76. Fish, "Why We Can't All Just Get Along," 21 (emphasis added); see "Mission Impossible," 406.

77. "Mission Impossible," 405. He acknowledges that, as a contingent possibility, cooperation may be achievable, but only "through the give and take of substantive agendas as they vie for the right to be supreme over this or that part of the public landscape" (*The Trouble with Principle*, 12).

78. Cf. James Skillen's review ("Toleration vs. Pluralism") of Stephen Carter, *The Culture of Disbelief*, in *Cross Currents* 44.2 (Summer 1994), 260-7.

79. Fish, "Mission Impossible," 403; see 407.

80. This is the title of Part 1 of his *The Trouble with Principle*.

81. Ibid., 394.

82. The term "agonism" suggests a conflictual, as opposed to a consensual, model of democracy.

83. Ashley Woodiwiss, "Deliberation or Agony? Toward a Postliberal Christian Democratic Theory," in *The Re-enchantment of Political Science*, eds. Heilke & Woodiwiss, 149-166. Cf. also his "Democracy Agonistes: Why Handwringing About Partisanship is Pointless," *Books & Culture* (March/April 2001), 22-25.

84. Such an "agonistic" conception of democracy, he proposes, comports well with an Augustinian view of human nature, which would lead us to expect continual conflict, absence of agreement about "virtue," and only modest political improvement.

85. Ibid., 162. "[S]pecific qualities of Christian citizenship in an agonistic democracy will be disclosed through the exercise of Christian political judgment in the negotiation of concrete particulars."

86. Ibid., 163.

87. Nor does it seem able to account for the fact that genuine public discourse, as opposed to mere sectional assertion and counter-assertion, does actually take place in contemporary liberal democracies, notwithstanding its obvious deficiencies.

88. Graham Walker, "Illusory Pluralism, Inexorable Establishment," in *Obligations of Citizenship and Demands of Faith*, ed. Rosenblum, 111-126. A similar position is entertained as legitimate and desirable (though neither essential nor mandatory) by Oliver O'Donovan in *The Desire of the Nations*, 224, 244.

89. He is responding to Michael McConnell, "Believers as Equal Citizens," in *Obligations of Citizenship and Demands of Faith*, ed. Rosenblum, 90-110. Cf. also McConnell's "Equal Treatment and Religious Discrimination," *Equal Treatment of Religion in a Pluralistic Society*, eds. Monsma & Soper, 30-54.

90. Walker, "Illusory Pluralism, Inexorable Establishment," 112.

91. Ibid., 114.

92. Ibid., 115.

93. Ibid., 115-116.

94. Ibid., 116.

95. Ibid., 118, 19.

96. Ibid., 119, 120.

97. Ibid., 119, 120.

98. He even concedes that a partial establishment of secular liberalism would be compatible with his model of a mixed constitution. Indeed he tells us that he, as a conservative Christian, would rather live under an open, constitutionally recognized partial establishment of secularism than "the present American scheme of unacknowledged secularist supremacy where a massive cultural transformation has been carried out by means of a strict separationist sleight of hand" (ibid., 122).

99. Ibid., 116.

100. Ibid., 116.

101. Cf. below, note 116.

102. As Skillen puts it (with an "Augustinian" echo): "The extent to which people of incompatible religions can, with some degree of peace, share a political order in common depends . . . on what they demand of the political order. An overlapping *political* consensus of some kind may be possible not because of an overlapping religious consensus . . . but because people of diverse religions agree to keep a pluralistic and constitutionally restricted political order subservient to their deepest and prior commitments . . . But political schism is entirely possible . . . if people with incompatible religious commitments choose to fight for exclusive control of the body politic." *Recharging the American Experiment*, 45. For an interesting treatment of this Augustinian theme, see Peter Meilaender, "The Problem of Having Only One City: An Augustinian Response to Rawls," *Faith and Philosophy* 20.2 (April, 2003), 170-189.

103. Some of these are cited in notes 9 and 10.

104. Galston, *Liberal Pluralism*, 4; see 94. Nor is the limited character of the state overridden by the fact that it is democratic (Galston, "Expressive Liberty," 892ff).

105. Monsma draws on both Catholic and Protestant notions in *Positive Neutrality*, 185ff., as does Luis Lugo in "Caesar's Coin and the Politics of the Kingdom: A Pluralist Perspective," in *Caesar's Coin Revisited: Christians and the Limits of Government*, ed. Michael Cromartie (Grand Rapids: EPPC/Eerdmans, 1996), 1-22. Skillen and Griffioen utilize especially the principle of "public justice," which I also examine in "Defining Public Justice in a Pluralist Society: Probing a Key Neo-Calvinist Insight," *Pro Rege* (March 2004).

106. The fact that the definitions of such terms is always contested, including among Christians, is sometimes taken to be a knock-down argument against invoking them. But it is no such thing. Every important political principle (religious or secular) is contested, and is formulated in concrete contexts out of various deliberative processes in which opposing sides argue their case. Lack of unanimity—indeed deep and pervasive disagreement—does not invalidate the appeal to such normative principles.

107. O'Donovan's "Christian liberalism" does no such thing, of course. I think it might be better termed 'Christian constitutionalism." See above, n8.

108. McConnell, "Equal Treatment," 44.

109. McConnell, "Believers as Equal Citizens," 105. He also says we need to "insist, in a rigorous and principled way, on the rights of all Americans, without regard to faith and ideology, to participate in public life on an equal basis" ("Equal Treatment," 32).

110. Hollinger, "Pluralism and Christian Ethics," 179.

111. For example, Monsma and Soper also invoke a similar understanding of directional neutrality: "Government policies should make it neither harder nor easier to follow the dictates of conscience; they should *neither burden nor favor* persons or groups whose consciences have been shaped by a particular faith tradition or by a secular belief structure" (emphasis added). ("Conclusion: The Implications of Equal Treatment," in *Equal Treatment of Religion in a Pluralistic Society*, eds. Monsma & Soper, 200; see 2-3.) Monsma's case is fully and compellingly stated in *Positive Neutrality*.

112. Kent Greenawalt, "Five Questions about Religion Judges Are Afraid to Ask," in *Obligations of Citizenship and Demands of Faith*, ed. Rosenblum, 197-244.
113. Mouw and Griffioen, *Pluralisms and Horizons*, 118.
114. Sander Griffioen, "Public Philosophy and Religious Pluralism," in *Political Theory and Christian Vision*, eds. Chaplin & Marshall, 177.
115. In my view, this will be situated somewhere in the vicinity of what Rawls calls a "constitutional consensus," which for him is an intermediate level of consensus, emerging in the course of the stabilization of an initially deeply divided society, between an initial stage of "modus vivendi" (the mere laying down of arms for the sake of peace) and the achievement of a full "overlapping consensus" where shared political principles of justice are widely endorsed across divisions of (reasonable) comprehensive doctrine. Cf. *Political Liberalism*, 144ff., 158ff. For constructive thoughts on this notion, see Paul Brink, "The Idea of a Constitutional Consensus: Pluralism and Consensus in Rawls's *Political Liberalism*," Christians in Political Science Conference, San Diego, June 7-10, 2001.
116. The term "overlapping political consensus" is Rawlsian, so let me be clear that Christian advocates for the political recognition of directional plurality do not necessarily endorse a Rawlsian understanding of such a consensus according to which it is "freestanding" with respect to diverse comprehensive doctrines. Some authors, notably Skillen and Mouw & Griffioen, make clear that they are commending their versions of the just treatment of directional plurality as specifically Christian (though not, of course, intended only for Christians).
117. Of course, some Christians will reject some of these supposed policy implications of a Christian pluralism (some will favor "pro-choice" or same-sex marriage laws; others will be pro-capitalist). They would set the boundaries of a Christian diversity state differently. But if they are seeking an authentically Christian pluralism (some may not be), the reasons for their boundary-settings will also necessarily appeal to specifically Christian political principles.
118. On this, see Julia Stronks, "Christians, Public Policy and Same-Sex Marriage: Framing the Questions Before We Shout Out the Answers," in *Christian Scholar's Review* 26.4 (1997), 540-562; Fred Van Geest, 'Homosexuality and Public Policy: A Challenge for Sphere Sovereignty," *Perspectives* (December 2002), and James Skillen's response, "Abraham Kuyper and Gay Rights" (April 2003); James Skillen, "Same-Sex Marriage is Not a Civil Right," *Public Justice Report* (2nd Quarter, 2004); Iain Benson, "When Injustice Uses the Law: The Missing Logic of the Claim for Same-Sex Marriage," and "The Future of Marriage in Canada: Is it Time to Consider 'Civil Unions'," both in *Centrepoints* (Winter/Spring 2003/4); Andrew Koppelman, "Civil Conflict and Same Sex Civil Union," *The Responsive Community* 14.2&3 (Spring/Summer 2004).
119. I am not arguing that Christian pluralism is generally more restrictive than secular liberalism. Liberals would (I'd guess) be more restrictive than many Christians on education policy or anti-discrimination law, while Christians (I'd hope) would be more restrictive on pornography and environmental protection. Paul Marshall's discussion is worth citing here. Marshall claims that Christianity can "provide more room for liberals and Christians than liberalism would for Christians and liberals." ("Liberalism, Pluralism and Christianity," in *Political Theory and Christian Vision*, eds. Chaplin & Marshall, 158.) Similar claims also appear in Monsma, *Positive Neutrality*, Mouw & Griffioen, *Pluralisms and Horizons*, Skillen, *Recharging the American Experiment*, and Walker, "Illusory Pluralism, Inexorable Establishment."
120. For some preliminary hints, see Jonathan Chaplin, "Silencing the Silencers: Reclaiming a Public Voice for Christian Faith," *Pro Rege* (September 2000), 1-10.
121. I am grateful to Stephen Monsma, Jeanne Heffernan, James Skillen, David Koyzis, John Hiemstra, Bruce Clemenger, Fred van Geest, Thomas Heilke, faculty at the Institute for Christian Studies, and two anonymous readers, for helpful comments on earlier drafts of this paper. They offered a liberal plurality of suggestions, but responsibility for any deficiencies in the final text is, of course, singularly mine.

21 A Pietist Perspective on Love and Learning in Cultural Anthropology (2006)

JENELL WILLIAMS PARIS

Rodney Sawatsky, former president of Messiah College, urges Christian scholars to consider not only faith and learning, but also faith, hope, and love as three dimensions of a full Christian approach to scholarship.[1] He and the other contributors to *Scholarship and Christian Faith: Enlarging the Conversation* promote an irenic approach to exploring intersections of scholarship and Christian identity.[2] This is, in his words, a "broadening of the conversation" beyond the dominant faith-integration approach which focuses on Christian philosophy and presuppositional analysis of the disciplines.[3]

Guided by my tradition, the pietist impulse within evangelicalism, I will explore love as a lens for understanding what Christians do with their scholarship in cultural anthropology. First, I argue that the integrationist model is not very helpful for making sense of the work of Christian anthropologists, because of its emphasis on philosophy and its prioritizing of faith as the element of Christianity that is to be integrated. Second, I show how a pietist perspective that focuses on love better illuminates the work of Christian anthropologists in the areas of basic research, mission, and applied anthropology. This analysis carries implications beyond the field of cultural anthropology, as I encourage a de-centering of the integrationist approach in favor of a broader conversation that includes numerous Christian traditions and diverse ways of understanding what Christian identity may mean for the scholarly vocation.

The dominant integrationist (or Kuyperian) model of faith integration emphasizes articulating the presuppositions of a Christian worldview and those of a discipline, and then comparing and contrasting these control beliefs. This approach is associated most closely with the Christian Reformed tradition, though its influence extends across Christian higher education.[4] An ultimate aim of this approach is to seek and speak Christian truth in all arenas, from the philosophy of a discipline to its teaching and public application. It involves "the effort to think like a Christian—to think within a specifically Christian framework—across the whole spectrum of modern learning."[5] This worldview approach encourages a systematic approach to faith-integration, usually relying on a biblical meta-narrative framework (creation- fall-redemption-consummation or something similar). Its advocates also emphasize the value of teaching, especially inculcating a Christian worldview and a strong sense of vocation in students. In scholarly analyses, however, integrationist approaches focus more on theoretical concerns than on method or application.

When viewed from this perspective, Christians in anthropology seem to be slow to consider the implications of their faith on their science. Eloise Hiebert Meneses, anthropologist at Eastern University, summarizes that "while social sciences such as sociology, psychology, and economics have wrestled much with faith-science integration, anthropology has not."[6] Some use the integrationist approach, but discussions are detached from the discipline's power centers, focused instead on Christian college and seminary classrooms, Christian networks, and Christian publications.[7] Such analyses usually show fundamental differences and hostilities between the faith and the discipline, allowing little room for cooperation or creative synergy at the level of philosophy.

Faith-integration approaches in many disciplines have strong grounding in and support from Christian colleges and universities. There is, however, a dearth of anthropology programs in Christian higher education, and this limits scholars' ability to amass resources for books, conferences, and the like.[8] Of the 105 North American institutions in the Council for Christian Colleges and Universities (CCCU), none have a stand-alone anthropology department. Nineteen colleges (18%) house anthropology within blended departments, most commonly including sociology and anthropology, as well as intercultural studies.[9] Others include missions and anthropology, sociology and social work, sociology, or some combination of social sciences. Only three colleges (2.8%) offer anthropology majors, and nine (8.6%) offer intercultural studies majors. Eight others (7.6%) offer anthropology embedded in some other major like sociocultural studies, missions and anthropology, or sociology with an anthropology concentration. In total, only 19% of CCCU schools offer a major that includes any anthropology. This survey also yielded a list of just thirty-five scholars holding Ph.D.s in anthropology working at Christian colleges and universities.[10] Secular universities and Christian seminaries are two other institutional sites in which Christians may be found, but here also, Christian anthropologists are marginal and few in number. This may help explain why, in comparison with other disciplines, integrationist efforts in anthropology are rare and poorly sustained over time.

Two articles regarding the relationship between Christianity and anthropology reveal limitations of the integrationist approach. Meneses offers her vision of a Christian anthropology, and concludes that anthropology and Christianity share little harmony at the level of worldview.[11] She describes secular anthropology as holding an ultimate commitment to humanity as god. Anthropology's penultimate commitments, and those of modern social science more generally, include naturalism (nature constitutes all that exists), evolution (human history has no meaningful *telos*), and humanism (an optimistic and elevated view of human nature and activity). In contrast, a Christian worldview is ultimately oriented toward God, not humanity. As such, it is holistic (the spiritual aspect of human life is not reducible to the natural) and Trinitarian (humans and human history have meaning and purpose as part of a larger narrative). She concludes that there cannot be harmony or synthesis between these two incompatible paradigms. "If one framework is chosen, then the other can be incorporated at a subordinate level, but only by 'chopping it up' and accepting or rejecting portions piecemeal."[12] From this perspective, then, one's commitment to anthropology must be subjugated to one's commitment to Christ.

Meneses' argument seems to show little appreciation for anthropology, describing it as hostile to Christian ideas about the nature of humanity and the world, yet she has worked in the field for years as teacher, scholar, and missionary. Her life commitments show that anthropology is well-suited for understanding missionary work and development, and for teaching responsibility and stewardship to first-world citizens, and that hostile disciplinary presuppositions need not hinder active Christian scholarship. Unfortunately, these rich areas of integration are nearly invisible in Meneses' article because of the integrationist emphasis on philosophy over practice.[13]

Anthropologist Robert Priest, associate professor of mission and intercultural studies and director of the doctoral program in intercultural studies at Trinity Evangelical Divinity School, analyzes the origins and meanings of the missionary position metaphor, including its use as a tool for exclusion of Christians in the discipline.[14] Anthropologists commonly reference Bronislaw Malinowski, an early ethnographer, as having documented the sexual regulation of indigenous people by missionaries. Priest shows instead that Alfred Kinsey, American biologist and sex researcher, misappropriated Malinowski's ethnography and that the "missionary position" is an ethnographic myth, never appearing in Malinowski's writings.

The missionary position is, instead, a core symbol in modernist and postmodernist discourse. In modern discourse, it distinguishes anthropologists as forward-looking and modern, and missionaries as conservative, ethnocentric, and pre-modern. In postmodern discourse, it synthesizes postmodernist objections to modernism. While anthropology has become increasingly open to diverse subject positions (identity of the speaker), the evangelical subject position continues to be maligned, in large part because such discriminations help define the field. Priest argues, in fact, that early anthropologists developed ideas about human nature as a modern replacement for Christian views of humankind, particularly the notion of original sin.[15] In his view, modernist and postmodernist anthropological theories do not merely ignore Christian narratives, but instead incorporate Christian narratives and symbols "in ways which dismantle, subvert, and desanctify Christian meta-narratives and justify uses of power that silence and exclude Christian voices."[16]

Thirteen anthropologists provided commentary following Priest's article, articulating common views of Christians held among many anthropologists. Michele Dominy argued that missionaries deserve disrespect because they are "engaged in an unending, unrelenting effort to foist their hegemonic projection onto the non-Western pagan Other."[17] Neville Hoad suggested that because of missionaries' ethnocentrism and exploitation of cultures, anthropologists have "an ethical and political obligation" to "have a little fun at the expense of the missionary position."[18] Several commentators argued that Christians in the academy are simply embarrassing, the "sibling similar in many ways but blunt and tactless."[19]

In addition to these expressions of anthropological ethnocentrism, commentators raised two points that advance my argument about the limitations of faith-integration. While Tanya Luhrmann resists prejudice and discrimination against religion and religious people in the academy, she notes that there is also some logic behind it. "Having a religious conviction is not like being of a different race, gender or sexual orientation, because faith—at least, devout Christian faith—entails a belief commitment about the fundamental nature of reality.... Religious faith ... tends to assert that there is a different kind of world, that it cannot be the case that both the atheist and the believer are correct in their understanding of their world."[20] Similarly, James Clifford argues that while religious views may be heard in the academy, they must conform to institutionalized protocols for professionalism. Thus, religious people cannot make claims about a different sort of reality based upon revelatory knowledge inaccessible to the unconverted. Clifford argues that Priest "does not (yet) offer an academic defense of religious content, an explicit Christian analysis rather than a discussion of the Christian academic predicament."[21]

Indeed, Priest produces knowledge and makes his argument in academically acceptable ways, but says the Christian subject position "gave me a perspective which helped me to see certain realities that were not as likely to be seen from another position but quite capable of being considered and evaluated once they were pointed out."[22] Meneses, on the other hand, makes her argument with explicitly Christian presuppositions. The revelatory knowledge she cites about the nature of humanity and the purpose of history cannot be accessed or critiqued with anthropological epistemologies and methodologies, and as theoretical underpinnings, are not shared with non-Christian scholars. Priest's argument, then, is shared broadly in a flagship journal, but does not rely upon or promote a Christian worldview. Meneses' work is thoroughly Christian in its perspective, and as such, is distributed mostly among Christian scholars.

These examples show that the integrationist project is limited in severe ways when used in cultural anthropology. Both Meneses and Priest describe some of the basic ideological hostilities and personal prejudices that exist between Christianity and anthropology, or between Christian anthropologists and secular anthropologists. Discussions of atheism, naturalism, evolution, and humanism take place regularly among Christian anthropologists, and have for over a century, honing the faith and the intellect of Christian scholars and anthropology students. Publications, conferences, and the Network of Christian Anthropologists have all been valuable for developing Christian thought and for building faith-sustaining relationships among scholars who work in a field so influenced by atheism and anti-Christian bias. Priest concludes, and I agree, that while Christian anthropologists are dependent upon the discipline, we must also "self-consciously stand in tension with many of the assumptions, paradigms, and values of the discipline."[23]

The discipline itself, however, is untouched by these discussions, and the integrationist project has not been fruitful as an avenue for redemptive change within the discipline. Scholars in other disciplines may consider such pragmatism to be irrelevant or even crass, but it matters greatly to Christian anthropologists. Because of the harmony between anthropology and mission, and because many Christian anthropologists come from activist faith traditions, the redemptive potential of one's career investments are considered important. Christian anthropologists simply have not prioritized the development of theoretical work for a hostile or disinterested audience when arenas for transformative cultural engagement, such as mission, have seemed more open to Christian efforts. Finally, many faith-integration efforts are more about the integration of Christian philosophy than the integration of faith itself. Scholars work with Christian philosophies, doctrines of creation, fall, and redemption, and other doctrines relevant to specific disciplines or issues. While such doctrines are broadly accepted across Christian traditions and are useful for some purposes, they are, nonetheless, systematic derivatives from the scriptural narrative of God and God's people. They are also thoughts potentially detached from practice. In this way, the practice of faith, that is, living a life yielded to God, is not even a prerequisite for faith-integration scholarship. A concern for praxis is often noted in prefaces or epilogues of faith-integration writings, but is not included as a substantive analysis. A non-Christian committed to understanding Christian philosophy could potentially analyze a subject with use of Christian doctrine, or a Christian committed to systematic theology or philosophy could do "faith integration" with little personal piety or faith. The faith-integration approach is surely valuable for addressing the secularizing socialization of graduate education, developing particular areas of systematic philosophy or theology, and for pedagogy in Christian colleges, universities, and seminaries. It does normally, but does not necessarily, engage the life of faith, however, and it too frequently limits the sphere of inquiry to matters of theory and philosophy. While redemption of disciplinary philosophy may be possible, it is not probable within anthropology, and is perhaps part of the reason why there are so few Kuyperian or Christian Reformed anthropologists. It seems to me that Christians in this field have found urgent and open areas for Christian witness, and have developed those areas rather than pursuing the seemingly closed venue of disciplinary philosophy and theory.

Rather than transforming or critiquing the discipline by analyzing its presuppositions, Christians have more often approached anthropology with a generous sense of commonality and agreement, developing anthropological insights for application in church, mission, society, and the discipline.[24] This is not apparent by reading faith-integration publications, because their focus on presuppositions highlights antagonisms between the faith and the discipline, and because they emphasize theoretical work over application.

In practice, however, many Christian anthropologists have developed careers that transcend traditional bifurcations between theory and practice: missionaries turned-scholars, missionaries-and-scholars, professors of missiology, mission trainers, and applied anthropologists. Indeed, an emerging movement in the discipline as a whole encourages an engaged anthropology that would move beyond the traditional prizing of basic research over application. Engaged anthropology makes social change and advocacy part of the scientific process. Nancy Scheper-Hughes, who currently studies and advocates against human organ theft, argues from a humanist perspective that to know about evil is to be responsible for trying to alleviate its effects on people.[25] In my areas of interest, race studies and queer theory, engaged anthropology is not without its pitfalls, as activist-scholars sometimes manipulate data to suit predetermined political ends. Nonetheless, there exists an interesting common ground between Christian and non-Christian scholars in anthropology in their shared concern for the social impact of science.

Other Christians have focused their non-mission-related scholarship on disenfranchised social groups or urgent social issues. This scholarship has contributed to the work of mission, to evangelical theology and church practice, to social change, and to anthropology as a whole, particularly in cultural and linguistic anthropology. Love for sharing the gospel and love for the disenfranchised have been important motivators for Christian anthropologists since the inception of the discipline. A pietist perspective focuses more on the generous, clever, and impactful areas of overlap between Christianity and anthropology, and less on philosophical antagonisms. While rigorous in methodology and theory, pietist approaches tend to be less systematic in terms of analyzing the intersections between Christian "control beliefs" and disciplinary presuppositions.

I refer to pietism in its broadest sense, as a non-institutional religious energy present across Christian traditions. It perhaps finds fullest institutional expression in America in the Wesleyan/Holiness tradition. Like its formal eighteenth-century German origins, the pietistic impulse may be broadly characterized as heart-focused, in contrast to head-focused approaches to religion that are excessively dogmatic, formalized, and lacking individual feeling and participation with God. In numerous denominations and traditions, the pietist impulse has promoted an individual relationship with God, moral living, outreach to the poor, mission, and participation in small group Bible study and accountability. *Pia Desideria* (1675) is commonly referred to as a first statement of pietism, in which German religious reformer Philipp Jakob Spener wrote that, among other things, Christianity should be a life practice more than a matter of knowledge, that ministers should preach understandable, practical sermons, and that all Christians should live moral lives and practice restraint and charity in their disagreements with unbelievers and with other Christians.[26]

When viewed in pietist perspective, love offers an interesting mode for scholarly integration. For pietists, faith is heart-felt, experiential, and not heavily doctrinal. While doctrine is not unimportant, pietists do not treat it with the reverence or precision of other traditions. John Wesley, a pietist, relied on Hebrews 11 in describing faith as "'the evidence' and conviction 'of things not seen.'"[27] It is a gift of God that is known and confirmed in the heart. Faith involves trusting in God with conviction, despite not having seen all of the things in which we believe. In a pietist view, faith is a way of life, not an ideology or a set of control beliefs.

In this view, faith is quite difficult to integrate with scientific rationalism. In extending the mention of Hebrews 11, the people commended by faith in that chapter are those who made choices with incomplete knowledge, walked into uncertain futures, and did not make full sense of things within their lifetimes. The Scientific Revolution promoted ways of knowing that were more empirical and experimental, and less revelatory and intuitive. In general, the scientific approach encourages control, predictability, measurement, and systematization. If faith is about believing without seeing, science is about seeing before believing. If faith is about living in trust without certain knowledge of the future, science is about predictability, explaining the present and predicting or controlling the future. If faith is about trust, science is about skepticism, privileging rational and sensory information.

In relating faith, love, and reason, Wesley said: "Let reason do all that reason can: employ it as far as it will go. But, at the same time, acknowledge it as utterly incapable of giving either faith, or hope, or love; and consequently, of producing either real virtue or substantial happiness."[28] For Wesley and other intellectual pietists, reason (scientific rationalism may be considered a subset of reason) is useful to a point, for understanding the world God made and in understanding some parts of religion. It is a limited good, however, because of its detachment to virtue.

Love is thus more amendable for pietists working to integrate scholarship with the Christian life because it is more visible and tangible than faith, and because it merges knowledge and practice. Love is faith in action, a demonstrated care for God, self, and neighbor. In Wesley's words again, love is "a calm, generous, disinterested benevolence to every child of man" and "an earnest, steady goodwill to our fellow-creatures."[29] Theologian Mildred Bangs Wynkoop explicates this Wesleyan emphasis in saying that Wesley's major contribution to the church "was not new dogma but a real, spiritual vitality infused into traditional, mainline Christianity. This vitality is love, and love is by its very nature dynamic."[30]

Next I will describe how the spiritual practice of love influences the work of Christian anthropologists in three areas: basic research, mission, and applied anthropology. In each of these spheres, many Christian anthropologists develop dual audiences, Christian and secular, for the dissemination of scholarly products.

Many Christian anthropologists contribute to the body of anthropological knowledge by doing basic research that is focused upon religious subject matter, or oppressed and marginal people. This work may be viewed as truth-telling, valuable in and of itself.[31] It may also be used to edify the church or the research subject's community. Judith Shapiro, an anthropologist who is not a Christian, argues that missionary linguists have contributed excellent basic research to the discipline "because they had the motivation to stay for very long periods of time in 'the field,' far longer than most academic anthropologists and linguists. Because they shared with their successful academic colleagues the intelligence and patience to grapple with a deeply unfamiliar language."[32] Kenneth Pike was such a Christian anthropologist, contributing to understandings of tone languages, the field of English as a Second Language, tagmemics, and innovating the concepts "emic" and "etic." Pike disseminated his academic and devotional insights to multiple audiences including the academy, the church, missionary trainers, and missionaries.[33]

Much basic research in anthropology involves marginal populations including the global poor, indigenous cultures, women, and other "Others." Many anthropologists, Christian and not, are motivated by love and a desire for social justice as they choose areas for study. Humanism as a common denominator offers rich areas for collaboration between Christians and non-Christians in the field, making philosophical antagonisms less important in arenas of engagement. While some Christians study populations with mission application in mind, others study religious subject matter unrelated to mission. Brian Howell (Wheaton College), for example, studies meaning-making among Protestants in the Philippines.[34] Still others study subjects that are neither religious nor related to mission. Laura Montgomery (Westmont College), for example, researched effects of new government agricultural policies and the North American Free Trade Agreement on Mexicali, Mexico. She has also researched religious subjects including short-term mission and gender equity in Christian higher education.[35] My work is similar in covering both religious and non-religious subjects. My research has related to race and ghetto formation, processes of urban neighborhood formation among Christian homosexuals, and successful corporate marketing strategies.[36]

In basic research, processes for producing knowledge are usually entirely secular in methodology and theory. Methodology for fieldwork has established codes of humanistic ethics that are entirely compatible with Christian ethics—in my view, they are a subset of a more inclusive and rigorous Christian ethic.[37] Anthropological theory is less compatible with Christianity, and Christian scholars live with tensions as they develop theoretical niches with secular colleagues. Secular anthropological theory can provide useful understandings of culture and cultural processes, though couched within larger frameworks of relativism, secular humanism, and evolution.

In a rare example, Eloise Hiebert Meneses and John Stapleford created an explicitly Christian theory to analyze three cultural types (egalitarian tribal, feudal peasant, and democratic capitalist) for ways in which each one manifests wealth, justice, love, spirituality, and humility.[38] This also makes a valuable contribution to Christian understandings of anthropological theory, but as with other explicitly and/or exclusively Christian points of view in anthropology, it is unlikely to influence mainstream theory in the field. This kind of work will contribute to pedagogy, and to inspiring other faith-integration efforts among Christian scholars.

Understanding the integrative aspects of basic research depends largely upon knowing the motivation and the full body of work of the scholar. Pike, for example, researched language partly to understand language, and partly to better communicate the Gospel cross-culturally. Some Christian scholars are motivated by love and care to research particular subjects. Others, however, do basic research with no application or dual audience and no explicitly Christian motivation. In basic research, the intensity or integrity of Christian integration is not necessarily apparent in the subject matter or in academic publications. The scholar's motivations may be known by considering her/

his broader agenda, which may include communicating with multiple audiences and exerting influence in areas including the academy, the church, and society.

Synchronicity between anthropology and mission was envisioned by missionaries since the inception of anthropology. In the nineteenth century, missionaries contributed first-hand knowledge of cultures to early "armchair" anthropologists, before the twentieth-century emphasis on first-hand fieldwork. Missionaries served as data-gatherers for European and American scholars who used the data to theorize about how societies evolved. Even today, missionaries and anthropologists still frequently help each other with access to populations, language, and other elements of fieldwork.[39]

Some early missionary anthropologists strove to reformulate mission strategy in ways that critically engaged colonial contexts. Many of these missionary anthropologists agreed with their secular colleagues' critiques of mission as colonial appendage. Some saw the tendency of some modern Christian groups toward anti-intellectualism and excessive subjectivity in mission, as evangelism and relief work were done without appropriate cross-cultural skills and knowledge. They turned to anthropology for insights and concepts that would help the missionary endeavor. Early missionary anthropologists sought to reformulate mission strategy to develop indigenous churches rather than colonial ones.[40]

A second generation of missionary anthropologists continued this emphasis, developing theories of contextualization. They used secular anthropology concepts such as functional equivalents, cultural cues, contextualization, and developed the field of ethnotheology. Their goal was to improve mission practice, especially in contextualizing the gospel and church planting. Sherwood Lingenfelter, anthropologist and provost of Fuller Theological Seminary, for example, offers missionaries models for doing analysis of the social order of a group, including understandings of property, economy, social exchange, family, community, authority, eating, and conflict. He explains how church planting must be done in culturally relevant ways that incorporate cultural patterns of property ownership, authority, conflict management, and so forth.[41]

Paul Hiebert is another example, devoting his career to both anthropology and missiology. He worked as a missionary in India, and later worked in higher education as professor and dean. He contributed to mission in his own work as a missionary, in teaching, and in writing books such as *Anthropological Insights for Missionaries* and *Missiological Implications of Epistemological Shifts: Affirming Truth in a Modern/Postmodern World*. He also wrote a cultural anthropology textbook in Christian perspective.[42]

Anthropology as a tool for mission has been institutionalized in Christian colleges, universities, and seminaries. Anthropology programs that prepare students for mission began at Wheaton College, Bethel University, and Hartford College in the mid-twentieth century, and now exist both as mission preparation and as the study of anthropology itself at some Christian colleges and universities. *Practical Anthropology*, a journal focused on the applications of anthropology for Christian theology and practice, mostly in the area of mission, was founded in 1953. The journal became *Missiology* in 1973 and continues on today as the journal of the *American Society of Missiology*.[43]

The activity of anthropologists in mission may be understood as an integration of love and learning. These anthropologists love people who do not know Christ, and devote their intellectual and vocational lives to better understanding how to communicate the Gospel and develop churches. They also express love for the field of mission in their efforts to engage critically the process of mission in colonial and post-colonial contexts.

A third arena in which Christian anthropologists express love in the discipline is in applied anthropology. Here, Christians have applied theoretical insights, method, and research findings in both church and society. Though some of the work referenced here would now be labeled "engaged anthropology," most was conceived of at the time as "applied," so I continue use of that term.

In the church, anthropologists have contributed to theology, church life, and teaching Christian adults in colleges and seminaries. In terms of theology, anthropologists have encouraged theologians and laypersons to consider culture when developing theology. Charles Kraft, for example, worked as a missionary, trainer of missionaries, and linguist. He applied anthropological insight to evangelical theology, presaging postmodern evangelical theology today. He argued that western evangelical theology is too heavily philosophical, and too oriented around academic concerns. He felt that an anthropological perspective and method could help theologians understand and better address people's questions in their communities, instead of esoteric issues of interest mostly only to themselves. He argued for the inclusion of non-philosophers and non-academicians in the making of theology, and for a theology that focuses on people (their understandings of God and their relationship with God in various culture) as much as it focuses on God. He also urged a relativism that situates all theological understandings in cultural contexts, with God alone existing outside of culture. Thus, he wrote that, "theologizing has been and is most appropriately done with specific reference to the concerns and needs of the audience addressed, rather than as a quest for a single set of once-for-all formulations of truth."[44] Kraft called this quest "ethnotheology," the need to understand the relationship between God and humans with both theological and cultural understanding.[45]

Many anthropologists make similar contributions today, and I offer just a few examples. Harold Recinos, at the Perkins School of Theology, wrote two books encouraging pastors and church members to use basic anthropology methods to do neighborhood and area surveys before starting outreach programs, and he uses theories of globalization to encourage contextualized urban ministry in the United States.[46] Both Miriam Adeney, anthropologist at Seattle Pacific University, and Laura Montgomery help churches critically analyze and formulate short-term mission programs, considering the paternalistic and neo-colonial aspects of too many mission encounters with the global poor.[47] Adeney encourages Christians to take social inequality seriously by writing and speaking about Christian concern for the oppressed in broader venues such as her post as board member for *Christianity Today*.[48]

Many Christian anthropologists contribute to the church by teaching in Christian colleges, universities, and seminaries. Some, like John Ahrensen, anthropologist at Houghton College, spend part of the year teaching at a U.S. college, and part outside the

U.S. with students in cross-cultural academic experiences. Many also teach and consult in churches on subjects of race and ethnicity, mission, and social inequality.

From a pietist perspective, of the faith-hope-love triad from 1 Corinthians, faith may be particularly difficult to integrate with scholarship. Jesus, for example, discusses faith with metaphors from nature. The birds and lilies express faith in the way they live without worry for the future. Though doctrinal, systematic readings of Scripture seem to be privileged among Christian scholars. Scripture may also be read as a narrative of people living lives of faith. In this view, faith is more way of life and less an ideology or a set of control beliefs. Thus, I think that what is generally referred to as "integration of faith and learning" may be more precisely called "integration of theology and learning" or "integration of Christian philosophy and learning." Though valuable, the doing of philosophy and the speaking of Christian thoughts is not faith itself. Systematized discussions of the world, religious practice, or religious doctrine are important, but they are derivative from faith itself, which is more often described biblically in narrative or figurative terms. Living a life of faith is, in pietist perspective, no different for a scientist than a nonscientist in that it involves trusting God in the uncertainty of human existence.

Love may provide a more powerful and concrete way of understanding ways in which some Christians live out the academic vocation. For example, Paul describes love in 1 Corinthians 13 as profoundly other-centered: patient, kind, not boastful or arrogant or rude. It rejoices in the truth, and bears with other people for the long haul. Jesus, as well as the prophets before him, emphasized the importance of care for the vulnerable and love for God, neighbor, and the self. Love, then, carries important implications for how Christian scholars engage in scholarly dialogue, their pedagogy, and their attitude toward subject matter. It highlights applications and teaching, aspects of the scholarly vocation that are too often devalued in the academy and at times neglected in faith-integration treatments. It offers a framework for engaged scholarship, moving beyond conventional divisions between theory and application, and concomitant privileging of theory.

On the other hand, a pietist perspective on love and learning has potential pitfalls. Though there have been many intellectual pietists and a strong institutionalized intellectual movement in the Wesleyan/Holiness tradition, the movement is sometimes mediocre in its intellectual life, at times even anti-intellectual.[49] An undue emphasis on experience and feeling over rationality and intellectual struggle has, at times, resulted in theological imprecision and social outreach efforts that fail for lack of forethought and/or assessment. Michael Emerson and Christian Smith, both Christian sociologists, critique this impulse with respect to evangelical (not specifically pietist) efforts toward racial reconciliation. They argue that the activist impulse combined with an anti-intellectual tradition often dooms well-intentioned efforts to failure.[50]

Pietism offers a valuable perspective, however, for Christians seeking integrity and wholeness in their scholarly lives. This pietist view of anthropology reveals that anthropologists have been integrating their Christian identity with their work in important ways since the discipline's inception, but the dominant faith-integration paradigm renders these efforts nearly invisible. In addition, the evangelical, fundamentalist, and pietist identities of many Christian anthropologists make them less likely to use Kuyperian frameworks to describe and shape what they do. Critical use of numerous faith traditions and broader use of spiritual concepts (love, hope, faith, trust, sin, and others) may expand and enrich our efforts to be faithful Christian scholars.[51]

Notes

1. Rodney Sawatsky, "Prologue: The Virtue of Scholarly Hope," in Douglas Jacobsen and Rhonda Hustedt Jacobsen, eds., *Scholarship and Christian Faith: Enlarging the Conversation* (New York: Oxford University Press, 2004), 3-14.
2. This essay first appeared in *CSR* 35.3 (Spring 2006): 371-86.
3. Scholars have explored faith-learning integration from numerous Christian traditions. See, for example, Richard Hughes and William Adrian, eds., *Models for Christian Higher Education: Strategies for Survival and Success in the 21st Century* (Grand Rapids, Mich.: Eerdmans, 1997); Ernest Simmons, *Lutheran Higher Education: An Introduction for Faculty* (Minneapolis: Augsburg Fortress Press, 1998).
4. General examples include Arthur Holmes, *Contours of a Worldview* (Grand Rapids, Mich.: Eerdmans, 1983); Cornelius Plantinga, *Engaging God's World: A Christian Vision of Faith, Learning, and Living* (Grand Rapids, Mich.: Eerdmans, 2002); Albert Wolters, *Creation Regained* (Grand Rapids, Mich.: Eerdmans, 1985). From sociology, see, for example, David Fraser and Tony Campolo, *Sociology Through the Eyes of Faith* (San Francisco: Harper San Francisco, 1992); Russell Heddendorf, *Hidden Threads: Social Thought for Christians* (Dallas: Probe Books, 1990).
5. Mark Noll, *The Scandal of the Evangelical Mind* (Grand Rapids, Mich.: Eerdmans, 1994).
6. Eloise Hiebert Meneses, "No Other Foundation: Establishing a Christian Anthropology," *Christian Scholar's Review* 29.3 (2000): 535.
7. Biola University, for example, sponsored a Network of Christian Anthropologists conference in 2000 that explored anthropological theory in Christian perspective. Similarly, in 2003 Wheaton College sponsored a symposium on Christian perspectives on postmodern theory in anthropology.
8. Jynell Brist surveyed the websites of 104 of the 105 colleges listed at www.cccu.org in September 2004, and called the remaining college whose website was down.
9. The phrase "intercultural studies" carries numerous meanings. Within Christian higher education, it usually refers to a blend of anthropology and missiology that is intended to prepare Christians for cross-cultural service.
10. This figure is approximate, because some faculty do not list credentials online.
11. Meneses, "No Other Foundation," 531-549.
12. Meneses, 531.
13. See, for example, Paul Hiebert and Eloise Hiebert Meneses, *Incarnational Ministry: Planting Churches in Band, Tribal, Peasant, and Urban Societies* (Grand Rapids, Mich.: Baker Books, 1995).
14. Robert J. Priest, "Missionary Positions: Christian, Modernist, Postmodernist," *Current Anthropology* 42.1 (2001): 29-68.
15. Robert J. Priest, "Cultural Anthropology, Sin, and the Missionary," in eds. D. A. Carson and John D. Woodbridge, *God and Culture: Essays in Honor of Carl F.H. Henry* (Grand Rapids, Mich.: Eerdmans, 1993), 85-105.
16. Ibid., 45.
17. Ibid., 50.
18. Ibid., 53.
19. Ibid., 46, 55.
20. Ibid., 55.
21. Ibid., 48.
22. Ibid., 44.
23. Ibid., 105.
24. I do not attempt a comprehensive history of Christians in anthropology in this article. For such history, see a special issue of *Missiology* titled *Missionaries, Anthropologists, and Human Rights* (April 1996), and Darrell Whiteman, "Anthropology and Mission: The Incarnational Connection," The Third Annual Louis J. Luzbetak, SVD Lecture on Mission and Culture, Catholic Theological Union, Chicago, Ill., May 5, 2003.
25. Nancy Scheper-Hughes, "The Primacy of the Ethical," *Current Anthropology* 36.3 (1995): 409-428.
26. James Nelson, "Pietism," BELIEVE Religious Information Source, http://mb-soft.com/believe, accessed July 26, 2004; Mark Noll, "Pietism: Advanced Information," BELIEVE Religious Information Source, http://mb-soft.com/believe, accessed July 26, 2004; Mark Noll, *The Rise of Evangelicalism: The Age of Edwards, Whitefield and the Wesleys* (Downers Grove, Ill.: InterVarsity Press, 2003).
27. John Wesley, "The Case of Reason Impartially Considered" (sermon 1781), Wesley Center Online, http://www.wesley.nnu.edu, accessed July 26, 2004.
28. Ibid.
29. Ibid.
30. Mildred Bangs Wynkoop, *A Theology of Love: The Dynamic of Wesleyanism* (Kansas City, Mo.: Beacon Hill Press of Kansas City 1972), 22.
31. George Marsden, *The Outrageous Idea of Christian Scholarship* (New York: Oxford University Press 1997).

32. Priest, "Missionary Positions," 57.

33. Among Pike's prolific publications are *Linguistic Concepts: An Introduction to Tagmemics* (Lincoln, Neb.: University of Nebraska Press 1982); "Christianity and Culture 1: Conscience and Culture," *Journal of the American Scientific Affiliation* 31(1979): 8-12; *With Heart and Mind: A Personal Synthesis of Scholarship and Devotion*, (Grand Rapids, Mich.: Eerdmans 1962) [Repub. 1996. Duncanville, Tex.: Adult Learning Systems].

34. Brian Howell, "Practical Belief and the Localization of Christianity: Pentecostal and Denominational Christianity in Global/Local Perspective," *Religion* 33 (2003): 233-248.

35. Laura Montgomery, "Irrigation and Social Reproduction in the Mexicali Valley of Northwest Mexico" in *Culture and Environment: A Fragile Coexistence*, ed. R. Jamieson (Calgary: University of Calgary Press, 1993).

36. Jenell Williams Paris, "Faith-Based Queer Space in Washington, D.C.: The Metropolitan Community Church-D.C. and Mount Vernon Square," with Rory Anderson, *Gender, Place and Culture* 8 (2001): 2: 149-168; "'We've Seen This Coming': Resident Activists Shaping Neighborhood Redevelopment in Washington, D.C.," *Transforming Anthropology* 10 (2001): 1:28-38.

37. Code of Ethics of the American Anthropological Association, accessed July 27, 2004, http://www.aaanet.org/committees/ethics/ethcode.htm.

38. Eloise Hiebert Meneses and John E. Stapleford, "Defeating the Baals: Balanced Christian Living in Different Cultural Systems," *Christian Scholar's Review* 30.1 (2000): 83-106.

39. Whiteman, "Anthropology and Mission: The Incarnational Connection."

40. See, for example, Louis Luzbetak, *The Church and Cultures: An Applied Anthropology for the Religious Worker* (Techny, Ill.: Divine Word Publications, 1963); Donald McGavran, *The Clash Between Christianity and Cultures* (Washington: Canon Press, 1974); Eugene Nida, *Customs and Cultures: Anthropology for Christian Missions* (New York: Harper & Row, 1954); Alan Tippett, ed., *God, Man, and Church Growth* (Grand Rapids, Mich.: Eerdmans, 1973).

41. Sherwood Lingenfelter, *Transforming Culture: A Challenge for Christian Mission* (Grand Rapids, Mich.: Baker Bookhouse, 1992). For other examples, see Stephen A. Grunlan and Marvin K. Mayers, eds., *Cultural Anthropology: A Christian Perspective* (Grand Rapids, Mich.: Zondervan, 1979); Charles Kraft, *Christianity in Culture: A Study in Dynamic Biblical Theologizing in Cross- Cultural Perspective* (Maryknoll, N.Y.: Orbis Books, 1979).

42. Paul Hiebert, *Anthropological Insights for Missionaries* (Grand Rapids, Mich.: Baker Book House, 1999); *Cultural Anthropology* (Grand Rapids, Mich.: Baker Book House, 1973); *Missiological Implications of Epistemological Shifts: Affirming Truth in a Modern/Postmodern World* (Harrisburg, Penn.: Trinity Press International, 1999).

43. Collections of articles from *Practical Anthropology* may be found in William Smalley, ed., *Readings in Missionary Anthropology* (Tarrytown, N.Y.: Practical Anthropology 1967); William Smalley, Ed., *Readings in Missionary Anthropology* II (South Pasadena, Cal.: William Carey Library, 1978).

44. Charles H. Kraft, "Can Anthropological Insight Assist Evangelical Theology?" *Christian Scholar's Review* 7 (1977): 165-203. Another example of pastoral application of anthropology, see Robert J. Priest, "Cultural Factors in Victorious Living," *Free and Fulfilled: Victorious Christian Living in the Twenty-First Century* (Nashville: Thomas Nelson, 1997).

45. Charles H. Kraft, "Toward a Christian Ethnotheology," in ed. A. R. Tippett, *God, Man and Church Growth* (Grand Rapids, Mich.: Eerdmans, 1973), 109-126.

46. Harold Recinos, *Hear the Cry!: A Latino Pastor Challenges the Church* (Louisville, Ky.: Westminster/John Knox Press, 1989); *Jesus Weeps: Global Encounters on our Doorstep* (Nashville: Abingdon Press, 1992).

47. Laura Montgomery, "Short-Term Medical Missions: Enhancing or Eroding Health," *Missiology: An International Review* 21 (1993): 30.

48. Miriam Adeney, *Daughters of Islam* (Downers Grove, Ill.: InterVarsity Press, 2002); *God's Foreign Policy* (Grand Rapids, Mich.: Eerdmans, 1984); *A Time for Risking: Priorities for Women* (Portland, Ore.: Multnomah Press, 1987).

49. Noll, *The Scandal of the Evangelical Mind*; John E. and Susie C. Stanley, "What Can the Wesleyan/Holiness Tradition Contribute to Christian Higher Education?", *Models for Christian Higher Education*, eds. Hughes and Adrian (Grand Rapids, Mich.: Eerdmans, 1997), 313-326.

50. Michael Emerson and Christian Smith, *Divided by Faith* (New York: Oxford University Press, 2000).

51. This paper was first presented at the Faith in the Academy conference at Messiah College in September 2004. It has benefited from feedback from conference participants, as well as from Carla Barnhill, C. Jeanne Serrao, Susie Stanley, Jynell Brist, Neil Lettinga, and two anonymous reviewers.

22 Does Mathematical Beauty Pose Problems for Naturalism? (2006)

Russell W. Howell

Numerous events occurred in 1960 whose effects could hardly have been predicted at the time: several African Americans staged a "sit-in" at a Greensboro lunch counter, the Soviet Union shot down Gary Powers while he was flying a U2 spy plane, the USFDA approved the use of the first oral contraceptive, AT&T filed with the Federal Communications Commission for permission to launch an experimental communications satellite, and four Presidential debates between John Kennedy and Richard Nixon aired on national television.[1]

Less well known was the publication of a paper by the physicist Eugene Wigner. Appearing in *Communications in Pure and Applied Mathematics*, a journal certainly not widely read by the general public, it bore the mysterious title "The Unreasonable Effectiveness of Mathematics in the Natural Sciences."[2] Like our cultural examples of the 1960's, it has had effects beyond what most people would have imagined. Our purpose here is to tease out some strains of an important question that has emerged from Wigner's work.

Wigner begins with a story about two friends who were discussing their jobs. One of them, a statistician, was working on population trends. He mentioned a paper he had produced, which contained a complicated-looking equation known as the Gaussian distribution. The statistician felt compelled to explain the meaning of various mathematical symbols. His friend was a bit incredulous and was not quite sure whether the statistician was pulling his leg. "How can you know that?" he repeatedly asked. "And what is this symbol here?"

"Oh," said the statistician, "this is pi."

"What is that?"

"The ratio of the circumference of a circle to its diameter."

"Well, now you are pushing your joke too far. Surely the population has nothing to do with the circumference of the circle."

Wigner uses this story to introduce two issues: (1) the surprising phenomenon that we have used mathematics so often to build successful theories; (2) the nagging

Kuhnian-like question, "How do we know that, if we made a theory which focuses its attention on phenomena we disregard and disregards some of the phenomena now commanding our attention, that we could not build another theory which has little in common with the present one but which, nevertheless, explains just as many phenomena as the present theory?"[3] Regarding Wigner's first point, he concedes that much of mathematics, such as Euclidean Geometry, was developed because its axioms were created on the basis of what appeared to be true of reality. From this viewpoint the applicability of mathematics to the physical world is hardly surprising. But how much of mathematics actually progresses in this manner? A strong argument can be made that other notions guide the formation of a large body of higher mathematical theories.

Take the field of complex analysis as just one example. It deals with imaginary numbers (more aptly called complex numbers), which are numbers that involve the square root of minus one. In the 1500's such notions seemed odd to mathematicians. Negative numbers by themselves were being treated with some suspicion, so taking square roots of them was all the more problematic. But mathematicians kept using their imagination and pressed forward. Serious investigation of complex numbers dates to the mid-fourteenth century, when Scipione del Ferro of Bologna solved the depressed cubic equation, which is a cubic equation without an x^2 term. (An example of a depressed cubic equation is $x^3 - 15x - 4 = 0$.) The solution was independently discovered some thirty years later by Niccolo Fontana. Girolamo Cardano subsequently extended the "Ferro-Fontana" formula to obtain a solution of the general cubic equation, which he published in *Ars Magna* in 1545. Then in 1572, Rafael Bombelli used Cardano's published work to interpret the form of solutions to some depressed cubic equations. Prior to Bombelli, this form had been impossible to decipher.

Bombelli derived his solutions by using complex numbers. For example, Bombelli's techniques, when applied to the depressed cubic equation $x^3 - 15x - 4 = 0$, yielded a solution of the form $x = (2 + i) + (2 - i)$, where i is a symbol that represents the square root of minus one. Simple arithmetic then gave $x = (2 + i) + (2 - i) = 4$. That $x = 4$ was a correct solution to the original equation was indisputable, as it could be checked easily. However, it was only arrived at via a detour through the uncharted territory of complex numbers.

The story that details the entire development of complex numbers is quite intricate, and it was not until the end of the nineteenth century that they became firmly entrenched in the corpus of mathematical literature. For our purposes, it is important to note that complex numbers were studied because they were useful for mathematical and not for physical purposes. To be sure, solving equations had the potential to be of great practical value, but no physical phenomenon guided the investigation of complex numbers. Success came mainly from abstraction, and the manipulation of mathematical symbols in accordance with specified rules of algebra.

Complex numbers, however, now play a pivotal role in helping physicists understand the quantum world. For Wigner, it is not just the utility of complex numbers in quantum mechanics that is surprising; it is that, time and time again, leaps of theory seem to be successfully guided by mathematical formalisms rather than experimentation. According to Wigner,

> Quantum mechanics originated when Max Born noticed that some rules of computation, given by Heisenberg, were formally identical with the rules of computation with matrices.... Born, Jordan, and Heisenberg then proposed to replace by matrices the position and momentum variables of the equations of classical mechanics.... The results were quite satisfactory. However, there was ... no rational evidence that their matrix mechanics would prove correct under more realistic conditions. As a matter of fact, the first application of their mechanics to a realistic problem, that of the hydrogen atom, was given several months later, by Pauli. This application gave results in agreement with experience. This was ... understandable because Heisenberg's rules of calculation were abstracted from problems which included the old theory of the hydrogen atom. The miracle occurred only when matrix mechanics ... was applied to problems for which Heisenberg's calculating rules were meaningless. Heisenberg's rules presupposed that the classical equations of motion had solutions with certain periodicity properties; and the equations of motion of the two electrons of the helium atom, or of the even greater number of electrons of heavier atoms, simply do not have these properties, so that Heisenberg's rules cannot be applied to these cases. Nevertheless, the calculation of the lowest energy level of helium, ... [agreed] with the experimental data within the accuracy of the observations, which is one part in ten million.

"Surely," Wigner concludes, "in this case we 'got something out' of the equations that we did not put in."[4] Wigner cites other examples: Newton's law of motion, formulated in terms that appear simple to mathematicians, but which proved to be accurate beyond all reasonable expectations; quantum electrodynamics; and the pure mathematical theory of the Lamb shift. He finally concludes his paper with the following observation: "The enormous usefulness of mathematics in the natural sciences is something bordering on the mysterious, and ... there is no rational explanation for it .... The miracle of the appropriateness of the language of mathematics for the formulation of the laws of physics is a wonderful gift which we neither understand nor deserve. We should be grateful for it and hope that it will remain valid in future research and that it will extend, for better or for worse, to our pleasure, even though perhaps also to our bafflement, to wide branches of learning."[5]

In 1980 Richard Wesley Hamming took up the effectiveness issue raised by Wigner, and offered four "partial explanations" that could account for the applicability of mathematics.[6] Following is a brief survey of Hamming's ideas. First, we see what we look for. Mathematicians craft postulates so that they will produce theories that conform to their prior observations. The Pythagorean theorem, Hamming claims, drove the formation of the geometric postulates, and not vice versa. Furthermore, if we insist on looking at the world through a mathematical lens, it is not entirely surprising that we wind up describing the world in mathematical terms. Second, we select the kind of mathematics to use. Hamming simply means here that we adopt the mathematical theories that seem, ahead of time, to be a good fit for a physical phenomenon being investigated. The same type of mathematical theory does not work everywhere; different theories are selected in accordance with the phenomenon they seem to describe. Because we habitually force mathematics onto particular situations, it is only natural that we subsequently find mathematics in general to be so widely applicable. These first two explanations are quite similar, and parts of each are in line with Wigner's Kuhnian-like question, which we will discuss later on. Regarding the selection of mathematics to fit our perception of reality, we have already acknowledged that some of mathematics develops this way. To the extent that not all applicable mathematical theories are generated out of concern for applicability, further work must be done, and Hamming indeed gives some additional food for thought.

Hamming's third response is that science in fact answers comparatively few problems. To the extent that this assertion is true, the less of a miracle the success of mathematics would appear to be. Wigner, as a physicist, certainly lived with mathematics as an indispensable tool, but other sciences do not share this same reliance on mathematics. Biology, it is often said, has not yet been successfully dissected by the mathematical scalpel. This position may have warrant, but upon reflection, some doubt can be cast as to whether it is entirely correct. Indeed, a great deal of mathematical attention has been focused of late on biological questions. A colleague of mine, for example, has looked at Coxeter Groups as models for DNA similarity. Knot theory, a newer branch of mathematics that deals with topological invariants, has had some success in the classification of DNA strands according to how they crinkle up under certain conditions. At the January 2006 annual joint meetings sponsored by the American Mathematical Society and the Mathematical Association of America, the prestigious Josiah Willard Gibbs Lecture was given by mathematical biologist Michael A. Savageau (University of California, Davis). His lecture, entitled *Function, Design, and Evolution of Gene Circuity*, was laced with mathematical models. It should be noted that this lecture was the only one on the four day program that had no competing presentations. Thus, the importance of this area to the mathematical community is unquestioned, and therefore it seems quite likely that mathematics will play a significant role in at least some areas of future biological studies. Indeed, there now exist various societies worldwide whose task is to investigate mathematical applications in biology. Certainly, though, Hamming has a point in that mathematics does not permeate all of science, at least to the extent that it does in physics. Even if we grant the argument that Hamming proposes here, the success of mathematics in physics itself is something that cannot be dismissed simply by pointing to slower progress in other areas. Are there any good explanations that fully account for this success?

One obvious candidate is Hamming's final suggestion, that the evolution of man provided the "model," meaning the explanation for why humans are able to mathematize the physical universe. At face value this claim may appear to be plausible, but it is not fleshed out beyond Hamming's comment that, "Darwinian evolution would naturally select for survival those competing forms of life which had the best models of reality in their minds—'best' meaning best for surviving and propagating."[7] It is interesting to note that Hamming concludes with the following remark: "If you recall that modern science is only about 400 years old, and that there have been from 3 to 5 generations per century, then there have been at most 20 generations since Newton and Galileo. If you pick 4,000 years for the age of science, generally, then you get an upper bound of 200 generations. Considering the effects of evolution we are looking for via selection of small chance variations, it does not seem to me that evolution can explain more than a small part of the unreasonable effectiveness of mathematics."[8] This observation seems hardly compelling. Just as an inclined block needs a critical slope to overcome its friction and start sliding, and once the sliding begins it proceeds rather rapidly, so too one might argue that once science started it progressed quickly, but any evolutionary development that occurred before this explosion was critical, and cannot be discounted.

But evolutionary accounts have problems as well. In fact, with respect to explaining our ability to apply higher mathematics to the physical world, they are sparse at best. In what follows I briefly examine three approaches that have been put forth as viable evolutionary accounts for various forms of cognition. Their proponents do not necessarily intend that their arguments should apply to mathematical cognition, so criticisms levied against them must be taken with the requisite grain of salt. The first explanation can be called the sexual selection hypothesis as argued by Geoffrey Miller.[9] He claims that excessive capacities or acquisition of resources of any kind may be a sexual display. If you have the energy or time or intrinsic capacity to do things that do not have direct adaptive value—carrying around a set of antlers that are so big they are more of a detriment than a defense, or a peacock walking around with a big colored tail, or possessing artistic or mathematical brains that are more than we need to solve the problems of survival—then that energy or time or intrinsic capacity by itself may attract mates. Physical attributes certainly seem to have some role in mate attraction, and artistic brains may as well insofar as they enable people to make attractive artifacts for display.

The argument for mathematical brains, however, does not seem to hold up as well. Although Miller does not specifically address the question of why mathematical reasoning is successful, there has been speculation that his thinking might be relevant. Miller states: "The healthy brain theory suggests that our brains are different from those of other apes not because extravagantly large brains helped us to survive or to raise offspring, but because such brains are simply better advertisements of how good our genes are. The more complicated the brain, the easier it is to mess up."[10] But how would a larger brain be evident, and how would one somehow conclude that this excess is evidence of good genes? In this regard one is reminded of the Gary Larson cartoon where, on a desert island, two men compete for the attention of women. The one winning the day is the one who is able to produce, on chalk board, a more impressive array of mathematical equations. These speculations, then, while certainly not disprovable, seem to have no good evidence in their support, at least insofar as they might relate to mathematical thinking.

Next is what we might call the module approach as argued by Stephen Mithin.[11] Mithin writes from the perspective of an anthropologist, and has an enormous amount of archaeological data upon which to draw. His thinking is that integrative and higher level (meta) cognitive processes grew out of the unification of specific evolutionary modules, such as a module for tool use, or a module for interpersonal relations. These modules seem to coincide with spurts of brain enlargement, which are caused by a variety of factors. For example, "in general larger animals have larger brains, simply because they have more muscles to move and coordinate."[12] Mithin further argues that in humans (and only in humans) we also find a structure on top of modules—a general purpose rationality. Says Mithin: "In summary science, like art and religion, is a product of cognitive fluidity. It relies on psychological processes which had originally evolved in specialized cognitive domains and only emerged when these processes worked together."[13] This last approach has been debated extensively. For example, Alvin Plantinga's celebrated essay, "An Evolutionary Argument against Naturalism"[14] claims that rationality is very unlikely a quality produced by survivability. Plantinga's approach, as he acknowledges, is similar to that found in C. S. Lewis's *Miracles*. (Lewis's argument, incidentally, was recently enhanced by Victor Reppert in his book *C. S. Lewis's Dangerous Idea*.) The thrust of their thinking here is that you cannot get (or are very unlikely to get) rationality out of a causally closed system that works solely on the basis of blind chance physical interactions operating in accordance with a "survival of the fittest" paradigm.

This brings us to the byproduct hypothesis, as exemplified by Pascal Boyer, who indirectly argues against Plantinga's, Lewis's and Reppert's view, at least as applied to religious cognition.[15] His main thesis is that many higher cognitive religious functions may not be evolutionary adaptations at all. Instead, they may be byproducts of things that are adaptive, and just piggyback on the adaptiveness of these other capacities. For Boyer, such cognition comes from many sources, which explains why religious claims, taken as a whole, produce so many false conclusions. Although Boyer is only speaking of religious sensibilities, in stating this view he seems to wave a magic wand and categorically pronounce that this piggyback model may be the case. On the one hand, if the piggyback model holds up, one may well be justified in extending Boyer's thinking to mathematical cognition. On the other hand, if one is going to argue for something using an evolutionary framework, it behooves that person to supply a detailed model or story that will support it. Such an account seems lacking in Boyer's work. More to the point, the argument becomes even more problematic if it were to be applied to mathematical cognition (a claim, to repeat, that Boyer does not make). How many false conclusions, for example, has mathematical cognition produced, whatever definitions one wants to give of "true" or "false?"

For the moment, let us suppose that evolutionary theory will be able, eventually, to come up with a plausible explanation of our rationality, notwithstanding the arguments we have mentioned challenging that possibility. If so, any such theory that also attempts to promote a naturalistic world view would still run up against the arguments of Mark Steiner, author of *The Applicability of Mathematics as a Philosophical Problem*.

Strictly speaking, Steiner's argument attempts to refute "nonanthropocentrism" rather than naturalism. But if Steiner is correct, the naturalist should not take comfort. For any form of naturalism, Steiner muses, is *ipso facto* non-anthropocentric, in that it would disallow a privileged status for humans in the scope of the universe. If, as Steiner argues, the success of mathematics can be shown to put humans in some sort of a privileged position, then naturalism has some problems to sort out.

How does the success of mathematics put humans in a privileged position? For Steiner, it is not so much the success of any one particular mathematical theory in an area of science. After all, there have been many failures of mathematics in addition to its successes. In this respect Steiner agrees with Hamming's third point and is thus critical of Wigner's approach in citing specific success examples from physics while ignoring error stories. The use of *pi* by the statistician in Wigner's opening line ignores all the failures in attempting to predict population trends. What Steiner is talking about is the success of mathematics as a grand strategy. It is a strategy that takes, for example, the raw formalisms of complex Hilbert space theory and boldly uses them as tools to make predictions about the quantum world, predictions that subsequently seem to be born out via experiment. And how is this phenomenon anthropocentric? An analogy may be helpful here. Most cultures use a base ten numbering system. There is no universal agreement as to why this is the case, but the general consensus is that it has to do with our having ten fingers. (The Mayas, incidentally, used base twenty, and to many this confirms the "appendage hypothesis.") Now, what if successful theories of how the universe operates were based on multiples of ten? That would be anthropocentric to an extreme, as the only reason the number ten is special to us is due to how we appear to ourselves.

Suppose, further, that not only did the number ten have special significance, but time and time again other human aesthetic criteria also played a significant role in understanding the universe. Such occurrences, when looked at from a meta-level, would surely make one wonder why such privilege seems to fall on the human species. Yet this situation is precisely analogous to what mathematicians and scientists actually do when they rely on human notions of beauty and symmetry in the development of their theories. In fact, such activity has been a longstanding and consistent strategy. Galileo, for example, pursued this tactic even though the best empirical evidence at the time did not support—indeed, it tended to disconfirm—his heliocentric theory.[16] He adopted it because it seemed much more elegant than the Ptolemaic model.[17] Most physicists generally admit that elegance, beauty, and symmetry hold primary sway in theory development. As Brian Green says in *The Elegant Universe*, "Physicists, as we have discussed, tend to elevate symmetry principles to a place of prominence by putting them squarely on the pedestal of explanation."[18] G. H. Hardy argues that mathematics itself, at least what constitutes good mathematics, is driven primarily by aesthetic criteria such as economy of expression, depth, unexpectedness, inevitability, and seriousness, qualities that also seem to form standards for good poetry.[19]

Two of these criteria, when taken together, appear paradoxical. In a beautiful mathematical theory, there is certainly the inevitable. A theorem marches on towards a conclusion that seems undeniable. But how can something inevitable also be unexpected? The answer lies in the proof of a theorem itself. A beautiful proof has, in its core, ideas that take the reader by surprise, almost like a series of brilliant moves in a chess match. And the surprises, when put in context, become stunningly beautiful. A good poem has that same effect. The pattern of words forms a symphony that contains many surprises to be sure, but when heard, seems paradoxically inevitable in that it had to be stated the way it was. For Hardy, the theories in mathematics that he deems "important" are precisely the ones that satisfy these aesthetic standards.

Steiner's book contains several examples of beautiful mathematical systems being used in applications to the physical world. His survey includes the use of complex analysis in fluid dynamics, relativistic field theory, thermodynamics, and quantum mechanics. Two of his examples are worth exploring in some detail. First, consider Schroedinger's use of the wave equation. He begins with the equation

$$E = \frac{p^2}{2m} + V(x,y,z)$$

where he makes an assumption that energy (represented by the symbol E in this equation) is constant, so he can eliminate it by a mathematical technique known as differentiating. After a series of manipulations he gets

$$i\hbar \frac{\partial \psi}{\partial t} = \left[-\frac{\hbar^2}{2m} \nabla^2 + V(x,y,z) \right] \psi$$

and then uses his result successfully in situations where energy is not constant. The reader unfamiliar with the above mathematical symbols may well wonder why they are included here, thinking that they are notational gimmicks only—designed to impress rather than educate, perhaps—and carry with them no valuable meaning. This is part of the point. To a mathematician, of course, the above symbols do carry meaning, but in manipulating them one is playing a game of sorts. As Steiner says, this is "a perfect example of allowing the notation to lead us by the nose."[20]

The second example is well known among mathematicians and physicists: Maxwell's anticipation of a physical reality. In 1871 James Clerk Maxwell made a remarkable prediction resulting from his work in electromagnetic theory. He noted that the experimentally confirmed laws of André-Marie Ampere, Charles Coulomb, and Michael Faraday, when put in a certain mathematical form (known as a differential form), contradicted the law of conservation of electrical charge. How could this contradiction be resolved? Maxwell decided to tinker with the mathematical equation that represented Ampere's law. He eventually realized that if he added a term to it, the resulting equation would not only be consistent with the conservation of charge law, it would actually logically imply it. With no other warrant, Maxwell then boldly predicted that his new term would be found to correspond with some physical phenomenon. Maxwell died in 1879. Nine years later Heinrich Hertz demonstrated the reality corresponding to Maxwell's term—electromagnetic radiation.

Richard Carrier (M.Phil., Ancient History, Columbia University), is a freelance writer who is unimpressed by this episode, claiming that what Maxwell did is entirely consistent with naturalism.[21] First, Carrier states that Maxwell's putting laws in differential form conforms to the naturalistic observation that nature works in continuous, not broken, processes. Second, Carrier argues that Maxwell took a logically sound hypothetical step: if charge is not being conserved, then it must be going somewhere. Carrier then states: "Maxwell rightly picked the simplest imaginable solution first, which due to human limitation is always the best place to start an investigation, and which statistically is the most likely [as] simple patterns and behaviors happen far more often than complex ones. [Thus] Maxwell's moves [that] anticipated EM radiation [were] therefore a natural conclusion from entirely naturalistic assumptions."[22] But with such language Carrier plays into Steiner's hands. Picking a simple solution in accordance with human limitations is precisely analogous to using the number ten as a means of unlocking secrets to the universe. It is quintessential anthropocentrism. Because of Carrier's background in history, one wonders if it is difficult for people who were not trained in science to appreciate how absolutely uncanny is the continued use of mathematical formalisms by physicists. Green, by contrast, seems to agree with Steiner's main point: at least unconsciously physicists have abandoned a raw naturalism in favor of a theory formation method that has principles of beauty embedded in its core. If they are correct, this approach certainly appears to be an anthropocentric—and by way of implication a non-naturalistic—strategy.

Or could it be naturalistic after all? Might it not be argued that evolutionary models can be devised that would explain, for example, the human preference for symmetry? Such constructs seem plausible, especially considering symmetries that might be adduced in examining our DNA code. But even if some model could be developed that would explain our preference for symmetry, how would a "blind chance" form of such thinking explain why such preferences are successful? After all, magical incantations are symmetrical, but they certainly do not work.

At least three strategies seem possible at this point. The first is to argue for some kind of probabilistic "weighting" that would drive physical processes towards the production of sentient life forms, and do so in such a way that their preferences for beauty coincide with the actual mechanisms of the universe. A second approach would involve an appeal to a primal basic position: it just so happens that the universe evolved in such a way that our notions for beauty work successfully in the development of theory formation. Finally, one might argue (along the lines of Wigner's second question) that what we call success came only because humans have invested a great deal of energy into science over the last 500 years. Who is to say that, if similar energies had been funneled in a different direction, there would be operating today a totally different paradigm, yet with the same degree of "success?" The success could be due to effort, not necessarily to some amazing connection humans have with reality. Thus, mathematical beauty poses no problems for naturalism whatsoever.

These are huge issues, and it would be presumptuous to think that a paper like this could settle them. Nevertheless, we can explore very quickly some tentative responses.

First, with respect to the probabilistic weighting hypothesis, one might legitimately ask where the evidence is for this claimed weighting. As Keith Ward comments: "A physical weighting ought to be physically detectable, . . . and it has certainly not been detected. . . . In this sense, a continuing causal activity of God seems the best explanation of the progress towards greater consciousness and intentionality that one sees in the actual course of the evolution of life on earth."[23] Furthermore, if some kind of weighting could eventually be hypothesized and then tested, it may still be asked why such a weighting is biased in favor of humans. To a theist, there is no *prima facie* reason why God could not work with what appears to be "chance" (although the problem of determining what exactly one means by "chance" is by no means trivial). For a theist, the position humans seem to have of being able to understand the workings of the universe is, by itself, the result of the creative and purposive activity of God, even if our coming to be this way arose out of some kind of probabilistic weighting scheme.

Next, although primal basic explanations are needed at some level, invoking them in an effort to explain the apparent privileged status for humans in the universe— this is just the way it is and no more needs to be said—appears akin to pulling a rabbit out of a hat. A naturalist may choose precisely this option. But for a theist, again, the conviction that human notions of beauty relate successfully to our knowledge of how the universe operates reinforces all the more the belief that human creation is the result of the purposive activity of an intelligent being.

Finally, the idea that our constructs of success are *ad hoc* appears to be an objection without any realistic alternative. It is almost like saying, "Well, your theory makes sense, but only if one buys into some of your commonly accepted cultural notions. Other (unspecified) theories would be able to show that the success you claim is really arbitrary, and thus not privileged." Such a position, unfortunately, almost shuts down discussion. Of course, it is possible that other theories could be successful, but where are they? And why is it the case that the development of mathematics seems to be universal across cultures? It is noteworthy, for example, that the mathematics of pre-modern China, an independent and isolated culture, exhibits an impressive list of mathematical theorems also found in ancient Greece and other cultures, including the Pythagorean theorem, the binomial theorem, the solution of polynomial equations via Horner's method, and Gaussian elimination for the solution of systems of linear equations.[24]

I would suggest, in summary, that a theistic explanation is the best one in accounting for the continuing success of mathematical theories that ultimately grow out of aesthetic criteria. In assessing these arguments the reader is encouraged to adopt an approach similar to Reppert's in his defense of C. S. Lewis; there are, of course, valid points to be made on the side opposing these ideas, which should be looked at not as final answers, but as a catalyst to weigh various options. Human aesthetic values, and their subsequent use in successful physical theories, dovetail nicely with a Christian view that humans are created in the image of God. Whatever being in God's image exactly entails, it seems to include a rational capacity reflective of his that enables humans to understand

and admire his creation. While not necessarily a final answer, such a perspective can be put confidently in the marketplace of ideas for appraisal, which is precisely what this discussion has attempted to do.

Notes

1. This essay first appeared in *CSR* 35:4 (Summer 2006): 493-504.
2. Available at www.dartmouth.edu/~matc/MathDrama/reading/Wigner.html; also at other sites.
3. Ibid.
4. Ibid.
5. Ibid.
6. R. W. Hamming, "The Unreasonable Effectiveness of Mathematics," *The American Mathematical Monthly* 87:2 (1980): 81-90. See also www.lecb.ncifcrf.gov/~toms/Hamming.unreasonable.html.
7. Ibid., 89.
8. Ibid., 89.
9. Geoffrey Miller, *The Mating Mind: How Sexual Choice Shaped the Evolution of Human Nature* (New York: Anchor Books, 2001).
10. Ibid, 104.
11. Stephen Mithin, *The Prehistory of Mind: The Cognitive Origins of Art, Religion, and Science* (New York: Thames and Huston, Ltd., 1996).
12. Ibid., 200.
13. Ibid., 215.
14. This essay has appeared in various forms. See, for example, Alvin Plantinga, *Warrant and Proper Function* (Oxford: Oxford University Press, 1993), Chapter 12.
15. Pascal Boyer, *Religion Explained: The Evolutionary Origins of Religious Thought* (New York: Basic Books, 2001).
16. For example, no stellar parallax shift could be detected from observed data, something that certainly would occur if the Earth revolved about the Sun. The problem, of course, is that stars are much further from the Earth than believed to be in Galileo's time, so the expected shift was not observed. In any case, detecting a shift would not have been possible with the technology then available.
17. For a good treatment of Galileo, see "Galileo, the Church, and the Cosmos," in David C. Lindberg, and Ronald L. Numbers, eds., *When Science and Christianity Meet* (Chicago: University of Chicago Press, 2003), 33-60, 291-94.
18. Brian Green, *The Elegant Universe* (New York: W. W. Norton & Company, 1999), 374.
19. See G. H. Hardy, *A Mathematician's Apology*, with foreword by C.P. Snow (Cambridge, U.K.: Cambridge University Press, 1967).
20. Mark Steiner, *The Applicability of Mathematics as a Philosophical Problem* (Cambridge, Mass.: Cambridge University Press, 1998), 80.
21. Richard Carrier, "Fundamental Flaws in Mark Steiner's Challenge to Naturalism in The Applicability of Mathematics as a Philosophical Problem." http://www.infidels.org/library/modern/richard_carrier/steiner.html.
22. Ibid.
23. Keith Ward, *God, Chance, & Necessity* (Oxford: Oneworld Publications, 1996), 78.
24. See Russell W. Howell and W. James Bradley, eds., *Mathematics in a Postmodern Age: A Christian Perspective* (Grand Rapids, Mich.: Eerdmans, 2001), ch. 2.

23 Mark and Aristotle
The Christ Embodied as Tragic Hero (2008)

Norman A. Bert

I sit in front of a blank computer screen, ready to write.[1] Maybe I am going to write the essay you are about to read. Maybe a short story. Maybe a poem. A play. A speech. The blank screen intimidates me, but at least I have an idea what essays are like, or short stories, or whatever I am going to write. After all, I have probably read hundreds of them. Likely I have studied them in school and written samples under the tutelage of teachers who, themselves, have read thousands of them. So I have an idea how to go about it.

I have an advantage over the writer we call Mark.[2] When Mark sat down to write his Gospel, that biblical form so familiar to us, he was about to write the very first one of its kind. He had never written a Gospel. He had never read a Gospel because no one had ever written a Gospel. No one had written a narrative account of Jesus' life or ministry ever before. Sitting in front of my empty screen, I marvel at the task that lay before Mark at that moment, and I marvel even more at the success with which he brought the task to fruition.

I want to know how he went about it. I want to know what principles guided him. Did he use a model? If so, what was it? And what effect did that model have on the picture of Jesus that he projected?

This essay attempts an answer to those questions. It proposes that Mark structured his story using Greco-Roman principles of narration, specifically the principles of tragedy and epic. Aristotle (384-322 B.C.E.) first set out these principles in his *Poetics*. Horace (c. 20-14 B.C.E.) adapted them to Roman tastes in his *Art of Poetry*. Recognizing the Aristotelian principles that underlie this first narrative about Jesus—analyzing it as a classical drama—elucidates Mark's Gospel and clarifies its portrayal of Jesus as a fully embodied human being who was both Judeo-Christian Messiah and also Greco-Roman tragic hero.

Forty years after Jesus' crucifixion, contrary to Christian expectations, the world had not ended, and it became clear that Christians needed to set about the business of creating lives. Fashioning a way of life would be facilitated greatly by having a model to follow. The Gentile Christian community already had a theology provided in expository form through preaching and epistolary writing. They had ideas and a few tantalizing details about the life of this Christ they worshipped—that he lived, died, and rose from the dead. But all the rest was philosophy. They did not have a living, breathing model to admire, to respect, to love, to emulate. Many of these Gentile believers were simple folk—slaves, the poor, the underclass—not intellectuals, many not even literate. They had ideas, but if they were to endure, even in the face of persecution and martyrdom, they needed a hero, a flesh-and-blood man to hold on to and to imitate. Mark would provide what they needed, Jesus the man, Jesus the doer of deeds.

As he set out to fashion a Christian hero, an exemplar for Christian living, Mark faced the immediate problem of how to go about the task. In classical rhetorical terms, having settled on a motivating vision, *conceptio*, he needed to solve three other compositional problems: *inventio* (What materials should be included?), *dispositio* (How should they be organized?), and *elecutio* (In what style should they be presented?).

As a writer in the classical period, Mark would naturally begin to solve this triad of problems by seeking a model to adapt for his purposes. Horace stated this impulse as a dictum: "Obey the conventions, or if you make something new, /Be sure it stays true to itself."[3] And he particularly advocated the use of Greek exemplars.[4] Present-day writers freely utilize a variety of approaches, including a romantically motivated insistence on radical originality, but classical writers in the first century naturally sought out models.[5] But where would Mark find an appropriate model? Christianity had not yet produced a narrative literary tradition. The Tanakh provided no usable model, and in any case Hebrew narrative would have little recognition factor or appeal for Gentile Christians. Greek models, however—those of tragedy and epic—existed and were understood and admired by Greeks and Romans. Mark could portray Jesus as a tragic hero in the Greek epic tradition. To accomplish this, he would use Aristotelian and Horatian principles, modified by Christian theology, to structure his Gospel.[6]

Mark's first task, *inventio*, was to select, create, and shape the material he would use. Where would he find information about Jesus' life, what specific materials would he use, and how would he treat his selected material? Would he be governed by his research, or would he shape his materials? And if he molded them, with what freedom would he do so?

As to the type of materials Mark should seek out, Aristotle gave clear guidance: the proper materials of drama are actions, deeds. Chapter 3 of the *Poetics* says, "Sophocles is the same sort of representational artist as . . . Aristophanes, since both represent men in action and doing things. That is why, some say, their works are called 'dramas,' because they represent men 'doing.'"[7]

This principle, the impulse to focus on deeds, immediately determined that Mark's picture of Jesus would differ from contemporary Christian views. While there may have been written collections of Jesus' sayings such as Q,[8] most of the information about Jesus' life likely was circulating in oral form. And, judging from the scant details one can glean from Paul's letters, these stories focused on Jesus as a teacher who otherwise was passive, not on Jesus as a doer of deeds.[9] Two observations emerge from a survey of materials about Jesus in Paul's letters. First, outside of the Gospels, the NT contains almost no details about the man Jesus. And secondly, the dominant picture these NT writers gave of Jesus of Nazareth was that he was not so much a doer of deeds as he was a passive recipient of the actions of others. Mark, writing in the tradition of Aristotle, would change this picture forever. Mark created the image of Jesus as a doer of marvelous deeds.[10]

The question of which elements in his Gospel Mark took from existing sources and which he created, as well as the question of how he molded the materials he found, have become the focus of considerable debate amongst scholars.[11] While a study of Aristotle cannot, of course, reveal the identity or content of Mark's sources, it can reveal the principles of the selection and shaping process. The fact that most of the tragedies Aristotle knew adapted preexisting materials makes his ideas particularly applicable to Mark's process.

Aristotle stated three principles for the selection and molding of materials for a tragedy. The first of these, the concept that poetry is truer than history, would encourage Mark to focus on the meaning of his Gospel rather than the factuality of its details. In Chapter 9 of the *Poetics*, Aristotle asserted that "poetry is a more philosophical and more serious thing than history" because, while history deals with the accidental and the particular, tragedy and epic deal with universal truths.[12] Although our modern commitment to scientism leads us to exactly the opposite conclusion, to value history as more important and valuable than fiction, Mark cannot be held to our standard. Following Aristotelian principles, he would have been more concerned to construct a work with poetic truth than to compile slavishly factual details about Jesus. He would, therefore, seek out traditions about Jesus that fit his argument, and he would carefully marshal his materials in order to present universal truths as he understood them.

Secondly, Aristotle's dictum that the poet's shaping process should not corrupt the original story would recommend that Mark fit his story into the received traditions about Jesus. In Chapter 14, Aristotle discussed the amount and nature of license the tragic poet properly exercises in turning preexisting materials into tragedy. He said that, on the one hand, the poet should not change the basic story, but on the other hand the poet's proper and central task is to mold the presentation of these materials into an effective play: "The poet cannot undo the traditional stories, I mean e.g. that Clytaemnestra is killed by Orestes or Eriphyle by Alcmeon; but he should invent for himself, i.e. use the inherited stories well."[13] In keeping with this principle, Mark maintained the broad framework of Jesus' life that is evident in Paul's writings: Jesus lived, died by crucifixion, and rose again.

Finally, Aristotle demonstrated that a tragedy's purpose, not external standards of factuality, governs a poet's selection of materials. Chapter 25 of the *Poetics* says that tragic and epic poets can represent life properly in three different ways: they can imitate life the way it really is, they can present life the way it should be, or they can represent it the way people fantasize it to be. Aristotle said that any and all of these approaches are equally valid, so long as the drama makes sense within itself. Since a play's internal structures are the means by which a poet creates and presents universals, the truth of a tragedy or epic should be judged not on the basis of its relationship to reality, but rather on the effectiveness of its own internal logic. For Mark, Aristotle's principle would permit the inclusion of miraculous deeds and theologically shaped sayings and incidents, regardless of his own judgment about the material's factuality. The question would not be whether the historical Jesus really did and said these things, but rather how Mark could best marshal these details to create his intended effect. Historical accuracy was not Mark's goal; his aim was to project a heroic Jesus.[14]

It is no stretch to say that Mark, as the author of the first Gospel, actually created the life of Jesus as we know it. He created this life in accord with Aristotle's principles. In order to create a suitable mode or style for telling the story of the Messiah, in other words, to solve the problem of *elecutio*, Mark created a new form, concise and impactive like tragedy yet narrated like epic rather than acted out. In the *Poetics*, Aristotle treated both dramatic tragedy and its related narrative form, epic. Although he judged tragedy the more elevated art form (Chapter 26), clearly he considered the two closely related in their basic principles (Chapter 24).

In spite of the advantages of drama, Mark had good reason not to choose theatrical tragedy as the sole mode for his Gospel. In tragedy's favor, it was revered, due to Aristotle's opinion, as superior to epic. Drama also had the virtue of brevity. As Aristotle put it, "Again, [tragedy] has the advantage that the end of the representation is in a smaller length. What is more concentrated is more pleasurable than what is diluted with a lot of time in performance."[15] However, Greek theatre had strong ties to paganism. Not only did the art form have its genesis within the cult of Dionysus, but the membership of contemporary actors in the Guild of Dionysus also maintained the connection. Mark therefore would have good reason to avoid fashioning Jesus' story for theatrical presentation.

Furthermore, epic presented some distinct advantages. First, it had a looser unity that permitted it to include more incidents and to cover a longer period of time. In Aristotle's words: "Again, with respect to length, tragedy attempts as far as possible to keep within one revolution of the sun or only to exceed this a little, but epic is unbounded in time."[16] Furthermore, epic could communicate better the miraculous or violent events that would be difficult to act out effectively on stage.[17]

Mark solved the problem of genre by creating a hybrid form that had the advantages of both tragedy and epic and the disadvantages of neither. Like a tragedian, he compressed his story into a length that could be absorbed at a single sitting. It takes about two hours to read the Gospel aloud. This length of story would be acceptable for a Christian rhetor to present to a gathering of believers, many of whom would not be able to read it for themselves.[18] While compressing his story into tragic magnitude, Mark utilized the expository, narrative mode of epic as well as epic's multiple incidents, its freedom to range across time and place, and its inclusion of "amazing" deeds and events.[19]

Along with conceptualizing a literary work (*conceptio*), collecting and selecting materials to include (*inventio*), and creating an appropriate style (*elecutio*), an author also has to devise suitable structures for a work (*dispositio*). Structuring a work includes the overall organization of the incidents into a powerful plot and the creation of effective characters. Classical narrative theory, based on Aristotle, would have provided Mark with useful models for these endeavors, and an examination of the Gospel demonstrates that, indeed, Mark followed these classical principles.

Aristotle devoted sizable portions of the *Poetics* to details about plot. He covered the importance of action-based unity in a good plot, the division of a plot into segments, the arc by which a plot moves from its beginning to its end, and the best ways to create probability. Mark's Gospel provides an exemplar of classical principles for each of these four topics while it also reveals how he adapted them to fit his source materials, his audience's belief structures, and his purpose.

A classical writer like Mark would have recognized the importance of action based unity. Aristotle decreed that the primary quality of a good plot is unity, and that the only appropriate unity for either a tragedy or an epic was action, the depiction of a single, clearly defined event.[20] For all its episodes and incidents, Mark's Gospel finds its unity in a single action: at the cost of his own life, Jesus establishes the Kingdom of God. Mark focused attention on this unifying event with his title, "The Beginning of the Gospel of Jesus Christ, the Son of God." The point of the title is that the good news of God's reign in the world begins with the tragic story of the heroic Messiah. This event—Jesus' unified act of describing, demonstrating, and founding the reign of God—gave shape to the major organizational units of Mark, dictated their order, and tied them into a coherent whole.

In addition to being unified, extended literary narratives are usually organized in units such as chapters and episodes, acts and scenes. An analysis of Mark's Gospel shows that he organized his work into units as well and that he drew his structures from both classical dramaturgy and also Hebraic traditions. Mark's melding of classical and Judeo-Christian traditions is perhaps more clearly evident in his handling of structure than in any other aspect of his work.

Aristotle's description of the four quantitative parts employed in Greek tragedy included the prologue that initiated the drama, episodes in which the actors performed the action, choral odes that divided the episodes and commented on them, and the exit of the actors and chorus that concluded the play (*Poetics*, Chapter 12). As the chorus faded in importance, plays came to include five units corresponding to the prologue, three episodes, and the exit. By the late first century B.C.E., classical theory solidified this development into the five act rule as expressed by Horace: "Let your play be five acts long, no more, no less, /If you ever want it staged a second time."[21]

Mark presented the incidents of his Gospel in accordance with Horace's five-unit structure. The sequence of quantitative parts clearly depicts the "beginning of the Gospel," the manner in which Jesus established the Kingdom of God. The following outline includes the major units—prologue, three acts, and exit:

- Prologue (1:1-15): Jesus enters proclaiming the Kingdom of God.
- Act 1 (1:16-8.21): Working under cover, Jesus lays the foundation for the Kingdom of God.

- Act 2 (8:22-10:52): In private, Jesus opens the eyes of the disciples to his identity, his destiny, and the implications of the Kingdom of God for them.
- Act 3 (11:1-15:39): Openly revealing his identity as Messiah, Jesus launches a frontal attack on the Jewish establishment, thus triggering his own death.
- Exit (15:40-16:8): The tragic messianic hero achieves apotheosis.

Mark's five-act structure provided an overall cause-and-effect progression in keeping with classical, logic-based principles.[22]

However, Mark's Judeo-Christian presuppositions led him to compromise the causality of classical structure by making the connections between the Gospel's units episodic. Aristotle's philosophical presupposition of a closed universe driven by natural law led him to call for a cause-and-effect structure for tragedy. In the Christian and Jewish cosmos, in contrast, the world is open, and God reaches in to alter the course of human history. Most typically, drama represents an open cosmos by an episodic sequence of scenes in which new events occur *de novo*.[23] Accordingly, Mark modified the overall Aristotelian inevitability of his story by ordering his scenes episodically. In dramatic parlance, it would be typical to accuse Mark of manipulating the structure artificially for his own purposes. Mark managed this progression, however, by attributing the manipulation to Jesus himself. Jesus initiates the events of Act 1 by his decision to leave Capernaum and broaden his ministry (1:35-39). He initiates the action of Act 2 by opening the topic of his identity (8:27-31). And he initiates Act 3 by organizing the symbolic spectacle of his entry into Jerusalem (11:1, 2). Jesus, thereby, becomes the agent of an immanent deity who reaches into human history and causes pivotal events to take place. Jesus moves history ahead according to a divine plan, the details of which lie beyond the purview of natural law but which are integral to the Kingdom of God.

Finally, Mark devised a probable conclusion that complied fully with the best expectations of classical dramaturgy, provided a logical resolution and avoided specifically the use of the *deus ex machina*. Aristotle, in keeping with his dicta on probability, insisted on conclusions that remained consistent with the tragic action of the play and did not soften the end by rescuing the sympathetic characters.[24] In tune with Aristotle, Horace advised against use of a *deus*: "And unless the crisis is really up to it, / Don't call upon a god to come in and solve it."[25]

Accordingly, at the point of his conclusion, perhaps more clearly than at any other point in the Gospel, Mark allowed his tragic model to take precedence over Christian doctrinal assertions. Centuries of Christians have found the shorter ending of the Gospel, the one generally accepted as authentic, unsatisfying because it includes no resurrection appearances. The ancient Christian community remedied this problem by adding longer, more positive conclusions—happy endings—while modern scholars have simply speculated about the abrupt conclusion. William Barclay, for instance, writes that the Gospel "cannot have been *meant* to stop at Mark 16:8," and he goes on to suggest reasons for the truncated ending, such as the possibility that Mark died before finishing the book.[26] It is more probable, however, that Mark intentionally ended the Gospel abruptly in keeping with his tragic model. He refrained from concluding his Gospel with resurrection appearances of Jesus, appearances that would ameliorate the tragic conclusion. Instead, after reminding the audience of Jesus' repeated predictions of his resurrection, he left his characters, as well as his audience, with the full impact of the suffering of the tragic messianic hero. This conclusion strikes an effective balance between classical tragic probability and Christian theology. While touching on the Messiah's resurrection, the conclusion emphasizes Jesus as a tragic hero, a human exemplar.

But Mark did not just plot out his story in accordance with classical principles. He also used tragic classical models to create his Gospel's central character. His portrayal of Jesus recast the divine Messiah of Pauline theology in the shape of the tragic hero of Aristotelian drama. Applying classical dramaturgical principles to Mark's Jesus clarifies the writer's process and reveals a long-overlooked source for his image of Christianity's central figure. Many have noticed that Mark's Jesus is particularly human—more so than the Jesus of Matthew and Luke.[27] And indeed, lifelikeness is a primary quality Aristotle called for in the construction of tragic heroes.[28] Although we cannot be sure what ideas about the man Jesus may have circulated amongst the Christian Diaspora prior to Mark's Gospel, lifelikeness was clearly not a significant component of Paul's image of Jesus. Paul wrote only two descriptions of Jesus in the flesh: that he was righteous, obedient, and without sin (Rom. 5:8, 9; 2 Cor. 5:21), and that he was meek and gentle (2 Cor. 10:1). Later New Testament writers repeat these assertions (1 Pet. 2:21-24; Heb. 2:10) but do not add to them. Mark's Gospel was directly responsible for subsequent perceptions about the behaviors, attitudes, motivations, thought processes, and decisional modes of Jesus. The evangelist established a lifelike Jesus by creating for him character as well as a personality, and he constructed these human traits on the model of the Greek tragic hero.

While personality is more a modern concept than a classical one, to the extent that ancient writers considered personality, they dealt with it in terms of dramatic characters being true to type. Aristotle, for instance, said that tragic characters "should be appropriate. It is possible to be manly in character, but it is not appropriate for a woman to be so manly or clever."[29] Expanding on that theme, Horace listed what he and his contemporaries considered appropriate to different ages of characters.

Since most of the central characters of tragedy were rulers or military heroes, and since additionally they had overblown self-perceptions, they were prone to personality traits that moderns do not find attractive, such as arrogance, anger, and impatience. Horace, for instance, said,

> If in your play
> You're bringing back the embassy to Achilles,
> Make him bitter, and stubborn, impetuous, irascible;
> If it's Medea, ferocious and implacable;
> Let Ino weep, Ixion be treacherous,
> Io a wanderer, Orestes mournful.[30]

And Aristotle pointed out that "Homer made Achilles good as well as stubborn."[31]

In tune with the practice of classical dramaturgy, Mark endowed Jesus with a personality appropriate to a kingly, tragic hero. Mark's Jesus is stern (3:12, 8:33), indignant (10:14), given to anger (3:5), impatient with his disciples (4:13, 8:21, and 9:19), and arrogant toward the Syrophoenician woman (7:27) and religious authorities (7:6-13). However, just as Sophocles' otherwise arrogant Oedipus is gentle and compassionate with petitioners, so Jesus shows pity toward the dispossessed, the weak, the sick, children, and the poor. In short, the personality Mark created for his central figure portrayed Jesus as a typical Greek tragic hero.[32]

However, Aristotle pointed out that regardless of their personalities, dramatic personages form character by making decisions.[33] So tragic heroes, though arrogant and angry, prove to be honorable characters as they make honorable decisions. Oedipus, arrogant though he may be, earns our respect because he keeps his word and pursues the truth—even when it becomes clear that the truth will crush him. Sophocles accented this decision by having Jocasta try to persuade Oedipus to give up his endeavors; Oedipus refuses her suggestion and perseveres while she goes inside to hang herself.

In tune with Aristotelian principles, Mark showed Jesus making good decisions with the result that, regardless of his abrasive personality, Jesus took shape as a person of truly good character. For example, much like Oedipus in the face of Jocasta's advice, Jesus forcefully refuses Peter's suggestion that he use his power to avoid his destiny (8:31-33). In several places, in fact, Mark went out of his way to manipulate his stories and language in order to focus attention on Jesus as a decision maker.[34] Repeatedly Mark portrayed Jesus making decisions that consistently established him as a good, compassionate character.

The picture Mark paints of Jesus—an impatient, even arrogant man, yet one who defines his good character by making good decisions—owes everything to Aristotle and nothing to Paul or other New Testament traditions.

Two questions about Mark's use of classical dramaturgy must be considered: How plausible is it that he had access to Aristotle's ideas about drama? And, assuming he did know about classical principles of tragedy, would he be inclined to use them? Richard Burridge has demonstrated that an awareness of literary genres and their structures was basic to the formal education of any literate person in the Mediterranean world from Hellenistic times onward.[35] Specifically, in the first century C.E., educated people throughout the Mediterranean world had considerable knowledge of Aristotelian dramatic principles. Aristotle's writings, including the *Poetics*, were widely available and widely read throughout the Greco-Roman region. Moreover, the fifth-century plays, on which Aristotle's analytical work was based, continued to be performed and read throughout the Roman world. Furthermore, Horace's *Art of Poetry*, heavily derivative of Aristotle, demonstrates the continued importance placed on Greek dramatic theory. The first-century-B.C.E. *Aeneid* of Virgil shows that epic continued to be a viable form. The first-century-C.E. tragedies of Seneca witness further to the continued availability of Aristotle's ideas and demonstrate their application to works that were intended for reading, not staging. It would, therefore, be reasonable to conclude that a writer of Mark's ability would have contact with Aristotelian ideas on literature; in fact, it would be unreasonable to suggest the contrary.

Furthermore, there is reason to believe that Jewish and Christian antagonism toward the theatre did not prevent members of those communities from contact with the art form. Fragments of *Exogoge*, a first-century-B.C.E. Greek tragedy about Moses, still survive. Scholars believe that this play, authored by an otherwise unknown Jew named Ezekiel, was intended for production in Hellenistic theatres. The existence of this play demonstrates that at least some Diaspora Jews knew classical principles of dramaturgy and that they were engaged with Greek culture closely enough that they even participated in its theatrical expressions.[36] Educated people in the Christian community, people like Mark, might easily have had contact with Greek drama.[37] To summarize, Aristotelian dramaturgical ideas were widely available and respected in the first-century Mediterranean world; Mark's level of education, evident in his writing, insures that he would have encountered these concepts; and the classical impulse toward use of models would have inclined a writer such as Mark to utilize these principles in his writing.

Mark's title announces his book to be "The Beginning of the Gospel of Jesus Christ, the Son of God." Indeed, the work fulfilled its promise in ways its author could not have imagined. Not only did it portray the beginning of Christianity, but also it established Christianity's image of its founder. And underlying all of this was a model explicated first by the pagan Greek philosopher, Aristotle. Mark's act of creation brought together in powerful synthesis the unlikely pair of the prophet from Galilee and the sage from Athens.

So what are the implications of that synthesis? What do we do with this Gospel? What do we do with this Jesus? I would sketch out four implications, one theological, one ethical, one political, and one evangelistic.

Theologically, acknowledging the synthesis of Christian belief with Greco-Roman dramatic principles, along with the impact of genre studies of the Gospels pursued over the past decades by scholars such as Bilezikian, Aune, and Burridge, should impact the present Christological controversies. The contemporary "Jesus wars," focused on attempts to identify the truly authentic Jesus Christ, have pitted radical scholars such as Robert Funk and John Dominic Crossan against more conservative ones such as Luke Timothy Johnson. Radicals, assuming that the Gospels have buried the historical Jesus under layers of Pauline and creedal theology, have attempted to excavate the Nazarene while conservatives have insisted the Christ of Paul and the creeds is the true messiah.

The present study, however, suggests that, in addition to the historical Jesus and the confessional Christ—the two polarizing images that provide the battle standards for the sides in these wars—scholars need to accept the existence and embrace the value of a third reality: the literary Jesus Christ. The Jesus wars tend to empower either Jesus' humanity or Christ's divinity at the cost of the other member of that duality. But the Gospels themselves give us a synthesis of these two viewpoints about Jesus Christ by combining the writers' faith-based content with their adopted literary forms. These portrayals of Jesus, synthetic in the best sense of the term, are all we have to go on; these Jesuses are each the *real* Jesus. Genre studies, such as the present one, recognize and embrace the impact of literary form on ideational content. Yes, Mark's Jesus, constructed according to the structures of Greek tragedy, is different from the Jesus of Luke and Matthew, formulated along the lines of Greco-Roman biography. These various Jesuses of the Gospels also differ from the actual man who lived in Galilee as well as the Christ of Paul and the creeds. But they are every bit as real—I would argue even more real—than those reductions. This is not to say, "Can't we all just get along?" It is rather to say: Let us recognize and embrace the unavoidable reality of the literarily constructed Jesus.

The Aristo-Markan Jesus has implications for ethics because this Gospel clearly has the rhetorical intent to set forth a model for Christian behavior. Indeed, the question Mark answers is "What would Jesus do?" The answer he gives, however, cuts across our typical expectations, including the assumptions of those of us whose bumpers bear a WWJD sticker. The Aristo-Markan Jesus, far from meek and mild, specializes in tough love. He is abrupt, moved by anger, arrogant to the point of being politically incorrect. Far from cozying up to authority, religious or otherwise, he triggers the opposition of an unholy alliance of conservative religion with political power. He redefines "family values" in a manner that empowers alliances of love and duty over traditional mores and biological ties. He consistently favors the poor, the weak, and the vulnerable young over those who are rich, powerful, and adult. When threatened, rather than taking up the weapons of violence and the strategies of coercion to protect himself and those he loves, he silently goes through interrogation, torture, and death. In his humanity he is every inch the tragic hero; in his heroic apotheosis, he exceeds the moral rectitude of his tragic forebears. He is a hero in the tradition of Oedipus and Antigone, but one whose heroism beggars theirs by comparison. And he calls us to follow him.

Mark's story—in its very story-ness—has political implications. As N. T. Wright has demonstrated, a story has authoritative power unavailable to theology and philosophy. Imperial Rome could absorb another philosophy; it would not tolerate a new story. Those who clung to this Jesus story were the ones martyred for their faith.[38] That Mark chose Greek tragic form as a model increased the political impact of his Gospel. As Hock pointed out, Greek new comedy represented social myth and the Greco-Roman novel projected personal myth, but Greek tragedy enacts political myth.[39] So it was not so much the theological Christ that challenged Rome as it was the Jesus of the Gospel story. Rome could ignore a set of arguments, but it would viciously attack the followers of a man-god whose story rivaled those of the Caesars. Realizing the power of the Jesus story, a story crafted first by Mark, should call the church back to a new, purified vision of its place in a world whose politics threaten to absorb it.

Finally, Mark's process of formulating the Jesus story by way of contemporary models has implications for the church's evangelistic mission. Those implications carry both a promise and a warning. In terms of promise, Mark's example recommends that, if future Christians follow suit, the positive results can be powerful indeed. Following this logic, the church should welcome, encourage, and sponsor efforts to share the Jesus story utilizing new, contemporary idioms. In terms of warning, Mark's use of classical tragedy demonstrates that the story itself is not left untouched by the form in which it is cast. Mark's Gospel is in the canon because the church recognized the validity of his portrayal of Jesus, including the manner in which Mark combined the messianic with the heroic. But not every contemporary icon fits the son of man. Recent paintings, for instance, of a muscled Jesus decked out in boxing gloves and trunks is altogether contrary to the Prince of Peace who, when Peter rejected his prediction of passive suffering, responded, "Get behind me, Satan! For you are setting your mind not on divine things but on human things" (8:33). Mark's example encourages us to re-create Jesus for our time and place; it warns us also to do so with care.

Mark adopted and adapted the model of classical tragedy to tell his story of Jesus. His synthesis of Hebraic and Greek traditions shaped the church's understanding of its founder. Mark's methodology is no less important than its result, his form no less important than his content. Through Mark's pages, because of Mark's synthesis, the hero messiah still calls his church to follow him.

Notes

1. This essay first appeared in *CSR* 37.2 (Winter 2008): 147-62.

2. The Gospel of Mark was written near the year 70 C.E. The Gospel's authorship has traditionally been attributed to John Mark, a Hellenistic Jew from a wealthy family in Jerusalem whom the Acts of the Apostles reports to be a relative of Peter and a traveling companion of Paul.

3. *To the Pisos (The Art of Poetry)*, in *The Epistles of Horace*, trans. David Ferry (New York: Farrar, Straus and Giroux, 2001), 161.

4. Horace criticized the poet Accius as "Battering the boards with pounding of ponderous verses . . . /because he knew too little about his craft. . . ." Horace's remedy for Accius' problem? "Study Grecian models night and day." Ibid., 170, 171.

5. The use of models fit the classical concept of poetry as imitation. This concept was stated first by Plato, modified by Aristotle, and summarized eventually by C. H. C. Wright as follows: "A sane and clear-sighted intellect, linked with an inbred or trained taste, seeking the inspiration of great masters of past literature who have themselves tried to interpret the universal laws of nature—this we may consider to be the foundation of true classicism" (*French Classicism* [Harvard Studies in Romance Languages 4, Cambridge: Harvard University Press, 1920], 97). Many scholars have noted similarities between the Gospels and various preexisting genres. Sample genres cited by these scholars include Hellenistic biography: Lawrence M. Wills, *The Quest of the Historical Gospel: Mark, John, and the Origins of the Gospel Genre* (New York: Routledge, 1997); Greco-Roman biography: David E. Aune, *The New Testament in Its Literary Environment* (Philadelphia: Westminster, 1987) and Richard A. Burridge, *What Are the Gospels? A Comparison with Graeco-Roman Biography* (Cambridge: Cambridge University Press, 1992); Greek tragedy: Gilbert G. Bilezikian, *The Liberated Gospel: A Comparison of the Gospel of Mark and Greek Tragedy* (Grand Rapids: Baker, 1977); epic: Marianne Palmer Bonz, *The Past as Legacy: Luke-Acts and Ancient Epic* (Minneapolis: Fortress, 2000); and Hellenistic novel: Ronald F. Hock, "The Greek Novel" in *Greco-Roman Literature and the New Testament: Selected Forms and Genres*, ed. David E. Aune (Atlanta: Scholars, 1988), 107-26. While these scholars have noted parallels, few have acknowledged the intentionality with which the Gospel writers would have modeled their work on those genres. The creative use of models by NT writers can be seen in the Gospels of Matthew and Luke who, in their aim to turn Mark's tragic hero into a cosmic imperial figure *vis-à-vis* the deified Roman emperor, combined Mark's literary model with that of the encomium, an Aristotelian biographical pattern (Robert W. Funk, *Honest to Jesus: Jesus for a New Millennium* [New York: HarperSanFrancisco, 1996], 282-92). And John the Revelator used the model of literary apocalypse to achieve the same goal as that of Matthew and Luke.

6. How likely is it that Mark would be familiar with Aristotle and classical dramatic principles? This question will be answered near the end of the essay.

7. Aristotle, Poetics I with the "Tractatus Coislinianus," A Hypothetical Reconstruction of "Poetics II," The Fragments of the "On Poets" trans. Richard Janko (Indianapolis: Hackett, 1987), 3-4.

8. Q, from the German *Quelle* (source), is a hypothetical document posited by NT scholars. Together with Mark's Gospel, Q served as the source for much of the material in Matthew and Luke. Like the apocryphal Gospel of Thomas, Q consisted almost exclusively of sayings and teachings attributed to Jesus, not his actions. N. T. Wright has pointed out that sayings Gospels like these were relatively inoffensive to the Roman hegemony because they were

unconnected to the story of Israel and Jesus and therefore lacked mythic impact. *The Last Word: Beyond the Bible Wars to a New Understanding of the Authority of Scripture* (New York: HarperSanFrancisco, 2005), 25-27.

9. According to Paul's letters, written prior to the Gospels, Jesus was a human being (Phil. 2:7, 8) genealogically descended from David (Rom. 1:3), and he was circumcised (Col. 2:11). His ministry was limited primarily to Israel (Rom. 15:7). He taught against divorce (1 Cor. 7:10-11) and that nothing is unclean in itself (Rom. 14:14). As to personality, he was meek and gentle (2 Cor. 10:1), and as to character, he was righteous, obedient (Rom. 5:8, 9), and knew no sin (2 Cor. 5:21). At the end of his life, on the night of his betrayal, he instituted the practice of the Lord's Supper (1 Cor. 11:23-26). Jesus died (Rom. 5:6, 6:1-11, 8:34, 14:9; 1 Cor. 15:3-8; 2 Cor. 4:10, 11; Gal. 2:19, 21; 3:1; Phil. 2:7-8; Col. 1:22; 1 Thess. 4:14) by crucifixion (Rom. 6:6; Gal. 3:13), and he suffered in the process (2 Cor. 1:5; 13:4). The ones who killed Jesus were the rulers and authorities of this age (1 Cor. 2:8; Col. 2:14, 15) and "the Jews" (1 Thess. 2:14, 15). After his death, Jesus was buried (Col 2:12; also see 1 Cor 15:3-8). Jesus was resurrected (Rom. 1:4, 6:1-11, 8:34, 14.9; 2 Cor. 4:14; Gal. 1:1; Phil. 2:7-8; 1 Thess. 4:14) and appeared to a variety of specified and unspecified persons after his death (1 Cor. 15:3-8) in a form that was spiritual, not fleshly (1 Cor. 15:35-49). This catalogue is the totality of what Paul had to say about the man Jesus.

10. Josephus' *Testimonium Flavianum* is one of the main early sources for information about Jesus. Scholars agree that, once the work's focal passage about Jesus is purged of accretions added by Christian scribes, it represents a summary of Jesus' life uncontaminated by Christian testimony. Scholars also agree that, among the genuine words of Josephus is the following sequence of sentences: "At this time there appeared Jesus, a wise man. For he was a doer of startling deeds, a teacher of people who receive the truth with pleasure." (Luke Timothy Johnson, *The Real Jesus: The Misguided Quest for the Historical Jesus and the Truth of the Traditional Gospels* [New York: HarperSanFrancisco, 1996], 114; Geza Vermes, *Jesus the Jew: A Historian's Reading of the Gospels* [Philadelphia: Fortress, 1981], 79.) It is possible, however, that the scribes who, influenced by Luke and Matthew, added Jesus' resurrection appearances to the *Testimonium*, drew also on the Gospel tradition to add "a doer of startling deeds." This phrase can be omitted without doing violence to the sentence structure, and the omission makes the sentence a clearer gloss on its predecessor: "At this time there appeared Jesus, a wise man. For he was a teacher of people who receive the truth with pleasure." Removing this phrase from Josephus eliminates all first-century, non-Gospel references to Jesus as a doer of deeds and suggests that this perception of him may have originated exclusively with Mark's portrayal.

11. Gilbert Bilezikian and Lawrence Wills, for instance, posit an ur-Gospel that Mark, acting as a redactor, edited to form his Gospel. Bilezikian seems to posit only an ur-Gospel tradition (16, 17, 140, 141). Wills argues for a well-developed proto-Gospel in written form (2-7); however, he admits that any attempt to reconstruct such a document, or even establish its probable existence, is problematic (156). In actuality, the primary features of the Gospel tradition, as sketched out by both Bilezikian and Wills, are present in Paul's kerygma: The preexistent Christ was born, suffered, died, and rose again. There is no reason to believe that anyone, prior to Mark, had pulled together a unified, detailed narrative of Jesus' life.

12. *Poetics*, 12.

13. *Poetics*, 18.

14. As a result of this methodology, arguments about the factuality of Jesus' deeds and words as reported in the Gospels are inconsequential as far as determining the authority of the Gospels for the life of the church. As N. T. Wright says, "There is a great gulf fixed between those who want to prove the historicity of everything reported in the Bible in order to prove that the Bible is 'true' after all and those who, committed to living under the authority of scripture, remain open to what scripture itself actually teaches and emphasizes" (95).

15. *Poetics*, 41.

16. Ibid., 7.

17. "The poet should put what is amazing into his tragedies; but what is improbable, from which amazement arises most, is more admissible in epic because the audience does not see the person in action" (Ibid., 35).

18. The effectiveness of Mark's compression has been demonstrated in modern times by British actor Alec McCowan, who successfully performed his one-man reading, St. Mark's Gospel, on Broadway and toured it around the world in the 1980s, and by Emmy-winning actor Wayne S. Turney who continued to offer touring productions of the performance in more recent years.

19. Note that Mark's merging of tragedy, epic, and Semitic literary forms fits clearly into Alastair Fowler's paradigm for the development of genres as outlined in his "The Life and Death of Literary Forms," *New Directions in Literary History*, ed. Ralph Cohen (Baltimore: Johns Hopkins University Press, 1974), 77-94. Accordingly, Mark's work was an innovative combination of old and new genres; Matthew's and Luke's Gospels fit with the second stage in which a genre settles into a classic unity; and John's Gospel would represent the final stage characterized by embellishment and inversion.

20. "A plot is not unified, as some suppose, if it concerns one single person. An indefinitely large number of things happens to one person, in which there is no unity. So too the actions of one person are many, but do not turn into a single action.... In composing the *Odyssey*, [Homer] did not put into his poem everything that happened to Odysseus.... But he constructed the *Odyssey* around a single action of the kind we are discussing.... So too the plot, since it is a representation of an action, ought to represent a single action" (*Poetics*, 11, 12).

21. *The Art of Poetry*, 165.

22. While Mark took his overall structure from classical dramaturgy, he drew on Hebraic traditions for the acts' internal organization. His primary Semitic literary device was the *chiasmus*, a configurative pattern that focuses on ideas and meanings rather than action. In a sophisticated chiasmus, the central concept may be framed by a series of convergent units: A, B, C, D, C', B', A'. Nils Wilhelm Lund traced the origins of the chiasmus to Middle Eastern sources (*Chiasmus in the New Testament: A Study in Formgeschichte* [Chapel Hill, N.C.: University of North Carolina Press, 1942], 128-36). He suggested that the Homeric writers may have borrowed the device from Mid-Eastern contacts, but he concluded that "the Greek idea of climax is expressed by the ladder (Greek, *kli max*), but the Hebrew

idea of climax, which seems to be the general Semitic idea, is that of two ladders" (136). Within the major units of his book Mark repeatedly arranged the subordinate units in chiasmic order. In Act 1, for instance, Mark used a chiasmus to focus the idea of Jesus becoming the new Moses:
A. Feeding the 5000 (6:30-34; cf. Moses and the manna)
B. Walking on the water (6:45-56; cf. Moses and the Red Sea)
C. Teaching about true righteousness (7:1-23; cf. Moses at Sinai)
B'. Healing Gentiles (7:24-37; contrast Moses and the desert raiders)
A'. Feeding the 4000 (8:1-10; cf. Moses and the manna)
Conclusion: A warning against the establishments (8:11-21; cf. the Mosaic blessings and curses). This chiasmus focuses attention on Jesus' establishment of the new standard of righteousness, framed by references to other Mosaic materials, with special attention to God's seal of approval on Moses and Jesus—the feeding of their two communities. It is concluded by a coda that warns against the hostility of other political and religious systems. Similar chiasmi provide the internal organization of Mark's other units as well.

23. Episodic structure was specifically criticized by Aristotle: "Among simple plots and actions, episodic tragedies are the worst. By 'episodic' I mean a plot in which there is neither probability nor necessity that the episodes follow one another. . . . It makes a great difference whether these events happen because of those or only after those" (*Poetics*, 13, 14).

24. "The second-best structure is that which some say is first, the tragedy which has a double structure like the *Odyssey*, and which ends in opposite ways for the better and worse persons. This structure would seem to be first because of the weakness of the audiences; the poets follow the spectators, composing to suit their wishes. But this is not the pleasure that comes from tragedy, but is more particular to comedy. There the bitterest enemies in the story, e.g. Orestes and Aegisthus, exit as friends at the conclusion, and nobody kills anyone else" (*Poetics*, 17).

25. *The Art of Poetry*, 165.

26. Barclay, *The Gospel of Mark*, rev. ed. (Philadelphia: Westminster, 1975), 5.

27. See, for instance, Barclay, 6; also Timothy J. Geddert, *Believers Church Bible Commentary: Mark* (Scottdale, Penn.: Herald, 2001), 16.

28. *Poetics*, Chapter 15.

29. Ibid., 19.

30. Ibid., 161.

31. *Poetics*, 20.

32. Interestingly, Matthew and Luke, who were guided more by Paul and less by Aristotle, typically modified Jesus' personality by removing or soft-pedaling the abrasive traits Mark ascribed to him.

33. *Poetics*, 19.

34. For instance, in reporting the cleansing of the leper (1:40-45), Mark made it clear that Jesus' physical contact with the pariah was a conscious decision; the leper says, "If you choose you can make me clean," and Jesus, reaching out to touch him, replies, "I do choose. Be made clean" (1:40-45). Again, in the walking on water incident, Mark manipulated the story to accent Jesus decision: inexplicably, Jesus intends to pass the struggling disciples and walk onward to land—until he detects their terror; then he modifies his plan, makes a decision motivated by pity, alters his course, and joins them (6:47-52).

35. Richard A. Burridge, *What Are the Gospels? A Comparison with Graeco-Roman Biography* (Cambridge: Cambridge University Press, 1992), 252.

36. Katharine B. Free, "Thespis and Moses: The Jews and the Ancient Greek Theatre" in *Theatre and Holy Script*, ed. Shimon Levy (Brighton: Sussex, 1999), 149-53. Bonz also mentions Ezekiel's play and, in addition, catalogues other late-B.C.E. dramatic and epic works by Jewish writers (*The Past as Legacy*, 27-29).

37. Bilezikian suggests that as a Greek speaker living in Rome, Mark would likely have attended the Greek tragedies that continued to be staged in the imperial capital throughout the 1st century C.E. similarly to the manner in which a Parisian living in London seeks out French productions of Racine (38).

38. Wright, 25-27, 62-64.

39. "The Greek Novel," 129.

24 Money or Business? A Case Study of Christian Virtue Ethics in Corporate Work (2008)

Scott Waalkes

What used to be called the Business section in my local paper and in *USA Today* is now called the Money section, and I suspect that these changes in nomenclature are not accidental but signal important shifts in postmodern business worth exploring.[1] The turn from business to money signals a process of abstraction away from the details of business operations toward the pursuit of financial goals as ends-in-themselves. Countering this trend, three virtues embedded in the Incarnation can encourage Christian businesspeople to work toward the Kingdom of God through attention to faithful, embodied work, to loving relationships, and to a hopeful humility.

The rest of this paper fleshes out the statements just made in two major sections. In the first section of the paper, I describe three problems: 1) The shift from business to money reflects the rise of monetary and financial measures over other aspects of business, which in turn reflects the ways in which "cash values" have become the measure of worth in affluent societies.[2] Although this problem has become increasingly apparent of late, Aristotle understood how the rise of money could lead to this outcome; thus, I will summarize his analysis briefly. 2) This shift intensifies the process of rationalization identified by Max Weber as a descent into the "iron cage" that reduces meaning and purpose in modern life to rational, instrumental means, to the exclusion of purposive ends.[3] 3) The shift from business to money suggests also that business managers might be learning to pursue goods external to the practice of business. As a result of the rise of monetary values and the growing emphasis on profitability, mangers are more likely to be distracted from the goods intrinsic to the success of their work. When tempted to pursue financial gain, business leaders will also be tempted to neglect the good of the business and of the larger community in which the business functions. They will attend less to their actual work than to the external goals of profits and shareholder values, whereas virtuous business requires attention to goods internal to the practice of good work—goods whose character it is to benefit all concerned.

In the second section of the paper, I argue that the virtues implicit in the Incarnation can offer potential remedies to each of our three problems, and I describe these remedies through a case study of the writings of Max DePree, the former CEO of Herman Miller, Inc. As Philippians 2 describes the Incarnation, Christ Jesus "made himself nothing, taking the very nature of a servant . . . [and] humbled himself and became obedient to death—even death on a cross" (Phil. 2:7-8). Imitating the humility of Christ, servant leaders can champion an embodied, relational and sacrificial model of business. A recognition of embodiment—a sense of "touch"—can help us focus on human persons and the building of long-term communities of work, in contrast to the short-term approach of valuing relationships in cash terms. The Incarnation reminds us to love people and attend to relationships as a central part of faithful discipleship. A sacrificial model of servant-leadership instills a sense of humility that runs counter to the pursuit of monetary gain. Instead of embodying an exclusive concern for the bottom line, Christian businesses can practice a humility that recognizes limits. I conclude that if business leaders, like all of us, "Seek first his kingdom and his righteousness" in daily work life, then material sufficiency should be added as well (Matt. 6:33). Although this vision of a Kingdom virtue ethic might sound utopian, ultimately it depends upon the theological virtues of faith, hope and love, divinely infused, in moral agents who promote more virtuous economic structures. The story of Max DePree suggests that it is possible to begin practicing Kingdom virtues with the infusion of divine grace even today.[4]

While this paper starts with deep and serious problems that caused the triumph of business over money, it ends with hope. By highlighting how Christian virtues can respond to these problems and how these virtues have been embodied in a real business by real people, we move from problems to constructive responses. In this spirit, the final section of the paper discusses conclusions and implications of this analysis for contemporary business practitioners. See Table 1 for a summary of the main argument.

Table 1. Summary of the Argument

Problem	Incarnational Christian Virtue that Responds to the Problem
Problem #1: The Rise of "Cash Values" in a Commercial Society	Practicing Embodiment and "Touch": Temperance Completed in Faith
Problem #2: Rationalization: Quantitative, Financial Measures of Worth	Practicing Covenantal Relationships: Justice Completed in Love
Problem #3: Seeking Goods External to Practice vs. Seeking Virtuous Work	Practicing Humility: Temperance Completed in Hope

Whether looking at the Enron scandal, the subprime mortgage mess or high gasoline prices, it is clear that we face a crisis of confidence in the financial systems driving so much of business in this postmodern age. Corporations fold and stock prices collapse; banks teeter on the brink of solvency; petroleum futures markets drive up the cost of driving and oil companies garner record profits, but ordinary people worry about the effects of corporations on their lives. Many have suggested corporate governance reforms or government programs to respond to the unease provoked by these crises. Yet the problems of business go deeper, into the role of money in our society, and possible solutions go deeper, into the role of virtuous persons who might resist the temptations of money. We will start by looking at three deep-rooted problems with the rise of money that Max Weber helps us to investigate.

Problem #1: The Rise of "Cash Values" in a Commercial Society: Thinking about the bottom line has become a societal preoccupation in modern, affluent societies, but this comes as no surprise to many observers. Just over a hundred years ago, Max Weber identified the spirit of capitalism as "the earning of more and more money, combined with the strict avoidance of all spontaneous enjoyment of life . . . ."[5] "Man is dominated by the making of money," writes Weber, "by acquisition as the ultimate purpose of his life. Economic acquisition is no longer subordinated to man as the means for the satisfaction of his material needs."[6] This triumph of money played no small part in Weber's worry that society was entering an iron cage. Weber noted that "in the United States, the pursuit of wealth, stripped of its religious and ethical meaning, tends to become associated with purely mundane passions, which often actually give it the character of sport."[7] Weber saw this pursuit as the logical outcome of a society that had secularized the Puritans' notion of an ascetic calling and lost any religious reasons for renunciation and hard work. While glorifying everyday pursuits, modern society had lost the teleological connection between work, self-denial and God.[8] Into the vacuum of meaning came the pursuit of the almighty dollar.

As Craig Gay illustrates clearly, other modern thinkers have worried about the ways in which "cash values" have intruded upon modern social life to the point that the "money metric" becomes the measure of all worth, filling the vacuum of meaning in secularized societies.[9] Similarly, Father John Kavanaugh worries that affluent societies have even begun to treat persons as commodities whose worth is dictated by their financial value, and Pope John Paul II increasingly stressed late in his life that a society in which "having" took precedence over "being" was devaluing human persons.[10] In such a society, it should come as no surprise that the poor and weak (whether unborn children, the handicapped, the unemployed or the aged) are in danger of being marginalized, since they contribute few tangible benefits to the monetary bottom line. By "cash value" standards, their worth is in question. Business executives, many of whom incidentally seek to employ the unemployed, handicapped or aged, are hardly unique in the habit of assessing their world around them in terms of monetary value, and they may resist this trend in order to support the idea of helping the weakest. But it is the growth of this habit of thinking—using money as the measure of worth, even of human persons—that concerns us, since it inculcates over time a dangerous temptation to measure worth (especially human worth) in monetary terms.[11]

A brief discussion of the philosopher Aristotle illustrates how the extensive use of money in a commercial society risks habituating its members into a process of abstraction away from the purpose of economic life and into the pursuit of money. In his *Politics*, Aristotle's ideal is that households or political communities should farm the land, fish the seas and cultivate the animals that nature provides, exchanging goods only when necessary to supplement what is lacking. Thus he makes a sharp distinction in his *Politics* between the legitimate acquisition of goods for household use (*oikonomia*) and the illegitimate pursuit of gain through exchange (*chremastistike*).[12] Aristotle contends that there is nothing wrong with barter exchanges and with households (or city-states) obtaining one type of useful goods by trading their own goods; for example, state A exchanging wheat for state B's corn. Such commerce seeks only "to re-establish nature's own equilibrium of self-sufficiency" and therefore fits the original goal and purpose (*telos*) of household management (economics).[13]

Unfortunately, in Aristotle's view, this rudimentary exchange brought about the need for currency, which quickly led to trade, in which people sought simply to gain wealth measured as coins. Such pursuit of monetary gain is contrary to nature, says Aristotle, because it seeks goals external to the production of goods for the welfare of the household or state and violates the purpose of money, which is to facilitate exchange. In his teleological account, one must always be attentive to the purposeful ends being pursued within the process of work itself, toward which the work is aiming. As Paul Wadell puts it, "the telos is not so much something toward which we move, but something in which we participate." He continues, "true, the telos represents the goal, the fulsome meaning of life. While it can be said that we advance toward that end through the virtues, the movement implied is not a change of place but a change of person. To Aristotle, a person moves toward the telos by being changed according to it."[14] All of the process in achieving the end is part of the end, and the dispositions of character (virtues or vices) formed along the way participate in achieving it.

Aristotle argues that the pursuit of monetary gain for its own sake as a *telos* can lead to some disturbing results: "And it will often happen that a man with wealth in the form of coined money will not have enough to eat; and what a ridiculous kind of wealth is that which even in abundance will not save you from dying with hunger!"[15] Holders of large amounts of Weimar German marks, Thai bahts, Indonesian rupiahs, Bolivian bolivianos or Argentine pesos—or any other currency that has suffered rapid devaluation or hyperinflation—can relate to the problem of money becoming meaningless paper. For that matter, holders of large amounts of Enron stocks or mortgage-backed bonds might relate also. Acquisition of credits or monetary gains can be wiped out easily by changes in the financial system that have little or nothing to do with tangible factors. Interestingly, many economists in the classical liberal tradition still distinguish between the purely financial and the "real" economy; Adam Smith's *Wealth of Nations* constantly presses the distinction between illusory financial wealth and real productive wealth. Similarly, the Consumer Price Index attempts to gauge the value of money relative to a basket of goods and services, and *The Economist* magazine ties exchange rates to the Big Mac as a tangible base, thereby distinguishing between currency fluctuations and real value.[16] On this question of real value versus currency value, modern economists follow

Aristotle, at least rhetorically, although in practice the pursuit of capital or money seems to be the point of capitalism.[17]

Although Adam Smith celebrated the benefits of trade and exchange based on money, Aristotle disdains such pursuits as harmful to virtue. He argues that trading that seeks monetary gain ends up encouraging people to seek wealth for the sake of wealth. Because there is no limit to the acquisitive impulse, the end is "sheer increase" rather than material provision for the community.[18] Of course, Smith argued that a person's pursuit of material gain will lead as if guided by an "invisible hand that was no part of his intention" to better material provision for the community.[19] But this increase is a byproduct and not a goal of private wealth seeking. By contrast, Aristotle's teleological approach is concerned with seeking the right goals (basic material needs) for the right reasons (for household or public provision) given a person's social role (as head of a household or a city) and with the right virtue (generosity) being embodied. Thus, he is concerned about the corrosive impact of greed on a community that allows extensive trade through currency usage, because money can allow one to seek an improper end (money for its own sake) rather than the proper ends of provision. Aristotle's comments echo contemporary concerns about modern business strikingly and therefore deserve more extensive quotation: "For where enjoyment consists in excess, men look for that which produces the excess that is enjoyed. And if they cannot procure it through money-making, they try to get it by some other means, using all their faculties for this purpose, which is contrary to nature: courage, for example, is to produce confidence, not goods; nor yet is it the job of military leadership and medicine to produce goods, but victory and health. But these people turn all skills into skills of acquiring goods, as though that were the end and everything had to serve that end."[20]

In an apt phrase, monetized societies run the risk of making "everything for sale," where the worth of health care, education or human personhood is measured in money terms.[21] When more and more skills are rewarded according to how well they help one obtain goods or acquire wealth (measured in currency), it ought not be surprising when students routinely ask in Christian college classrooms, "How will this help me get a job?" rather than "How is this part of my calling?" In a commercialized society, many such students will value education as a means to develop skills in order to acquire money, which is extrinsic to the practices of education, rather than entering with a willingness to develop virtuous habits intrinsic to the practices of education.[22] Similarly, Aristotle worries that a commercial society will be concerned with gaining material wealth for its own sake, without attention to goods internal to practices such as medicine. Such a society will reward the pursuit of extrinsic rather than intrinsic rewards, and money will be the measure of extrinsic reward. Doctors then become significant more because of their high salaries than because of their craft of healing. By seeking monetary gain as a major corporate goal, businesses have merely joined the dominant trend in a highly commercialized society (a trend anticipated by Aristotle). Their habits are our habits. We are all tempted to think about the bottom line and thus abstract ourselves away from the concrete contexts and purposes of shared activities such as education, health care or manufacturing. We are all tempted to assess worth in terms of monetary value.

Problem #2: Rationalization: Quantification and Profit as the Measure of Worth: A second harmful habit of modern business also relates to Max Weber's description of the iron cage of rationality: the triumph of a trend of rationalization. At the same time Weber was writing, Thorstein Veblen began to worry about the impact of capitalist industrialization upon society.[23] Already then, Veblen detected a trend toward the use of abstract and impersonal measures in management, criticizing the trend among large corporations to pursue financial gain rather than productive benefit for society; clearly, the drift from business to money started quite some time ago.[24] The same era saw the birth of Frederick Winslow Taylor's scientific management, which marked a crucial early use of quantitative measures to pursue rationalization and efficiency in business.[25] Cut off from concrete work oriented toward divine purposes, such quantitative measures became the standards of value for business and even society at large. Robert McNamara's mid-century story may well mark the apex of this trend. McNamara—a corporate star at Ford Motor Company, Secretary of Defense in the Kennedy administration and then president of the World Bank—got his start teaching at the Harvard Business School before he later applied quantitative techniques to studies of strategic bombing during World War II and to "body counts" during the Vietnam War. However, it was at the Ford Motor Company that McNamara made his major contribution to American business through the use of powerful quantitative tools.

McNamara's use of quantification to measure market share is illustrated vividly in his description of the adoption of the Ford Falcon in Errol Morris' documentary film, *The Fog of War*:

> They didn't have a market research organization [at Ford]. I set one up. The manager said to me, "What do you want me to study?" I said, "Find out who in the hell's buying the Volkswagens. Everybody says it's a no good car. It was only selling about twenty thousand a year, but I want to know what's going to happen. Is it going to stay the same, or go down, or go up? Find out who buys it."
>
> He came back six months later, he said, "Well, they're professors, and they're doctors and they're lawyers, and they're obviously people who can afford more."
>
> Well, that set me to thinking about what we in the industry should do. Was there a market we were missing? At this time nobody believed that Americans wanted cheaper cars. They wanted conspicuous consumption. Cadillac, with these huge ostentatious fins, set the style for the industry for ten or fifteen years. And that's what we were up against.
>
> We introduced the Falcon as a more economical car, and it was a huge success profitwise. We accomplished a lot.[26]

This story appears under the heading of Lesson Number 6 from McNamara in the film, significantly entitled "Get the Data." Quantitative measures are extremely important to him, and he draws readily on numbers here, as he does throughout the interviews in the film. Today the kind of market research that went into the Ford Falcon is so common that it is unremarkable, suggesting that we have become accustomed to quantitative, market-driven estimates of demand. But there may be a danger in seeking habitually to cater to demand outside the corporation without attending to internal habits of doing excellent work that meets societal needs naturally. When Ford's new Edsel model sold poorly, the response was to commission a buyers' survey to recruit customer loyalty to the brand, when the car itself might have been the problem.[27]

It is significant also that in telling his story, McNamara defines success "profitwise" rather than in terms of the teamwork that produced the car, the quality of the car itself, or the ecological benefits of smaller cars. Profit focuses on results but not the work going into the results. On this note, the journalist David Halberstam contrasts McNamara's (and the Ford Motor Company's) emphasis with Japanese business practices in his book *The Reckoning*. In Halberstam's account, McNamara is blamed for an obsessive focus on production numbers and quantitative measures of efficiency—to the detriment of the physical craft of making cars: "Numbers were not just a belief but more like a theology to him. Cars themselves were almost secondary."[28] Instead of factory men running the company, according to Halberstam, the financial "whiz kids" gained the power to run the organization under McNamara's influence. "The realities of manufacturing meant less and less; what those realities should be, according to Detroit's numbers, meant more and more."[29] By contrast, the Nissan company, according to one former Ford executive who was hired by Nissan to run its first Tennessee plant, "had learned long ago that manufacturing was basic to quality."[30] Instead of allowing short-term financial considerations to dictate the building of a manufacturing plant, Nissan was willing to take five years before the plant turned a profit. Surely stock market analysts would put more pressure for short-term profits on a publicly traded American corporation. But the point here is about the culture of leadership that Robert McNamara helped to instill at Ford Motor Company— the culture that focused on meeting quantitative targets for production, market share and profit, the culture that promoted short-term efficiency goals to minimize waste and maximize earnings—all types of rationalization in Weberian terms. Weber worried that it could be said of people in his age that they were "specialists without spirit, sensualists without heart."[31] Unfortunately, as we will see, former business executive Max DePree likely would concur that such a description applies to many executives today.

McNamara's Weberian practices—notably the quantification of profits as a "rational" indicator of corporate health and maximum efficiency—have only increased since the 1970s, when financial investors began to take back influence from the managerial class that was largely in control of American corporations until that time.[32] Whereas McNamara was concerned with financial controls over business operations, it is clear that the contemporary era has made financial goals its central concern.[33] As just one example of such a contemporary emphasis, Jim Collins' study *Good to Great* used stock values and profits as measures of business improvement.[34] Lawrence Mitchell cites "a recent survey of more than four hundred chief financial officers of major corporations [that] revealed that almost 80 percent of them would have at least moderately mutilated their businesses in order to meet analysts' quarterly profit estimates."[35] Not only does the common use of profit benchmarks reflect the triumph of rationalized finance over other aspects of business management, but it also reflects convenience. Such measures are attractive, in part, because they are understood easily and are easy to communicate, whereas qualitative descriptions of physical work are more cumbersome to understand and communicate. Yet when financial goals become ends in themselves, there is the danger that leaders are not only diverted to pursue goods outside the daily operation of the business, but are also diverted from attending to critical factors within daily operations. They may even "mutilate" those daily operations, losing sight of their main purposes. It is no accident that by the 1980s Ford ran a national advertising campaign claiming that at Ford, "Quality is Job One." Many in Detroit believed that the triumph of "bean counters" over the "car guys" had led to the erosion of quality in the cars themselves due to a focus on profits and increasing value for shareholders.[36]

At the same time, however, the practices of finance can (although not necessarily will) accomplish moral aims in business through stewardship of resources. Maximizing efficiency, calculating profits, discovering hidden markets and increasing value for owners all might be desirable goods in assisting the primary process of crafting one's products or services and serving needs. No one is recommending that financial stewardship be ignored. But the practical and moral effect of pursuing financial goods habitually over time should worry Christian ethicists, especially if such goods become the most important goals and detach themselves from the practices of the work itself. When the goal of profit becomes detached from the pursuit of proper goals, businesses may turn away from serving customers well and stop providing excellent goods and services that benefit society. They will then contribute to a "speculation economy," where "business management focused on production is replaced with business management focused on stock price."[37] When executives at Enron and MCI/WorldCom detached financial considerations from underlying fundamentals, for instance, they were falling prey to such speculative thinking with disastrous results. Although more effective corporate governance structures and better audits would help to prevent such disasters, these measures fail to address the underlying trend toward the pursuit of monetary gain—a trend that schools executives in non-virtuous habits. Consider stock options, whose value varies depending on the date on which they are exercised. Executives can arrange to have those options back-dated so that they are cashed in at the time when the stock value is highest. Equities, then, no longer become ways of owning part of an enterprise; they become ways of maximizing wealth.

Some of these techniques might be defended as mechanisms of healthy rationalization. Creative executive compensation plans or the quantification of stock prices might be ways of bringing rational discipline to an organization. While some discipline is desirable, however, there is a danger that the bottom line can become the major purposive aim driving the work instead of the aim of providing excellent goods or services that benefit neighbors. Rationalization can backfire if it is not kept in check by a commitment to the larger societal good and divine teleology.

Problem #3: Seeking Goods External to Practice vs. Virtuous Work: Today, then, we worry that profit, increased stock values and (closely related) executive compensation win out all too often over good work and attention to the work itself. So I want to focus here on what I consider the root problem for postmodern business: the lack of attention to the more tangible goods internal to the practice of business, the loss of purposive attention to actual work. What alternatives can a Christian virtue ethic offer?

If we consider the Sermon on the Mount, Christian businesspeople ought to believe in faith that if they seek the Kingdom within their day-to-day activities, business success will be added. If they seek to improve the bottom line too much, they contravene the advice of Jesus not to worry (Mt. 6:25-34), and out of fear they may well lose their focus on the actual work of their business. Certainly those corporations that attend more to financial increase than to the warp and woof of daily operations risk losing attentiveness to their main purposes for existing as a business. They are pursuing goods external to the practice of their work and are neglecting goods internal to its practice, and that may well have something to do with losing sight of the role of business in the larger world. For those committed to biblical faith in God the Creator, after all, business is embedded within that larger reality of God's economy of the Kingdom. Wendell Berry evokes this embeddedness beautifully in his essay "Two Economies," where he writes:

> Work that is authentically placed and understood within the Great Economy moves virtue toward virtuosity: skill and technical competence.... When they are rightly practiced within the Great Economy, we do not call the virtues virtues; we call them good farming, good forestry, good carpentry, good husbandry, good weaving and sewing, good housewifery, good parenthood, good neighborhood, and so on. The general principles are submerged in the particularities of their engagement with the world.... The work of the small economy, when it is understandingly placed within the Great Economy, minutely particularizes the virtues, carries principle into practice, and to the extent that it does so it escapes specialization.[38]

Berry suggests that specialization—say, the separation of business activity into the functions of marketing, public relations, accounting finance, management and so on—is linked closely with the loss of seeing the Great Economy (or household) of God's Kingdom. It is also linked with the loss of attentiveness to the mission of a business. When functions are compartmentalized, it is easy for workers within different departments to lose sight of their larger organizational mission in the Great Economy of God. Indeed, it is possible that different departments will be evaluated and compensated by quantitative standards that conflict with each other.[39]

In a vacuum of purpose or a clash of purposes, it is then easy for one part of the business to hijack the mission. If we accept David Halberstam's diagnosis of the Ford

Motor Company's problems, the finance division hijacked Ford's mission by the early 1960s. Certainly this story has been replicated frequently within our own day.

The problem is that monetary goals are goods external to the practice of work, and this harms the "work of the small economy" itself. Alasdair MacIntyre notes that a key characteristic of external goods is that "they are always some individual's property and possession . . . [and] therefore characteristically objects of competition in which there must be losers as well as winners."[40] By pursuing increased stock value over other goods, executives with stock options profit personally, often to the detriment of workers who are paid a tiny fraction of executive compensation. Clearly this is pursuit of an external good by MacIntyre's definition. By contrast, he argues, goods internal to practices "are indeed the outcome of competition to excel, but it is characteristic of them that their achievement is a good for the whole community who participate in the practice."[41] Good farming, good carpentry, or good weaving, to evoke Wendell Berry again, benefits the farmers, the carpenters, the weavers, and the whole community. Yet if "good business" is defined solely in terms of profits, then that harms the larger community by taking resources that may or may not be employed for the productive gain of the community. Here again Aristotle would be concerned about the possibility of vice, returning to the distinction between legitimate household provision and illegitimate monetary gain.

Among other business ethicists, Dennis McCann and Robert Solomon have advanced helpful versions of Aristotle's business ethics to describe the possibility of both corporate vice and corporate virtue.[42] While the idea of corporate vice is familiar in light of the Microsoft antitrust case, the Enron scandal or the WorldCom collapse, the idea of corporate virtue might sound unusual. Yet it is essential to assessing any positive mission for business in a postmodern world. D. Stephen Long suggests that "we would expect a good and faithful corporation to contribute directly or indirectly to the theological virtues of faith, hope, and charity . . . ."[43] If we can imagine such an operation, how would we assess it? Later we will add a theological element, but first, because all moral action for Aristotle is teleological, we can only assess whether actions are virtuous in relation to their immediate and ultimate ends within a context.[44] MacIntyre characterizes these immediate ends as goods internal to practices, defining virtue as "an acquired human quality the possession and exercise of which tends to enable us to achieve those goods . . . and the lack of which effectively prevents us from achieving any such goods."[45] In Aristotle's view, one must find the mean when pursuing the good within any given activity, avoiding the extremes that are either deficiencies or excesses of character and that deter one from achieving the good.[46]

What might virtuous business look like? MacIntyre uses the hypothetical example of someone founding "a school, a hospital, or an art gallery," to illustrate.[47] We can take this example to refer to the founders of any other kind of business. The founders or their successors, he writes, "would need to value—to praise as excellences—those qualities of mind and character which would contribute to the realization of their common good or goods."[48] These would be the virtues inherent in the pursuit of the good. In addition, the founders would need "to identify certain types of action as the doing or the production of harm of such an order that they destroy the bonds of community in such a way as to render the doing or achieving of good impossible in some respect at least for some time."[49] These would be defined as vices. MacIntyre points out that harmful vices could be either deficiencies (sins of omission or falling short) or offenses (sins of commission). Both types of offenses, he writes, "injure the community to some degree and make its shared project likely to be less successful."[50] Conversely, virtues are those actions that build the community and allow its shared project to be more successful (in the long run) by contributing to the larger social good. The nascent school, hospital, or art gallery community would compile descriptions of both categories to teach its members the positive goods to seek and what to avoid. Although these descriptions sound much like corporate mission statements and codes of conduct, without a real commitment to shared mission, such documents will not have life within an organization. The organization must be a true community. With this strong understanding of communal mission, it might be hard to imagine rugged American individualists or business students talking in such terms.[51] Yet, as we will see, the writings of Max DePree illustrate a business leader thinking in ways consonant with MacIntyre's description.

The implications of virtue ethics for business managers are obvious. If leaders are to be ethical, they must cultivate their own virtuous character, seek the goods intrinsic to the unique practice of their business, promote the habits that foster the success of their communities, and find the proper balance of considerations in their actions along the way. But what would all this really mean for them? Solomon argues that business ethics is a matter of individual character and social responsibility, of the well-being of the person, and the well-being of the corporation-as-community, writing that an Aristotelian "approach to business ethics is, perhaps, just another way of saying that people come before profits."[52]

But Solomon's approach falls short in two ways. First, it falls short of a true virtue ethic. The "people" to whom Solomon refers appear to be those within the corporation, but a virtue ethic must include the community as a whole.[53] After all, Aristotle defines the political community as an extension of the friendships that he thinks are essential for the virtues to flourish. In other words, the city-state—the locus of virtue for Aristotle—ideally should "be a community of friends, the locus of civic friendship."[54] If leaders and followers in business are to work virtuously, in Aristotle's view, they must foster such friendship. But do they view their work as fostering friendships among their co-workers? A focus on profits alone fails to wrestle with this question. Does the business foster friendship with communities outside it? Aristotle says at the very beginning of the *Nicomachean Ethics* that ethical inquiry is a kind of political science because politics deals with the highest question: What is good for the people and the city? Are corporations good for the wider community?

Second, what about the Kingdom? A Christian virtue ethic must bring us closer to the Great Economy of the Kingdom, but Solomon's account ignores the wider theological community within which the corporation is embedded. A Christian virtue ethicist must not neglect the ultimate ends toward which our actions are aiming or the contexts in which they are embedded. We can only understand our immediate ends as they are embodied in larger social, political, ethical, and theological contexts. For Aristotle, the city-state was the highest form of community that gave shape to ethics, but for Christians the Kingdom of God (or communion with God) is the highest form of community and any business that fails to operate without attention to that community will fall short of the mark.[55] Can we imagine corporations as communities that foster friendship with God? Without this locus of virtue, it seems, corporations cannot participate fully in the Great Economy of the Kingdom.

But even if they participate partially in that economy, can we imagine how that would look? To quote Wendell Berry again, if the work of the business could be "understandingly placed within the Great Economy," which is the Kingdom of God, it might be possible for "the general principles [of virtue to be] submerged in the particularities of their engagement with the world."[56] It might then be possible to imagine a situation where successful businesses were ethical businesses, where excellent business practice might also flourish financially, where those who "race to the bottom" globally with environmentally harmful or harsh labor practices might no longer be rewarded with rising profit rates. Would greater concern for the tangible practices of producing goods or services within a business help business people work virtuously within their crafts? The next section will describe how three virtues closer to the Kingdom might be realized in business—business understood as attentive work rather than the pursuit of money.

But business ethicists will protest: we do not need to imagine a situation in which ethical businesses attentive to their tangible work succeed; such businesses exist already and they do succeed (sometimes).[57] It is indeed possible to find examples of some business practices that represent God's holiness, justice and love more faithfully than others.[58] So far, the argument has depended on Aristotle's ethics, but at this point I turn to the story of the Incarnation to ground theologically an alternative ethic to the pursuit of money. I want to describe virtuous business practices based upon the more distinctly Christological truth of the Incarnation— a supreme expression of the economy of God's Kingdom—thereby showing how an Aristotelian virtue approach is completed in a Christian theology that takes business closer to true faith, hope and love.[59] Acting on this faith, hope, and love, a Christian executive should come closer to the self-emptying, servant leadership of Christ in Philippians 2 than to the spirit of the aggressive, self-confident, highly compensated CEO of popular culture.[60]

This may sound like a high ideal or an unrealistic vision. But the writings of Max DePree suggest that it is possible to embody parts of this vision, just as it is possible for many Christians to be relatively faithful disciples in a number of callings in a wide variety of settings (even though their walk as disciples also might call them into conflict with those settings). DePree makes his Christian faith no secret, and it is evident that this faith informed his approach to business life, offering a compelling challenge to the dominance of financial goals over business and a call to return to something closer to the vision of the Great Economy. In this section, I will highlight three aspects of the Incarnation that DePree models, demonstrating how they respond to the three problems identified earlier.

When the church celebrates the mystery of the Incarnation at Christmas, it is reenacting a deep truth that goes to the heart of the faith—the truth that the Word of God became flesh in the womb of a Virgin, only to suffer and die an unjust death, before being raised to new life and ascending to heaven, from where he reigns over a Kingdom that already exists on earth but is not yet fully come. Without reducing the meaning of Christ's Incarnation to any one theme, this story schools us in at least three virtues that challenge the ascendance of money in business practice and promote hopeful alternatives. Each of these can be illustrated in DePree's writings.

First, God creates humans in his image out of dust (Gen. 1:26-27; Gen. 2:7, Gen. 3:19), an earthiness that Jesus' birth affirms and echoes. This earthiness suggests that God valued the dust of humanity enough to enter Mary's womb, and likewise he values us enough to send his Holy Spirit to blow into our frail frames of dust; God is attentive to human embodiment. Therefore, business practices that pursue "cash values" to the neglect of the physical details of the actual provision of goods or services disdain our earthiness. They are abstracted, averting attention from daily work. Crafting widgets with a team of fellow workers and spending time with clients, after all, appear much less glamorous than divvying up profits. But which is closer to the core functions of a business? And which is more in tune with the work of the Spirit in blowing within our dusty frames?

Max DePree strongly advocates a philosophy of "touch" that responds to such questions. This attention to touch aligns with DePree's close attention to the daily work environment, which surely stems from the nature of Herman's Miller's business of designing and building office furniture systems. "At the core of becoming a leader," says DePree, "is the need always to connect one's voice and one's touch."[61] In *Leadership is an Art*, DePree writes: "In a difficult and fractured and complex world, in problems of failure and success, but especially in the joys and tragedies of our personal lives, we touch each other. This 'touching' is at the heart of who we are."[62] And this sense of touch is part of a holistic and integrative understanding of work: "We need to understand and be 'at home' in our working environment—both the human environment and the physical environment. There needs to be a visible order and a 'sense of place' so that we may know who we are and where we fit."[63] DePree returns to the link between touch and the social purpose of work when discussing buildings: "A facility should be a place of realized potential. It should be a 'high touch' place."[64] With attention to social purpose and context, he writes: "It is important that everyone understand the context in which our facilities function and the context and value they create for us."[65] Here we see attentiveness to human embodiment, rather than the abstraction advocated by leaders like Robert McNamara. Attention to the larger social and physical context means that DePree regularly criticizes a narrow focus on financial measures only:

> We don't have to connect every decision about our environment or product design or trees or signage solely to first costs or return on assets or the eternal shortage of parking. Achieving a prescribed return on assets is not part of the

law of the Medes and Persians, you know. It's only one of a long list of items for which we are accountable. Decisions on the beauty and harmony of an environment are not the province of the financial department or the developer or even the person who owns the land. These decisions are the proper concern of an enormous public, since no one can walk through the results of such decisions without encountering the consequences. Once a building is up or a tree is grown, it belongs to all of us.[66]

Closer to Wendell Berry than to McNamara, DePree attends here to the "high touch" context in which his business operated. Attending to "touch," we might say, is a way of resisting the abstract pursuit of money and having faith in the goodness of the material creation. For Aquinas, sensory touch is the basis of our embodied senses and part of the virtue of temperance.[67] We must trust our embodied-ness, since surely God did. In response, we handle our embodied selves with care and "creational joy" through the gift of faith.[68]

Second, the Incarnation shows how God values an embodiment that requires community and harmonious relationships, challenging the pursuit of abstract notions such as profits. Being created in the image of the Trinitarian God implies that we are created for relationships, just as the Godhead—Father, Son and Holy Spirit—is a relational community of persons. Furthermore, since Jesus was born of a woman, born into a family, born into a village, and born into friendships, the Incarnation affirmed social life. Therefore, Christian financial practices should reflect the operation of God's relational economy, an operation summed up by D. Stephen Long this way: "The principle is quite simple: money does no work; people do. So when we assume our money to be working for us to make more money, we have not accurately described God's economy."[69] And yet by detaching money from relational contexts, we are putting our money to work for us—without bothering to figure out who our money is affecting or how it is affecting them, without attending to the internal goods and ultimate purposes toward which money is being put. Thus, writes Long: "We lose the ability to describe how our lives are embedded in the narratives of others. The food that we eat, the clothes we wear, the transportation available to us, clean restrooms, floors, etc.—all these things are provided for us without any awareness on our part of the practices that make such external goods possible. We cannot name our debts; thus we cannot pray well."[70] Both churches and businesses ought to be places where we embed money within relationships to real people rooted in time and place who bring us the food, the clothes, the transportation, the clean restrooms, and all the rest. A church that rehearses the story of Christmas rightly will form people who care about what money does for or to others. They ought to be attentive to the relationships that their money and business activity support or fail to support.

DePree contends in his writings that humans are created for relationship and function better when relationships take precedence over profit. He makes a sharp distinction between short-term, contractual and long-term, covenantal relationships, strongly advocating the latter.[71] Hence, he writes, "I am convinced that the best management process for today's environment is participative management based on covenantal relationships. Look for the 'good goods' of quality relationships that prevail in a corporation as you seek to serve."[72] One might expect a biblical emphasis on covenantal relationships to be exclusive, sectarian, or divisive, but DePree echoes regularly the Apostle Paul's elegant metaphors about the diversity of gifts in the body (Rom. 12:3-10; 1 Cor. 12; Eph. 4:11-16). DePree treasures the diversity of gifts that people can bring to work. "We are God's mix," he writes. "We are made in His image."[73] A leader is one who "cherishes heterogeneity and diversity."[74] Bringing harmony out of this diversity, like leading a jazz band, requires work. But the results can be exciting: "When we think about the people with whom we work, people on whom we depend, we can see that without each individual we are not going to get very far as a group. By ourselves we suffer serious limitations. Together we can be something wonderful."[75] Unlike many executives, DePree contends that "relationships count more than structure."[76] Friendships and "intimacy" between employees were something he sought to encourage in practice at Herman Miller.[77] Yet achieving intimacy is difficult: "In our group activities, intimacy is betrayed by such things as politics, short-term measurements, arrogance, superficiality, and an orientation toward self rather than toward the good of the group."[78] Hence, "Leadership is more tribal than scientific, more a weaving of relationships than an amassing of information."[79] Viewing a business as a set of friendships and relationships oriented toward shared goods sounds more like a Christian version of Aristotle than arrogant "top-down" leadership. Such a view recognizes the Incarnational reality of our relationships to God and to each other.

This attention to relationships was put into practice under DePree's leadership. One of the most striking manifestations of Herman Miller's commitment to building relationships came in its employee stock ownership plans and profit sharing plans. In discussing these plans, DePree says, "There is a certain morality in connecting shared accountability as employees with shared ownership. This lends a rightness and a permanence to the relationship of each of us to our work and to each other."[80] Such plans create a situation where "ownership demands a commitment to be as informed about the whole as one can be."[81] Is it possible for businesses to structure pay plans that weave relationships together around the common purpose of the organization? Aristotle would call this good politics, in the sense of governing the whole community in ways that contribute to the flourishing of all in relation to the larger good for all—quite a contrast from the common story of heavily compensated CEOs who care little for how that looks to ordinary workers and how that undermines the common mission of the organization. It is no accident that DePree advocated Herman Miller's policy of limiting the CEO's annual cash compensation to no more than twenty times the average pay of a factory worker.[82] The starting point, in DePree's view, is to view people as persons and not as quantities to be manipulated for the bottom line.[83] "Likewise," writes DePree, "a short-term look at the financial status of a corporation or a dependence on immediate financial results will lead to a partial and perhaps twisted view of the whole picture."[84] Here we have a clear picture of the importance of attending to long-term relationships with whole persons taking precedence over profits.

And these relationships are not limited to those within the corporation. They extend to the larger society. "It seems to me," writes DePree, "that our value system and world view should be as closely integrated into our work lives as they are integrated into our lives with our families, our churches, and our other activities and groups"[85] To conserve those values, DePree argues that every group needs a "tribal storyteller" and that, "the penalty for failing to listen [to tribal storytellers] is to lose one's history, one's historical context, one's binding values."[86] Not only must a business be a storied people, in DePree's view, but it must practice the virtue of justice.[87] Two expressions of justice outside of Herman Miller that DePree cites are its commitment to environmental stewardship and to voluntary work for agencies "whose purpose is the common good. We cannot live our lives isolated from the needs of society."[88] Living in just relationships that extend to the larger society helps us to re-embed business practices within a larger context of the common good, thereby helping us escape the iron cage of blind pursuit of money. Instead of loving money, a Christian business person loves her neighbors and the Creator God who initiates and sustains that love.[89]

A third virtue implicit in the Incarnation is the virtue of humility, the exercise of which helps one to attend to the goods internal to the practice of business rather than seek financial gain arrogantly for its own sake. Humility can be defined as having a realistic appraisal of oneself in relation to God, the world, and others.[90] And certainly such humility should extend to one's appraisal of financial goals relative to other goals in a corporation's mission—and relative to society and God. Certainly the humility embodied between the members of the Body of Christ can inform how those members work so that their work should look more like virtuous work that contributes to the Kingdom. We have a model for these practices, the ultimate mystery of self-imposed limitation: The Creator of the universe is willing to enter Mary's womb and be born as a human child, to grow as a child, and to die as a young adult. We are reminded here that we are called to humility and self-emptying. To evoke Philippians 2 again, profits and advantage are not "something to be grasped," but only something that flows from self-sacrificing service. Aristotle worried that a commercial society that used money would free itself from the limited purposes of business (material provision) and would pursue monetary gain arrogantly for its own sake, but the church in its Christmas pageants, sermons, and hymns rehearses Christ's story of emptying himself and embracing limits. Thomas Merton writes, "if we accept this Infant as our God, then we accept our own obligation to grow with Him in a world of arrogant power and travel with Him as He ascends to Jerusalem and to the Cross, which is the denial of power."[91] Paul invokes God's self-emptying embrace of limitations specifically in order to illustrate an attitude of humility (Phil. 2:1-4). A church that lives out of the Incarnation should inculcate self-sacrificial humility in its members, including those members that enter the business world.

DePree advocates an other-centered style of leadership, epitomized by his metaphor of a jazz band: "The leader of a jazz band has the beautiful opportunity to draw the best out of the other musicians . . . . [T]he leader must become a servant and a debtor."[92] After returning to the Christ-like virtues of service to others, he writes, "the measure of leadership is not the quality of the head, but the tone of the body. The signs of outstanding leadership appear primarily among the followers."[93] Hence, his advice: "Try to think about a leader, in the words of the gospel writer Luke, as 'one who serves.'"[94] Using Christian language, DePree says that leaders must practice "reconciliation," and that such a process cannot be hierarchical.[95] He seemed to practice what he preached. Throughout his books, he describes ordinary Herman Miller employees whose work he admired or who came to him with problems. He made it a practice to meet once a month with twelve to fifteen employees with no agenda other than to listen.[96] Humility emerges in some of the questions that leaders should ask themselves (according to DePree): "How long ago was it that I actually saw the products my business sells being made?" And, "How often do I say 'I don't know'?"[97] He links humility to attentiveness to the actual process of making goods or providing services, closer to the "good carpentry" that Berry advocates. Instead of pursuing goods external to practice such as profits, humble service to the mission of an organization at least imitates Christlike service to the Kingdom. While profits are "normal and essential . . . Why we get those results is more important."[98] Vince Lombardi said once that winning wasn't everything; it was the only thing. But DePree worries about business managers who think that profit is the only thing: "Profit gives us the chance to make a difference in the world, but profit is never more than a by-product."[99] The humble pursuit of servant leadership comes first and then results should be added to us.[100] Such humility is a kind of high-minded temperance that recognizes that one is not God, relying on "an unshakable firmness of hope . . . and the perfect peace of a fearless heart."[101] Knowing that we are not God liberates us. But to sustain humility we must receive the infused virtue of hope, trusting that the humble self-sacrifice of the Cross does in fact redeem the world through divine love and that our own sacrifices are not in vain. The question is whether our business practices are hopeful enough to participate in and emulate divine love. One hopes they could be.

In contrast to proud managers who would emulate the likes of Robert McNamara, DePree argues that humble leaders should realize that financial success is only a byproduct of success in work, not a central concern. Perhaps for this reason, he states: "Being faithful is more important than being successful. If we are successful in the world's eyes but unfaithful in terms of what we believe, then we fail."[102] As he puts it in *Leadership Jazz*, "good work is the goal; recognition is a consequence."[103] It is hard to imagine a clearer defense of the idea that one should seek goods internal to practices for the right reasons. Thus, DePree's work and writings form a contrast to those business leaders who have become enamored with monetary gain as a good external to the daily practices of good work. Instead, he argues for attention to one's work that will find one's character developed along the way. First, he champions an incarnational approach to "touch" that attends to the physical work environment and the embodied human persons in a business. Second, he supports an incarnational imperative to orchestrate harmony out of long-term relationships within the corporation, within the larger society and within Creation, in relation to shared purposes. And third, he promotes an incarnational form of servant leadership with humility. In short, his attention to the development of the virtues within business itself, rather than to the pursuit of money, suggests that the pursuit of Kingdom virtues is partially realizable even in American business today.

Through the DePree case study, I sought to demonstrate that a "good and faithful corporation" (to quote Long again) can contribute to virtue and thereby bring business practice closer to the Great Economy of the Kingdom. In contrast to the pursuit of monetary values, a Kingdom business approach practices the Incarnational virtue of embodiment and attentiveness to physical realities—a virtue completed in faith in the goodness of Creation. In contrast to rationalization trends that focus on profits, a Kingdom business approach practices the Incarnational virtue of engaging in covenantal relationships that include wider communities—a virtue completed in receiving and sharing the gift of love of God and our neighbors. In contrast to the pursuit of financial goods external to the practice of sound work, a Kingdom business approach practices the Incarnational virtue of humility and servant leadership—a virtue completed in the Christian hope that the greatest sacrifice of self-emptying ends in exaltation.

If the story of the Kingdom has any meaning, we can hope that Christian business leaders would embody the virtues of the Incarnation chapter of that story, thereby challenging the "cash values" of profit-driven workplaces that neglect the mundane matters of work in favor of external goods that harm communities and Creation. Instead of thinking about business as making money, we might once again think of it as doing good work that participates in divine work.

If Christian business leaders began to operate with such a model of good and virtuous Kingdom work, what might that look like? In the so-called human resources area, it would start with friendships oriented toward common virtuous purposes within companies. Fostering friendship recognizes both our embodiment and our need for life in just and loving communities. I believe we know these when we see these and when we do not see these in the organizations within which we work. Dennis Bakke quotes an Oxford professor who says, "There's a real difference between saying to your workers, 'We care about your welfare because we do,' and saying, 'We care about your welfare because that will make you work harder for us.' Employees can tell when values are genuine and when they're adopted for ulterior purposes."[104] Promoting genuine friendships around shared moral purposes will bypass such hypocrisy altogether. Organizations driven by a strong mission that is devoted to justice and the good of others can bond groups of friends together in pursuing the mission. The proper analogy here, of course, is the church at its best. Corporations must never replace the work of the church, but surely they can learn from it by analogy and participate in the Kingdom.

Practicing Christian virtue in business would also require taking risks rooted in the faith and hope that the Kingdom will triumph. It would entail making decisions primarily on the grounds of whether they promote virtue rather than on short-term or even long-term financial grounds. The real test here is whether businesspeople have the faith to make virtuous decisions even when such decisions are financially risky or guaranteed to cut into profits: Is it worth doing the right thing even when it causes you to lose money (at least in the short-term)? We must admit that sometimes moral excellence may get in the way of business effectiveness.[105] If you are competing against Machiavelli, who has no scruples, you may lose out. While there are often situations where companies can "do well (financially) by doing good," the tricky cases are those where doing the right thing will cause a loss of profits or risk the closure of a business. Fully aware that sometimes "nice guys do finish last" and fully aware of what happened to Jesus for his steadfast attention to the end of his work—death on a cross—I would not want to claim that all ethical businesses succeed.

But here is where faith and hope—trust in the economy of God's Kingdom—enter the discussion and challenge the fear that rules business life all too often. The great fear in all market systems is that cheating and ethical shortcuts will win out, a fear modeled in the "defectors" in the game theory matrix of the Prisoners' Dilemma. To use the language of game theory, if two competing companies, one Christian and one non-Christian, act for short-run material gain, the strategy of defecting (forsaking virtue) will be the dominant one in this scenario (cell 4 in Table 2).

Table 2. A Prisoners' Dilemma Model of Market Logic

	Machiavelli Company practices virtue	Machiavelli Company seeks profit without virtue
Christian Company practices virtue	1	2
Christian Company seeks profit without virtue	3	4

To explicate the logic behind this last statement—and the logic of this table—let us say that our Christian Company practices virtue in the hope that it and the Machiavelli Company both end up in cell 1; this is the best of all possible worlds, with both companies practicing virtue. But the Christian Company knows that the Machiavelli Company likely will put aside moral scruples to benefit the bottom line; after all, the name alone should be a cue! Likely this will put the Christian Company at a competitive disadvantage relative to the Machiavelli Company, locking up Christian Company in cell 2, the worst possible situation, since it hamstrings the company against competition. In fact, it might put the Christian Company out of business while the Machiavelli Company rakes in record profits. So, for the sake of effectiveness, for the sake of keeping the business alive, for the sake of being relevant to the system by staying in it, what is to prevent the Christian Company from sacrificing ethical practices for the sake of financial gains? Indeed, the temptation is great, because the worst that could happen for Christian Company would be that both companies go straight for profit and compete on an equal basis (cell 4)—even though this is the worst outcome from the standpoint of virtue. And if the Machiavelli Company suddenly has an epiphany and starts implementing socially and environmentally responsible practices that cut into profits, Christian Company might be able to seize a competitive advantage (putting it in cell 3). Virtue may not be its own reward, and virtue might lead to failure. Therefore, it is safer to let profits trump it.

Of course, this highly simplified, purely hypothetical scenario assumes that Christian Company and Machiavelli Company have a choice, which means that they are privately held companies. But the problem is that both actors are constituted within a competitive system called the market that encourages vice over virtue in prioritizing profits as a measure of success and survival.[106] And any publicly traded corporations in the United States must seek profits as part of their charters with the Securities and Exchange Commission (SEC). In fact, Christian businessman Dennis Bakke reports that his AES energy company conflicted with the SEC precisely because it sought other goals besides profit.[107] Seeking first the Kingdom does not always breed success; sometimes it breeds conflict with other kingdoms.

Which brings us to the most radical thought of all, but one that is at the center of the Kingdom: it may be that some Christian businesspeople will be called to be exemplary martyrs whose virtuous efforts fail in such a way that they point the world to Christ. To return briefly to our scenario, it may take Christian Company being spectacularly crushed by Machiavelli Company to help show others the economy of the Kingdom. Failure is a tall order to request of businesspeople, but it would reflect the faith and trust in God's provision that is essential to living out the Kingdom ethics of Jesus in the Sermon on the Mount and on the cross. After all, what looked like a failure on Good Friday turned out to be part of God's economy. Without such radical steps of obedience, we may remain in the Iron Cage of the market's Prisoners' Dilemma for some time to come. With such courageous moves of obedience, it might be possible to live for the Kingdom within the business world of today.[108]

Notes

1. This essay first appeared in *CSR* 38.1 (Fall 2008): 14-40.
2. Craig M. Gay, *Cash Values: Money and the Erosion of Meaning in Today's Society* (Grand Rapids: Eerdmans, 2003).
3. Max Weber, *The Protestant Ethic and the Spirit of Capitalism*, trans. Talcott Parsons (New York: Charles Scribner's Sons, 1958), 181–83. On Weber, also see Alasdair MacIntyre, *After Virtue: A Study in Moral Theory*, 2nd ed. (Notre Dame, Ind.: University of Notre Dame Press, 1984), 26–30, 74–75, 86, 109, 114–15.
4. On the infusion of divine grace, see Frederick Christian Bauerschmidt, *Holy Teaching: Introducing the Summa Theologiae of St. Thomas Aquinas* (Grand Rapids, Mich.: Brazos Press, 2005), 122–29.
5. Weber, *The Protestant Ethic*, 53.
6. Ibid.
7. Ibid., 182. On Weber, also see Bruno Dyck and David Schroeder, "Management, Theology and Moral Points of View: Towards an Alternative to the Conventional Materialist-Individualist Ideal-Type of Management," *Journal of Management Studies* 42 (June 2005): 705–35.
8. Also see Hannah Arendt, *The Human Condition* (New York: Doubleday Anchor, 1958), 27–69; and Charles Taylor, *Sources of the Self: The Making of the Modern Identity* (Cambridge, Mass.: Harvard University Press, 1989), 3–24, 211-33.
9. Gay, 21–72. On the eclipse of sacred meaning, see Charles Taylor, *A Secular Age* (Cambridge, Mass.: Belknap Press, 2007).
10. John F. Kavanaugh, *Following Christ in a Consumer Society: The Spirituality of Cultural Resistance*, rev. ed. (Maryknoll, N.Y.: Orbis Books, 1991), 34–35; Angelo Matera, "The Pope and St. Joseph on Wall Street," *National Catholic Register* (May 11-19, 2003), http://www.ncregister.com (accessed May 19, 2003); George Weigel, *Witness to Hope: The Biography of John Paul II* (New York: Cliff Street/HarperCollins, 1999), 420–21; John Paul II, Encyclical Letter Veritatis Splendor (August 6, 1993), sections 98–100, http://www.vatican.va/holy_father/john_paul_ii/encyclicals/documents/hf_jp-ii_enc_06081993_veritatissplendor_en.html (accessed June 16, 2008); John Paul II,

Encyclical Letter *Centesimus Annus* (May 1, 1991), section 39, http://www.vatican.va/holy_father/john_paul_ii/encyclicals/documents/hf_jp-ii_enc_01051991_centesimus-annus_en.html (accessed June 16, 2008).

11. Philip Goodchild, *Theology of Money* (London: SCM Press, 2007), 5, writes that money has become the "value of values" or the measurement of worth.

12. Aristotle, *The Politics*, trans. T. A. Sinclair (New York: Penguin, 1981), I.9–10, 81–85.

13. Ibid., 81.

14. Paul J. Wadell, *Friendship and the Moral Life* (Notre Dame, Ind.: University of Notre Dame Press, 1989), 42–43.

15. Aristotle, *Politics* I.9, 83.

16. The latter index is based on the theory of purchasing power parity, which starts from the assumption that the price of a Big Mac should be roughly the same when we control for exchange rates, thereby distinguishing mere fluctuations in currency value from other factors that affect pricing.

17. See Frances Hutchinson, Mary Mellor, and Wendy Olsen, *The Politics of Money: Towards Sustainability and Economic Democracy* (London: Pluto Press, 2002), 82–90.

18. Aristotle, *Politics*, I.9, 84.

19. Adam Smith, *An Inquiry into the Nature and Causes of the Wealth of Nations*, 5th ed., ed. Edwin Canaan (London: Methuen, 1904), Book IV, chapter 2 http://www.econlib.org/LIBRARY/Smith/smWN.html (accessed June 16, 2008).

20. Aristotle, *Politics*, I.9, 85.

21. Robert Kuttner, *Everything for Sale: The Virtues and Limits of Markets* (New York: Alfred A. Knopf, 1997), 39–67; also see Goodchild, 64, on how the pursuit of money overpowers "all existing values."

22. Shawn Floyd reflects on this problem in "Morally Serious Pedagogy," *Christian Scholar's Review* 36.3 (Spring 2007): 245–61, at 255–56.

23. For a description of a generation of management theorists who responded to this problem, see Eugene McCarraher, "Me, Myself, and Inc.: 'Social Selfhood,' Corporate Humanism, and Religious Longing in Management Theory, 1908-1956," in *Figures in the Carpet: Finding the Human Person in the American Past*, ed. Wilfred E. McClay (Grand Rapids, Mich.: Eerdmans, 2007).

24. Christopher Shannon, *Conspicuous Criticism: Tradition, the Individual, and Culture in Modern American Social Thought*, rev. ed. (Scranton, Penn.: University of Scranton Press, 2006), 14–15; Robert L. Heilbroner, *The Worldly Philosophers*, 6th ed. (New York: Touchstone, 1986), 234–40.

25. Alfred D. Chandler, Jr., *The Visible Hand: The Managerial Revolution in American Business* (Cambridge, Mass.: Belknap Press, 1977), 274–82; Lee Hardy, *The Fabric of This World: Inquiries into Calling, Career Choice, and the Design of Human Work* (Grand Rapids, Mich.: Eerdmans, 1990), 128–40; and Robert Kanigel, *The One Best Way: Frederick Winslow Taylor and the Enigma of Efficiency* (New York: Penguin, 1997).

26. Errol Morris, "The Fog of War: Transcript," *Errol Morris Website*, http://www.errolmorris.com/film/fow_transcript.html (accessed June 14, 2007). This account is mostly corroborated in Deborah Shapley, *Promise and Power: The Life and Times of Robert McNamara* (Boston: Little, Brown, 1993), 60–62. David Halberstam, *The Reckoning* (New York: Avon Books, 1987), 206-07, 365–66, 373, offers a critical account based on Lee Iacocca's "car guy" perspective.

27. Shapley, 55.

28. Halberstam, *The Reckoning*, 206. Also see Halberstam, *The Best and the Brightest* (New York: Fawcett Crest, 1972), 263–95. In fairness, one must note that Halberstam held a grudge against McNamara for playing a large role in the Vietnam War and blamed his focus on body counts. Shapley's biography and Morris's film, however, corroborate the thesis that McNamara emphasized quantitative data.

29. Halberstam, *The Reckoning*, 240, 371.

30. Ibid., 635.

31. Weber, 182. Thanks to an anonymous reviewer for pointing to this passage.

32. Chandler, 476–83; Lawrence E. Mitchell, *The Speculation Economy: How Finance Triumphed Over Industry* (San Francisco: Berrett-Koehler, 2007), 271–79.

33. Shapley, 21, 24.

34. Jim Collins, *Good to Great: Why Some Companies Make the Leap and Others Don't* (New York: Collins, 2001).

35. Mitchell, 1.

36. I am indebted to Fred Thomas for this point.

37. Mitchell, x.

38. Wendell Berry, "Two Economies," in *On Moral Business: Classical and Contemporary Resources for Ethics*, eds. Max L. Stackhouse, Dennis P. McCann, Shirley Roels, and Preston Williams (Grand Rapids, Mich.: Eerdmans, 1995), 836.

39. Thanks to Fred Thomas for this point.

40. MacIntyre, 190.

41. Ibid., 190–91.

42. Robert C. Solomon, "Virtues and the Virtuous Manager: An Aristotelean [sic] Approach to Business Ethics," in Thomas Donaldson and Patricia H. Werhane, eds., *Ethical Issues in Business: A Philosophical Approach*, 5th edition, (Upper Saddle River, N.J.: Prentice-Hall, 1996), 45–59; Dennis P. McCann and M. L. Brownsberger, "Management as a Social Practice: Rethinking Business Ethics after MacIntyre," in, *On Moral Business*, 508–13.

43. D. Stephen Long, Nancy Ruth Fox and Tripp York, *Calculated Futures: Theology, Ethics, and Economics* (Waco, Tex.: Baylor University Press, 2007), 113.

44. Aristotle, *Nicomachean Ethics*, trans. Roger Crisp (New York: Cambridge University Press, 2000).

45. MacIntyre, 191.

46. Aristotle, *Nicomachean Ethics*, II.7, 32.

47. MacIntyre, 151.

48. Ibid.

49. Ibid.
50. Ibid., 152.
51. However, for positive appraisals of MacIntyre in business ethics, see Charles M. Horvath, "Excellence vs. Effectiveness: MacIntyre's Critique of Business," *Business Ethics Quarterly* 5:3 (July 1995): 499–532; and Daryl Koehn, "A Role for Virtue Ethics in the Analysis of Business Practice," *Business Ethics Quarterly* 5:3 (July 1995): 533–39. For a more skeptical account of the possibility of virtue in management theory, see McCarraher.
52. Solomon, "Virtues and the Virtuous Manager," 59. Aristotle, *Politics*, I.13, 94: "It is clear then that in household-management [economics] the people are of greater importance than the inanimate property, and their virtue is of more account than that of the property which we call their wealth...."
53. Robert Solomon, *A Better Way to Think about Business* (New York: Oxford University Press, 1999), xxii, 46–48. Although Solomon mentions Aristotle's focus on social and political context, he discusses this only in terms of relationships within the firm—not outside it. Also see Solomon, *Ethics and Excellence: Cooperation and Integrity in Business* (New York: Oxford University Press, 1993), 97–190. Koehn, 537–38, commends MacIntyre's work for its attention to social context.
54. Wadell, 47.
55. St. Augustine, *Concerning the City of God Against the Pagans*, trans. John O'Meara (New York: Penguin Books, 1984), XIV.17, pp. 877–79.
56. Berry, 836.
57. However, see Horvath, 524, on the tension between excellence and effectiveness.
58. Alexander Hill, *Just Business: Christian Ethics for the Marketplace* (Downers Grove, Ill.: InterVarsity Press, 1997), ch. 1–4. For another case study of Christian business that challenged a profit-driven approach, see Dennis Bakke, *Joy at Work: A Revolutionary Approach to Fun on the Job* (Seattle: PVG, 2005).
59. Thomas Aquinas, *Summa Theologiae* I-II, question 62, on the "theological virtues," in *The Summa Theologica of St. Thomas Aquinas*, 2nd ed., trans. Fathers of the English Dominican Province (1920), online edition: http://www.newadvent.org/summa/2062.htm.
60. See the critique of "Jesus CEO" in Michael Budde, "God Is Not a Capitalist," in *God Is Not: Religious, Nice, "One of Us," an American, a Capitalist*, ed. D. Brent Laytham (Grand Rapids, Mich.: Brazos Press, 2004).
61. Max DePree, *Leadership Jazz* (New York: Dell, 1992), 3.
62. Max DePree, *Leadership Is an Art* (New York: Dell, 1987), 76.
63. Ibid., 34.
64. Ibid., 113.
65. Ibid., 114.
66. DePree, *Leadership Jazz*, 89.
67. Josef Pieper, *The Four Cardinal Virtues* (Notre Dame, Ind.: University of Notre Dame Press, 1966), 186–88.
68. Ibid., 188.
69. Long, *Divine Economy*, 239.
70. Ibid.
71. DePree, *Leadership Is an Art*, 25, 32–33, 50–53.
72. Ibid., 52.
73. Max DePree, "Reflections on Some Preserving Principles of Capitalism in a Democracy," in *The Heart of a Business Ethic*, ed. Donald D. Holt (Lanham, Md.: University Press of America, 2005), 81. See also DePree, *Leadership is an Art*, 23 and *Leadership Jazz*, 90–92.
74. DePree, *Leadership Is an Art*, 119.
75. Ibid., 43.
76. Ibid., 26.
77. James O'Toole, "Foreword: History, Leadership, and a Vision for Corporate Life," in *Leadership is an Art*, xx-xxi, says that when he visited a Herman Miller factory he could not tell managers from workers. On "intimacy," see DePree, *Leadership Is an Art*, 45–53.
78. DePree, *Leadership Is an Art*, 47–48.
79. Ibid, 3.
80. Ibid., 85.
81. Ibid., 87
82. DePree, *Leadership Jazz*, 131.
83. DePree, *Leadership Is an Art*, 7, 130–31.
84. Ibid., 131.
85. Ibid., 24.
86. Ibid., 72.
87. Ibid., 62, 130–34; also see DePree, *Leadership Jazz*, 11, 27–28; and Pieper, 43–113.
88. *Leadership Is an Art*, 76. For theorizing on relational approaches, see Nicola Baker, ed., *Building a Relational Society: New Priorities for Public Policy* (Burlington, Vt.: Arena, 1996).
89. Piper, 112–13, cites Aquinas saying that justice without charity or love is not enough.
90. For an attempt to ground humility theologically, see Stephen K. Moroney, Matthew P. Phelps, and Scott Waalkes, "Cultivating Humility in Students: Teaching Practices Rooted in Christian Anthropology," in *The Schooled Heart: Moral Formation in American Higher Education*, eds. Michael Beaty and Douglas V. Henry (Waco, Tex.: Baylor University Press, 2007).
91. Thomas Merton, *Love and Living* (New York: Harvest, 1979), 231.
92. DePree, *Leadership Jazz*, 9; *Leadership Is an Art*, 9.
93. DePree, *Leadership Is an Art*, 10.

94. Ibid.; also see DePree, *Leadership Jazz*, 10–11.
95. DePree, "Reflections," 87.
96. DePree, *Leadership Jazz*, 132–33.
97. Ibid., 119.
98. DePree, *Leadership Is an Art*, 2.
99. DePree, *Leadership Jazz*, 191. Strikingly, DePree's only major negative comments in his books end up excoriating managers who are obsessed with quantification and financial yardsticks and who lose sight of the larger purpose and meaning of business. See DePree, *Leadership Jazz*, 137; and *Leadership Is an Art*, 47, 63, 99–100, 137.
100. DePree, *Leadership Is an Art*, 83.
101. Pieper, 190.
102. DePree, *Leadership Is an Art*, 61, 129–32; also see DePree, *Leadership Jazz*, 137–39.
103. DePree, *Leadership Jazz*, 107.
104. Bakke, 27; the name of the professor is John Kay.
105. Horvath, 524.
106. On "anarchic" systems as structures, see Kenneth Waltz, *The Theory of International Politics* (New York: McGraw-Hill, 1979), 79–128.
107. Bakke, 38–40.
108. Some portions of this paper were presented at the International Studies Association Annual Meeting in New Orleans in March 2002. I am indebted to specific comments from an anonymous reviewer, from Fred Thomas, and from Maria Lam that greatly improved the final draft. Thanks also to Becky Albertson and Jay Case for reading and responding to earlier versions. Jack Harris, Mike Ophardt, Ken Stoltzfus and Kenman Wong also offered helpful comments in response to the thesis of the paper. Steve Long and Mike Budde provided inspiration and helpful reading suggestions at the Calvin College Seminar in Christian Scholarship on Liturgical Identities in the summer of 2007. My thanks go out to Joel Carpenter, Marilyn Rottman, and the staff at the Calvin Seminars office for providing the space to complete the research in business ethics.

Afterword

Alister McGrath

How should Christians relate to their culture? How can they be salt and light within the academy, without being overwhelmed by the prevailing spirit of the age on the one hand, or on the other becoming completely isolated from it, like a circle of wagons defensively huddling together for comfort and mutual protection?

Post-war American evangelicalism tended towards the second of these options, anxious lest an engagement with academy and culture might lead to the secularization of Christianity, rather than the evangelization of culture. It is an understandable concern and is to be taken seriously. Yet this disengagement simply meant that American culture was robbed of any possibility of being enriched, challenged, or redirected by evangelical insights and wisdom. It was not a satisfactory situation.

There is, however, an alternative approach, which is deeply grounded in Scripture and in the long history of Christian reflection on this vital text. In his major work *On Christian Doctrine*, Augustine of Hippo compares the church to the people of Israel, who had escaped from Egypt and were on their way to the promised land. Using the exodus from Egypt as his informing paradigm, Augustine argues that there is no reason why Christians should not extract all that is good from secular culture and put it to the service of preaching the gospel. Just as Israel carried off the treasures of the Egyptians as it fled from their bondage, so the church can make use of what is good in academic culture, without becoming enslaved to it.

For Augustine, the church can thus engage critically yet positively with the academy and with culture. It rejoices in what is good, and filters out what is bad. It is this model that I see in the *Christian Scholar's Review*, which encourages and models a faithful, critical, yet positive engagement between Christian scholars and the world of academic culture. What academic can love God without wanting to make connections with the academy—with literature, art, or the sciences? And how do we think about our fields of study and research in an intentionally Christian way? As I read (and in many cases re-read) these essays, I found myself thrilled to see how the Christian gospel can enrich our engagement with culture, allowing the light of the gospel to illuminate some of the shadowlands of the human soul.

Yet there is another point, perhaps too easily overlooked. Engaging with our culture allows us to expand our vision of the gospel itself—not by adding to it, but by helping us develop points of contact, ways of speaking, and modes of illustration which allow us both to appreciate its intellectual and imaginative rigor, while at the same time enabling us to communicate its "spiritual excellencies" (Jonathan Edwards) to this important element of our culture. The *CSR* vision of an "enriching perspective of divine revelation" captures this point perfectly. Perhaps this is the most important lesson that North American evangelicalism has learned from C. S. Lewis, who has proved a remarkably fertile and stimulating dialogue partner for the movement, as it seeks to engage the academy for Christ and his gospel.

I salute the vision that lies behind *CSR*, which is so evident throughout this volume. We need more evangelicals to be actively present within our academic culture, and I hope that younger scholars will be encouraged and challenged by the role models we find within the pages of this book. The highly significant contributions of Alvin Plantinga and others in the philosophy of religion show how a specific academic discipline can take new and better directions when evangelicals engage it, positively yet critically. The same is increasingly true of other disciplines, as this volume attests. Perhaps a rising generation of evangelicals might catch the vision of these authors, and choose to become living witnesses for faithful scholarship within the academy. Yes, there are risks—but there are also great opportunities.

I have always saluted those who feel called to the pastoral ministry, honoring and respecting those who believe that this is what God wants them to do with their lives. Yet God calls us to other fields of witness and mission as well. My hope and prayer is that this collection of essays, and the evangelical vision that undergirds it, will lead many to realize the importance of this engagement. Christ "plays in ten thousand places" (Gerard Manley Hopkins); perhaps you, gentle reader, might feel called to play for him in one of them.

Contributors

Nancy T. Ammerman is Professor of Sociology of Religion at Boston University's School of Theology and Chair of the Department of Sociology in the College of Arts and Sciences. She has spent much of her career studying American religious organizations, especially congregations and denominations. Her 2005 book, *Pillars of Faith: American Congregations and Their Partners*, describes the organizational patterns that shape America's diverse communities of faith. She has also written extensively on conservative religious movements, including *Bible Believers: Fundamentalists in the Modern World* and *Baptist Battles: Social Change and Religious Conflict in the Southern Baptist Convention*.

Norman A. Bert teaches playwriting and drama at Texas Tech University, and formerly taught theater at Messiah College and Montana State University-Billings. He earned a B.D. from Goshen College Biblical Seminary and a Ph.D. in dramatic theory from Indiana University. His play scripts include *Riders of the Golden Sphinx* published by Baker's Plays, *America Shows Her Colors*, produced by Inner Voices Social Issues (University of Illinois), and *Scenes from a Romance: A Play on the Book of Hosea*, showcased by the Association for Theatre in Higher Education. His most recently produced script is *The Gospel According to Jesse*. His books include *Theatre Alive!* and *One-Act Plays for Acting Students*.

Steven Bouma-Prediger is Professor of Religion and Director of the Environmental Studies Program at Hope College in Holland, Michigan. A graduate of Hope College, his Ph.D. is in religious studies from the University of Chicago. His publications include *For the Beauty of the Earth: A Christian Vision for Creation Care*, revised second edition, *Beyond Homelessness: Christian Faith in a Culture of Displacement*, co-authored with Brian Walsh, and *The Greening of Theology*. He has won numerous teaching awards, including the recipient of the Hope Outstanding Professor-Educator Award (1999) and Hope's Favorite Faculty Award (2001).

Jonathan Chaplin is the first Director of the Kirby Laing Institute for Christian Ethics, Cambridge, a member of the Divinity Faculty of Cambridge University, and Visiting Lecturer at the VU University, Amsterdam. He was Associate Professor of Political Theory at ICS from 1999-2006, holding the Dooyeweerd Chair of Social and Political Philosophy from 2004-2006. He is author of *Herman Dooyeweerd: Christian Philosopher of State and Civil Society* (2011), and of the think-tank report *Talking God: The Legitimacy of Religious Public Reasoning*. He has edited or co-edited five books, including *God and Global Order: The Power of Religion in American Foreign Policy*, and authored many articles on Christian political thought.

Paul de Vries is President of the New York Divinity School, with twenty-five years of leadership in Christian higher education administration, including at Wheaton College, Northern Baptist Theological Seminary, and the Seminary of the East. He earned his M.A. and Ph.D. at the University of Virginia, specializing in applied ethics, critical thinking, and hermeneutics. He is the lead author of three books: *The Taming of the Shrewd*, *Ethics Applied*, and *Business Ethics Applied*. He is also a contributing author to a dozen other books. He is founder of the Office of Community Service at the University of Virginia and founder of the Center for Applied Christian Ethics at Wheaton College, the first ethics center of any Christian college.

William Hasker is Professor Emeritus of Philosophy at Huntington University, where he taught from 1966 until 2000. He holds a Ph.D. from the University of Edinburgh. He was the editor of *Christian Scholar's Review* from 1985 to 1994, and the editor of *Faith and Philosophy* from 2000 until 2007. He has contributed numerous articles to journals and reference works, and is the author of *Metaphysics: Constructing a World View, God, Time, and Knowledge , The Emergent Self, Providence, Evil, and the Openness of God* , and, most recently, *The Triumph of God over Evil: Theodicy for a World of Suffering* (2008).

Stanley Hauerwas is the Gilbert T. Rowe Professor of Theological Ethics at the Divinity School of Duke University and holds a joint appointment in the Duke Law School. He holds a Ph.D. from Yale University and a D.D. from the University of Edinburgh. In 2001 *Time* magazine named him "America's Best Theologian." His book, *A Community of Character: Toward a Constructive Christian Social Ethic*, was selected as one of the hundred most important books on religion in the twentieth century. Recent books include *Matthew: Brazos Theological Commentary on the Bible* and *The State of the University: Academic Knowledges and the Knowledge of God*.

Carl F. H. Henry (1913 – 2003) was perhaps the leading American Evangelical theologian of the twentieth century. His magnum opus was the six-volume *God, Revelation, and Authority* (1976 – 1983). He was the author of many other books, including *The Uneasy Conscience of Modern Fundamentalism, Toward a Recovery of Christian Belief*, and *Twilight of a Great Civilization: The Drift toward Neo-Paganism*. He was the founding editor of *Christianity Today* magazine and served as its editor-in-chief until 1968. He earned a Ph.D. from Boston University in 1949.

Arthur F. Holmes is Professor Emeritus at Wheaton College, where he taught philosophy from 1951 to 1994. He holds a Ph.D. from Northwestern University, and has lectured at many colleges, universities, and conferences. During his long tenure at Wheaton, he championed the cause of Christian higher education and the field of Christian philosophy. His book, *The Idea of a Christian College* (1975, 1987), has been a seminal contribution to Christian higher education. His other books include *All Truth Is God's Truth, Building the Christian Academy*, and *Contours of a World View*.

Russell W. Howell earned a Ph.D. in mathematics from Ohio State University and an MS.C. in computer science from the University of Edinburgh. He did his undergraduate work at Wheaton College, which instilled in him an interest in both mathematics and philosophy. He currently serves on the faculty at Westmont College, having had temporary stints along the way at Calvin College, University of Maryland, and a visiting appointment at Oxford University. He takes delight in working with college students who are making important decisions regarding their future service. He also enjoys tennis, hiking, ocean kayaking, and playing the piano.

Roger Lundin is the Blanchard Professor of English at Wheaton College. Twice named Teacher of the Year at Wheaton, Lundin has written and edited ten books, including *Believing Again: Doubt and Faith in A Secular Age, Emily Dickinson and the Art of Belief,* and *The Culture of Interpretation: Christian Faith and the Postmodern World*. He has received major research fellowships from the Erasmus Institute at the University of Notre Dame, the Pew Charitable Trusts, and the Evangelical Scholarship Initiative. Lundin has an M.A from Gordon-Conwell Theological Seminary and an M.A. and Ph.D. in English from the University of Connecticut. From 1986 to 1991 he served as the Humanities Editor for the *Christian Scholar's Review*.

Alister McGrath is Professor of Theology, Ministry, and Education at King's College London, and is Director of its Center for Theology, Religion, and Culture. Before moving to London, he served for many years as Professor of Historical Theology at Oxford University. He is the author of many books, including the recent, *The Passionate Intellect: Christian Faith and the Discipleship of the Mind*. A former atheist, McGrath has a close interest in the relation of Christian faith and contemporary culture, and has been a leading critic of the New Atheism. He is at work on a biography of C. S. Lewis, due to be published in 2013 to mark the fiftieth anniversary of Lewis's death.

George A. Marsden is Francis A. McAnaney Professor of History Emeritus, University of Notre Dame. He taught history at Calvin College from 1965 to 1986; the history of Christianity in America at The Divinity School of Duke University from 1986 to 1992; and history at Notre Dame from 1992 to 2008. He earned a B.D. from Westminster Theological Seminary and an M.A. and Ph.D. from Yale University. His books include *Fundamentalism and American Culture, The Soul of the American University, The Outrageous Idea of Christian Scholarship, Jonathan Edwards: A Life,* and *A Short Life of Jonathan Edwards*.

Richard J. Mouw has served as President of Fuller Theological Seminary since 1993, after having served four years as Provost and Senior Vice President. A philosopher, scholar, and author, Mouw joined the Fuller faculty as professor of Christian philosophy and ethics in 1985. Prior to that he served seventeen years as professor of philosophy at Calvin College. In 2007, Mouw was awarded the Kuyper Prize at Princeton Theological Seminary, awarded annually to a scholar who has made a major contribution to Reformed public theology. As the 2007 recipient he delivered a lecture entitled "Culture, Church and Civil Society: Kuyper for a New Century" to scholars from the United States, Canada, and the Netherlands.

Elizabeth Newman holds a Ph.D. from Duke University and is Professor of Theology and Ethics at the Baptist Theological Seminary at Richmond. She is the author of *Untamed Hospitality: Welcoming God and Other Strangers,* and is currently completing *Attending to the Wounds on Christ's Body: Teresa's Scriptural Vision* (forthcoming). She currently serves on the editorial board of *Studies in Baptist History and Thought* and is a participant in the Baptist World Alliance Conversations with the Pontifical Council for Christian Unity. In 2009, she was named a Henry Luce III Fellow in Theology.

Mark A. Noll is the Francis A. McAnaney Professor of History at the University of Notre Dame. His books include *The Scandal of the Evangelical Mind*; *American Evangelical Christianity: An Introduction*; *The Rise of Evangelicalism: The Age of Edwards, Whitefield and the Wesleys*; and *Jesus Christ and the Life of the Mind*. He is the co-editor of *Evangelicals and Science in Historical Perspective*, and co-author of *Is the Reformation Over? An Evangelical Assessment of Contemporary Catholicism*. The essays in this volume were published when he was on the history faculty of Wheaton College. Although now at a Catholic institution, he remains deeply committed to the development of evangelical higher education.

Jenell Williams Paris is Professor of Sociology and Anthropology at Messiah College in Grantham, Pennsylvania. She received a B.A. from Bethel University and a Ph.D. from American University in Washington, DC. Extending the work of the essay in this volume, she is co-author (with Brian Howell) of *Introducing Cultural Anthropology: A Christian Perspective* (2010). She has also authored *Sex Is (Not) a Big Deal: Why Sex Is Too Important to be Central in Human Identity* and *Birth Control for Christians: Making Wise Choices about Fertility*.

Alvin Plantinga is the first occupant of the William Harry Jellema Chair in Philosophy at Calvin College, having retired recently as John A. O'Brien Professor of Philosophy at the University of Notre Dame. He earned an A.B. at Calvin College, an M.A from the University of Michigan, and a Ph.D. from Yale University. His work in epistemology, metaphysics, and philosophy of religion has earned him a global reputation as one of the leading philosophers of his generation. Among his many books are *God, Freedom and Evil*, *The Nature of Necessity*, and a three-volume examination of the concept of warrant as a criterion for knowledge. His work is also the subject of numerous articles, anthologies, and critical studies.

Luke Reinsma has been devoted to Christian education his entire life—first as a student at a Christian school in north Seattle; then at Calvin College, class of 1970; then as a teacher in Memphis at a Baptist private school; then at East Grand Rapids Christian High School; then as a student at the University of Michigan, where he wrote his dissertation on the Old English homilies of the Benedictine monk Aelfric and graduated in 1978; and then, for several more years at Gustavus Adolphus College in Minnesota. Finally, he returned to the Northwest in 1985, where he's been hiking the Pacific Crest Trail, teaching medieval literature, and directing the honors program at Seattle Pacific University.

Ronald J. Sider is a professor, director of the Sider Center, and president of Evangelicals for Social Action, all three at Palmer Theological Seminary. He holds a Ph.D from Yale University. He has spoken on six continents, published thirty-one books, and scores of articles. His *Rich Christians in an Age of Hunger* was recognized by *Christianity Today* as one of the one hundred most influential religious books of the twentieth century. His most recent book is *The Scandal of Evangelical Politics: Why Are Christians Missing the Chance to Really Change the World?* Sider is a contributing editor of *Christianity Today* and *Sojourners* and has lectured at scores of colleges and universities around the world, including Yale, Harvard, Princeton, and Oxford.

Mary Stewart Van Leeuwen earned her Ph.D. from Northwestern University and is currently Professor of Psychology and Philosophy at Eastern University in St. Davids, Pennsylvania. She taught at Calvin College for many years, and she has been a senior editor of *Christianity Today*. She is a contributing editor for *Books & Culture*. Her books include *Gender and Grace: Love, Work & Parenting in a Changing World*, *My Brother's Keeper: What the Social Sciences Do (and Don't) Tell Us about Masculinity*, and *A Sword between the Sexes?: C. S. Lewis and the Gender Debates*.

Scott Waalkes is Professor of International Politics at Malone University in Canton, Ohio. He is the author of a recent book, *The Fullness of Time in a Flat World: Globalization and the Liturgical Year*, as well as articles, book chapters, and book reviews in international studies. His research and teaching focus on Christian approaches to globalization and the market economy, international affairs, and the Middle East. A former Fulbright Scholar in the Middle Eastern nation of Bahrain, Waalkes holds a B.A. in Political Science from Calvin College and M.A. and Ph.D. degrees in Foreign Affairs from the University of Virginia.

Brian J. Walsh serves as a Christian Reformed campus minister at the University of Toronto. He is also Adjunct Professor of Theology of Culture at Trinity and Wycliffe Colleges. He has published six articles over the years in *CSR* and is the co-author of *The Transforming Vision: Shaping a Christian Worldview*, *Truth Is Stranger than It Used to Be: Biblical Faith in a Postmodern Age*, *Colossians Remixed: Subverting the Empire* and *Beyond Homelessness: Christian Faith in a Culture of Displacement*. His most recent book is *Kicking at the Darkness: Bruce Cockburn and the Christian Imagination* (2011). Walsh lives at Russet House Farm, a solar and wind-powered organic farm in Cameron, Ontario.

Dallas Willard is Professor of Philosophy at the University of Southern California. His B.A. is from Baylor University and his Ph.D. is from the University of Wisconsin. His areas of interest are metaphysics, contemporary European philosophy, ethics and the history of ethics, and the status of moral knowledge (absence thereof) in contemporary society. His many books include *A Place for Truth: Leading Thinkers Explore Life's Hardest Questions*, *Knowing Christ Today: Why We Can Trust Spiritual Knowledge*, *The Spirit of the Disciplines: Understanding How God Changes Lives*, and *The Divine Conspiracy: Rediscovering Our Hidden Life in God*.

Nicholas Wolterstorff is Noah Porter Professor Emeritus of Philosophical Theology, Yale University and Senior Fellow at the Institute for Advanced Studies in Culture, at the University of Virginia. He received his A.B. from Calvin College and his Ph.D. in philosophy from Harvard University. He taught philosophy at Calvin (1959-1989) and at Yale 1957-59, 1989-2001). He is the author of many books, including *Art in Action, Until Justice and Peace Embrace, Reason within the Bounds of Religion, Justice: Rights and Wrongs*, and *Justice in Love*. He has served as president of the American Philosophical Association (Central Division) and of the Society of Christian Philosophers, and is a Fellow of the American Academy of Arts and Sciences.